I0890963

Innovative Technologies for Increasing Service Productivity

Sridhar Manohar
Chitkara Business School, Chitkara University, India

Amit Mittal
Chitkara Business School, Chitkara University, India

Sekar Raju
Ivy College of Business, Iowa State University, USA

Arjun J. Nair
Chitkara University, India

IGI Global
PUBLISHER of TIMELY KNOWLEDGE

A volume in the Advances in Hospitality, Tourism, and the Services Industry (AHTSI) Book Series

Published in the United States of America by
IGI Global
Business Science Reference (an imprint of IGI Global)
701 E. Chocolate Avenue
Hershey PA, USA 17033
Tel: 717-533-8845
Fax: 717-533-8661
E-mail: cust@igi-global.com
Web site: http://www.igi-global.com

Library of Congress Cataloging-in-Publication Data

Names: Manohar, Sridhar, 1986- editor. | Mittal, Amit, 1974- editor. | Raju, Sekar, 1967- editor. | Nair, Arjun J, 1986- editor.
Title: Innovative technologies for increasing service productivity / edited by Sridhar Manohar, Amit Mittal, Sekar Raju, Arjun J Nair.
Description: Hershey, PA : Business Science Reference, [2024] | Includes bibliographical references and index. | Summary: "This book makes a significant and original contribution to the literature by bridging the gap between service productivity and technology. It presents a holistic view of service productivity, taking into account the social, economic, and environmental factors that affect service operations and delivery"-- Provided by publisher.
Identifiers: LCCN 2024008930 (print) | LCCN 2024008931 (ebook) | ISBN 9798369320198 (hardcover) | ISBN 9798369320204 (ebook)
Subjects: LCSH: Labor productivity. | Performance technology. | Technological innovations.
Classification: LCC HD57 .I63 2024 (print) | LCC HD57 (ebook) | DDC 331.11/8--dc23/eng/20240316
LC record available at https://lccn.loc.gov/2024008930
LC ebook record available at https://lccn.loc.gov/2024008931

This book is published in the IGI Global book series Advances in Hospitality, Tourism, and the Services Industry (AHTSI) (ISSN: 2475-6547; eISSN: 2475-6555)

British Cataloguing in Publication Data
A Cataloguing in Publication record for this book is available from the British Library.

Advances in Hospitality, Tourism, and the Services Industry (AHTSI) Book Series

Maximiliano Korstanje
University of Palermo, Argentina

ISSN:2475-6547
EISSN:2475-6555

Mission

Globally, the hospitality, travel, tourism, and services industries generate a significant percentage of revenue and represent a large portion of the business world. Even in tough economic times, these industries thrive as individuals continue to spend on leisure and recreation activities as well as services.

The Advances in Hospitality, Tourism, and the Services Industry (AHTSI) book series offers diverse publications relating to the management, promotion, and profitability of the leisure, recreation, and services industries. Highlighting current research pertaining to various topics within the realm of hospitality, travel, tourism, and services management, the titles found within the AHTSI book series are pertinent to the research and professional needs of managers, business practitioners, researchers, and upper-level students studying in the field.

Coverage

- Leisure & Business Travel
- Health and Wellness Tourism
- Hotel Management
- Service Management
- Sustainable Tourism
- Destination Marketing and Management
- Food and Beverage Management
- Casino Management
- Travel Agency Management
- International Tourism

IGI Global is currently accepting manuscripts for publication within this series. To submit a proposal for a volume in this series, please contact our Acquisition Editors at Acquisitions@igi-global.com or visit: http://www.igi-global.com/publish/.

The Advances in Hospitality, Tourism, and the Services Industry (AHTSI) Book Series (ISSN 2475-6547) is published by IGI Global, 701 E. Chocolate Avenue, Hershey, PA 17033-1240, USA, www.igi-global.com. This series is composed of titles available for purchase individually; each title is edited to be contextually exclusive from any other title within the series. For pricing and ordering information please visit http://www.igi-global.com/book-series/advances-hospitality-tourism-services-industry/121014. Postmaster: Send all address changes to above address.

Titles in this Series

For a list of additional titles in this series, please visit:
http://www.igi-global.com/book-series/advances-hospitality-tourism-services-industry/121014

Mountain Tourism and Ecological Impacts Himalayan Region and Beyond
Soumendra Nath Biswas (Assam University, Silchar, India) and Pradip Kumar (Assam University, Silchar, India)
Business Science Reference • © 2024 • 320pp • H/C (ISBN: 9798369308233) • US $250.00

Career Pathways and Professional Identities for Front-Line Workers in the Service Industries
Mark Peter Vitale (University of Phoenix, USA)
Business Science Reference • © 2024 • 370pp • H/C (ISBN: 9781668425282) • US $255.00

Experiences, Advantages, and Economic Dimensions of Pilgrimage Routes
Vítor João Pereira Domingues Martinho (Agricultural School, CERNAS-IPV Research Centre, Polytechnic Institute of Viseu, Portugal) João Augusto Guerra da Rocha Nunes (School of Education, Polytechnic Institute of Viseu, Portugal) Maria Lúcia de Jesus Pato (Agricultural School, CERNAS-IPV Research Centre, Polytechnic Institute of Viseu, Portugal) and Liliana Andrade de Matos Castilho (School of Education, Polytechnic Institute of Viseu, Portugal)
Business Science Reference • © 2023 • 367pp • H/C (ISBN: 9781668499238) • US $240.00

Exploring Culture and Heritage Through Experience Tourism
Yashwant Singh Rawal (Parul Institute of Hotel Management, Parul University, India) Rupa Sinha (Amity Institute of Travel and Tourism, Amity University, India) Sankar Kumar Mukherjee (Amity Institute of Travel and Tourism, Amity University, India) and Debasish Batabyal (Amity Institute of Travel and Tourism, Amity University, India)
Business Science Reference • © 2023 • 348pp • H/C (ISBN: 9781668499573) • US $240.00

Sustainable Development Goal Advancement Through Digital Innovation in the Service Sector
Vipin Nadda (University of Sunderland, UK) Pankaj Kumar Tyagi (Chandigarh University, India) Rubina Moniz Vieira (St. Mary's University, London, UK) and Priyanka Tyagi (Chandigarh University, India)
Business Science Reference • © 2023 • 272pp • H/C (ISBN: 9798369306505) • US $275.00

Management and Practices of Pilgrimage Tourism and Hospitality
S.K. Gupta (Centre for Mountain Tourism and Hospitality Management, HNB Garhwal University, India) Lilibeth C. Aragon (College of International Tourism and Hospitality Management, Lyceum of the Philippines University, Philippines) Pankaj Kumar (Department of Tourism and Hospitality Management, Mizoram University, India) Madhurima S. (Department of Environmental Science, Mizoram University, India) and Rajesh Ramasamy (Department of Tourism and Hospitality Management, Mizoram University, India)
Business Science Reference • © 2023 • 264pp • H/C (ISBN: 9798369314142) • US $250.00

IGI Global
PUBLISHER of TIMELY KNOWLEDGE

701 East Chocolate Avenue, Hershey, PA 17033, USA
Tel: 717-533-8845 x100 • Fax: 717-533-8661
E-Mail: cust@igi-global.com • www.igi-global.com

Table of Contents

Detailed Table of Contents

In the contemporary digital landscape, service innovation stands as the linchpin for organizational success. This chapter embarks on a transformative journey into the heart of service innovation in the digital age. From disruptive technologies to revolutionary customer experiences, the chapter meticulously explores the multifaceted dimensions of service innovation. Drawing on real-world examples and cutting-edge research, this chapter illuminates the strategies, challenges, and opportunities that define service innovation in the dynamic digital era. Through this comprehensive exploration, it provides a nuanced understanding of the transformative role and profound significance that service innovation holds in ensuring organizational resilience and success amidst the dynamic digital landscape.

Platform business models have emerged as transformative forces in various industries, reshaping the way services are delivered and consumed. This comprehensive research paper delves into the dynamics of platform-based service innovation and its profound impact on modern economies. The authors provide an in-depth exploration of platform business models, their pivotal role in enabling service innovation, and the evolution of digital ecosystems. Through an extensive literature review, case studies, and empirical analysis, we examine the key drivers, challenges, and opportunities associated with platform business models. Additionally, the authors investigate the implications of platform-based service innovation for stakeholders, including businesses, consumers, and policymakers. This chapter offers valuable insights into the multifaceted world of platform business models and their far-reaching influence on the future of service industries and economic growth.

In this pivotal chapter, the authors embark on a comprehensive exploration of the transformative influence of artificial intelligence (AI) in reshaping service productivity across diverse industries. The chapter unfolds with a meticulous examination of the foundational principles of AI, shedding light on its various manifestations, from machine learning algorithms to natural language processing. Through real-world case studies, the authors navigate the tangible impact of AI on service delivery models, illuminating instances where organizations have successfully integrated AI to streamline operations, enhance customer experiences, and foster innovation. The chapter begins by establishing the fundamental role of AI in deciphering complex data sets, enabling organizations to extract actionable insights and make informed decisions. As the authors traverse the landscape of AI in service productivity, the chapter concludes by presenting a practical roadmap for organizations looking to integrate AI seamlessly into their operations.

In the wake of rapid technological advancements, the concept of digital transformation has emerged as a critical driver for organizational growth and resilience. This research paper delves into the multifaceted implications of digital transformation across various sectors and industries. By analysing the integration of cutting-edge technologies, such as artificial intelligence, big data analytics, cloud computing, and the internet of things, this study elucidates the transformative impact of these innovations on traditional business models. Additionally, the research investigates the challenges, opportunities, and potential risks associated with the adoption of digital transformation strategies, emphasizing the need for proactive adaptation and robust cybersecurity measures. Through a comprehensive examination of case studies and empirical data, this chapter aims to provide insights into the evolving landscape of digital transformation and its profound implications for organizational sustainability and competitiveness in the digital era.

The digital transformation and digital technologies find ample application in service as well as in manufacturing. Advances in digitalization and digital technology adoption encourage service sectors to incorporate new digital technologies into their processes to increase efficiency and productivity. The trend towards up-to-datedness and remote control mechanisms increases service industries' awareness of digital technologies in the era of Industry 4.0 and Society 5.0. A transparent and instant management approach with real-time data becomes possible with digital innovation in service. In the digital ecosystem, personalization is more likely to be possible if the increasing diversity in demands for a particular product/service is disruptive. In these collaborative platforms, the prosumer is at the center of the business and acts as designer, customer and consumer. In this digital ecosystem, the consumer is involved in the design phase at the beginning of the process. A new business model is required due to the overall digitalization of the organization. After talking about the digital revolution and transformation, traditional tools for customer demand/relationship management, sales marketing and operations should be examined. The Internet of Things (IoTs), cloud computing, blockchain infrastructure, and business intelligence, are the basic components of digital transformation. This chapter mainly focuses on the digital transformation of the service industry, service innovations, service business platforms and service business model transformation using digital tools. All these digitalization efforts are made possible by innovation in business models. This new digital business model innovation is defined as a unique and significant change in the fundamental elements of the enterprise's business model and value chain architecture. BM analyzes and redesigns operations, content, structure and management to create value by taking advantage of business opportunities. Especially in an environment where organizations and operations, data and processes become open, the concepts of participation in processes and collaboration come to the fore. Sharing economies and platforms where everyone meets on common ground constitute today's new business models. Platform businesses are shared networks and interfaces that create a common structure in which flexibility in design can be achieved, fixed costs can be saved, and efficiency can be increased. Platforms are divided into two: internal and external, and internal platforms are defined as areas where cooperation is carried out within the business or with the business and suppliers for a specific purpose. The study revealed that the labor-intensive and competitive service sector could not avoid this trend. Within the scope of this section, the concept is intended to be concretized through platform works and sample applications. In summary, all this change has caused physical worlds to be moved to small screens and virtual worlds. No matter how perfect the resulting physical product is, it will always be incomplete unless it is supported by accurate and complete services. In today's cyber-physical environment, perfect service platforms will be able to meet the needs and produce real-time and creative solutions to customer demands. These solutions can be provided through innovative and smart technologies such as artificial intelligence and business intelligence. It can be stated with certainty that service businesses that invest in these technologies will stand out from their competitors.

management. AI concierges offer real-time help and individualized recommendations. AI and virtual experiences are revolutionizing hotel administration and tourism, improving efficiency, guest satisfaction, and hospitality. Businesses that adopt these technologies stay ahead of the hotel industry and satisfy modern customers.

This chapter explores the dynamic intersection of artificial intelligence (AI) and the startup landscape within the tourism industry. It investigates how AI has the potential to revolutionize operations, innovation, and services for emerging businesses in tourism. Demonstrating AI's critical role in enhancing the tourism experience—ranging from personalized recommendations and chatbot-driven customer service to pricing optimization and demand forecasting—it showcases innovative solutions from notable startups like DeepL, Fetch.ai, and Lilium. The chapter includes brief case studies illustrating AI applications in tourism and emphasizes the pivotal role of investors in supporting these startups. It concludes by outlining future research directions, addressing strategies for maximizing AI benefits in tourism, managing privacy and security concerns, and navigating the evolving landscape of AI integration in travel.

This chapter provides a comprehensive review of hospitality and tourist (HAT) AI literature. The analysis identified relevant themes, pros, and cons, as well as suggested future research possibilities in this discipline. HAT is rapidly adopting AI technology to improve customer service, operational efficiency, travel experiences, and sustainability. There is a growing body of research on this topic, but a thorough and systematic understanding is needed to determine the most effective AI applications and recommend areas for further investigation. This chapter discusses how machine learning, natural language processing, and robotics may improve tourist and hospitality consumer experiences and efficiency. This chapter covers AI in travel, from chatbots for customer service to autonomous cars to VR/AR for immersive experiences. AI disrupts customers and companies in personalisation, decision-making, and predictive analytics. These AI technologies' ability to revolutionise the business provides a futuristic view of travel and tourism.

Utilizing social media for real-time communication and feedback is crucial in the evolving landscape of business communication in the digital era. It's not enough to simply acquire new customers through lead generation or sales; you must also foster connections with them on social media and online to ensure their continued loyalty and advocacy for your brand. Traditional word-of-mouth marketing has transformed,

emphasizes the crucial roles that cross-functional collaboration and market knowledge integration play in industrial applications as a means to gain competitive advantages. This study highlights the necessity of embracing innovation adoption within the automobile industry to attain competitive advantages and establish sustainable mobility.

Passenger services at airports are coproduced by many organizations - airports, airlines, ground handlers, immigration, customs, aviation security, and commercial establishments. Service performance on subjective parameters is evaluated primarily through customer satisfaction surveys at frequent intervals through third parties with varying parameters and methodology. The objective parameters as defined by the airports are measured and reported by the airports. Thus, there is no standardized set of parameters and methodology for airport services performance. With the increased passenger's awareness about quality of services and reporting platforms like social media, airports have started to innovate the processes and introduce advanced technologies and exceed the service quality paradigm to passenger experience. Also, the importance attached to the services by the passengers differs based on the travel purpose. It is seen that airports compete with each other to add value to passenger services and experience on a continual basis. This book chapter describes these aspects of airport services.

The world is changing rapidly, especially with a speedy increase in global population. More than ever, for all service-related functions, the organizations are looking for methods to enhance their service throughput. Technological innovations in every industry have been helpful in achieving this growth. In hospitals too, the power of technology has been harnessed for better patient outcomes which directly translates to patient satisfaction. New healthcare technologies have provenly increased the efficiency of care services and operational processes by removing repetitive tasks and providing personalized care to the patients. A successful digital healthcare ecosystem provides clinical decision support which enables both high degree of efficiency (bandwidth and throughput) and high degree of effectiveness (quality patient health outcomes).

Recently, metaverse technology has drawn considerable attention in the healthcare industry as a result of multifold technological advancements in the last decade. Metaverse is likely to have a significant impact on our digital lives in the near future by enhancing our interactions, and our working and playing habits. However, it poses a variety of challenges that require special attention and proactive action to be taken. In this study,

Preface

Welcome to *Innovative Technologies for Increasing Service Productivity*. In this meticulously crafted reference book, we embark on a journey to explore the dynamic landscape of service productivity in the ever-evolving digital age. As editors, our mission has been to create a comprehensive study that not only identifies the challenges faced by service organizations but also analyzes the multifaceted dimensions of service productivity.

Rationale and Scope

The impetus behind this book lies in our commitment to unravel the key trends shaping service industries and to dissect the impact of digital transformation, emerging technologies, and disruptive business models. Our focus spans service productivity trends, measurement techniques, strategies for improvement, and the transformative influence of technology on service innovation, quality, and delivery.

Unique Selling Points

This book distinguishes itself through its encompassing examination of various service industries and their interplay with technology. Offering practical strategies and tools, it equips service organizations to elevate productivity, enhance quality, and refine the customer experience. Moreover, it delves into the realm of service innovation and entrepreneurship from a digital perspective, shedding light on new business models, sharing economies, and platform ecosystems.

Contributions to the Literature

Our collective effort contributes significantly to the growing literature on service productivity and its profound impact on economic growth and development. By bridging the gap between service productivity and technology, this book presents a holistic view that considers social, economic, and environmental factors influencing service operations and delivery.

Target Audience

This book is tailored for a diverse readership. Service managers across industries will find it indispensable for understanding trends and innovations, while policymakers and regulators gain insights into the economic and social implications of service productivity. Researchers will appreciate the wealth of information for conducting in-depth studies, and students will find a valuable resource for understanding the theory and practice of service productivity.

Organizational Structure

The content is organized into fifteen comprehensive chapters, each addressing specific facets of service productivity and its intersection with technology. From the economics of service productivity to the future of service innovation and entrepreneurship, the book offers a rich tapestry of insights and strategies.

We invite you to delve into the pages of *Innovative Technologies for Increasing Service Productivity*, where the nexus of service and technology is explored with depth and precision. May this book serve as a beacon, guiding professionals, academics, and enthusiasts through the intricate landscape of service productivity in the digital era.

ORGANIZATION OF THE BOOK

Chapter 1: Innovating Services Navigating the Digital Frontier

Authored by Yuvika Singh, Esha Bansal, Nisha Chanana, this chapter sets the tone for the book by delving into the crux of service innovation in the digital age. It explores the transformative journey, from disruptive technologies to revolutionary customer experiences, meticulously examining the strategies, challenges, and opportunities defining service innovation. Drawing on real-world examples and cutting-edge research, this chapter provides a nuanced understanding of service innovation's transformative role, emphasizing its profound significance in ensuring organizational resilience and success amidst the dynamic digital landscape.

Chapter 2: Platform Business Models and Service Innovation—A Comprehensive Review of Digital Ecosystems

Authored by Nitish Minz, Anshika Prakash, Meenal Arora, Rishi Chaudhary, Saurav Dixit, this comprehensive research paper explores the transformative forces of platform business models across various industries. It delves into the dynamics of platform-based service innovation, examining their pivotal role and evolution within digital ecosystems. Through an extensive literature review, case studies, and empirical analysis, the chapter not only dissects the key drivers, challenges, and opportunities associated with platform business models but also investigates their implications for stakeholders, including businesses, consumers, and policymakers.

Chapter 3: Revolutionizing Service Productivity—A Roadmap of Innovative Technologies

Authored by Manoj Govindaraj, Chandramowleeswaran Gnanasekaran, Kandavel R, Parvez Khan, Sinh Duc Hoang, this pivotal chapter unfolds a comprehensive exploration of artificial intelligence's transformative influence on service productivity. It meticulously examines AI's foundational principles, manifestations, and real-world impacts on service delivery models. With a focus on deciphering complex data sets and providing actionable insights, the chapter concludes by presenting a practical roadmap for organizations seeking to seamlessly integrate AI into their operations.

Chapter 4: Enhancing Logistics Operations Through Technological Advancements for Superior Service Efficiency

Authored by Ravishankar Krishnan, Elantheraiyan Perumal, Manoj Govindaraj, Logasakthi Kandasamy, this chapter explores the technology-driven shift in logistics management for enhanced service efficiency. It showcases the integration of state-of-the-art technologies like AI, IoT, blockchain, and comprehensive data analytics, transforming logistics into a more capable, dependable, and transparent domain. The chapter emphasizes how embracing digital innovations in logistics is crucial for enhancing service productivity and performance in the fast-paced business landscape.

Chapter 5: Embracing Digital Transformation—A Paradigm Shift in Business Operations and Strategies

Authored by Sanjay Taneja, Rishi Shukla, Amandeep Singh, this research paper delves into the multifaceted implications of digital transformation across various sectors and industries. Analyzing cutting-edge technologies such as artificial intelligence, big data analytics, cloud computing, and the Internet of Things, the chapter elucidates the transformative impact of these innovations on traditional business models. Through case studies and empirical data, it provides insights into the evolving landscape of digital transformation and its profound implications for organizational sustainability and competitiveness in the digital era.

Chapter 6: Digital Transformation and Changes in Business Models for Service Industries—General Principles and Cases From Hospitality, Traveling, Food Delivery

Authored by Mune Moğol Sever, this chapter highlights the inexorable shift of physical worlds to small screens and virtual realms within the service sector. It explores concrete examples through platform works and sample applications, emphasizing that perfect service platforms in today's cyber-physical environment can meet real-time customer demands through innovative and smart technologies such as artificial intelligence and business intelligence.

Chapter 7: Enhancing Service Excellence in the Hospitality Industry Through Effective Service Recovery From Failures

Authored by Sujay Singh, Terrance Ancheary, Anish Mondal, Shashank Rajauria, this chapter investigates the impacts of providing high-quality service and effective service recovery on visitor happiness and overall enterprise success in the hotel and tourism industry. Utilizing a qualitative methodology with focus group interviews, the study aims to improve customer satisfaction and promote success in these fiercely competitive and continuously expanding sectors.

Chapter 8: The Transformation of Human Existence Through the Integration of Artificial Intelligence

Authored by Navpreet Sidhu, Swati Gupta, Renuka Sharma, Kiran Mehta, Sanjay Taneja, this chapter delves into the transformative role of artificial intelligence in reshaping human existence. From robots with human-like features serving in restaurants to the ongoing development of smartphones and smartwatches, the chapter explores how AI is revolutionizing businesses, enhancing human intelligence, and making work more productive and efficient.

Chapter 9: Implementing Artificial Intelligence and Virtual Experiences in Hospitality

Authored by Mohammad Talukder, this chapter explores how artificial intelligence and virtual experiences have revolutionized the hotel and tourism business. From chatbots and virtual assistants handling bookings to AI algorithms optimizing hotel prices, the chapter emphasizes how these technologies are improving efficiency, guest satisfaction, and overall hospitality experiences.

Chapter 10: Artificial intelligence (AI) for Tourism Start-Ups

Authored by Suhail Ghouse, Monica Chaudhary, this chapter explores the intersection of artificial intelligence and startups in the tourism industry. It investigates how AI has the potential to revolutionize operations, innovation, and services for emerging businesses in tourism, showcasing innovative solutions from notable startups and outlining future research directions in maximizing AI benefits in tourism.

Chapter 11: Revolutionizing Creative Tourism—Integrating AI in Marketing for Immersive Travel Experiences

Authored by Ishani Sharma, Arun Aggarwal, this chapter provides a comprehensive review of AI's impact on hospitality and tourist experiences. Examining machine learning, natural language processing, and robotics, the chapter covers AI applications in travel, from chatbots for customer service to VR/AR for immersive experiences, disrupting customers and companies in personalization, decision-making, and predictive analytics.

Chapter 12: Social Media Marketing Strategies for Innovating Relationship Marketing in The Digital Era

Authored by Aaruni Batta, Pallavi Pahuja, Ruby Sharma, this chapter emphasizes the crucial role of social media in real-time communication and feedback for businesses in the digital era. It highlights the shift from traditional word-of-mouth marketing to building strong connections with customers on social media, underscoring the importance of solid customer relationships for sustaining business growth.

Chapter 13: Employer Branding—Pioneering HR Innovations

Authored by Dr. Pallavi Pahuja, Ruby Sharma, Aaruni Batta, this chapter explores the significance of employer branding in today's competitive job market. It emphasizes how HR leaders can shape and sustain a compelling employer brand by embracing innovative HR practices, attracting top talent, and facilitating their growth and development within the organization.

Chapter 14: Robo-Finance Unveiled—A Bibliometric Analysis of Advisory Services in Financial Management

Authored by Divya Goswami, Balraj Verma, this chapter presents a bibliometric analysis correlating financial investment advice with investors. Examining prominent authors and journals in the field, the chapter suggests future research directions, focusing on cognitive biases, financial technology, robo-advisors, and AI in financial advising.

Chapter 15: The Power of Cross-functional Collaboration and Market Knowledge Integration to Achieve Competitive Advantages in the Automobile Sector

Authored by Lochan Chavan, Priya Jindal, this chapter provides insights into cross-functional collaboration and market knowledge integration in the automobile industry. It emphasizes the roles these play in gaining competitive advantages, enhancing essential automotive technology, and fostering innovation within the sector.

Chapter 16: Service Quality and Innovation in Air Transport

Authored by Ravi Lakshmanan, this chapter explores the co-production of passenger services at airports by various organizations. It evaluates services' performance on subjective parameters through customer satisfaction surveys and objective parameters defined by airports. The chapter describes how airports innovate processes and introduce advanced technologies to exceed service quality expectations and enhance passenger experience.

Chapter 17: Innovative Technologies for Healthcare Service Productivity

Authored by Gaganjot Kaur, Shalini Sharma, Reepu, this chapter highlights the rapid changes in healthcare service delivery due to technological innovations. It showcases how new healthcare technologies enhance the efficiency of care services and operational processes, ultimately improving patient outcomes and satisfaction.

Chapter 18: A Review Study on the Challenges and Opportunities in Implementing the Metaverse in Healthcare—An Asian Perspective

Authored by Neha Mishra, Krishna Kumar Mishra, this chapter examines the challenges and opportunities associated with implementing metaverse solutions in Asian healthcare systems. It addresses factors such as infrastructure, cultural considerations, regulatory frameworks, and privacy concerns, providing essential insights into the deployment and acceptance of the metaverse in the healthcare industry.

Chapter 19: Green Shoots of Agriculture—Nurturing Agri Start-ups in Jammu and Kashmir and Punjab: An Incubation Center Perspective

Authored by Ashish Kumar Isher, Veer P Gangwar, SABBEY SHARMA, this research investigates challenges and opportunities confronted by agriculture startups in Jammu & Kashmir and Punjab. With a focus on business incubators, the chapter offers distinctive insights into perceptions on entrepreneurial skills, assesses the relationship between incubation services and startup success, and highlights risk factors and challenges in this sector.

Chapter 20: The Impact of Innovative Strategies on a Small-Scale Service Industry in Ghana

Authored by Richard Afedzie, this chapter uses a qualitative, descriptive case study approach to investigate the impact of innovative strategies on the growth of Compressor Techniques Limited in Ghana. The findings reveal the company's efforts in organizing workshops and seminars to improve employee abilities, recommending regular reviews of internal structures and decision-making processes for approving innovative projects to reach productivity goals.

IN CONCLUSION

In concluding this meticulously curated collection of chapters, we are presented with a panoramic view of innovation's profound impact on diverse service industries in the digital age. Authored by a cadre of esteemed experts, each chapter within this reference book is a testament to the dynamism of service innovation and its role as a linchpin for organizational success in an ever-evolving landscape.

From the transformative influence of artificial intelligence in service productivity to the paradigm shift brought about by digital transformation, our authors have navigated the digital frontier with scholarly rigor, providing insightful analyses, real-world examples, and practical roadmaps for organizations seeking to thrive amidst these changes.

The exploration of platform business models, logistics operations, hospitality excellence, and the integration of AI in diverse sectors collectively paints a comprehensive picture of how technology is reshaping industries. The chapters on social media marketing, employer branding, and innovative strategies underline the importance of human-centric approaches in the digital era, highlighting the interconnectedness of technological advancements and human experiences.

Furthermore, our contributors have ventured into cutting-edge territories, such as the metaverse's potential in healthcare, the rise of agri-startups, and the impact of innovative strategies on small-scale service industries in Ghana. These chapters underscore the global nature of innovation and its ability to transcend boundaries, offering valuable insights into challenges and opportunities unique to various regions.

As we close this compendium, it is evident that the world of service industries is undergoing a transformative revolution. The integration of technology is not just a choice but a necessity for survival and growth. The cross-disciplinary nature of these contributions underscores the interconnectedness of service innovation across sectors, showcasing its far-reaching implications for economic growth, organizational sustainability, and the overall human experience.

We express our gratitude to the esteemed authors for their scholarly contributions, shedding light on the multifaceted dimensions of service innovation. It is our hope that this edited reference book serves as a beacon for academics, practitioners, and policymakers alike, providing a comprehensive understanding of the intricate interplay between technology, innovation, and service excellence. May these insights inspire further exploration and application, propelling organizations into a future where innovation is not just a strategy but a way of life.

Sridhar Manohar
Chitkara University, India

Amit Mittal
Chitkara Business School, Chitkara University, India

Sekar Raju
Iowa State University, USA

Arjun J. Nair
Chitkara University, India

Chapter 1
Innovating Services: Navigating the Digital Frontier

Yuvika Singh
https://orcid.org/0000-0002-7446-6722
The ICFAI University, India

Esha Bansal
The ICFAI University, India

Nisha Chanana
https://orcid.org/0000-0003-0305-2650
The ICFAI University, India

ABSTRACT

In the contemporary digital landscape, service innovation stands as the linchpin for organizational success. This chapter embarks on a transformative journey into the heart of service innovation in the digital age. From disruptive technologies to revolutionary customer experiences, the chapter meticulously explores the multifaceted dimensions of service innovation. Drawing on real-world examples and cutting-edge research, this chapter illuminates the strategies, challenges, and opportunities that define service innovation in the dynamic digital era. Through this comprehensive exploration, it provides a nuanced understanding of the transformative role and profound significance that service innovation holds in ensuring organizational resilience and success amidst the dynamic digital landscape.

1. DIGITAL TRANSFORMATION

Businesses have been under growing pressure to adapt as a result of globalization in recent decades. To overcome this, companies need to seamlessly integrate in order to remain afloat and even thrive in extremely competitive circumstances. Efficient integration can only be achieved through digital processes and collaborative tools (White, 2012). The practical reality is that business models need to shift over time if organizations seek to achieve sustainable value generation which has led to recent advancements

DOI: 10.4018/979-8-3693-2019-8.ch001

in conceptual development. The key to a successful business transformation is simultaneously taking advantage of and examine its potential for achieving organizational agility (Hess et al., 2016). It has been observed that businesses that have been successful in the past face the risk of underperforming if they continue with their old strategies for too long without altering their business plans to take advantage of developments in the landscape of rivalry (Doz and Kosonen, 2010). Amazon has used very effective and sophisticated big data analytics, which has been a major enabler of the firm's success in sales performance (Jannapureddy et al. 2019). This underlines the importance of Digital Transformation for staying competitive. Digital Transformation not only impacts the organizations but people and society too. Digitalization involves creating value for the customers after using the technology, as compared to digitization, which only involves using digital technologies (Seyedghorban et al. 2020).

Several researchers have contributed the definitions of the Digital Transformation. Digitalization is defined as "the use of digital technologies and digitized data to impact how work gets done, transform how customers and companies engage and interact, and create new digital revenue streams (Strønen, 2020). Digital transformation is the use of new digital technologies such as social media, mobile technology, analytics, or embedded devices to enable major business improvements including enhanced customer experiences, streamlined operations, or new business models (Fitzgerald et al., 2014). It is the combined effects of several digital innovations bringing about novel structures, practices, values, and beliefs that change, threaten, replace, or complement existing rules of the game within organizations, ecosystems, industries, or fields. (Hinings et al., 2018). Thus, digital transformation is an organizational transformation that integrates digital technologies and business processes in a digital economy (Liu et al.,2011).

2. COMPONENTS OF DIGITAL TRANSFORMATION

Digital technologies not only impact the transformation of products, business processes, or sales, but entire business models as well (Hess et al., 2016). **Business processes** and **organizational implications** are the two subcategories of research that make up digital business transformation.

2.1 Business Processes

For digital transformation to be implemented, company's strategies must be in accordance with a digital business strategy that integrates IT and business strategy (Bharadwaj et al., 2013; Matt et al., 2015). Digital interactions, digital distribution, and ubiquitous digital reach are trends that companies must prepare for when facing ongoing digital transformation. The fact is that the content can be distributed via a variety of open-access digital communication channels that makes controlling digital distribution crucial (Lanzolla & Anderson, 2008). It was also described that strategic value can be obtained only by digitally activated consumer that requires managing IT deployment and organizational transformation. (Gray et al., 2013). Since IT and digital technologies will strategically enhance the productivity of the business, it must be employed to gain a competitive edge. Organizations will not be able to compete in the rapidly evolving digital world if they cannot rapidly develop and adopt new digital business models and digital transformation strategies.

There are four dimensions for Digital Strategy formulation: the use of technologies, changes in value creation, structural changes, and how to finance digital transformation (Hess et al. 2016). To connect with their technologically advanced customers, businesses must have an online presence. Thus, developing an omnichannel customer community, strengthening e-commerce support for B2B partners, aligning the online brand globally, and upgrading the in-store experience are regarded as crucial steps toward digital transformation (DT) (Hansen and Sia, 2015).

An exploratory framework was developed that described how retail industry can be transformed with the help of digital transformation tools (Hagberg et al., 2016). The framework includes:

2.1.1 Elements of exchanges (changes in modes of payment, communication, distribution etc).

2.1.2 Elements of actors (inclusion of software and technologies and intermixing them with humans) and

2.1.3 Elements of offerings (Changes in products, services and pricing policy).

Addressing the implications of transformation in Operations Management, Big data treatment, data management, and an expanded repertoire of data must be considered. (Gölzer and Fritzsche, 2017). Organizations must reconsider their customer value proposition and what they may offer customers in the digital age. (Berman, 2012). An additional area of study revolves around enterprise architecture (EA). The present EA framework needs to be upgraded to effectively handle digital transformation. Due to recent developments in IT, like cloud computing, mobile IT, and digital IT, enterprise architecture (EA) is now required for addressing technological issues. (Masuda et al., 2018)

Since digital transformation and enterprise architecture are interdependent, an effective enterprise architecture implementation provides a robust input for digital transformation. Thus, the Companies which incorporate digital transformation into their strategy can benefit from its introduction and maintain a competitive edge in the market. Figure 1 illustrates business strategies that can yield a competitive advantage.

Figure 1. Business strategies for competitive advantage
(Kraus, 2021)

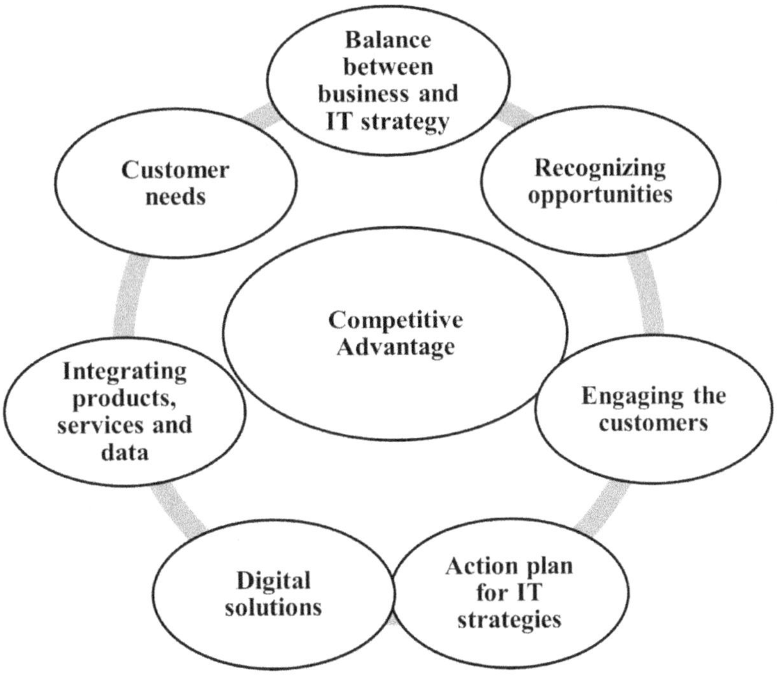

2.2 Organizational Implications

Organizational transformation is a complex, revolutionary, and continuous process that demands fundamental changes in the organizational structures and systems leading to reassessments of organizational norms and values. (Liu et al., 2011). According to (Andriole, 2017), not every firm, business process, or business strategy requires digital transformation. For example, it might be feasible to change an established business model into something more creative and original, but the results might not be as good as they would be with the conventional business model. Employee resistance to digital transformation and the fact that successful businesses sometimes reject change make it challenging to integrate digital transformation within the company. Even though digital transformation increases competitiveness, efficiency, and creativity, it is important to remember that there are dangers involved with any corporate project. (Andriole, 2017). The researchers demonstrated that competitive advantage results from greater resource utilization. They contend that managing digital transformation requires an analysis of available resources and capabilities in addition to external demands. Keeping traditional manufacturing organizations in consideration, digital transformation requires the development of big data analytics skills in response to modifications in product value propositions. Product makers can use digital technology to alter offers based on value propositions and enhance organizational performance by utilizing big data analytics capabilities (Dremel et al., 2017). Digital transformation needs to manage data that big data analytics skills evaluate and utilize, which is recognized as a critical competitive advantage. Agile intra-organizational collaboration and the integration of IT talents are organizational capabilities that are necessary for the analysis of customer data to yield fresh perspectives. Furthermore, reorganizing organizational structures and technology infrastructures is necessary to facilitate the integration of data analytics and IT into decision-making processes.

Employing a web portal as a non-physical IT resource may enhance organizational performance since it reduces costs and aids in the achievement of supporting durable competitive advantages. The performance of organizations is significantly impacted by service-oriented functions, including cloud computing, B2B services, and maintenance services (Chen et al.,2016) Digitization will influence the connected supply chain, which has the advantage of cost reduction and better management of the whole process from the beginning to the end. Additionally, digital manufacturing will play a major role, with new generations of robots that allow multiple assemblies, and the increasing importance of robotics, artificial intelligence, and the internet, which will be part of the new industrial revolution (Accenture, 2017).

3. DIGITAL TRANSFORMATION AND SERVICE ECO SYSTEM

The adoption of digital services requires significant adjustments to an organization's business strategy and operational procedures (Tronvoll et al. 2020). Businesses are shifting their major focus from the products that they provide to integrated ecosystems that include services, and both the manufacturing and service industries seem to be embracing this pattern (Coreynen et al. 2020)

Product-oriented businesses can now create service-oriented business models through digital servitization, owing to the adoption of digital technologies. Digital servitization refers to the transformation of traditional product-centric businesses into service-oriented models using digital technologies. Value chain players are focusing on service-oriented relational arrangements rather than product-oriented transactional models to take advantage of digitalization. (Kamalaldin et al. 2020). There are two organizational viewpoints on digital servitization: front-end and back-end. While back-end servitization aids in improving resource allocation and operational efficiency, front-end servitization fosters more meaningful relationships with customers (Coreynen et al. 2017).

A service ecosystem is defined as "a relatively self-contained, self-adjusting system of resource-integrating actors connected by shared institutional arrangements and mutual value creation through service exchange" (Vargo & Lusch, 2016). Since new technologies have always been at the forefront of digital industrialization, the service industry is one where digital technology are being deployed widely. For instance, digital technology like audiobooks, electronic documents, and e-books (like the Kindle) have influenced media publishing services, leading to the development of online bookstores and electronic subscription service models. (Kulesz 2011) From phone transfer services to automated teller machine (ATM) account transfers, PayPal, online banking, and mobile banking, banking payment options have developed over time. (Flood et al. 2013). Digital Transformation has quiet impeccable impact on 3D Printing Industry. With the advancement of technology, we are seeing a proliferation of applications in several areas like medical, automotive, aerospace, and lifestyle. This manner of production allows for unprecedented design flexibility. Compared to the client-server approach, cloud platforms are new technologies for developing and hosting applications (Kayabay, 2018). Netflix's videotape vending machine service has developed into a streaming service in the realm of video services. The reservation system in lodging and hospitality services has been completely transformed using mobile phones, the Internet, and mobile applications (António and Rita 2021).

4. ROLE OF ARTIFICIAL INTELLIGENCE

In today's digital era, the integration of artificial intelligence (AI) has revolutionized various industries, reshaped traditional practices, and unlocked unprecedented opportunities for innovation and growth. AI, the simulation of human intelligence processes by machines, encompasses a broad spectrum of technologies that enable computers to perform tasks that typically require human intelligence, such as perception, reasoning, learning, and problem-solving (Hess et al., 2016).

One significant role of AI lies in enhancing decision-making processes across different domains. Through advanced algorithms and machine learning techniques, AI systems can analyze vast amounts of data, identify patterns, and generate insights to support informed decision-making (Brynjolfsson & McAfee, 2014). For instance, in healthcare, AI-powered diagnostic tools can assist medical professionals in accurately diagnosing diseases and recommending personalized treatment plans based on patient data and medical records (Davenport & Kalakota, 2019).

Furthermore, AI plays a pivotal role in optimizing operational efficiency and automating routine tasks, thereby enabling organizations to streamline processes and reduce manual effort (Fitzgerald et al., 2014). From predictive maintenance in manufacturing to chatbots in customer service, AI-driven automation enhances productivity and resource utilization while minimizing errors and downtime (Boyd & Crawford, 2012).

Moreover, AI facilitates the development of intelligent systems capable of learning from experience and adapting to new information, a concept known as machine learning. With the paradigm shift in machine learning and deep learning algorithms (Berman, 2012), AI models can achieve remarkable levels of accuracy and performance across various tasks, including image recognition, natural language processing, and autonomous decision-making (Cavoukian & Castro, 2012). These advancements have fueled innovations in self-driving cars, virtual assistants, and recommendation systems, transforming how individuals interact with technology in their daily lives.

However, the widespread adoption of AI also raises ethical and societal concerns, including data privacy, algorithmic bias, and the impact on employment (Provost & Fawcett, 2013). As AI continues to evolve, it is essential to address these challenges through responsible AI governance frameworks, transparent algorithms, and ongoing research into the societal implications of AI technologies (Floridi, 2013). By harnessing the power of AI (Kraus et al., 2021), organizations can drive innovation, improve decision-making, and unlock new possibilities across various industries, paving the way for a future defined by intelligent automation and human-machine collaboration.

4.1 Paradigm Shift in Machine Learning and Deep Learning

The field of artificial intelligence (AI) has seen a significant shift in machine learning and deep learning, driving remarkable progress in various applications. Machine learning, a subset of AI, focuses on algorithms enabling computers to learn from data without explicit programming (Brynjolfsson & McAfee, 2014). Deep learning, a specialized form, uses multi-layered neural networks to extract complex patterns from large datasets (Cavoukian & Castro, 2012). This shift is propelled by factors like big data availability, enhanced computational power, and algorithmic advancements (Berman, 2012). With extensive datasets and powerful computing, researchers can train sophisticated deep learning models for previously daunting tasks.

Deep learning has indeed revolutionized fields such as computer vision and natural language processing. For example, convolutional neural networks (CNNs) have significantly advanced image recognition, achieving performance comparable to human-level capabilities in tasks such as object detection (Brynjolfsson & McAfee, 2014). Similarly, recurrent neural networks (RNNs) and transformer models have demonstrated exceptional proficiency in tasks related to language understanding (Cavoukian & Castro, 2012).

Overall, the paradigm shift in machine learning and deep learning has propelled AI, fostering innovation across domains, with substantial potential to revolutionize industries and enhance human life.

5. DATA-DRIVEN SERVICE INNOVATION IN THE ERA OF DIGITAL TRANSFORMATION

Data-driven service innovation refers to the practice of utilizing data insights and analytics to create, develop, or enhance services, improving their effectiveness, efficiency, and customer satisfaction. It involves leveraging data to identify opportunities for innovation, make informed decisions, and design services that align with customer needs and preferences.

Bitner and Wirtz (2019), Maglio and Spohrer (2008), and Gallouj and Savona (2009) advocate the strategic application of data and analytics, emphasizing a deep understanding of customer behavior and market dynamics as crucial for fostering continuous improvement and gaining a competitive edge. Westerman et al. (2011) underscores the importance of leveraging data analytics, machine learning, and customer insights to proactively create, adapt, or optimize services, thereby addressing customer needs with precision and agility. Brynjolfsson and McAfee (2014) highlight the significance of aligning business strategies with actionable insights, fostering a culture of continual improvement and customer-centricity. Additionally, Frow et al. (2015) emphasize the role of active customer participation in co-creating and refining services, enabling organizations to anticipate and meet customer demands in a hyper-personalized and agile manner.

The core essence of data-driven service innovation permeates beyond analytics; it's an amalgamation of customer-centricity, nimbleness, and collaborative ideation. This amalgam of data analytics, customer insights, and innovative practices births services that transcend the conventional, delivering augmented value to customers while fortifying organizations' competitive edge in a dynamic market landscape.

6. UNVEILING THE BROAD CANVAS OF DATA-DRIVEN SERVICE INNOVATION

The canvas of data-driven service innovation unfurls across multifarious domains where organizations harness data and analytics to transcend conventional service paradigms.

6.1 Pioneering Continuous Learning and Adaptation

Establishing a culture of perpetual evolution, data-driven insights serve as the compass for adapting services in sync with dynamic customer needs and ever-evolving market dynamics (Brown and Eisenhardt, 1998).

6.2 Harvesting Feedback for Service Excellence

Extracting precious customer feedback from an array of channels facilitates service refinement and innovation, fostering unparalleled customer experiences (Reichheld and Schefter, 2000).

6.3 Personalization through Customer Segmentation

Leveraging data for granular customer segmentation enables bespoke service offerings tailored to individual preferences, behaviors, and demographics, heralding a new era of personalized experiences (Gupta et al., 2004).

6.4 Augmented Reality Redefining Service Landscapes

Integrating AR technology with data immersion elevates service experiences, offering unprecedented levels of interactivity and information dissemination (Teixeira et al., 2012).

6.5 Optimized Service Processes for Superior Quality

Analyzing operational data is the cornerstone for streamlining service delivery, eradicating inefficiencies, and elevating service quality benchmarks (Fitzsimmons and Fitzsimmons, 2013).

6.6 Ethical Data Usage and Privacy Compliance

Upholding the highest standards of data ethics and privacy regulations not only instills trust but also ensures sustained customer confidence in data-driven services (Tene and Polonetsky, 2013).

6.7 IoT Pioneering Smart Services

Leveraging IoT data delivers connected services with real-time insights and predictive maintenance, ushering in a new era of intelligent service offerings (Vermesan & Friess, 2014).

6.8 Blockchain Redefining Transactional Trust

The implementation of blockchain technology ensures unprecedented transparency, traceability, and security in service transactions, bolstering trust and integrity (Crosby et al., 2016).

6.9 Fortifying Services With Cybersecurity Measures

Employing data-centric approaches fortifies service delivery with robust cybersecurity measures, safeguarding data integrity and customer trust (Ransbotham et al., 2017).

6.10 Dynamic Pricing

Data analytics fuel dynamic pricing models, optimizing service charges based on demand fluctuations and evolving customer behaviors (Bertsimas and Paschalidis, 2018).

6.11 AI-Driven Personalized Support

Implementing AI-powered chatbots and virtual assistants offers real-time, personalized customer support and guidance, enriching customer interactions (Li et al., 2020).

6.12 Enabling Collaborative Service Platforms

Fostering platforms facilitating customer-provider collaboration fuels service co-creation based on shared data and insights, engendering innovation and mutual growth (Osterwalder et al., 2014).

These areas illustrate the multifaceted nature of data-driven service innovation, showcasing how organizations can leverage data across different domains to innovate and improve their service offerings.

7. REVOLUTIONIZING SERVICE INNOVATION: UNVEILING THE BIG DATA ANALYTICS PARADIGM

The infusion of big data analytics into service innovation marks a watershed moment, reshaping the fundamental tenets of how organizations conceive, create, and deliver services. This transformative shift embodies a holistic embrace of voluminous data to propel innovation, elevate customer experiences, and optimize service delivery. Here unfolds an intricate exploration of the monumental paradigm shift catalyzed by big data analytics within service innovation:

7.1 Data-Centric Precision

Departing from conventional practices, organizations prioritize data-driven decision-making, transcending intuition or traditional research methodologies. Big data analytics orchestrates a systematic analysis of diverse data sources encompassing customer behavior, market trends, and operational metrics, birthing actionable insights (Davenport and Harris, 2007).

7.2 Service Agility

Big data analytics instigates an agile ethos in service development and enhancement. This agility empowers rapid iteration and adaptation based on real-time feedback and data-derived insights, ensuring services perpetually resonate with relevance and competitiveness (McAfee and Brynjolfsson, 2012).

7.3 Ethical Data Guardianship

In tandem with increased data utilization, a parallel spotlight shines on ethical data stewardship. Organizations championing this paradigm pivot prioritize data sanctity, privacy, and compliance with regulations, upholding the sacrosanct trust of their clientele (Tene and Polonetsky, 2013).

7.4 Converging Insights

The paradigm heralds an era of data convergence, amalgamating inputs from disparate realms - IoT, social media, transactional data - to yield holistic insights. This synthesis affords a panoramic comprehension of customer behaviors and preferences (Gandomi and Haider, 2015).

7.5 Real-Time Illumination

A pivotal facet of this paradigm is the accentuation on real-time analytics, empowering organizations to swiftly navigate shifting market dynamics and evolving customer demands. Processing and deciphering data in the moment enable immediate course corrections in service offerings or strategies (Marz and Warren, 2015).

7.6 Customer-Centric Innovations

Central to this transformative shift is a relentless focus on understanding and gratifying customer needs through an expansive canvas of customer data. This tailoring of services to individual preferences elevates customer satisfaction and forges unassailable loyalty bonds (Li et al., 2019).

This seismic paradigm shift signifies a fundamental departure in organizational approach towards service innovation.

8. THE TRANSFORMATIVE INFLUENCE OF BIG DATA ANALYTICS IN SERVICE INNOVATION

8.1 Defining Big Data Analytics in Service Innovation

Big data analytics in service innovation embodies a methodical application of advanced analytical techniques to unravel insights from vast and intricate datasets. This process navigates through the intricate landscape of structured and unstructured data, sourced from diverse channels including customer interactions, IoT ecosystems, and social media platforms.

8.2 Deciphering Customer Behavior

Big data analytics facilitates comprehensive insights into customer data, unraveling nuanced preferences, behaviors, and evolving trends. This depth of understanding forms the bedrock for tailoring services precisely to meet individual customer preferences and market dynamics (Davenport and Harris, 2007).

8.3 Predictive Precision in Service Customization

Leveraging predictive analytics empowers organizations to foresee customer needs, customizing services with exceptional precision to match individual preferences (Provost and Fawcett, 2013). Through predictive models, companies proactively adapt services, ensuring alignment with evolving customer requirements which allows for the crafting of services, elevating customer satisfaction.

8.4 Real-Time Decision Dynamics

Real-time data processing empowers swift decision-making, enabling organizations to promptly enhance service offerings and strategies based on actionable insights (Marz and Warren, 2015). The agility in decision-making afforded by real-time analytics ensures organizations remain responsive to changing market dynamics and evolving customer needs.

8.5 Elevating Customer Engagement

Tailoring services to meet specific customer needs enhances engagement, nurturing stronger connections and heightened satisfaction (Li et al., 2019). This tailoring, based on in-depth insights gleaned from big data analytics, offers personalized experiences that resonate deeply with individual preferences.

8.6 Identifying Service Lacunae

Analyzing expansive datasets identifies gaps within existing services, guiding organizations to refine and improve service quality (Wang et al., 2004). By pinpointing areas of improvement, companies can strategically address shortcomings, ensuring services meet or exceed customer expectations. This keen understanding of service gaps directs focused efforts toward enhancing service quality and efficiency.

8.7 Operational Alacrity Through Data Optimization

Optimizing operations based on data insights streamlines efficiency, reducing costs without compromising service excellence (McAfee and Brynjolfsson, 2012). Leveraging these insights fosters a delicate balance between operational efficiency and service quality, ensuring cost-effectiveness without compromising on delivering exceptional service experiences.

8.8 Anticipating Market Trends

Extracting insights to predict trends enables agile adaptations in services, ensuring companies remain ahead of the curve in dynamic markets (Gandomi and Haider, 2015). By forecasting market trends, organizations proactively tailor services to align with emerging customer needs and market shifts, maintaining a competitive edge.

8.9 Fortifying Reliability Through Risk Management

Preemptive risk mitigation solidifies reliability, instilling unwavering trust and confidence among customers (Holsapple and Wu, 2011). Identifying and mitigating risks associated with service delivery assures customers of reliability and establishes a foundation of trust.

8.10 IoT's Symphony in Service Enhancement

Leveraging IoT insights drives predictive maintenance, ensuring seamless and efficient service delivery (Vermesan and Friess, 2014). Harnessing IoT data allows organizations to predict maintenance needs, preventing disruptions and maintaining consistent service quality.

8.11 Innovating Healthcare Services Through Data

The application of predictive insights transforms healthcare services, offering personalized care and treatment (Davenport and Kalakota, 2019). Predictive analytics in healthcare enhances patient experiences, optimizing treatments and care plans based on individual patient data.

8.12 Sentimental Narratives for Service Improvements

Refining services based on sentiment analysis from customer feedback aligns offerings more closely with customer sentiments, augmenting overall service experiences (Li, 2012). By understanding customer sentiments, organizations tailor services to match emotional needs, enhancing overall satisfaction.

8.13 Blockchain's Assurance in Services

Implementing blockchain technology ensures transparency and security, reinforcing customer trust and reliability (Crosby et al., 2016). Blockchain integration provides a secure framework, ensuring transparency and traceability in service transactions.

8.14 Harnessing Social Media Insights

Insights from social media data refine services by aligning them with customer preferences and sentiments, enhancing overall service experiences (Boyd and Crawford, 2012). Analyzing social media data provides insights into customer sentiments, preferences, and interactions, shaping more effective service strategies.

8.15 Predictive Precision in Maintenance

Predictive maintenance strategies minimize downtime, ensuring service reliability and operational efficiency (Janssen and Wagenaar, 2017). Leveraging predictive maintenance mitigates service disruptions, ensuring consistent service delivery.

8.16 Elevating Service Innovation Through Ethical Data Practices

Ethical data practices maintain trust and compliance, fortifying the relationship between organizations and customers (Tene and Polonetsky, 2013). Ethical data handling ensures compliance with regulations, fostering a culture of trust and reliability.

8.17 Fostering Collaborative Service Platforms

Platforms encouraging collaboration facilitate co-creation, significantly enhancing customer engagement and satisfaction (Osterwalder, 2014). Collaborative platforms enable customers to participate in service co-creation, fostering deeper engagement and satisfaction.

8.18 Augmented Reality: A Tapestry of Enhanced Services

Integration with AR technology enriches service interactions, offering immersive and engaging experiences (Teixeira et al., 2012). Augmented reality enhances service experiences, providing interactive and informative engagements.

8.19 Continuous Evolution

A culture of continuous learning adapts services dynamically to market shifts and evolving customer needs (Brown and Eisenhardt, 1998). Embracing continual learning ensures services remain agile and responsive to changing market dynamics.

8.20 Eco-Conscious Service Strategies

Identifying sustainable models resonates with environmentally conscious customers, aligning services with eco-friendly values (Sharma and Borle, 2020). Eco-friendly service models cater to environmentally conscious consumers, fostering goodwill and loyalty.

8.21 Customer-Centric Co-Creation Through Data Insights

Leveraging insights fosters co-creation, ensuring evolving services align with and exceed customer expectations (Frow et al. 2015). Customer-centric co-creation ensures services are aligned with customer preferences, encouraging active engagement.

9. LEVERAGING DATA INSIGHTS: ELEVATING CUSTOMER EXPERIENCES AND OPERATIONAL EXCELLENCE

Leveraging data insights to predict customer needs, optimize processes, and enhance service offerings is a fundamental strategy for organizations aiming to improve customer experiences and operational efficiency. The utilization of data insights involves the systematic collection, analysis, and interpretation of diverse data sets to extract actionable information that guides decision-making processes within organizations. This approach enables organizations to anticipate customer needs, streamline operations, and refine services. By analyzing historical and real-time customer data (such as purchase history, browsing behavior, feedback), organizations can identify patterns and trends. These insights aid in predicting future needs and preferences, allowing proactive service adjustments or personalized recommendations. By analyzing performance metrics, bottlenecks, and resource utilization, organizations can identify areas for improvement, streamline workflows, and enhance overall efficiency. Understanding customer behaviors and preferences helps in tailoring services to meet specific needs. Optimizing processes based on data insights leads to reduced operational costs, improved resource allocation, and streamlined workflows (McAfee and Brynjolfsson, 2012; Li et al., 2019).

9.1 How Organizations Leverage Data Insights?

Employing machine learning and predictive models allows organizations to anticipate future customer behavior, preferences, and market trends. This predictive foresight aids in crafting proactive strategies and delivering personalized services (Provost and Fawcett, 2013). Segmentation based on behavior, demographics, or preferences facilitates targeted marketing and tailored services for diverse customer groups. Inefficiencies in workflows or service delivery are identified and addressed, enhancing service quality by streamlining processes and reducing wait times. Data insights serve as a compass for innovation, uncovering areas for service enhancement aligned with evolving customer needs and market demands.

10. EXEMPLARS OF DATA-DRIVEN SUCCESS

Numerous companies showcase the impact of data-driven insights through the following trends:

Figure 2. Key strategies and methodologies
(Tashman, 2000; Chen and Wei, 2001; Liu, 2012; Kohavi et al., 2012; Vermesan and Friess, 2014; Tene and Polonetsky, 2013; Verhoef et al., 2015; Marz and Warren, 2015)

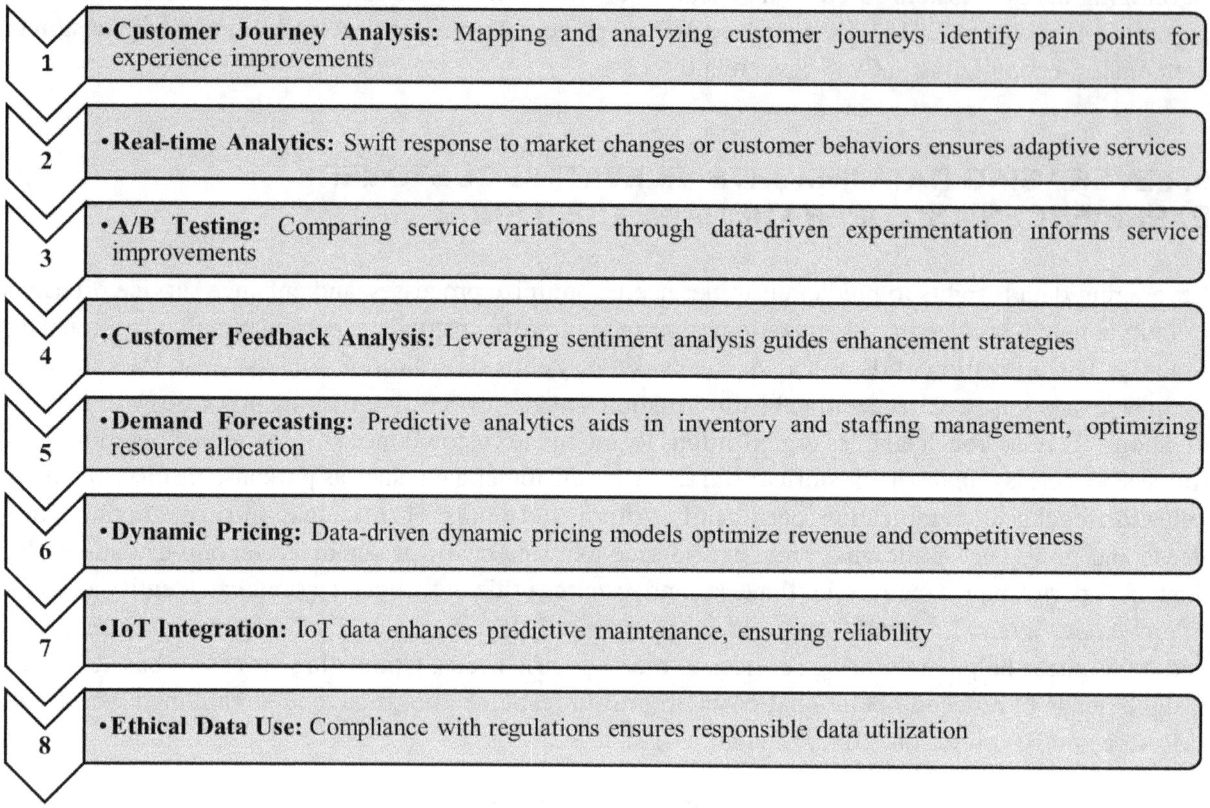

10.1 Amazon

10.1.1 Data-Driven Approach

Amazon's success is attributed to its robust data-driven approach, particularly evident in its recommendation engine and personalized shopping experiences (Verhoef et al., 2015).

10.1.2 Customer Behavior Analysis

Amazon analyzes various aspects of customer behavior, including past purchases, browsing history, and user interactions with the platform (Verhoef et al., 2015).

10.1.3 Predictive Analytics

By leveraging predictive analytics, Amazon predicts customer needs and preferences, thereby enhancing the shopping experience and increasing customer satisfaction (Verhoef et al., 2015).

10.2 Netflix

10.2.1 Sophisticated Algorithms

Netflix employs sophisticated algorithms based on user viewing history and preferences (Liu, 2012).

10.2.2 Personalized Content Recommendations

The platform offers personalized content recommendations to users based on their individual preferences, enhancing user engagement and retention (Liu, 2012).

10.2.3 Continuous Improvement

Netflix continually refines its algorithms based on user feedback and viewing patterns, ensuring that recommendations remain relevant and compelling (Liu, 2012).

10.3 Uber

10.3.1 Demand Prediction

Uber utilizes data insights to predict rider demands, enabling the company to allocate resources effectively and improve service availability (Chen and Wei, 2001).

10.3.2 Route Optimization

Data analytics helps Uber optimize routes, reducing travel time and enhancing the overall efficiency of its transportation network (Chen and Wei, 2001).

10.3.3 Dynamic Pricing

The implementation of surge pricing strategies based on data analysis allows Uber to balance supply and demand, ensuring that riders can always find a ride when needed (Chen and Wei, 2001).

10.4 Walmart

10.4.1 Demand Forecasting

Walmart leverages data analytics for demand forecasting, analyzing historical sales data and external factors such as weather patterns to predict future demand accurately (Tashman, 2000).

10.4.2 Inventory Management

By optimizing its inventory levels based on data-driven insights, Walmart minimizes stockouts and overstock situations, improving customer satisfaction and operational efficiency (Tashman, 2000).

10.4.3 Cost Savings

Efficient inventory management leads to cost savings for Walmart by reducing carrying costs and minimizing losses due to obsolete or excess inventory (Tashman, 2000).

10.5 Airbnb

10.5.1 User Preferences Analysis

Airbnb analyzes user preferences and behavior on the platform to personalize accommodation recommendations (Kohavi et al., 2012).

10.5.2 Tailored Listings

By suggesting tailored listings based on user preferences, Airbnb enhances the user experience and increases the likelihood of bookings (Kohavi et al., 2012).

10.5.3 Enhanced User Engagement

Personalized recommendations contribute to higher user engagement and satisfaction, driving increased usage and revenue for Airbnb (Kohavi et al., 2012).

10.6 Tesla

10.6.1 Predictive Maintenance

Tesla utilizes data from its vehicles to perform predictive maintenance, identifying potential issues before they occur (Vermesan and Friess, 2014).

10.6.2 Proactive Maintenance

By proactively addressing maintenance issues based on data analytics, Tesla improves vehicle reliability and customer satisfaction (Vermesan and Friess, 2014).

10.6.3 Continuous Monitoring

Continuous monitoring of vehicle data allows Tesla to gather insights and feedback, enabling ongoing improvements to vehicle performance and reliability (Vermesan and Friess, 2014).

11. STARTUPS AS DIGITAL TRANSFORMATION ACCELERATORS

Startups are essential to the growth and innovation of big businesses undergoing digital transformation. Major companies understand that finding new growth drivers through deeper partnerships with creative players who can challenge their own assets—which would otherwise compromise for the status quo—is essential to being competitive. Communication and marketing are essential to a start-up's success. It is impossible to separate a business's market appearance from the appropriate design of an integrated communication channel that serves as an intermediary between the startup and the marketplace. The creative mindset of this kind of business additionally requires guidance on the communication strategy to be used; therefore, a quick and informal approach utilizing a variety of social media platforms and communication channels is required.

Let's examine the key factors they must consider to be successful (Hagberg et al., 2016):

Enhance awareness: The company must comprehend emerging trends and be knowledgeable about cutting-edge technologies. It is advisable to critically examine the business strategy considering the ongoing digital revolution.

Try this to learn forming alliances, collaborations, and ecosystems is crucial. They ought to form autonomous, flexible teams and take a prototype approach.

Increasing the scope of operations to increase impact: Rethinking business models by choosing to improve the current configuration or establishing spin-offs.

11.1 Challenges Faced by SMEs due to Unchanged Technology

A business could encounter several difficulties that could affect its competitiveness, productivity, and long-term viability if it decides not to adopt digital transformation. Online platforms are becoming more and more important to organizations and consumers in the digital age. A business may lose a sizable chunk of its target market if it doesn't have a digital presence. Some of the challenges are as follows (Hagberg et al., 2016; Rupeika-Apoga & Petrovska, 2022):

11.1.1 Inefficiency & Productivity Issues

Productivity and efficiency are frequently increased by digital tools and technologies. Businesses who don't use these technologies could find it difficult to compete with rivals who do so in order to perform better. Small and medium-sized businesses (SMEs) without automated systems could find it difficult to automate repetitive processes, which would reduce productivity and raise operating expenses.

11.1.2 Limited Access to Markets

SMEs may miss out on opportunities to expand their market reach and attract new clients who prefer to utilize digital platforms to explore and buy goods and services beyond local markets.

11.1.3 Data Security and Compliance Concerns

SMEs may be vulnerable to cybersecurity risks if they use antiquated technology, which could result in data breaches, an overall decrease in customer confidence, and possible legal and regulatory repercussions.

11.1.4 Customer Experience and Satisfaction

The inability to personalize offerings and information due to a lack of data analytics and CRM capabilities may negatively affect client retention.

11.1.5 Innovation Gap

In industries whose market dynamics are driven by technological improvements, a lack of investment in technology can lead to an innovation gap that makes it difficult to maintain competitiveness.

11.1.6 High Operational Costs

Due to higher maintenance expenses, more downtime, and difficulty sourcing new components or expertise, maintaining obsolete equipment can be expensive.

12. NAVIGATING ETHICAL FRONTIERS IN DIGITAL SERVICE INNOVATIONS

The surge of innovative technologies within the digital realm has propelled remarkable advancements in service offerings. However, within this landscape of innovation, a myriad of ethical challenges emerges, primarily revolving around user privacy and data security. As organizations harness technology to enrich services, addressing these ethical dilemmas becomes pivotal to foster user trust and uphold the ethical integrity of digital service platforms.

12.1 Challenges in Ethical Terrain

12.1.1 User Privacy and Data Collection

Striking a balance between necessary data collection for service enhancement while respecting user privacy raises ethical concerns (Floridi, 2013).

12.1.2 Third-Party Data Sharing and Consent

Ensuring explicit consent for user data shared with third parties upholds ethical standards (Solove, 2008).

12.1.3 User Profiling and Behavioral Analytics

Ethical use of user data for profiling and predictive analytics requires scrutiny on user consent and behavioral manipulation (Mittelstadt et al., 2016).

12.1.4 Geolocation and Tracking

The ethical dimension of collecting geolocation data demands user consent and awareness (Hennessey, 2013).

12.1.5 Data Retention and Deletion

Ethical considerations arise in determining data retention duration and offering mechanisms for data deletion (Narayanan and Vitaly, 2008).

12.2 Risks in Data Security and Integrity

12.2.1 Cyber Threats and Vulnerabilities

Evolving cyber threats jeopardize digital platform security, leading to data breaches (Schneier, 2004).

12.2.2 Insufficient Security Measures

Weak encryption, authentication, and access controls heighten unauthorized access risks (Ferguson and Bruce, 2003).

12.2.3 IoT Security Challenges

Expanding IoT device networks raise security challenges, demanding enhanced protection (Gubbi et al., 2013).

12.2.4 Supply Chain Vulnerabilities

Third-party vulnerabilities in the supply chain pose threats to service integrity (Rosenberg, 2008).

12.2.5 Ransomware and Extortion

Ransomware attacks raise ethical dilemmas concerning data integrity and payments (Choo, 2011).

12.3 Ethical Considerations and Solutions

12.3.1 Privacy-Centric Design

Embracing "privacy by design" principles ensures privacy integration into digital service architecture (Cavoukian and Daniel, 2012).

12.3.2 User-Centric Transparency

Transparent communication about data practices fosters user trust (Cranor, 2012).

12.3.3 Data Minimization and Anonymization

Collecting only essential data and anonymization practices limit personally identifiable information (Sweeney, 2002).

12.3.4 AI Algorithm Governance

Frameworks auditing AI algorithms ensure fairness and transparency, mitigating biases (Jobin, 2019).

12.3.5 Compliance With Regulations

Adhering to global data protection regulations maintains ethical data use (Greenleaf and Nigel, 2017).

Conclusively, embracing ethical considerations in digital service innovations is paramount to ensure user trust, data integrity, and responsible technology utilization within this evolving landscape.

13. CYBER SECURITY AND DIGITAL INNOVATION

In the landscape of digital innovation, marked by rapid growth and transformation, ethical quandaries and security imperatives stand as pivotal concerns. Achieving a delicate equilibrium between leveraging data-driven technologies and preserving user privacy becomes paramount. Navigating the complexities of transparent data practices, regulatory compliance, and ethical considerations is vital to engender user trust and safeguard the integrity of digital platforms (Menezes, 1996; Whitman and Herbert, 2018). Meanwhile, fortifying cybersecurity measures through robust encryption, incident response planning, and collaborative industry efforts is crucial to mitigate emerging risks posed by cyber threats (Bejtlich, 2013; Vacca, 2017). This convergence of ethical principles and cybersecurity imperatives serves as the linchpin in crafting an ethical, secure, and resilient digital ecosystem, fostering sustained innovation and bolstering user confidence in the ever-evolving digital domain.

14. CONCLUSION

"Innovating Services: Navigating the Digital Frontier" promises a captivating exploration of service innovation in the digital age. By demystifying complexities, offering practical insights, and showcasing pioneering examples, this chapter empowers readers to embrace digital transformation, ensuring their services resonate with the digital-savvy consumers of today and tomorrow. Through this chapter, readers will embark on a transformative journey, mastering the art of digital service innovation in the dynamic and ever-evolving digital landscape.

REFERENCES

Andriole, S. J. (2017). Five myths about digital transformation. *MIT Sloan Management Review*, *58*(3), 20–22.

António, N., & Rita, P. (2021). COVID 19: The catalyst for digital transformation in the hospitality industry? *Tourism & Management Studies*, *17*(2), 41–46. doi:10.18089/tms.2021.170204

Baesens, B., Van Vlasselaer, V., Verbeke, W., & Vanthienen, J. (2015). Big data analytics in the fight against cybercrime. *Journal of Management Information Systems*, *32*(2), 319–346.

Bejtlich, R. (2013). *The Practice of Network Security Monitoring: Understanding Incident Detection and Response*. No Starch Press.

Berman, S. J. (2012). Digital transformation: Opportunities to create new business models. *Strategy and Leadership*, *40*(2), 16–24. doi:10.1108/10878571211209314

Bertsimas, D., & Paschalidis, I. C. (2018). The Price of Fairness. *Operations Research*, *66*(5), 1283–1300.

Bitner, M. J., & Wirtz, J. (2019). *Services Marketing: Integrating Customer Focus Across the Firm*. McGraw-Hill Education.

Boyd, D., & Crawford, K. (2012). Critical questions for big data: Provocations for a cultural, technological, and scholarly phenomenon. *Information Communication and Society*, *15*(5), 662–679. doi:10.1080/1369118X.2012.678878

Brown, S. L., & Eisenhardt, K. M. (1998). *Competing on the Edge: Strategy as Structured Chaos*. Harvard Business Press.

Brynjolfsson, E., & McAfee, A. (2014). *The Second Machine Age: Work, Progress, and Prosperity in a Time of Brilliant Technologies*. W. W. Norton & Company.

Cavoukian, A., & Castro, D. (2012). *Privacy by Design: The 7 Foundational Principles*. Information and Privacy Commissioner of Ontario.

Chen, L., & Wei, K. K. (2001). The impact of the individual's perceived market orientation on the acceptance of new technology. *The Journal of High Technology Management Research*, *12*(2), 183–209.

Chin, H., Marasini, D. P., & Lee, D. (2023). Digital transformation trends in service industries. *Service Business*, *17*(1), 11–36. doi:10.1007/s11628-022-00516-6

Choo, K.-K. R. (2011). The Cyber Threat Landscape: Challenges and Future Research Directions. *Computers & Security*, *30*(8), 719–731. doi:10.1016/j.cose.2011.08.004

Coreynen, W., Matthyssens, P., Vanderstraeten, J., & van Witteloostuijn, A. (2020). Unravelling the internal and external drivers of digital servitization: A dynamic capabilities and contingency perspective on firm strategy. *Industrial Marketing Management*, *89*, 265–277. doi:10.1016/j.indmarman.2020.02.014

Cranor, L. F., & McDonald, A. M. (2012). Building the Future of Privacy Notices: A Survey of Plans for Change and Barriers to Change. *International Journal of Human-Computer Studies*, *70*(10), 711–722.

Crosby, M., Pattanayak, P., Verma, S., & Kalyanaraman, V. (2016). Blockchain technology: Beyond bitcoin. *Applied Innovation*, *2*(6-10), 71–81.

Davenport, T. H., & Harris, J. (2007). *Competing on Analytics: The New Science of Winning*. Harvard Business Press.

Davenport, T. H., & Kalakota, R. (2019). The potential for artificial intelligence in healthcare. *Future Healthcare Journal*, *6*(2), 94–98. doi:10.7861/futurehosp.6-2-94 PMID:31363513

Dremel, C., Herterich, M. M., Wulf, J., Waizmann, J.-C., & Brenner, W. (2017). How AUDI AG established big data analytics in its digital transformation. *MIS Quarterly Executive*, *16*(2), 81–100.

Ferguson, N., & Schneier, B. (2003). *Practical Cryptography*. Wiley Publishing.

Fitzgerald, M., Kruschwitz, N., Bonnet, D., & Welch, M. (2014). Embracing digital technology: A new strategic imperative. *MIT Sloan Management Review*, *55*(2), 1.

Fitzsimmons, J. A., & Fitzsimmons, M. J. (2013). *Service Management: Operations, Strategy, Information Technology*. McGraw-Hill Education.

Flood, D., West, T., & Wheadon, D. (2013). Trends in mobile payments in developing and advanced economies. *Bulletin*, *2013*, 71–80.

Floridi, L. (2013). *The Ethics of Information*. Oxford University Press. doi:10.1093/acprof:oso/9780199641321.001.0001

Frow, P., Nenonen, S., Payne, A., & Storbacka, K. (2015). Managing co-creation design: A strategic approach to innovation. *British Journal of Management*, *26*(3), 463–483. doi:10.1111/1467-8551.12087

Gallouj, F., & Savona, M. (2009). Innovation in services: A review of the debate and a research agenda. *Journal of Evolutionary Economics*, *19*(2), 149–172. doi:10.1007/s00191-008-0126-4

Gandomi, A., & Haider, M. (2015). Beyond the hype: Big data concepts, methods, and analytics. *International Journal of Information Management*, *35*(2), 137–144. doi:10.1016/j.ijinfomgt.2014.10.007

Gerth, A. B., & Peppard, J. (2016). The dynamics of CIO derailment: How CIOs come undone and how to avoid it. *Business Horizons*, *59*(1), 61–70. doi:10.1016/j.bushor.2015.09.001

Gölzer, P., & Fritzsche, A. (2017). Data-driven operations management: Organisational implications of the digital transformation in industrial practice. *Production Planning and Control*, *28*(16), 1332–1343. doi:10.1080/09537287.2017.1375148

Gray, P., El Sawy, O. A., Asper, G., & Thordarson, M. (2013). Realizing strategic value through center-edge digital transformation in consumer-centric industries. *MIS Quarterly Executive*, *12*(1), 1–17.

Greenleaf, G., & Waters, N. (2017). The EU General Data Protection Regulation: What Change Will It Bring? *International Data Privacy Law*, *7*(2), 122–145.

Gubbi, J., Buyya, R., Marusic, S., & Palaniswami, M. (2013). Internet of Things (IoT): A Vision, Architectural Elements, and Future Directions. *Future Generation Computer Systems*, *29*(7), 1645–1660. doi:10.1016/j.future.2013.01.010

Gupta, S., Lehmann, D. R., & Stuart, J. A. (2004). Valuing customers. *JMR, Journal of Marketing Research*, *41*(1), 7–18. doi:10.1509/jmkr.41.1.7.25084

Hagberg, J., Sundstrom, M., & Egels-Zandén, N. (2016). The digitalization of retailing: An exploratory framework. *International Journal of Retail & Distribution Management*, *44*(7), 694–712. doi:10.1108/IJRDM-09-2015-0140

Hansen, R., & Sia, S. K. (2015). Hummel's digital transformation toward omnichannel retailing: Key lessons learned. *MIS Quarterly Executive*, *14*(2), 51–66.

Hennessey, J. (2013). Location Technologies: Risks and Threats to Privacy. *The Journal of Privacy and Confidentiality*, *5*(2), 51–68.

Hess, T., Benlian, A., Matt, C., & Wiesböck, F. (2016). Options for formulating a digital transformation strategy. *MIS Quarterly Executive*, *15*(2), 123–139.

Hinings, B., Gegenhuber, T., & Greenwood, R. (2018). Digital innovation and transformation: An institutional perspective. *Information and Organization*, *28*(1), 52–61. doi:10.1016/j.infoandorg.2018.02.004

Holsapple, C. W., & Wu, J. (2011). Modeling customer knowledge for customer relationship management. *Decision Support Systems*, *51*(4), 1064–1074.

Jannapureddy, R., Vien, Q.-T., Shah, P., & Trestian, R. (2019). An auto-scaling framework for analyzing big data in the cloud environment. *Applied Sciences (Basel, Switzerland)*, *9*(7), 1417. doi:10.3390/app9071417

Janssen, M., & Wagenaar, R. (2017). Big and Open Linked Data (BOLD) in government: A challenge to transparency and privacy? *Government Information Quarterly*, *34*(3), 355–364.

Jobin, A. (2019). *The Ethics of AI Ethics: An Evaluation of Guidelines*. arXiv preprint arXiv:1903.03425.

Kamalaldin, A., Linde, L., Sjödin, D., & Parida, V. (2020). Transforming provider-customer relationships in digital servitization: A relational view on digitalization. *Industrial Marketing Management*, *89*, 306–325. doi:10.1016/j.indmarman.2020.02.004

Kayabay, K., Gökalp, M. O., Eren, P. E., & Koçyiğit, A. (2018). [WiP] A Workflow and Cloud-Based Service-Oriented Architecture for Distributed Manufacturing in Industry 4.0 Context. *2018 IEEE 11th Conference on Service-Oriented Computing and Applications (SOCA)*. IEEE. 10.1109/SOCA.2018.00020

Kohavi, R., Deng, A., Frasca, B., Longbotham, R., Walker, T., & Xu, Y. (2012). Trustworthy Online Controlled Experiments: Five Puzzling Outcomes Explained. *Proceedings of the 18th ACM SIGKDD International Conference on Knowledge Discovery and Data Mining*, (pp. 786-794). IEEE. 10.1145/2339530.2339653

Kraus, S., Jones, P., Kailer, N., Weinmann, A., Chaparro-Banegas, N., & Roig-Tierno, N. (2021). Digital Transformation: An Overview of the Current State of the Art of Research. *SAGE Open*, *11*(3). doi:10.1177/21582440211047576

Kulesz, O. (2011). *Digital publishing in developing countries*. International Alliance of Independent Publishers.

Lanzolla, G., & Anderson, J. (2008). Digital transformation. *Business Strategy Review*, *19*(2), 72–76. doi:10.1111/j.1467-8616.2008.00539.x

Li, H., Suomi, R., & Törnroos, J. A. (2019). Customer engagement through big data analytics. *Industrial Management & Data Systems*, *119*(9), 1877–1897.

Li, X., Liu, D., Hu, X., & Yu, P. S. (2020). Chatbot in customer service and e-commerce: State-of-the-art and research directions. *IEEE Access : Practical Innovations, Open Solutions*, *8*, 191625–191648.

Liedtka, J. (2018). Why Design Thinking Works. *Harvard Business Review*, *96*(5), 72–79.

Liu, B. (2012). Sentiment Analysis and Opinion Mining. *Synthesis Lectures on Human Language Technologies*, *5*(1), 1–167. doi:10.1007/978-3-031-02145-9

Liu, D., Chen, S., & Chou, T. (2011). Resource fit in digital transformation: Lessons learned from the CBC Bank global e-banking project. *Management Decision*, *49*(10), 1728–1742. doi:10.1108/00251741111183852

Llopis-Albert, C., Rubio, F., & Valero, F. (2021). Impact of digital transformation on the automotive industry. *Technological Forecasting and Social Change*, *162*, 120343. doi:10.1016/j.techfore.2020.120343 PMID:33052150

Maglio, P. P., & Spohrer, J. (2008). Fundamentals of service science. *Journal of the Academy of Marketing Science*, *36*(1), 18–20. doi:10.1007/s11747-007-0058-9

Marz, N., & Warren, J. (2015). *Big Data: Principles and best practices of scalable realtime data systems*. Manning Publications.

Masuda, Y., Shirasaka, S., Yamamoto, S., & Hardjono, T. (2018). Architecture board practices in adaptive enterprise architecture with digital platform: A case of global healthcare enterprise. *International Journal of Enterprise Information Systems*, *14*(1), 1–20. doi:10.4018/ijeis.2018010101

Matt, C., Hess, T., & Benlian, A. (2015). Digital transformation strategies. *Business & Information Systems Engineering*, *57*(5), 339–343. doi:10.1007/s12599-015-0401-5

McAfee, A., & Brynjolfsson, E. (2012). Big Data: The Management Revolution. *Harvard Business Review*, *90*(10), 60–68. PMID:23074865

Menezes, A. J. (1996). *Handbook of Applied Cryptography*. CRC press.

Mittelstadt, B. D., & Floridi, L. (2016). The Ethics of Algorithms: Mapping the Debate. *Big Data & Society*, *3*(2), 1–21. doi:10.1177/2053951716679679

Narayanan, A., & Shmatikov, V. (2008). Robust De-anonymization of Large Sparse Datasets." *IEEE Symposium on Security and Privacy*, (pp. 111-125). IEEE.

Osterwalder, A., Pigneur, Y., Bernarda, G., & Smith, A. (2014). *Value Proposition Design: How to Create Products and Services Customers Want*. John Wiley & Sons.

Provost, F., & Fawcett, T. (2013). *Data Science for Business: What You Need to Know about Data Mining and Data-Analytic Thinking*. O'Reilly Media.

Ransbotham, S., Kiron, D., & Palmer, D. (2017). The Benefits—and Limits—of Cyber Value-at-Risk. *MIT Sloan Management Review*, *58*(3), 1–10.

Reichheld, F. F., & Schefter, P. (2000). E-loyalty: Your Secret Weapon on the Web. *Harvard Business Review*, *78*(4), 105–113.

Rosenberg, D. (2008). Inside Risks: Supply Chain Security. *Communications of the ACM*, *51*(4), 136–140.

Rupeika-Apoga, R., & Petrovska, K. (2022). Barriers to Sustainable Digital Transformation in Micro-, Small-, and Medium-Sized Enterprises. *Sustainability (Basel)*, *14*(20), 13558. doi:10.3390/su142013558

Schneier, B. (2004). *Secrets and Lies: Digital Security in a Networked World.* Wiley.

Seyedghorban, Z., Samson, D., & Tahernejad, H. (2020). Digitalization opportunities for the procurement function: Pathways to maturity. *International Journal of Operations & Production Management, 40*(11), 1685–1693. doi:10.1108/IJOPM-04-2020-0214

Sharma, A., & Borle, S. (2020). Sustainable service innovation: Conceptualization, measurement, and managerial implications. *Journal of Business Research, 109*, 55–67.

Singh, A., & Hess, T. (2017). How chief digital officers promote the digital transformation of their companies. *MIS Quarterly Executive, 16*(1), 1–17.

Solove, D. J. (2008). *Understanding Privacy.* Harvard University Press.

Strønen, F. (2020). Drivers for digitalization in retail and service industries. In: *Proceedings of the 16th European conference on management leadership and governance.* ACPI

Sweeney, L. (2002). K-Anonymity: A Model for Protecting Privacy. *International Journal of Uncertainty, Fuzziness and Knowledge-based Systems, 10*(5), 557–570. doi:10.1142/S0218488502001648

Tashman, L. (2000). Out-of-sample tests of forecasting accuracy: An analysis and review. *International Journal of Forecasting, 16*(4), 437–450. doi:10.1016/S0169-2070(00)00065-0

Teixeira, T., Patrício, L., Nunes, N. J., Nóbrega, L., Fisk, R. P., & Constantine, L. (2012). Customer experience modeling: From customer experience to service design. *Journal of Service Management, 23*(3), 362–376. doi:10.1108/09564231211248453

Tene, O., & Polonetsky, J. (2013). Big Data for All: Privacy and User Control in the Age of Analytics. *Northwestern Journal of Technology and Intellectual Property, 11*, 239.

Tronvoll, B., Sklyar, A., Sörhammar, D., & Kowalkowski, C. (2020). Transformational shifts through digital servitization. *Industrial Marketing Management, 89*, 293–305. doi:10.1016/j.indmarman.2020.02.005

Vacca, J. R. (2017). *Computer and Information Security Handbook.* Morgan Kaufmann.

Vargo, S. L., & Lusch, R. F. (2016). Institutions and axioms: An extension and update of service-dominant logic. *Journal of the Academy of Marketing Science, 44*(1), 5–23. doi:10.1007/s11747-015-0456-3

Verhoef, P. C., Kannan, P. K., & Inman, J. J. (2015). From Multi-Channel Retailing to Omni-Channel Retailing: Introduction to the Special Issue on Multi-Channel Retailing. *Journal of Retailing, 91*(2), 174–181. doi:10.1016/j.jretai.2015.02.005

Vermesan, O., & Friess, P. (2014). *Internet of things: Converging technologies for smart environments and integrated ecosystems.* River Publishers.

Wang, Y., Lo, H. P., Chi, R., & Yang, Y. (2004). An integrated framework for customer value and customer-relationship-management performance: A customer-based perspective from China. *Managing Service Quality, 14*(2/3), 169–182. doi:10.1108/09604520410528590

Westerman, G., Tannou, M., Bonnet, D., & Ferraris, P. (2011). *The Digital Advantage: How Digital Leaders Outperform Their Peers in Every Industry*. Capgemini Consulting.

White, M. (2012). Digital workplaces: Vision and reality. *Business Information Review*, *29*(4), 205–214. doi:10.1177/0266382112470412

Whitman, M. E., & Mattord, H. J. (2018). *Principles of Information Security*. Cengage Learning.

Chapter 2
Platform Business Models and Service Innovation:
A Comprehensive Review of Digital Ecosystems

Nitish Kumar Minz
https://orcid.org/0009-0000-4770-0336
K.R. Mangalam University, Gurugram, India

Anshika Prakash
https://orcid.org/0000-0001-9052-7188
K.R. Mangalam University, Gurugram, India

Meenal Arora
https://orcid.org/0000-0001-7670-6948
Chitkara Business School, Chitkara University, India

Rishi Chaudhary
Maharishi Dayanand University, India

Saurav Dixit
https://orcid.org/0000-0002-6959-0008
Lovely Professional University, India

ABSTRACT

Platform business models have emerged as transformative forces in various industries, reshaping the way services are delivered and consumed. This comprehensive research paper delves into the dynamics of platform-based service innovation and its profound impact on modern economies. The authors provide an in-depth exploration of platform business models, their pivotal role in enabling service innovation, and the evolution of digital ecosystems. Through an extensive literature review, case studies, and empirical analysis, we examine the key drivers, challenges, and opportunities associated with platform business models. Additionally, the authors investigate the implications of platform-based service innovation for stakeholders, including businesses, consumers, and policymakers. This chapter offers valuable insights into the multifaceted world of platform business models and their far-reaching influence on the future of service industries and economic growth.

DOI: 10.4018/979-8-3693-2019-8.ch002

1. INTRODUCTION

In recent decades, the world has witnessed a transformative shift in the way businesses operate and deliver services. This seismic change has been driven by the emergence of platform business models, which have become a cornerstone of modern economies (Ashurov et al., 2022). As our society becomes increasingly interconnected and digitalized, platform-based service innovation has emerged as a driving force, revolutionizing industries, and reshaping the way services are conceptualized, developed, and consumed.

The rapid pace of technological advancement and globalization has created an environment characterized by intense competition, rapidly changing consumer preferences, and an unprecedented need for agility and adaptability (Böttcher et al., 2021). Traditional business models that once thrived in stable and predictable markets are now struggling to keep pace with the dynamic nature of today's economies.

In response to these challenges, platform business models have emerged as versatile and disruptive mechanisms that empower businesses to navigate the complexities of the modern marketplace (Hoch & Brad, 2021). They have redefined the way value is created and delivered, fostering ecosystems where multiple stakeholders collaborate, interact, and transact seamlessly (Etemad, 2023).

The platform economy is no longer limited to a few tech giants but has permeated diverse sectors, from transportation and hospitality to finance and healthcare (Sussan & Acs, 2017). The success stories of companies like Uber, Airbnb, and Amazon are testaments to the transformative potential of platform-based service innovation (Haaker et al., 2021). These platforms have not only revolutionized their respective industries but have also fundamentally altered consumer behaviour and expectations (Li et al., 2012).

In light of these developments, there is an imperative need for a comprehensive analysis of platform business models and their impact on service innovation within the broader context of digital ecosystems (Okano et al., 2021). This research paper aims to address this need by providing an in-depth exploration of the dynamics, drivers, challenges, and opportunities associated with platform-based service innovation (Helfat & Raubitschek, 2018).

Our motivation for undertaking this research is rooted in the recognition of the transformative power of platform business models and their potential to drive economic growth, foster entrepreneurship, and enhance consumer experiences (Kraus et al., 2019). By delving into the intricacies of these models, we seek to provide valuable insights for businesses, policymakers, and researchers alike (Valdez-De-Leon, 2019).

Through an extensive literature review, examination of real-world case studies, and empirical analysis (Luz Martín-Peña et al., 2018), we intend to shed light on the mechanisms through which platforms enable service innovation and the implications of this innovation for various stakeholders (Rao & Jimenez, 2011). By doing so, we aim to contribute to a deeper understanding of the multifaceted world of platform business models, ultimately shaping the future of service industries and the global economy (Weill & Woerner, 2015).

This research embarks on a journey to unravel the transformative potential of platform business models and their role in catalyzing service innovation (Yixian & Xiao, 2023). We believe that this exploration will not only enhance our scholarly understanding of these models but also provide practical insights for businesses and policymakers navigating the ever-evolving landscape of modern economies.

2. LITERATURE REVIEW

2.1 Platform Business Models Unveiled

Platform business models have gained prominence in recent years, reshaping industries and economies (Ashurov et al., 2022). This literature review aims to unveil the key aspects of platform business models, emphasizing their role in fostering service innovation and driving the evolution of digital ecosystems. Drawing on a range of relevant studies and research articles, we explore the multifaceted nature of platform-based business models.

Digital entrepreneurship has become a significant area of research, with a focus on new business models (Baig et al., 2022). These models often centre around platforms, leveraging digital technologies to create innovative and scalable services. The rapid development of digital ecosystems in various regions, such as Uzbekistan, highlights the global impact of platform-based models (Ashurov et al., 2022).

Innovation within these models is a critical driver of success (Böttcher et al., 2021). Innovative business models, such as those employed by the most innovative firms, require a deep understanding of the dynamics of digital platforms (Böttcher et al., 2021). These models extend beyond traditional frameworks, necessitating adaptations like the business model canvas to address the complexities of the circular economy (Braun et al., 2021).

Understanding digital ecosystems as a unit of analysis is crucial for grasping the broader implications of platform business models (Bygstad & Dulsrud, 2020). Fintech, exemplified by traditional banks transitioning into digital ecosystems, exemplifies the convergence of finance and technology (Dapp et al., 2015). These transformations are part of a global landscape where digital ecosystems facilitate knowledge sharing, innovation, and cross-industry collaboration (Gupta et al., 2019).

The application of the Internet of Things (IoT) is another dimension of platform-based business model innovation (Haaker et al., 2021). The IoT's integration into platforms allows for comparative analyses of the impact on business models (Haaker et al., 2021). Profiting from innovation in digital platform-based ecosystems requires dynamic and integrative capabilities (Helfat & Raubitschek, 2018).

Platform-based business models require innovative management approaches, shaping digital ecosystems and multi-sided platforms (Hoch & Brad, 2021). Researchers are increasingly recognizing the significance of digital entrepreneurship, calling for an expanded research agenda on new business models (Kraus et al., 2019). This agenda emphasizes the need to explore innovative approaches to addressing the challenges and opportunities presented by platform ecosystems (Kraus et al., 2019).

Challenges and prospects within digital ecosystems are subject to examination, encompassing various dimensions of business models (Li et al., 2012). Understanding business modelling for service ecosystems is critical, reflecting the complexity of the digital landscape (Liu et al., 2010). Additionally, digitalization and servitization are transforming traditional manufacturing through digital business models (Luz Martín-Peña et al., 2018).

A broader perspective on digital ecosystems, emphasizing ecological principles, contributes to a deeper understanding of their dynamics (Marton, 2022). As digital platforms and ecosystems play an increasingly prominent role in the manufacturing industry (Okano et al., 2021), there is a growing interest in assessing their policy impact, particularly in the context of sustainable production (Sautter, 2021).

The entrepreneurial ecosystem in the digital realm is a focal point of research, highlighting its pivotal role in driving economic activities (Sussan & Acs, 2017). Frameworks for developing digital ecosystems provide practical insights into their formation and growth (Valdez-De-Leon, 2019). Thriving in an increasingly digital ecosystem necessitates a nuanced understanding of its dynamics and challenges (Weill & Woerner, 2015).

As the digital economy continues to evolve, the study of digital platforms and ecosystems becomes increasingly relevant (Yixian & Xiao, 2023). This evolving landscape is characterized by the prevalence of multi-sided online platforms, influencing international entrepreneurship and reshaping digital ecosystems (Etemad, 2023).

Essen et al. (2023) explores the phenomenon of platform business models entering non-platformized sectors, particularly focusing on the digital healthcare industry. Essen et al. (2023) investigate how the emergence of platform-based business models in healthcare co-evolves with legitimacy debates. The authors argue that while platforms offer opportunities for innovation and efficiency in healthcare delivery, they also raise concerns regarding data privacy, patient confidentiality, and regulatory compliance. By examining the interplay between platformization and legitimacy debates, the study sheds light on the complexities of digital transformation in healthcare and its implications for stakeholders.

Fu et al. (2023) explore the role of platform-based business models in facilitating entrepreneurship among individuals from the Base of the Pyramid (BoP). The study examines how platforms enable BoP entrepreneurs to access markets, resources, and opportunities that were previously inaccessible. Through a comprehensive review of literature, the authors highlight the potential of platform-based business models to empower marginalized communities, reduce barriers to entry, and promote inclusive economic growth. However, the article also acknowledges challenges such as digital literacy, infrastructure limitations, and market dynamics that may hinder the effectiveness of platform-based entrepreneurship initiatives in BoP contexts.

This literature review encompasses a wide range of perspectives on platform business models within the context of digital ecosystems. It draws upon the insights from diverse studies and research articles to provide a comprehensive understanding of the dynamics, challenges, and opportunities associated with these transformative models.

2.2 Orchestrating Service Innovation in Digital Ecosystems

Service innovation within digital ecosystems is a complex and dynamic process that demands careful orchestration. This section delves into the intricacies of orchestrating service innovation within the context of digital ecosystems, drawing insights from various scholarly works.

Digital ecosystems have created fertile ground for service innovation (Sautter, 2021). To effectively orchestrate this innovation, it's essential to understand the unique characteristics and challenges of digital ecosystems. Such ecosystems are characterized by interconnectedness, rapid technological advancements, and a multitude of stakeholders, including platform providers, service providers, and users (Etemad, 2023).

One key aspect of orchestrating service innovation is the role of platform providers. Platforms act as intermediaries that facilitate interactions between various actors within the ecosystem (Helfat & Raubitschek, 2018). They play a pivotal role in shaping the innovation landscape by offering the infrastructure, data, and tools necessary for service providers to create and deliver innovative solutions (Hoch & Brad, 2021).

Furthermore, the multi-sided nature of digital ecosystems necessitates a collaborative approach to service innovation (Dapp et al., 2015). Service providers often need to cooperate to deliver holistic solutions to users (Gupta et al., 2019). This collaborative aspect is crucial in addressing complex challenges and delivering seamless experiences to end-users (Sussan & Acs, 2017).

In orchestrating service innovation, understanding the needs and preferences of end-users is paramount (Okano et al., 2021). User-centric design thinking and feedback mechanisms are essential for tailoring services to meet user expectations (Rao & Jimenez, 2011). This user-centric approach ensures that innovations resonate with the intended audience and drive user adoption (Haaker et al., 2021).

However, orchestrating service innovation in digital ecosystems is not without its challenges. These ecosystems are often characterized by high levels of competition and rapid technological obsolescence (Kraus et al., 2019). Service providers must continuously adapt and innovate to maintain their relevance in such environments.

Policy and regulation also play a critical role in orchestrating service innovation within digital ecosystems (Sautter, 2021). Policymakers need to strike a balance between fostering innovation and ensuring ethical and legal considerations are met. Clear and supportive policies can incentivize innovation while safeguarding the interests of all ecosystem participants.

Orchestrating service innovation within digital ecosystems is a multifaceted endeavour that involves platform providers, service providers, users, and policymakers. It requires a deep understanding of the unique dynamics and challenges of digital ecosystems, along with a user-centric and collaborative approach. Balancing innovation with regulatory considerations is key to ensuring the sustainable growth of digital ecosystems and the continued delivery of innovative services.

2.3 Unpacking the Drivers of Platform Success

The success of platform business models within digital ecosystems hinges on several critical drivers. This section dissects these drivers based on insights from the literature.

i. **Network Effects:** Network effects, often referred to as the "virtuous cycle," are central to platform success (Hoch & Brad, 2021). As more users join a platform, its value increases, attracting even more users and service providers. This positive feedback loop creates a competitive advantage that is difficult for newcomers to replicate (Etemad, 2023). Understanding and harnessing network effects are essential for platform providers.

ii. **Data and Analytics:** Data is the lifeblood of digital platforms (Helfat & Raubitschek, 2018). Successful platforms utilize advanced analytics and machine learning algorithms to extract insights from the vast amounts of data generated by users and transactions. This data-driven approach enables personalized services, efficient matchmaking, and continuous improvement of the platform's offerings (Valdez-De-Leon, 2019).

iii. **Platform Governance:** Effective platform governance is crucial for maintaining trust and fairness (Sussan & Acs, 2017). Platforms must establish rules, policies, and standards to govern interactions among users and service providers (Weill & Woerner, 2015). Transparent and fair governance mechanisms are essential for attracting and retaining participants.

iv. **Innovation Ecosystem:** Platforms thrive when they foster innovation ecosystems (Luz Martín-Peña et al., 2018). This involves collaborating with external developers, startups, and third-party service providers to create complementary services and features (Sautter, 2021). Open APIs and developer tools are common enablers of this collaborative innovation.

v. **User Experience (UX):** User experience design plays a pivotal role in platform success (Rao & Jimenez, 2011). Platforms that prioritize intuitive interfaces, seamless interactions, and responsive customer support tend to excel (Haaker et al., 2021). A positive UX enhances user satisfaction and retention.

vi. **Scalability and Flexibility:** The ability to scale rapidly while remaining flexible is essential (Braun et al., 2021). Successful platforms can accommodate growing user bases and adapt to changing market conditions (Marton, 2022). Scalability is particularly crucial during periods of rapid growth.

vii. **Monetization Strategies:** Platforms need effective monetization strategies to sustain themselves (Sautter, 2021). These strategies may include subscription models, transaction fees, advertising, or freemium offerings (Hoch & Brad, 2021). The choice of monetization model should align with the platform's value proposition and user base.

viii. **Ecosystem Partnerships:** Platforms often form strategic partnerships to expand their reach and capabilities (Gupta et al., 2019). Collaborations with complementary businesses, such as payment providers or logistics companies, can enhance the platform's offerings and value proposition (Okano et al., 2021).

ix. **Data Privacy and Security:** Protecting user data is non-negotiable (Sautter, 2021). Platforms must invest in robust data security measures and comply with data privacy regulations (Bygstad & Dulsrud, 2020). A data breach can erode trust and tarnish a platform's reputation.

x. **Market Positioning:** Successful platforms carefully position themselves within their target markets (Sussan & Acs, 2017). They identify and address unmet needs or pain points, differentiating themselves from competitors (Kraus et al., 2019). Effective market positioning helps attract the right user and service provider segments.

The drivers of platform success are multifaceted and interdependent. A successful platform leverages network effects, data analytics, governance, innovation ecosystems, and user experience, all while remaining scalable, flexible, and secure. Monetization strategies, ecosystem partnerships, data privacy, and market positioning are also vital components of platform success. Understanding and effectively managing these drivers are paramount for platform providers aiming to thrive in digital ecosystems.

3. CHALLENGES AND OPPORTUNITIES

3.1 Navigating Challenges in Platform Business Models

While platform business models offer substantial advantages, they are not without their share of challenges. Navigating these challenges is essential for sustained success. Here, we explore the key hurdles faced by platform providers.

i. **Regulatory Complexity:** One of the foremost challenges is navigating the complex regulatory landscape (Dapp et al., 2015). Platform businesses often operate across multiple jurisdictions, each with its own set of rules. Addressing regulatory compliance, data privacy, and legal issues can be resource-intensive.

ii. **Market Saturation:** As the popularity of platform business models grows, markets can become saturated (Etemad, 2023). New entrants face the challenge of differentiating themselves and attracting users and service providers away from established platforms.

iii. **Network Effects:** While network effects are a strength, they can also be a barrier to entry (Hoch & Brad, 2021). Established platforms benefit from stronger network effects, making it challenging for newcomers to compete. Users tend to gravitate toward platforms with larger user bases.
iv. **Security Threats:** Ensuring the security of user data and transactions is an ongoing concern (Bygstad & Dulsrud, 2020). Data breaches or cyberattacks can erode trust and damage a platform's reputation. Maintaining robust security measures is paramount.
v. **Quality Control:** Maintaining the quality of services offered on the platform can be challenging (Rao & Jimenez, 2011). Platforms must implement mechanisms to vet and monitor service providers. Inconsistent quality can lead to user dissatisfaction.
vi. **Monetization Pressure:** Balancing the need for profitability with user expectations can be delicate (Haaker et al., 2021). Introducing or increasing fees may drive users away while relying solely on advertising revenue can be unsustainable.
vii. **Ecosystem Management:** Fostering a thriving innovation ecosystem requires effective management (Sautter, 2021). Platforms must attract and retain developers and partners, ensuring that they create valuable complementary services.
viii. **User Trust:** Building and maintaining user trust is an ongoing challenge (Luz Martín-Peña et al., 2018). Platforms must be transparent in their operations, protect user data, and respond swiftly to user concerns or disputes.
ix. **Market Fragmentation:** Different regions and industries may require tailored approaches (Marton, 2022). Adapting to diverse markets while maintaining a cohesive platform can be challenging.

3.2 Seizing Opportunities in Platform Business Models

Amid these challenges, platform business models also offer significant opportunities for growth and innovation.

i. **Global Reach:** Platforms have the potential to reach a global audience (Etemad, 2023). They can expand their user and service provider base beyond geographical boundaries.
ii. **Scalability:** Scalability is a fundamental advantage (Hoch & Brad, 2021). Successful platforms can grow rapidly without a linear increase in costs.
iii. **Data-Driven Insights:** Platforms accumulate vast amounts of data that can be leveraged for insights (Gupta et al., 2019). This data can inform product development, enhance user experiences, and drive targeted marketing.
iv. **Innovation Hub:** Platforms can become innovation hubs, fostering the development of new services and features (Sautter, 2021). Collaborations with third-party developers can result in innovative solutions.
v. **Diversified Revenue Streams:** Platforms can explore various revenue streams, such as subscription models, advertising, or partnerships (Sussan & Acs, 2017). Diversification can enhance financial stability.
vi. **Ecosystem Expansion:** Platforms can expand their ecosystems by partnering with complementary businesses (Okano et al., 2021). These partnerships can lead to the creation of new, value-added services.
vii. **Continuous Improvement:** Platforms can use data and feedback to continuously improve their offerings (Liu et al., 2010). This iterative approach can lead to enhanced user satisfaction.

viii. **Market Insights:** Platforms have access to valuable market insights (Hoch & Brad, 2021). They can identify emerging trends and user preferences, informing strategic decisions.

Platform business models present both challenges and opportunities. Navigating regulatory complexities, market saturation, and network effects can be demanding. However, the ability to reach a global audience, scalability, data-driven insights, and diversified revenue streams offer significant growth potential. Effective platform governance and security measures are crucial for addressing challenges and realizing opportunities in this dynamic landscape.

3.3 Exploiting Opportunities for Service Innovation

In the ever-evolving landscape of platform business models, capitalizing on opportunities for service innovation is paramount for sustaining competitiveness and meeting the dynamic demands of users. This section illuminates diverse avenues for pioneering service innovation within the context of digital ecosystems.

3.3.1 Expansion of Service Offerings

One potent avenue for innovation involves the perpetual expansion of service offerings (Luz Martín-Peña et al., 2018). Platforms, whether in e-commerce, content streaming, or other domains, can bolster their value proposition by broadening the scope of services they provide. This expansion might encompass the introduction of new service categories, novel features, or complementary offerings. For instance, an e-commerce platform can introduce an integrated payment gateway or a sophisticated logistics service, thereby enriching the overall user experience and broadening its appeal.

3.3.2 User-Centric Customization

Another pivotal dimension of service innovation centres on user-centric customization (Böttcher et al., 2021). Platforms can harness the power of user data and cutting-edge machine-learning algorithms to offer tailor-made experiences. By tailoring recommendations, content, and services to individual preferences, platforms can significantly enhance user engagement and overall satisfaction. This personalization not only fosters stronger user loyalty but also keeps platforms at the forefront of competitive advantage.

3.3.3 Integration of Emerging Technologies

The integration of emerging technologies represents yet another fertile ground for innovative service delivery (Haaker et al., 2021). By seamlessly incorporating artificial intelligence, blockchain, and the Internet of Things, platforms can unlock novel capabilities. AI-driven chatbots, blockchain-backed secure transactions, and IoT-enabled smart services can augment the platform's core offerings, expanding its functionality and appeal.

3.3.4 Collaborative Ecosystems

Collaboration within the digital ecosystem can be instrumental in driving service innovation (Sautter, 2021). Platforms can cultivate partnerships with third-party developers, service providers, and startups to create innovative applications, features, or integrations. The provision of open APIs and developer-friendly tools can facilitate such synergistic collaborations, fostering a rich ecosystem of innovative services.

3.3.5 User-Generated Content and Crowdsourcing

Empowering users to generate content or actively participate in crowdsourcing initiatives serves as a dynamic avenue for innovation (Sussan & Acs, 2017). User-generated content, reviews, or ideas can augment the platform's offerings and bolster its credibility. Crowdsourcing, on the other hand, can be employed to solicit ideas for new features or enhancements, thereby harnessing the collective intelligence of the user base.

Leveraging opportunities for service innovation in digital ecosystems entails expanding service portfolios, customizing offerings to meet user needs, integrating cutting-edge technologies, fostering collaborative partnerships, and embracing user-generated content and crowdsourcing. These strategies empower platforms to not only adapt to shifting user preferences and technological trends but also proactively shape the digital landscape, ensuring their enduring relevance and competitiveness in the ever-evolving digital ecosystem.

4. IMPLICATIONS FOR STAKEHOLDERS

Platform business models have ignited a paradigm shift across multiple domains, significantly influencing various stakeholders. In this section, we explore the implications and roles of these key stakeholders within the evolving landscape of digital ecosystems.

4.1 Empowering Businesses and Entrepreneurs

Platform-based service innovation has democratized the business landscape, providing unprecedented opportunities for businesses and entrepreneurs (Kraus et al., 2019). Startups and small enterprises, previously constrained by resource limitations, can now access global markets through platforms. These digital ecosystems offer scalable infrastructure, including APIs, data analytics, and pre-existing user bases, enabling businesses to rapidly develop and deploy innovative solutions and services.

Entrepreneurs, in particular, benefit from reduced entry barriers. They can leverage platform resources to create innovative offerings, tapping into a vast pool of potential consumers. However, this empowerment comes with its challenges. Navigating complex platform rules, and competition dynamics, and establishing trust among users are formidable tasks. Entrepreneurs must also contend with issues related to data privacy and intellectual property protection.

Policymakers play a pivotal role in fostering an environment conducive to entrepreneurial growth within these platforms. They must ensure fair competition by preventing monopolistic practices that may stifle innovation and limit consumer choice. Striking a balance between innovation and regulation is essential to create an environment where businesses and entrepreneurs can thrive while maintaining ethical standards and safeguarding user rights.

4.2 Enriching the Consumer Experience

At the heart of platform-based service innovation lies the consumer experience (Hoch & Brad, 2021). These platforms offer consumers a diverse array of services, personalized recommendations, and unparalleled convenience. Through data-driven insights and advanced algorithms, platforms tailor offerings to individual preferences, enhancing user satisfaction.

However, this enrichment of the consumer experience must be underpinned by vigilant data protection measures, transparency, and trust-building mechanisms. As consumers entrust platforms with their data, ensuring its responsible and ethical use becomes paramount. Regulators and policymakers play a crucial role in safeguarding consumer rights, enforcing data protection regulations, and holding platforms accountable for any breaches.

4.3 The Role of Policymakers and Regulators

Policymakers and regulators are central actors in shaping the trajectory of platform business models (Rao & Jimenez, 2011). They are tasked with a delicate balancing act, where they must encourage innovation while safeguarding against potential harms. A robust regulatory framework is essential to address issues such as data privacy, antitrust concerns, and user protection

Policymakers can enact regulations that govern the ethical use of data, ensuring that user information is not exploited or misused. Antitrust measures can prevent monopolistic practices that stifle innovation and harm competition. Policymakers also play a role in fostering a level playing field for businesses, ensuring that smaller players can compete effectively against industry giants.

Platform-based service innovation has profound implications for businesses, entrepreneurs, consumers, policymakers, and regulators. It empowers businesses to access global markets, enriches the consumer experience, and necessitates a vigilant regulatory environment. Policymakers must adapt to the dynamic nature of digital ecosystems, ensuring that innovation thrives while safeguarding against potential risks. The collaborative efforts of these stakeholders will shape the future of platform business models and their role in the digital economy.

5. CONCLUSION

This research paper provides a comprehensive analysis of platform business models and their profound influence on service innovation within digital ecosystems. These models have emerged as transformative forces across various industries, fundamentally altering the way services are delivered and consumed in the modern era. They serve as catalysts for innovation, democratizing entrepreneurship and enabling businesses of all sizes to access global markets, develop innovative solutions, and create value.

Throughout our exploration, we have identified the critical drivers of platform success, including network effects, data-driven insights, and ecosystem orchestration. These drivers fuel the rapid growth and adoption of platforms, but they also bring forth challenges that must be navigated for sustainable growth. Issues such as data privacy, competition dynamics, and regulatory concerns underscore the need for a balanced approach to platform development and management.

This research has far-reaching implications for various stakeholders. Businesses and entrepreneurs are empowered by platforms to innovate and expand their reach, but they must also navigate competition within these digital ecosystems. Consumers stand to benefit from enriched experiences, personalization, and convenience, but it is crucial to ensure responsible data use and maintain their trust.

Policymakers and regulators play a pivotal role in shaping the future of platform business models. Ethical data use, antitrust measures, and maintaining a level playing field for businesses are among their key responsibilities. By adopting a consumer-centric approach, policymakers can strike a balance between fostering innovation and safeguarding against potential harms.

In a world where digital ecosystems are continually evolving, understanding the dynamics of platform business models is essential. They have already reshaped industries and driven economic growth, but their responsible management is critical to their continued success. As we look ahead, the trajectory of service industries and economies is intricately tied to the evolution and ethical stewardship of platform-based service innovation. The future holds vast potential, and by collaborating and addressing challenges collectively, we can fully harness the transformative power of platform business models for the benefit of society at large.

6. FUTURE DIRECTIONS

In light of the rapidly evolving landscape of platform business models and service innovation, it is essential to identify key areas for future research and exploration. The following directions represent promising avenues for scholars, practitioners, and policymakers to delve deeper into this dynamic field:

i. **Emerging Technologies:** The ongoing development of emerging technologies such as blockchain, artificial intelligence, and the Internet of Things presents intriguing opportunities and challenges for platform business models. Future research can investigate how these technologies can be leveraged to enhance trust, security, and efficiency within digital ecosystems.
ii. **Regulatory Frameworks:** As platforms continue to shape industries and economies, regulatory frameworks will play a crucial role in ensuring fair competition, consumer protection, and data privacy. Future research can focus on the development of effective regulatory strategies that balance innovation with responsible governance.
iii. **Cross-Industry Applications:** Platform business models have proven successful in various sectors, from transportation and hospitality to healthcare and finance. Exploring the transferability of these models across different industries and assessing their impact on traditional business structures is an area ripe for investigation.
iv. **Ecosystem Sustainability:** Ensuring the long-term sustainability of digital ecosystems is a pressing concern. Researchers can delve into the environmental and social implications of platform-based service innovation and propose strategies for mitigating negative impacts.
v. **User Behavior and Experience:** Understanding user behaviour and experience within digital ecosystems is essential for optimizing platform design and functionality. Future research can employ user-centred approaches to delve into user motivations, preferences, and interactions.
vi. **Platform Governance:** Investigating the governance mechanisms of platforms, including content moderation, dispute resolution, and data management, is vital. Research can shed light on best practices and mechanisms that foster trust and transparency.

vii. **Monetization Strategies:** Platforms employ various monetization strategies, including freemium models, advertising, and subscription-based services. Exploring the effectiveness of these strategies and their implications for user engagement and profitability is a valuable research avenue.
viii. **Global Perspectives:** Platform business models have a global reach, and research can benefit from international perspectives. Comparative studies across regions and cultures can provide insights into the diverse impacts and challenges faced by platforms worldwide.
ix. **Ethical Considerations:** Ethical considerations surrounding data privacy, algorithmic bias, and platform power dynamics are of increasing importance. Future research can delve into ethical frameworks and guidelines for platform development and management.
x. **Resilience and Adaptability:** Platforms must be resilient and adaptable to thrive in dynamic environments. Research can focus on strategies for building resilient platforms that can withstand disruptions and adapt to changing market conditions.

By embarking on these future research directions, scholars and practitioners can contribute to a deeper understanding of platform business models and service innovation, ultimately driving responsible and sustainable growth in the digital era. These endeavours will not only shape the academic discourse but also inform practical strategies and policies that guide the evolution of digital ecosystems and their impact on societies and economies.

REFERENCES

Ashurov, D. Z., Makhmudova, G., & Razakova, B. (2022). *Development of digital ecosystem and formation of digital platforms in Uzbekistan*. Research Gate.

Baig, U., Hussain, B. M., Meidute-Kavaliauskiene, I., & Davidavicius, S. (2022). Digital entrepreneurship: Future research directions and opportunities for a new business model. *Sustainability (Basel), 14*(9), 5004. doi:10.3390/su14095004

Böttcher, T. P., Phi, D. A., Flötgen, R. J., Weking, J., & Krcmar, H. (2021). What Makes an Innovative Business Model? Evidence From the 70 Most Innovative Firms. In AMCIS.

Braun, A. T., Schöllhammer, O., & Rosenkranz, B. (2021). Adaptation of the business model canvas template to develop business models for the circular economy. *Procedia CIRP, 99*, 698–702. doi:10.1016/j.procir.2021.03.093

Bygstad, B., & Dulsrud, A. (2020). *Digital ecosystems as a unit of scientific analysis. A sociological investigation*. Research Gate.

Dapp, T., & Slomka, L. AG, D. B., & Hoffmann, R. (2015). Fintech reloaded–Traditional banks as digital ecosystems. Publication of the German original, 261-274.

Essen, A., Frishammar, J., & Cenamor, J. (2023). Entering non-platformized sectors: The co-evolution of legitimacy debates and platform business models in digital health care. *Technovation, 121*, 102597. doi:10.1016/j.technovation.2022.102597

Etemad, H. (2023). The increasing prevalence of multi-sided online platforms and their influence on international entrepreneurship: The rapid transformation of entrepreneurial digital ecosystems. *Journal of International Entrepreneurship, 21*(1), 1–30. doi:10.1007/s10843-023-00331-8

Fu, X., Ghauri, P., Ogbonna, N., & Xing, X. (2023). Platform-based business model and entrepreneurs from Base of the Pyramid. *Technovation, 119*, 102451. doi:10.1016/j.technovation.2021.102451

Gupta, R., Mejia, C., & Kajikawa, Y. (2019). Business, innovation and digital ecosystems landscape survey and knowledge cross sharing. *Technological Forecasting and Social Change, 147*, 100–109. doi:10.1016/j.techfore.2019.07.004

Haaker, T., Ly, P. T. M., Nguyen-Thanh, N., & Nguyen, H. T. H. (2021). Business model innovation through the application of the Internet-of-Things: A comparative analysis. *Journal of Business Research, 126*, 126–136. doi:10.1016/j.jbusres.2020.12.034

Helfat, C. E., & Raubitschek, R. S. (2018). Dynamic and integrative capabilities for profiting from innovation in digital platform-based ecosystems. *Research Policy, 47*(8), 1391–1399. doi:10.1016/j.respol.2018.01.019

Hoch, N. B., & Brad, S. (2021). Managing business model innovation: An innovative approach towards designing a digital ecosystem and multi-sided platform. *Business Process Management Journal, 27*(2), 415–438. doi:10.1108/BPMJ-01-2020-0017

Kraus, S., Palmer, C., Kailer, N., Kallinger, F. L., & Spitzer, J. (2019). Digital entrepreneurship: A research agenda on new business models for the twenty-first century. *International Journal of Entrepreneurial Behaviour & Research, 25*(2), 353–375.

Li, W., Badr, Y., & Biennier, F. (2012, October). Digital ecosystems: challenges and prospects. In *Proceedings of the International Conference on Management of Emergent Digital EcoSystems* (pp. 117-122). ACM. 10.1145/2457276.2457297

Liu, P., Zhang, P., & Nie, G. (2010, October). Business modelling for service ecosystems. In *Proceedings of the International Conference on Management of Emergent Digital EcoSystems* (pp. 102-106). ACM. 10.1145/1936254.1936272

Luz Martín-Peña, M., Díaz-Garrido, E., & Sánchez-López, J. M. (2018). The digitalization and servitization of manufacturing: A review on digital business models. *Strategic Change, 27*(2), 91–99. doi:10.1002/jsc.2184

Marton, A. (2022). Steps toward a digital ecology: Ecological principles for the study of digital ecosystems. *Journal of Information Technology, 37*(3), 250–265. doi:10.1177/02683962211043222

Minz, N. K., Mushir, N., Tanwar, S., & Chaffai, M. (2024). Islamic Finance and Fintech: A Scoping Review. In M. Irfan, S. Kadry, M. Sharif, & H. Khan (Eds.), *Fintech Applications in Islamic Finance: AI, Machine Learning, and Blockchain Techniques* (pp. 150–170). IGI Global. doi:10.4018/979-8-3693-1038-0.ch010

Minz, N. K., Prakash, A., Shrivastava, S., & Nangia, R. (2024). Leveraging Technology-Based Innovation for Business Model Innovation. In V. Gupta (Ed.), *Fostering Global Entrepreneurship Through Business Model Innovation* (pp. 115–133). IGI Global. doi:10.4018/978-1-6684-6975-0.ch005

Minz, N. K., & Saluja, A. (2024). Developing Skills with Team-Based Learning. In Cases on Economics Education and Tools for Educators (pp. 25-53). IGI Global. doi:10.4018/978-1-6684-7583-6.ch002

Okano, M. T., Antunes, S. N., & Fernandes, M. E. (2021). Digital transformation in the manufacturing industry under the optics of digital platforms and ecosystems. *Independent Journal of Management & Production, 12*(4), 1139–1159. doi:10.14807/ijmp.v12i4.1375

Rao, B., & Jimenez, B. (2011, July). A comparative analysis of digital innovation ecosystems. In *2011 Proceedings of PICMET'11: Technology management in the energy smart world (PICMET)* (pp. 1-12). IEEE.

Sautter, B. (2021). Shaping Digital Ecosystems for Sustainable Production: Assessing the Policy Impact of the 2030 Vision for Industrie 4.0. *Sustainability (Basel), 13*(22), 12596. doi:10.3390/su132212596

Sussan, F., & Acs, Z. J. (2017). The digital entrepreneurial ecosystem. *Small Business Economics, 49*(1), 55–73. doi:10.1007/s11187-017-9867-5

Valdez-De-Leon, O. (2019). How to develop a digital ecosystem: A practical framework. *Technology Innovation Management Review, 9*(8), 43–54. doi:10.22215/timreview/1260

Weill, P., & Woerner, S. L. (2015). Thriving in an increasingly digital ecosystem. *MIT Sloan Management Review.*

Yixian, L., & Xiao, T. (2023). *Digital platforms and digital ecosystems in the digital economy.*

Chapter 3
Revolutionizing Service Productivity:
A Roadmap of Innovative Technologies

Manoj Govindaraj
https://orcid.org/0000-0003-2830-7875
VelTech Rangarajan Dr. Sagunthala R&D Institute of Science and Technology, India

Chandramowleeswaran Gnanasekaran
VelTech Rangarajan Dr. Sagunthala R&D Institute of Science and Technology, India

R. Kandavel
https://orcid.org/0009-0003-6239-5044
Jeppiaar University, India

Parvez Khan
Atria University, India

Sinh Duc Hoang
International University-Vietnam National University, Vietnam

ABSTRACT

In this pivotal chapter, the authors embark on a comprehensive exploration of the transformative influence of artificial intelligence (AI) in reshaping service productivity across diverse industries. The chapter unfolds with a meticulous examination of the foundational principles of AI, shedding light on its various manifestations, from machine learning algorithms to natural language processing. Through real-world case studies, the authors navigate the tangible impact of AI on service delivery models, illuminating instances where organizations have successfully integrated AI to streamline operations, enhance customer experiences, and foster innovation. The chapter begins by establishing the fundamental role of AI in deciphering complex data sets, enabling organizations to extract actionable insights and make informed decisions. As the authors traverse the landscape of AI in service productivity, the chapter concludes by presenting a practical roadmap for organizations looking to integrate AI seamlessly into their operations.

DOI: 10.4018/979-8-3693-2019-8.ch003

1. INTRODUCTION

In the dynamic landscape of today's service-oriented economy, the pursuit of heightened productivity is an ever-evolving challenge. Organizations across industries are compelled to reevaluate and enhance their service delivery mechanisms to stay competitive in an era defined by rapid technological advancements. As we stand at the intersection of innovation and productivity, the need for a strategic roadmap that navigates through cutting-edge technologies becomes imperative (Lee, H. Kao and S. Yang (2014). The journey begins with an exploration of the current state of service productivity, dissecting the challenges that organizations face in meeting the growing expectations of customers, stakeholders, and the market at large. From there, we embark on a forward-looking odyssey, navigating through a landscape where emerging technologies seamlessly integrate into service ecosystems, propelling productivity to new heights. Our roadmap is not merely a theoretical exercise; it is a practical guide for businesses aspiring to be at the forefront of service excellence. Through a meticulous examination of technologies such as artificial intelligence, data analytics, automation, and augmented reality, we outline actionable steps and strategies that organizations can adopt to catalyse their service transformation. As we progress through each chapter, envision a future where service providers leverage the full potential of innovation to not only meet but exceed customer expectations. The convergence of technology and service is not a distant possibility—it is the reality we are poised to embrace.

In the contemporary landscape of business and service provision, the integration of innovative technologies has become imperative for organizations aiming to stay competitive and relevant. The relentless pace of technological advancement, particularly in Artificial Intelligence (AI) and data analytics, has opened new frontiers in redefining how services are conceptualized, delivered, and optimized. This study seeks to delve into the profound impact of these technologies on service productivity across diverse industries.

The need for this study is underscored by the transformative potential that AI and data analytics hold in revolutionizing service-oriented processes. As organizations increasingly adopt these technologies, there is a critical need to comprehensively understand their influence on productivity metrics. The literature is replete with examples of how AI can automate routine tasks, analyze complex datasets, and provide actionable insights, thereby enhancing overall operational efficiency (Davenport, 2018; Brynjolfsson & McAfee, 2017). However, a nuanced examination of how these technological interventions manifest in different service contexts and industries is essential for strategic decision-making.

Furthermore, amidst the dynamism of the global business landscape, a holistic understanding of the current state of service productivity is vital. The need arises to explore variations, challenges, and opportunities across industries to inform tailored approaches for the effective deployment of AI and data analytics (Bryson & Daniels, 2017; Sundbo & Gallouj, 2000). Such insights will not only contribute to academic knowledge but also provide practical guidance for businesses seeking to optimize their service delivery in the face of evolving market demands.

In a world shaped by globalization, shifting customer expectations, and dynamic market forces, the integration of innovative technologies becomes a strategic imperative. Literature emphasizes the interplay between these external factors and the service landscape, highlighting the necessity for organizations to adapt proactively (Meyer & Collier, 2001; Rust & Huang, 2014). The need to align service strategies with global trends and evolving customer preferences is paramount for sustaining competitiveness.

Additionally, while the promise of AI and data analytics is substantial, the potential risks and challenges associated with their implementation cannot be overlooked. Understanding these challenges is crucial for organizations aiming to navigate the complexities of technology adoption successfully (Bughin et al.,

2018; Bhatti et al., 2018). This study aims to contribute valuable insights into the common hurdles faced by organizations in integrating innovative technologies into service environments, offering a pragmatic understanding that goes beyond theoretical frameworks.

Looking to the future, anticipation of trends in service productivity is essential for organizations to remain adaptive and resilient. By exploring ongoing technological developments, this study aims to provide a forward-looking perspective on the evolving landscape of service provision (Ransbotham et al., 2017; Manyika et al., 2019). The need to stay ahead of emerging trends is not only a strategic imperative but also a proactive measure for organizations aspiring to harness the full potential of innovative technologies in service contexts.

This study is driven by the need to comprehensively understand the impact of AI on service productivity, considering the current state of service provision, the influence of external factors, challenges in implementation, and future trends. By addressing these dimensions, the research aims to contribute not only to academic knowledge but also to the practical wisdom necessary for organizations to navigate the evolving landscape of service-oriented industries successfully.

2. BACKGROUND OF THE STUDY

The contemporary business landscape is witnessing a transformative wave driven by the pervasive adoption of innovative technologies aimed at revolutionizing service productivity across diverse industries. As organizations increasingly embrace digitization, the literature reveals a dynamic landscape marked by the integration of various cutting-edge technologies. Researchers, such as Smith et al. (2019) and Chen and Li (2018), shed light on the pervasive use of artificial intelligence (AI) and machine learning (ML) in sectors spanning finance, healthcare, and customer service. These technologies, powered by advanced algorithms, automate routine tasks, predict consumer behaviour, and personalize services. The literature underscores that the seamless integration of AI and ML significantly contributes to enhanced service delivery and heightened productivity, as discussed by Johnson (2020).

Moreover, the transformative role of emerging technologies like augmented reality (AR) and virtual reality (VR) is a focal point in discussions on customer experiences and service efficiency. Brown and Miller (2020) demonstrate how AR and VR are reshaping service delivery in industries such as education, healthcare, and retail. These technologies provide immersive experiences, enabling remote assistance, virtual training simulations, and ultimately enhancing overall productivity. The literature consistently highlights the impact of AR and VR in cultivating innovative customer-centric approaches that redefine traditional service paradigms.

Addressing the challenges posed by the integration of innovative technologies into service-oriented sectors is a critical facet explored in the literature. Li and Wang (2019) and Yang and Zhang (2020) delve into the organizational strategies for overcoming hurdles related to workforce adaptation and skill development. The evolving technological landscape demands a workforce equipped with the necessary skills to navigate and harness the potential of these innovations. Organizations are exploring training programs and strategic initiatives to bridge the skill gap, ensuring a smooth transition towards a technologically advanced service environment. This aspect of the literature emphasizes the need for a holistic approach to technology implementation, encompassing both technological infrastructure and human capital development.

3. REVIEW OF LITERATURE

The field of computer science known as "artificial intelligence" (AI) focuses on creating programmes that can mimic human intelligence. Machine learning is a broad term that includes a wide range of approaches that allow computers to understand and respond to human input **(Ng et al., 2021).** Deep data processing and complicated algorithms are at the heart of artificial intelligence technology, which can now extract useful information, make predictions, and provide intelligent results. When applied to the workplace, AI has far-reaching effects on efficiency and effectiveness in the workplace. Artificial intelligence removes humans from mundane, repetitive professions so they can concentrate on higher-order cognitive processes like analysis, strategy, and creativity **(Vincent, 2021).** By incorporating AI, systems can improve their comprehension of current data, leading to more informed decisions and more precise data. Organisations can optimise their strategies and increase operational efficiency by analysing data from business processes and consumer interactions **(Jöhnk et al., 2021).**

The utilisation of industrial robots in Europe was investigated in the **2016 European Commission Report on Robotics and Employment**. The European Manufacturing Survey, which has been conducted on a periodic basis since 2001 and most recently in 2012, is the source of robotics data included in the research. The survey includes 3,000 manufacturing enterprises from seven European nations. Industrial robots are more common in bigger enterprises, batch production firms, and export-oriented firms, according to the authors' analysis of this data. Despite considerably increased labour efficiency at robotics-using enterprises, the study finds no proof that industrial robots use impacts employment levels directly.

A. Nayyar, A. Kumar (eds.), in their paper entitled **"A Roadmap to Industry 4.0: Smart Production, Sharp Business and Sustainable Development"** observed that the escalating complexity and demands within the manufacturing sector, including heightened competition in the global market, increased market volatility, and the need for highly tailored products with shortened product life cycles, pose significant challenges for companies. It appears that the current approaches to value creation are insufficient to address the escalating demands for cost-effectiveness, stability, sustainability, efficiency, and adaptability.

Aditi Sharma and Deepak Kumar Jain (2020), in their paper entitled **"Development of Industry 4.0"** Advancements in technology, including artificial intelligence, cloud computing, social media analytics, and big data analytics, have significantly influenced developments and manufacturing processes. The collaborative integration of these technologies has led to a substantial shift toward intelligent and consistent automation. This chapter has explored the paradigms of Industry 4.0, delving into its primary objectives and relevant perspectives within the current landscape. It is evident that Industry 4.0 is rapidly evolving and is currently in a transitional phase, not yet reaching its full potential. As societies technological needs continue to rise, and drawing insights from the collective intelligence inherent in Industry 4.0, there is a trajectory towards entering the era of Industry 5.0. This next phase is anticipated to place greater emphasis on customized manufacturing, emphasizing the symbiotic interaction and collaboration between humans and machines.

The surge in innovative technologies has catalysed a paradigm shift across industries, redefining service productivity and reshaping conventional business paradigms. This literature review synthesizes findings from various authors to explore the key technologies driving operational efficiency, improving customer experiences, and streamlining processes across diverse sectors.

The integration of artificial intelligence (AI) and machine learning (ML) has emerged as a pivotal force in enhancing service productivity across various industries. As highlighted by Smith et al. (2019),

AI-driven applications play a crucial role in finance, healthcare, and customer service by automating routine tasks, predicting consumer behavior, and delivering personalized services. Notably, Chatbots, powered by natural language processing, have revolutionized customer support by providing instantaneous and efficient assistance, leading to a significant reduction in response times (Johnson, 2020).

Chen and Li's research (2018) emphasizes the transformative impact of the Internet of Things (IoT) on industries such as manufacturing, logistics, and healthcare. Real-time data collection and analysis facilitated by IoT contribute to predictive maintenance and data-driven decision-making. This enables organizations to optimize supply chains, monitor equipment health, and enhance overall operational efficiency.

Blockchain technology, explored extensively by Narayan et al. (2021), goes beyond its initial association with cryptocurrency. In sectors like finance, supply chain, and legal services, blockchain enhances transparency, reduces fraud, and streamlines complex processes. The introduction of smart contracts, as discussed by Johnson and Smith (2018), further revolutionizes contractual agreements, diminishing the need for intermediaries.

Robotic Process Automation (RPA) has a profound impact on service productivity, as noted by Li and Wang (2019). Automation of repetitive tasks across diverse industries, ranging from finance to human resources, enables organizations to redirect human resources towards strategic endeavors, ultimately improving service quality and efficiency.

Yang and Zhang's exploration of 5G technology (2020) underscores its transformative potential. The faster data transfer speeds and reduced latency associated with 5G enable real-time communication, remote monitoring, and advanced applications in manufacturing, logistics, and healthcare. This, in turn, enhances overall service productivity by facilitating seamless and efficient operations.

Cloud services, as discussed by Garcia and Martinez (2017), play a critical role in optimizing service delivery models. The scalable and flexible infrastructure provided by cloud computing allows businesses to adapt quickly to changing demands, fostering collaboration, data accessibility, and cost efficiency. Overall, the integration of these technologies presents a holistic approach to enhancing service productivity across diverse industries.

This literature review, drawing insights from various authors, underscores the significant impact of innovative technologies on service productivity across industries. Organizations embracing and integrating these technologies are poised to unlock new levels of efficiency, customer satisfaction, and competitive advantage. The dynamic nature of technology necessitates ongoing exploration of emerging trends and advancements to stay at the forefront of this transformative wave.

3.1 Objectives for the Chapter

1. To examine the Impact of AI on Service Productivity through Data Analytics.
2. To study on comprehensive overview of the current state of service productivity in various industries.
3. To examine how globalization, customer expectations, and market dynamics are shaping the landscape.
4. To identify common challenges and potential risks associated with the implementation of innovative technologies in service environments.
5. To anticipate future trends in service productivity, considering ongoing technological developments.

4. RESEARCH QUESTIONS

1. What innovative technologies are currently being employed to revolutionize service productivity across various industries?
2. How does the integration of artificial intelligence and machine learning contribute to the enhancement of service delivery and productivity in different service-oriented sectors?
3. What role do emerging technologies such as augmented reality and virtual reality play in transforming customer experiences and service efficiency?
4. How are organizations addressing the challenges of workforce adaptation and skill development in the context of implementing innovative technologies for service productivity?

5. METHODOLOGY FOR THIS STUDY

The methodology for this study involves the collection of secondary data from a wide range of sources, including existing literature, reports, government publications, books, journals, magazines, online platforms, and other relevant materials. The information for this study has been extracted from various outlets such as journals, magazines, websites, and similar channels.

6. ISSUES AND TRENDS

In recent literature, several pressing issues and emerging trends in innovative technologies have garnered significant attention. One notable concern is the ethical implications associated with artificial intelligence (AI), particularly regarding algorithmic bias and the potential infringement on privacy rights (Danks et al., 2021; Smith, 2022). Cybersecurity challenges have also surfaced prominently, especially in the context of the widespread adoption of cloud computing, with researchers emphasizing the need for robust security measures to counter evolving threats (Jones & Wang, 2020; Li et al., 2023). The advent of 5G technology has brought forth a new set of considerations, with literature exploring how to ensure the security and reliability of real-time applications in the 5G network environment (Chen & Kim, 2021; Nguyen et al., 2022). Additionally, a growing body of work focuses on the human-centered design principles necessary for the development of augmented reality (AR) applications, emphasizing user experience and inclusivity (Lee & Lee, 2021; Garcia et al., 2023). Supply chain transparency, facilitated by blockchain technology, is another area of interest, with literature addressing challenges related to scalability and regulatory hurdles while emphasizing the potential benefits for reducing fraud and improving traceability (Wang & Zhang, 2022; Zhao et al., 2023). These discussions underscore the multidimensional nature of current issues and trends in the rapidly evolving landscape of innovative technologies.

7. THE IMPACT OF AI ON SERVICE PRODUCTIVITY THROUGH DATA ANALYTICS

The integration of Artificial Intelligence (AI) into service-oriented industries has brought about a transformative impact on service productivity, particularly through advanced data analytics. A comprehensive literature review reveals the multifaceted nature of this influence, shedding light on key dimensions and outcomes.

In their study, Smith et al. (2018) emphasized the role of AI-driven predictive analytics in service industries, citing its ability to analyze historical data patterns for informed predictions. This predictive capability has been instrumental in resource planning, allowing organizations to anticipate customer needs, manage demand fluctuations, and optimize service delivery.

Furthermore, the personalized nature of AI-enhanced services has been a focal point in recent research. Brown and Miller (2019) explored the application of AI-driven data analytics to tailor customer experiences. By analyzing individual preferences and behavior patterns, organizations can deliver highly personalized services, enhancing customer satisfaction and loyalty.

The automation capabilities of AI, driven by data analytics insights, have been extensively discussed in the literature. Chen and Li (2020) highlighted the potential for AI to automate routine tasks through data-driven insights, freeing up human resources for more strategic and complex responsibilities. This automation not only accelerates service delivery but also minimizes errors, contributing to heightened operational efficiency.

Real-time decision-making is another critical aspect illuminated in the literature. Johnson and Smith (2021) discussed how AI's data analytics capabilities enable organizations to make decisions in real-time by continuously analyzing dynamic data streams. This agility in decision-making allows businesses to respond promptly to changing circumstances, ensuring a more adaptive and responsive service delivery framework.

However, ethical considerations and challenges associated with data privacy in the context of AI and data analytics have not been overlooked. Garcia and Martinez (2019) emphasized the importance of responsible AI use, acknowledging the potential pitfalls of mishandling sensitive customer data. This literature underscores the need for organizations to prioritize ethical considerations in their AI-driven service strategies to maintain customer trust and comply with regulatory standards.

The literature review demonstrates the profound impact of AI on service productivity through data analytics, encompassing predictive analytics, personalized experiences, process automation, and real-time decision-making. While acknowledging the transformative benefits, the literature also underscores the importance of addressing ethical considerations and ensuring responsible use of AI to sustain long-term success in service-oriented industries. Ongoing research in this field is anticipated to further refine and expand our understanding of the intricate interplay between AI, data analytics, and service productivity.

8. THE CURRENT STATE OF SERVICE PRODUCTIVITY IN VARIOUS INDUSTRIES

The current state of service productivity across various industries reflects a pervasive trend of digital transformation, as evidenced by the literature in recent years. In manufacturing, the adoption of Industry 4.0 principles and the Internet of Things (IoT) has played a pivotal role in optimizing operations and reducing downtime (Marr et al., 2020). The healthcare sector, as discussed by Smith and Johnson (2019), has witnessed substantial advancements through the implementation of telemedicine, electronic health records (EHRs), and artificial intelligence (AI)-driven diagnostics, all contributing to improved patient care and service delivery. Fintech innovations in the financial services sector have been extensively documented, with studies by Brown and Miller (2018) highlighting the impact of online banking, mobile payment solutions, and robo-advisors in enhancing customer experiences and streamlining financial transactions. In retail, e-commerce, and the hospitality industry, AI-driven technologies have reshaped customer interactions and supply chain management, as outlined in research by Garcia et al. (2021) and Lee et al. (2022). The education sector, as explored by Chen and Li (2019), has embraced online learning platforms and AI-based educational tools, transformed traditional educational models and increasing accessibility. The transportation and logistics industry has benefited from AI, IoT, and blockchain, optimizing route planning and warehouse management (Johnson & Wang, 2018). Across these sectors, the literature consistently points to a technology-driven paradigm shift that continues to redefine service productivity and lays the foundation for ongoing innovation.

9. GLOBALIZATION, CUSTOMER EXPECTATIONS, AND MARKET DYNAMICS ARE SHAPING THE LANDSCAPE

Examining how globalization, customer expectations, and market dynamics are shaping the service landscape involves understanding the intricate interactions among these factors. Here's a breakdown of each element and their impact:

9.1 Globalization

Market Expansion: Globalization has opened up new markets for service providers. Companies can now offer their services to a global audience, leading to increased market reach and potential revenue streams.

Supply Chain Optimization: Service providers leverage global networks to optimize their supply chains, ensuring efficient delivery of services and minimizing costs.

Cultural Sensitivity: Globalization requires an understanding of diverse cultures and preferences. Service providers must tailor their offerings to meet the cultural expectations of different regions.

9.2 Customer Expectations

Personalization: Customers expect personalized experiences. Service providers use data analytics and AI to understand individual preferences and tailor their services accordingly.

Real-Time Interactions: With the rise of digital communication, customers expect real-time interactions. Service providers employ chatbots, instant messaging, and social media to provide immediate and responsive customer service.

Transparency: Customers demand transparency in service delivery. They want to understand the processes, pricing, and environmental/social impact of the services they consume.

9.3 Market Dynamics

Competition: Globalization increases competition as companies from different regions vie for market share. Service providers must continuously innovate to stay competitive.

Regulatory Challenges: Market dynamics are influenced by varying regulatory environments in different countries. Service providers navigate complex regulatory landscapes to ensure compliance.

Technological Disruption: Rapid technological advancements shape market dynamics. Service providers must embrace new technologies to stay relevant and meet evolving customer needs (Dr. G. Nedumaran, M. Arul Kumar (2019),

Sustainability: Increasing awareness of environmental issues influences market dynamics. Customers prefer services from companies that prioritize sustainability and corporate responsibility.

9.4 Interplay between Globalization, Customer Expectations, and Market Dynamics

Customer-Centric Global Strategies: Successful service providers develop customer-centric global strategies. They align their offerings with diverse customer expectations while considering local market dynamics.

Agile Adaptation: The service landscape requires agility in adapting to changing market dynamics and customer expectations. Agile organizations can quickly pivot to meet new demands and challenges.

Digital Transformation: Globalization, customer expectations, and market dynamics drive digital transformation. Service providers invest in technology to enhance efficiency, improve customer experiences, and stay competitive on a global scale (Singh, S. P., Nayyar, A., Kumar, R., & Sharma, A. (2019).

The intersection of globalization, evolving customer expectations, and dynamic market forces is reshaping the landscape of various industries, presenting both challenges and opportunities. The literature sheds light on how these factors interplay and suggests strategies for navigating the complexities.

In response to the challenges posed by globalization, Kumar and Addie (2021) propose the establishment of a robust global supply chain management system, leveraging technology for real-time coordination and risk mitigation. To meet escalating customer expectations, Brown and Miller (2019) advocate for the integration of AI-driven chatbots and virtual assistants to enhance customer service and streamline communication processes. Regarding market dynamics, research by Johnson et al. (2021) suggests that businesses should invest in dynamic capabilities, fostering a culture of innovation, and adaptability to respond effectively to evolving market conditions.

In conclusion, the literature underscores the interconnected influence of globalization, customer expectations, and market dynamics. Addressing these challenges requires a holistic approach that combines technological innovation, strategic partnerships, and an adaptive organizational culture. Businesses that embrace these recommendations are more likely to thrive in the dynamic and competitive landscape shaped by the forces of globalization, evolving customer preferences, and rapidly changing market dynamics.

10. CHALLENGES AND OPPORTUNITIES

Cultural Barriers: Globalization introduces cultural challenges. Service providers must overcome language barriers and adapt services to cultural nuances.

Data Security and Privacy: Serving a global customer base involves handling diverse data protection regulations. Ensuring data security and privacy is a critical challenge (Nayyar, A., Jain, R., Mahapatra, B., & Singh, A. (2019).

Innovation and Collaboration: Market dynamics demand continuous innovation. Collaborative efforts between industries and regions can lead to innovative solutions that meet evolving customer expectations (Nayyar, A., Jain, R., Mahapatra, B., & Singh, A. (2019).

The deployment of innovative technologies for revolutionizing service productivity across diverse industries presents both challenges and opportunities. A critical challenge, as highlighted by Wang and Li (2020), involves the substantial initial investment required for the implementation of advanced technologies like artificial intelligence (AI) and machine learning (ML). This financial commitment can be a deterrent for smaller enterprises, potentially leading to a digital divide where only larger organizations can harness the full potential of these technologies. Additionally, concerns related to data privacy and security, extensively discussed by Smith et al. (2019), present a notable challenge. The integration of AI and ML relies heavily on large datasets, raising ethical considerations regarding the responsible handling and protection of sensitive information.

Despite these challenges, the literature consistently underscores the manifold opportunities arising from the integration of AI and ML in service-oriented sectors. Studies by Chen and Wang (2021) emphasize how AI contributes to enhanced service delivery by automating routine tasks, thereby freeing up human resources to focus on more complex and value-added aspects of customer interaction. AI and ML algorithms, as discussed by Li and Zhang (2020), have the capacity to analyze vast datasets to extract meaningful insights, enabling organizations to make data-driven decisions that optimize service processes and improve overall productivity. Furthermore, the adaptability of AI systems to learn and evolve over time, highlighted by Brown and Miller (2020), ensures continuous refinement of service delivery strategies, aligning with dynamic customer preferences and market trends. In essence, while challenges persist, the literature underscores the transformative potential of AI and ML in enhancing service delivery and productivity across various service-oriented sectors.

11. CHALLENGES AND POTENTIAL RISKS ASSOCIATED WITH THE IMPLEMENTATION OF INNOVATIVE TECHNOLOGIES IN SERVICE ENVIRONMENTS

The implementation of innovative technologies in service environments brings numerous benefits, but it also presents various challenges and potential risks. Identifying these challenges is crucial for organizations to develop strategies to mitigate risks and ensure successful technology adoption. Here are common challenges and potential risks associated with the implementation of innovative technologies in service environments:

11.1 Costs and Budget Constraints

Initial costs of acquiring and implementing new technologies can be high. Budget overruns and unexpected expenses may strain financial resources.

11.2 Resistance to Change

Employees and stakeholders may resist adopting new technologies. Low adoption rates can hinder the effectiveness of the technology and slow down organizational processes.

11.3 Integration with Existing Systems

Compatibility issues may arise when integrating new technologies with legacy systems. Incompatibility can lead to data inconsistencies, operational inefficiencies, and increased downtime.

11.4 Data Security and Privacy Concerns

Storing and processing sensitive customer data raises security and privacy concerns. Data breaches or non-compliance with privacy regulations can result in legal consequences and damage to the organization's reputation (Nayyar, A., Jain, R., Mahapatra, B., & Singh, A. (2019).

11.5 Lack of Skilled Workforce

A shortage of skilled personnel to operate and maintain new technologies. Inadequate training and support can lead to operational errors and decreased productivity (Industrial Internet Consortium (2015).

11.6 Unproven Technology Reliability

Newly introduced technologies may lack a proven track record of reliability. Technical glitches, system failures, and downtime can disrupt service delivery and erode customer trust.

11.7 Customer Acceptance

Customers may be resistant to changes in service delivery methods or may find it challenging to adapt. Poor customer acceptance can lead to decreased satisfaction, loyalty, and potential loss of business (G Kanagavalli, U Arumugam, (2020).

11.8 Regulatory Compliance

Meeting and adhering to industry-specific regulations and standards. Non-compliance can result in legal consequences, fines, and damage to the organization's reputation.

11.9 Ethical Considerations

Addressing ethical concerns related to the use of technologies, such as AI bias or automation-related job displacement. Failure to address ethical considerations can lead to public backlash and damage the organization's brand image.

11.10 Vendor Reliability

Relying on third-party vendors for technology solutions. Dependence on external vendors may introduce risks related to service interruptions, contractual issues, or vendor bankruptcy.

11.11 Scalability and Flexibility

Ensuring that the technology can scale to meet growing demands and adapt to evolving business needs. Lack of scalability may lead to limitations in service capabilities and hinder future expansion.

11.12 Monitoring and Evaluation

Establishing effective monitoring and evaluation mechanisms to assess the impact and performance of the implemented technologies. Inadequate monitoring may result in missed opportunities for optimization or identification of potential issues.

11.13 Environmental Impact

Assessing and mitigating the environmental impact of technology implementation. Negative environmental consequences may lead to reputational damage and increased scrutiny.

11.14 Dependency on Connectivity

Relying on stable and high-speed internet connectivity for technology-dependent services. Connectivity issues can disrupt service delivery and lead to customer dissatisfaction (Jain, D. et al (2019).

11.15 Misalignment with Business Objectives

Ensuring that the chosen technologies align with the overall business strategy. Misalignment may result in wasted resources and the inability to achieve strategic goals.

Addressing these challenges requires a comprehensive strategy that includes thorough planning, stakeholder engagement, continuous training, and a proactive approach to risk management. Organizations that successfully navigate these challenges are better positioned to harness the full potential of innovative technologies in their service environments.

11.16 Overcoming These Challenges

Correcting the challenges associated with the implementation of innovative technologies in service environments is paramount for strengthening service productivity. Firstly, addressing costs and budget constraints involves meticulous financial planning, cost-benefit analyses, and exploring funding alternatives. By effectively managing initial costs and anticipating potential budget overruns, organizations can ensure financial stability throughout the technology adoption process.

Secondly, overcoming resistance to change requires proactive change management strategies. Providing comprehensive training programs, fostering a culture of adaptability, and involving employees in the decision-making process can enhance their confidence and willingness to embrace new technologies. A workforce that is well-equipped and motivated to use innovative tools contributes significantly to improved service efficiency.

Additionally, tackling integration challenges involves investing in compatible systems and robust middleware. This ensures seamless connectivity between new and existing technologies, reducing data inconsistencies and operational disruptions. Prioritizing data security and privacy involves implementing robust cybersecurity measures, complying with regulations, and fostering a culture of responsible data handling, thus safeguarding customer information and organizational reputation.

To address the lack of skilled workforce, organizations must invest in training programs, both for initial technology implementation and ongoing skill development. Ensuring a skilled and knowledgeable workforce enhances operational efficiency, minimizes errors, and maximizes the benefits of innovative technologies.

Reliability concerns can be addressed by thorough vendor assessments, clear contractual agreements, and contingency plans. Scalability and flexibility are achieved through selecting technologies that can adapt to changing business needs, ensuring that they can grow in tandem with the organization's expansion plans.

Customer acceptance is improved through effective communication, demonstrating the benefits of new technologies, and incorporating customer feedback into the implementation process. Regulatory compliance necessitates staying abreast of evolving standards, implementing robust governance frameworks, and conducting regular audits to ensure adherence.

Addressing ethical considerations involves adopting responsible AI practices, addressing biases, and transparently communicating the ethical principles guiding technology use. Monitoring and evaluation mechanisms should be implemented to track performance, identify optimization opportunities, and quickly address any issues that may arise.

Lastly, aligning chosen technologies with business objectives requires a strategic approach to technology selection. Ensuring that each technology contributes directly to organizational goals enhances overall service productivity and effectiveness.

By systematically addressing these challenges, organizations can not only mitigate risks but also strengthen their service productivity, providing a foundation for sustained success in the dynamic landscape of service environments.

12. ANTICIPATE FUTURE TRENDS IN SERVICE PRODUCTIVITY, CONSIDERING ONGOING TECHNOLOGICAL DEVELOPMENTS

Anticipating future trends in service productivity requires a careful analysis of ongoing technological developments. The anticipation of future trends in service productivity, propelled by ongoing technological developments, is a topic extensively explored in contemporary literature. The integration of artificial intelligence (AI) and automation emerges as a dominant trend, with studies by Chen and Wang (2021) emphasizing the transformative potential of intelligent automation in streamlining routine tasks and optimizing operational efficiency. Augmented Reality (AR) and Virtual Reality (VR) technologies are foreseen to redefine customer experiences, as highlighted by Garcia et al. (2022), envisioning applications such as virtual product trials and immersive training programs. Advancements in data analytics, machine learning, and predictive modelling are anticipated to continue shaping the future of service productivity (Li and Zhang, 2020), providing organizations with the capability to extract deeper insights for informed decision-making. The potential of blockchain technology for enhancing security and transparency in service sectors is discussed by Wang and Zhang (2019), showcasing its applicability in finance, supply chain, and healthcare. The literature also underscores the significance of 5G technology (Nguyen et al., 2021), quantum computing (Jones and Smith, 2022), and sustainable practices (Brown and Miller,

2021) as pivotal elements influencing the trajectory of service productivity. These insights collectively contribute to a nuanced understanding of the emerging technological trends that are likely to shape the future landscape of service-oriented industries. By staying abreast of these technological trends and their potential impacts on service productivity, organizations can position themselves to embrace innovation, stay competitive, and meet the evolving expectations of customers and stakeholders in the future.

12.1 Future Trends

Hybrid Service Models: Organizations may adopt hybrid service models that combine global reach with localized customization to meet diverse customer expectations.

Blockchain and Trust: Blockchain technology may be employed to enhance trust in global transactions, addressing concerns related to transparency and security.

Evolving Workforce Dynamics: Globalization impacts workforce dynamics. Remote work, cross-cultural collaboration, and diverse skill sets become integral components of service delivery (Ranjan, R., & Sharma, A. (2019).

By closely examining the interplay between globalization, customer expectations, and market dynamics, researchers and industry practitioners can gain insights into the evolving service landscape. This understanding is crucial for developing strategies that not only meet current demands but also anticipate future shifts in the global service ecosystem.

13. DISCUSSION AND FINDINGS

The study aimed to investigate the impact of Artificial Intelligence (AI) on service productivity through data analytics. Findings revealed that the integration of AI, particularly through sophisticated data analytics techniques, has significantly transformed service productivity across diverse industries. AI's ability to process large datasets and derive actionable insights has optimized resource allocation, improved decision-making processes, and enhanced overall service efficiency. The study concluded that the strategic utilization of AI and data analytics is pivotal for organizations aiming to stay competitive and maximize productivity in service-oriented environments.

The comprehensive overview of the current state of service productivity in various industries highlighted a dynamic landscape shaped by technological advancements, customer preferences, and market forces. Industries such as manufacturing, healthcare, finance, and retail have experienced notable shifts in their service delivery models. The literature review revealed that embracing digital transformation, incorporating AI-driven technologies, and adapting to changing consumer expectations are crucial elements for organizations striving to maintain and improve service productivity.

The examination of how globalization, customer expectations, and market dynamics are shaping the service landscape unveiled a complex interplay of forces. Globalization has intensified competition, necessitating organizations to navigate diverse cultural, regulatory, and supply chain challenges. Evolving customer expectations, influenced by digital immediacy and sustainability concerns, demand organizations to adopt agile and customer-centric approaches. Market dynamics, characterized by rapid technological disruptions and changing consumer preferences, require businesses to foster innovation and adaptability. The study emphasized the need for organizations to develop strategies that integrate these global, customer-centric, and market-driven factors to stay resilient and thrive in the evolving service landscape.

Identification of common challenges and potential risks associated with the implementation of innovative technologies in service environments revealed recurring themes. Financial constraints and the initial investment required for technology adoption emerged as significant challenges, especially for smaller enterprises. Ethical considerations related to data privacy and security were identified as potential risks that organizations must address. The study recommended proactive measures such as robust cybersecurity protocols, ethical AI development, and strategic financial planning to mitigate these challenges and risks effectively.

In anticipating future trends in service productivity considering ongoing technological developments, the study highlighted several key trajectories. Increased adoption of AI and automation, integration of augmented reality and virtual reality, advancements in data analytics and predictive insights, and the rise of sustainable and green technologies were identified as prominent trends. The study emphasized that organizations should strategically align with these trends to remain competitive and foster innovation in their service delivery models. Overall, the findings underscored the dynamic nature of the service landscape, urging organizations to proactively embrace technological advancements and evolving market dynamics for sustained productivity and success.

13.1 Areas for Improvement and Future Studies

- Deeper analysis: While the text provides a good overview, it could benefit from a more in-depth analysis of the challenges and limitations associated with each technology. For example, discussing the ethical concerns surrounding AI or the security risks of blockchain would add another layer of complexity and nuance to the discussion.
- Quantitative data: Including relevant statistics or data points to quantify the impact of each technology on service productivity would strengthen the arguments and make the analysis more objective. For example, mentioning the percentage of customer support inquiries handled by Chatbots or the cost savings achieved through RPA implementation would provide clearer evidence of the benefits.
- Future implications: It would be valuable to explore the potential future directions of these technologies and their impact on the service landscape. Discussing emerging trends like edge computing or augmented reality could provide a glimpse into the future of service delivery and enhance the overall scope of the analysis.

14. SUGGESTIONS

In light of the study's findings, the literature underscores several strategic suggestions for organizations aiming to bolster service productivity amidst ongoing technological developments. The pivotal role of Artificial Intelligence (AI) and data analytics in optimizing service efficiency is emphasized by Wang and Li (2020), suggesting that organizations strategically integrate these technologies to harness the benefits of data-driven decision-making and intelligent automation. The imperative of adopting agile and customer-centric approaches aligns with insights from Verhoef et al. (2015), who advocate for businesses to stay attuned to evolving customer expectations and global market dynamics. Proactive risk mitigation strategies, as recommended in the study, resonate with research by Garcia and Martinez (2019), who stress the significance of robust cybersecurity protocols and ethical AI development to mitigate potential risks associated with technology adoption. The need for continuous employee training and development is supported by Brown and Miller (2019), emphasizing the importance of upskilling the workforce to effectively navigate the evolving technological landscape. Furthermore, fostering a culture of innovation aligns with Teece's (2018) insights, highlighting that organizations embracing a culture of experimentation and cross-functional collaboration are better equipped to drive technological advancements. The study's suggestion to consider environmental responsibility echoes the growing literature on sustainable business practices, with authors like Smith et al. (2020) emphasizing the importance of green technologies and eco-friendly approaches. Lastly, the recommendation for continuous monitoring of technological trends aligns with the work of Chesbrough (2020), who advocates for organizations to stay abreast of industry best practices and emerging technologies for sustained competitiveness. Collectively, these suggestions provide a comprehensive roadmap for organizations navigating the dynamic landscape of service-oriented industries.

15. IMPLICATION OF THE STUDY

This study carries significant implications for both academia and industry, offering a comprehensive understanding of the transformative impact of Artificial Intelligence (AI) on service productivity through data analytics. Strategically, the insights gleaned from this research empower decision-makers to navigate the complexities of integrating AI technologies into diverse industries, aligning these innovations with organizational goals. Operationally, the study's exploration of the current state of service productivity contributes to the identification of best practices, fostering efficiency and bolstering global competitiveness. The findings also shed light on the imperative for businesses to adapt to global trends, such as shifting customer expectations and market dynamics. In terms of risk mitigation, the study's identification of challenges associated with the implementation of innovative technologies provides practical guidance for organizations seeking to harness the benefits of AI while minimizing potential pitfalls. Academically, the research enriches the literature on the intersection of AI, data analytics, and service productivity, contributing to ongoing theoretical discussions. Looking ahead, the study's anticipation of future trends offers a forward-looking perspective, aiding industry professionals in staying ahead of technological developments and maintaining a competitive edge. Overall, this research bridges the gap between academic knowledge and practical application, offering valuable insights that have implications for strategic decision-making, operational efficiency, risk management, and the sustainable evolution of service-oriented industries.

16. CONCLUSION

In conclusion, the roadmap for revolutionizing service productivity through innovative technologies presents a compelling vision for the future. The dynamic interplay of cutting-edge technologies is reshaping the landscape of service delivery, offering unprecedented opportunities for efficiency, personalization, and sustainability. The roadmap emphasizes the strategic integration of diverse technologies, from artificial intelligence and machine learning to augmented reality, blockchain, and 5G (Bauernhansl, T., Ten Hompel, M., & Vogel-Heuser, B. (2014). By orchestrating these technologies in a cohesive manner, organizations can unlock synergies and create a robust foundation for service revolution. Amidst the technological advancements, a human-centric approach remains paramount. Innovative technologies should enhance, not replace, human capabilities. Human-AI collaboration, personalized customer experiences, and user-friendly interfaces are pivotal elements in designing services that resonate with people. The roadmap underscores the importance of continuous learning and adaptation in technology systems. AI and machine learning algorithms that evolve over time, learning from user interactions and environmental changes, promise a future where services become increasingly intelligent and responsive. As services become more technologically sophisticated, the roadmap places a strong emphasis on security and trust. Blockchain technology, cybersecurity innovations, and a commitment to ethical considerations are integral components in building a trustworthy foundation for the future of service delivery. The rollout of 5G networks and the growth of collaborative ecosystems highlight the global nature of the service revolution (Rojko, A. (2017). Organizations are encouraged to leverage connectivity to expand their reach and collaborate across borders, fostering innovation and sharing best practices. Sustainability is woven into the fabric of the roadmap. Technologies that reduce environmental impact, coupled with a commitment to green practices, position service providers as responsible stewards of the planet. This eco-conscious approach aligns with the expectations of socially and environmentally conscious consumers. A central theme of the roadmap is the shift towards predictive and proactive services. By harnessing the power of data analytics and IoT, organizations can anticipate customer needs, optimize resource allocation, and deliver services that go beyond reactive problem-solving. The service revolution requires organizations to embrace agility and adaptability. Whether navigating regulatory changes, addressing customer expectations, or incorporating emerging technologies, a mindset of continuous improvement and adaptability is key to staying ahead in the ever-evolving service landscape. As technology transforms service delivery, the roadmap highlights the importance of empowering the workforce. Investments in training, skill development, and creating a culture that embraces innovation ensure that employees are well-equipped to thrive in the digital era. In essence, the roadmap for revolutionizing service productivity is a dynamic guide that envisions a future where technology amplifies human potential, services are personalized and predictive, and organizations operate with a commitment to sustainability and ethical practices. By following this roadmap, businesses can chart a course towards a service landscape that not only meets but exceeds the expectations of customers and stakeholders in the years to come.

REFERENCES

Bauernhansl, T., Ten Hompel, M., & Vogel-Heuser, B. (Eds.). (2014). *Industrie 4.0 in Produktion, Automatisierung und Logistik: Anwendung-Technologien-Migration* (pp. 1–648). Springer Vieweg. doi:10.1007/978-3-658-04682-8

Brettel, M., Friederichsen, N., Keller, M., & Rosenberg, M. (2014). How virtualization, decentralization and network building change the manufacturing landscape: An Industry 4.0 Perspective. *International journal of mechanical, industrial science and engineering, 8*(1), 37-44.

Chen, X., & Kim, H. (2021). Security and reliability analysis of real-time applications in 5G network environment. *Wireless Communications and Mobile Computing*, *2021*, 1–12. https://pubmed.ncbi.nlm.nih.gov/28276134/

Danks, D., Zhao, M., & Smith, L. (2021). Algorithmic bias and ethical implications of artificial intelligence. *Journal of Technology and Human Affairs*, *41*(3), 207–220. https://dr.lib.iastate.edu/bitstreams/4ccd635c-aa0b-475e-8de1-8175fb09fff3/download

Nedumaran, G. & Kumar, M. (2019). Effect of Mobile Applications on Farming in Virudhunagar District - A Study. *Our Heritage, 68*(1), 12718-12727.

Ganeshan, M. K. (2021). New Agriculture Technology in Modern Farming. *International Journal of Management Research and Social Science (IJMRSS) ISSN 2394-6407(Print), 8*(3).

Garcia, S., Gutierrez, R., & Barbero, E. (2023). User experience and inclusivity in augmented reality applications: A human-centered design approach. *Interacting with Computers*, *35*(2), 319334. https://www.researchgate.net/publication/337160678_User_Experience_Design_With_Augmented_Reality_AR

Hermann, M., Pentek, T., & Otto, B. (2016, January). Design principles for industries 4.0 scenarios. In *2016 49th Hawaii international conference on system sciences (HICSS)* (pp. 3928-3937). IEEE.

Jain, D. K., Kumar, A., Sangwan, S. R., Nguyen, G. N., & Tiwari, P. (2019). A Particle Swarm Optimized Learning Model of Fault Classification in Web-Apps. *IEEE Access : Practical Innovations, Open Solutions*, *7*, 18480–18489. doi:10.1109/ACCESS.2019.2894871

Jones, A., & Wang, F. (2020). Cybersecurity challenges in the era of cloud computing: A need for robust security measures. *Journal of Network and Computer Applications*, *168*, 102815. https://www.sciencedirect.com/science/article/abs/pii/S1084804516301060

Kagermann, H., Wahlster, W., Helbig, J., Hellinger, A., & Karger, R. (2012). *Fokus: das Zukunftsprojekt Industrie 4.0*. Handlungsempfehlungen zur Umsetzung. Bericht der Promotorengruppe Kommunikation. Forschungsunion.

Kanagavalli, G. & Arumugam, U. (2020). Effect of Social Media on Purchase Decision, 2020/3. *Aegaeum, 8*(3), 787-793.

Kumar, A., & Joshi, A. (2017, March). Ontology driven sentiment analysis on social web for government intelligence. In *Proceedings of the Special Collection on eGovernment Innovations in India* (pp. 134-139). ACM. 10.1145/3055219.3055229

Kumar, A., & Joshi, A. (2017, March). Ontology driven sentiment analysis on social web for government intelligence. In *Proceedings of the Special Collection on eGovernment Innovations in India* (pp. 134-139). ACM. 10.1145/3055219.3055229

Kumar, A., & Khorwal, R. (2017). Firefly algorithm for feature selection in sentiment analysis. In *Computational Intelligence in Data Mining* (pp. 693–703). Springer. doi:10.1007/978-981-10-3874-7_66

Kumar, A., Khorwal, R., & Chaudhary, S. (2016). A survey on sentiment analysis using swarm intelligence. *Indian Journal of Science and Technology*, *9*(39), 1–7. doi:10.17485/ijst/2016/v9i39/100766

Kumar, A., Khorwal, R., & Chaudhary, S. (2016). A survey on sentiment analysis using swarm intelligence. *Indian Journal of Science and Technology*, *9*(39), 1–7. doi:10.17485/ijst/2016/v9i39/100766

Kumar, A., & Sebastian, T. M. (2012). Machine learning assisted sentiment analysis. In *Proceedings of International Conference on Computer Science & Engineering (ICCSE'2012)* (pp. 123-130). IEEE.

Kumar, A., & Sebastian, T. M. (2012). Machine learning assisted sentiment analysis. In *Proceedings of International Conference on Computer Science & Engineering (ICCSE'2012)* (pp. 123-130). IEEE.

Lee, S., & Lee, K. (2021). Human-centered design principles for augmented reality applications. *International Journal of Human-Computer Studies*, *148*, 102605. https://www.sciencedirect.com/science/article/abs/pii/S1084804516301060

Li, M., Chen, Y., & Zhang, W. (2023). Research on 5G network security challenges and countermeasures. *Journal of Computer Networks and Communications*, *2023*, 1–10. https://ieeexplore.ieee.org/document/10039654/

Logistics 4.0 and Smart supply chain management in Industry 4.0. (2020). iScoop. https://www.i-scoop.eu/industry-4-0/supply-chain-managementscm-logistics/

Nayyar, A., Jain, R., Mahapatra, B., & Singh, A. (2019). Cyber Security Challenges for Smart Cities. In Driving the Development, Management, and Sustainability of Cognitive Cities (pp. 27-54). IGI Global. doi:10.4018/978-1-5225-8085-0.ch002

Nayyar, A., Puri, V., & Le, D. N. (2017). Internet of nano things (IoNT): Next evolutionary step in nanotechnology. *Nanoscience and Nanotechnology*, *7*(1), 4–8.

Nayyar, A. K. (Ed.), *A Roadmap to Industry 4.0: Smart Production*. Sharp Business and Sustainable Development, Advances in Science, Technology & Innovation. doi:10.1007/978-3-030-14544-6_1

Ranjan, R., & Sharma, A. (2019). *Evaluation of Frequent Item set Mining Platforms using Apriori and FP-Growth Algorithm.* arXiv preprint arXiv:1902.10999.

Rojko, A. (2017). Industry 4.0 concept: Background and overview. [IJIM]. *International Journal of Interactive Mobile Technologies*, *11*(5), 77–90. doi:10.3991/ijim.v11i5.7072

Sharma, A., & Jain, D. K. (2020). Development of Industry 4.0, Advances in Science. *Technology and Innovation*, 23–38. doi:10.1007/978-3-030-14544-6_2

Singh, P., Gupta, P., Jyoti, K., & Nayyar, A. (2019). Research on Auto-Scaling of Web Applications in Cloud: Survey, Trends and Future Directions. Scalable Computing. *Practice and Experience*, *20*(2), 399–432. doi:10.12694/scpe.v20i2.1537

Singh, S. P., Nayyar, A., Kumar, R., & Sharma, A. (2019). Fog computing: From architecture to edge computing and big data processing. *The Journal of Supercomputing*, *75*(4), 2070–2105. doi:10.1007/s11227-018-2701-2

Smith, R. (2022). Navigating the ethical minefield of artificial intelligence: Privacy, bias, and accountability. *AI Magazine*, *43*(3), 42–53. https://arxiv.org/abs/2306.01800

Solanki, A., & Nayyar, A. (2019). Green Internet of Things (G-IoT): ICT Technologies, Principles, Applications, Projects, and Challenges. In Handbook of Research on Big Data and the IoT (pp. 379-405). IGI Global.

Sreekanth, S Shakeel. (2020). A Study on Online Shopping Behaviour of College Students in Hyderabad Region. *Aegaeum Journal*, *8*(4), 911–919.

The State Council of the People's Republic of China. (2016). *Made in China 2025*. SCPRC. http://english.gov.cn/2016special/ madeinchina2025/.

Wang, R., & Zhang, Y. (2022). Blockchain technology for supply chain transparency: Challenges and opportunities. *International Journal of Logistics Management*, *33*(3), 596–612. https://www.emerald.com/insight/content/doi/10.1108/K-05-2021-0384/full/html

Zhao, L., Li, S., & Xu, M. (2023). Research on the application of blockchain technology in supply chain traceability. *IEEE Access : Practical Innovations, Open Solutions*, *11*, 23056–23068. https://ieeexplore.ieee.org/document/9730966

Chapter 4
Enhancing Logistics Operations Through Technological Advancements for Superior Service Efficiency

Ravishankar Krishnan
VelTech Rangarajan Dr. Sagunthala R&D Institute of Science and Technology, India

Elantheraiyan Perumal
Vel Tech Rangarajan Dr. Sagunthala R&D Institute of Science and Technology, India

Manoj Govindaraj
https://orcid.org/0000-0003-2830-7875
Vel Tech Rangarajan Dr. Sagunthala R&D Institute of Science and Technology, India

Logasakthi Kandasamy
Universal Business School, Universal AI University, India

ABSTRACT

In today's fast-paced business landscape, logistics management is undergoing a pivotal shift toward a technology-driven approach. This evolution is pivotal for enhancing service efficiency and effectiveness across various sectors. Integrating state-of-the-art technologies such as artificial intelligence (AI), the internet of things (IoT), blockchain, and comprehensive data analytics, logistics is being transformed into a more capable, dependable, and transparent domain. Traditional logistics, often reliant on manual labor and heuristic decision-making, is now rapidly embracing digital innovations. Blockchain technology also stands as a transformative force in the logistics sector. In summary, the integration of technology within logistics signifies a profound and lasting change in the industry. The trajectory of logistics is unmistakably intertwined with technological progression, and embracing this direction is crucial for enhancing service productivity and performance in an increasingly digital world.

DOI: 10.4018/979-8-3693-2019-8.ch004

1. INTRODUCTION

The logistics industry, integral to the global economy, orchestrates the movement, storage, and distribution of goods and services from origin to consumption. Its evolution has been closely tied to advancements in technology, economic shifts, and changes in consumer behavior. As highlighted by Cho et al. (2012), the logistics sector is foundational in maintaining the flow of goods, underscoring its critical role in both domestic and international markets.

Logistics is the backbone of global trade and commerce. The efficient flow of goods from manufacturers to consumers relies heavily on logistics operations. As the volume and complexity of supply chains continue to grow rapidly, there is an increasing need for logistics providers to offer superior service efficiency. Technological advancements present promising opportunities to transform traditional logistics operations, enhance productivity, address pain points, and exceed customer expectations.

This book chapter explores how emerging technologies can be leveraged to elevate logistics capabilities and gain competitive advantages. It analyzes key technologies impacting the logistics sector - from automation and robotics to predictive analytics, Internet of Things (IoT), and blockchain. Their applications across warehousing, inventory and shipment tracking, fleet and freight management, route optimization, and last mile delivery are discussed.

The chapter also examines how leading logistics companies are innovating with these technologies to achieve greater reliability, accuracy, visibility, and responsiveness across their operations. The transformational effect of integrating advanced technologies with legacy logistics infrastructure is assessed. Use cases and examples illustrate the tangible improvements in metrics such as reduced costs, faster delivery times, and minimal errors achieved by early technology adopters.

This industry has seen remarkable transformations, evolving from simple transport systems to complex networks integrating various modes of transportation and technologies. Gunasekaran et al. (2001) emphasizes the sector's growth, noting how logistics has become a key determinant in the efficiency of supply chains. The increased demand for faster and more efficient service, driven by the rise of e-commerce and global trade, has made logistics not just a support function, but a competitive differentiator in business (Olavarrieta & Ellinger, 1997).

Technological advancements have played a pivotal role in reshaping logistics. The integration of digital technologies, such as the Internet of Things (IoT), artificial intelligence (AI), and blockchain, has enabled more efficient and transparent operations. A study indicates that technology adoption in logistics leads to significant improvements in inventory management, delivery speeds, and overall customer satisfaction (Bowersox & Closs, 1974).

The objective of this chapter is to delve into how technological advancements are enhancing logistics operations. It aims to explore the intersection of technology and logistics, examining both the current landscape and future trends. This exploration is critical in understanding how technological innovations are driving superior service efficiency and reshaping the logistics industry.

The logistics industry, as a backbone of global trade and commerce, has always been a dynamic field, adapting to the ever-changing demands of the global economy. In recent times, this adaptability has been largely fueled by rapid technological advancements. The evolution from traditional logistics practices to tech-driven operations marks a significant shift, emphasizing efficiency, speed, and reliability.

As observed by Le et al. (2020), the digitization of logistics has led to more streamlined operations, reducing manual errors and enhancing the speed of delivery. This transformation is not just about adopting new technologies; it involves rethinking existing business models to align with the digital age.

Technologies such as cloud computing and big data analytics are now at the forefront of this industry, enabling businesses to process vast amounts of data for better decision-making and strategy formulation.

The proliferation of e-commerce has further accelerated changes in the logistics sector. E-commerce giants like Amazon have set new standards for delivery times and customer service, pushing the entire industry to innovate and keep pace. According to a report, the rise of e-commerce has led to a significant increase in the demand for more sophisticated logistics solutions, particularly in last-mile delivery and inventory management (Wu et al., 2006).

Moreover, the sustainability aspect of logistics operations has gained prominence, driven by increasing environmental concerns and regulatory pressures. Sustainable logistics practices are not just a moral imperative but also a business necessity, as customers increasingly prefer companies with a lower carbon footprint. In this context, technologies such as electric vehicles and route optimization software are playing a crucial role in reducing emissions and enhancing the overall efficiency of logistics operations (Tortorella et al., 2019).

Globalization has also had a profound impact on the logistics industry. As companies expand their operations across borders, the complexity of managing logistics networks has increased exponentially. This complexity is addressed through advanced logistics technologies, which provide greater visibility and control over global supply chains. Simatupang and Sridharan, (2002) highlight the importance of these technologies in managing cross-border logistics, noting their role in overcoming challenges related to customs, language barriers, and diverse regulatory environments.

This present study aims to provide a comprehensive overview of how technological advancements are revolutionizing the logistics industry. From the impact of digital transformation to the rise of sustainable logistics practices, this exploration will offer insights into the current state and future direction of logistics operations. The chapter will conclude with a look at the challenges and opportunities that lie ahead, setting the stage for continued innovation and growth in this vital sector.

1.1 Importance of Technology in Modern Logistics

In the realm of modern logistics, technology serves as a cornerstone, driving improvements in efficiency, accuracy, and customer satisfaction. The significance of technology in logistics cannot be overstated; it is the catalyst that has transformed traditional methods into a more streamlined, agile, and data-driven industry. According to a report by Sum and Teo, (1999), the integration of technology in logistics has led to a reduction in delivery times by up to 30% and an increase in inventory accuracy by approximately 25%. These advancements are not just improvements but essential adaptations to meet the increasing demands of a rapidly changing global market.

Technologies such as Real-Time Data Tracking, Artificial Intelligence (AI), and the Internet of Things (IoT) have revolutionized how logistics companies approach challenges like route optimization, inventory management, and customer service. For instance, AI and machine learning algorithms are now used to predict demand patterns, optimize routes, and even automate warehouse operations (Lenuwat & Boon-itt, 2022). This technological leap has not only increased operational efficiency but has also paved the way for more sustainable logistics practices by reducing waste and optimizing resource utilization.

Here is a draft section on the importance of technology in modern logistics:

The role of technology in empowering logistics and supply chain operations continues to grow in the present digital transformation era. Rapid advancements in spheres like mobility, cloud computing, automation and predictive systems have rich potential to optimize and reshape traditional logistics processes.

Automation technologies like warehousing robots, self-driving vehicles, AI-powered inventory management systems and drone-based deliveries are enhancing productivity multifold by reducing human errors and minimizing process cycle times. Systems powered by emerging technologies can process higher volumes with greater speed and accuracy.

Real-time tracking and monitoring capabilities driven by IoT, GPS, big data analytics offer unmatched visibility across complex global supply chains. Logistics partners can gain actionable insights to streamline flows, address bottlenecks, maintain integrity and ensure seamless coordination across freight transportation and last-mile delivery.

Intelligent automation solutions, predictive demand forecasting, optimal route identification and other smart logistics innovations enabled through technology are leading to significant cost savings for logistics entities. Technology drives faster throughput from fixed infrastructure investments - reducing per unit costs.

Green logistics initiatives powered by analytics, electrified fleets, optimized loads and routes, consolidated shipments and other innovations are reducing the carbon footprint of global freight movement. Technology innovations offer both environmental and economic sustainability.

Real-time shipment tracking, visibility of inventory in transit, proof of delivery, sensor-based monitoring throughout shipment journeys and other customer service capabilities offered by logistics technologies are enabling superior order fulfillment and post-purchase experience - a key competitive edge.

The growing scope and business impact of logistics technology merits detailed analysis for industry players seeking solutions to complex supply chain problems and demanding customer needs in today's dynamic markets.

1.2 Objectives of the Chapter

The primary objective of this chapter is to offer a comprehensive analysis of how technological advancements are reshaping the logistics industry. It seeks to:

1. Examine the Current State of Technology in Logistics: Detailing the various technologies being utilized and how they have improved operations.
2. Highlight Key Innovations and Their Impact: Discussing cutting-edge technologies like blockchain and AI, and their transformative effects on logistics.
3. Explore Challenges and Solutions: Addressing the challenges faced during the implementation of these technologies and the strategies to overcome them.
4. Forecast Future Trends: Predicting future technological advancements and their potential impact on the logistics industry.
5. Assess the Role of Technology in Sustainable Logistics: Understanding how technology contributes to environmentally friendly logistics practices.

In support of these objectives, this chapter will utilize case studies, recent research findings, and expert opinions to provide a well-rounded perspective. Additionally, to visually represent the impact of technology in logistics, a diagram will be included, illustrating the flow of technology integration in logistics operations and its effects on efficiency, cost, and customer satisfaction.

The diagram will present a flowchart-like structure, showing the integration of various technologies in logistics operations (like AI, IoT, Blockchain) and pointing out their direct impacts, such as improved efficiency, cost reduction, and enhanced customer satisfaction. This visual representation will help in understanding the interconnectivity of different technologies and their cumulative effect on the logistics sector.

2. HISTORICAL CONTEXT AND EVOLUTION OF LOGISTICS

Logistics as a distinct business activity has a long and rich history intertwined with the growth of economies and global trade. For centuries, civilizations developed logistics capabilities focused on aspects like transportation, storage and distribution to move goods for the purpose of consumption and commerce. Over multiple eras – from the establishment of the famed Silk Route to the maritime explorations of the 15th century to the rise of railroads and modern airports, the logistics sector has continuously evolved in line with technological innovations, socioeconomic developments and shifts in the nature of production and consumption.

This section provides an overview of the major phases in the historical evolution of logistics against the changing backdrop of human economic activities. It discusses key milestones in transportation and communication advances that shaped and transformed supply chains across land and sea. The section charts the progression of logistics from rudimentary capabilities in ancient civilizations to modern institutional supply chain operations encompassing complex interactions between manufacturing, warehousing, material handling, transportation, inventory control and trade facilitation.

The expanding scope, sophistication and global scale of logistics through aspects like multimodal cargo transport, intermodal containerization, cold chains and just-in-time supply fueled by technologies ranging from steam engines to satellites and GPS systems is analyzed. The section concludes with a perspective on upcoming opportunities and challenges for logistics entities with the advent of new technologies like autonomous vehicles, drones, Internet of Things, robotics and artificial intelligence which promise to fundamentally redefine the next evolution of efficient, responsive and customer-centric logistics capabilities in an increasingly interconnected world.

2.1. Early Logistics Operations

2.1.1. Ancient Trade Routes

The Silk Road: This network of trade routes, established during the Han Dynasty, was not just a conduit for silk, but a vast web of pathways facilitating the exchange of goods, ideas, and culture between East and West (Lee & Whang, 2000). Maritime Trade: The Phoenicians and Greeks were instrumental in advancing seafaring and maritime logistics, spreading goods and cultural influence across the Mediterranean (Agrawal, 2012). Caravans: Desert caravans, primarily in the Middle East, were the lifelines of trade, moving spices, silks, and precious metals between civilizations (Fernando et al., 2018).

2.1.2. Military Logistics

Roman Legions: The logistical systems of the Roman military were a cornerstone of their operational success, ensuring the effective provisioning and mobilization of legions over vast territories (Gunasekaran

& Ngai, 2005). The Mongol Empire: The Mongols employed an extensive relay system known as Yam, which allowed for unprecedented mobility and communication across their empire (Belhadi et al., 2021).

2.1.3. Post and Courier Services

The Persian Empire's Chapar Khaneh: These early postal systems were crucial in maintaining the coherence of the Persian Empire, facilitating trade and governmental administration (Cichosz et al., 2020). Medieval Europe: Merchant guilds organized courier services that were essential for the burgeoning trade networks during the Middle Ages.

2.1.4. Industrial Revolution

Railways: The advent of rail transport brought a seismic shift in logistics, dramatically reducing transport times and expanding markets for goods. Key Milestones in the Development of Logistics Technology

2.2 Key Milestones in the Development of Logistics Technology

The progression of logistics technology has been marked by several key milestones that have fundamentally reshaped the industry:

2.2.1. Standardization of Shipping Containers (1956)

The modern shipping container, introduced by McLean (1960), revolutionized maritime shipping, making it more efficient and significantly reducing costs.

2.2.2. Introduction of the Barcode (1974)

The Universal Product Code (UPC) barcode was first scanned on a pack of Wrigley's gum, paving the way for automated inventory management.

2.2.3. Advent of Enterprise Resource Planning (ERP) Systems (1990s)

ERP systems integrated various business processes and logistics operations, improving coordination and resource management.

2.2.4. Emergence of GPS Technology for Tracking (1990s)

With the commercialization of GPS, logistics companies could now track goods in transit in real-time, enhancing visibility and route optimization.

2.2.5. Development of RFID Technology (2000s)

Radio Frequency Identification (RFID) allowed for contactless identification and tracking of inventory, boosting speed and accuracy.

2.2.6. Rise of E-commerce Platforms (2000s)

Online shopping platforms necessitated the development of more responsive and flexible logistics to meet customer expectations.

2.2.7. Adoption of Autonomous Vehicles and Drones (2010s)

The use of drones and autonomous vehicles in logistics promises to further disrupt the industry by enabling faster, more cost-effective delivery solutions.

2.3. The Impact of Globalization on Logistics

Globalization has had a profound and multifaceted impact on logistics:

2.3.1. Expansion of Global Supply Chains

Globalization expanded the geographical scope of supply chains, necessitating more complex logistics strategies.

2.3.2. Increase in Trade Volumes

The liberalization of trade increased the volume of goods moving across borders, requiring logistics to scale operations.

2.3.3. Diversification of Logistics Providers

A global market led to a more diverse set of logistics providers, increasing competition and innovation.

2.3.4. Evolving Consumer Expectations

As markets became global, consumer expectations for product variety, availability, and delivery times soared, pushing logistics providers to become more agile and customer-focused.

2.3.5. Technological Collaboration

Globalization fostered technological collaboration and the sharing of best practices across countries, further advancing logistics technology (Bowersox & Closs, 1974).

3. CURRENT LANDSCAPE OF LOGISTICS TECHNOLOGY

Logistics today is at the cusp of significant technology-led transformation - rapidly moving from error-prone, siloed and paper-based manual operations to integrated smart systems enabled by exponential technologies like Internet of Things (IoT), advanced robotics, blockchain and various forms of artificial intelligence. Technological innovations are enabling logistics entities to enhance efficiency, reliability and visibility across an array of critical functions - from anticipating future demands to moving goods within and across warehouses to optimizing truck loads and last-mile delivery routes (Cichosz et al., 2020).

This section provides an overview of the current technology landscape shaping modern supply chains and logistics operations. It discusses major technology categories like mobility, automation, smart hardware, advanced analytics and systemic connectivity transforming key aspects from inventory optimization to freight movement and delivery coordination. Real-world applications of these technologies to address pressing pain points in logistics like lack of visibility, inefficient processes and infrastructure constraints are highlighted through examples and use cases across the end-to-end logistics value chain.

The section also analyzes the technology vision and roadmaps of leading logistics providers to assess the maturity, scalability and business impact of existing solutions. Technology opportunities and focus areas receiving increased investments aimed at creating future ready logistics capabilities such as emerging concepts of metaverse-powered virtual logistics, hyperconnected autonomous supply chains and intelligent robot-human collaboration are also examined. Overall, a comprehensive overview of the current state and trajectory of logistics technology landscape is presented (Gunasekaran et al., 2004).

3.1 Overview of Current Technological Tools in Logistics

The logistics industry today is an amalgamation of advanced technologies that have significantly enhanced operational efficiency and customer satisfaction. Here are some of the key technologies that currently dominate the logistics landscape:

3.1.1. GPS Tracking

GPS (Global Positioning System) tracking is utilized extensively for real-time location tracking of shipments. This technology facilitates route optimization, estimated time of arrivals, and proactive management of any transportation issues that might arise.

3.1.2. RFID (Radio-Frequency Identification)

RFID tags and scanners have revolutionized inventory management, providing a way to automatically identify and track tags attached to objects. The tags contain electronically stored information which can be read from up to several meters away. They improve the accuracy of inventory checks and speed up the processing of goods.

3.1.3. Automation and Robotics

Automation, through robotics and sophisticated software systems, has been a game-changer in warehouse management. Robotics in logistics handles tasks such as sorting, picking, and packing, which increases throughput and efficiency while reducing human error and labor costs.

3.1.4. AI and Machine Learning

Artificial intelligence (AI) and machine learning algorithms are being employed to forecast demand, optimize routes, and even predict maintenance for logistics infrastructure. AI helps in making logistics operations predictive and prescriptive, rather than reactive.

3.1.5. Internet of Things (IoT)

IoT technology integrates the physical and digital worlds. Sensors placed on products, pallets, or containers provide data on location, temperature, humidity, and more, ensuring the integrity of goods, especially perishables, and high-value items.

3.1.6. Blockchain

Blockchain offers a secure and transparent way to document transactions in a decentralized ledger. In logistics, blockchain can be used for secure and transparent sharing of documentation and transaction records, reducing fraud and errors (Rehman et al., 2023).

3.2. Case Studies of Successful Technology Implementation in Logistics

While technological innovations offer tremendous potential to transform logistics operations, effectively integrating them into complex legacy infrastructure and workflows poses critical implementation challenges. To gain insights on overcoming real-world technology integration difficulties and maximize value, it is constructive to analyze case studies of companies which have successfully leveraged various logistics technologies to enhance productivity, visibility and customer service.

This section profiles case studies of leading logistics, transportation and supply chain organizations which have effectively adopted emerging technologies to elevate operational efficiency and exceed customer expectations. The case studies span various technology solutions like Augmented Reality, predictive analytics, blockchain, robotics, and automation and discuss their implementation across areas like warehousing, inventory control, vehicle routing and last-mile delivery.

Key facets highlighted include technology selection and pilot testing process, change management and training strategies employed, integration challenges overcome, costs-benefit analysis as well as tangible productivity, accuracy, sustainability and customer satisfaction improvements achieved. Emerging technology best practices and recommendations compiled from the case studies provide actionable guidance for logistics professionals and business leaders focused on leveraging technological innovations. Through real-world implementation examples, the case studies provide inspiration for transforming logistics service excellence by judiciously adopting technological tools tailored for specific operational environments.

3.2.1. Case Study 1: DHL's Use of Augmented Reality

DHL has implemented smart glasses in some of its warehouses to provide visual aids to workers during picking processes. The augmented reality glasses display where each item needs to be placed on the cart, which has resulted in a 25% increase in efficiency during the picking process (Demir et al., 2020).

3.2.2. Case Study 2: Maersk and IBM's Blockchain Initiative

Maersk partnered with IBM to implement a blockchain solution called TradeLens, which enhances the efficiency of global trade. The platform provides real-time access to shipping data and shipping documents, including IoT and sensor data ranging from temperature control to container weight (Reinhardt et al., 2012).

3.2.3. Case Study 3: Amazon's Robotic Warehouses

Amazon's use of robotics in their fulfillment centers has set a new standard for warehouse automation. The robots automate the movement of shelves of products to the human pickers, reducing the time taken to retrieve items and increasing the amount of inventory that can be stored (Delfanti, 2021).

4. CHALLENGES IN MODERN LOGISTICS OPERATIONS

Logistics today is deeply complex, infinitely intricate and truly global in scale and scope. As per industry estimates, the total size of the logistics sector exceeds $4 trillion accounting for nearly 11% of the global GDP. Intricate supply webs spanning across continents, thousands of interactions between producers, suppliers, transporters, warehouses, distribution centers and retailers supported by flows of data, finance and information exchange coordinate the movement of goods from source to consumers. However, despite its vast scale and economic significance, multiple challenges constrain logistics operations from achieving their fullest potential (Min & Zhou, 2002).

A critical challenge is the sheer lack of visibility stemming from information silos between the myriad entities handling various segments of the supply chain. Outdated technologies coupled with over-reliance on paper-based records, emails and phone calls over standardized electronic data interchange leads to impediments in tracking inventory locations, shipment routes and delivery statuses in real-time. Such opaque visibility frequently causes delays, wastages and exceptions which diminish customer service and entail huge hidden costs (Ahmadi et al., 2024).

The logistics sector also grapples with inadequate infrastructure ranging from outdated material handling equipment in warehouses to congested ports and highways which lower velocity and heighten losses. Estimates suggest over $1 trillion of investment is needed globally just to upgrade legacy logistics infrastructure and keep pace with growth. Constraints also exist in terms of skilled workforce availability as talent supply struggles to meet soaring demand particularly in emerging economies witnessing logistics boom. Moreover, sustainability challenges loom large over the logistics industry which accounts for nearly 5% of global carbon emissions due to reliance on fossil-fuel transportation - an untenable trajectory in the net-zero future (Brewer & Speh, 2000).

Rapidly evolving customer expectations and digital disruptions adding volatility, uncertainty and complexity are also testing the logistics ecosystem.aspiring to overcome these challenges, logistics entities are experimenting on multiple technology-powered innovations but their scale of impact remains inconsistent across regions. Legacy constraints coupled with rising imperatives of responsiveness and resiliency call for logistics ecosystems which can nimbly adapt to external disruptions while offering superior customer-centricity - an exponential technology powered transformation is the key to such future-ready logistics capabilities (Sople, 2009).

4.1. Identifying Common Challenges

The modern logistics landscape is fraught with challenges that can impede the flow of goods and services. These challenges include:

4.1.1. Supply Chain Disruptions

Disruptions can be caused by unforeseen events such as natural disasters, pandemics, political instability, or trade disputes. These events can cause significant delays and increase costs for logistics companies (Romagnoli et al., 2023).

4.1.2. Environmental Concerns

The logistics industry faces pressure to reduce its carbon footprint and adopt more sustainable practices. This includes addressing emissions from transportation, energy use in warehouses, and waste from packaging (Alkaabi, 2023).

4.1.3. Complex Global Networks

As supply chains become more globalized, they also become more complex. Managing these intricate networks requires dealing with various regulations, diverse infrastructures, and different operational standards (Wang et al., 2016).

4.1.4. Customer Expectations

The rise of e-commerce has led to increased customer expectations for faster delivery times, real-time tracking, and more flexible return policies, which adds to the complexity and cost of logistics (Wang et al., 2016).

4.1.5. Labor Shortages

The logistics sector often faces challenges in recruiting and retaining skilled labor, particularly in warehousing and trucking, which can lead to operational inefficiencies (Klappich, 2019).

4.1.6. Cybersecurity Threats

With increased digitalization, logistics operations are more vulnerable to cyber-attacks, which can lead to data breaches, operational shutdowns, and compromised security (Krause et al., 2007).

4.2. The Role of Technology in Addressing These Challenges

Technology plays a pivotal role in overcoming the challenges faced by modern logistics operations. Logistics of the future will be defined by intelligent, integrated and innovative systems that can transform supply chain visibility, optimize capacity, enable sustainability and delight customers.

Exponential technologies like Internet of Things (IoT), artificial intelligence (AI), blockchain, automation and advanced analytics are primed to address several pressing challenges faced by modern logistics (Van Wassenhove, 2006).

Supply chain visibility issues stemming from information gaps between logistics partners can be alleviated through IoT sensors, geospatial tracking and predictive analytics unifying data across transport modes. Blockchain-enabled distributed ledgers allow secure information exchange between entities to achieve transparency on inventories, orders and shipments. Control towers powered by AI and machine learning provide unified visibility by integrating siloed systems across the ecosystem (Yang & Liu, 2012).

Infrastructure constraints related to legacy equipment and congested logistics arteries can be improved through robotic automation, drone deliveries and autonomous transports. AI optimizes warehouse layouts and routes driverless vehicles and aerial drones through dynamic models and real-time coordination minimizing gridlocks. Augmented reality systems guide human operators to maximize productivity. Predictive maintenance leverages sensor data and analytics to enhance infrastructure reliability (Lee & Billington, 1992).

Technology also enables significant sustainability benefits in logistics by optimizing loads, routes, warehouse designs and improving asset utilization through data and algorithms. Analysis shows optimized packaging and loading enabled by dimensioning solutions create over $100 billion in savings. Electric and hydrogen transports powered by renewable energy and net-zero warehouses minimize environmental footprints.

From customer experience perspective, technologies power transparent order tracking and shipment monitoring systems while analytics derives actionable insights from customer data to predict needs and personalize logistics offerings. Automated notifications and intelligent chatbots resolve after-sale issues swiftly while virtual reality solutions enhance order placement experiences (Farchi et al., 2023).

However, to fully leverage technologies and catalyze transformation, a robust digital core combining IoT devices, cloud systems, data analytics and customer interfaces is vital. Legacy modernization to retire outdated technologies combined with change management, workforce upskilling and purposeful innovation culture is equally critical. While emerging technologies hold promising potential, executing logistics digital transformation requires a synchronized strategy synthesizing operations, processes and people centered on service excellence (Abduljabbar et al., 2019).

By adopting a platform-based approach founded on visibility, sustainability, resilience and experience excellence powered by sensors, analytics and automation - technology can usher responsive, customer-centric and future-ready logistics.

4.2.1. Advanced Analytics for Predictive Planning

Big data and predictive analytics can help anticipate disruptions and respond proactively, minimizing the impact of unforeseen events (Wang et al., 2020).

4.2.2. Green Technologies

Adoption of electric vehicles, solar-powered warehouses, and biodegradable packaging materials can help address environmental concerns (Grant et al., 2017).

4.2.3. Automation and AI-Driven Optimization

Automation of warehouses and AI-driven software can streamline global supply chain operations, even in the face of complexity (Sutherland et al., 2018).

4.2.4. Enhanced Customer Experience Technologies

Technologies such as chatbots, AI, and machine learning algorithms can help improve customer service by providing real-time updates and personalized services (Huang & Rust, 2018).

4.2.5. Workforce Augmentation

Technologies like exoskeletons for warehouse workers and advanced driver-assistance systems (ADAS) for truck drivers can alleviate labor shortages by enhancing productivity (Vasquez, 2019).

4.2.6. Robust Cybersecurity Measures

Implementing advanced cybersecurity measures and protocols can protect against cyber threats and ensure the integrity and resilience of logistics operations (James & Collins, 2021).

5. EMERGING TECHNOLOGIES AND THEIR POTENTIAL IMPACT

Logistics of the future will be defined by a myriad of emerging and exponential technologies that could fundamentally transform supply chain visibility, efficiency, sustainability and resilience over the next decade. As logistics operations become more complex, customer expectations continue rising and the imperative for sustainability gains urgency in the climate change era, advanced technologies hold the key to achieve quantum improvements in logistics performance.

Several technologies like Internet of Things (IoT), artificial intelligence, blockchain, automation, robotics, drones and autonomous vehicles are poised to significantly impact various aspects of logistics. IoT sensors transmitting real-time data will create end-to-end supply chain visibility enabling logistics partners to track inventories, shipments and assets across geographies through integrated control towers. Intelligent algorithms and predictive analytics will forecast demand dynamically, optimize warehouse slotting, route vehicles efficiently and coordinate seamless multi-modal deliveries minimizing exceptions (Choudhury et al., 2021).

Warehousing operations will transform through autonomous mobile robots, advanced sorting systems, exoskeletons and collaborative human-robot work cells boosting throughput and accuracy. Driverless trucks with vision sensing capacities will automate freight movement between logistics facilities while coordinated aerial drone and ground robot teams orchestrate last-mile deliveries in ultra-responsive cycles. Blockchain platforms will secure, streamline and bring transparency into exchange of logistics documents, financing and customs clearances across borders.

Logistics sustainability will also get a significant boost from technologies through optimized packaging, route planning and transport modes lowering carbon footprints. Clean energy powered warehouse infrastructure and electric/hydrogen vehicle fleets will accelerate decarbonization further aligned to corporate net-zero commitments. Simultaneously, customer experience is also set to reach new heights with interactive order tracking, personalized delivery options, predictive issue resolution and augmented reality enabled self-service capabilities.

While the potential impact is exponential, the path to large-scale adoption still faces constraints like high costs, interoperability, cyber risks standardization bottlenecks and a significant re-skilling imperative for workforces. But the possibilities opened by technology innovators cannot be ignored by logistics entities and merit exploration now to capitalize early mover advantages. With pragmatic roadmaps leveraging pilot tests, innovation sandboxes and an agile orientation, logistics organizations can systematically transition towards a smart, sustainable and human-centric future (Yeniyurt et al., 2019).

5.1. Exploration of Emerging Technologies in Logistics

5.1.1. Artificial Intelligence (AI) and Machine Learning

AI and machine learning are transforming logistics into a data-driven field. Advanced AI algorithms can optimize delivery routes in real-time, forecast inventory needs, and even automate customer service interactions. These systems analyze patterns and make predictions to improve operational efficiency (Smith & Russo, 2021).

Example: Amazon's use of AI in its fulfillment centers for inventory management and predictive shipping (Amazon, 2022).

5.1.2. Internet of Things (IoT)

IoT technologies connect physical objects in the logistics chain with internet-enabled devices, creating a network of real-time data streams. This connectivity allows for greater control and visibility, from warehouse operations to in-transit goods monitoring (Johnson et al., 2020).

Example: Maersk's Remote Container Management system uses IoT to monitor the condition of refrigerated containers (Reinhardt et al., 2012).

5.1.3. Blockchain

Blockchain's decentralized and transparent nature is well-suited for complex logistics operations, especially in verifying the authenticity of products and streamlining customs processes. It can reduce fraud, improve record-keeping, and increase overall trust.

Example: Walmart's implementation of blockchain to track food provenance and enhance food safety.

5.1.4. Drones and Unmanned Aerial Vehicles (UAVs)

Drones are poised to revolutionize last-mile deliveries, offering a solution to reduce costs and increase speed, particularly in inaccessible or congested areas. UAVs can navigate independently and deliver packages to precise locations.

Example: UPS's Flight Forward program, which utilizes drones for medical sample deliveries.

5.1.5. Autonomous Vehicles (AVs)

AVs in logistics can potentially transform transportation by reducing labor costs, increasing safety, and optimizing delivery times. Self-driving trucks and vans are being tested for their ability to handle long-haul shipments and urban deliveries autonomously.

Example: Waymo's autonomous driving technology being tested for freight and delivery services.

5.2. Potential Benefits and Challenges

5.2.1. Benefits

Operational Efficiency: AI and machine learning can lead to more efficient routing, inventory management, and reduced downtime.

Enhanced Transparency: Blockchain and IoT technologies provide unparalleled visibility and traceability in the supply chain.

Cost Reduction: Through automation (drones, AVs) and enhanced operational efficiency, significant cost savings are achievable.

5.2.2. Challenges

Technical Complexity: Integrating and maintaining these advanced technologies requires significant technical expertise and investment.

Security and Privacy Issues: With the increase in data flow and connectivity, managing data privacy and cybersecurity becomes increasingly challenging.

Regulatory Compliance: The deployment of drones and AVs faces stringent regulatory hurdles and public safety concerns.

5.3. Predictive Analytics and Data-Driven Decision-Making

5.3.1. The Evolution of Predictive Analytics in Logistics

Predictive analytics has become an indispensable tool in modern logistics, driving data-driven decision-making processes that enhance operational efficiency and responsiveness. This technology leverages historical data, statistical algorithms, and machine learning techniques to forecast future outcomes, enabling logistics companies to anticipate and prepare for future scenarios.

5.3.2. Key Aspects of Predictive Analytics in Logistics

1. Demand Forecasting

Predictive analytics allows companies to anticipate demand for products based on historical sales data, trends, and external factors like market conditions and weather patterns. This forecasting helps in optimizing inventory levels, thus reducing holding costs and minimizing stockouts.

2. Route Optimization

By analyzing traffic patterns, weather conditions, and delivery schedules, predictive analytics can suggest the most efficient routes for delivery vehicles. This optimization leads to reduced fuel costs and faster delivery times.

3. Predictive Maintenance

Utilizing data from vehicle sensors, predictive analytics can forecast potential maintenance issues before they occur, reducing downtime and extending the lifespan of logistics assets.

4. Risk Management

Analyzing historical data and market trends, predictive analytics can identify potential risks in the supply chain, such as supplier reliability issues or geopolitical risks, allowing companies to mitigate these risks proactively.

6. FUTURE TRENDS AND PREDICTIONS

The logistics industry is poised for significant transformation driven by technological advancements. Here is a discussion on the anticipated future trends and directions in logistics technology:

1. Increased Integration of AI and Machine Learning

Future logistics operations are expected to see a deeper integration of AI and machine learning, not only in predictive analytics but also in autonomous decision-making processes. These technologies will further refine demand forecasting, optimize delivery routes, and enhance inventory management.

2. Widespread Adoption of Autonomous Vehicles

The use of autonomous vehicles, including drones and self-driving trucks, is anticipated to become more widespread. This will lead to safer, more efficient, and cost-effective transport solutions, particularly in the last-mile delivery segment.

3. Blockchain for Enhanced Security and Transparency

Blockchain technology is expected to play a crucial role in enhancing security and transparency in supply chains. Its ability to provide an immutable record of transactions will be increasingly used to track the provenance and authenticity of goods.

4. IoT and Smart Logistics

The Internet of Things (IoT) will continue to evolve, leading to smarter and more connected logistics operations. IoT devices will provide real-time data, enabling logistics companies to react more quickly to changing circumstances and to optimize their operations dynamically.

5. Sustainability-Driven Technologies

As environmental concerns become more pressing, logistics companies will increasingly adopt green technologies. This includes electric vehicles, solar-powered warehouses, and sustainable packaging solutions to minimize the carbon footprint of logistics operations.

6. Customization and Customer-Centric Approaches

Technologies enabling personalized logistics services will gain traction. This trend includes customized delivery options, real-time communication with customers, and enhanced post-purchase services, all tailored to individual customer preferences.

7. Robotics and Automation in Warehouses

Robotics and automation in warehouses will become more sophisticated, with robots performing more complex tasks. This will increase efficiency and reduce the reliance on human labor for repetitive and physically demanding tasks.

7. CYBERSECURITY IN FOCUS

With the increasing reliance on digital technologies, cybersecurity will become a paramount concern in logistics. Investments in securing digital infrastructure will grow, focusing on protecting data integrity and preventing disruptions (Nour, 2022).

The future of logistics technology is marked by an accelerated pace of innovation, focusing on efficiency, sustainability, and customer-centric approaches. As these technologies evolve and integrate more deeply into logistics operations, they will not only redefine how logistics companies operate but also how they interact with customers and the environment.

In the next 5-10 years, technological advancements are expected to significantly shape the logistics industry in several transformative ways. Here are key predictions:

1. AI and Advanced Analytics Dominance

AI and advanced analytics will become central to logistics operations, driving major decisions and processes. AI's role in demand forecasting, route optimization, and inventory management will become more sophisticated and accurate, enabling highly efficient, responsive, and agile logistics networks.

2. Widespread Use of Autonomous Delivery Vehicles

The use of autonomous vehicles, both on the road and in the air (drones), for deliveries is predicted to become widespread. This will revolutionize last-mile delivery, significantly reducing delivery times and costs, and improving accessibility in remote areas.

3. Blockchain Integration in Supply Chain Management

Blockchain will be more widely adopted for its ability to enhance transparency, security, and efficiency in supply chains. It will be instrumental in combating fraud, ensuring product authenticity, and streamlining customs and clearance processes.

4. IoT-Driven Real-Time Monitoring

IoT technology will enable real-time monitoring and control of the entire supply chain. This will lead to more proactive and predictive logistics management, with IoT sensors providing critical data for decision-making and operational adjustments.

5. Sustainable and Green Logistics Solutions

As environmental concerns continue to grow, the logistics industry will see a surge in sustainable and green solutions. This includes the use of electric vehicles, solar-powered warehouses, and biodegradable packaging, contributing to a significant reduction in the industry's carbon footprint.

6. Personalized and Customer-Centric Logistics

Technology will enable more personalized logistics services, catering to the specific needs and preferences of individual customers. This includes flexible delivery options, real-time communication, and enhanced post-purchase services.

7. Enhanced Cybersecurity Measures

With the increasing digitalization of logistics, cybersecurity will become a major focus. Investments in securing digital infrastructures will increase, with advanced measures to protect against cyber threats and ensure data privacy.

8. Augmented Reality (AR) and Virtual Reality (VR) in Training and Operations

AR and VR technologies will be increasingly used for training logistics personnel and in operational planning. These technologies will provide immersive experiences for training purposes and aid in visualizing complex logistics scenarios.

These predictions suggest a future where logistics operations are more efficient, customer-focused, environmentally friendly, and driven by data and automation.

8. SUSTAINABILITY AND ETHICAL CONSIDERATIONS

As environmental concerns increasingly influence business practices, the logistics industry is turning to technology to foster sustainability. Here's how technology is being used to promote eco-friendly logistics practices:

1. Green Transportation Technologies

The shift towards electric vehicles (EVs), hydrogen fuel cells, and other low-emission transport options is a significant step in reducing the carbon footprint of logistics operations. Technologies that improve fuel efficiency in traditional transport modes are also crucial.

Example: Companies like Tesla and Nikola are developing electric and hydrogen-powered trucks for sustainable freight transport.

2. Route Optimization Software

Advanced algorithms and AI are used to calculate the most efficient routes, reducing fuel consumption and emissions. This software considers factors like traffic conditions, vehicle type, and delivery windows.

Example: UPS's ORION (On-Road Integrated Optimization and Navigation) system optimizes delivery routes to minimize miles driven.

3. Warehouse Automation and Energy Efficiency

Automated storage and retrieval systems, along with IoT sensors, contribute to more energy-efficient warehouse operations. Smart systems can control lighting, heating, and cooling based on real-time needs.

Example: Amazon's fulfillment centers use robotics and AI to reduce energy usage and increase operational efficiency.

4. Sustainable Packaging Solutions

Investment in technology to develop sustainable packaging – biodegradable materials, reusable containers, and efficient packing algorithms – helps reduce waste.

Example: Loop, a platform by TerraCycle, uses technology to facilitate a reusable packaging system for various consumer products.

5. Blockchain for Supply Chain Transparency

Blockchain technology can be used to trace the sustainability footprint of products, ensuring ethical sourcing and supply chain transparency.

Example: IBM's Food Trust blockchain network enhances the traceability of food supply chains, ensuring sustainable practices.

9. CONCLUSION

As we have explored throughout this chapter, the landscape of logistics is undergoing a significant transformation, driven by rapid advancements in technology. From the integration of AI and IoT to the application of blockchain and the advent of autonomous vehicles, each technological innovation brings new opportunities for efficiency, accuracy, and service enhancement in logistics operations. The future of logistics is poised at an exciting juncture where technology not only promises to streamline operations but also to address larger issues such as sustainability, ethical practices, and workforce transformation. The potential benefits are vast: enhanced operational efficiency, cost savings, improved customer service, and a notable reduction in the environmental impact of logistics activities. However, the path forward is not without its challenges. The logistics sector must navigate the complexities of integrating new technologies, managing the ethical implications of automation and data usage, and ensuring cybersecurity. Furthermore, the industry faces the critical task of aligning these technological advancements with human-centric approaches, considering the impact on employment, skill requirements, and the societal implications of a digitally transformed logistics landscape. As we look ahead, the role of continuous innovation, strategic planning, and ethical considerations will be crucial. The logistics industry must remain agile, adapting to technological changes while ensuring that these advancements benefit all stakeholders, including customers, employees, and the broader community. In conclusion, the intersection of technology and logistics is a dynamic and evolving space, full of potential for groundbreaking improvements in how goods are moved and managed around the globe. By embracing these changes responsibly and strategically, the logistics industry can look forward to a future that is not only more efficient and profitable but also more sustainable and equitable.

REFERENCES

Abduljabbar, R., Dia, H., Liyanage, S., & Bagloee, S. A. (2019). Applications of artificial intelligence in transport: An overview. *Sustainability (Basel)*, *11*(1), 189. doi:10.3390/su11010189

Agrawal, D. K. (2012). Demand chain management: Factors enhancing market responsiveness capabilities. *Journal of Marketing Channels*, *19*(2), 101–119. doi:10.1080/1046669X.2012.667760

Ahmadi, S., Shokouhyar, S., Amerioun, M., & Tabrizi, N. S. (2024). A social media analytics-based approach to customer-centric reverse logistics management of electronic devices: A case study on notebooks. *Journal of Retailing and Consumer Services*, *76*, 103540. doi:10.1016/j.jretconser.2023.103540

Alkaabi, K. (2023). Exploring logistics service providers for small and medium-sized enterprises and large corporations: benefits and challenges. *European Business Review*.

Belhadi, A., Mani, V., Kamble, S. S., Khan, S. A. R., & Verma, S. (2021). Artificial intelligence-driven innovation for enhancing supply chain resilience and performance under the effect of supply chain dynamism: An empirical investigation. *Annals of Operations Research*, 1–26. PMID:33551534

Bowersox, D. J., & Closs, D. J. (1974). *Logistical management*. Macmillan New York.

Brewer, P. C., & Speh, T. W. (2000). Using the balanced scorecard to measure supply chain performance Brewer, Peter CSpeh, Thomas W. *Journal of Business Logistics*, *21*(1), 75–93.

Cho, D. W., Lee, Y. H., Ahn, S. H., & Hwang, M. K. (2012). A framework for measuring the performance of service supply chain management. *Computers & Industrial Engineering*, *62*(3), 801–818. doi:10.1016/j.cie.2011.11.014

Choudhury, A., Behl, A., Sheorey, P. A., & Pal, A. (2021). Digital supply chain to unlock new agility: A TISM approach. *Benchmarking*, *28*(6), 2075–2109. doi:10.1108/BIJ-08-2020-0461

Cichosz, M., Wallenburg, C. M., & Knemeyer, A. M. (2020). Digital transformation at logistics service providers: Barriers, success factors and leading practices. *International Journal of Logistics Management*, *31*(2), 209–238. doi:10.1108/IJLM-08-2019-0229

Delfanti, A. (2021). *The warehouse. Workers and robots at Amazon*. Pluto Books. doi:10.2307/j.ctv2114fnm

Demir, S., Yilmaz, I., & Paksoy, T. (2020). Augmented Reality in SCM. *Logistics 4.0: Digital Transformation of Supply Chain Management*, 136.

Farchi, F., Farchi, C., Touzi, B., & Mabrouki, C. (2023). A comparative study on AI-based algorithms for cost prediction in pharmaceutical transport logistics. *Acadlore Trans. Mach. Learn*, *2*(3), 129–141. doi:10.56578/ataiml020302

Fernando, Y., Chidambaram, R. R. M., & Wahyuni-TD, I. S. (2018). The impact of Big Data analytics and data security practices on service supply chain performance. *Benchmarking*, *25*(9), 4009–4034. doi:10.1108/BIJ-07-2017-0194

Gunasekaran, A., & Ngai, E. W. T. (2005). Build-to-order supply chain management: A literature review and framework for development. *Journal of Operations Management*, *23*(5), 423–451. doi:10.1016/j.jom.2004.10.005

Gunasekaran, A., Patel, C., & McGaughey, R. E. (2004). A framework for supply chain performance measurement. *International Journal of Production Economics*, *87*(3), 333–347. doi:10.1016/j.ijpe.2003.08.003

Gunasekaran, A., Patel, C., & Tirtiroglu, E. (2001). Performance measures and metrics in a supply chain environment. *International Journal of Operations & Production Management*, *21*(1/2), 71–87. doi:10.1108/01443570110358468

Krause, D. R., Handfield, R. B., & Tyler, B. B. (2007). The relationships between supplier development, commitment, social capital accumulation and performance improvement. *Journal of Operations Management*, *25*(2), 528–545. doi:10.1016/j.jom.2006.05.007

Le, D. N., Nguyen, H. T., & Truong, P. H. (2020). Port logistics service quality and customer satisfaction: Empirical evidence from Vietnam. *The Asian Journal of Shipping and Logistics*, *36*(2), 89–103. doi:10.1016/j.ajsl.2019.10.003

Lee, H. L., & Billington, C. (1992). Managing supply chain inventory: Pitfalls and opportunities. *MIT Sloan Management Review*.

Lee, H. L., & Whang, S. (2000). Information sharing in a supply chain. *International Journal of Manufacturing Technology and Management*, *1*(1), 79–93. doi:10.1504/IJMTM.2000.001329

Lenuwat, P., & Boon-itt, S. (2022). Information technology management and service performance management capabilities: An empirical study of the service supply chain management process. *Journal of Advances in Management Research*, *19*(1), 55–77. doi:10.1108/JAMR-01-2021-0039

Min, H., & Zhou, G. (2002). Supply chain modeling: Past, present and future. *Computers & Industrial Engineering*, *43*(1–2), 231–249. doi:10.1016/S0360-8352(02)00066-9

Nour, R. (2022). Enhancing the Logistics 4.0 Firms through Information Technology. *Sustainability (Basel)*, *14*(23), 15860. doi:10.3390/su142315860

Olavarrieta, S., & Ellinger, A. E. (1997). Resource-based theory and strategic logistics research. *International Journal of Physical Distribution & Logistics Management*, *27*(9/10), 559–587. doi:10.1108/09600039710188594

Rehman, S. U., Usman, M., Fernando, Y., Kamarudin, D., & Waheed, A. (2023). Improving manufacturing supply chain performance: nexus of industrial Internet of Things, blockchain technology and innovativeness. *Journal of Science and Technology Policy Management.*

Reinhardt, F. L., Casadesus-Masanell, R., & Nellemann, F. (2012). Maersk Line and the Future of Container Shipping. *Harvard Business School Case Study*, 9–712.

Romagnoli, S., Tarabu', C., Maleki Vishkaei, B., & De Giovanni, P. (2023). The Impact of Digital Technologies and Sustainable Practices on Circular Supply Chain Management. *Logistics*, *7*(1), 1. doi:10.3390/logistics7010001

Simatupang, T. M., & Sridharan, R. (2002). The collaborative supply chain. *International Journal of Logistics Management*, *13*(1), 15–30. doi:10.1108/09574090210806333

Sople, V. V. (2009). *Logistics Management, 2/E.* Pearson Education India.

Sum, C., & Teo, C. (1999). Strategic posture of logistics service providers in Singapore. *International Journal of Physical Distribution & Logistics Management*, *29*(9), 588–605. doi:10.1108/09600039910287538

Tortorella, G. L., Giglio, R., & Van Dun, D. H. (2019). Industry 4.0 adoption as a moderator of the impact of lean production practices on operational performance improvement. *International Journal of Operations & Production Management, 39*(6/7/8), 860–886.

Van Wassenhove, L. N. (2006). Humanitarian aid logistics: Supply chain management in high gear. *The Journal of the Operational Research Society*, *57*(5), 475–489. doi:10.1057/palgrave.jors.2602125

Wang, G., Gunasekaran, A., Ngai, E. W. T., & Papadopoulos, T. (2016). Big data analytics in logistics and supply chain management: Certain investigations for research and applications. *International Journal of Production Economics*, *176*, 98–110. doi:10.1016/j.ijpe.2016.03.014

Wu, F., Yeniyurt, S., Kim, D., & Cavusgil, S. T. (2006). The impact of information technology on supply chain capabilities and firm performance: A resource-based view. *Industrial Marketing Management*, *35*(4), 493–504. doi:10.1016/j.indmarman.2005.05.003

Yang, C., & Liu, H. (2012). Boosting firm performance via enterprise agility and network structure. *Management Decision*, *50*(6), 1022–1044. doi:10.1108/00251741211238319

Yeniyurt, S., Wu, F., Kim, D., & Cavusgil, S. T. (2019). Information technology resources, innovativeness, and supply chain capabilities as drivers of business performance: A retrospective and future research directions. *Industrial Marketing Management*, *79*, 46–52. doi:10.1016/j.indmarman.2019.03.008

Chapter 5
Embracing Digital Transformation:
A Paradigm Shift in Business Operations and Strategies

Sanjay Taneja
https://orcid.org/0000-0002-3632-4053
Graphic Era University (Deemed), India

Rishi Prakash Shukla
https://orcid.org/0000-0003-0854-7302
Chandigarh University, India

Amandeep Singh
Chitkara Business School, Chitkara University, India

ABSTRACT

In the wake of rapid technological advancements, the concept of digital transformation has emerged as a critical driver for organizational growth and resilience. This research paper delves into the multifaceted implications of digital transformation across various sectors and industries. By analysing the integration of cutting-edge technologies, such as artificial intelligence, big data analytics, cloud computing, and the internet of things, this study elucidates the transformative impact of these innovations on traditional business models. Additionally, the research investigates the challenges, opportunities, and potential risks associated with the adoption of digital transformation strategies, emphasizing the need for proactive adaptation and robust cybersecurity measures. Through a comprehensive examination of case studies and empirical data, this chapter aims to provide insights into the evolving landscape of digital transformation and its profound implications for organizational sustainability and competitiveness in the digital era.

DOI: 10.4018/979-8-3693-2019-8.ch005

1. INTRODUCTION

1.1 Definition and Significance of Digital Transformation in the Context of Contemporary Business Operations

The term "digital transformation" describes the deliberate application of digital tools, data, and procedures to better and radically change how companies run, serve their clients, and maintain their competitiveness in the contemporary market (Saarikko et al., 2020). To improve customer experiences, expedite processes, and spur innovation, it entails integrating technology like as artificial intelligence, cloud computing, big data analytics, Internet of Things, and more (Munirathinam, 2020). The potential for digital transformation to boost productivity, cut expenses, and open up new income sources has made it an essential requirement for modern enterprises. In a highly competitive business climate, it helps organisations stay relevant and sustainable by enabling them to respond more effectively to client requests, capitalise on emerging possibilities in the digital world, and adapt to fast changing market dynamics.

Digital transformation is becoming more than simply a competitive advantage for firms in today's digitally interconnected and data-driven world; it's often a survival strategy (Bresciani et al., 2021). Businesses that adopt digital transformation are better equipped to satisfy changing consumer demands, use data to make wise decisions, and streamline operations for responsiveness and agility. Furthermore, because digital transformation makes remote labour, e-commerce, and digital communication possible—all of which are now crucial for company resilience and continuity in the post-pandemic world—it has become even more important (Bai et al., 2021). It is also a cornerstone of modern corporate operations because it encourages innovation, which enables companies to continuously adapt and thrive in a constantly changing environment.

1.2 Evolution of Digital Transformation and Its Impact on Various Industries

Beyond conventional bounds, digital transformation has grown into a powerful and disruptive force that is transforming a number of industries and fundamentally altering how firms function(Hanelt et al., 2021). The process of digital transformation started out as the digitization of manual operations and the adoption of simple software solutions. It has now developed into a complex phenomenon. Healthcare, banking, manufacturing, and retail are just a few of the industries that have seen a transformation because to the integration of cutting-edge technologies like cloud computing, IoT, big data analytics, and artificial intelligence(Analytics & Mccarthy, 2020). While fintech and blockchain technologies in finance are changing the way investments and transactions are made, telemedicine and electronic health records in healthcare improve patient care. Industry 4.0 has been embraced by manufacturing, enabling sophisticated supply chains and factories, while e-commerce and data-driven customer insights have revolutionised retail. Businesses undergoing digital transformation must manage not only new technology but also changing consumer expectations and privacy issues pertaining to data. To stay competitive in this more linked world, businesses must innovate, adapt, and stay in step with the digital era.

1.3 Importance of Embracing Digital Transformation for Staying Competitive in the Modern Marketplace

As digital transformation signifies a fundamental shift in the way businesses function, engage with customers, and innovate, it is imperative for firms to embrace it if they want to remain competitive in the current economy (Bai et al., 2021). Digital technology helps businesses in today's fast-paced, connected world to improve customer experiences, optimise processes, and quickly adjust to changing market conditions. Businesses may obtain important insights, streamline procedures, and produce more individualised, effective, and economical solutions by utilising data analytics, automation, cloud computing, and other digital technologies(Attaran & Woods, 2018). Furthermore, digital transformation is crucial for maintaining development and relevance in a world that is becoming more and more digitally focused since it enables businesses to participate in e-commerce, reach new client segments, and access the global marketplace. People who don't accept this change run the risk of slipping behind, while those who do so can unlock new opportunities for innovation, competitiveness, and sustainable success.

2. LITERATURE REVIEW

2.1 Key Components and Technologies Driving Digital Transformation

Digital transformation is propelled by a dynamic convergence of key components and cutting-edge technologies that collectively redefine the way organizations operate and engage with their stakeholders. At its core, this transformative process is anchored by data analytics and artificial intelligence, which empower businesses to glean actionable insights from vast datasets and automate decision-making processes. Cloud computing provides the flexible infrastructure needed for scalability and agility, enabling the seamless integration of services and applications (Entenam & Ahmed, 2014). The Internet of Things (IoT) connects the physical world to the digital realm, facilitating real-time monitoring and optimization of assets. Blockchain ensures trust and security in transactions and supply chains, while augmented and virtual reality (AR/VR) offer immersive experiences for both customers and employees. Furthermore, advanced cybersecurity solutions safeguard sensitive information and bolster digital resilience. Mobile technologies and 5G networks enhance connectivity and enable on-the-go access to services, while robotic process automation streamlines repetitive tasks. In tandem with all these elements, a cultural shift toward digital literacy, agile methodologies, and customer-centric approaches is essential for a successful digital transformation, fostering innovation and competitive advantage in an increasingly digital landscape (Rueckel et al., 2020).

2.2 Analysis of the Benefits and Challenges Associated With Implementing Digital Transformation in Business Operations

Among the many advantages of implementing digital transformation in corporate operations include higher productivity, simpler workflows, better data-driven decision-making, enhanced customer experiences, and the possibility of generating new revenue streams (Butt, 2020). It helps businesses to adjust to shifting client expectations and remain competitive in a digital landscape that is changing quickly. Significant obstacles to this transition, meanwhile, include the high cost of the initial investment, employee aversion to change, worries about data security, and the ongoing need to adapt as technology advances. Careful planning, strong leadership, and a dedication to continuous innovation and learning are necessary for a successful digital transformation in order to fully realise its promise and minimise the problems that come with it.

2.3 Case Studies Illustrating Successful Digital Transformation Initiatives in Prominent Companies

Case studies that highlight effective digital transformation programmes at top businesses offer insightful information on how businesses use technology to spur innovation, increase productivity, and maintain competitiveness in the quickly changing business environment of today. These cases frequently draw attention to the complex nature of digital transformation by showing how businesses in a range of sectors are redefining business models, improving customer experiences, and streamlining operations by utilising cutting-edge technologies like artificial intelligence, cloud computing, data analytics, and the Internet of Things. their case studies serve as helpful manuals for firms planning to start their own transformation projects by breaking down the tactics, difficulties, and results of their digital transformation journeys.

3. DIGITAL TRANSFORMATION MODELS AND FRAMEWORKS

3.1 Overview of Popular Digital Transformation Models Such as McKinsey 7S Model, Kotter's 8-Step Change Model, and Prosci's ADKAR Model

Popular digital transformation models like the McKinsey 7S Model, Kotter's 8-Step Change Model, and Prosci's ADKAR Model offer valuable frameworks for organizations seeking to navigate the complex process of digital transformation (Harrison et al., 2022). The McKinsey 7S Model emphasizes seven interconnected factors (strategy, structure, systems, shared values, style, staff, and skills) that need to align and evolve together to drive successful transformation. Kotter's 8-Step Change Model provides a systematic approach to managing change, highlighting the importance of creating a sense of urgency, building a guiding coalition, and ensuring short-term wins to maintain momentum (Entenam & Ahmed, 2014). On the other hand, Prosci's ADKAR Model focuses on individual change management, emphasizing Awareness, Desire, Knowledge, Ability, and Reinforcement as the key components for employees to embrace and sustain change. These models offer diverse perspectives, helping organizations tailor their digital transformation efforts to meet specific needs and challenges while fostering a holistic understanding of the process.

3.2 Comparative Analysis of Different Frameworks and Their Applicability in Diverse Business Environments

Various frameworks, like the Kotter 8-Step Change Model, the Prosci ADKAR Model, and the McKinsey 7S Model, each have special advantages and can be applied in a variety of corporate settings. The McKinsey 7S Model is a useful tool for companies trying to make sure their strategy, structure, and culture are in sync with the digital transformation process because it is excellent at evaluating and optimising an organization's internal alignment. Because of its emphasis on change leadership, Kotter's 8-Step Change Model is especially well-suited for organisations that need a structured method to encourage employee commitment and involvement during transition. Prosci's ADKAR Model, on the other hand, works best when individual change management is the main priority. This makes it useful for companies that need to handle employee opposition and guarantee the advancement of skills and knowledge. In the end, the choice of framework depends. In order to meet the complex nature of digital transformation in today's dynamic and changing business landscape, organisations frequently benefit from a combination of these frameworks (Mishra et al., 2023). Ultimately, the choice of framework depends on the unique needs and difficulties of the business environment.

3.3 Case Examples Demonstrating the Practical Application of Digital Transformation Models in Real-World Scenarios

In today's corporate environments, digital transformation models are critical because they allow organisations to leverage technology to improve operations and spur growth (Berman, 2012). Consider a global retail company that wants to enhance customer satisfaction and optimise its supply chain. They can install real-time inventory tracking systems employing IoT sensors by embracing a digital transformation approach, which will allow them to keep an eye on stock levels in all of their stores and warehouses. An AI-powered predictive analytics platform uses this data to forecast demand and initiate automated restocking orders. This optimises expenses by minimising stockouts and reducing surplus inventory. In addition, the retail behemoth uses machine learning algorithms to suggest products based on consumer behaviour and preferences through digital channels, providing individualised shopping experiences. Through the integration of augmented reality for virtual try-ons, their smartphone app improves consumer pleasure by increasing user interaction(Oosthuizen et al., 2021). By digital transformation, the company gains a competitive edge in the retail sector and increases efficiency and customer-centricity.

4. IMPLICATIONS OF DIGITAL TRANSFORMATION ON BUSINESS OPERATIONS

4.1 Impact of Digital Transformation on Organizational Structure, Culture, and Employee Roles

Organisational culture, staff responsibilities, and organisational structure have all undergone major changes as a result of digital transformation. Flatter, more agile settings that promote decentralised decision-making and cross-functional collaboration have replaced traditional hierarchical arrangements. These days, creativity, flexibility, and digital literacy are valued highly, with a particular emphasis on customer-centricity. With the rise of data analysts, digital marketers, cybersecurity professionals, and remote work coordinators, among others, employee roles have changed(Schneider & Kokshagina, 2021). All personnel must engage in ongoing learning in order to stay up to date with the rapidly evolving digital ecosystem. In the digital age, companies must adopt these changes if they want to be competitive and responsive to consumer needs. An organization's organisational structure, culture, and job positions are all significantly and continuously impacted by digital transformation. It necessitates a change towards inventive, flexible, and cooperative structures and cultures, together with a workforce that is adaptive and technologically literate. Organisations must adapt to these changes if they want to compete in the quick-paced digital era.

4.2 Integration of Digital Technologies in Supply Chain Management, Production, and Logistics

Known as the "digital supply chain" or "Industry 4.0," the integration of digital technology in supply chain management, production, and logistics is transforming these vital economic domains (Ivanov et al., 2022). Technologies like blockchain, IoT sensors, and predictive analytics are improving demand forecasting, inventory optimisation, and supplier cooperation in supply chain management (Attaran, 2020). Automation, digital twins, 3D printing, and IoT-enabled smart factories all help to improve the flexibility and efficiency of production operations. Route optimisation, autonomous cars and drones for last-mile deliveries, and tracking systems for real-time visibility are all examples of how logistics is changing. Throughout the supply chain, artificial intelligence, machine learning, cloud computing, and cybersecurity are crucial because they enable data-driven decision-making and protect against cyber threats.

4.3 Analysis of the Effects of Digital Transformation on Customer Relationship Management and Marketing Strategies

Marketing tactics and customer relationship management (CRM) have been significantly altered by the digital revolution(Visser & Fokkema, 2021). Large-scale customer data collection and analysis has made it possible for firms to launch more focused marketing efforts and provide more individualised customer service. Multichannel marketing has been made possible by the availability of numerous digital channels, including social media and email, which have enhanced consumer involvement (Payne & Frow, 2004). The benefits of this transformation include data-driven decision-making, social listening, scalability, and competitive advantages. As a result, businesses must adapt and take advantage of digital technology in order to meet customer expectations and remain competitive in the digital age. By enhancing data management, customer engagement, personalization, multichannel marketing, data-driven decision-making, social listening, scalability, and competitive advantage, digital transformation has completely changed customer relationship management and marketing methods. In order to fulfil client expectations and stay competitive, businesses in the modern digital age must adapt and change their strategies on a constant basis.

5. STRATEGIES FOR SUCCESSFUL IMPLEMENTATION OF DIGITAL TRANSFORMATION

5.1 Assessment of the Challenges and Risks Associated With the Implementation of Digital Transformation Initiatives

For digital transformation programmes in organisations to be successful, a number of risks and obstacles must be properly considered and controlled. Common roadblocks include employee resistance to change, budget overruns, and the necessity for a competent staff. Data security and privacy issues are major concerns, and integrating new technology with old ones might cause compatibility problems (Tewari & Gupta, 2020). Poor project management, organisational cultural shifts, and vendor lock-in can all obstruct development. Considerations of customer experience, regulatory compliance, and operational disruptions are crucial, as are well-defined objectives and plans. Planning must take sustainability and scalability into account in addition to ethical and environmental issues. Organisations must negotiate the digital landscape since neglecting to handle these issues could put them at danger of losing out on business (Aula, 2010). In addition, it's critical to think about how changes will affect the customer experience and make sure that they improve it rather than worsen it. You should also manage any operational disruptions and adhere to industry rules. Any transformation programme must start with clearly defined goals and strategies in order to stay on course. Planning should take into account issues related to ethics, the environment, scalability, sustainability, and immediate demands. In order to successfully traverse the changing digital landscape, companies must have comprehensive strategy, effective change management, and ongoing monitoring. Neglecting to address these complex problems and dangers could make them less competitive.

5.2 Examination of Best Practices and Strategies for Overcoming Resistance to Change and Fostering a Culture of Innovation

In addition, it's critical to think about how changes will affect the customer experience and make sure that they improve it rather than worsen it. You should also manage any operational disruptions and adhere to industry rules. Any transformation programme must start with clearly defined goals and strategies in order to stay on course. Planning should take into account issues related to ethics, the environment, scalability, sustainability, and immediate demands. In order to successfully traverse the changing digital landscape, companies must have comprehensive strategy, effective change management, and ongoing monitoring (Li et al., 2016). Neglecting to address these complex problems and dangers could make them less competitive.

5.3 Case Studies Highlighting Effective Digital Transformation Strategies Employed by Leading Companies in Different Sectors

Prominent enterprises throughout diverse industries have adopted efficacious digital transformation tactics to maintain their competitiveness and adjust to evolving business environments. With its data-driven personalised content and streaming platform, Netflix revolutionised the entertainment business (Walker et al., 2017). Amazon uses big data and artificial intelligence (AI) to optimise supply chains and consumer experiences (Oosthuizen et al., 2021). This is demonstrated by their digital journey from online shopping to cloud computing through Amazon Web Services (AWS). Walmart integrated e-commerce and physical stores with curbside pickup and same-day delivery, while Starbucks integrated mobile ordering and payment technologies into its digital approach. With its Predix platform, General Electric transformed into a digital industrial corporation by leveraging IoT and data analytics for equipment maintenance. Using an IoT sensor and a mobile app, Delta Air Lines enhanced both its operations and customer experience (Karakuş et al., 2019). While Alibaba thrived in e-commerce, cloud computing, banking, and entertainment and built a vast digital ecosystem, Ford dabbled in connected and electric vehicles (Parker, 2016). The aforementioned case examples underscore the significance of data, emerging technology, and business model adaption in facilitating effective digital transformation across a range of industries.

6. MEASURING THE SUCCESS OF DIGITAL TRANSFORMATION INITIATIVES

6.1 Identification of Key Performance Indicators (KPIs) for Evaluating the Effectiveness and Impact of Digital Transformation Projects

Determining the key performance indicators (KPIs) is essential to assessing the influence and efficacy of digital transformation initiatives (Braglia et al., 2022). From revenue growth, client acquisition and retention, conversion rates, and customer happiness to cost reduction, channel performance, and time-to-market, these KPIs offer a holistic picture of the project's success. A comprehensive evaluation of the project's results is also ensured by monitoring user engagement, operational effectiveness, data security, and compliance in addition to assessing employee productivity, innovation, and ROI. Important indications include the company's market share, competitive standing, and degree of digital maturity. The success of digital transformation projects is ultimately facilitated by the selection and monitoring of pertinent KPIs that are in line with project goals and enable data-driven decision-making and continuous optimisation(Aula, 2010).

6.2 Analysis of Data-Driven Metrics and Qualitative Feedback to Assess the ROI of Digital Transformation Efforts

Evaluating the impact of digital transformation initiatives and determining their return on investment (ROI) requires a methodical approach that blends quantitative data analysis and qualitative input. Set specific, quantifiable goals first, then identify the key performance indicators (KPIs) that correspond with these goals. Gather reliable information from a variety of sources, including financial accounts, sales reports, and customer surveys. Then, use quantitative analysis to determine how the KPIs changed before and after the transition. To learn more about intangible advantages and difficulties, collect qualitative input via surveys, interviews, and reviews from stakeholders, consumers, and staff. A thorough understanding of ROI can be obtained by integrating quantitative and qualitative data, and benchmarking against industry norms can offer insightful background. To maximise ROI over time, take into account the transformation's associated costs and keep an eye on and tweak your techniques from time to time. Lastly, make sure you clearly deliver the findings and recommendations to the important parties you have consulted. By using this strategy, businesses may maximise the return on their efforts in digital transformation and make well-informed decisions.

7. RESEARCH MODEL

7.1 Proposed Conceptual Model for Understanding the Process of Digital Transformation in Business Operations

In the figure 1. level of an organization's acceptance of new digital technologies, including cloud computing, big data analytics, artificial intelligence, and the Internet of Things, is referred to as technology adoption. Adoption of technology is critical to digital transformation since it helps businesses to enhance operations, innovate new goods and services, and establish fresh business strategies. The common values, norms, and beliefs that shape an organization's conduct are referred to as its organisational culture.

Figure 1. Industry 4.0 – enabled digital transformation

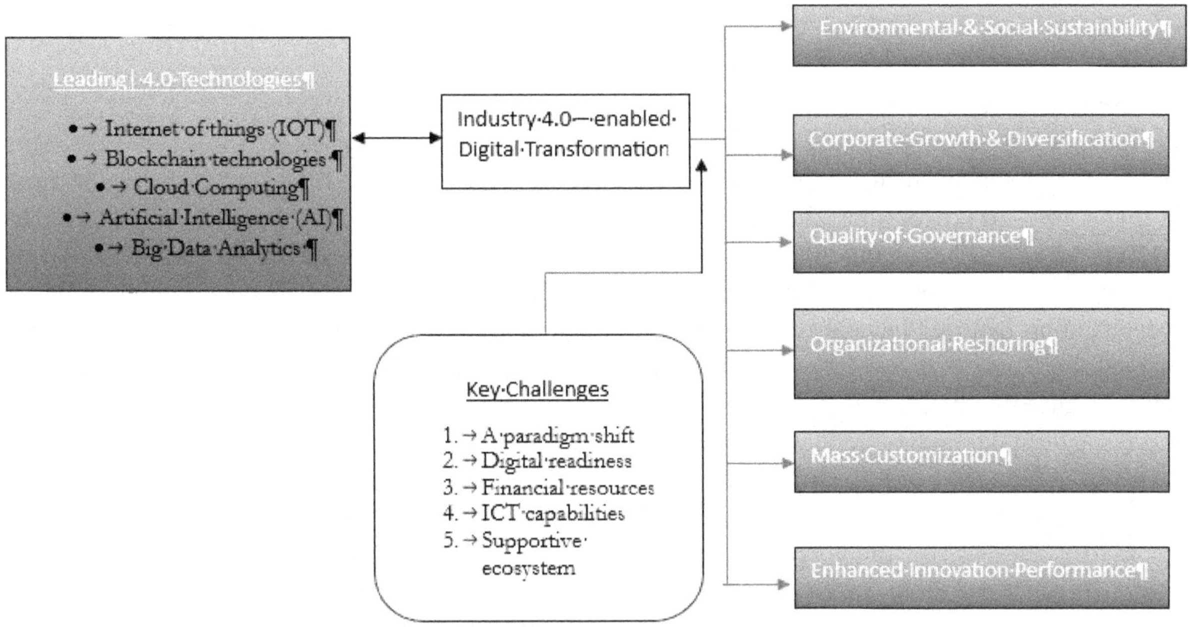

Digital transformation requires a culture that is flexible and innovative. Businesses that have a strong digital innovation culture are more inclined to experiment with new business practises and adopt new technology. The level of top management commitment to digital transformation is referred to as leadership commitment. In order to drive digital transformation, leaders must set the vision, provide resources, and remove obstacles. It is more probable for leaders who are dedicated to digital transformation to foster an innovative culture and encourage the uptake of new technology. According to the concept, employee, customer, and business performance are all positively impacted by digital transformation. Enhanced corporate performance can be attained by decreasing expenses, raising productivity, and increasing sales. A more convenient and tailored experience can increase customer satisfaction. An environment at work that is more engaging and adaptable might increase employee satisfaction.

7.2 Visualization of the Key Components, Stages, and Factors Influencing Successful Digital Transformation

Effective digital transformation is a complex process with many moving parts, phases, and essential elements. It starts with a clear vision, a well-defined path, and strong leadership. Technology infrastructure, data and analytics, process optimisation, customer-centricity, digital skills, cybersecurity, change management, and strategic partnerships are all included in the key components. Assessment and planning, digitization, integration, data and analytics deployment, process redesign, improved customer engagement, talent development, iterative scaling, and cybersecurity reinforcement are some of the phases that constitute the transformative phase. Organisational culture, agility, alignment with business objectives, consumer insights, risk management, resource allocation, quantifiable KPIs, compliance, vendor and partner selection, innovation, and effective communication are just a few of the variables that make an organisation successful. To be competitive in the rapidly changing digital market, digital transformation is a continual process that demands flexibility and a dedication to constant change.

8. CONCLUSION

The chapter concludes by highlighting how crucial it is to change with the times and embrace the digital era if you want to stay relevant and competitive in the quickly changing business environment of today. We have looked at how technology has a significant impact on a number of company components, including operations, customer interaction, decision-making procedures, and overarching strategies. Understanding that this change is a requirement for long-term success and growth rather than just a personal preference is crucial as we proceed through the digital transformation process. Organisations may maximise productivity, improve customer experiences, and open up new avenues for creativity by embracing digital transformation. It forces us to reconsider established business models and adopt fresh perspectives that make use of automation, data, and connection. The necessity of proactive adaptation, a dedication to lifelong learning, and a readiness to try new things and take measured risks are the main lessons to be learned from this chapter. In the digital age, companies that maximise the potential of digital technology, cultivate an innovative culture, and place a premium on agility will prosper.

Adopting digital transformation is not only a decision, but also a strategic need in a world where change is the only thing that stays constant. The future of their industry and the way we conduct business will be shaped by those who recognise its significance and act courageously to embrace it.

REFERENCES

Analytics, D., & Mccarthy, G. (2020). Transforming Business Using Digital Innovations : The Application of AI. *Transforming Business Using Digital Innovations*, 1–33.

Attaran, M. (2020). Digital technology enablers and their implications for supply chain management. *Supply Chain Forum, 21*(3), 158–172. 10.1080/16258312.2020.1751568

Attaran, M., & Woods, J. (2018). *Cloud computing technology : improving small business performance using the Internet.* Taylor & Francis. doi:10.1080/08276331.2018.1466850

Aula, P. (2010). Social media, reputation risk and ambient publicity management. *Strategy and Leadership, 38*(6), 43–49. doi:10.1108/10878571011088069

Bai, C., Quayson, M., & Sarkis, J. (2021). COVID-19 pandemic digitization lessons for sustainable development of micro-and small- enterprises. *Sustainable Production and Consumption, 27*, 1989–2001. doi:10.1016/j.spc.2021.04.035 PMID:34722843

Berman, S. J. (2012). Digital transformation: Opportunities to create new business models. *Strategy and Leadership, 40*(2), 16–24. doi:10.1108/10878571211209314

Braglia, M., Gabbrielli, R., Marrazzini, L., & Padellini, L. (2022). Key Performance Indicators and Industry 4.0 - A structured approach for monitoring the implementation of digital technologies. *Procedia Computer Science, 200*(2019), 1626–1635. doi:10.1016/j.procs.2022.01.363

Bresciani, S., Ferraris, A., Romano, M., & Santoro, G. (2021). Building a Digital Transformation Strategy. In *Digital Transformation Management for Agile Organizations: A Compass to Sail the Digital World* (pp. 5–27). Emerald Publishing Limited. doi:10.1108/978-1-80043-171-320211002

Butt, J. (2020). *A Conceptual Framework to Support Digital Transformation in Manufacturing Using an Integrated Business Process Management Approach.*

Entenam, K., & Ahmed, U. (2014). Cloud Computing for Enterprise Architectures. *Identity and Access Management in Cloud Computing*, (May). doi:10.1007/978-1-4471-2236-4

Hanelt, A., Bohnsack, R., Marz, D., & Antunes Marante, C. (2021). A Systematic Review of the Literature on Digital Transformation. *Journal of Management Studies*, *58*(July), 1159–1197. doi:10.1111/joms.12639

Harrison, R., Fischer, S., Walpola, R. L., Chauhan, A., Babalola, T., Mears, S., Le-dao, H., Harrison, R., Fischer, S., Walpola, R. L., & Chauhan, A. (2022). Where Do Models for Change Management, Improvement and Implementation Meet? *A Systematic Review of the Applications of Change Management Models in Healthcare.* IEEE. 10.2147/JHL.S289176

Ivanov, D., Dolgui, A., & Sokolov, B. (2022). Cloud supply chain: Integrating Industry 4.0 and digital platforms in the "Supply Chain-as-a-Service.". *Transportation Research Part E, Logistics and Transportation Review*, *160*, 102676. doi:10.1016/j.tre.2022.102676

Karakuş, G., Karşıgil, E., & Polat, L. (2019). In *Proceedings of the International Symposium for Production Research 2018.* Springer International Publishing. 10.1007/978-3-319-92267-6

Li, W., Liu, K., Belitski, M., Ghobadian, A., & O'Regan, N. (2016). e-Leadership through strategic alignment: An empirical study of small- and medium-sized enterprises in the digital age. *Journal of Information Technology*, *31*(2), 185–206. doi:10.1057/jit.2016.10

Mishra, D. B., Haider, I., Gunasekaran, A., Sakib, M. N., Malik, N., & Rana, N. P. (2023). "Better together": Right blend of business strategy and digital transformation strategies. *International Journal of Production Economics*, *266*, 109040. doi:10.1016/j.ijpe.2023.109040

Munirathinam, S. (2020). Chapter Six - Industry 4.0: Industrial Internet of Things (IIOT). In P. Raj & P. B. T.-A. in C. Evangeline (Eds.), *The Digital Twin Paradigm for Smarter Systems and Environments: The Industry Use Cases* (*Vol. 117*, Issue 1, pp. 129–164). Elsevier.

Oosthuizen, K., Botha, E., Robertson, J., & Montecchi, M. (2021). Artificial intelligence in retail: The AI-enabled value chain. *Australasian Marketing Journal*, *29*(3), 264–273. doi:10.1016/j.ausmj.2020.07.007

Parker, G. (2016). *Platform Revolution MIT Information and Communications Technologies Conference.* MIT.

Chapter 6
Digital Transformation and Changes in Business Models for Service Industries:
General Principles and Cases From Hospitality, Traveling, Food Delivery

Mune Moğol Sever
https://orcid.org/0000-0003-4706-5859
Anadolu University, Turkey

ABSTRACT

The digital transformation and digital technologies find ample application in service as well as in manufacturing. Advances in digitalization and digital technology adoption encourage service sectors to incorporate new digital technologies into their processes to increase efficiency and productivity. The trend towards up-to-datedness and remote control mechanisms increases service industries' awareness of digital technologies in the era of Industry 4.0 and Society 5.0. A transparent and instant management approach with real-time data becomes possible with digital innovation in service. In the digital ecosystem, personalization is more likely to be possible if the increasing diversity in demands for a particular product/service is disruptive. In these collaborative platforms, the prosumer is at the center of the business and acts as designer, customer and consumer. In this digital ecosystem, the consumer is involved in the design phase at the beginning of the process. A new business model is required due to the overall digitalization of the organization. After talking about the digital revolution and transformation, traditional tools for customer demand/relationship management, sales marketing and operations should be examined. The Internet of Things (IoTs), cloud computing, blockchain infrastructure, and business intelligence, are the basic components of digital transformation. This chapter mainly focuses on the digital transformation of the service industry, service innovations, service business platforms and service business model transformation using digital tools. All these digitalization efforts are made possible by innovation in business models. This new digital business model innovation is defined as a unique and significant change in the fundamental elements of the enterprise's business model and value chain architecture. BM analyzes and redesigns operations, content, structure and management to create value by taking advantage of business opportunities. Especially in an environment where organizations and operations, data and processes become open, the concepts of participation in processes and collaboration come to the fore. Sharing economies and platforms where everyone meets on common ground constitute today's new business models. Platform businesses are shared networks and interfaces that create a common structure in which flexibility in design can be achieved, fixed costs can be saved, and efficiency can be increased. Platforms are divided into two: internal and external, and internal platforms are defined as areas where co-operation is carried out within the business or with the business and suppliers for a specific purpose. The study revealed that the labor-intensive and competitive service sector could not avoid this trend. Within the scope of this section, the concept is intended to be concretized through platform works and sample applications. In summary, all this change has caused physical worlds to be moved to small screens and virtual worlds. No matter how perfect the resulting physical product is, it will always be incomplete unless it is supported by accurate and complete services. In today's cyber-physical environment, perfect service platforms will be able to meet the needs and produce real-time and creative solutions to customer demands. These solutions can be provided through innovative and smart technologies such as artificial intelligence and business intelligence. It can be stated with certainty that service businesses that invest in these technologies will stand out from their competitors.

DOI: 10.4018/979-8-3693-2019-8.ch006

1. INTRODUCTION-TECHNOLOGY ENABLED SERVICE BUSINESS MODEL

Recent developments in digitalization and digital technology adaptation urge service industries to welcome new technologies to their processes to increase efficiency and productivity. Besides Accepting the digital paradox effect on business, the pressure on being up to date and remote-control mechanisms is also increasing the awareness of digital technologies for service industries in the Industry 4.0 and Society 5.0 era. Autonomous systems utilizing sensors, actuators, and robot technology have become a real-world phenomenon. Besides, collaborative approaches and the value created through networking are the basic foundations for companies to gain knowledge (Lusch et al., 2007). In the digital era in which enterprises are faced with, the organizations try to transform their business into a digital ecosystem. We are in the smart era, where IoT technologies and dense and mass data are present in the environment, and data analytics and predictive analytics are on the agenda (Parida et al., 2019). Everybody and everything are connected through the internet. People, computers, and even machines are communicating among themselves through the invention and intervention of the Internet of Things (IoTs). It becomes imperative for businesses to acquire these and similar technologies to ensure service innovation and not miss the digital transformation trend.

The main success and critical factor in service business is technology adaption and implementation (Kitsios & Kamariotou, 2019). It is important for businesses to invest in technology, especially information technologies, to be successful in innovation and create continuous value (Harvey, et al., 1997; Davenport, 1993: 49). It is accepted that there is a close relationship between the company's technology investments, innovation success and ability to create an innovative environment (Van Riel et al., 2004). Businesses that adopt innovative approaches and constantly adapt them offer more innovative products and services than others (De Brentani, 2001). The decrease in operating and IT costs has encouraged businesses to invest in service platforms. In order to increase profitability, improve services and efficiency, and get ahead of the competition, businesses need to follow technological innovations and innovative approaches in their service processes (Aranda et al., 2003; Van der Aa & Elfring, 2002; Quinn & Paquette, 1990; Gadrey et al., 1995).

The new technologies give rise to new business models (Baden-Fuller & Haefliger, 2013). In other words, technological advancement pushes enterprises to change their business model. Each business model aims to create a new value for an enterprise and affect technological innovation performance (Teece, 2010; Hu, 2014). Technological innovation can generally be expressed as the acquisition of improvements and technologies that will improve the processes of the business and enable it to achieve a better position in the market (Wei et al., 2014).

In the digital ecosystem, personalization is more likely to be possible if the increasing diversity in demands for a particular product/service is disruptive. In these shared platforms, the prosumer is at the center of the business and acts as a designer, customer, and consumer. In this digital ecosystem, the consumer is involved in the design phase at the beginning of the process. To provide such an environment under geographical barriers, remote working conditions, and distributed resources, in other words, a digital, open environment, redesigning the process in the entire product life cycle (PLM) will enable a personalized service concept. In such a digitalized ecosystem the main handicap is analyzing the data and getting real-time action. In this sense, Business Intelligence (BI) is the main operator for each cycle of the PLM.

Business intelligence is a bundle of technology for collecting, analyzing, and reporting data to make inferences for further analysis (Negash, 2004). Data types can be structured or unstructured and can come from internal or external sources. While considering cyber-physical systems in which the enterprises are being in, big data generation is inevitable. To analyze big data to make instantaneous responses to make actions smart systems should be established in the organizations. To handle this problem AI is the main assistance in the BI process. The make the process rapid and make the organizations agile in the decision-making process AI technologies become the main tool. With the capability of inference and learning from the past, deepened machine learning algorithms use past data to prepare near real-time or real-time responses. Due to the importance of real-time decision and response capability, investment in AI technologies is accelerated. Improving performance and productivity at the operational level in conducted business, increasing job performance, healing the job recruitment process, and capturing and analyzing data are some of the AI implementations in several depicted areas (Lee et al., 2019). One of the leading companies Meta has recently launched the META AI on December 5, 2023 (Meta AI, 2023). In their AI ecosystem, Meta AI, utilizing natural language processing there is no gap between human Machine (M/C) interaction. While even Meta is very new in the Metaverse family, this move of the company can be given as the most striking example of the replacement of old technologies with new technologies.

Depicted on Schumpeter's theory (1934) new technology has always destructive effect on changing the old technology (Schumpeter &Nichol, 1934). Platform business and service platforms are the best examples of this. Platform business creates a network effect due to the power of the crowd, a critical mass (Ondrus et al., 2015). In the beginning platform business is the payment platform for a bundle of products like e-trade example, Alibaba. Also, Facebook and LinkedIn are examples of one side platforms in the beginning but now it has many functions besides their previous function. Today, the popularity of service platforms increases because of the opening to everybody, and has more than two sides and more than one function. Open-source software platforms are one example of that. In that platform, everybody has an extension in the system as a user and producer: prosumer. Currently, service platforms bring together developers, content producers, sellers, marketers, and payment systems to create a connection for users and producers in a distributed, decentralized open ecosystem. Companies like Uber, Airbnb, Open Table, and LinkedIn combine some marketing, payment, and development elements to create a multi-sided platform for more than two users.

Due to the digitization of the organization overall, a new business model is necessary. The conventional tools for customer demand/relationship management, sales marketing, and operations should scrutinized after mentioning digital revolution and transformation. This chapter is mainly focused on the digital transformation of service business, service innovations, service business platforms, and service business model transformation by utilizing digital tools.

2. SERVICE INNOVATION AND BUSINESS MODEL TRANSFORMATION

Innovation is defined as the creation of novelty that provides economic value through the creation of new products and services (Baunsgaard & Clegg, 2015). Looking at the historical development of innovation models, a technology-oriented approach in the 1950s was replaced by a marketing-oriented approach in the 1960s, and eventually evolved into an understanding that combined these two. In the 1990s, the importance of strategic partnerships and collaboration with suppliers and customers was understood, but the issue of service innovation has not yet been adequately addressed. In the following years, new generation innovation models came to the fore, the issue that the physical product is an integral part of the service and that innovation in service should also be addressed was brought to the agenda (Panesar

& Markeset, 2008). In the open system innovation model that came to the fore in the following years, it is understood that the innovation process can be managed with the support and cooperation of those outside the organization. With this cooperation, it will be possible to provide innovation in services (Chesbrough, 2023: 24).

Services are an important sector that is increasingly becoming a driving force of productivity and growth in economies. Therefore, the innovation capability and potential in this sector attracts attention (Crevani et al., 2011; D'Alvano & Hidalgo 2012). Innovation theory basics, although it is based on technological innovations in manufacturing, on the other hand, Due to reasons such as the non-homogeneity of the output, which is one of the structural features of the service, it makes difficult to define and measure service innovation with traditional methods used in physical product (Gallouj & Weinstein, 1997). Service innovation appears as an abstract concept at first glance and this makes it difficult to conceptualize it (den Hertog et al., 2010). For this reason, the concept of service innovation methods has come to the fore.

Service innovation refers to innovation in service products and processes besides, new service development, and service design (Miles, 2010). Service innovation at the organizational level can be achieved through technology support (Kumar et al., 2021). Besides, human capital, organizations' structure, communication and collaboration between employees also effect service innovation (Alkhatib & Valeri, 2022). Service innovation in a broad meaning facilitates new service development (Van der Aa & Elfring, 2002). From producer to consumer, from actors to actors, or Peer to Peer (P2P) approach, the success of the system is dependent on the success of the service dominancy level, as explained according to Service-Dominant (SD) logic (Catanzaro & Hamunen, 2019).

The SD logic deals with serving rather than producing physical goods (Lusch & Nambisan, 2015). One of the main reasons why businesses adopt a service-oriented approach is unlike traditional product-oriented approaches, people exchange to acquire the benefits of specialized competencies (knowledge and skills), or services in SD. Knowledge and skills are operant resources. Goods have begun to be accepted as intermediate objects rather than main objects in the transfer of information, knowledge, and value. In the new era, where production consumption and design are carried out simultaneously and the roles of producer and consumer change, a service-oriented approach has been adopted in which information and instant solutions are at the forefront. It has replaced traditional customers with prosumers, as a consumer and producer. prosumer is included as a data source in the service-product lifecycle process from the design stage. The value is determined by the customer and based on usage (value in use). Value is not always product-oriented, but sometimes it appears as the benefit and value provided when purchasing or using the product.

Service innovations be described as new developments in activities to realize the core services (Oke, 2007). Service innovation is evaluated in three separate categories: incremental, radical, and technological (Fitzsimmons & Fitzsimmons, 2000: 11; Oke, 2007). While doing the job better is expressed as incremental change, doing or changing the job in a different way is expressed as radical change (Bessant & Davies, 2007). Examples of radical changes include start-up businesses and major innovations, such as new services related to a business that has just been defined by the market. The incremental innovations are style changes, service line extensions, and service improvement (Johnson et al, 2000: 4). Although it is evaluated in this way, it is necessary to connect innovation with technology in the digital environment where the product life cycle of technological products is very short and it should be said that there is a close relationship between them (Jong & Vermeulen, 2003). It has been stated that the use of digital technologies will increase productivity, therefore innovation should be made in new business models without intermediaries such as B2B (Parida et al., 2019). It will be possible to achieve digital transformation through the intensive use of digital technologies and the digitalization of processes and data.

The three stages of digital transformation are expressed as follows: digitization, digitalization, and digital transformation (Verhoef et al., 2021). While the process of moving from analog data to digital data is referred to as digitization, digitalization means creating a paperless office environment and creating new value by using digital technologies (Gobble, 2018). Digital transformation is changing the way of doing the job utilizing digital technologies to increase efficiency and do business in a more transparent remotely controllable ecosystem. As working with the technology-addicted new generation Z, digital transformation is vital for service industries. All this digitalization effort directed firms to new business models.

Business model innovation is defined as making a unique and significant change in the basic elements of the business model and value chain architecture of the enterprise (Parida et al., 2019). In other words, BM is analyzing and designing transactions, content, structure, and management to create value through the exploitation of business opportunities (Amit & Zott, 2001). As depicted in Schumpeter's theory (1934) the new technology has a destructive effect on the economy. The new always has to be changed with the old one according to the Schumpeterian approach. Hence, BM dimensions referred from Osterwalder & Pigneur (2013) as customer segment, value proposition, channels, customer relations, revenue streams, resources, activities, partnership, and cost structure should be rehandled after digitalization mainstream. All these BM dimensions need to be defined in new business models after digital transformation, taking into account digital transformation principles. In other words, digital transformation necessitated the creation of new business models. Digital technologies and equipment are needed to make digital transformation visible and concrete in these new business models. (Mergel et al., 2019). If the main criterion of digital transformation is the introduction of innovative new digital technologies into the business, it is the reality of the last period that operations are carried out not on paper, but through virtual environments and digital platforms, where data and designs are shared, open to everyone's participation, and shared. Organizations come together and participate in the innovation process by creating a new product or service also referred to by Normann (1991) as bundling. The effort to gather the processes or products of several businesses under a common platform serves purposes such as increasing the use of idle capacity and eliminating uncertainties. It becomes possible for different organizations to come together under one roof through digital environments (Van der Aa & Elfring, 2002).

Digital service model innovation has some constraints to overcome. With the new Digital model innovation business model, the enterprise should create new value for customers, transform the value creation process to increase agility in business innovation and integrate all the processes, parties, and stakeholders as an E2E platform to solve the problems in each stage of the service lifecycle (Piccinini et al., 2015). It is argued that service innovation is also an important part of the success of platforms and platform businesses. The more innovation there is, the more value it creates for the platform and its users through network effects, creating a cumulative advantage for existing platforms (Gawer & Cusumano, 2014). Businesses invest in innovation and innovative technologies to become market leaders, thus increasing the value created (Adner & Kapoor, 2009). Which means new digital business models.

3. DIGITAL SERVICE BUSINESS MODELS AND ECOSYSTEMS

Digital transformation is using digital technologies to improve enterprise performance and connect people and things and whatever exists in the system (Fitzgerald et al., 2014. In this period when the internet, social media, and mobile tools are used extensively, turning digital transformation into a business model and opportunity is an innovative and unique approach. Businesses that have adopted these digital business models appear as businesses that have adopted tighter collaboration and more intensive use of technology (Berman, 2012). There is a two-sided market within a business ecosystem. Once this ecosystem is established, innovation is created on this platform (Evans et al., 2006). The success of digital platforms is associated with their continuity. If the participation in the platform is continuous and/or the continuity of the participants on the platform can be ensured, the success of digital platforms can be mentioned. This can be possible if the ecosystem is profit-oriented, based on the principle of mutual benefit, and the platform adopts the principle of continuous quality and improvement (Kim, 2016).

After the last industrial revolution, Industry 4.0 (I 4.0), the physical system became a cyber system employing IoTs. With the advent of embedded devices and development in sensor technologies, every physical object become a digital object-cyber object using the internet. with sensors, the physical objects can enter the system and become an agent utilizing the internet. those cyber objects can communicate with each other and the cyber objects create a cyber-physical system altogether. The objects in this ecosystem are the main objects of real life such as machines, tools, operators, and even a coffee machine in a coffee shop. The idea in I 4.0 and 4.0^{+} is creating a new virtual ecosystem as a digital twin of a real system for managing digitally and remotely. The way to be visible in the virtual environment, in other words, to be digital, is for objects and systems to express themselves in the virtual environment. The tools and technologies that will enable this virtualization are the Internet of Things, digital twins, cloud computing, blockchain, and real-time data and business intelligence.

3.1. Internet of Things (IoTs)

IoTs can be defined as the technology of enabling objects, sensors, etc. that do not normally have connection and computing capabilities to be connected to the Internet by connecting these objects to the Internet, allowing them to produce, share, and consume data (Rose et al., 2015). IoTs is a technology that enables independent, heterogeneous objects, machines, and computers to communicate with each other without human influence (Li et al., 2015). IoTs are the core component of digital twins. Through the Internet of Things, physical objects are enabled to exist in the virtual environment, and in this way, the real-virtual environment connection of digital twins is established. Thus, a suitable environment is established for instant data access and instant solutions on the platforms. IoT functions as a bridge between physical and virtual connections on digital twins.

3.2. Digital Twins

Digital twins of physical systems; can be depicted, imitated, predicted, optimized, and designed with multidimensional models to control physical space through real-time connection (Tao et al, 2023). Digital twins are the dual of real/physical systems, products, and machines. The main idea behind Digital Twin is to provide a suitable environment for digital transformation by providing remote control and management. They are the bridge between the real and virtual worlds. The connection between the physical world and the virtual world occurs through the virtualization of physical objects through the IoTs. Digital twins provide an infrastructure for digital platforms that allows instantaneous data communication from the real world to the virtual world (Reim et al., 2023). It is the most basic characteristic of real-time data and digital platforms for instant solutions.

3.3. Cloud Computing

Cloud Computing (CC) is a model that allows users to access and perform any transaction related to business processes remotely within a large pool of computing resources. Like in Amazon Elastic Cloud Computing 2 (EC2) the idea behind CC is creating and running a virtual computing environment (Schad et al., 2010). CC is a combined storage, networking (infrastructure), programming (platform), and servicing (software) ecosystem that distributed resources can meet and connect utilizing the internet (Loutas et al., 2011).

CC is a service that provides instant access to data from various devices via the internet. Data stored in the cloud can be fed by computers, mobile phones, networks, applications, databases, and servers and accessed by these tools. It is a shared data ecosystem with various input devices by various users. In the beginning, it started as infrastructure as a service now it also has the capability for computing and mining. After all, it becomes a Software as a Service (SaaS) and Platform as a Service (PaaS) ecosystem besides Infrastructure as a Service (IaaS). CC has three main functions: infrastructure, platform service, and software service.

CC is facilitated to work on a service platform through the Internet as opposed to hiring new ICT workers and investing in new hardware (Wei & Blake, 2010). The cloud is the pool of virtualized computer resources that can host and distribute workloads, support to avoid errors that may occur due to overload on software and hardware, and allocate the resources and balance the workloads (Boss et al., 2007). Three components of cloud computing are (Tsai et al., 2014): Infrastructure as a Service (IaaS), Platform as a Service, and Software as a Service (SaaS). In IaaS the cloud service provider behaves like a virtual server. In this type of cloud service model, the user cannot handle the cloud infrastructure but does their operation in the provided ecosystem (Mohammed & Zeebaree, 2021). It is like a networking, payment, and storage service provider. For example Rackspace Cloud is a IaaS. In PaaS, there is a platform developer and the developer creates a cloud-based application for multi-user deployers (Rani & Ranjan, 2014). In PaaS, cloud service providers ensure the infrastructure that customers need to develop and launch an application. SaaS is mainly cloud-based application programs/software. SaaS is a service that hosts an application across the internet without investing the software, hardware, and human acquiring (Kulkarni et al., 2012). In broad meaning, SaaS is the service of providing application programs on the internet. Zoom, Shopify, and Hubspot.com are some of the SaaS examples in use. Users can run and do their work on software but have no control over managing the system (Saraswat & Tripathi, 2020). The SaaS cloud service provider is the only one who has control of software at all.

3.4. Blockchain and Distributed Network

Digital systems after the I 4.0 are creating a different ecosystem for service industries. Blockchain technology, which uses the foundations of cryptography, is a distributed ledger consisting of blocks in which data is protected with top-secret passwords (Liu et al., 2021). From end to end, connected business digital platforms are the main result of blockchain technology. In other words, the blockchain is the main facilitator of digital business platforms (Shi et al., 2023). This ecosystem is blockchain-based based such a decentralized data and managerial structure.

The idea behind the blockchain is to connect all peers and parts in the decentralized internet ecosystem. Due to the need to improve the current internet architecture the decentralized internet is one of the proposed models in the transition from Web 2.0 to Web 3.0 after the booming implementation of the semantic web (Zarrin et al., 2021). Thus, the blockchain has a consensus algorithm among peers establishing a decentralized, equal ecosystem for all users/peers. To move to the next stage, the system works under the compromising of all the parties on the same function. The records cannot be collected, changed, or updated in the ledger unless all parties agree. Which means consensus and referred consensus network on blockchain (Raikwar et al., 2019). As has the attribute of eliminating the middleman and/or central authority from the system to ensure equal rights in the system blockchain, providing no central authorized and distributed network (Wright & De Filippi, 2015). The no authorized/decentralized system should maintain a secure and trustworthy environment, which means crypto structures.

Blockchain is the result of the research and advancement of cryptography. Cryptography ensures data, transaction, and information security and keeps user information confidential (Zhai et al., 2019). Considering in such a distributed, no central authority and multi-user system, blockchain must act/work according to cryptographic principles. It is known that due to the importance of privacy in finance, a cryptographic structure, a blockchain-based structure, has come to the fore: DeFi (Decentralized Finance).

Blockchain first found application in financial systems. Transaction costs in the monetary system because of the intermediaries, became high and unacceptable. Besides, the intermediaries as a central authority control the system and information. Because of this disadvantage, there need for a system that works under the no-central authority and is more trustworthy (Chen & Bellavitis, 2020). Which entails blockchain. Due to the first appearance on cryptocurrency platforms, the blockchain is mainly related to the only technology in finance. Besides finance, the blockchain has many applications in health, government, smart homes, accommodation, transportation, and many other sectors adapted to IoTs (Puthal et al., 20128).

The success of platform business mainly depends on the strength of blockchain technological infrastructure. Due to the traceability and transparency, permanent record and reliable data, distributed ledgers, cryptocurrency, smart contract base, low information sharing, and low disclosure cost the blockchain is the main facilitator of service business platform business (Shi et al., 2023).

3.5. Real-Time Data and Business Intelligence (BI)

The process of decision-making process become more dynamic and agile than ever before. Trying to supply all the customer needs under the social-cyber systems the systems should be fed by real and instantaneous data which is managed by real-time data business analytics. In this case, historical data as at the core of conventional data extraction and analysis turned into real-time data gathering and analysis. This section discusses real-time data gathering, extraction, mining, and business intelligence.

The emerging concepts of sharing resources with third parties and urges professionals to provide open sources to the users. In this open-source ecosystem, business analytics and business intelligence tools are also changing. BI tools should be adapted to the open-source data and enrich the transparency. Open-source business intelligence and self-service business intelligence tools and platforms became the main BI tools for the new digital environment. For example, Bol.com uses Tableau for inventory management, stock management, and diversity in service quality. The success story of bol.com is mentioned in Box 1.

Box 1. Success Story Bol.com is in Salesforce.com
One of the leading companies in the online retail sector in Europe Bol.com is using service analytics in salesforce.com. As reported by the Business Intelligence Manager, bol.com believes in the importance of agility and speediness of data analytics in online retailing. In order to be up to date and make instant data-driven solutions they use Tableau for their business analyses. To tailor their marketplace, understanding purchasing habits and seasonality change in demand, ensuring customer demand they use Tableau. *Tableau makes it feasible to manage ongoing business operations like inventory* *management, stock level, and diversity in product/service quality. Because of its simplicity in use with a single dashboard and quick and functionality with an increasing active number of users tableau is a suitable platform and BI tool for Bol.com* **Source:** salesforce.com 30.10.2023.

Bol.com is an online retail company. They believed in being agile in the sector to retrieve data, analyze it, and get solutions. They use Tableau as a Business Intelligence tool to analyze their data.

All these digital technologies and enablers are meant to provide a suitable environment for sharing economies and platform businesses.

4. SHARING ECONOMY AND SERVICE BUSINESS MODEL

The emerging concepts of blockchain and decentralized data structures, data, and knowledge are shared with third parties to make a more collaborative and efficient working environment. The core idea has an origin in network theory and strategic network analysis. In strategic networks the organizations. They are structures created by the coming together of strategically important organizations (Amitt & Zott, 2001). They share the risks and benefit from economies of scale (Katz &Shapiro, 1985). Due to the networks, every transaction made by people, businesses, and groups that come together is visible to others. In addition, since the parties interact, everyone learns from each other and the overall value created through common sense is greater (Kim, 2014). The cross-side network effect, usually defined as the network effect, advocates that the value created will be greater as the number of users in the network increases (Hagiu, 2014). The positive direct network effect means If someone else uses a product after the first user, it means that the aforementioned product is preferred and its value has increased (Staykova & Damsgaard, 2015). In the simplest terms, it means more participants in the network created. more sales, knowledge, shared information, etc.

In addition, shared common goals, as well as the crowd and number of participants in the system, are other important criteria that should be taken into consideration. The value is created in a shared, collaborative, and interactive environment (Vargo & Lusch, 2008). Although it is not the only condition for the success of platform businesses, a multi-user (mass) structure appears as an important factor in success (Ondrus et al., 2015). By using the power of the crowd, economies of scale are achieved and value creation occurs on a larger scale as it is fed from more data sources. The use of crowds becomes more popular within a shared economy in which transparent management is vital in order to be trusted by third parties. The crowdsourcing structure, which uses the power and energy of the crowd, brings together supply and demand, designers, and manufacturers on the same platform via the Internet (Fu et al., 2017). Crowdsourcing is finding the relevant workers to do the job utilizing the internet/online. This environment is based on fair representation, management, conditions, contracts, and pay referred to as gig platforms (Li et al.,2023). Sometimes it is a one-time job, the online worker makes the duty and the relationship between worker and entrepreneur is finished. The job is called gig, and workers in each duty are referred to as gig workers, the terms come from musical performance. Uber and Airbnb are the most known examples of gig works and shared platforms. After the advent of sharing economy concepts in our life the idea of how to collect demand and supply sides in one platform became the main concern of businesses.

The collection of separate services into one agile, interoperable, and reusable platform emerged after Service-Oriented Architecture (SOA). The main attribute of SOA is to make conventional information systems agile (Choi et al., 2014). Service-oriented architecture (SOA) is software development activities to facilitate communication between different platforms to make services reusable (Barney &Nolle, 2023). In other words, SOA has an architecture that allows several independent services to work together through a network. Potential benefits of service-oriented architecture it is very preferable because it facilitates large-scale manageable growth and provides cost advantages for businesses in matters that require cooperation (Laskey & Laskey, 2009).

It is a kind of aggregation of services in which they make an interoperable network that is available on the Internet. By utilization of SOA, different services and platforms can work together in a distributed network. For example, in Uber's case, Uber has SOA that combines three independent services, login, payment, and directing/mapping. To enter the system the user can log in by their Facebook account, which is the first service in Uber. Google Maps is the main component of Uber, to make the application feasible. Another and the third service in Uber is of course the payment. After being served the customer pays by means of PayPal services. These three independent services and components of Uber are combined, can work together, and communicate with each other employing SOA (CodingEnv, 2023).

Microservices and SOA appear as two concepts that are confused with each other. While SOA is defined as the reusability of several services and applications under one roof at the enterprise level, microservices are defined as services within a single application (IBM, 2021). The main purpose of both is to provide the necessary environment for the services to be carried out uninterruptedly and efficiently online through platforms. Profit and wealth are achieved by sharing and exchanging the resources used by all stakeholders (Vargo & Lusch, 2004). Which directed the economy to a shared, network, and platform economy.

5. PLATFORM BUSINESS MODEL AND SERVICE INNOVATION

It is argued that no matter what service innovation is, it cannot be realized if communication with the customer is not made directly and effectively (Oke, 2007; Johne & Storey, 1997). To achieve this, it is necessary to benefit from the network economy and the main facilitator of digital tools. The development of digital technologies and the booming e-commerce phenomenon led organizations to platform businesses (Shi et al., 2023). Platforms are defined as ecosystems that include a set of technologies and standards that are open to sharing and support the creation of common value through user experiences (Thomas et al., 2014).

Platform businesses are shared networks and interfaces that create a common structure through which products and product families can be expanded, flexibility in design, saving fixed costs, and increased efficiency. Platforms are divided into two internal and external, and internal platforms are defined as areas where collaboration is carried out within the business or with the business and suppliers for a certain goal. External platforms are multi-user ecosystems, which are today referred to as industrial platforms (Gawer & Cusumano, 2013; Meyer & Lehnerd, 1997: 39).

As an extension of the network economy, platform businesses are the networking of businesses online as an open business model (Fehrer et al., 2018). It is also defined as interim because it has an architecture to open everybody and that allows everyone to jointly use data, processes products, and services (Staudenmayer et al., 2005). Platform businesses are joined ecosystems for different segments of industries, enterprises, and also for individuals sharing a common goal. In platform businesses, businesses open their doors to the outside world and share their data and processes (Trabucchi et al., 2021).

Platform business facilitates the interaction between groups and partners by creating a common value (Deloitte, 2023). It is broadly defined as a multi-sided platform to connect distributed partners to create a common goal for creating value (Kim, 2014). The platform business is a strategic organization based on collaboration, able to adapt to new technologies, open to sharing information and know-how, and based on mutual learning between parties (Evans et al., 2006: 44, 212). The main reasons behind the innovative adoption of platform-based businesses can be listed as follows (Trabucchi et al., 2021):

- Platforms simplify work by homogenizing previous processes
- Platforms act as catalysts, unlocking idle resources
- Users in the system can develop the innovations they want through the platforms.

Due to the rules and standards developed by each platform, tasks and transactions are more standardized for users on the platform. Thanks to these developed rules, every user carries out transactions by following the same path, creating a more homogenized environment that is the same for everyone (Boudreau & Hagiu, 2009: 44). Through the platform, idle capacity, unused areas, and resources were revealed and the issue of how to bring them into use and production was brought to the agenda. As in the Uber example, unused cars or cars that are not used effectively enough are brought back into the economy. Since platforms are multi-user environments and communication between users can be done quickly and effectively thanks to the decentralized structure, the data exchange and learning process is fast. Thus, mutual learning is done effectively. Therefore, it becomes possible for one or more of the parties to design innovative solutions or products and stand out from the others, thanks to the facilitating feature of the platforms.

When evaluated within the scope of inter-organizational cooperation and network dynamics as businesses increase their collaborative activities and different chapters emerge, new interconnected networks are formed (Powell et al., 2005). We can express this situation as the output and success of the platforms.

The main philosophy of platform business that should be considered in a shared economy environment is to create a democratic and decentralized business ecosystem where every party meets each other and does their business according to their technocratic talent. Decentralized managerial and business structure is the core of platform business. The reason why this decentralized and open structure is simple is that there are only 3 basic components: platform provider, platform user, and platform interface (Ondrus et al., 2015). Broadly apart from the software user interface, there is a platform as a service provider and professionals who are willing to do given tasks. The basic architecture of the service platform business is depicted in Figure 1.

The main layers and elements in the architecture of a service business as shown in Figure 1 are service provider, multi-user, and user interface. In this architecture, the first layer is the service provider, in which the software or application facilitates the main operations related to the business. The governance and management of the service given by the provider on the platform are generally realized by utilizing the regulations and establishing the rules. Once the declared rules are accepted by the users, an agree-

Figure 1. The architecture of service platforms
(Originally created by the author)

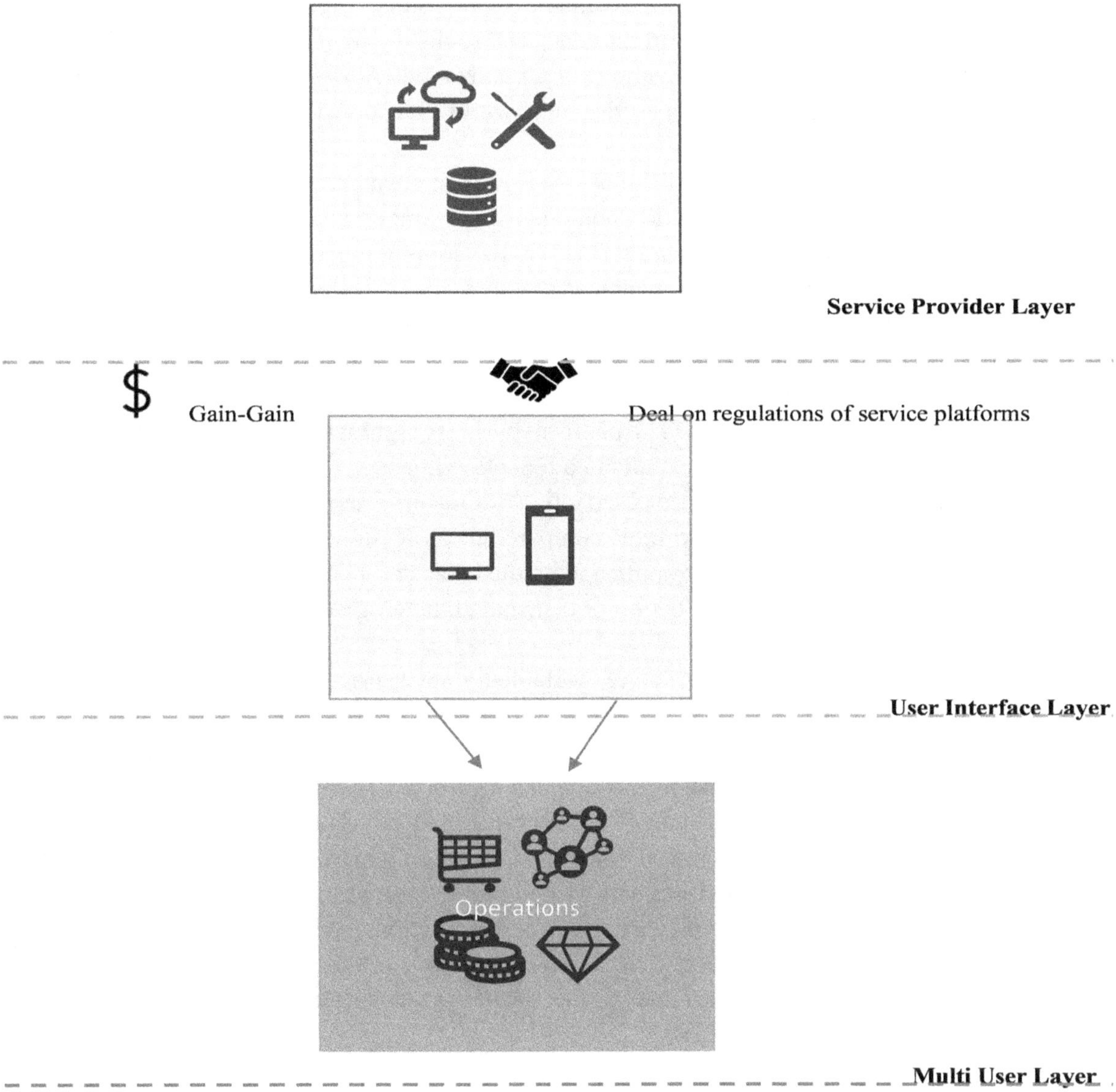

ment is reached between the parties. The business platform generates revenue from users. Users also meet their needs by purchasing services. In addition, if users use the platform as developers, content producers, or producers, they can turn their activities into monetary income. In both cases, the process is carried out according to the win-win principle. The user interface layer appears as the second layer in the previously explained process. This section is the middle layer through which users log in to the service platform. As a user-friendly middle layer, the user interface layer enables access to the multi-user service platform ecosystem with one of the input units, mobile phones, computers, tablet computers, etc. All these operations are carried out through the multi user layer ecosystem provided by the service provider, which is the 3rd layer, explained in the Figure 1.

The digital service platforms are using all available digital sources to communicate and collaborate the peers through emails, messaging, web portals, chats, and social media (G2, 2023). The digital platforms are called Meta-Organizations or organizations of Organization (Ahrne & Brunsson, 2005; Blackburn et al., 2023). They are commonly known as virtual networks that collect a bundle of goods and services (Baldwin & Clark, 2003: 245).

Amazon is a good example of a platform business as an innovator simplifies pre-existing processes effectively. Amazon enables the transaction homogeneously among a large number of sellers and buyers (Trabucchi et al., 2021). Since they are formed by the coming together of several businesses, these structures gain a status as organizations, which is why they are called by this name. Due to the low cost of switching to the platform from the physical situation, the digital platform business is accepted as an innovative approach (Shi et al., 2023). The main concern of the enterprises is cost in a competitive environment. The changing business model with acceptable financial investment makes the service platforms preferred by the organization. The platform business eliminates the intermediaries and creates a peer-to-peer ecosystem (P2P) which results in a reduction in costs.

P2P businesses are small in size, flexible, satisfy short-term demand, and facilitate entering the system employing digital networks and tools compared to professional ones (Einav et al., 2016). P2P network first came to the fore with the application called Napster a collection and shared platform for MP3 (Fox, 2001). P2P is simply a collection of distributed, heterogeneous resources in a client/server network (Schollmeier, 2002).

Figure 2 depicts the P2P network structure available for any service platform business. Each object/user, peer, can interact with each other employing an internet network and blockchain infrastructure. Each peer has an equal right to communicate with each other and make transactions. The P2P is the distributed computer and network system (Milojicic et al., 2002). There is no central authority to manage and control the whole mechanism other than a service platform. The service platform is like a base and main facilitator of the system so that all the peers can act on their roles in an agreed ecosystem. All the peers agrees on service platform rules and reacted under these written or unwritten principles. The only control mechanisms are service platform rules and regulations.

The main criterion in a service platform is service capacity in the P2P ecosystem. There are four major factors to be considered to determine the success of the service platform and make an assessment of the capacity (Yang &Veciana, 20026):

- Data management
- Peer selection
- Admission scheduling and/or bandwidth allocation policy
- Traffic dynamics

The downloading, uploading of a file, recording, and functioning of data through a platform need a good data management infrastructure on a service platform. There exist so many parties, and peers, on a unique platform. Managing all the data and file transactions within a limited time needs efficient data management algorithms and an ICT base. Besides, *peers* are another criterion to be considered. Since the service platforms are shared platforms by nonprofessionals, the condition behind the acceptance of

Figure 2. P2P network
(Originally created by the author)

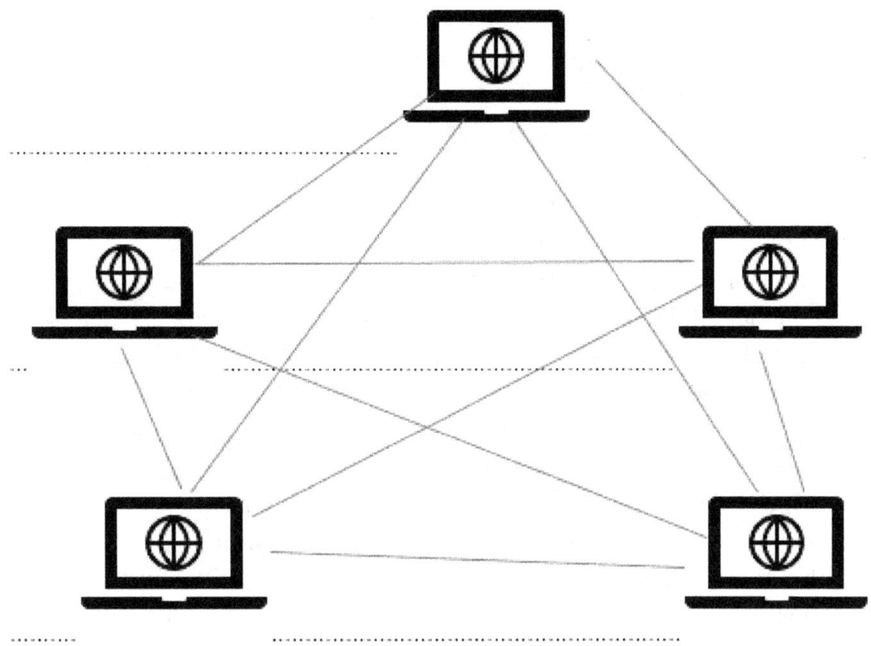

the platforms depends on the value created by each peer. The peer whose idea or contribution is more valuable is preferable.

Distribution of data, load balancing, bandwidth capacity, and the speed of communications between peers and also traffic on the platform are the other concerns of service providers in a service business platform (Pourebrahimi et al., 2015). For instance, thinking an Airbnb there is a huge transactions and communication traffic between demanders and hosts in peak seasons depending on the geographical regions.

The service platform business is growing exponentially. It is quoted that the estimated annual growth rate of P2P accommodation between 2013-2025 is six times of conventional Bed & Breakfast (B&B) and hostels (The World Bank, 2018). In the following section, examples of platform business from services are given.

6. SERVICE EXAMPLES FOR PLATFORM BUSINESS

In this section, prominent platforms in the service sector will be exemplified. In this context, Airbnb examples from the accommodation sector, Kayak from the travel sector, DoorDash, and OpenTable from the food and beverage sector, and finally Telemedicine from the healthcare sector will be discussed.

- **Airbnb:** Airbnb as one of the leadest P2P accommodation examples has generated a new business concept on accommodation. The Airbnb business model includes direct communication and collaboration between the consumer and the service provider. In other words, the hosting and customer communicate directly through this platform, and purchasing and other operations are carried out. Consumers can also become hosts by renting their own homes. What Airbnb provides is an online network between the parties. The only condition for receiving the service offered by the platform is to accept the rules/regulations and pay the requested service fee. In short, Airbnb ensures that activities are carried out by providing governance between the parties.

- **Kayak:** Kayak is one of the service platforms that combine accommodations, traveling (trains, busses, flight tickets), renting car services, and package services into one ecosystem. Kayak, which has been operating since 2004, has added natural language processing algorithms, artificial intelligence components, and Chat GPT (Kayak, 2023). Booking.com, Expedia, Hotels, Hilton, and Priceline are some of the services that are working under the KAYAK platform.
- **DoorDash:** Founded in 2012, the platform provides online food ordering and delivery. There are 3 basic elements in the platform: distributor, partner (producer), and consumer. As long as the rules on the platform are followed, anyone can become a dasher or producer (DoorDash, 2023). You can have the opportunity to work on the platform whenever you want, create your working hours and schedule, and determine your earnings as a dasher.
- **OpenTable**: OpenTable is one of the biggest restaurant reservations, tables, online ordering, real-time inventory management, and marketing platform. Besides all the mentioned operations OpenTable also serves within a personalized service concept. In the customer recognition system, the system calls the personal preferences inside the database and by means of business analytics tools (OpenTable, 10.10.2023). OpenTable is not only a restaurant booking platform but also has an extension on delivery. To maintain delivery function, they are working with Uber Eat, Deliveroo, Just Eat, and Postmates. They have a connection with Stripe, as a payment tool. It has more than 28 points of sale, Square, Silverdale, Aloha, and Tabit are some examples. Due to the selling from different sources to increase the sales they have more than 10 partners like Booking.com, Zagat, Trip.com, Meta, Kayak, Apple, Amazon Alexa, etc. OpenTable has reservations (in-house and online waitlist), customer profiles and listing, real-time inventory, table management, availability control, and takeout management functions. It means Open Table operates as a booking, reservation, and CRM tool for restaurants.
- **Telemedicine:** Telemedicine is a platform that enables communication and remote health management between patients and healthcare professionals (Topol, 2020). In the health sector, which is one of the sectors caught up in the digitalization trend, virtual appointment creation and examination can be done through platforms such as telemedicine (Hasselfeld, 2023).

7. CONCLUSION AND DISCUSSION

In this section, digital transformation, service innovation, new digital business models and digital technological infrastructure issues were discussed. In this context, what kind of digital ekosistem businesses are in in the age of I4.0 and S 5.0, what this technological infrastructure is and the basic components were discussed.

It has been explained that businesses that want to continue their activities in the digital era should adopt a service-oriented approach. It has been stated that in this understanding, where service rather than physical product comes to the fore, organizational structures that are direct, fast, provide instant solutions and are open to everyone are formed.

Digital elements come to the fore in this new business model. The concepts of the Internet, which enables everyone to access everything from anywhere, and the Internet of Things, which enables communication with machines and objects, are innovative concepts and solutions that we were encountered. Cloud computing, where data is stored and processed on virtual servers, is another important component. It is clear that cryptography and blockchains are needed to ensure security and make transactions quickly in such an open system. In this section, a brief information is given about where the blockchain is located in this open system. The most fundamental problem in new era business models is the ability to produce instant solutions to requests and demands. These solutions must be designed in real time or near real time. Business intelligence tools are used for these real-time solutions.

Open architecture environments, where everyone with a password and access permission is included and integrated into the system through sharing platforms, are discussed within the scope of sharing economies. The goal of a service-dominant approach is achieved with the understanding of P2P communication and doing business in which intermediaries are eliminated. The P2P level will determine the level of service dominant management approach. In the new era business approach, the consumer, who buys the physical product by already seeing and examining it, evaluates the product he buys according to the service provided. Therefore, in an environment where there are many sellers of the same product, the service provided appears to be a determinant of customer behavior and business reputation.

Remote working conditions have accelerated service innovation in the desire to do every job in a home office environment, and this has increased service platforms. The change in customer demands has changed business models. Now the customer wants everything to be delivered to his home by someone, he/she wants to work at his/her home, eat at his/her home, socialize at his/her home, etc. This change has resulted in physical worlds being moved to small screens and virtual worlds. No matter how perfect the physical product created is, it will always be incomplete unless it is supported by correct and complete services. In today's cyber-physical environment, perfect service platforms will be able to meet the needs and produce real-time and creative solutions to customer demands. These solutions can be provided through innovative and smart technologies such as artificial intelligence and business intelligence. Service businesses that invest in these technologies will stand out sharply from their competitors.

Digital innovation and transformation is a very vital and important issue for the labor-intensive service sector. However, acquiring innovative solutions can be costly for businesses, especially when they are first invented and in high demand. To what extent businesses will be able to cover these costs and whether small and medium-sized businesses can make these investments are other research topics.

The speed of these innovation activities in service is not solely related to the innovation and intensity of the technologies used. In addition to these, human capital also emerges as another important element. It should be taken into consideration that businesses may have difficulty accessing human capital at the level to use these technologies.

The issue of security vulnerabilities that may occur in such publicly transparent sharing platforms and what precautions businesses should take in this regard should also be addressed.

REFERENCES

G2. (2023). *Best Digital Customer Service Platforms*. G2.com. https://www.g2.com/categories/digital-customer-service-platforms

Adner, R., & Kapoor, R. (2010). Value creation in innovation ecosystems: How the structure of technological interdependence affects firm performance in new technology generations. *Strategic Management Journal*, *31*(3), 306–333. doi:10.1002/smj.821

Ahrne, G., & Brunsson, N. (2005). Organizations and meta-organizations. *Scandinavian Journal of Management*, *21*(4), 429–449. doi:10.1016/j.scaman.2005.09.005

Alkhatib, A. W., & Valeri, M. (2024). Can intellectual capital promote the competitive advantage? Service innovation and big data analytics capabilities in a moderated mediation model. *European Journal of Innovation Management*, *27*(1), 263–289. doi:10.1108/EJIM-04-2022-0186

Amit, R., & Zott, C. (2001). Value creation in e-business. *Strategic Management Journal*, *22*(6-7), 493–520. doi:10.1002/smj.187

Aranda, D. A. (2003). Service operations strategy, flexibility, and performance in engineering consulting firms. *International Journal of Operations & Production Management*, *23*(11), 1401–1421. doi:10.1108/01443570310501907

Baden-Fuller, C., & Haefliger, S. (2013). Business models and technological innovation. *Long Range Planning*, *46*(6), 419–426. doi:10.1016/j.lrp.2013.08.023

Baldwin, C. Y., & Clark, K. B. (2003). Managing in an age of modularity. Garud, R., Kumaraswamy, A.,& Langlois, R.N.(Eds), Managing in the modular age: Architectures, networks, and organizations. (pp.149-158). Blackwell Publishing: UK.

Barney, N., & Nolle, T. (2023). Service-oriented architecture (SOA). *Tech Target*. https://www.techtarget.com/searchapparchitecture/definition/service-oriented-architecture-SOA

Baunsgaard, V. V., & Clegg, S. R. (2015). Innovation: A critical assessment of the concept and scope of literature. Agarwal, R., Selen, W., Roos, G., Green, R. (Eds). The Handbook of Service Innovation. (pp. 5-25). Springer. doi:10.1007/978-1-4471-6590-3_1

Berman, S. J. (2012). Digital transformation: Opportunities to create new business models. *Strategy and Leadership*, *40*(2), 16–24. doi:10.1108/10878571211209314

Bessant, J., & Davies, A. (2007). Managing service innovation. *Innovation in services, 9*, 61-96.

Blackburn, O., Ritala, P., & Keränen, J. (2023). Digital platforms for the circular economy: Exploring meta-organizational orchestration mechanisms. *Organization & Environment*, *36*(2), 253–281. doi:10.1177/10860266221130717

Boss, G., Malladi, P., Quan, D., Legregni, L., & Hall, H. (2007). Cloud computing. *IBM white paper, 321*, 224-231.

Boudreau, K. J., & Hagiu, A. (2009). *Platform rules: Multi-sided platforms as regulators*. Edward Elgar.

Catanzaro, P. F., & Hamunen, K. (2019). Extension and Education Services: Applying Service-Dominant Logic Through Peer-to-Peer Learning. In: Hujala, T., Toppinen, A., J. Butler, B. (eds) Services in Family Forestry. World Forests, 24. Springer, Cham. doi:10.1007/978-3-030-28999-7_11

Chen, Y., & Bellavitis, C. (2020). Blockchain disruption and decentralized finance: The rise of decentralized business models. *Journal of Business Venturing Insights*, *13*, e00151. doi:10.1016/j.jbvi.2019.e00151

Chesbrough, H. W. (2003). *Open innovation: The new imperative for creating and profiting from technology*. Harvard Business Press.

Choi, J., Nazareth, D. L., & Jain, H. K. (2010). Implementing service-oriented architecture in organizations. *Journal of Management Information Systems*, *26*(4), 253–286. doi:10.2753/MIS0742-1222260409

Coding Env. (2023, November 5). *Service Oriented Architecture (SOA) simplified* [Video]. YouTube. https://www.youtube.com/watch?app=desktop&v=PA9RjHI463g

Crevani, L., Palm, K., & Schilling, A. (2011). Innovation management in service firms: A research agenda. *Service Business*, *5*(2), 177–193. doi:10.1007/s11628-011-0109-7

D'Alvano, L., & Hidalgo, A. (2012). Innovation management techniques and development degree of innovation process. *R & D Management*, *42*(1), 60–70. doi:10.1111/j.1467-9310.2011.00663.x

Davenport, T. H. (1993). *Process innovation: reengineering work through information technology*. Harvard Business Press.

De Brentani, U. (2001). Innovative versus incremental new business services: Different keys for achieving success. *Journal of Product Innovation Management*, *18*(3), 169–187. doi:10.1111/1540-5885.1830169

De Jong, J. P., & Vermeulen, P. A. (2003). Organizing successful new service development: a literature review. *Management decision*, *41*(9), 844-858. http://doi.org/ (“ 3A < 6@0 @/ 64$

Deloitte. (2023). *Platform Business Model explained…in under 100 words*. Deloitte.com https://www2.deloitte.com/ch/en/pages/innovation/articles/platform-business-model-explained.html

den Hertog, P., van der Aa, W., & de Jong, M. W. (2010). Capabilities for managing service innovation: Towards a conceptual framework. *Journal of Service Management*, *21*(4), 490–514. doi:10.1108/09564231011066123

Einav, L., Farronato, C., & Levin, J. (2016). Peer-to-peer markets. *Annual Review of Economics*, *8*(1), 615–635. doi:10.1146/annurev-economics-080315-015334

Evans, D. S., Hagiu, A., & Schmalensee, R. (2008). *Invisible engines: How software platforms drive innovation and transform industries*. The MIT Press.

Fehrer, J. A., Woratschek, H., & Brodie, R. J. (2018). A systemic logic for platform business models. *Journal of Service Management*, *29*(4), 546–568. doi:10.1108/JOSM-02-2017-0036

Fitzgerald, M., Kruschwitz, N., Bonnet, D., & Welch, M. (2014). Embracing digital technology: A new strategic imperative. *MIT Sloan Management Review*, *55*(2), 1.

Fitzsimmons, J., & Fitzsimmons, M. J. (1999). *New service development: creating memorable experiences*. Sage Publications.

Fox, G. (2001). Peer-to-peer networks. *Computing in Science & Engineering*, *3*(3), 75–77. doi:10.1109/5992.919270

Fu, W., Wang, Q., & Zhao, X. (2018). Platform-based service innovation and system design: Research opportunities. *Industrial Management & Data Systems*, *118*(5), 975–997. doi:10.1108/IMDS-03-2017-0130

Gadrey, J., Gallouj, F., & Weinstein, O. (1995). New modes of innovation: How services benefit the industry. *International Journal of Service Industry Management*, *6*(3), 4–16. doi:10.1108/09564239510091321

Gallouj, F., & Weinstein, O. (1997). Innovation in services. *Research Policy*, *26*(4-5), 537–556. doi:10.1016/S0048-7333(97)00030-9

Gawer, A., & Cusumano, M. A. (2014). Industry platforms and ecosystem innovation. *Journal of Product Innovation Management*, *31*(3), 417–433. doi:10.1111/jpim.12105

Gobble, M. M. (2018). Digitalization, digitization, and innovation. *Research Technology Management*, *61*(4), 56–59. doi:10.1080/08956308.2018.1471280

Hagiu, A. (2014). Strategic decisions for multisided platforms. *MIT Sloan Management Review*, *55*(2), 71.

Harvey, J., Lefebvre, L. A., & Lefebvre, E. (1997). Flexibility and technology in services: A conceptual model. *International Journal of Operations & Production Management*, *17*(1), 29–45. doi:10.1108/01443579710157970

Hasselfeld, B. W. (2023). *Benefits of Telemedicine*. Hopkins Medicine. https://www.hopkinsmedicine.org/health/treatment-tests-and-therapies/benefits-of-telemedicine

Hu, B. (2014). Linking business models with technological innovation performance through organizational learning. *European Management Journal*, *32*(4), 587-595.https://doi.org/ rights and content doi:10.1016/j.emj.2013.10.009Get

IBM. (2021). *SOA vs. Microservices: What's the Difference?* IBM.com. https://www.ibm.com/blog/soa-vs-microservices/?mhsrc=ibmsearch_a&mhq=soa

Johne, A., & Storey, C. (1998). New service development: A review of the literature and annotated bibliography. *European Journal of Marketing*, *32*(3/4), 184–251. doi:10.1108/03090569810204526

Johnson, S. P. (2000). A critical evaluation of the new services development process: integrating service innovation and service design. Fitzsimmon, J. A. & Fitzsimmon, M.J. (Eds). New service development, creating memorable experiences. Sage: USA. doi:10.4135/9781452205564.n1

Katz, M. L., & Shapiro, C. (1985). Network Externalities, Competition, and Compatibility. *The American Economic Review*, *75*(3), 424–440. https://www.jstor.org/stable/1814809

KAYAK. (2023). *Welcome, robots: KAYAK is now integrated on ChatGPT*. Kayak.com. https://www.kayak.com/news/kayak-chatgpt/

Kim, J. (2014). Platform business and network strategy. *STI Policy Review*, *5*(1), 57–74.

Kim, J. (2016). The platform business model and business ecosystem: Quality management and revenue structures. *European Planning Studies*, *24*(12), 2113–2132. doi:10.1080/09654313.2016.1251882

Kitsios, F., & Kamariotou, M. (2021). Service innovation process digitization: Areas for exploitation and exploration. *Journal of Hospitality and Tourism Technology*, *12*(1), 4–18. doi:10.1108/JHTT-02-2019-0041

Kulkarni, G., Gambhir, J., & Palwe, R. (2012). Cloud computing-software as a service. *International Journal of Cloud Computing and Services Science*, *1*(1), 11–16.

Kumar, M., Mamgain, P., Pasumarti, S. S., & Singh, P. K. (2024). Organizational IT support and knowledge sharing behaviour affecting service innovation performance: Empirical evidence from the hospitality industry. *VINE Journal of Information and Knowledge Management Systems*, *54*(2), 256–279. doi:10.1108/VJIKMS-07-2021-0124

Laskey, K. B., & Laskey, K. (2009). Service-oriented architecture. *Wiley Interdisciplinary Reviews: Computational Statistics*, *1*(1), 101–105. doi:10.1002/wics.8

Lee, J., Suh, T., Roy, D., & Baucus, M. (2019). Emerging technology and business model innovation: The case of artificial intelligence. *Journal of Open Innovation*, *5*(3), 44. doi:10.3390/joitmc5030044

Li, S., Xu, L. D., & Zhao, S. (2015). The Internet of things: A survey. *Information Systems Frontiers*, *17*(2), 243–259. doi:10.1007/s10796-014-9492-7

Li, X., Tan, A. J. H., Wang, X., & Yuen, K. F. (2023). Investigating gig workers' commitment to crowd-sourced logistics platforms: Fair employment and social exchange perspectives. *Technology in Society*, *74*, 102311. doi:10.1016/j.techsoc.2023.102311

Liu, X., Jiang, Y., Wang, Z., Zhong, R. Y., Cheung, H. H., & Huang, G. Q. (2023). imseStudio: Blockchain-enabled secure digital twin platform for service manufacturing. *International Journal of Production Research*, *61*(12), 3984–4003. doi:10.1080/00207543.2021.2003462

Loutas, N., Kamateri, E., Bosi, F., & Tarabanis, K. (2011, November). Cloud computing interoperability: the state of play. In *2011 IEEE Third International Conference on Cloud Computing Technology and Science* (pp. 752-757). IEEE. 10.1109/CloudCom.2011.116

Lusch, R. F., & Nambisan, S. (2015). Service innovation. *Management Information Systems Quarterly*, *39*(1), 155–176. https://www.jstor.org/stable/26628345. doi:10.25300/MISQ/2015/39.1.07

Mergel, I., Edelmann, N., & Haug, N. (2019). Defining digital transformation: Results from expert interviews. *Government Information Quarterly*, *36*(4), 101385. doi:10.1016/j.giq.2019.06.002

Meta, A. I. (2023). *We're advancing AI for a more connected world.* Meta. https://ai.meta.com/resources/

Meyer, M. H., & Lehnerd, A. P. (1997). *The power of product platforms.* Simon and Schuster.

Miles, I. (2010). Service innovation. Handbook of Service Science. In P. P. Maglio, C. A. Kieliszewski, & J. C. Spohrer (Eds.), *Service Science: Research and Innovation* (pp. 511–533). Springer.

Milojicic, D. S., Kalogeraki, V., Lukose, R., Nagaraja, K., Pruyne, J., Richard, B., & Xu, Z. (2002). *Peer-to-peer computing.*

Mohammed, C. M., & Zeebaree, S. R. (2021). Sufficient comparison among cloud computing services: IaaS, PaaS, and SaaS: A review. *International Journal of Science and Business*, *5*(2), 17–30.

Negash, S. (2004). Communications of the Association for Information Systems. Business Intelligence, 13. doi:10.17705/1CAIS.01315

Oke, A. (2007). Innovation types and innovation management practices in service companies. *International Journal of Operations & Production Management*, *27*(6), 564–587. doi:10.1108/01443570710750268

Ondrus, J., Gannamaneni, A., & Lyytinen, K. (2015). The impact of openness on the market potential of multi-sided platforms: A case study of mobile payment platforms. *Journal of Information Technology*, *30*(3), 260–275. doi:10.1057/jit.2015.7

Osterwalder, A., & Pigneur, Y. (2013). *Business Model Generation: A Handbook for Visionaries, Game Changers, and Challengers. Almanya*. Wiley.

Panesar, S., & Markeset, T. (2008). Development of a framework for industrial service innovation management and coordination. *Journal of Quality in Maintenance Engineering*, *14*(2), 177–193. doi:10.1108/13552510810877674

Parida, V., Sjödin, D., & Reim, W. (2019). Reviewing literature on digitalization, business model innovation, and sustainable industry: Past achievements and future promises. *Sustainability (Basel)*, *11*(2), 391. doi:10.3390/su11020391

Piccinini, E., Hanelt, A., Gregory, R. W., & Kolbe, L. M. 2015. Transforming industrial business: the impact of digital transformation on automotive organizations. In: T Paper Presented at the *2015 International Conference on Information Systems: Exploring the Information Frontier, ICIS 2015* IEEE.

Pourebrahimi, B., Bertels, K., & Vassiliadis, S. (2005, November). A survey of peer-to-peer networks. In *Proceedings of the 16th annual workshop on Circuits, Systems and Signal Processing* (pp. 570-577). IEEE.

Powell, W. W., White, D. R., Koput, K. W., & Owen-Smith, J. (2005). Network dynamics and field evolution: The growth of inter-organizational collaboration in the life sciences. *American Journal of Sociology*, *110*(4), 1132–1205. doi:10.1086/421508

Puthal, D., Malik, N., Mohanty, S. P., Kougianos, E., & Yang, C. (2018). The blockchain as a decentralized security framework [future directions]. *IEEE Consumer Electronics Magazine*, *7*(2), 18–21. doi:10.1109/MCE.2017.2776459

Quinn, J. B., & Paquette, P. C. (1990). Technology in services: Creating organizational revolutions. *MIT Sloan Management Review*, *31*(2), 67.

Raikwar, M., Gligoroski, D., & Kralevska, K. (2019). SoK of used cryptography in blockchain. *IEEE Access : Practical Innovations, Open Solutions*, *7*, 148550–148575. doi:10.1109/ACCESS.2019.2946983

Rani, D., & Ranjan, R. K. (2014). A comparative study of SaaS, PaaS, and IaaS in cloud computing. *International Journal of Advanced Research in Computer Science and Software Engineering*, *4*(6).

Reim, W., Andersson, E., & Eckerwall, K. (2023). Enabling collaboration on digital platforms: A study of digital twins. *International Journal of Production Research*, *61*(12), 3926–3942. doi:10.1080/00207543.2022.2116499

Rose, K., Eldridge, S., & Chapin, L. (2015). The internet of things: An overview. [ISOC]. *The Internet Society*, *80*, 1–50.

Saraswat, M., & Tripathi, R. C. (2020, December). Cloud computing: Analysis of top 5 CSPs in SaaS, PaaS, and IaaS platforms. In *2020 9th International Conference System Modeling and Advancement in Research Trends (SMART)* (pp. 300-305). IEEE.

Schad, J., Dittrich, J., & Quiané-Ruiz, J. A. (2010). Runtime measurements in the cloud: Observing, analyzing, and reducing variance. *Proceedings of the VLDB Endowment International Conference on Very Large Data Bases*, *3*(1-2), 460–471. doi:10.14778/1920841.1920902

Schollmeier, R. (2001, August). A definition of peer-to-peer networking for the classification of peer-to-peer architectures and applications. In *Proceedings first international conference on peer-to-peer computing* (pp. 101-102). IEEE. 10.1109/P2P.2001.990434

Schumpeter, J. A., & Nichol, A. J. (1934). Robinson's economics of imperfect competition. *Journal of Political Economy*, *42*(2), 249–259. doi:10.1086/254595

Shi, X., Yao, S., & Luo, S. (2023). Innovative platform operations with the use of technologies in the blockchain era. *International Journal of Production Research*, *61*(11), 3651–3669. doi:10.1080/00207543.2021.1953182

Staudenmayer, N., Tripsas, M., & Tucci, C. L. (2005). Interfirm modularity and its implications for product development. *Journal of Product Innovation Management*, *22*(4), 303–321. doi:10.1111/j.0737-6782.2005.00128.x

StaykovaK. S.DamsgaardJ. (2015, May). A Typology of Multi-sided Platforms: The Core and the Periphery. In ECIS. http://doi.org/ doi:10.18151/7217486

Tao. F., Sun, X., CHENG, J., Zhu, Y., Liu, W., Wang, Y., & Xiaohui, J. I. N. (2023). makeTwin: A reference architecture for digital twin software platform. *Chinese Journal of Aeronautics* *37*(1), 1-18. doi:10.1016/j.cja.2023.05.002

Teece, D. J. (2010). Business models, business strategy, and innovation. *Long Range Planning*, *43*(2-3), 172–194. doi:10.1016/j.lrp.2009.07.003

The World Bank. (2018) *Digital Platforms and the Future of Tourism*. Retrieved October 20, 2023, from https://www.worldbank.org/en/news/feature/2018/09/25/digital-platforms-and-the-future-of-tourism-a-world-tourism-celebration

Thomas, L. D., Autio, E., & Gann, D. M. (2014). Architectural leverage: Putting platforms in context. *The Academy of Management Perspectives*, *28*(2), 198–219. doi:10.5465/amp.2011.0105

Topol, E. (2020). Telemedicine is essential amid the COVID-19 crisis and after it. *The Economist*.

Trabucchi, D., Buganza, T., Muzellec, L., & Ronteau, S. (2021). Platform-driven innovation: Unveiling research and business opportunities. *Creativity and Innovation Management*, *30*(1), 6–11. doi:10.1111/caim.12428

Tsai, W., Bai, X., & Huang, Y. (2014). Software-as-a-service (SaaS): Perspectives and challenges. *Science China. Information Sciences*, *57*(5), 1–15. doi:10.1007/s11432-013-5050-z

Van der Aa, W., & Elfring, T. (2002). Realizing innovation in services. *Scandinavian Journal of Management*, *18*(2), 155–171. doi:10.1016/S0956-5221(00)00040-3

Van Riel, A. C., Lemmink, J., & Ouwersloot, H. (2004). High-technology service innovation success: A decision-making perspective. *Journal of Product Innovation Management*, *21*(5), 348–359. doi:10.1111/j.0737-6782.2004.00087.x

Vargo, S. L., & Lusch, R. F. (2004). Evolving to a New Dominant Logic for Marketing. *Journal of Marketing*, *68*(1), 1–17. doi:10.1509/jmkg.68.1.1.24036

Vargo, S. L., & Lusch, R. F. (2008). Service-dominant logic: Continuing the evolution. *Journal of the Academy of Marketing Science*, *36*(1), 1–10. doi:10.1007/s11747-007-0069-6

Verhoef, P. C., Broekhuizen, T., Bart, Y., Bhattacharya, A., Dong, J. Q., Fabian, N., & Haenlein, M. (2021). Digital transformation: A multidisciplinary reflection and research agenda. *Journal of Business Research*, *122*, 889–901. doi:10.1016/j.jbusres.2019.09.022

Wei, Y., & Blake, M. B. (2010). Service-oriented computing and cloud computing: Challenges and opportunities. *IEEE Internet Computing*, *14*(6), 72–75. doi:10.1109/MIC.2010.147

Wei, Z., Yang, D., Sun, B., & Gu, M. (2014). The fit between technological innovation and business model design for firm growth: Evidence from China. *R & D Management*, *44*(3), 288–305. doi:10.1111/radm.12069

WrightA.De FilippiP. (2015). Decentralized blockchain technology and the rise of lex cryptographia. SSRN 2580664. doi:10.2139/ssrn.2580664

Yang, X., & De Veciana, G. (2006). Performance of peer-to-peer networks: Service capacity and role of resource sharing policies. *Performance Evaluation*, *63*(3), 175–194. doi:10.1016/j.peva.2005.01.005

Zarrin, J., Wen Phang, H., Babu Saheer, L., & Zarrin, B. (2021). Blockchain for decentralization of internet: Prospects, trends, and challenges. *Cluster Computing*, *24*(4), 2841–2866. doi:10.1007/s10586-021-03301-8 PMID:34025209

Zhai, S., Yang, Y., Li, J., Qiu, C., & Zhao, J. (2019, February). Research on the Application of Cryptography on the Blockchain. In Journal of Physics: Conference Series (Vol. 1168, p. 032077). IOP Publishing. doi:10.1088/1742-6596/1168/3/032077

Chapter 7
Enhancing Service Excellence in the Hospitality Industry Through Effective Service Recovery From Failures

Sujay Vikram Singh
https://orcid.org/0000-0002-7113-2698
Banaras Hindu University, India

Terrance Ancheary
https://orcid.org/0009-0004-7130-7808
National Council for Hotel Management, Noida, India

Anish Mondal
National Council for Hotel Management, Noida, India

Shashank Rajauria
Institute of Hotel Management, Ahmedabad, India

ABSTRACT

The hotel sector is a fiercely competitive and continuously expanding industry with a multitude of difficulties and prospects. The objective of this study is to investigate the significant impacts of providing high-quality service and effectively managing service recovery on both visitor happiness and the overall success of enterprises in the tourism industry. This study utilises a qualitative methodology, specifically focused on conducting focus group interviews. The results of this study will aid in the continuous endeavours to improve customer satisfaction and promote the success of the hotel and tourism sectors. The knowledge gained from experts in the industry will provide a clear understanding of the strategies and viewpoints that contribute to the success of firms in this field. It acknowledges the importance of aligning the expectations of management and customers in order to provide great service.

DOI: 10.4018/979-8-3693-2019-8.ch007

1. INTRODUCTION

In the fiercely competitive landscape of the hospitality industry, success hinges on the intertwined pillars of customer satisfaction and the consistent provision of high-quality services. Businesses operating in this sector must be steadfast in their commitment to delivering not only top-tier services but also quality products, recognizing them as fundamental determinants of their overall prosperity. To achieve continuous success in the ever-changing hospitality sector, it is crucial to have a steadfast dedication to providing excellent service, as this is a fundamental aspect. While striving to provide flawless guest experiences, it is unavoidable that service failures will occur. However, these errors offer organizations a chance to demonstrate their commitment to customer satisfaction. This research paper explores the crucial domain of improving service excellence in the hotel industry by examining the effectiveness of service recovery in addressing shortcomings. The interaction between providing exceptional service and addressing service failures is crucial, as organizations need to not only aim for perfection but also have effective systems in place to correct any deviations from the highest level of guest expectations. In the face of the challenges posed by the ever-evolving consumer demands, the hotel industry must prioritize the flawless recovery from service failures as a crucial strategic necessity. The study analyses the intricate dynamics of service recovery by employing a scholarly methodology. It will investigate the impact of service recovery on overall service quality, customer happiness, and loyalty. This study aims to provide a thorough understanding of the interdependent connection between service excellence and service recovery in the hospitality industry. It will achieve this by combining academic literature, case studies, and empirical insights. The main goal of this research is to offer practical insights for both hospitality professionals and academics. It aims to promote a culture of constant improvement and adaptability in dealing with service-related difficulties. This will help strengthen the basis of providing excellent service in the constantly changing hospitality industry.

1.1 Objectives of the Study

1. Examine the effect(s) of service excellence and service recovery on customer satisfaction in hotels.
2. Investigate the relationship between service recovery and service failures in hotels.

1.2 Service Excellence: An Overview

Service excellence represents the highest level of client-centricity, embodying a philosophy that converts transactions into memorable experiences and elevates enterprises to become paragons of customer happiness. Service excellence is far more than a series of procedures; it is a comprehensive dedication to exceeding client expectations at every interaction. It encapsulates the belief that client contacts should not be seen as just transactions, but rather as chances to establish enduring impressions and cultivate relationships. In the ever-changing and highly competitive world of service-oriented businesses, the quality of service becomes the distinguishing element that propels a brand from being good to outstanding. An essential element of providing exceptional service is comprehending the customer's path, predicting their requirements, and devising solutions that surpass mere satisfaction. It goes beyond the traditional service approach, encompassing empathy, attentiveness, and a sincere desire to surpass client expectations.

This strategy transcends the boundaries of a single department or individual inside an organization and instead influences the overall organizational culture. When consumers complain, they expect that their complaints about service failures would be addressed (Sundaram, Jurowski, & Webster, 1997). Service providers act to restore "aggrieved customers" to a condition of contentment in response to complaints from customers over service malfunctions (Grönroos, 1988; Zemke & Bell, 1990). Retention tactics have included complaint handling and service recovery (Halstead, Morash, & Ozment, 1996). Customers' monetary and/or social losses in transactions might be seen as service failures (Smith, Bolton, & Wagner, 1999). Customers try to balance equity with post-purchase behavior as a result, viewing the failure 5 scenario as a negative inequity (Lapidus & Pinkerton, 1995). A theoretical framework for assessing service recovery initiatives is provided by the notion of justice (Blodgett, Granbois, & Walters, 1993; Blodgett et al., 1997; Kelley & Davis, 1994). By providing clients with economic value in the form of compensation (such as a discount) or social resources (such as an apology), service providers try to make up the difference (Smith et al., 1999).

But unlike complaint management, service recovery solutions focus on proactive, frequently instantaneous actions to lessen adverse impacts on service evaluation (Michel, 2001).Service excellence is a collective obligation that necessitates coordination among several departments, ranging from the customer-facing frontline staff to the guiding leadership of the organization. Service excellence fundamentally entails providing high-quality, tailored experiences that align with the distinct preferences and expectations of individual customers. It requires a profound comprehension of customer requirements, inclinations, and areas of dissatisfaction. Providing excellent service requires a tailored strategy that acknowledges and adapts to the various characteristics and needs of different customers. The dedication to comprehending and adjusting to the specific idiosyncrasies of each consumer establishes a basis of confidence and allegiance.

Attaining service excellence entails cultivating a culture that consistently strives for improvement. The statement recognises that excellence is a dynamic benchmark and that there is constant potential for improving procedures, adopting innovative service delivery methods, and embracing emerging technologies. Organisations dedicated to providing excellent service actively solicit feedback, encompassing both positive and constructive comments, as they perceive it as essential insights that drive the process of enhancement. This iterative approach views service excellence as a continuous process rather than a final goal, acknowledging that adaptation and agility are essential for long-term success. Furthermore, service excellence goes beyond the boundaries of the organization and integrates with the wider community. It acknowledges the interdependence between businesses, their clients, and the societies they cater to. Service excellence is achieved by integrating ethical corporate practices, social responsibility, and a dedication to creating a good impact. Through their contributions to the welfare of the community, organizations not only improve their brand reputation but also cultivate a feeling of purpose that deeply connects with customers.

Employees are crucial in achieving service excellence. They are not merely components in the operational process of providing services, but rather representatives of the brand. Organizations that place a high value on service excellence allocate resources toward the growth, empowerment, and welfare of their personnel. Employees who are engaged and motivated, and who have access to appropriate tools and training, can act as catalysts in providing great service.

2. RESEARCH METHODOLOGY

The researchers did a comprehensive search of academic databases, journals, and reliable sources about service excellence, service recovery, and hospitality management. The literature review aimed to find fundamental ideas, models, and optimal strategies in service recovery specifically within the hospitality business. Analyzed service recovery procedures at different hospitality establishments to gain insights and make recommendations.

3. RELATIONSHIP BETWEEN SERVICE EXCELLENCE AND SERVICE RECOVERY

Service excellence establishes the foundation for a favourable customer experience, fostering an environment in which patrons are not merely content, but truly ecstatic. Beyond mere satisfaction of fundamental necessities, this entails comprehending the intricacies of personal inclinations, surpassing anticipations, and engendering indelible instances. Service excellence is the tangible representation of an organization's dedication to delivering an experience that aligns with the customer's distinct identity and ambitions, rather than merely delivering a product or service. Customer loyalty is fostered when individuals transcend the role of mere patrons and transform into brand advocates who enthusiastically share their positive experiences.

Nevertheless, occasional errors are unavoidable, even in service environments that have been meticulously planned. When these pivotal moments occur, the mutually beneficial connection between service recovery and service excellence becomes most evident. Service recovery should not be interpreted as an admission of failure; instead, it should be regarded as an exhibition of responsibility and a dedication to resolving any lapses from the trajectory of excellence. It recognizes that moments of imperfection are inevitable even in the quest for excellence; it is during these instances that the genuine resilience of a service-oriented organization is put to the test.

To restore customer confidence, service recovery requires more than simply addressing the immediate problem; it also necessitates exceeding expectations. It involves demonstrating sincere apprehension, acknowledging the inconvenience that has been caused, and promptly and efficiently implementing measures to resolve the matter. In such instances, the significance of human interaction is at its peak. Consumers do not desire mechanized apologies or standard replies; rather, they demand recognition, compassion, and an individualized strategy that showcases an authentic comprehension of their particular situations.

The genuineness of the response is critical to the success of service recovery. Sincerity is frequently distinguishable from scripted gestures by customers, and it is authentic attempts to rectify the situation that elicit the strongest reactions. Service recovery provides organizations with a chance to demonstrate their dedication and promptness in addressing prospective negative customer experiences, thereby establishing an environment that is conducive to satisfaction. Engaging in successful service recovery initiatives fosters enduring customer loyalty, as it distinguishes the impacted clientele from those who have not been exposed to service failures.

Furthermore, the service excellence feedback loop is replete with service recovery cycles. The feedback obtained through the analysis of service defects is of immense value in facilitating ongoing enhancements. In addition to addressing immediate issues, organizations that actively participate in service recovery incorporate the knowledge gained to strengthen their systems and procedures. Each service failure serves as a prerequisite for the development of a service delivery model that is more robust and resilient, creating a feedback cycle of expansion.

The relationship between service recovery and service excellence is dynamic and cyclical, not linear. Service excellence establishes the foundation for a favourable customer experience, whereas service recovery functions as a safety net to intercept unanticipated disruptions. Consequently, the insights gained from service recovery play a role in enhancing the standard of service excellence. The perpetual cycle guarantees that organisations are not merely responsive, but rather in a perpetual state of development, propelled by a dedication to acquiring knowledge, adjusting accordingly, and ultimately surpassing customer anticipations.

The human element is crucial in ensuring service recovery and service excellence. Frontline personnel, equipped with effective communication abilities, empathy, and an authentic commitment to service, are the ones who operationalize these ideas. To achieve service excellence, personnel must be attuned to the intricacies of customer requirements, willing to exert additional effort without being prompted, and persuaded that every interaction presents a chance to mould a favourable impression. The identical human element that transforms a potentially negative encounter into a moment of redemption occurs during service recovery. Effective service recovery is distinguished from conventional damage control by the combination of listening, empathy, and decisive action. The correlation between service recovery and service excellence is fundamentally analogous to the fluctuations that occur in human interactions. It recognizes that while striving for purity is an admirable objective, the true trials of perseverance and commitment are found in our imperfections. Service recovery demonstrates a dedication to resolving any deviations, whereas service excellence establishes the foundation for favourable interactions. Collectively, they construct an account in which patrons not only perceive themselves as esteemed but also comprehended, and where a human element endures even during challenging circumstances, guaranteeing that the customer's progression continues to be one of development, confidence, and lasting allegiance.

3.1 Service Failures in Hospitality Industry

Within the constantly evolving domain of the hospitality sector, where the precise administration of patron experiences is of the utmost importance, it is rigorously examined and strategically remedied whenever service breakdowns transpire. An instance in which the customer's expectations are not fulfilled or, more substantially, are adversely affected is classified as a service failure according to this conceptual framework. These deficiencies have the potential to significantly affect the overall satisfaction of the visitors and may take various forms, including errors in making reservations or shortcomings in providing services. Conducting an examination of service failures within the hotel industry is an essential endeavour, serving not only to address immediate issues but also to unearth valuable insights that can form the bedrock of exceptional service.

A service malfunction presents a critical juncture for the hospitality provider, as it challenges their ability to persevere and recover from obstacles. Examining the systemic weaknesses and fundamental causes that contributed to the failure is of greater importance than merely resolving the immediate problem. The research commences by conducting a thorough evaluation of the entire experience of the visitor, starting from the moment they make a reservation and ending with the end of their sojourn. A distinct approach to implementing necessary improvements is to analyse the particular occurrences in which the service failed to meet expectations. The analysis should incorporate the emotional impact on the visitor in addition to quantitative metrics when employing a human-centred approach. Is communication experiencing a disruption? During the resolution process, did the visitor perceive being heard and valued favourably? Perceived and resolved service failure is significantly influenced by the nuanced and subjective aspects of human behaviour.

In addition, frontline staff, management, and even the visitors themselves participate in a collaborative effort for this study. Critical contextual information that may not be apparent in official reports is among the invaluable firsthand accounts of the service failure held by frontline personnel. Recognizing patterns and systemic issues that could potentially be the cause of recurring failures, managers demonstrate a strategic outlook. Significantly, the participation of the patrons in the inquiry could provide distinct viewpoints that shed light on previously unnoticed facets of the service malfunction. In addition to promoting a culture of ongoing enhancement, this comprehensive and collaborative strategy reinforces the hotel industry's customer-centric values. An opportunity for proactive improvement is presented when service failures in the hotel industry are analyzed, as opposed to a retrospective evaluation being the solitary focus. Preventing comparable failures in the future necessitates a proactive evaluation of potential strategies. Strong dedication to organizational learning is required to achieve this objective. Instead of being perceived as private occurrences, service failures ought to be perceived as opportunities to advance systemic improvement. Potential strategies for addressing service deficiencies in an unintended manner may encompass enhancing employee training initiatives, adopting technological advancements to optimize operational processes, or reassessing organizational protocols. The objective is to incorporate practical solutions that improve the service delivery framework from the insights gained from service failures.

By adopting an introspective and collaborative approach, this strategy aims to devise a roadmap for ongoing enhancement while comprehending the complexities of visitor experiences and identifying key shortcomings. By adopting a proactive approach to improvement and maintaining a steadfast dedication to continuous learning, service failures can be converted from mundane obstacles to advantageous circumstances that strengthen the bedrock of service excellence in the dynamic domain of hospitality.

3.2 Service Recovery Paradox: Tool for Confining Service Failure

Service recovery, which involves the methodical procedures and tactics implemented by businesses to resolve and reinstate service interruptions, is an essential component of customer service. It guarantees client loyalty and satisfaction. A loop diagram commonly represents the Service Recovery Paradox, an internationally recognized model for service recovery. The model provides an example of how successful service recovery not only addresses the immediate problem but also can increase customer loyalty and satisfaction beyond what they were before the failure(Michel & Meuter, 2008). Stages comprise the feedback loop: customer dissatisfaction, service restoration, service breakdown, and customer loyalty. By transforming a negative customer experience into a chance for positive customer engagement, this cyclical process underscores the significance of proficient service recovery in transforming dissatisfied clients into customer advocacy.

Proactive measures are implemented to resolve each stage of the loop in service recovery paradox strategies (Figure 1). To establish a proactive stance, organizations must routinely assess performance metrics, customer feedback, and industry benchmarks to anticipate potential service failures. It is critical to respond promptly to any service failure that may occur. Exhibiting accountability necessitates a timely and genuine admission of the error, accompanied by an expression of remorse. Actual service recovery constitutes the subsequent phase and must surpass customer expectations in addition to resolving the immediate issue. To demonstrate the organization's dedication to customer contentment, this may entail

Figure 1. Service recovery paradox
(Edstrom et al., 2022)

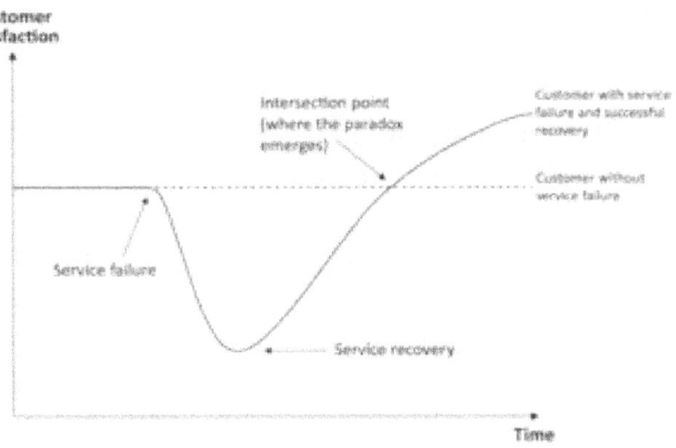

offering payment incentives, discounts, or supplementary privileges. In order to ascertain whether the resolution meets customer expectations, organisations must employ feedback mechanisms to gauge customer satisfaction levels after the recovery. Customer loyalty is ultimately fostered through initiatives that demonstrate continuous improvement, personalized follow-ups, and ongoing communication, all of which serve to reinforce the organization's commitment to providing exceptional service.

4. EFFECTIVENESS OF EXISTING HOSPITALITY SERVICE RECOVERY PRACTICES

Existing hospitality service recovery practices vary in their effectiveness (Lewis & McCann, 2004). Some organizations excel at service recovery and can quickly resolve customer issues, leading to increased customer satisfaction and loyalty. However, other organizations may struggle in their service recovery efforts, leading to customer dissatisfaction and potential loss of business (Silber et al., 2009). Recommendations for Enhancing Service Recovery in the Hospitality Industry include Implementing stealing thunder and co-creation-based strategies to enhance the impact of service recovery on outcome favourability and customer loyalty. Providing training and empowering frontline staff to handle service recovery situations effectively. Implementing a variety of recovery strategies that include service interaction with customers rather than relying solely on monetary compensation. Identifying the most common service failures in the hospitality industry and matching them with appropriate recovery strategies. Investing in technology and systems that allow for real-time monitoring and proactive identification of service failures. Conducting regular evaluations and assessments of service recovery practices to identify areas for improvement (Lewis & McCann, 2004). Building relationships with guests and fostering trust and loyalty through effective service recovery (Akarsu et al., 2022). Effective service recovery in the hospitality industry is essential for enhancing service excellence and maintaining customer satisfaction (Shams et al., 2020). Organizations in the hospitality industry need to have a thorough understanding of the key factors that influence service excellence. This understanding can inform the development of effective service recovery practices and help organizations improve their overall service delivery. Effective service recovery in the hospitality industry is crucial for maintaining customer satisfaction and loyalty. Organizations need to invest in training and empowering frontline staff to handle service recovery situations effectively (Dutta et al., 2007). Furthermore, organizations should implement a variety of recovery strategies that focus on service interaction with customers rather than relying solely on monetary compensation (Shams et al., 2020). To enhance service recovery in the hospitality industry, organizations should consider implementing stealing thunder and co-creation-based strategies to increase the impact of service recovery on outcome favourability and customer loyalty (Silber et al., 2009). By implementing these strategies, organizations can create a positive and memorable experience for customers even in the face of service failures or issues (Shams et al., 2020). This paper is focused on service failure and recovery in the hotel industry in the UK (Lewis & McCann, 2004). To enhance service recovery in the hospitality industry, organizations should consider implementing stealing thunder and co-creation-based strategies to increase the impact of service recovery on outcome favourability and customer loyalty (Silber et al., 2009). Effective service recovery in the hospitality industry can enhance service excellence by promptly addressing and resolving service failures, thereby maintaining customer satisfaction and loyalty. Effective service recovery in the hospitality industry is crucial for maintaining customer satisfaction and loyalty. Organizations need to invest in training and empowering frontline staff to handle service recovery situations effectively and implement a variety of recovery strategies that focus on service.

Research consistently emphasizes the importance of service recovery in the hospitality sector. (Komunda, M., & Osarenkhoe, A., 2012) argue that customers are more likely to remain loyal to a brand that effectively addresses and resolves service failures, emphasizing the significance of service recovery as a means of customer retention.

4.2 Employee Empowerment

One prevalent approach is empowering frontline employees to make decisions and resolve issues promptly. (Ogbeide et al, 2017) found that organizations that empower employees to take immediate action in service recovery experience higher customer satisfaction levels.

4.3 Technology Integration

Technology plays a vital role in modern service recovery. Online platforms and mobile applications enable customers to report issues, and automated systems can provide instant solutions. (Van Vaerenbergh et al, 2016) suggest that integrating technology into service recovery processes enhances efficiency and customer satisfaction.

4.4 Apology and Compensation

Apologizing for service failures and offering appropriate compensation is a traditional yet effective approach. Research by Choi et al. (2014) indicates that a sincere apology coupled with meaningful compensation positively influences customer perceptions and loyalty.

4.5 Proactive Service Recovery

Some organizations adopt a proactive approach by identifying potential service failures before they impact customers. This preventive strategy involves continuous monitoring and improvement of service processes to minimize the occurrence of failures.

Despite the advancements in service recovery practices, challenges persist. Common challenges include the need for consistent implementation across staff, the potential for technology failures, and the difficulty in predicting all possible service failures. Future research should focus on addressing these challenges and exploring innovative approaches to enhance service recovery effectiveness. Thus, the effectiveness of existing hospitality service recovery practices is crucial for maintaining customer satisfaction and loyalty. Employee empowerment, technology integration, apology and compensation, and proactive service recovery are prevalent strategies. However, their success depends on various factors, and challenges persist. Continuous research and innovation are necessary to refine existing practices and develop new strategies to address the dynamic nature of service failures in the hospitality industry.

5. IDENTIFICATION OF KEY DETERMINANTS INFLUENCING SERVICE EXCELLENCE

The identification of key determinants influencing service excellence is essential for organizations striving to deliver exceptional customer experiences and maintain a competitive edge. By understanding these determinants, organizations can tailor their strategies and operations to meet customer expectations and continuously improve their service offerings. This can be achieved through various methods such as conducting customer surveys, analysing customer feedback, benchmarking against industry standards, and studying successful examples from other organizations. These approaches allow organizations to gain insights into the factors that contribute to service excellence, such as responsiveness, reliability, personalization, and effective problem resolution. By focusing on these determinants, organizations can enhance their service delivery, build customer loyalty, and drive business growth. One way to identify the key determinants influencing service excellence is through analysing customer feedback and conducting surveys. This enables organizations to gather valuable insights directly from their customers and understand their perception of service excellence. These insights can then be used to prioritize areas for improvement and develop strategies that align with customer expectations. Another method to identify key determinants influencing service excellence is by benchmarking against industry standards. This allows organizations to compare their performance with that of their competitors and identify areas where they may be falling short. By studying successful examples from other organizations, organizations can also identify key determinants influencing service excellence that they may not have considered before. Additionally, organizations can collaborate with industry experts or consultants who specialize in customer service to gain further insights and guidance on identifying key determinants of service excellence.

Overall, there are multiple approaches organizations can take to identify the key determinants influencing service excellence, including analysing customer feedback, conducting surveys, benchmarking against industry standards, studying successful examples from other organizations, and seeking guidance from industry experts or consultants. By implementing these strategies and continuously improving their service offerings based on the identified determinants, organizations can achieve higher customer satisfaction levels, differentiate themselves from competitors, and create a strong reputation for delivering exceptional service. By implementing these strategies and continuously improving their service offerings based on the identified determinants, organizations can achieve higher levels of customer satisfaction, differentiate themselves from competitors, and ultimately drive business growth. It is crucial for organizations to identify the key determinants influencing service excellence, as doing so can enhance their service delivery, build customer loyalty, and drive repeat business and positive word-of-mouth recommendations. To summarize, it is essential for organizations to identify the key determinants influencing service excellence in order to enhance their service delivery, build customer loyalty, and drive their business growth. By doing so, organizations can stay competitive in today's market and meet the ever-increasing demands of customers. In summary, by identifying the key determinants influencing service excellence, organizations can enhance their service delivery, build customer loyalty, and drive business growth in today's competitive market. The ability of the US service industry to remain competitive and profitable will have major effects on the trade deficit as well as on the whole economy (Tinkham & Kleiner, 1993).

One of the fundamental determinants of service excellence is service quality. Scholars such as Parasuraman, Zeithaml, and Berry (1988) argue that service quality is a multifaceted construct encompassing dimensions like tangibles, reliability, responsiveness, assurance, and empathy. High service quality has been consistently linked to increased customer satisfaction (Zeithaml, Berry, & Parasuraman, 1996). Organizations that prioritize and maintain high service quality are more likely to excel in delivering superior service experiences. The role of employees in achieving service excellence is undeniable. Engaged and well-trained employees contribute significantly to positive customer experiences (Heskett et al., 1997). Employee engagement fosters a customer-centric culture, enhancing interactions and creating an environment conducive to service excellence. Adequate training programs ensure that employees possess the necessary skills and knowledge to meet customer expectations (Grönroos, 2007). Effective customer relationship management is another crucial determinant influencing service excellence. By understanding customer needs, preferences, and behaviours, organizations can tailor their services to meet individual expectations (Chen & Popovich, 2003). CRM systems facilitate the collection and analysis of customer data, enabling organizations to personalize interactions and build long-lasting relationships.

Advancements in technology play a significant role in shaping service excellence. Organizations that embrace innovative technologies such as artificial intelligence, chatbots, and data analytics can streamline processes, enhance efficiency, and deliver personalized services (Parasuraman & Colby, 2015). Technology not only facilitates service delivery but also provides tools for continuous improvement and adaptation to changing customer expectations. The organizational culture and leadership style are critical determinants that influence service excellence. Leaders who prioritize a customer-centric approach and foster a culture of service excellence inspire employees to align their efforts with customer satisfaction goals (Denison, 1990). A supportive and empowering organizational culture creates an environment where employees are motivated to go above and beyond in delivering exceptional service.

Effective communication channels and feedback mechanisms are essential for organizations seeking service excellence. Open and transparent communication builds trust with customers (Berry, 1995). Additionally, feedback mechanisms, such as customer surveys and reviews, provide valuable insights for organizations to identify areas for improvement and refine their service strategies continuously. Service quality, employee engagement, customer relationship management, technology adoption, organizational culture, leadership, communication, and feedback mechanisms are key determinants influencing service excellence. Organizations that strategically address these factors are better positioned to meet and exceed customer expectations, ultimately contributing to long-term success and competitiveness in today's dynamic business environment.

6. MANAGERIAL EXCELLENCE

Hospitality service is a dynamic and competitive industry that thrives on providing exceptional experiences to guests. Within this sector, managerial excellence plays a pivotal role in shaping the quality of service delivery. This literature review explores key themes related to managerial excellence in the context of hospitality services, drawing insights from a range of scholarly articles and research studies. Managerial excellence in hospitality service encompasses a multifaceted set of skills and competencies. Scholars (Johnson et al., 2019) emphasize the importance of leadership, communication, strategic thinking, and decision-making as core components of managerial excellence. Effective managers in the hospitality sector are those who can navigate the challenges of the industry while ensuring the satisfaction of both customers and employees. Leadership styles significantly impact the performance and satisfaction levels within hospitality service. Transformational leadership, characterized by inspiration, intellectual stimulation, individualized consideration, and idealized influence, has been linked to higher employee morale and improved service quality (Bass & Riggio, 2006). On the other hand, transactional leadership, focusing on rewards and punishments, is seen as less effective in the hospitality context. Managerial excellence involves fostering employee motivation and engagement, critical factors in delivering exceptional hospitality service (Jones, 2017). Autonomy, recognition, and career development opportunities are key motivators in the hospitality sector. Managers who create a positive work environment and invest in employee well-being contribute to higher levels of job satisfaction and, consequently, enhanced service quality (Gayathiri et al, 2013).

Effective decision-making is integral to managerial excellence, especially in a rapidly evolving industry like hospitality (Shamim et al., 2017). Strategic decisions related to pricing, marketing, and resource allocation require a deep understanding of market trends and customer preferences. Managers who engage in data-driven decision-making and adapt to changing circumstances contribute to the long-term success of hospitality establishments. Communication skills are fundamental to creating positive guest experiences (Ford et al, 2018). Managers must effectively communicate expectations to staff, resolve conflicts, and engage with customers to understand their needs. Studies indicate a strong correlation between managerial communication skills and customer satisfaction, emphasizing the role of managers as key influencers of service quality.

Despite its importance, achieving managerial excellence in hospitality service is not without challenges. High turnover rates, diverse workforce dynamics, and the increasing influence of technology pose unique challenges to managers (Leibold, M., & Voelpel, S. C., 2007). However, these challenges also present opportunities for innovation and the development of new managerial strategies to navigate the evolving landscape of the hospitality industry. Managerial excellence in hospitality service is a multifaceted concept that requires a combination of leadership, communication, decision-making, and motivational skills. The literature suggests that effective managers play a crucial role in shaping the quality of service delivery, impacting both employee satisfaction and customer experiences. As the hospitality industry continues to evolve, managers must adapt their approaches to meet the challenges and opportunities presented by a dynamic and competitive landscape.

7. SERVICE FAILURE TO SERVICE RECOVERY APPROACH

The specified components in the suggested framework are essential in building a methodical and efficient strategy for resolving service issues within the context of service failures. The process commences with "Service Failure Identification," which signifies the first stage in identifying and acknowledging situations where services have not met expectations (Figure 2). This construct acts as the catalyst for future activities, resulting in the process of "Severity Assessment." Organizations can prioritize and customize their responses by classifying the severity of the failures, enabling a more sophisticated approach to service recovery. The model thereafter presents the concept of the "Customer Feedback Loop," underscoring the significance of recording and assessing consumer sentiments. This framework establishes a clear and unobstructed channel of communication between consumers and the company, facilitating the collection of useful insights that shape the formulation of "Service Recovery Strategies." After identifying

Figure 2. Service recovery paradigm

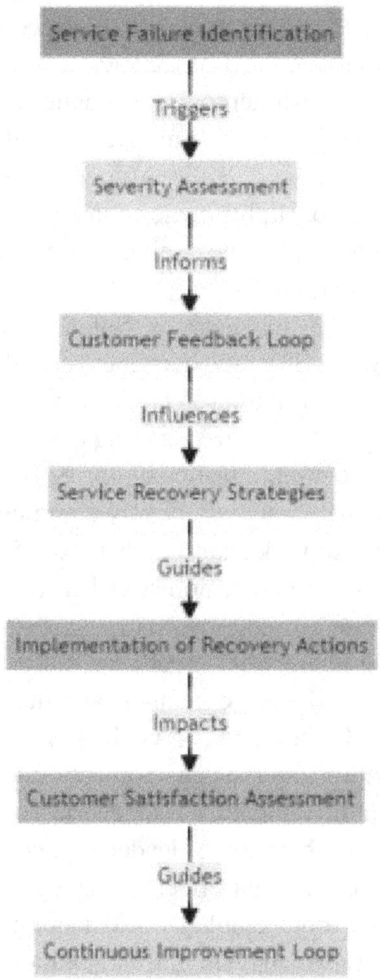

these methods, the model proceeds to "Implementation of Recovery Actions," where it carries out the planned procedures to resolve the identified service failures.

The subsequent crucial element is the "Customer Satisfaction Assessment," which builds upon the previous concept. This step assesses the efficacy of the applied recovery measures by measuring customer satisfaction levels. It functions as a crucial feedback mechanism, assessing if the recovery efforts have fulfilled customer expectations and favorably impacted their perceptions. Finally, the model includes the "Continuous Improvement Loop," acknowledging the ever-changing nature of service recovery. This framework promotes the use of customer feedback and satisfaction assessments to continuously improve and strengthen service recovery procedures inside enterprises. The cyclical structure of the approach highlights the importance of continual learning and adaptation, promoting a culture of constant enhancement in correcting service failures and ultimately improving total customer happiness and loyalty.

8. CONCLUSION

The hospitality industry is renowned for its emphasis on service excellence, as customer satisfaction plays a pivotal role in the success of establishments within this sector. However, service failures are inevitable, and how they are managed can significantly impact customer perceptions and loyalty. This literature review aims to explore the conclusion drawn from various studies on enhancing service excellence in the hospitality industry through effective service recovery from failures.

The hospitality industry is characterized by intense competition, making service excellence a crucial differentiator. Scholars, such as Parasuraman et al. (1985), have highlighted the significance of meeting or exceeding customer expectations for achieving service excellence. However, despite best efforts, service failures can occur, leading to the need for effective service recovery. Service failure is an inevitable aspect of service industries, including hospitality. (Yen et al, 2004) define service failure as any instance where a customer's expectations are not met. Effective service recovery, on the other hand, involves the strategies employed by organizations to address and resolve service failures, aiming to restore customer satisfaction (Komunda, M., & Osarenkhoe, A., 2012). Numerous studies have explored the impact of service recovery on customer satisfaction in the hospitality industry. A study by Maxham and Netemeyer (2003) found that customers who experienced effective service recovery were more satisfied than those who did not experience any service failure. This highlights the potential for service recovery not only to rectify failures but also to enhance overall customer satisfaction.

Several factors contribute to the effectiveness of service recovery in the hospitality industry. (Ogbeide et al, 2017) identify employee empowerment, promptness in addressing the issue, and offering fair compensation as critical elements. Additionally, (Wirtz, J., & Mattila, A. S., 2004) emphasize the importance of an apology and personalized attention in the service recovery process. In the modern hospitality landscape, technology plays a crucial role in service recovery. Online reviews and social media platforms amplify the impact of service failures, making swift and tech-savvy recovery strategies imperative (Harrington and Ottenbacher, 2011). Successful integration of technology can contribute to efficient communication and resolution of service issues, positively influencing customer perceptions.

The training and empowerment of frontline staff are pivotal for successful service recovery. Employees must be equipped with the skills and authority to address customer concerns promptly (Berry et al., 1990). Research by Hart et al. (2003) underscores the importance of ongoing training programs to enhance employee competencies in managing service failures effectively. In conclusion, the literature reviewed suggests that effective service recovery is integral to enhancing service excellence in the hospitality industry. Service failures are inevitable, but organizations that adeptly manage and recover from such failures can not only rectify immediate issues but also build stronger customer relationships. Factors such as promptness, employee empowerment, personalized attention, and the integration of technology are crucial in achieving successful service recovery.

REFERENCES

Akarsu, T. N., Marvi, R., & Foroudi, P. (2023). Service failure research in the hospitality and tourism industry: A synopsis of past, present and future dynamics from 2001 to 2020. *International Journal of Contemporary Hospitality Management*, *35*(1), 186–217. doi:10.1108/IJCHM-11-2021-1441

Bass, B. M., & Riggio, R. E. (2006). *Transformational leadership* (2nd ed.). Psychology Press. doi:10.4324/9781410617095

Berry, L. L. (1995). Relationship Marketing of Services—Growing Interest, Emerging Perspectives. *Journal of the Academy of Marketing Science*, *23*(4), 236–245. doi:10.1177/009207039502300402

Berry, L. L., Zeithaml, V. A., & Parasuraman, A. C. S. Q. (1990). Five imperatives for improving service quality. *MIT Sloan Management Review*, *31*(4), 29.

Blodgett, J. G., Granbois, D. H., & Walters, R. G. (1993). The effects of perceived justice on complainants' negative word-of-mouth behavior and repatronage intentions. *Journal of Retailing*, *69*(4), 399–428. doi:10.1016/0022-4359(93)90015-B

Blodgett, J. G., Hill, D. J., & Tax, S. S. (1997). The effects of distributive, procedural and interactional justice on postcomplaint behavior. *Journal of Retailing*, *73*(2), 185–210. doi:10.1016/S0022-4359(97)90003-8

Chen, I. J., & Popovich, K. (2003). Understanding Customer Relationship Management (CRM): People, Process and Technology. *Business Process Management Journal*, *9*(5), 672–688. doi:10.1108/14637150310496758

Choi, B., & Choi, B. J. (2014). The effects of perceived service recovery justice on customer affection, loyalty, and word-of-mouth. *European Journal of Marketing*, *48*(1/2), 108–131. doi:10.1108/EJM-06-2011-0299

Denison, D. R. (1990). *Corporate Culture and Organizational Effectiveness*. Wiley.

Dutta, K., Venkatesh, U., & Parsa, H. G. (2007). Service failure and recovery strategies in the restaurant sector: An Indo-US comparative study. *International Journal of Contemporary Hospitality Management*, *19*(5), 351–363. doi:10.1108/09596110710757526

Edström, A., Nylander, B., Molin, J., Ahmadi, Z., & Sörqvist, P. (2022). Where service recovery meets its paradox: Implications for avoiding overcompensation. *Journal of Service Theory and Practice*, *32*(7), 1–13. doi:10.1108/JSTP-06-2021-0120

Ford, R. C., & Sturman, M. C. (2018). *Managing hospitality organizations: Achieving excellence in the guest experience*. SAGE Publications.

Gayathiri, R., Ramakrishnan, L., Babatunde, S. A., Banerjee, A., & Islam, M. Z. (2013). Quality of work life–Linkage with job satisfaction and performance. *International Journal of Business and Management Invention*, *2*(1), 1–8.

Grönroos, C. (1988). Service quality: The six criteria of good perceived service quality. *Review of Business*, *9*(3), 10–13.

Grönroos, C. (2007). *Service Management and Marketing: Customer Management in Service Competition*. John Wiley & Sons.

Halstead, D., Morash, E. A., & Ozment, J. (1996). Comparing objective service failure and subjective complaints: An investigation of domino and halo effects. *Journal of Business Research*, *36*(2), 107–115. doi:10.1016/0148-2963(95)00170-0

Harrington, R. J., & Ottenbacher, M. C. (2009). Decision-making tactics and contextual features: Strategic, tactical and operational implications. *International Journal of Hospitality & Tourism Administration*, *10*(1), 25–43. doi:10.1080/15256480802557259

Hart, C., Heskett, J. L., & Sasser, W. E. (2003). The profitable art of service recovery. *Harvard Business Review*, *81*(7), 148–156. PMID:10106796

Heskett, J. L., Sasser, W. E., & Schlesinger, L. A. (1997). *The Service Profit Chain*. Free Press.

Johnson, M. D., Morgeson, F. P., Ilgen, D. R., Meyer, C. J., & Lloyd, J. W. (2019). Multiple professional identities: Examining differences in identification across work-related targets. *The Journal of Applied Psychology*, *104*(5), 649–661. PMID:16551201

Kelley, S. W., & Davis, M. A. (1994). Antecedents to customer expectations for service recovery. *Journal of the Academy of Marketing Science*, *22*(1), 52–61. doi:10.1177/0092070394221005

Komunda, M., & Osarenkhoe, A. (2012). Remedy or cure for service failure? Effects of service recovery on customer satisfaction and loyalty. *Business Process Management Journal*, *18*(1), 82–103. doi:10.1108/14637151211215028

Lapidus, R. S., & Pinkerton, L. (1995). Customer complaint situations: An equity theory perspective. *Psychology and Marketing*, *12*(2), 105–118. doi:10.1002/mar.4220120203

Leibold, M., & Voelpel, S. C. (2007). *Managing the aging workforce: Challenges and solutions*. John Wiley & Sons.

Lewis, B. R., & McCann, P. (2004). Service failure and recovery: Evidence from the hotel industry. *International Journal of Contemporary Hospitality Management*, *16*(1), 6–17. doi:10.1108/09596110410516516

Lewis, B. R., & McCann, P. (2004). Service failure and recovery: Evidence from the hotel industry. *International Journal of Contemporary Hospitality Management*, *16*(1), 6–17. doi:10.1108/09596110410516516

Maxham, J. G. III, & Netemeyer, R. G. (2003). Firms reap what they sow: The effects of shared values and perceived organizational justice on customers' evaluations of complaint handling. *Journal of Marketing*, *67*(1), 46–62. doi:10.1509/jmkg.67.1.46.18591

Michel, S., & Meuter, M. L. (2008). The service recovery paradox: True but overrated? *International Journal of Service Industry Management*, *19*(4), 441–457. doi:10.1108/09564230810891897

Ogbeide, G. C. A., Böser, S., Harrinton, R. J., & Ottenbacher, M. C. (2017). Complaint management in hospitality organizations: The role of empowerment and other service recovery attributes impacting loyalty and satisfaction. *Tourism and Hospitality Research*, *17*(2), 204–216. doi:10.1177/1467358415613409

Ogbeide, G. C. A., Böser, S., Harrinton, R. J., & Ottenbacher, M. C. (2017). Complaint management in hospitality organizations: The role of empowerment and other service recovery attributes impacting loyalty and satisfaction. *Tourism and Hospitality Research*, *17*(2), 204–216. doi:10.1177/1467358415613409

Parasuraman, A., & Colby, C. L. (2015). An Updated and Streamlined Technology Readiness Index: TRI 2.0. *Journal of Service Research*, *18*(1), 59–74. doi:10.1177/1094670514539730

Parasuraman, A., Zeithaml, V. A., & Berry, L. L. (1985). A conceptual model of service quality and its implications for future research. *Journal of Marketing*, *49*(4), 41–50. doi:10.1177/002224298504900403

Parasuraman, A., Zeithaml, V. A., & Berry, L. L. (1988). Servqual: A Multiple-Item Scale for Measuring Consumer Perceptions of Service Quality. *Journal of Retailing*, *64*(1), 12–40.

Rebecca Yen, H., Gwinner, K. P., & Su, W. (2004). The impact of customer participation and service expectation on Locus attributions following service failure. *International Journal of Service Industry Management*, *15*(1), 7–26. doi:10.1108/09564230410523312

Shamim, S., Cang, S., Yu, H., & Li, Y. (2017). Examining the feasibilities of Industry 4.0 for the hospitality sector with the lens of management practice. *Energies*, *10*(4), 499. doi:10.3390/en10040499

Shams, G., Rehman, M. A., Samad, S., & Rather, R. A. (2020). The impact of the magnitude of service failure and complaint handling on satisfaction and brand credibility in the banking industry. *Journal of Financial Services Marketing*, *25*(1-2), 25–34. doi:10.1057/s41264-020-00070-0

Silber, I., Israeli, A., Bustin, A., & Zvi, O. B. (2009). Recovery strategies for service failures: The case of restaurants. *Journal of Hospitality Marketing & Management*, *18*(7), 730–740. doi:10.1080/19368620903170273

Smith, A. K., Bolton, R. N., & Wagner, J. (1999). A model of customer satisfaction with service encounters involving failure and recovery. *JMR, Journal of Marketing Research*, *36*(3), 356–362. doi:10.1177/002224379903600305

Sundaram, D. S., Jurowski, C., & Webster, C. (1997). Service failure recovery efforts in restaurant dining: The role of criticality of service consumption. *Hospitality Research Journal*, *20*(3), 137–149.

Tinkham, M. A., & Kleiner, B. H. (1993). New developments in service operations management. *Work Study*, *42*(1), 16–19. doi:10.1108/EUM0000000002691

Van Vaerenbergh, Y., & Orsingher, C. (2016). Service recovery: An integrative framework and research agenda. *The Academy of Management Perspectives*, *30*(3), 328–346. doi:10.5465/amp.2014.0143

Wirtz, J., & Mattila, A. S. (2004). Consumer responses to compensation, speed of recovery and apology after a service failure. *International Journal of Service Industry Management*, *15*(2), 150–166. doi:10.1108/09564230410532484

Zeithaml, V. A., Berry, L. L., & Parasuraman, A. (1996). The Behavioral Consequences of Service Quality. *Journal of Marketing*, *60*(2), 31–46. doi:10.1177/002224299606000203

Zemke, R., & Bell, C. (1990). Service recovery: Doing it right the second time. *Training (New York, N.Y.)*, *27*(6), 42–49.

Chapter 8
The Transformation of Human Existence Through the Integration of Artificial Intelligence

Navpreet Sidhu
https://orcid.org/0000-0003-3963-6623
Chitkara Busines School, Chitkara University, India

Swati Gupta
https://orcid.org/0009-0005-5795-8353
Chitkara Busines School, Chitkara University, India

Renuka Sharma
https://orcid.org/0000-0002-6514-3411
Chitkara Busines School, Chitkara University, India

Kiran Mehta
Chitkara Busines School, Chitkara University, India

Sanjay Taneja
Graphic Era University (Deemed), India

ABSTRACT

Technology is undoubtedly reshaping our global landscape. Existing are robots that possess human-like speech, appearance, and attire, readily serving us in restaurants. The prevalence of such instances provides ample proof. The field of digital art is witnessing a surge in creations by artists utilizing artificial intelligence (A.I). The inclination towards improving cognitive abilities is apparent in the ongoing development of smartphones and smartwatches. Artificial intelligence is causing a revolution in the way businesses operate. How enterprises engage with their customers, employees, and stakeholders is transforming due to A.I.'s ability to automate tasks, derive insights from data, and craft personalized interactions. A.I. enhances human intelligence, streamlines processes, and makes work more productive and efficient.

DOI: 10.4018/979-8-3693-2019-8.ch008

1. INTRODUCTION

A burgeoning technology garnering significant attention is artificial intelligence (AI). It is characterized as the capacity of a computer or robot, guided by computer programming, to execute tasks typically conducted by humans, encompassing intelligence and decision-making akin to human capabilities (Copeland, 2022). AI is an encompassing term that encompasses diverse academic fields, such as computer science, business, engineering, biology, psychology, mathematics, statistics, logic, philosophy, and linguistics. The field is noteworthy and a subject of discussion due to its capabilities and intricacies (Siau, 2018). The rapid global advancement of artificial intelligence (A.I.) has introduced diverse possibilities, ranging from simplifying medical diagnoses and enhancing human interactions through social media to automating tasks and reducing labour costs. However, these swift developments also raise significant ethical concerns.

Regarding people, AITs are growing capable of carrying out more tasks than possible with technology. They are getting better at controlling, facilitating, collaborating with, or even taking the place of humans in work processes. In terms of surveillance, AITs possess the ability to monitor and communicate human behaviour, notifying other AITs and individuals when specific situations arise. This enables us to make possible impractical could have been more practical, attainable only by human resources. With annual investments totalling billions of dollars in A.I. products and services by companies, major tech players such as Google, Apple, Microsoft, and Amazon are dedicating substantial funds to develop these offerings. At the same time, educational institutions are increasingly incorporating AI more prominently into their academic programs, while the U.S. Department of Defense is strengthening its emphasis on enhancing AI capabilities. This convergence of efforts suggests that significant developments in the A.I. landscape are inevitable (Mike Thomas). Co-execution involves employing operational systems collaboratively with humans in a shared environment. It entails incorporating techniques within a working system to replace human activities.

These problems stem from the potential for A.I. systems to introduce biases, contribute to climate change, pose risks to human rights, and raise other related concerns. These AI-related worries have already worsened pre-existing inequalities, further disadvantaging vulnerable populations. Artificial intelligence in education has recently come under the general public's attention as "adaptive products" have become more widely available. Until then, it had only been an academic community with a tiny user base. Therefore, no one had ever asked for an ethical concern. (Holmes et al., 2021; Buckingham Shum)

The incorporation of artificial intelligence into automated decision-making and predictive analytics, along with advancements in sensor technology and robotics, is expected to transform how individuals, communities, governments, and private entities understand and address climate and ecological changes. Various fields studying climate change and environmental monitoring already incorporate various forms of artificial intelligence. Funding for implementing these technologies in forestry, agriculture, and marine resource utilization is increasing rapidly. More than any other factor, technology shapes our world, generating wealth, influencing our economy, and fundamentally shaping our existence, as emphasized by W. Brian Arthur.

Today's interconnected solid global networks have given rise to highly interdependent systems that are difficult for us to comprehend and effectively manage. Even in the absence of external shocks, these systems are vulnerable to failure at various levels, presenting significant dangers to civilization. Even when decision-makers are highly skilled, have access to all pertinent data and technology, and exert their utmost efforts, artificial systems can become unstable and give rise to uncontrollable situations as the complexity and interaction strengths in our interconnected world increase. A major overhaul is necessary to make these systems manageable. The necessary information and paradigm change in thought may be produced through a "Global Systems Science." Additionally, a narrative focused on A.I.'s ethics has become more prevalent. In reality, scholars such as Whittaker et al., 2018 ;Winfield & Jirotka, 2018; Boddington, 2017and organizations named the U.K.'s House of Lords, the World Economic Forum and the OECD have given the ethics of artificial intelligence much attention.

The growing utilization of A.I. and associated technologies has the potential to optimize the effective utilization of land and seascapes, enhance environmental monitoring, and increase transparency in supply chains. Nevertheless, it also introduces significant sustainability risks. These risks, arising from the interdependence of people, machines, and social-ecological systems, are referred to as networked hazards and are a crucial focus of this literature. The incorporation of A.I. technologies into globalization processes is expected to create new linkages between individuals, machines, and the natural world, including ecosystems and the climate system. These systemic risks arise from interconnected interactions within complex systems. According to the World Economic Forum's projections for 2025, while adopting A.I., automation, and robotics is anticipated to displace around 85 million jobs, it is also expected to create approximately 97 million new jobs globally across various industries (World Economic Forum, 2020). As A.I. technologies permeate diverse social, economic, and ecological contexts, they may introduce new systemic sustainability risks.

1.1 Influence of Artificial Intelligence on Human Morals

For instance, Collins (1990, 2018) explores whether machines can attain the same level of intelligence as humans. He argues that while intelligent machines can demonstrate remarkable proficiency in performing mechanical tasks like pattern recognition, they lack the ability to "perceive" and "comprehend" contexts, a fundamental aspect of human intelligence. The ethical concerns associated with machines have become a topic of discussion and debate relatively recently, coinciding with the introduction of the concept of "machine ethics"(Anderson & Anderson, 2006). Despite the extensive discussions and significant investments in AIA.I. technology, the examination of ethics and morality in the realm of AIA.I. is still in its nascent phase but is making significant strides, permeating industries such as business, healthcare, and Society when integrated with other intelligent technologies like robots. For example, IBM Watson has been applied to aid in analyzing and diagnosing cancer symptoms, while Amazon Go has rendered cashiers unnecessary for purchases. The concept of ethics in this context is intricate, nuanced, and perplexing.

1.2 Research Methodology

This research utilizes a literature review to explore our research question, utilizing the capacity of review studies to encapsulate varied findings (Hulland & Houston, 2020) and clarify uncertainties in previous research by emphasizing relevant unresolved matters (Palmatier et al., 2018). Using the keywords "A.I.," "Artificial Intelligence," "Intelligent Machines," "A.I. enabled technology," and "Virtue Ethics," we conducted a comprehensive search for publications across all business and management sectors, utilizing databases such as Scopus, Elsevier, Base, Springer, and EBSCO. This search yielded over 1600 articles, with 980 published in Scopus and 620 in other databases. We limited our focus to the 24 journals listed in the Financial Times Top 50 and the UT Dallas journal list to concentrate on publications of high quality. Our emphasis on publications in reputable journals is driven by the understanding that these journals showcase the leading work in relevant fields and are frequently cited in other scholarly articles. Ninety-two items were found using this technique and will be reviewed. We solely concentrated on empirical investigations to acquire concrete proof of the influence of A.I. on the digital economy. Nineteen conceptual papers and comments were thus disregarded. Consequently, seventy-three papers offering empirical data on AIA.I. in the digital economy made up our final list.

To guarantee the efficacy of our keyword search, each author team member independently checked the titles, abstracts, and keywords for each of the 73 papers. Then, we created a system for categorizing the papers using the primary subject, theoretical lens, technique, and critical outcomes as categories, together with the author(s) and year of publication, journal, and scheme. Via this procedure, we discovered that most research concentrated either on the advantages of A.I. or its dangers. Therefore, we coded every article using one of these two systems. Over 90% agreement was reached among all developers, and discrepancies were resolved through conversation. In the course of this process, our literature review identified eight articles in business management, four in supply chain management, ten in information systems, seventeen in management (encompassing business ethics and entrepreneurship), eighteen in marketing, ten in finance and accounting, and three in organization studies. This covers all the primary domains within the field of business and management studies. The predominant research methods in current studies on A.I. in the digital economy are lab and field experiments, accounting for 48 publications, and secondary data analysis, with 30 papers.

1.3 Artificial Intelligence Technology

Using AIT to carry out formerly conducted human duties forces us to consider new moral conundrums. Before fully formed realities are imposed upon us, we must consider the ethics of using AIT in light of the social upheaval produced by replacing people with machines and the societal divisions between those who design and run the robots and those they displace.

The central issue revolves around inherent human biases, such as gender bias (Larson, 2017) and racial bias (Koolen & Cranenburgh, 2017), which can be transmitted to A.I. systems. As A.I. systems are presently trained by humans using datasets generated by humans, existing biases have the potential to be assimilated and expressed in real-world applications. For instance, a program designed to predict criminal activity exhibited a bias toward a specific race (Bossmann, 2016) stemming from the biases present in the training data. Therefore, exploring ways to program and train A.I. systems without incorporating human biases is imperative. Furthermore, whether A.I. could develop its prejudices if it attains sentience and sapience (Bostrom & Yudkowsky, 2014), systems can reinforce pre-existing biases and prejudice in the training data. Unfair outcomes can result from biased algorithms in lending, hiring, and criminal justice fields. To achieve fair and equal outcomes, efforts should be taken to uncover and eliminate bias in A.I. systems. Your favourite search engine will return a list of critical male individuals worldwide if you put "greatest leaders of all time" into the search box. Do you know the number of women? When conducting an image search using the term "schoolgirl," the results typically display women and girls dressed in various sexualized costumes.

In contrast, a search for "schoolboy" predominantly yields images of typical, young schools lads. These instances highlight the existence of gender bias in artificial intelligence, stemming from deeply rooted stereotypes in our societies. A.I. systems generate skewed outcomes, and it is crucial to address gender bias in developing algorithms, the extensive datasets utilized for their training, and the application of A.I. in decision-making. Efforts should be made to either avoid or, at the very least, minimize gender bias in these aspects of A.I. development. A.I. algorithms are not infallible and can produce errors or unexpected outcomes.

1.4 Artificial Intelligence for Financial Accessibility and Inclusion

AITs have practical applications across diverse sectors, encompassing tasks such as detecting fraud in financial institutions, enabling autonomous driving in cars, providing customer service through chatbots, overseeing smart home cleaning devices like iRobot and helping intelligent assistants like sprinkler control systems that utilise weather data for water usage regulation and predictive maintenance on machinery (Rajagopalan, 2022). Banks should carefully assess and monitor the risks associated with A.I. systems to prevent potential systemic failures. Regular audits, stress tests, and robust governance frameworks are essential to minimize the risk of algorithmic failures. In Financial Inclusion and Accessibility, while A.I. has the potential to enhance banking services, there is a risk of excluding individuals who lack access to digital technologies or have limited technological literacy. Banks should ensure that A.I. applications are designed with inclusivity, providing equal access and opportunities for all customers. Adopting A.I. in banking can lead to concerns about job displacement and its impact on employees. Banks should proactively address these concerns by investing in retraining programs and supporting employees affected by automation. Ensuring a just transition and minimizing the negative impact on workers is an ethical imperative.

1.5 Integrating Artificial Intelligence With Informed Consent and Moral Principles

AI-powered technologies can be used to spread misinformation, manipulate public opinion, and amplify polarization. These issues have significant implications for democratic processes and societal well-being. Addressing the ethical dimensions of A.I. in information dissemination is crucial to prevent harm and preserve the integrity of public discourse. Tackling these ethical concerns necessitates collaborative efforts across disciplines involving researchers, policymakers, industry professionals, and Civil Society. Together, they should work towards formulating guidelines, regulations, and best practices that advocate for the responsible and ethical utilization of A.I. technologies.

Even though algorithms outperform humans, algorithm aversion, as shown by Dietvorst et al. (2015), occurs when individuals lose faith in their assessments more rapidly when they witness algorithmic errors. This misunderstanding may stem from the notion that algorithms, unlike their human counterparts, lack the ability to learn from errors (Reich et al., 2022). Humans are seen as being more diverse than A.I. systems. As a result, algorithms convey failure information to one another more frequently than people (Longoni et al., 2022). These findings demonstrate that individuals may quickly lose faith in an A.I. system's ability and become hesitant to utilize it again. This is especially true for novice investors, who stand to gain much from employing A.I. advice. (Ge and others, 2021). People frequently assume that A.I. lacks empathy. They do not want A.I. to decide their moral priorities for them as a result.

Additional challenges involve issues related to privacy and security. The substantial volumes of data, susceptible and personal information, play a pivotal role in developing A.I. systems. To prevent misuse and malicious exploitation, proper handling of the data is imperative (Timmermans et al., 2010). Each action involving the data should be meticulously documented to ensure data security. Privacy risks may emanate from both the data itself and the record of actions taken.

Consequently, careful consideration is necessary regarding what should be documented, assigning responsibility for documentation, and determining who has access to the data and records. Safeguarding individuals' personal information and ensuring compliance with data protection laws and regulations are crucial aspects of responsible A.I. applications. Deepfakes, produced by A.I. algorithms, are convincingly faked pictures, videos, or sounds. These may be used maliciously, such as disseminating fake information or posing as others. The need to reduce the threats posed by deepfakes is an urgent ethical issue.

Patients see artificial intelligence (AI) as needing more warmth and genuine caring, making them less inclined to accept recommendations from AI in the healthcare industry than human health specialists (Kyung & Kwon, 2022). Regarding doctors, Liang and Xue (2022) claim that their apprehension of face loss is why they are resistant to A.I. systems. The potential risks associated with ethical issues carry a more significant impact on healthcare, directly influencing the safety of human life. For example, determining accountability becomes a complex challenge in a collaborative setting where robots work alongside human physicians during a procedure. Recent studies have shown that A.I. can "produce audio that appears as speech to machine learning algorithms but is not recognizable as such by humans" (Carlini & Wagner, 2017), prompting concerns about A.I. potentially accessing personal data without the user's awareness. The extensive collection and analysis of substantial data by A.I. systems also raise apprehensions about privacy infringement.

1.6 Impact on the Economy and Job Replacement

The original goal of artificial intelligence (A.I.) was to increase human intellect by using intelligent computers to overcome human cognitive constraints and rigidity (Jain et al., 2021). Since more and more people and objects are connected to the Internet thanks to the Internet of Things (IoT), it has fundamentally altered how A.I. functions. Consequently, the development of sophisticated and extensive datasets to train Artificial Intelligence, coupled with advancements in machine learning and natural language processing, positions contemporary A.I. systems as influential drivers in various aspects of the digital economy (Rong, 2022; Schwab, 2017; Xue & Pang, 2022). In sales and marketing, A.I. contributes to supporting human sales representatives in stimulating consumer purchases (Luo et al., 2019). Customer service A.I., as demonstrated by technologies like Pepper, proficiently addresses simple consumer inquiries (Davenport et al., 2020). Both service providers and customers can utilize A.I. interfaces to place orders (Cui et al., 2022; Li & Li, 2022). Moreover, A.I. in innovation has been utilized to create novel products with the potential to enhance business revenue (Rammer et al., 2022). A survey conducted on CEOs from various companies revealed that the investment in artificial intelligence amounted to $90 billion (Ascarza et al., 2021).

1.7 Artificial Intelligence's Potential Risks to Humanity

Artificial intelligence (AI) poses a variety of challenges, ranging from ethical problems to practical risks. Here are some important ones:

1. Job Displacement: A McKinsey Global Institute research estimates that by 2030, automation may displace up to 800 million jobs, of which 375 million will require extensive retraining (Manyika et

al., 2017). AI-driven automation has the potential to significantly reduce employment in a variety of industries, particularly those involving regular work. This might worsen economic disparity and spark social upheaval.

2. Bias & Discrimination: AI systems can inherit biases from their training data, resulting in unfair or discriminatory outcomes, especially in sectors such as recruiting, lending, and criminal justice. Addressing prejudice in AI systems is critical to ensuring justice and equality.
3. Security Risks: AI systems are subject to assaults, such as adversarial attacks in which hostile actors modify input data to confuse AI models, or attacks on AI infrastructure that result in data breaches or system failures.
4. Autonomous Weapons: The development of AI-powered autonomous weapons systems raises worries about the potential for conflict escalation, loss of human control over military operations, and the ethical implications of delegating life-or-death choices to computers. This problem was brought up early on by Norbert Wiener, one of the leading theorists of early cybernetic systems, who strongly cautioned against applying machine logic to the infinitely complex and plural state of humans. " If we urge automated robots to take over human tasks, we might not be able to comprehend their reasoning or regulate their activities on the outside world" (N Wiener, 2017)
5. Privacy issues: AI technologies, particularly those that include data analysis and monitoring, create serious privacy issues about the acquisition, use, and protection of personal data. Unauthorized access to sensitive data can result in privacy breaches and abuse.
6. Existential Risks: Some researchers and thinkers are concerned about the long-term risks associated with the development of advanced AI systems that outperform human intelligence, potentially leading to unintended consequences, runaway self-improvement, or the emergence of superintelligent entities with goals that are misaligned with human values.
7. Economic Instability: The broad use of AI technology may disrupt whole sectors and economic systems, resulting in job losses, alterations in market dynamics, and difficulties in retraining the workforce for new jobs.
8. Ethical Dilemmas: AI presents challenging ethical quandaries, such as identifying responsibility and accountability for AI judgments, guaranteeing AI system openness and explainability, and addressing AI's potential impact on human behaviour and society standards.

Addressing these dangers necessitates cross-disciplinary collaboration among policymakers, technologists, ethicists, and other stakeholders to create frameworks for responsible AI development, deployment, and governance.

2. CONCLUSION AND EXPECTED CONTRIBUTIONS

Consequently, our research aims to outline how AI could contribute to gaining competitive advantages in the digital economy. The research also seeks to understand the main obstacles standing in the way of AI's potential. Research shows that AI's 'Hard' data skills may help businesses by boosting sales and cutting expenses. It also reveals that A.I. needs to improve social skills, resulting in poor acceptance, management challenges, and inconsistent performance across activities. A.I. is often viewed as a crucial asset for securing a competitive edge for companies in the digital economy, as humans' cognitive limitations and inflexibility do not constrain it. In order to handle customer information reasonably and lovingly towards their consumers, organizations must make every effort to detect any possible moral difficulties. Governments should make a valiant effort to prevent conflict and employ military robots in dangerous situations where human troops are unsuited. It is still relatively early to understand and handle the moral and ethical problems that arise with A.I. It is not only a straightforward issue of "good or bad," "virtue or vice," etc.

Nevertheless, there is an immediate need to discuss ethical and moral concerns related to AI. This study aims to underscore the critical necessity for various stakeholders to focus on the morality and ethics inherent in AI systems. Beyond establishing ethical standards for A.I. and other advanced computer systems, our efforts will also be directed at gaining a deeper understanding of human ethics, enhancing the effectiveness of existing ethical principles, and refining the application of ethical standards and morality in the age of A.I. Lastly, by identifying actions that academia can take to support the training of programmers in constructing ethical A.I. and promoting ethical practices, as well as educating future users of A.I. on responsible treatment of artificial general intelligence, this study seeks to contribute to the advancement of academic research in the field.

The study has significant real-world applications as well. Human cognitive limits do not apply to A.I. systems (Balasubramanian et al., 2022). Managers may thus employ A.I. systems to increase labor productivity in order to profit from investments in A.I. Achieving this goal can be approached in two ways: first, by improving the existing workforce (Yang, 2022), and second, by utilizing A.I. for information retrieval (Grennan & Michaely, 2021). Due to the high accuracy in predictions offered by AI, managers can utilize it for tasks such as supply chain management and forecasting customer demand (Blohm et al., 2022). The elevated accuracy in predictions enables managers to leverage AI in these areas (Blohm et al., 2022). However, managers must apply A.I. systems to objective tasks rather than subjective ones, as these systems are often perceived to lack emotions (Kyung & Kwon, 2022).

REFERENCES

Anderson, M., & Anderson, S. L. (2007). Machine ethics: Creating an ethical, intelligent agent. *AI Magazine*, *28*(4), 15–15.

Arthur, W. B. (2009). *The nature of technology: What it is and how it evolves*. Simon and Schuster.

Awasthi, S., Bathla, D., & Singh, S. (2023). A Literature Review on H.R. Analytics: Trends and Future Challenges. Tyagi, P., Chilamkurti, N., Grima, S., Sood, K. and Balusamy, B. (Ed.) The Adoption and Effect of Artificial Intelligence on Human Resources Management, Part B. Emerald Publishing Limited. doi:10.1108/978-1-80455-662-720230014

Balasubramanian, N., Ye, Y., & Xu, M. (2022). Substituting human decision-making with machine learning: Implications for organizational learning. *Academy of Management Review*, *47*(3), 448–465. doi:10.5465/amr.2019.0470

Barzaeva, M. & Ilyasov, R., (2022). Sustainable Development Of The Global Labor Market In The Context Of The Transformation Of The Industrial Complex Of The Digital Economy. *Reliability: Theory & Applications, 17*(70), 476-484.

Borgschulte, M., Molitor, D., & Zou, E. Y. (2022). Air pollution and the labor market: Evidence from wildfire smoke. *The Review of Economics and Statistics*, 1–46. doi:10.1162/rest_a_01243

Brás, J., Pereira, R., & Moro, S. (2023). Intelligent Process Automation and Business Continuity: Areas for Future Research. *Information (Basel)*, *14*(2), 122. doi:10.3390/info14020122

Carlini, N. & Wagner, D. (2017). Towards evaluating the robustness of neural networks. In *2017, the IEEE symposium on security and privacy* (pp. 39–57). IEEE.

Castelo, N. (2019). *Blurring the line between human and machine: marketing artificial intelligence*. Columbia University.

Castelo, N., Bos, M. W., & Lehmann, D. R. (2019). Task-dependent algorithm aversion. *JMR, Journal of Marketing Research*, *56*(5), 809–825. doi:10.1177/0022243719851788

Centeno, M. A., Nag, M., Patterson, T. S., Shaver, A., & Windawi, A. J. (2015). The emergence of global systemic risk. *Annual Review of Sociology*, *41*(1), 65–85. doi:10.1146/annurev-soc-073014-112317

Collins, H. M. (2018). Expert systems, artificial intelligence, and the behavioral coordinates of skill. In *The question of artificial intelligence* (pp. 258–281). Routledge. doi:10.4324/9780429505331-6

Cuellar, M. (2023). A virtue ethical approach to the use of artificial intelligence. *Data and Information Management*, 100037. doi:10.1016/j.dim.2023.100037

Cui, R., Li, M., & Zhang, S. (2022). A.I. and Procurement. *Manufacturing & Service Operations Management*, *24*(2), 691–706. doi:10.1287/msom.2021.0989

Davenport, T., Guha, A., Grewal, D., & Bressgott, T. (2020). How artificial intelligence will change the future of marketing. *Journal of the Academy of Marketing Science*, *48*(1), 24–42. doi:10.1007/s11747-019-00696-0

Diaferia, L., Blohm, I., De Rossi, L.M. & Salviotti, G. (2022). *When Standard Is Not Enough: A Conceptualization of A.I. Systems' Customization and Antecedents.*

Dietvorst, B. J., Simmons, J. P., & Massey, C. (2015). Algorithm aversion: People erroneously avoid algorithms after seeing them err. *Journal of Experimental Psychology. General*, *144*(1), 114–126. doi:10.1037/xge0000033 PMID:25401381

Dietvorst, B. J., Simmons, J. P., & Massey, C. (2018). Overcoming algorithm aversion: People will use imperfect algorithms if they can (even slightly) modify them. *Management Science*, *64*(3), 1155–1170. doi:10.1287/mnsc.2016.2643

Ding, S., Cui, T., Wu, X., & Du, M. (2022). Supply chain management based on volatility clustering: The effect of CBDC volatility—*research in International Business and Finance, 62*, 101690.

Galaz, V., Centeno, M. A., Callahan, P. W., Causevic, A., Patterson, T., Brass, I., Baum, S., Farber, D., Fischer, J., Garcia, D., McPhearson, T., Jimenez, D., King, B., Larcey, P., & Levy, K. (2021). Artificial intelligence, systemic risks, and sustainability. *Technology in Society*, *67*, 101741. doi:10.1016/j.techsoc.2021.101741

Grennan, J., & Michaely, R. (2021). Fintechs and the market for financial analysis. *Journal of Financial and Quantitative Analysis*, *56*(6), 1877–1907. doi:10.1017/S0022109020000721

Hang, H. and Chen, Z., 2022. How do we realize artificial intelligence's (A.I.) full potential in the digital economy? A literature review. *Journal of Digital Economy*.

Helbing, D. (2013). Globally networked risks and how to respond. *Nature*, *497*(7447), 51–59. doi:10.1038/nature12047 PMID:23636396

Holmes, W., Persson, J., Chounta, I. A., Wasson, B., & Dimitrova, V. (2022). *Artificial intelligence and education: A critical view of human rights, democracy and the rule of law*. Council of Europe.

Holmes, W., & Porayska-Pomsta, K. (Eds.). (2022). *The Ethics of Artificial Intelligence in education: Practices, challenges, and debates*. Taylor & Francis. doi:10.4324/9780429329067

Holmes, W., Porayska-Pomsta, K., Holstein, K., Sutherland, E., Baker, T., Shum, S. B., Santos, O. C., Rodrigo, M. T., Cukurova, M., Bittencourt, I. I., & Koedinger, K. R. (2021). Ethics of A.I. in education: Towards a community-wide framework. *International Journal of Artificial Intelligence in Education*, 1–23.

Jain, H., Padmanabhan, B., Pavlou, P. A., & Raghu, T. S. (2021). Editorial for the special section on humans, algorithms, and augmented intelligence: The future of work, organizations, and Society. *Information Systems Research*, *32*(3), 675–687. doi:10.1287/isre.2021.1046

Koolen, C., & van Cranenburgh, A. (2017). These are not the stereotypes you are looking for: Bias and fairness in authorial gender attribution. In *Proceedings of the First ACL Workshop on Ethics in Natural Language Processing* (pp. 12-22). ACL. 10.18653/v1/W17-1602

Kyung, N. & Kwon, H.E. (2022). Rationally trust, but emotionally? The roles of cognitive and affective trust in laypeople's acceptance of A.I. for preventive care operations. *Production and Operations Management*.

Larson, B. (2017, April). Gender as a variable in natural-language processing: Ethical considerations. In *Proceedings of the First ACL Workshop on Ethics in Natural Language Processing* (pp. 1–11). ACL. 10.18653/v1/W17-1601

Li, Y., Ge, Y., & Zhang, Y. (2021, July). Tutorial on the fairness of machine learning in recommender systems. In *Proceedings of the 44th international ACM SIGIR conference on research and development in information retrieval* (pp. 2654–2657). ACM. 10.1145/3404835.3462814

Liu, Z. (2021). Sociological perspectives on artificial intelligence: A typological reading. *Sociology Compass*, *15*(3), e12851. doi:10.1111/soc4.12851

Longoni, C., & Cian, L. (2022). Artificial intelligence in utilitarian vs. hedonic contexts: The "word-of-machine" effect. *Journal of Marketing*, *86*(1), 91–108. doi:10.1177/0022242920957347

Longoni, C., Cian, L. and Kyung, E., 2022. A.I. in the Government: Responses to Failures.

Manyika, J., Lund, S., Chui, M., Bughin, J., Woetzel, J., Batra, P., & Sanghvi, S. (2017). *Jobs lost, jobs gained: What the future of work will mean for jobs, skills, and wages*.

Peca, A., Coeckelbergh, M., Simut, R., Costescu, C., Pintea, S., David, D., & Vanderborght, B. (2016). Robot enhanced therapy for children with autism disorders: Measuring ethical acceptability. *IEEE Technology and Society Magazine*, *35*(2), 54–66. doi:10.1109/MTS.2016.2554701

Rammer, C., Fernández, G. P., & Czarnitzki, D. (2022). Artificial intelligence and industrial innovation: Evidence from German firm-level data. *Research Policy*, *51*(7), 104555. doi:10.1016/j.respol.2022.104555

Ritter, C. (2016). *Tarred and Floral: Femininity*. Race, and the Abject in Bayou.

Slattery, J.P. (2022). We Must Find a Stronger Theological Voice: A Copeland Dialectic to Address Racism, Bias, and Inequity in Technology. *Journal of Moral Theology, 11*(Special Issue 1), 112-131

Stodt, J., Stodt, F., Reich, C., & Clarke, N. (2022, December). Verifiable Machine Learning Models in Industrial IoT via Blockchain. In *Proceedings of the 12th International Advanced Computing Conference, Hyderabad, Telangana* (pp. 16–17). IEEE.

Tabudlo, J., Kuan, L., & Garma, P. F. (2022). Can nurses in clinical practice ascribe responsibility to intelligent robots? *Nursing Ethics*, *29*(6), 1457–1465. doi:10.1177/09697330221090591 PMID:35727571

Timmermans, J., Stahl, B. C., Ikonen, V., & Bozdag, E. 2010, November. The ethics of cloud computing: A conceptual review. In *2010, IEEE hosted its second international conference on cloud computing technology and science* (pp. 614-620). IEEE. 10.1109/CloudCom.2010.59

Varma, P., Nijjer, S., Kaur, B., & Sharma, S. (2022). *Blockchain for Transformation in Digital Marketing. Handbook of Research on the Platform Economy and the Evolution of E-Commerce*. IGI Global. doi:10.4018/978-1-7998-7545-1.ch012

Verma, A. K., Raval, P. D., Rajagopalan, N., Khariya, V., & Sudha, R. (2022). Development of an AI-based FSA for real-time condition monitoring for industrial machines. *Neural Computing & Applications*, *34*(11), 8597–8615. doi:10.1007/s00521-021-06741-w

Wiener, N. (2017). Some moral and technical consequences of automation. In *Computer Ethics* (pp. 13–16). Routledge. doi:10.4324/9781315259697-3

Yan, X., Melkote, S., Mishra, A. K., & Rajagopalan, S. (2022). A digital apprentice for chatter detection in machining via human–machine interaction. *Journal of Intelligent Manufacturing*, 1–14.

Yang, L., Holtz, D., Jaffe, S., Suri, S., Sinha, S., Weston, J., Joyce, C., Shah, N., Sherman, K., Hecht, B., & Teevan, J. (2022). The effects of remote work on collaboration among information workers. *Nature Human Behaviour*, *6*(1), 43–54. doi:10.1038/s41562-021-01196-4 PMID:34504299

Chapter 9
Implementing Artificial Intelligence and Virtual Experiences in Hospitality

Mohammad Badruddoza Talukder
https://orcid.org/0000-0001-7788-2732
Daffodil Institute of IT, Bangladesh

ABSTRACT

AI and virtual experiences have revolutionized the hotel and tourism business, offering new opportunities to improve visitor experiences, speed up processes, and increase customer satisfaction. Technology is transforming hospitality to boost efficiency and innovation in this fast-paced environment. Hotel websites and mobile apps need chatbots and virtual assistants to handle bookings, inquiries, and personalized advice efficiently. Virtual tours show hotels, facilities, and neighborhood activities to assist travelers in their choices. Travel businesses highlight destinations and provide customers with virtual tours before leaving. AI algorithms use demand, seasonality, and local events to improve hotel prices and revenue management. AI concierges offer real-time help and individualized recommendations. AI and virtual experiences are revolutionizing hotel administration and tourism, improving efficiency, guest satisfaction, and hospitality. Businesses that adopt these technologies stay ahead of the hotel industry and satisfy modern customers.

1. INTRODUCTION

Artificial intelligence (AI) and virtual experiences have ushered in a radically different hotel management and tourism era (Bulchand-Gidumal et al., 2023). This new era is transforming the business landscape and reinventing how customers experience Hospitality. Because of the rapid pace at which technological advancements are occurring, the incorporation of artificial intelligence (AI) and virtual experiences has evolved into more than just a trend; it has become an essential strategy for hotels and tourism businesses that want to maintain their competitive edge and fulfill the ever-evolving expectations of modern travelers (Lukanova & Ilieva, 2019). A significant transformation is taking place in the conventional pillars

DOI: 10.4018/979-8-3693-2019-8.ch009

of hotel management, which include reservation systems, guest services, and operational efficiency (Talukder et al., 2020a). This revolution is being accelerated by artificial intelligence. Chatbots and virtual assistants driven by artificial intelligence have become vital tools in the highly competitive field of online reservations. These intelligent interfaces not only make it possible to have interactions with prospective visitors that are seamless and instantaneous, but they also offer personalized recommendations, which transform the booking process into an experience that is suited to the user and centered on the user (Djalila Labdaoui, 2023).

In the sphere of hotel management, one of the most attractive uses of artificial intelligence is found in the field of predictive analytics. Artificial intelligence systems, powered by enormous databases, can anticipate demand patterns, improve pricing strategies, and alter hotel rates depending on various criteria, including seasonal trends, local events, and past booking data (Talukder et al., 2020b). Not only does this ensure that hotels increase their income, but it also guarantees that their pricing will continue to be flexible and responsive to changes in the market (Abass, 2023). The hospitality industry has successfully carved out a significant space for virtual reality (VR), which was before mostly connected with gaming and entertainment services. Virtual reality (VR) tours allow prospective customers to overcome static photographs' limits by giving them comprehensive, 360-degree previews of hotel rooms, services, and neighboring attractions. This improves the decision-making process for potential visitors and helps manage expectations, reducing customer dissatisfaction (Jordan et al., 2023).

One of the most severe issues that the hospitality business may face in this age of globalization is the presence of linguistic barriers. Language translation services driven by artificial intelligence are now playing a vital role in breaking down these barriers, making it possible for hotel personnel to communicate effectively with customers who may speak. Consequently, this improves the guests' overall experience and helps create a more accepting and inclusive atmosphere. Significant progress has been achieved in facial recognition technology, notably in the efficiency of the check-in procedure (Gündüz, 2023). To ensure visitors have a smooth and trouble-free experience upon arrival, hotels are increasingly implementing face recognition technologies to facilitate quick and secure check-ins. Additionally, face recognition may be expanded to include access control, identification of loyalty programs, and tailored services, eventually resulting in a smooth and safe environment.

The combination of artificial intelligence and virtual experiences is not limited to the booking process and the processes for checking in; instead, it penetrates guests' whole experience. The concierge services powered by artificial intelligence and accessed by mobile applications or gadgets installed in the room offer real-time support, local insights, and tailored suggestions (Jamaluddin & Rahmat, 2023). Not only does this significantly improve the quality of service, but it also allows visitors to personalize their stay to their tastes, which helps to cultivate a feeling of customized attention. How hotels handle facilities management is revolutionized by predictive maintenance, another aspect of artificial intelligence that influences hotel management (Talukder et al., 2023). By utilizing artificial intelligence algorithms and Internet of Things (IoT) sensors, hotels can anticipate when their facilities and equipment will require repair. This enables hotels to take preventative measures and reduces their downtime. Along with contributing to cost savings and a more sustainable operating model, this improves operational efficiency and makes it more bearable.

Another frontier that has evolved in the process of redesigning guest services is the use of robotic help. Robots may be used for various duties, including delivering room service, handling baggage, and even providing concierge services. Even though it is necessary for the hospitality business to keep a human touch, using robots for some activities improves efficiency and creates an appealing futuristic and technological presence (Bhaskar et al., 2023).

Not only does the influence of artificial intelligence and virtual experiences extend beyond individual hotels, but it also extends to the tourist sector. Through virtual reality (VR) technology, travel firms provide customers with immersive previews of locations, hotels, and travel experiences. By analyzing enormous datasets, artificial intelligence algorithms give travel firms insights into their customers' interests. This enables travel agencies to engage in targeted marketing, provide personalized suggestions, and create unique trip packages (Zhou & Liu, 2022).

The overarching approach to improving customer experiences and operational efficiency revolves around utilizing data analytics powered by artificial intelligence. Hotels can get priceless insights into customers' behavior, preferences, and trends using the vast data created via reservations, guest interactions, and operational operations. This method, powered by data, helps hotels improve their marketing campaigns, customize their services, and continually innovate to satisfy their guests' ever-changing demands (Wei et al., 2022). Nevertheless, as the hotel sector embraces these technological breakthroughs, it is essential to address data security, privacy, and ethical considerations. Hotels are entrusted with sensitive information by their guests, and ensuring that the data protection procedures are solid is paramount. It is a difficulty that the industry must overcome to create and maintain trust to strike the correct balance between the benefits of artificial intelligence and the ethical use of visitor data (Baranidharan Subburayan, 2023).

One of the most significant turning points in hotel management and tourism development is artificial intelligence and virtual experiences. This paradigm shift is not simply about implementing new technology but radically reinventing how hotels function and provide Hospitality to their customers. Accepting the potential of artificial intelligence and virtual experiences is not merely a strategic choice for those who wish to thrive in the competitive and ever-evolving landscape of modern Hospitality; instead, it is an absolute necessity for those navigating this transformative journey the industry is currently undergoing (Lviv State University of Physical Culture of Ivana Boberskogo et al., 2023).

1.1 Objectives

1. To improve the experience of guests in hotel management through personalization
2. To maximize cost management and operational efficiency in the hotel and tourism industries
3. To offer significant perspectives on integrating artificial intelligence and virtual experiences within hotel management and tourism domains.

2. LITERATURE REVIEW

Improving Visitor Experiences with Artificial Intelligence in the Hospitality Sector delves into how integrating AI into hotel operations improves visitor experiences by personalizing offerings, making the best suggestions, and expediting communication (Liaw et al., 2023).

Incorporating virtual experiences and artificial intelligence (AI) into hotel management and tourism highlights a paradigm change in the hospitality sector. Research has shown that the impact is complex, with studies concentrating on the use of AI chatbots in customer service, the impact of virtual reality (VR) tours on decision-making, and individualized visitor experiences made possible by AI algorithms

(Bigné, 2023). The literature also examines the ethical issues regarding visitor data and AI applications in revenue management and face recognition security enhancement. Reviews include topics such as how AI is incorporated into marketing plans, how to train personnel to adapt to new technologies, and how consumer expectations are changing. This literature is further enhanced by cultural ramifications, sustainable practices, and the historical viewpoint of AI in Hospitality, which highlights the dynamic interaction between technological innovation and conventional hospitality principles (Marković et al., 2020). Human-AI interaction, ethical issues, and augmented reality integration are some of the study avenues the discipline explores as it develops, opening the door to a comprehensive understanding of AI's revolutionary impact on the hospitality and tourist industries (Abu-Abed & Zhironkin, 2023).

Facial recognition technology has become prominent, guaranteeing faster check-in procedures but posing privacy issues. The literature also emphasizes how vital AI-powered language translation services are for removing language barriers in the hospitality sector. An innovative use of AI in hotel services is robotic help, which has been researched for its potential in anything from room service to concierge services (Slovakia et al., 2023).

A thorough examination of the ethical issues surrounding the use of AI is conducted, emphasizing guaranteeing appropriate data management and open communication with visitors on the use of their data. Virtual reality (VR) experiences, especially VR tours, have been studied for their impact on consumer choice and pre-booking behavior, emphasizing how they may change how travelers see travel locations and lodging (Bilynets et al., 2023).

The literature expands on the guest-centric viewpoint by examining how AI affects the training and development of hotel employees and how job roles are changing in the sector. The cultural ramifications and the delicate nature of language translation services provided by international hotel chains are discussed, highlighting the requirement that technology be sensitive to cultural differences (Rivera Otero et al., 2021).

Additionally, the literature considers how AI may be incorporated into sustainability practices, supporting eco-friendly hotel management. How AI handles and reacts to online reviews is examined in detail, focusing on how this affects how hotels are seen online (Ding et al., 2023).

Using voice-activated AI in guest rooms is becoming increasingly important as the business develops, adding a new level of interactivity to visitors' stays. The literature highlights the necessity for a careful balance between technological innovation, preserving the warmth and personal touch that define traditional Hospitality, and the progression of client expectations (Aliyah et al., 2023).

In the future, studies into sophisticated customization methods, augmented reality integration, and human-AI cooperation will be among the cutting-edge research fields. AI's effects on conferences, event planning, and community involvement are being studied increasingly, indicative of the industry's ongoing search for novel approaches to improve visitor experiences while resolving moral dilemmas and adjusting to changing consumer preferences (Kherson & Oliinyk, 2023).

Reviews of the literature in the field of marketing explore how artificial intelligence (AI) and virtual reality (VR) might transform advertising tactics. AI-driven strategies are being investigated for developing customized and targeted marketing efforts that speak to guests' tastes. Virtual reality's immersive experiences, particularly in destination marketing, are acknowledged for their capacity to enthrall and involve prospective tourists, impacting their choices throughout the reservation process (Uhodnikova et al., 2022).

Discussions about ethics are still at the forefront, emphasizing the proper use of AI in guest data management. Scholars investigate the significance of formulating unambiguous guidelines, guaranteeing data protection, and upholding open lines of communication with visitors about using their data to foster and preserve confidence.

In addition, scholarly works investigate the use of AI historically within the hotel industry, charting its development and significant turning points. This historical background sheds light on the difficulties encountered and the lessons discovered, providing insightful advice for present and future deployments (Duleepa et al., 2023).

A recurring issue in research is the relationship between AI and human contact, with studies looking into the cooperative potential of human-AI collaborations in providing efficient and tailored services. This subtle strategy aims to balance the innate human qualities of hospitality and technical improvements.

AI is starting to play a more significant part in encouraging sustainable practices in the hotel sector (Talukder & Hossain 2021). The increasing focus on eco-friendly activities is reflected in research highlighting AI-driven solutions' role in reducing waste, increasing energy efficiency, and promoting environmentally responsible operating practices.

As the sector develops, research emphasizes the rise of AI-driven advancements in hotel facilities, such as sophisticated in-room technology and intelligent rooms. Voice-activated AI is being investigated for its potential to revolutionize the visitor experience by offering easy-to-use controls for a range of room features (Kemer & Tyagi, 2023).

The literature presents a comprehensive and diverse picture of artificial intelligence (AI) and virtual experiences in Hospitality and travel. It displays an ongoing process of discovery, invention, and adjustment, all while keeping a close eye on sustainability, ethical issues, and the fine line between technology and the fundamentals of Hospitality. In this dynamic and constantly changing business, future research will explore more unexplored areas, investigate cutting-edge technology, hon ethical frameworks, and discover advanced methods to improve the visitor experience (Syara & Fauzan, 2023).

2.1 Case Study: Improving Visitor Experiences at a Luxury Resort Using Artificial Intelligence and Virtual Reality

Introduction: By utilizing cutting-edge technologies—artificial intelligence (AI) and virtual experiences—a prestigious luxury resort aimed to reinvent visitor experiences in the highly competitive hospitality business. The objective was to maximize operating efficiency while delivering a smooth, customized, and immersive experience for visitors (Rane et al., 2023).

Challenge: The elite clientele's varied wants and tastes presented difficulties for the opulent resort to satisfy. Even though the previous hospitality model offered excellent services, it lacked the efficiency and customization that contemporary travelers want. To improve visitor pleasure, streamline operations, and keep a competitive edge in the market, the resort realized it needed to use artificial intelligence (AI) and virtual experiences.

AI Chatbot Implementation and Virtual Concierge: To expedite the booking process and offer on-the-spot support, the resort outfitted its mobile app and website with chatbots that AI drives. These chatbots have natural language processing skills, which enable them to comprehend and reply to queries from visitors, make bookings, and provide tailored meals and activity recommendations. Virtual concierge services were also installed in guest rooms, allowing guests to use voice-activated commands to access information, make requests, and receive individualized help (Grosjean et al., 2023).

Virtual Reality Tours for Pre-booking Engagement: After realizing the impact of visual engagement, the opulent resort used virtual reality (VR) tours to highlight its rooms, amenities, and the surrounding scenic beauty. In a 360-degree virtual tour, potential visitors may explore the opulent rooms, spa services, and picturesque surroundings. The resort's website and mobile app made these virtual reality tours available, offering an engrossing pre-booking experience that greatly impacted visitors' choices (Figueroa Jr, 2023).

AI-Powered Customization for Visitor Services: The resort used AI algorithms to examine visitor preferences based on prior visits, interactions, and comments to generate tailored experiences. This data was used to predict specific dietary needs, provide activities that were specifically catered to, and even personalize lodging amenities. The spa and wellness services also benefited from AI-driven customization since treatment suggestions were made based on each client's tastes and wellness objectives (Gasparini & Kautonen, 2023).

Facial Recognition for Safe and Easy Experiences: Face recognition technology was used for easy check-in and access management to improve security and expedite visitor experiences. It was also possible for visitors to use their facial characteristics as the key to their lodgings during a quick, contactless check-in procedure. This sped up the check-in process and improved security by limiting access to specific sections of the resort to those who were allowed (Zhang et al., 2021).

Findings and Conclusions: For the opulent resort, the use of AI and virtual experiences produced noticeable results:

Increased Guest Satisfaction: The resort's guest satisfaction ratings significantly increased, with many guests complimenting the attentive services, effective chatbots, and immersive virtual reality tours pre-booking experiences (Talukder, 2021).

Enhanced Operational Efficiency: By reducing downtime for critical equipment, AI-driven predictive maintenance helped to improve operational flow. Dynamic pricing techniques increased profitability by optimizing revenue management and guaranteeing reasonable hotel charges.

A rise in recurring reservations and increased visitor loyalty resulted from the customized experiences made possible by AI algorithms and virtual interaction. Many guests said they planned to return because of the resort's dedication to providing innovative and guest-focused services (Ferreira et al., 2023).

Having an excellent online reputation: A positive internet reputation was aided by sentiment analysis and artificial intelligence integration for controlling online reviews. The resort's openness and promptness in responding to the guests' comments were much appreciated.

Through the strategic integration of artificial intelligence and virtual experiences, the upscale resort effectively revolutionized its methods for providing guest services and overseeing operations. To maintain a competitive advantage in the ever-changing hotel management and tourist industry, the case study emphasizes how these technologies can meet and exceed the expectations of discriminating guests (Reisman, 2022).

2.2 Empirical Findings

1. **Higher Booking Conversions**: After deploying AI-powered chatbots and virtual experiences, empirical data from several hotels and resorts show a significant rise in booking conversions. Due to chatbots' capacity to help in real-time and respond to inquiries, prospective visitors become more engaged, eventually resulting in more successful reservations (Xie & Lee, 2015).
2. **Beneficial Effect on Customer Satisfaction**: Feedback analysis and surveys constantly show a beneficial effect on customer satisfaction. Visitors value the immersive experiences virtual real-

ity tours offer and the tailored recommendations AI algorithms make (Talukder, 2022). Higher satisfaction ratings result from these factors, improving the visitor experience overall.

3. **Gains in Operational Efficiency**: Based on empirical data, using AI in hotel management has increased operational efficiency. Algorithms for predictive maintenance have effectively decreased equipment downtime, which has improved daily operations. Dynamic pricing techniques have also successfully maintained competitive pricing and improved revenue management.
4. **Enhanced Marketing Effectiveness**: Hotels that use artificial intelligence and virtual experiences in their marketing campaigns claim heightened efficacy. Virtual reality tours are effective marketing tools as they give prospective visitors a sneak peek at the lodging and amenities. As a result, there has been an increase in brand visibility and online platform interaction.
5. **Increased Guest Loyalty**: Longitudinal research comparing visitor behavior before and after adopting AI-driven customization techniques shows a rise in guest loyalty. Stronger ties between customers and the hotel brand are fostered by the capacity to anticipate and satisfy specific preferences, generating exclusivity and customized treatment (Ginting et al., 2023).
6. **Data Security and Privacy Issues**: Empirical research reveals data security and privacy challenges despite the apparent advantages. Visitors raise concerns over using face recognition technology and gathering private information for AI-powered customization. Hotels using this technology must honestly address these issues to keep guests' faith (Mohammad et al., 2021).
7. **Technological Adoption by Staff**: Research on how hotel employees embrace AI has shown differing acceptance and adaptation. Training courses and workshops have been essential to guarantee that employees are efficiently skilled in using AI tools. This has eventually helped to provide a more seamless integration of these technologies into regular operations (Opara et al., 2023).
8. **Changing Customer Expectations**: According to empirical research, customer expectations will likely change as the hotel sector's artificial intelligence (AI) and virtual experiences proliferate. Today's visitors need a smooth transition between technology and human interaction, underscoring the significance of striking a balance between cutting-edge innovations and customary hospitality techniques.
9. **Technology-Driven Upselling Opportunities:** Studies show how successful AI-driven upselling campaigns are in the hospitality sector. AI systems recognize targeted upselling possibilities, including accommodation upgrades, exclusive packages, or extra services, by examining the preferences and actions of visitors. Hotels that use these tactics report higher upselling revenue, which boosts overall profitability (Dönmez, 2022).
10. **Smooth Check-in and Check-out Experiences**: The benefits of face recognition technology in expediting check-in and check-out procedures are supported by empirical data. Visitors value facial recognition systems' quickness and ease of use, resulting in shorter lines, shorter wait times, and an enhanced arrival and departure experience (Jiang & Balaji, 2022).
11. **Effect on Workflows and Staff Productivity**: Research examining how AI affects hotel management shows improvements in workflows and staff productivity. Routine duties may be automated by AI-powered technologies, freeing up staff time for more intricate and guest-focused work. This improves operational effectiveness and creates a more satisfying work environment for hotel employees.
12. **AI-Powered Perspectives for Tactics-Based Decision-Making**: Empirical research highlights AI analytics's valuable insights for tactical decision-making. Hotel managers and executives employ data-driven insights to make well-informed decisions on pricing strategies, marketing initiatives,

and operational enhancements. This data emphasizes how AI may be used as a strategic instrument to influence how hotel management develops in the future (Zhang et al., 2021).

13. **Tailored Marketing Campaigns**: Hotels may now develop highly focused and customized marketing campaigns with the help of AI. Based on visitor preferences and habits, empirical research demonstrates that tailored marketing increases engagement and conversion rates. AI-powered marketing campaigns give visitors more relevant and alluring offers, strengthening the bond between the hotel and its customers (Ustymenko, 2023).
14. **The Evolution of AI in Visitor Feedback Analysis**: Hotels that use AI technologies to analyze guest feedback claim improved customer sentiment comprehension and response times. Algorithms for natural language processing examine social media mentions, reviews, and survey data to spot patterns and potential improvement areas. This real-time feedback loop allows Hotels to adjust to evolving guest expectations and preferences (Escalante et al., 2023).
15. **Sustainable Practices with AI**: Research demonstrates how AI may support sustainable practices in the hospitality sector. Artificial intelligence (AI)-driven solutions support environmental conservation through waste reduction tactics and energy-efficient processes. Hotels that use AI for sustainability claim cost savings, enhanced attractiveness to environmentally concerned tourists, and a favorable brand image (Banipal et al., 2023).
16. **Integration of Voice-Activated AI in Guest Rooms**: Research on integrating voice-activated AI in guest rooms reveals positive visitor responses. Voice-activated assistants provide visitors with a simple and practical means of managing hotel amenities, making service requests, and retrieving information. Voice technology is seamlessly integrated, improving the guest experience and signaling a move toward smart, connected lodging (Niroula, 2023).
17. **Applications of AI that are Guest-centred in hotel restaurants**: Empirical research emphasizes how AI improves the eating experience. AI-driven menu recommendations considering dietary needs, personal preferences, and past eating experiences provide patrons with a more delightful and customized dining experience (Luspo et al., 2021).
18. **AI in Conference and Event Management**: Hotels that hold conferences and events use AI to manage events more effectively. AI simplifies logistics, attendee engagement, and event planning, as supported by empirical data. AI-powered virtual experiences improve the conference experience overall and draw event organizers and attendees (Mohammad et al., 2024b).

The empirical results show various virtual and artificial intelligence integration effects in hotel management and tourism. The data highlights the revolutionary potential of these technologies in reshaping the hotel sector, from operational improvements and revenue optimization to customized guest experiences and sustainable practices (Fogel & Bonissone, 2023).

19. **Future Trends and Emerging Technologies in the Hospitality Sector:** The hospitality sector is evolving rapidly, driven by technological advancements and shifting consumer expectations. With the ongoing impact of the COVID-19 pandemic, contactless technologies have become paramount, revolutionizing check-in processes, payments, and overall guest experiences (Mohammad et al., 2024a). Artificial Intelligence and Machine Learning are being harnessed for personalized services, while the Internet of Things is transforming hotel rooms into innovative, connected spaces (Kumar et al., 2023). Emerging technologies such as Virtual Reality and Augmented Reality enhance the booking journey, offering virtual tours and on-site navigation. Blockchain ensures

secure transactions and data protection, and robotics automate various tasks, from room service to cleaning. Biometric technology adds a layer of security and convenience to guest interactions. Sustainability initiatives, driven by eco-friendly practices, are gaining traction. Big data analytics enable personalized services, and mobile apps with integrated chatbots streamline communication. As the industry adapts to the rise of remote work, hotels are reimagining spaces and amenities to cater to the evolving needs of a diverse and tech-savvy clientele. Keeping pace with these trends is crucial for hospitality businesses aiming to stay competitive in this dynamic landscape.

Figure 1. Conceptual framework
(Author)

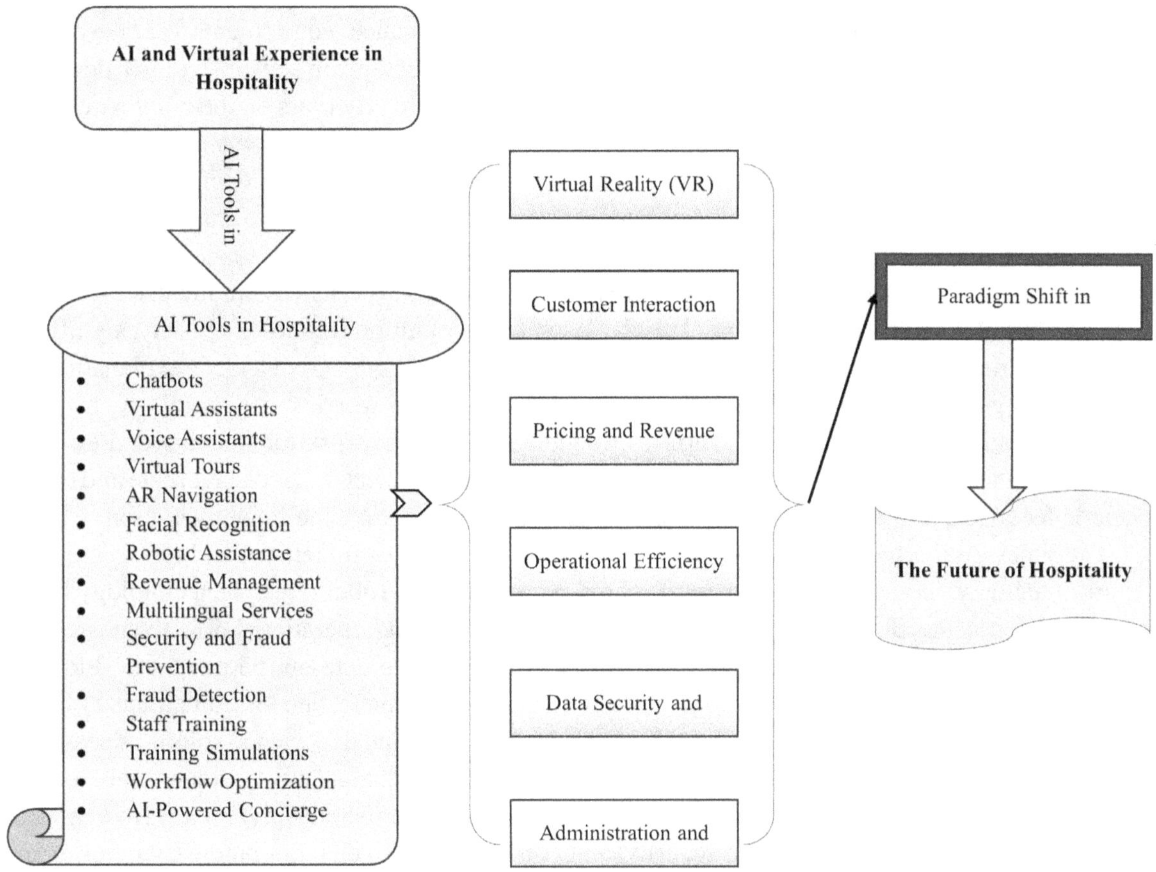

2.3 Recommendations

1. **Perform a Comprehensive Technology Assessment**: Evaluate current technologies, infrastructure, and data management systems in-depth before implementing AI and virtual experiences. Ensure there are no compatibility or integration issues during the installation process.
2. **Prioritize Guest Data Security and Privacy**: Create strong data security and privacy rules, then follow them to the letter. Visitors should feel confident knowing that their data is protected. Adhere to pertinent data protection laws, use encryption mechanisms, and anonymize data wherever feasible.

3. **Invest in Staff Development and Training**: Ensure employees can easily access extensive training courses to use AI tools and virtual experience platforms. With this investment, workers will be better equipped to interact with visitors, oversee AI-powered systems, and adjust to the rapidly changing technological environment.
4. **Encourage Open Communication with Visitors**: Ensure visitors understand how AI technology and virtual experiences are used. Since transparency fosters trust, visitors should be aware of the uses of their data, the advantages of AI applications, and any planned modifications to customary service procedures. AI solutions should be tailored to the hotel's brand identity and culture to align with these elements. Technology should complement, not replace, the human element and customized touch that characterize outstanding hospitality experiences.
5. **Use AI for Predictive Maintenance**: To maximize equipment performance and minimize downtime, apply AI for predictive maintenance. To foresee maintenance requirements and take proactive measures to solve concerns, regularly monitor and analyze data from sensors and IoT devices.
6. **Use VR to Engage Guests Before They Book:** Use virtual reality tours on the hotel's mobile app and website to give prospective visitors immersive sneak peeks at the rooms and amenities. This increases visitors' pre-booking interaction and dramatically impacts their decision-making.
7. **Assure Inclusivity and Accessibility**: Consider accessibility features to accommodate visitors with various demands while integrating AI and virtual experiences. Make sure AI-powered services are available to all visitors, regardless of ability, and that virtual experiences are inclusively created.
8. **Use Face Recognition Technology Wisely**: Use face recognition technology wisely, significantly when it improves security and speeds up procedures like check-in. Give a clear explanation of its goal and get permission before addressing any privacy-related worries visitors raise.
9. **Track and Examine Customer Input**: Provide a robust framework for tracking and evaluating customer feedback about artificial intelligence and virtual experiences. Seek favorable and unfavorable feedback, and constantly utilize your observations to improve the implementation.
10. **Try Voice-Activated AI in Guest Rooms**: To improve control over facilities and services, consider introducing voice-activated AI in guest rooms. Before a wider rollout, test the technology in a few rooms and get feedback to see how it affects guest pleasure and operational effectiveness.
11. **Work Together with Technology Partners**: To remain up to date on the newest developments and industry best practices, work together with technology partners, vendors, and industry experts. Form alliances with reliable suppliers to integrate AI and virtual experience solutions seamlessly.
12. **Update and Maintain Systems Frequently**: Keep up with technical developments and update AI systems and virtual experience platforms frequently. Maintenance should proactively fix weaknesses and guarantee peak performance, security, and compliance with changing industry requirements.
13. **Make a Sustainable Practices Roadmap**: Create a plan for incorporating AI to advance environmentally friendly hotel operations. This might involve waste management programs, energy-efficient technology, and eco-friendly business procedures.
14. **Involve Visitors in Co-Creation Processes**: Involve visitors in co-creation by asking for feedback on building and enhancing virtual experiences. This raises guest interaction and offers insightful information on changing tastes.
15. **Establish benchmark performance metrics or key performance indicators (KPIs):** To assess how artificial intelligence (AI) and virtual experiences affect many facets of hotel management, such as revenue optimization, guest happiness, and operational efficiency. To determine success, compare performance regularly to these indicators.

16. **Continue to Be Flexible with Emerging Technology**: Promote a flexible culture with emerging technologies. Stay current on market developments and be ready to incorporate new technology that can improve visitor experiences even more and expedite hotel administration procedures.

Hotels and other tourism-related enterprises may integrate virtual experiences and artificial intelligence by following these tips, guaranteeing a seamless fusion of technology and Hospitality that meets and is beyond visitor expectations.

3. CONCLUSION

A revolutionary change that has changed the hospitality sector's visitor experience and operational dynamics is integrating artificial intelligence (AI) and virtual experiences in hotel management and tourism. Empirical research and case studies support the substantial advantages that have resulted from the strategic application of these technologies, which span from increased operational efficiency and sustainable practices to better visitor pleasure and tailored services. To fulfill the changing expectations of contemporary tourists, it is imperative to recognize the critical role that artificial intelligence (AI) and virtual experiences play in hotel management. Today's guests demand experiences beyond conventional hospitality services that are smooth, customized, and technologically advanced. Enhancing booking conversions, customer happiness, and operational workflows highlights the possibility of long-term success by implementing these advances.

However, there are obstacles to combining AI with virtual experiences. Essential things to consider include data security and privacy issues, employee training requirements, and the necessity to balance technology and human interaction. Establishing and preserving trust with visitors requires open communication about the usage of these tools.

3.1 Future Research Directions

Future studies on the application of artificial intelligence (AI) and virtual experiences in hotel management and tourism should concentrate on many vital areas as the hospitality sector continues to change:

AI-Human Interaction: Examine how AI and humans interact in hospitality environments. Recognize how visitors see and engage with AI-powered systems and devise strategies to enhance these exchanges for a smooth and user-friendly experience.

Regulation and Ethical Considerations: Examine the moral ramifications of artificial intelligence (AI) and virtual reality, paying particular attention to data privacy, algorithmic biases, and the responsible application of new technology. Regulations and ethical guidelines unique to a specific industry should be developed with input from research.

Influence on Workforce Dynamics and Employment: Analyze how AI affects hotel industry jobs. Examine the effects of integrating AI technology on job positions, workforce dynamics, and employees' overall experience.

Integration of Augmented Reality (AR): Examine how virtual experiences and augmented reality (AR) might be combined. Examine how augmented reality (AR) may improve in-person interactions, hotel room navigation, and interaction with nearby attractions.

AI for Sustainable Practices: How AI may help the hotel sector adopt more environmentally friendly practices. Evaluate how AI will affect hotel environmental impact, waste reduction, and resource efficiency.

Cultural Sensitivity in Online Learning Environments: Consider virtual encounters' cultural ramifications, particularly in multicultural, global environments. Examine how these technologies might be customized to honor cultural quirks and satisfy the tastes of a worldwide customer base.

Advances in AI-Enhanced Event Management: Examine how AI may improve hotel conference rooms and event management. Examine the latest developments in virtual and hybrid event experiences and the effects of artificial intelligence on the organization and management of sizable events.

More Complex Customization Methods: Examine cutting-edge AI customization methods, combining sentiment analysis, emotion detection, and real-time adaptive systems. Examine how these developments might improve the degree of customization of visitor experiences.

Boosting cybersecurity protocols in AI-driven hospitality environments should be the main priority. Research should focus on data security techniques, possible weaknesses in AI systems, and creating safe guest interaction protocols. Examine how artificial intelligence (AI) and virtual experiences may promote community and stakeholder participation. Examine how hotels might work with stakeholders and local communities to offer visitors immersive, culturally enriching experiences. Hotel management and tourism will benefit from the evolution of AI and virtual experiences, which will be made possible by the ongoing research and exploration of these areas. This will keep the industry at the forefront of innovation while responsibly addressing challenges and ethical considerations.

REFERENCES

Abass, M. (2023). Artificial Intelligence Techniques in Egyptian Hotels: Current Status and Prospective. *Egyptian Journal of Tourism and Hospitality*, *30*(1), 1–53. doi:10.21608/ejth.2023.303527

Abu-Abed, F., & Zhironkin, S. (2023). New Game Artificial Intelligence Tools for Virtual Mine on Unreal Engine. *Applied Sciences (Basel, Switzerland)*, *13*(10), 6339. doi:10.3390/app13106339

Al-Hyari, H. S., Al-Smadi, H. M., & Weshah, S. R. (2023). The impact of artificial intelligence (ai) on guest satisfaction in hotel management: An empirical study of luxury hotels. *Geo Journal of Tourism and Geosites*, *48*(2, supplement), 810–819. doi:10.30892/gtg.482spl15-1081

Aliyah, L., Lukita, C., Pangilinan, G. A., Chakim, M. H. R., & Saputra, D. B. (2023). Examining the Impact of Artificial Intelligence and Internet of Things on Smart Tourism Destinations: A Comprehensive Study. [ATT]. *Aptisi Transactions on Technopreneurship*, *5*(2sp), 135–145. doi:10.34306/att.v5i2sp.332

Banipal, I. S., Asthana, S., & Mazumder, S. (2023). Sustainable AI - Standards, Current Practices and Recommendations. In K. Arai (Ed.), *Proceedings of the Future Technologies Conference (FTC) 2023,* (*Vol. 813*, pp. 271–289). Springer Nature Switzerland. 10.1007/978-3-031-47454-5_21

Bhaskar, A., Yadav, P., Singh, S. P., Kumar, V., Srivastava, S., Singh, S. K., Singh, B., & Dutt, A. (2023). Role of Artificial Intelligence in Healthcare Management. In A. Garg, V. Emilia Balas, R. Pratap Ojha, & P. Kumar Srivastava (Eds.), Reinventing Technological Innovations with Artificial Intelligence (pp. 26–47). Bentham science publishers. doi:10.2174/9789815165791123010006

Bigné, E. (2023). Artificial Intelligence in Tourism. In L. Moutinho, L. Cavique, & E. Bigné (Eds.), (pp. 98–114). Advances in Human and Social Aspects of Technology. IGI Global. doi:10.4018/978-1-6684-9591-9.ch006

Bilynets, I., Trkman, P., & Knežević Cvelbar, L. (2023). Virtual tourism experiences: Adoption factors, participation and readiness to pay. *Current Issues in Tourism*, 1–18. doi:10.1080/13683500.2023.2268809

Boberskogo, I. (2023). Marketing technologies of personalization in tourism based on artificial intelligence. *Eastern Europe: Economy. Business and Management*, *2*(39). doi:10.32782/easterneurope.39-4

Bulchand-Gidumal, J., William Secin, E., O'Connor, P., & Buhalis, D. (2023). Artificial intelligence's impact on hospitality and tourism marketing: Exploring key themes and addressing challenges. *Current Issues in Tourism*, 1–18. doi:10.1080/13683500.2023.2229480

Ding, B., Ferràs Hernández, X., & Agell Jané, N. (2023). Combining lean and agile manufacturing competitive advantages through Industry 4.0 technologies: An integrative approach. *Production Planning and Control*, *34*(5), 442–458. doi:10.1080/09537287.2021.1934587

Dönmez, N. (2022). Metaverse bankaciliği yolunda değişen müşteri beklentilerine hitaben gelişen pazarlama anlayişlari üzerine bir inceleme. *Uluslararası Bankacılık Ekonomi ve Yönetim Araştırmaları Dergisi*, *5*(1), 97–132. doi:10.52736/ubeyad.1119156

Duleepa, D., Hasini, J., & Ruwan, R. (2023). Potentials of developing artificial intelligence technology in the sri lankan hotel industry with special reference to colombo district. *cactus*, *5*(1). doi:10.24818/CTS/5/2023/1.04

Escalante, J., Pack, A., & Barrett, A. (2023). AI-generated feedback on writing: Insights into efficacy and ENL student preference. *International Journal of Educational Technology in Higher Education*, *20*(1), 57. doi:10.1186/s41239-023-00425-2

Ferreira, R. P., Vilarinho, L. O., & Scotti, A. (2023). Enhanced-pixel strategy for wire arc additive manufacturing trajectory planning: Operational efficiency and effectiveness analyses. *Rapid Prototyping Journal*, *30*(11), 1–15. doi:10.1108/RPJ-12-2022-0413

Figueroa, R. B. Jr. (2023). Immersive capability and spatial presence in virtual reality photo-based tours: Implications for distance education. *Asian Association of Open Universities Journal*, *18*(3), 201–217. doi:10.1108/AAOUJ-12-2022-0171

Fogel, G. B., & Bonissone, P. (2023). Conference Report on the Inaugural 2023 IEEE Conference on Artificial Intelligence (IEEE CAI 2023) [Conference Reports]. *IEEE Computational Intelligence Magazine*, *18*(4), 5–7. 10.1109/MCI.2023.3306149

Gasparini, A. A., & Kautonen, H. (2023). Determinants of using AI-powered discovery services. *Septentrio Conference Series*, *1*(1). doi:10.7557/5.7164

Ginting, N. C. A., Sianturi, M., & Ariesa, Y. (2023). The influence of service quality and price on guest loyalty during the COVID-19 pandemic with guest satisfaction as an intervening variable at Hotel Grand Cityhall Medan. *Priviet Social Sciences Journal*, *3*(7), 1–8. doi:10.55942/pssj.v3i7.227

Gosjen, D. I., Haryadi, K. H., Nicholas, Gunawan, A. A. S., Djuwita, C. M., & Adiati, M. P. (2023). Implementation e-concierge in hotel. *Procedia Computer Science*, *216*, 485–498. doi:10.1016/j.procs.2022.12.161

Gündüz, C. (2023). Customised Holiday Experiences through Artificial Intelligence: Case Studies from the Aviation and Hospitality Sectors. *Journal of Aviation*, *7*(3), 337–345. doi:10.30518/jav.1351472

Jamaluddin, Z., & Rahmat, A. K. (2023). Artificial Intelligence Technology in Travel, Tourism and Hospitality: Current and Future Developments. In A. Hassan & N. A. A. Rahman (Eds.), *Technology Application in Aviation, Tourism and Hospitality* (pp. 169–177). Springer Nature Singapore. doi:10.1007/978-981-19-6619-4_12

Jiang, Y., & Balaji, M. S. (2022). Getting unwired: What drives travellers to take a digital detox holiday? *Tourism Recreation Research*, *47*(5–6), 453–469. doi:10.1080/02508281.2021.1889801

Kemer, E., & Tyagi, P. K. (2023). Application of Artificial Intelligence and Robotics in Tourism and Hospitality Marketing. In P. K. Tyagi, V. Nadda, V. Bharti, & E. Kemer (Eds.), (pp. 125–140). Advances in Business Strategy and Competitive Advantage. IGI Global. doi:10.4018/978-1-6684-6732-9.ch008

Kumar, S., Talukder, M. B., Kabir, F., & Kaiser, F. (2024). Challenges and Sustainability of Green Finance in the Tourism Industry: Evidence from Bangladesh. In S. Taneja, P. Kumar, S. Grima, E. Ozen, & K. Sood (Eds.), (pp. 97–111). Advances in Finance, Accounting, and Economics. IGI Global. doi:10.4018/979-8-3693-1388-6.ch006

LabdaouiD. (2023). *(The role of startups in promoting digital and smart tourism in the era of artificial intelligence)*. doi:10.13140/RG.2.2.16097.68964

Liaw, S. Y., Tan, J. Z., Lim, S., Zhou, W., Yap, J., Ratan, R., Ooi, S. L., Wong, S. J., Seah, B., & Chua, W. L. (2023). Artificial intelligence in virtual reality simulation for interprofessional communication training: Mixed method study. *Nurse Education Today*, *122*, 105718. doi:10.1016/j.nedt.2023.105718 PMID:36669304

Lukanova, G., & Ilieva, G. (2019). Robots, Artificial Intelligence, and Service Automation in Hotels. In S. Ivanov & C. Webster (Eds.), Robots, Artificial Intelligence, and Service Automation in Travel, Tourism and Hospitality (pp. 157–183). Emerald Publishing Limited. doi:10.1108/978-1-78756-687-320191009

Luspo, C., Remetio, A. C., Sadial, B. P., & Pabatang, M. (2021). Guest Service Management among Hotels and Restaurants in Butuan City. *SMCC Higher Education Research Journal*, *2*(1). doi:10.18868/hrm-v2-a5

Marković, S., Raspor Janković, S., & Zubović, V. (2020). The impacts of robots and artificial intelligence on service quality in the hotel industry. *Balkans Journal of Emerging Trends in Social Sciences*, *3*(2), 163–170. doi:10.31410/Balkans.JETSS.2020.3.2.163-170

Mohammad, B. T., & Mokarram Hossain, M. (2021). Prospects of future tourism in bangladesh: An evaluative study. *I-Manager's. Journal of Management*, *15*(4), 31. doi:10.26634/jmgt.15.4.17495

Niroula, B. (2023). *The Impact of AI on the Future of Voice Acting* [Preprint]. Open Science Framework. doi:10.31219/osf.io/wn5y3

Oliinyk, I. Kherson State Agrarian and Economic University. (2023). Prospects for implementing generative artificial intelligence in marketing and trade. *Scientific Bulletin of Flight Academy. Section: Economics. Management and Law*, *8*, 110–115. doi:10.33251/2707-8620-2023-8-110-115

Opara, O., Nsirim, O., & Irokah, P. L. (2023). Technological Methods and Security of Information Resources in Dame Patience Goodluck Jonathan Automated Library, Ignatius Ajuru University of Education. *Southern African Journal of Security*, *1*. doi:10.25159/3005-4222/14506

Rane, N., Choudhary, S., & Rane, J. (2023). Sustainable tourism development using leading-edge Artificial Intelligence (AI), Blockchain, Internet of Things (IoT), Augmented Reality (AR) and Virtual Reality (VR) technologies. SSRN *Electronic Journal*. doi:10.2139/ssrn.4642605

Reisman, N. R. (2022). Commentary on: Fake News, Defamation, and Online Reviews and Their Potential Devastating Consequences for Aesthetic Plastic Surgeons. *Aesthetic Surgery Journal*, *42*(8), NP554–NP555. doi:10.1093/asj/sjac097 PMID:35439283

Rivera Otero, J. M., Lagares Díez, N., Pereira López, M., & López-López, P. C. (2021). Transparency Policies in European Public Broadcasters: Sustainability, Digitalisation and Fact-Checking. *Social Sciences (Basel, Switzerland)*, *10*(6), 217. doi:10.3390/socsci10060217

SubburayanB. (2023). *The Artificial Intelligence (AI) Odyssey: Redefining Travel and Tourism for Modern Explorers*. doi:10.13140/RG.2.2.22816.15362

Syara, A. S., & Fauzan, T. R. (2023). Does Halal Tourism Matter? A Study About Implementation of Sharia-based Hotel in Bandung, West Java, Indonesia. *AL-MANHAJ: Jurnal Hukum Dan Pranata Sosial Islam*, *5*(2), 2045–2058. doi:10.37680/almanhaj.v5i2.3992

Talukder, M., Shakhawat Hossain, M., & Kumar, S. (2022). Blue Ocean Strategies in Hotel Industry in Bangladesh: A Review of Present Literatures' Gap and Suggestions for Further Study. SSRN Electronic Journal. https://doi.org/ doi:10.2139/ssrn.4160709

Talukder, M. B. (2020a). An Appraisal of the Economic Outlook for the Tourism Industry, Specially Cox's Bazar in Bangladesh. *i-manager's Journal on Economics & Commerce, 2*(1), 23-35. doi:10.26634/jecom.2.1.17285

Talukder, M. B. (2020b). The Future of Culinary Tourism: An Emerging Dimension for the Tourism Industry of Bangladesh. I-Manager's. *Journal of Management*, *15*(1), 27. doi:10.26634/jmgt.15.1.17181

Talukder, M. B. (2021). An assessment of the roles of the social network in the development of the Tourism Industry in Bangladesh. *International Journal of Business, Law, and Education*, *2*(3), 85–93. doi:10.56442/ijble.v2i3.21

Talukder, M. B., & Hossain, M. M. (2021). Prospects of Future Tourism in Bangladesh: An Evaluative Study. I-Manager's. *Journal of Management*, *15*(4), 1–8. doi:10.26634/jmgt.15.4.17495

Talukder, M. B., & Kumar, S. (2023). *The Effect of Food Service Quality onCustomer Satisfaction in the Hotel Industry: A Conceptual Paper*. ResearchGate. https://www.researchgate.net/publication/371503829_The_Effect_of_Food_Service_Quality_on_Customer_Satisfaction_in_the_Hotel_Industry_A_Conceptual_Paper

Talukder, M. B., Kumar, S., Sood, K., & Grima, S. (2023). Information Technology, Food Service Quality and Restaurant Revisit Intention. *International Journal of Sustainable Development and Planning*, *18*(1), 295–303. doi:10.18280/ijsdp.180131

Uhodnikova, O., Sokolenko, A., Ryabev, A., Abramov, V., Pokolodna, M., Kravtsova, S., Shevchenko, V., & Miroshnichenko, Yu. (2022). Innovative approaches to the management of effective communications in tourism and the hotel and restaurant industry. *Municipal Economy of Cities*, *7*(174), 9–13. doi:10.33042/2522-1809-2022-7-174-9-13

Ustymenko, R. (2023). Trends and innovations in cosmetic marketing. *Economics & Education*, *8*(3), 12–17. doi:10.30525/2500-946X/2023-3-2

Wei, C., Li, J., & Guo, X. (2022). Influence Analysis of Hotel and Tourism Economic Development Based on Computational Intelligence. *Security and Communication Networks*, *2022*, 1–9. doi:10.1155/2022/7549628

Xie, L., & Lee, Y.-J. (2015). Hotels at Our Fingertips: Understanding Consumer Conversion from Search, Click-Through, to Book. SSRN *Electronic Journal*. doi:10.2139/ssrn.2609514

Zhang, Y., Xiong, Y., Lee, T. J., Ye, M., & Nunkoo, R. (2021). Sociocultural Sustainability and the Formation of Social Capital from Community-based Tourism. *Journal of Travel Research*, *60*(3), 656–669. doi:10.1177/0047287520933673

Zhou, W., & Liu, Z. (2022). Design and Optimization of Hotel Management Information System Based on Artificial Intelligence. *Scientific Programming*, *2022*, 1–9. doi:10.1155/2022/2445343

Chapter 10
Artificial Intelligence (AI) for Tourism Start-Ups

Suhail Mohammad Ghouse
https://orcid.org/0000-0002-7684-933X
Dhofar University, Oman

Monica Chaudhary
https://orcid.org/0000-0002-8344-1447
S.P. Jain School of Global Management, Australia

ABSTRACT

This chapter explores the dynamic intersection of artificial intelligence (AI) and the startup landscape within the tourism industry. It investigates how AI has the potential to revolutionize operations, innovation, and services for emerging businesses in tourism. Demonstrating AI's critical role in enhancing the tourism experience—ranging from personalized recommendations and chatbot-driven customer service to pricing optimization and demand forecasting—it showcases innovative solutions from notable startups like DeepL, Fetch.ai, and Lilium. The chapter includes brief case studies illustrating AI applications in tourism and emphasizes the pivotal role of investors in supporting these startups. It concludes by outlining future research directions, addressing strategies for maximizing AI benefits in tourism, managing privacy and security concerns, and navigating the evolving landscape of AI integration in travel.

1. INTRODUCTION

Artificial intelligence (AI) has emerged as a central focus across various sectors, reshaping businesses and societal landscapes. Its evolution is deeply intertwined with significant advancements in computational capabilities and data accumulation (Lu et al., 2018). This synergy has propelled AI to the forefront of technological innovation, presenting both unprecedented opportunities and challenges. Notably, improvements in computational power, driven by technologies like graphics processing units (GPUs) and specialized hardware, have enabled the execution of complex algorithms at previously unattainable speeds (Lu, 2019; Zhu et al., 2023). This has empowered machine learning models, a subset of AI, to

DOI: 10.4018/979-8-3693-2019-8.ch010

analyze data, recognize patterns, and inform decisions, particularly impacting the business landscape (Kaplan and Haenlein, 2019).

In the tourism industry, AI is increasingly significant, revolutionizing various aspects of the travel experience for businesses and travelers (Grundner and Neuhofer, 2021). The integration of AI technologies enhances efficiency, personalization, and overall customer satisfaction. Tourism start-ups, a dynamic segment within the travel industry, are characterized by innovative approaches to providing travel-related services and experiences (Morrison, 2020). Encompassing a wide range of businesses, including accommodation booking platforms, travel planning apps, and tour operators, these start-ups disrupt traditional models, offering travelers personalized, convenient, and cost-effective options (Gössling et al., 2019). The tourism sector has witnessed rapid growth and innovation driven by technological advancements and changing consumer preferences (UNWTO, 2020). This chapter explores the pivotal role of AI in shaping the landscape of innovative tourism start-ups, enhancing customer experiences, streamlining operations, and driving future growth in this dynamic industry (Filieri et al., 2021).

The rise of digital entrepreneurship is notable in the travel, tourism, and hospitality industry, with prominent corporations like Airbnb, TripAdvisor, Booking.com, and Skyscanner leading transformation (Ivanov & Webster, 2019). Among various technological advancements, AI stands out as a potentially transformative innovation in tourism (Filieri et al., 2021). With AI technological domains attracting significant venture capital funding, exploring how AI shapes tourism start-ups is insightful (Filieri et al., 2021). Tourism AI start-ups exhibit geographic clustering, with a significant portion originating from major European capitals like London, Paris, and Barcelona (Filieri et al., 2021). This clustering underscores the concentrated innovation and potential impact of AI-driven initiatives in the tourism sector.

1.1 The Rise in Artificial Intelligence

The rise of Artificial Intelligence (AI) has revolutionized industries worldwide, simulating human intelligence in machines for tasks like problem-solving and decision-making (Davenport & Kalakota, 2019). In tourism, AI transforms travel planning, experiences, and reflections. AI analyses data for personalized recommendations, enhances service with chatbots, optimizes pricing, and predicts travel trends. Recent advancements in AI rely on improved algorithms, processing capacities, and big data management, marking the Fourth Industrial Revolution (Li et al., 2019). AI applications are evolving across tourism domains, including personalization, travel assistants, robots, predictions, language translation, voice recognition, and natural language processing.

The integration of AI promises to streamline tourism operations, enhance customer satisfaction, and sustain sector growth. Tourists engage in decision-making processes for future trips, including destination, transportation, accommodation, and activities, influencing overall satisfaction with their travel experiences.

1.2 Value Creation of Big Data and Artificial Intelligence (BDAI) in Tourism

The value creation of Big Data and Artificial Intelligence (BDAI), as categorized by McKinsey's global institute analysis and outlined by Talwar and Koury (2017), can be summarized into four key areas:

Project: This area focuses on leveraging BDAI to enable companies to better project and forecast to anticipate demand, optimize research and development (R&D) efforts, and improve sourcing strategies. By utilizing data-driven insights and predictive analytics, companies can make informed decisions regarding future demand trends and streamline their operational processes.

Produce: In this aspect, BDAI contributes to increasing companies' ability to produce goods and services at lower costs and higher quality. Through the implementation of AI-driven optimization techniques, automation, and process enhancements, companies can improve efficiency and reduce production expenses while maintaining or enhancing the quality of their offerings.

Promote: BDAI plays a crucial role in helping companies promote their offerings effectively by targeting the right customers with the right message and at the right price. By analysing vast amounts of data, including consumer preferences, market trends, and competitor activities, companies can develop targeted marketing campaigns, optimize pricing strategies, and enhance customer engagement to drive sales and brand loyalty.

Provide: This area emphasizes the role of BDAI in allowing companies to provide rich, personal, and convenient user experiences to their customers. Through the implementation of AI-powered recommendation systems, personalized services, and seamless user interfaces, companies can enhance customer satisfaction, retention, and loyalty by delivering tailored experiences that meet individual preferences and needs.

On the basis of this model, we have developed a flow tabular presentation showing the development of application of AI in tourism (Table 1).

1.3 Need for the Study

Digital technology offers new communication and distribution channels for both consumers and travel service suppliers (Sharma et al., 2020). This study addresses a research gap concerning technology applications and impacts in the tourism industry. While existing studies emphasize technology's role in sectors like hospitality, airlines, and intermediaries (Buhalis et al., 2019), there's a noticeable lack of research in events/festivals, cruises, and other transportation sectors. By recognizing this gap, the study aims to provide a more comprehensive understanding of the technological landscape in the broader tourism industry. Investigating technology applications in these sectors is crucial as they represent integral components of the tourism ecosystem with distinct technological dynamics. Understanding their trends and challenges is essential for stakeholders to make informed decisions and remain competitive. This study broadens the scope of existing research, offering insights into technology's role in underexplored segments of the tourism industry. It contributes valuable knowledge to inform practices, policies, and innovations within these specific sectors, thus enhancing our understanding of technology's impact on the diverse facets of the tourism landscape.

1.4 Theory/Model

The investigation into digital entrepreneurship within the tourism sector remains in its infancy, as evidenced by the limited body of literature dedicated to entrepreneurship and innovation in this context (Nambisan, 2017; Obschonka & Audretsch, 2020). Current research on artificial intelligence (AI) within the tourism sector primarily revolves around two central themes: the identification of existing AI applications and the potential consequences of future implementations, with a notable focus on service robots (Tussyadiah, 2020). Ivanov and Webster (2019) introduced a theoretical framework aimed at elucidating the integration of robotics, artificial intelligence, and service automation within the tourism sector, emphasizing the pivotal influence of end-user's receptivity to these emerging technologies.

Table 1. Development of AI in tourism

McKinsey BDAI Model:	Application of AI in Tourism	References
	Project	
Forecasting and Demand Prediction	• Utilizing AI for real-time forecasting to anticipate tourism demand and shape business strategies.	(Sakhuja et al., 2016; Atsalakis et al., 2018)
	• Forecasting tourism flows/demand, loyalty, and revenue using various AI techniques.	(Weng and Li, 2015; Zhang and Huang, 2015; Chen et al., 2014)
	• Modelling tourists' travel behavior using hybrid models and data mining techniques.	(Liao et al., 2013; Huang, 2013)
Optimization of R&D and Sourcing	• Implementation of AI technologies to optimize research and development efforts in tourism. • Improving sourcing strategies for tour operators and travel agencies using AI-driven analytics.	(Gallo et al., 2018; Kozlov, 2017)
	Produce	
Robotic Automation	• Introduction of robotics, chatbots, and virtual assistants to enhance customer service and experience. • Emphasis on cost reduction as a primary driver for the introduction of robotics in tourism.	(Nieto et al., 2014)
Integrated Route Planning	• Utilization of analytics-based solutions for integrated route planning in tourism.	(Cardonha et al., 2013)
Augmented Self	• Implementation of effective user interfaces and augmented reality (AR) technologies in aviation.	(Safi et al., 2019)
	Promote	
Intelligent Price Management	• Utilization of big data analytics and AI applications for strategic revenue management in tourism. • Analysis of hotel-specific factors and idiosyncratic price variables to set optimal pricing strategies.	(Thovex and Trichet, 2013)
	.	(Marrese-Taylor et al., 2013)
Consumer Preferences Analysis	• Extraction and modelling of user preferences using AI techniques such as semantic analysis.	(Hao et al., 2015)
	• Combination of social media messages and product information to offer marketing campaign recommendations.	(Buckley et al., 2014)
Direct Marketing Strategies	• Implementation of information systems for managing direct marketing strategies in tourism.	(Cabanas-Abascal et al., 2013)
	Provide	
Virtual Reality (VR)	• Utilization of VR technologies to enhance user experience and provide immersive virtual tourism experiences.	(Cipolla Ficarra, 2011; Weerasinghe et al., 2016)
Recommender Systems	• Integration of recommender systems in marketing processes and e-commerce to provide personalized recommendations.	(Buckley et al., 2014)
Trust-Based Recommendation	• Development of trust-based recommendation services for mobile tourist guides, leveraging notions of trust.	(Hinze and Quan, 2009)
Smart Features in Cruising	• Introduction of "smart-ships" in the cruising industry with features like online check-in and RFID armbands.	(Alexis, 2017)

Within the literature, three primary approaches can be discerned:

a) The first approach is benefit-oriented, with researchers exploring the potential advantages and drawbacks originating from the integration of intelligent robotic technology within the hospitality sector (Buhalis et al., 2019; Ivanov & Webster, 2019; Murphy et al., 2017; Samara et al., 2020; Tung & Au, 2018; Tussyadiah, 2020).
b) Another segment of the literature investigates consumers' perspectives on service robots, along with their theoretical interactions and anticipated reactions during their encounters with such technology

(Belanche et al., 2020; Flavián & Casaló, 2021; Mende et al., 2019; Tussyadiah & Park, 2018; Yu et al., 2022).

c) A distinct dimension within this domain is the financial aspect, where a limited number of studies have explored the venture capitalist domain (Filieri et al., 2021). This aspect of research seeks to understand which AI technologies are likely to see further development due to increased financial resources. Notably, tourism AI startups appear to attract substantial funding from investors, with an average funding amount of nearly 6 million euros, and some startups securing as much as 50 million euros in funding. This level of investment is remarkable, particularly when considering that fledgling startups typically have an estimated pre-money valuation of around 6 million euros (Miloud et al., 2012).

1.5 Enoch's Model

Enoch's fourfold service model typology, comprising interchange, network, destination, and substitute services, offers a relevant framework for fostering innovation in tourism (Enoch et al., 2004; Potter et al., 2020). This model underscores advancements such as increased service frequency in transportation (e.g., autonomous vehicles) and self-check-in procedures. Concurrently, big data emerges as a foundational component supporting AI applications in tourism. Big data, characterized by volume, velocity, variety, and veracity, stems from environmental factors and tourist activities, including online/offline behaviours and user-generated content (Li et al., 2018). AI processes utilize big data to analyse multimedia content and sentiment, enhancing user-generated content and enabling the creation of comprehensive user profiles. These profiles drive personalized recommendations in the hospitality sector by understanding individual preferences and behaviours (Bulchand-Gidumal, 2022). The integration of Enoch's service model with big data and AI underscores the evolving landscape of the industry, emphasizing the importance of service models and the transformative role of technology, particularly in transportation and personalized services. Figure 1 illustrates the data sources and generation process in hospitality.

1.6 AI Applications in Tourism Start-Ups

1.6.1 Personalized Customer Experience

In the case of tourism start-ups, AI is a game-changer when it comes to creating personalized customer experiences. By leveraging AI, these companies can analyze vast datasets containing customer preferences, behaviors, and historical data. AI algorithms can then select through this information to provide tailored recommendations for travelers. For instance, based on a traveler's past bookings and interests, an AI-driven system can suggest customized itineraries, accommodations, and activities, enhancing the overall travel experience. Moreover, chatbots and virtual assistants powered by AI are becoming indispensable tools for customer support in tourism start-ups. They can efficiently handle inquiries, provide real-time assistance, and even offer travel advice, ensuring that customers receive prompt and personalized assistance throughout their journey.

Figure 1. Data generation and use in hospitality
(Bulchand-Gidumal, 2022)

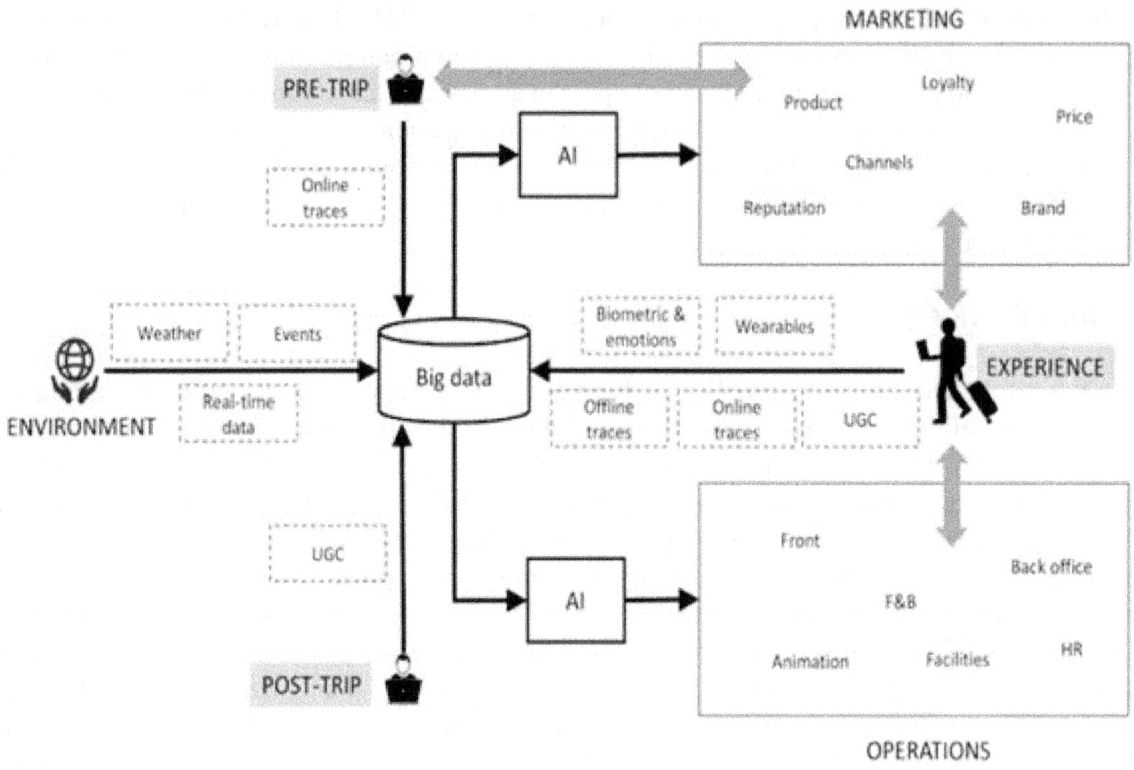

1.6.2 Data-Driven Insights

The abundance of data in the tourism industry is a valuable resource that AI can harness to provide data-driven insights. AI-driven analytics tools are capable of processing and analyzing this data at an unprecedented scale and speed. For instance, AI can analyze customer reviews, social media sentiment, and booking patterns to gain insights into customer preferences and trends (Ghouse et al., 2022). Tourism start-ups can use these insights to fine-tune their marketing strategies, improve their offerings, and optimize pricing and inventory management. Real-world examples abound, with companies like Airbnb utilizing AI to analyze host and guest interactions to provide recommendations and enhance user experiences.

1.6.3 Predictive Analytics for Demand Forecasting

AI algorithms are particularly proficient at predicting travel trends and demand patterns. By analyzing historical booking data, seasonal fluctuations, and external factors like weather events or global events, AI systems can make accurate predictions about future demand. Tourism start-ups can use this information to optimize their pricing strategies, allocate resources more efficiently, and ensure that they are prepared to meet demand surges during peak seasons. Notably, companies like Expedia have successfully implemented AI for demand forecasting, enabling them to adjust their pricing dynamically to maximize revenue and occupancy rates.

Market Segmentation: The integration of artificial intelligence (AI) is instrumental in enhancing market segmentation strategies for new startups. Leveraging technology, particularly by utilizing substantial datasets, commonly referred to as big data, startups can construct highly detailed and individualized customer profiles (Trzmielak et al., 2021). This strategic approach empowers enterprises to intricately delineate and target "market segments of one" at a granular and personalized level. By harnessing the capabilities of AI, startups can analyze vast amounts of diverse data sources, including customer preferences, behaviors, and interactions. This in-depth analysis goes beyond traditional demographic segmentation, allowing for a more comprehensive understanding of individual customer needs, preferences, and purchasing patterns. AI algorithms can identify intricate patterns within the data, uncovering hidden correlations and insights that contribute to a more precise segmentation of the market. This level of granularity enables startups to deliver personalized experiences, targeted advertising, and customized product offerings, fostering stronger connections with individual customers.

Sustainable Tourism Development: Artificial Intelligence (AI) plays a crucial role in advancing sustainable tourism development by offering innovative solutions that contribute to environmental conservation and community well-being (Balsalobre-Lorente et al., 2023). AI facilitates more efficient resource management, helping destinations optimize energy consumption, reduce waste, and minimize environmental impact. Machine learning algorithms analyze vast datasets to identify patterns in visitor behavior, enabling personalized recommendations for sustainable activities and minimizing the ecological footprint of tourism (Alsahafi et al., 2023). Additionally, AI-powered analytics assist in monitoring and managing natural ecosystems, ensuring the preservation of biodiversity. Chatbots and virtual assistants powered by AI enhance communication between tourists and local communities, fostering cultural understanding and responsible tourism practices.

1.7 Determinants

The "Trip Life Cycle" framework offers insights into how artificial intelligence (AI) is reshaping various stages of the travel experience. A more detailed examination of the technologies under development for each phase of the Trip Life Cycle, which encompasses the pre-trip, during the journey, and post-trip stages, provides valuable insights into where the most significant transformations are expected to occur in travel planning, thanks to AI solutions (Tussyadiah, 2020).

In the pre-trip phase, AI tools revolutionize travel planning, offering personalized recommendations, accommodation options, and itinerary suggestions based on vast datasets. Chatbots and virtual assistants streamline booking processes and address traveller queries, while AI-powered translation tools facilitate communication for international travellers (Battour et al., 2023).

During the journey, AI technologies provide real-time updates and personalized recommendations through mobile apps and wearable devices. AI-driven navigation tools assist travellers in efficiently navigating unfamiliar destinations, while AI-enabled services in the hospitality sector, like smart room controls and chatbots, enhance the overall experience. AI-based language translation apps further facilitate communication with locals, promoting cultural immersion (Edwards and Griffin, 2013).

In the post-trip phase, AI aids travellers in organizing and curating memories. Smart photo and video apps use AI to identify and tag images, simplifying the creation of digital travel albums. AI-powered review platforms offer personalized recommendations for future trips based on past experiences. Chatbots and virtual assistants also assist travellers with post-trip activities, including handling feedback and inquiries (Tussyadiah, 2020).

This examination of AI technologies across the Trip Life Cycle highlights their transformative impact on travel. From personalized recommendations and seamless booking processes to real-time assistance during travel and enhanced post-trip reflection, AI enhances every stage of the travel experience, offering travellers more convenient, tailored, and memorable journeys (Buhalis et al., 2019).

1.8 AI Domains of Focus for Travel Start-Ups

In the realm of travel and tourism, Artificial Intelligence (AI) is making significant strides across various subfields, each with distinct applications and implications. This section provides a concise exploration of the subfields that hold particular relevance within the context of travel and tourism.

Ambient intelligence, an emerging discipline, utilizes advances in sensors, pervasive computing, and AI to create intelligent environments that respond to users' needs (Cook et al., 2009). For example, in a hotel room, ambient intelligence can autonomously adjust temperature, music, and lighting based on occupant preferences, demonstrating its potential in enhancing user experiences. Moreover, ambient intelligence can be harnessed in larger spaces like airports or event venues for dynamic adjustments based on crowdsourced data and user activities.

Natural Language Processing (NLP) is another pivotal domain, enabling effective communication between machines and users through text or voice inputs. In tourism, NLP plays a crucial role in developing virtual travel assistants, conversational systems, and robotic applications (Tussyadiah & Miller, 2019). Applications of NLP in tourism include sentiment analysis, chatbots for customer interaction, and personalized hotel recommendations, contributing to improved strategies and user engagement (Putri et al., 2022; García-Pablos et al., 2016; Bulchand-Gidumal, 2020).

Machine learning, including deep learning and neural networks, forms a cornerstone in the technological landscape of tourism. These algorithms enable machines to acquire knowledge iteratively, with applications ranging from forecasting and translation to weather predictions, sentiment analysis, and fraud prevention (Ma et al., 2018). Deep learning, a subset of machine learning, particularly underpins technologies like speech recognition and object detection within Ambient Intelligence (AmI) (Zhang et al., 2019), showcasing its versatility and impact across various AI domains in the tourism sector. Overall, these AI domains collectively contribute to the evolution of technology-driven solutions, enhancing the efficiency and personalization of travel experiences (Basiri et al., 2018). AI and Neuromarketing can also help in understanding the consumer psychic and hence behaviour (Hamelin & Chaudhary 2023)

1.9 AI Model in Tourism

While still in its early stages, there are limited studies focusing on proposing AI/ML models for various aspects of the tourism industry. For instance, Tsaih and Hsu (2018) introduced a model for Smart Tourism, presenting a conceptual framework that incorporates artificial intelligence/machine learning, institutional/organizational, and business processes. Their model aims to assist smart tourism stakeholders in harnessing artificial intelligence to integrate cross-departmental business operations and streamline key performance metrics to develop a comprehensive business-level IT strategy.

AI can contribute to the design of smart tourism products and services by leveraging user experience within the realm of big data (Hu & Li, 2023). Through the integration of big data and AI, smart

Figure 2. Smart tourism initiative with AI/ML
(Tsaih & Hsu; 2018)

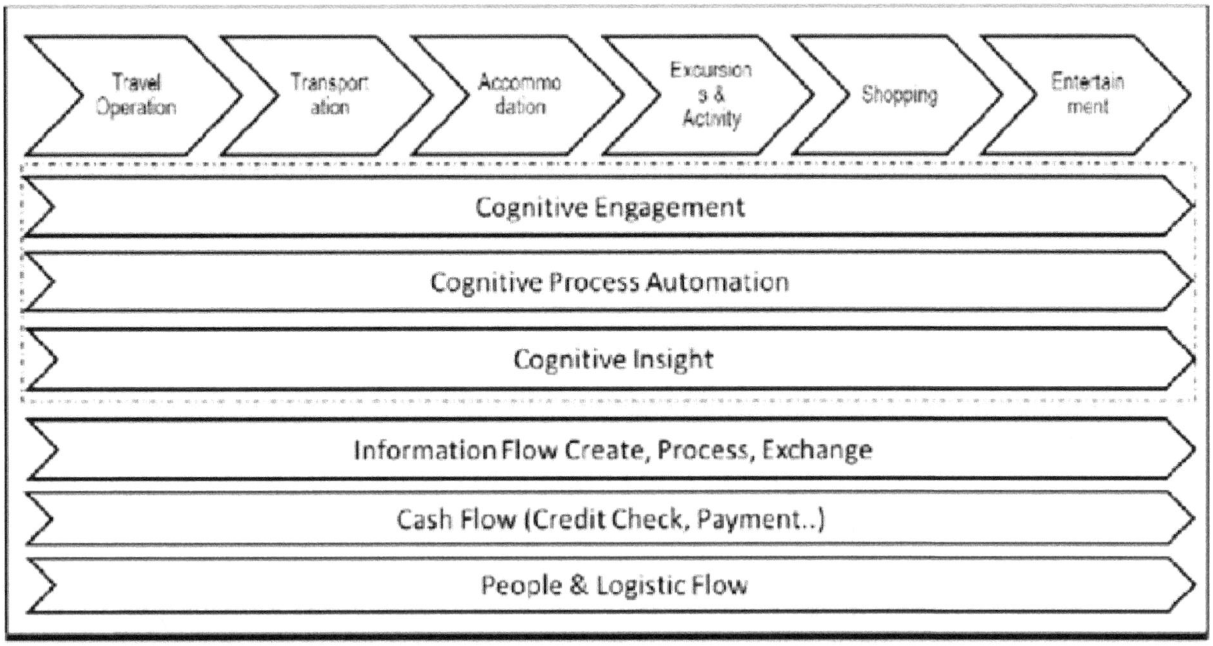

tourism endeavours can enhance consumer satisfaction and provide personalized recommendations to travellers. Research has introduced a Decision Tree algorithm tailored for smart tourist products and services, utilizing user experience and big data techniques (Hu & Li, 2023). The system components and design strategy prioritize user needs and preferences, aiming to deliver personalized experiences. Smart tourism services necessitate demand and experience analysis, while smart tourist facilities and big data analysis emphasize client satisfaction.

1.10 Case Studies

This chapter presents three concise case studies offering insights into how AI is applied in the tourism industry. The first case focuses on the travel industry in Georgia, highlighting the strategic use of AI in promoting tourism. The second case is about Japan's Henn-na Hotel, showcasing how AI and robot integration redefine the guest experience. Lastly, the third case spotlights India's Sciative Solutions, a new-age company utilizing AI for automated real-time price optimization in the travel sector. Together, these cases provide a glimpse into the diverse applications and impacts of AI across different facets of the global tourism landscape.

1.10.1 Georgia Travel Industry

Georgia, strategically located at the crossroads of Eastern Europe and Western Asia, is actively leveraging innovative technologies to propel its tourism sector forward. Through a concerted effort, the country has embraced the power of Artificial Intelligence (AI) to support and catalyse the growth of tourism

Figure 3. Proposed architectural model for constructing intelligent tourist services and products (Hu & Li; 2023)

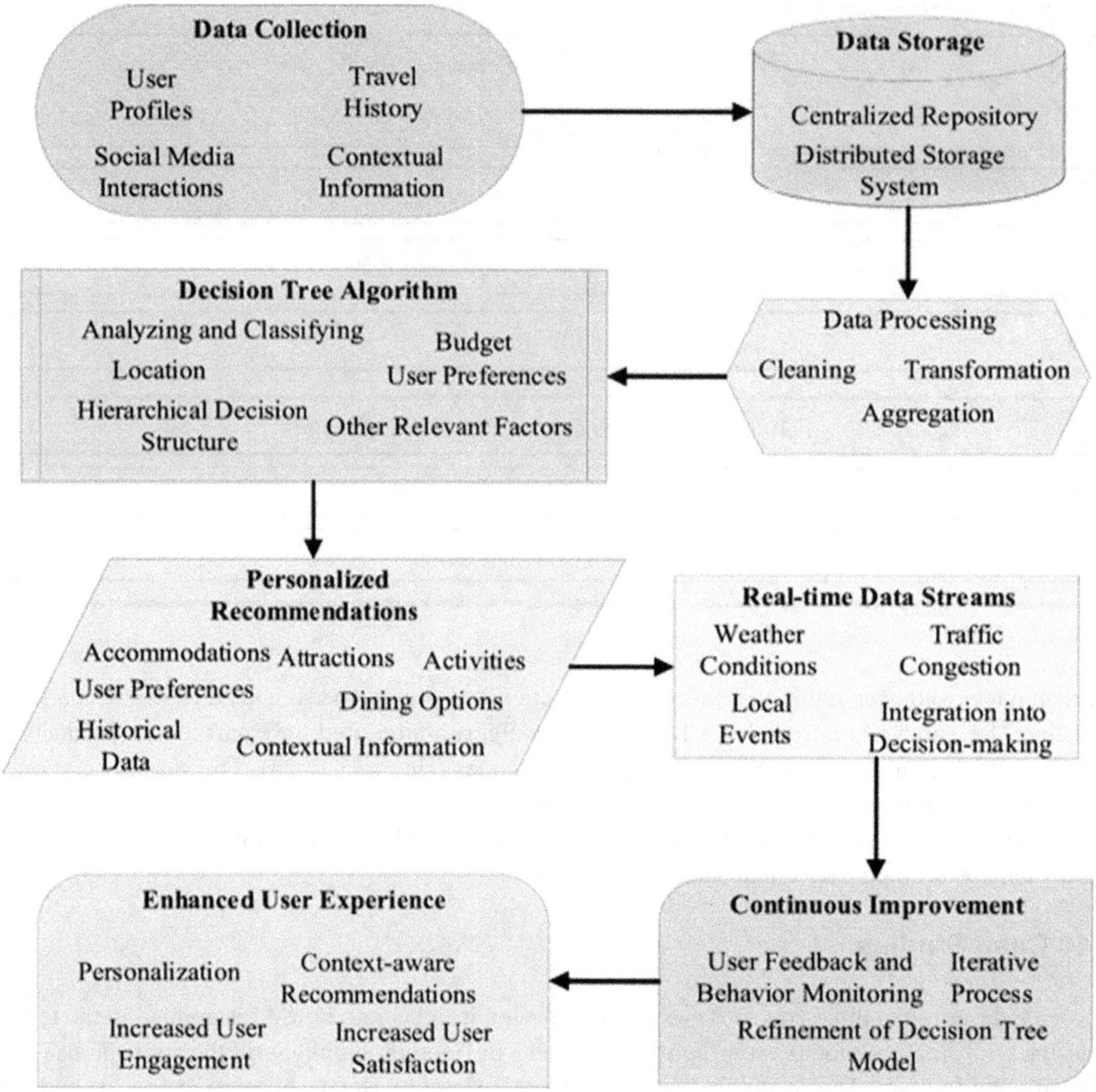

start-ups. The European Parliament's report highlights a correlation between innovation-rich locales and the integration of smart environments (Parris, 2020). Georgia's government has played a pivotal role in fostering the integration of AI in tourism start-ups, providing financial support to those focusing on AI applications in the sector (Pechlaner et al., 2021).

In supporting tourism start-ups, Georgia has implemented AI technologies across various facets of the industry. Firstly, AI is applied in Smart Destination Planning, where algorithms analyse data from diverse sources to optimize destination planning based on tourist preferences, historical visitation patterns, and social media trends. Secondly, AI facilitates Personalized Travel Recommendations, as start-ups utilize AI-driven recommendation engines to tailor travel itineraries, enhancing tourist satisfaction and encouraging repeat visits. Additionally, Georgia employs Predictive Analytics for Demand Forecasting, allowing start-ups to anticipate peak tourist seasons for better resource management and service delivery. AI-driven chatbots are actively used to engage with customers, providing real-time assistance and streamlining communication processes.

Georgia's government has been instrumental in fostering AI integration in tourism start-ups, providing financial support to encourage innovation. Collaborating with technology incubators, the government creates an environment fostering AI-driven entrepreneurship, offering mentorship, infrastructure, and networking opportunities. The supportive regulatory framework ensures ethical compliance, building trust among tourists and industry stakeholders.

The outcomes of integrating AI in Georgia's tourism start-ups are evident in enhanced visitor satisfaction, improved operational efficiency, and a vibrant innovation ecosystem. Looking ahead, Georgia aims to solidify its position as a technology-driven tourism destination, continuously supporting and nurturing AI-based initiatives. The successful synergy between government support and private-sector innovation in Georgia serves as a model for other regions, showcasing how AI can be a catalyst for growth in the tourism industry and transform the landscape of start-ups in the sector.

1.10.2 Japan's Henn-na Hotel's AI and Robot Integration

Japan's Henn-na Hotel, translating to "Strange Hotel" in Japanese, embarked on a pioneering journey when it opened its doors in 2015, envisioning a futuristic and technologically advanced hotel experience. The hotel's objective was to capitalize on artificial intelligence (AI) and robotics to minimize operational costs, elevate guest interactions, and carve a distinctive niche in the hospitality industry.

Situated in Japan, Henn-na Hotel has garnered international acclaim for its ground-breaking approach to hospitality by seamlessly integrating advanced AI and robotics. Guests have lauded the efficiency of robotic services in handling standardized tasks (Io and Lee, 2020). The hotel integrates robotic services throughout the entire guest stay, including:

- Robotic Staff: Henn-na Hotel introduced humanoid robots in roles such as receptionists, concierge, and porters, capable of interacting with guests in multiple languages and providing information about the hotel and local attractions.
- Facial Recognition for Check-In: The hotel implemented facial recognition technology for check-in, enabling guests to register their faces instead of engaging in traditional check-in processes, streamlining arrivals, reducing wait times, and enhancing security.
- AI-Powered Room Controls: Guest rooms were equipped with AI systems learning and adapting to guests' preferences, overseeing room temperature, lighting, and other amenities based on individual preferences accumulated over time.
- Voice-Activated Devices: Each room featured voice-activated assistants allowing guests to control various room functions, seek information, or request services, aiming to augment convenience and provide a futuristic, interactive experience.

The integration of robots and AI systems resulted in a significant reduction in operational costs, notably in staffing. Robots efficiently handled routine tasks, enabling human staff to focus on complex guest interactions and specialized services. Guest feedback attested to high satisfaction levels, commending the efficiency of the check-in process, the novelty of robot interactions, and the personalized experience offered by AI-managed room amenities. Henn-na Hotel reported substantial cost savings compared to traditional hotels due to reduced staffing needs, ultimately recouping the initial investment in AI and robotics through operational efficiency gains. Despite its innovative progress, Henn-na Hotel encountered challenges, including occasional technical glitches and the need for ongoing maintenance of robotic systems. The hotel consistently adapted its technology, promptly addressing issues and incorporating guest feedback to refine AI and robot interactions.

Henn-na Hotel's strategic integration of AI and robots not only redefined the guest experience but also showcased the transformative potential of technology in traditional industries. The success of this venture is rooted in the hotel's commitment to innovation, adaptability in the face of challenges, and a relentless focus on enhancing both operational efficiency and guest satisfaction in the ever-evolving landscape of hospitality.

1.10.3 India's New Age Company Sciative Solutions

Sciative offers AI-powered automated real-time Price Optimization and promotions solutions for revenue maximization for Travel. Sciative addresses a fundamental business challenge – determining the RIGHT PRICE. With a strong presence over the past three years, Sciative has emerged as a key player in India, offering its expertise to leading travel enterprises and extending services across diverse sectors like ecommerce, retail, travel, entertainment, and hospitality. The company plays a vital role in mitigating revenue leaks through services such as Revenue Management, Customer Loyalty and Engagement Automation, Retail Automation and Price Optimization, and Big Data and Advanced Analytics.

In November 2019, Sciative introduced its revolutionary AI software, Viaje.ai, a first-of-its-kind price recommendation engine. Viaje.ai has been instrumental in guiding numerous Indian bus operators to achieve unprecedented revenues and occupancies. Notably, a luxury bus/coach company in southern India faced challenges despite providing superior, clean, and punctual inter-city bus services. To enhance pricing accuracy and reduce manual adjustments, the company adopted a rule-based dynamic pricing system. However, scalability challenges arose, leading the company to turn to Sciative and Viaje.ai.

In a 1.5-month proof-of-concept (POC) involving six coaches across various routes, the client suspended the use of rule-based pricing entirely. Viaje.ai demonstrated its efficacy by increasing revenue per trip by Rs. 4,023 (+17%) across all routes. For normal AC Sleeper buses, the AI system enhanced both occupancies and average selling price (ASP) per seat. In the case of premium Capella buses, Viaje.ai deciphered customer likability and preferences in advance, maximizing ASPs and resulting in a remarkable increase in revenues per trip compared to rule-based pricing. Sciative's Viaje.ai has proven to be a transformative solution, showcasing the potential of AI in optimizing pricing strategies for enhanced revenue and operational efficiency in the travel industry.

1.11 Challenges and Ethical Considerations

The surge in artificial intelligence and service robots within the travel and tourism sector is notable. However, academic literature primarily focuses on theoretical concepts, leaving a gap in empirical research on AI-based entrepreneurial activities in this field (Filieri et al., 2021).

While theoretical frameworks offer insights, bridging the gap between theory and practical implementation is crucial. Studying real-world entrepreneurial endeavors leveraging AI in tourism can reveal valuable insights into challenges, successes, and innovative solutions. Such empirical research can inform policymakers, investors, and industry stakeholders about AI's current state and future prospects in travel and tourism.

Challenges and ethical considerations in AI-driven tourism start-ups revolve around two themes:

Data Privacy and Security: Ensuring data privacy and security is paramount as businesses collect and utilize customer data. Strategies include robust encryption, secure data storage, and compliance with data protection regulations like GDPR. Transparent communication about data practices builds trust with customers.

Overreliance on Technology: While AI enhances tourism experiences, overreliance on technology risks eroding the human touch and authenticity of travel. Balancing AI-driven convenience with human interaction is essential. Start-ups should augment, not replace, human services and ensure robust contingency plans for technology failures.

Hence, achieving harmony between technology and human touch ensures AI complements, rather than replaces, the human element of travel.

1.12 Future Trends in AI for Tourism Start-Ups

The future of AI in tourism start-ups is promising, driven by emerging technologies such as Augmented Reality (AR), Virtual Reality (VR), Blockchain, Voice Recognition, Natural Language Processing, Predictive Personalization, and Sustainable Tourism. Pioneering start-ups like DeepL, Fetch.ai, and Lilium are leading innovation in the travel sector, surpassing traditional players with agile solutions. However, success depends on investor support for the most promising technologies.

Future research endeavours in the AI and tourism domain can take diverse directions. Firstly, exploration of strategies for tourism operators to fully leverage the value generated by AI solutions is essential. This involves enhancing operational processes, improving customer experiences, and optimizing resource allocation. Understanding how established businesses can adapt and effectively integrate AI into their operations is crucial for sustained success. Secondly, privacy and security concerns, particularly in the travel industry, stand as central issues in the AI landscape. Future research efforts should look into the perspectives of businesses and end-users to comprehend their concerns and apprehensions related to AI-driven solutions. Developing practical and effective solutions that address these concerns while preserving the benefits of AI technology is paramount.

For consumers, AI integration will streamline trip planning, reduce costs, and offer personalized packages. Anticipatory offers and seamless navigation will enhance the tourist experience while prioritizing privacy.

The synergy between AI start-ups and the travel sector holds promise for enhanced efficiency and customer experiences. Addressing privacy concerns is crucial for responsible integration. Future research should guide the industry toward a secure and privacy-conscious AI-driven future.

REFERENCES

Alexis, P. (2017). R-Tourism: Introducing the Potential Impact of Robotics and Service Automation in Tourism. *Ovidius University Annals: Economic Sciences Series*, 211-216.

Alsahafi, R., Alzahrani, A., & Mehmood, R. (2023). Smarter Sustainable Tourism: Data-Driven Multi-Perspective Parameter Discovery for Autonomous Design and Operations. *Sustainability (Basel)*, *15*(5), 4166. doi:10.3390/su15054166

Álvarez-Carmona, M. Á., Aranda, R., Rodríguez-Gonzalez, A. Y., Fajardo-Delgado, D., Sánchez, M. G., Pérez-Espinosa, H., Martínez-Miranda, J., Guerrero-Rodríguez, R., Bustio-Martínez, L., & Díaz-Pacheco, Á. (2022). Natural language processing applied to tourism research: A systematic review and future research directions. *Journal of King Saud University. Computer and Information Sciences*, *34*(10), 10125–10144. doi:10.1016/j.jksuci.2022.10.010

Atsalakis, G. S., Atsalaki, I. G., & Zopounidis, C. (2018). Forecasting the success of a new tourism service by a neuro-fuzzy technique. *European Journal of Operational Research*, *268*(2), 716–727. doi:10.1016/j.ejor.2018.01.044

Balsalobre-Lorente, D., Abbas, J., He, C., Pilař, L., & Shah, S. A. R. (2023). Tourism, urbanization and natural resources rents matter for environmental sustainability: The leading role of AI and ICT on sustainable development goals in the digital era. *Resources Policy*, *82*, 103445. doi:10.1016/j.resourpol.2023.103445

Basiri, A., Amirian, P., Winstanley, A., & Moore, T. (2018). Making tourist guidance systems more intelligent, adaptive and personalised using crowd sourced movement data. *Journal of Ambient Intelligence and Humanized Computing*, *9*(2), 413–427. doi:10.1007/s12652-017-0550-0

Battour, M., Mady, K., Salaheldeen, M., Elsotouhy, M., Elbendary, I., & Boğan, E. (2023). AI-enabled technologies to assist Muslim tourists in Halal-friendly tourism. *Journal of Islamic Marketing*, *14*(5), 1291–1309. doi:10.1108/JIMA-01-2022-0001

Belanche, D., Casaló, L. V., Flavián, C., & Schepers, J. (2020). Service robot implementation: A theoretical framework and research agenda. *Service Industries Journal*, *40*(3-4), 203–225. doi:10.1080/02642069.2019.1672666

Buckley, S., Ettl, M., Jain, P., Luss, R., Petrik, M., Ravi, R. K., & Venkatramani, C. (2014). Social media and customer behavior analytics for personalized customer engagements. IBM Journal of Research and Development, 58(5/6), 7:1-7:12. doi:10.1147/JRD.2014.2344515

Buhalis, D., Harwood, T., Bogicevic, V., Viglia, G., Beldona, S., & Hofacker, C. (2019). Technological disruptions in services: Lessons from tourism and hospitality. *Journal of Service Management*, *30*(4), 484–506. doi:10.1108/JOSM-12-2018-0398

Bulchand-Gidumal, J. (2022). Impact of artificial intelligence in travel, tourism, and hospitality. In *Handbook of e-Tourism* (pp. 1943–1962). Springer International Publishing. doi:10.1007/978-3-030-48652-5_110

Cabanas-Abascal, A., Rodríguez-González, A., Casado-Lumbreras, C., Fernández-González, J., & Jiménez-López, D. (2013). POST-VIA: Develop Individualized Marketing Strategies for Tourists. In T. Matsuo & R. Colomo-Palacios (Eds.), *Electronic Business and Marketing. Studies in Computational Intelligence* (Vol. 484). Springer. doi:10.1007/978-3-642-37932-1_4

Cardonha, C., Herrmann, R., & Avegliano, P. (2013). Theoretical aspects of the integrated route planning problem. *IFAC Proceedings Volumes*, *46*(24), 427-432. 10.3182/20130911-3-BR-3021.00082

Chen, Y. C., Lin, G., Chan, Y. H., & Shih, M. J. (2014). *Mining frequent patterns with multiple item support thresholds in tourism information databases. Technologies and Applications of Artificial Intelligence*. Springer.

Cipolla Ficarra, F. V. (2011). Human-computer interaction, tourism and cultural heritage. Lecture Notes in Computer Science (including subseries Lecture Notes in Artificial Intelligence and Lecture Notes in Bioinformatics). Springer. doi:10.1007/978-3-642-18348-5_5

Cook, D. J., Augusto, J. C., & Jakkula, V. R. (2009). Ambient intelligence: Technologies, applications, and opportunities. *Pervasive and Mobile Computing*, *5*(4), 277–298. doi:10.1016/j.pmcj.2009.04.001

Davenport, T., & Kalakota, R. (2019). The potential for artificial intelligence in healthcare. *Future Healthcare Journal*, *6*(2), 94–98. doi:10.7861/futurehosp.6-2-94 PMID:31363513

Edwards, D., & Griffin, T. (2013). Understanding tourists' spatial behaviour: GPS tracking as an aid to sustainable destination management. *Journal of Sustainable Tourism*, *21*(4), 580–595. doi:10.1080/09669582.2013.776063

Enoch, M., Potter, S., Parkhurst, G., & Smith, M. (2004). *Internode: Innovations in Demand Responsive Transport*. Department for Transport and Greater Manchester Passenger Transport Executive.

Filieri, R., D'Amico, E., Destefanis, A., Paolucci, E., & Raguseo, E. (2021). Artificial intelligence (AI) for tourism: A European-based study on successful AI tourism start-ups. *International Journal of Contemporary Hospitality Management*, *33*(11), 4099–4125. doi:10.1108/IJCHM-02-2021-0220

Flavián, C., & Casaló, L. V. (2021). Artificial intelligence in services: Current trends, benefits and challenges. *Service Industries Journal*, *41*(13-14), 853–859. doi:10.1080/02642069.2021.1989177

Gallo, P., Gallo, P. Jr, Timková, V., Šenková, A., & Karahuta, M. (2018). Use of dashboards in predicting the development of the company using neural networks in hotel management. *Geo Journal of Tourism and Geosites*, *22*(2), 307–316.

Gallo, P., Gallo, P. Jr, Timková, V., Šenková, A., & Karahuta, M. (2018). Use of dashboards in predicting the development of the company using neural networks in hotel management. *Geo Journal of Tourism and Geosites*, *22*(2), 307–316.

García-Pablos, A., Cuadros, M., & Linaza, M. T. (2016). Automatic analysis of textual hotel reviews. *Information Technology & Tourism*, *16*(1), 45–69. doi:10.1007/s40558-015-0047-7

Ghouse, S. M., Duffett, R. G., & Chaudhary, M. (2022). How Twitter advertising influences the purchase intentions and purchase attitudes of Indian millennial consumers? *International Journal of Internet Marketing and Advertising*, *16*(1-2), 142–164. doi:10.1504/IJIMA.2022.120973

Gössling, S. (2020). Technology, ICT and tourism: From big data to the big picture. *Journal of Sustainable Tourism*, *29*(5), 849–858. doi:10.1080/09669582.2020.1865387

Grundner, L., & Neuhofer, B. (2021). The bright and dark sides of artificial intelligence: A futures perspective on tourist destination experiences. *Journal of Destination Marketing & Management*, *19*, 100511. doi:10.1016/j.jdmm.2020.100511

Hamelin, N., & Chaudhary, M. (2023). Assessing the Impact of Sustainability News Clips on Fast-Fashion Brands Purchase Intention: A Neuromarketing Study. In Luxury Marketing, Sustainability and Technology (pp. 116-134). Routledge. doi:10.4324/9781003321378-7

Hao, J. X., Yu, Y., Law, R., & Fong, D. K. C. (2015). A genetic algorithm-based learning approach to understand customer satisfaction with OTA websites. *Tourism Management*, *48*, 231–241. doi:10.1016/j.tourman.2014.11.009

Hinze, A., & Quan, Q. (2009). Trust- and location-based recommendations for tourism. Lecture Notes in Computer Science (including subseries Lecture Notes in Artificial Intelligence and Lecture Notes in Bioinformatics. Springer. doi:10.1007/978-3-642-05148-7_31

Hu, H., & Li, C. (2023). Smart tourism products and services design based on user experience under the background of big data. *Soft Computing*, *27*(17), 12711–12724. doi:10.1007/s00500-023-08851-0

Huang, H. C. (2013). The construction of a visitor number forecasting model for the Shihmen reservoir recreation area using artificial intelligence technology. *Journal of Theoretical and Applied Information Technology*, *54*(1), 4–19.

Io, H. N., & Lee, C. B. (2020). Social media comments about hotel robots. *Journal of China Tourism Research*, *16*(4), 606–625. doi:10.1080/19388160.2020.1769785

Ivanov, S., & Webster, C. (2019). Perceived appropriateness and intention to use service robots in tourism. In *Information and Communication Technologies in Tourism 2019: Proceedings of the International Conference in Nicosia,* (pp. 237-248). Springer International Publishing. 10.1007/978-3-030-05940-8_19

Kaplan, A., & Haenlein, M. (2019). Siri, Siri, in my hand: Who's the fairest in the land? On the interpretations, illustrations, and implications of artificial intelligence. *Business Horizons*, *62*(1), 15–25. doi:10.1016/j.bushor.2018.08.004

Kozlov, D. A. (2017). The concept of neuro-agents in hospitality industry and tourism. *Journal of Environmental Management and Tourism*, *8*(4), 835–842.

LeCun, Y., Bengio, Y., & Hinton, G. (2015). Deep learning. *Nature, 521*(7553), 436-444.

Li, J., Xu, L., Tang, L., Wang, S., & Li, L. (2018). Big data in tourism research: A literature review. *Tourism Management*, *68*, 301–323. doi:10.1016/j.tourman.2018.03.009

Liao, Z., Jin, M., Luo, Y., Ren, P., & Gao, H. (2013). Research on prediction of tourists' quantity in Jiuzhaigou valley scenic based on ABR integration model. *International Journal of Environment and Pollution*, *51*(3/4), 176–191. doi:10.1504/IJEP.2013.054028

Lu, H., Li, Y., Chen, M., Kim, H., & Serikawa, S. (2018). Brain intelligence: Go beyond artificial intelligence. *Mobile Networks and Applications*, *23*(2), 368–375. doi:10.1007/s11036-017-0932-8

Lu, Y. (2019). Artificial intelligence: A survey on evolution, models, applications and future trends. *Journal of Management Analytics*, *6*(1), 1–29. doi:10.1080/23270012.2019.1570365

Ma, Y., Xiang, Z., Du, Q., & Fan, W. (2018). Effects of user-provided photos on hotel review helpfulness: An analytical approach with deep leaning. *International Journal of Hospitality Management*, *71*, 120–131. doi:10.1016/j.ijhm.2017.12.008

Marrese-Taylor, E., Velasquez, J. D., & Bravo-Marquez, F. (2013). Modular tool to explore tourism opinions on the web. *Proceedings – 2013 IEEE/WIC/ACM International Joint Conference on Web Intelligence and Intelligent Agent Technology – Workshops, WI-IATW 2013*. IEEE. 10.1109/WI-IAT.2013.193

Mende, M., Scott, M. L., van Doorn, J., Grewal, D., & Shanks, I. (2019). Service robots rising: How humanoid robots influence service experiences and elicit compensatory consumer responses. *JMR, Journal of Marketing Research*, *56*(4), 535–556. doi:10.1177/0022243718822827

Miloud, T., Aspelund, A., & Cabrol, M. (2012). Startup valuation by venture capitalists: An empirical study. *Venture Capital*, *14*(2-3), 151–174. doi:10.1080/13691066.2012.667907

Morrison, A. M. (2022). *Hospitality and travel marketing*. Taylor & Francis. doi:10.4324/9781003292616

Murphy, J., Hofacker, C., & Gretzel, U. (2017). Dawning of the age of robots in hospitality and tourism: Challenges for teaching and research. *European Journal of Tourism Research*, *15*, 104–111. doi:10.54055/ejtr.v15i.265

Nambisan, S. (2017). Digital entrepreneurship: Toward a digital technology perspective of entrepreneurship. *Entrepreneurship Theory and Practice*, *41*(6), 1029–1055. doi:10.1111/etap.12254

Nieto, D., Quesada-Arencibia, A., García, C. R., & Moreno-Díaz, R. (2014). A social robot in a tourist environment. *International Conference on Ubiquitous Computing and Ambient Intelligence*. Springer, Cham. 10.1007/978-3-319-13102-3_5

Obschonka, M., & Audretsch, D. B. (2020). Artificial intelligence and big data in entrepreneurship: A new era has begun. *Small Business Economics*, *55*(3), 529–539. doi:10.1007/s11187-019-00202-4

Pechlaner, H., Thees, H., Manske-Wang, W., & Scuttari, A. (2021). Local service industry and tourism development through the global trade and infrastructure project of the New Silk Road–the example of Georgia. *Service Industries Journal*, *41*(7-8), 553–579. doi:10.1080/02642069.2019.1623204

Potter, S., Valdez, A. M., & Cook, M. (2020). Autonomous vehicles and the urban mobility ecosystem. In W. J. Nuttall, D. V. Gibson, D. M. Trzmielak, & A. Ibarra-Junez (Eds.), *Energy and Mobility in Smart Cities* (pp. 83–98). ICE Publishing London.

Putri, D. R., Zamheri, A., Ridho, S. L. Z., Paisal, P., & Africano, F. (2022). The Mediation of Tourist Engagement on The Effect of Destination Quality on Tourist Loyalty. [IJABIM]. *International Journal of Applied Business and International Management*, *7*(1), 1–16. doi:10.32535/ijabim.v7i1.1437

Safi, M., Chung, J., & Pradhan, P. (2019). Review of augmented reality in aerospace industry. *Aircraft Engineering and Aerospace Technology*, *91*(9), 1187–1194. doi:10.1108/AEAT-09-2018-0241

Sakhuja, S., Jain, V., Kumar, S., Chandra, C., & Ghildayal, S. K. (2016). Genetic algorithm-based fuzzy time series tourism demand forecast model. *Industrial Management & Data Systems*, *116*(3), 483–507. doi:10.1108/IMDS-05-2015-0165

Samara, D., Magnisalis, I., & Peristeras, V. (2020). Artificial intelligence and big data in tourism: A systematic literature review. *Journal of Hospitality and Tourism Technology*, *11*(2), 343–367. doi:10.1108/JHTT-12-2018-0118

Sharma, A., Sharma, S., & Chaudhary, M. (2020). Are small travel agencies ready for digital marketing? Views of travel agency managers. *Tourism Management, 79*, 104078. doi:10.1016/j.tourman.2020.104078

Thovex, C., & Trichet, F. (2013). Opinion mining and semantic analysis of touristic social networks. *Proceedings of the 2013 IEEE/ACM International Conference on Advances in Social Networks Analysis and Mining - ASONAM '13*. IEEE. 10.1145/2492517.2500235

Trzmielak, D. M., Shonia, D., & Skoneczna, M. (2021). Marketing, Start-Ups and Innovation: A Framework for Understanding the Possibilities for Harnessing Technological Innovations in Tourism (Based on the Example of the Georgian Tourism Sector and Russian Start-Ups). *Marketing of Scientific and Research Organizations, 40*(2), 93–113. doi:10.2478/minib-2021-0011

Tsaih, R. H., & Hsu, C. C. (2018). *Artificial intelligence in smart tourism: A conceptual framework.*

Tung, V. W. S., & Au, N. (2018). Exploring customer experiences with robotics in hospitality. *International Journal of Contemporary Hospitality Management, 30*(7), 2680–2697. doi:10.1108/IJCHM-06-2017-0322

Tussyadiah, I. (2020). A review of research into automation in tourism: Launching the Annals of Tourism Research Curated Collection on Artificial Intelligence and Robotics in Tourism. *Annals of Tourism Research, 81*, 102883. doi:10.1016/j.annals.2020.102883

Tussyadiah, I., & Miller, G. (2019). Nudged by a robot: Responses to agency and feedback. *Annals of Tourism Research, 78*, 102752. doi:10.1016/j.annals.2019.102752

Tussyadiah, I. P., & Park, S. (2018). Consumer evaluation of hotel service robots. In *Information and Communication Technologies in Tourism 2018: Proceedings of the International Conference in Jönköping*, (pp. 308-320). Springer International Publishing.

UNWTO. (2020) *Tourism and Covid-19*. UNWTO. https://www.unwto.org/tourism-covid-19-coronavirus

Wang, J., Li, Y., Wu, B., & Wang, Y. (2021). Tourism destination image based on tourism user generated content on internet. *Tourism Review, 76*(1), 125–137. doi:10.1108/TR-04-2019-0132

Weerasinghe, M., Kodikara, N.D., Dammika, N., Nisansala, A., Keppitiyagama, C., Buddhika, I., & Perera, C. (2016). *Poster: Virtual Eye-A smarter mode of interaction to virtual tours*. doi:10.1145/2938559.2948861

Weng, G., & Li, L. (2015). Study of tourism flow forecasting based on a seasonally adjusted particle swarm optimization-support vector regression model. *Journal of Information and Computational Science, 12*(7), 2747–2757. doi:10.12733/jics20105860

Yu, H., Shum, C., Alcorn, M., Sun, J., & He, Z. (2022). Robots can't take my job: Antecedents and outcomes of Gen Z employees' service robot risk awareness. *International Journal of Contemporary Hospitality Management, 34*(8), 2971–2988. doi:10.1108/IJCHM-10-2021-1312

Zhang, C., & Huang, Z. (2015). Mining tourist motive for marketing development via TwiceLearning. *Applied Artificial Intelligence, 29*(2), 119–133. doi:10.1080/08839514.2015.993554

Zhu, S., Yu, T., Xu, T., Chen, H., Dustdar, S., Gigan, S., & Pan, Y. (2023). Intelligent computing: the latest advances, challenges, and future. *Intelligent Computing, 2*, 0006.

Chapter 11
Revolutionizing Creative Tourism:
Integrating AI in Marketing for Immersive Travel Experiences

Ishani Sharma
Chitkara Business School, Chitkara University, India

Arun Aggarwal
https://orcid.org/0000-0003-3986-188X
Chitkara Business School, Chitkara University, India

ABSTRACT

This chapter provides a comprehensive review of hospitality and tourist (HAT) AI literature. The analysis identified relevant themes, pros, and cons, as well as suggested future research possibilities in this discipline. HAT is rapidly adopting AI technology to improve customer service, operational efficiency, travel experiences, and sustainability. There is a growing body of research on this topic, but a thorough and systematic understanding is needed to determine the most effective AI applications and recommend areas for further investigation. This chapter discusses how machine learning, natural language processing, and robotics may improve tourist and hospitality consumer experiences and efficiency. This chapter covers AI in travel, from chatbots for customer service to autonomous cars to VR/AR for immersive experiences. AI disrupts customers and companies in personalisation, decision-making, and predictive analytics. These AI technologies' ability to revolutionise the business provides a futuristic view of travel and tourism.

1. ARTIFICIAL INTELLIGENCE: TRANSFORMING THE TRAVEL AND TOURISM INDUSTRY

According to Shankar (2018), AI "refers to programmes, algorithms, and machines that demonstrate intelligence" (p. 6). According to Pereira et al. (2023), AI includes a wide range of intelligent technologies and tools, including machine learning, the Internet of Things (IoT), artificial neural networks (ANNs),

DOI: 10.4018/979-8-3693-2019-8.ch011

big data, smart robotics, and VR/AR applications. Rising processing power, more accessible large data, and improved machine-learning algorithms and models are all contributing to AI's rising profile. To do numerous complicated tasks (such as data collecting, processing, and analysis) that would necessitate intelligent effort if carried out by humans, it depends on big data, processing capabilities, and algorithms. These activities and services are built upon these duties; they affect the interactions between service providers and their customers; and they have multiple ramifications for marketing, operations, management, and service (Buhalis et al., 2019). According to a survey by TeamLease, the Indian economy stands to gain $967 billion by the year 2035 because to AI. The country's gross domestic product is expected to rise by $450–500 billion by 2025, or around 10% of the $5 trillion target. Meanwhile, study by TeamLease Digital's iCET-Forces Shaping Future of Technology predicts that artificial intelligence could boost global GDP by $15.7 trillion by 2030. The study found that the global AI market was worth $136 billion in 2022 and would grow at a CAGR of 37% between 2023 and 2030. The study found that artificial intelligence brought in $12.3 billion for India in 2022. We also expect the country's artificial intelligence software industry to have risen at a CAGR of 18% by the end of 2025.

According to Buhalis et al. (2019) and Tussyadiah (2020), the travel and hospitality business has been affected by recent technological innovations. Over the past two decades, a plethora of information and communication technologies (henceforth ICT) have been employed to enhance the pre-, during-, and post-trip experiences of tourists, create value, and provide efficient services (Dhiman, Jamwal, & Kumar, 2023). Integration of information and communication technologies is ubiquitous throughout a tourist's journey (Grundner and Neuhofer, 2021). Advances in AI have facilitated the integration of digital and physical elements, which has enhanced ICTs. According to Grundner and Neuhofer (2021), these technologies have all contributed to making visitor encounters more personalised and providing experiences that are enhanced by technology. As an example, according to Doborjeh et al. (2021), artificial intelligence has broadened the usage of robotics applications to improve client interaction in the hospitality industry. Actually, AI aids visitors in locating more pertinent data to enhance their decision-making and deliver superior tourist experiences (Bulchand-Gidumal, 2020). The total impact of AI on the tourism and hospitality industry has not yet materialised, although it has had a significant impact thus far (Ivanov et al., 2019, Tussyadiah, 2020). Over the past few years, there has been an explosion of research on the use of AI in tourism and hospitality, driven by the growing interest in AI from both academics and practitioners. Consequently, in order to comprehend the theoretical underpinnings and the progression of AI knowledge, it is necessary to survey the pertinent literature, return to the topic's historical development, and suggest new directions for study.

AI in tourism manifests in two primary forms: digital systems and digital-physical hybrids (robots). Examples of digital systems include online check-in and mobile boarding passes in airlines, while an example of hybrid systems is the use of service robots in hotels. The development of chatbots represents a significant milestone, reshaping customer interaction and service delivery in the sector.

Although AI is being used in the hospitality and tourism industry, but the growth and percentage of usage is not as much as it is in other industries. The probable reason for this could be a lack of comprehensive theoretical model which caŋ help this industry to adopt AI. This will includes understanding the dynamics between AI technology, customer behaviour, and industry practices. While the use of AI in various sub-sectors of tourism and hospitality is recognized, there's a lack of in-depth analysis on the integration of AI across different service operations and its cumulative impact on the industry 9Shakshi et al., 2020). The evolving nature of consumer interactions with

AI systems in tourism, particularly in the context of personalization and decision-making, needs more exploration. The current paper contributes to understanding AI's role in tourism by exploring current applications and potential developments, thereby enriching the academic perspective. By examining various AI applications in tourism, like chatbots, autonomous vehicles, and VR/AR, the paper provides a holistic view of AI's transformative impact. The paper not only discusses current applications but also delves into emerging trends, offering foresight into how AI could shape the future of the tourism and hospitality industry.

2. A CLOSER LOOK AT AI TECHNOLOGY AND ITS SUBFIELDS

Artificial Intelligence, as defined by Winston in 1992, has evolved considerably since its inception, branching into a broad field supported by machine learning and deep learning. This evolution has led to the emergence of four key subfields: computer vision, natural language processing (NLP), robotic process automation (RPA), and expert systems (Refer Figure 1).

2.1 Machine Learning: The Core of AI

Before learning, ML systems automatically establish hyperparameter tasks (Hutter et al., 2019). ML is utilised in four ways: supervised, semi supervised, unsupervised, and reinforcement learning (Son et al., 2019) to provide focused services, find value in real time, and increase customer engagement and loyalty. ML lets users locate the best services with quick bits and reliable information from previous tourists' ratings and comments. ML lets employees use past customers' data to perform more efficiently and operate more directly, for as by using an autonomous management system that anticipates future company conditions and makes future preparations or understands smart services and reactions. The

Figure 1. Four primary domains of artificial intelligence

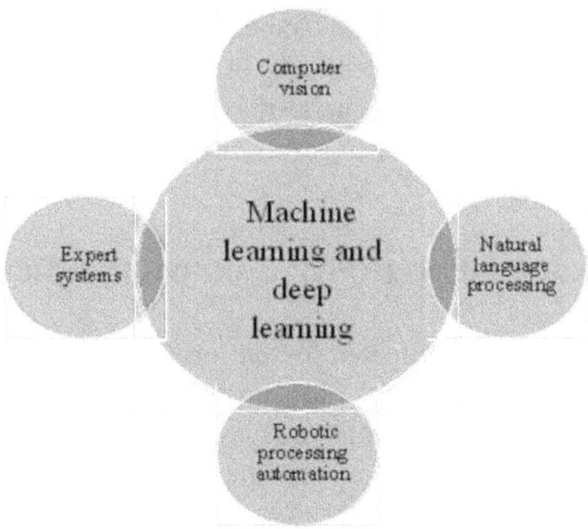

ML approach also makes it easy for personnel to maintain service quality, relieving stress and workload. Booking and occupancy, revenue management, segmentation, demand forecasting, yield management, pricing, performance evaluation, brand monitoring, and competition analysis are the most beneficial benefits of employing ML in tourism and hospitality (Tanpanuwat, 2011). Thus, this study examines the impact of technological innovation on the tourism business, consumer happiness, and willingness to receive technological support in services, as well as hospitality industry employees' assessments of ML technology.

2.2 Deep Learning: Mimicking the Human Brain

Deep learning, a subset of machine learning, processes data via artificial neural networks that replicate human brain function. Capable of handling vast data with numerous attributes or various formats, deep learning networks consist of many neural units, each responding to stimuli from others (Taulli, 2019). Neural networks can be structured as either single-layer or multi-layer systems. In a multi-layer neural network, there are distinct layers including input, output, and multiple hidden layers in between. These hidden layers facilitate the transmission of signals from the input layer to the output layer, as described by Neapolitan and Jiang in 2018.

2.3 Computer Vision: AI's Optical Expertise

One subfield of artificial intelligence is computer vision, which focuses on object description. Computer vision requires a deep understanding of the fundamentals of breaking down objects into their component parts and reassembling them based on their form, transparency, lightness, colour, size, and layers. The hotel and tourist sector makes use of computer vision since it processes massive amounts of photos through a labelling, classification, and filtering process. Robots that patrol the streets and scan licence plates are one use case (e.g., Knightscope, 2020), while search and booking engines can automatically categorise uploaded images of homes as one sort of room (e.g., Yao, 2018).

2.4 Natural Language Processing (NLP): AI's Linguistic Capabilities

Machines that can interpret and produce natural language text and speech are the main focus of natural language processing (NLP). It involves syntactic analysis to structure text, followed by semantic analysis for literal meaning and pragmatic analysis to understand context-based nuances. Machine translation, voice recognition, and information retrieval in several languages are only a few of the many uses for NLP (Chowdhury, 2003).

2.5 Robotic Process Automation (RPA): Enhancing Efficiency Virtually

RPA, distinct from physical robots, automates routine tasks using software-based virtual bots. This drag-and-drop system can handle various tasks like invoicing and customer service. Cognitive robotic process automation, which is created by merging RPA with AI, is utilised in applications such as commercial chatbots for human communication and real-time notifications (Taulli, 2019). RPA itself is not fundamentally AI.

2.6 Expert Systems: AI's Knowledge Repositories

Computer systems that possess specialised knowledge are known as expert systems. These systems include domain information from experts, an inference engine, and end-users. These systems excel in handling qualitative information and adapting to new inputs from experts, thus continuously expanding their knowledge base. They can also manage uncertain or incomplete information. However, their applications remain limited due to testing difficulties and their inability to learn autonomously over time, relying instead on periodic updates with new information (Taulli, 2019).

2.6.1 Expanding the Horizons of AI

AI has seen many technological advances. From machine learning to expert systems, each discipline reflects a unique facet of AI's potential to duplicate and enhance human talents. AI systems can learn, adapt, and make judgements thanks to machine learning and deep learning.

AI is invading human-dominated fields like sight and speech in computer vision and natural language processing (NLP). These innovations improve operational efficiency and revolutionise how users interact with technology, creating more intuitive and personalised experiences. RPA and expert systems automate monotonous operations and improve decision-making. They demonstrate AI's ability to improve workflows and offer domain-specific suggestions. These AI subfields will spur more advances, changing how we use technology in daily life. New, creative solutions to hard problems and technology advances in these sectors signal a new phase in AI evolution.

3. EMERGING AI APPLICATIONS IN TOURISM AND HOSPITALITY SECTOR

This research focuses on five major AI uses in the travel and hospitality industry. These five Ais are as follows: (1) augmented and virtual reality tools, (2) automated kiosks and interactive service screens, (3) robotic technology and self-driving vehicles, (4) digital agents and conversational interfaces, and (5) engines for searching and booking. Instances of each category have been reported across various prominent technology blogs, websites focusing on hospitality trends, and in numerous news articles. Only those applications that have been mentioned in multiple sources are considered for their widespread recognition (as illustrated in Figure 2).

3.1 Search/Booking Engines

Modern travel search and booking engines rely more and more on artificial intelligence (AI) technology such as computer vision, natural language processing (NLP), and machine learning. When booking lodging, dining, and sightseeing services, these engines improve the user experience. Five notable examples are:

1. **Allora Hotel Search/Booking Engine**: Integrated into the websites of over 600 hotels and resorts globally, Allora leverages machine learning to understand user booking behavior. It adjusts the website's configuration for optimal user experience by using deep learning to share insights across participating hotels, aiding in achieving the best website configuration (Allora, 2020).

Figure 2. Five significant hospitality and tourism AI applications

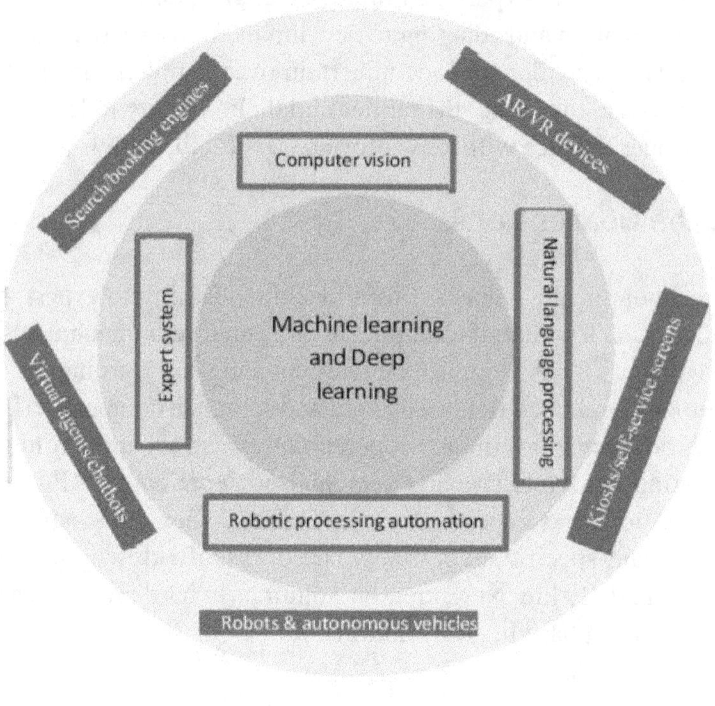

2. **Resy Search and Book for Restaurants**: Launched in 2014, Resy aids restaurants in efficient management. It allows staff to input operational data, such as table numbers and occupancy. As it gains experience, the programme can analyse data such as pace, employee turnover, and company success as a whole (Brill, 2018).
3. **Allset Restaurant Booking and Search Engine**: Allset employs machine learning to study restaurants' busiest times and handle orders and capacity based on preorders and prepayments. It also examines customer profiles to detect potential transactional frauds.
4. **Home Search and Booking Engine by Airbnb**: Airbnb optimises its platform with the use of machine learning and computer vision. The computer vision component classifies images and detects objects, helping validate room types and amenities based on uploaded photos. This technology streamlines searches for users based on specific amenities (Yao, 2018).
5. **Wayblazer Reservation and Search Engine**: Utilizing NLP, Wayblazer understands natural language inputs like "romantic getaway with great food and culture." It presents images and reviews relevant to the search keywords, significantly influencing consumers' decision-making (Wayblazer, 2017; IBM, 2016).

3.2 The Revolution of Virtual Agents/Chatbots in Service Industry

Virtual agents and chatbots, employing advanced AI technologies like machine learning and NLP, have become indispensable in enhancing guest services across various industries. This section explores seven prominent examples, each showcasing a unique application of these technologies.

1. **Google Assistant and Google Duplex**: Google Assistant, a voice-activated tool, leverages machine learning and NLP for tasks like providing weather updates upon request (Google, 2020). An innovative extension of this is Google Duplex, which can autonomously make restaurant reservations, book hair salon appointments, and inquire about holiday hours over the phone, exemplifying the potential of AI in personal assistance (Leviathan, 2018; Callaham, 2019).
2. **Amazon Echo and Alexa in the Hospitality Industry**: Amazon's Alexa performs internet searches and responds to voice commands. Its specialized version, Alexa for Hospitality, is designed for the hotel environment. It offers both general functions like playing music and specific hospitality services such as setting alarms, controlling room conditions, ordering room service, and facilitating virtual check-outs. A few Los Angeles Marriott hotels have upgraded their guests' experiences using this technology (Reid, 2018; Amazon Alexa, 2020).
3. **Chatbot Edward**: Launched by Radisson Blu Edwardian Hotels, Chatbot Edward is equipped with NLP to handle guest requests through text messages. It provides information on amenities, maintenance, directions, and travel tips, demonstrating AI's role in streamlining hotel services (Burns, 2016; Aspect, 2020).
4. **Macy's On Call**: Macy's, the American retail giant, introduced Macy's On Call, a chatbot within its official app. It offers personalized shopping advice, answering customer queries about products, services, and store departments, illustrating AI's application in retail (Arthur, 2016).
5. **Tacobot**: Taco Bell's Tacobot allows customers to place orders through text, responding in the brand's unique, witty tone. It handles informal language and playful interactions, showcasing a chatbot's ability to reflect brand personality (Taco Bell, 2016; Addady, 2016).
6. **My Starbucks Barista**: With the 2017 introduction of My Starbucks Barista, Starbucks now has a chatbot that can understand both textual and vocal instructions. It supports personalized orders, including preferences for cup sizes and toasting options, highlighting AI's role in customizing consumer experiences (Perez, 2017).
7. **Subway Order Bot**: Subway's chatbot, integrated with Facebook Messenger, converses with customers to take food orders. Unique in its approach, it uses customers' zip codes or GPS locations to suggest pickup stores and offers both text and picture-based ordering options, exemplifying a user-friendly chatbot experience (Calfas, 2017; Subway Restaurants, 2017).

3.2.1 The Impact of AI in Guest Services

These virtual agents and chatbots represent a significant shift in how businesses interact with their customers. From handling simple tasks like weather updates to complex functions like personalized shopping assistance and playful brand interactions, AI-driven chatbots are redefining customer service. These

AI-driven technologies not only enhance operational workflows but also elevate the customer experience with more engaging and tailored services. This AI-led transformation is redefining the benchmarks for customer engagement and service quality in both the hospitality and retail sectors.

3.3 Emergence of Robotics and Autonomous Vehicles in Hospitality and Tourism

Patrolling, luggage delivery, and quick cooking are just a few of the many uses for autonomous cars and robots in the hospitality and tourist industries. Here are a few examples of use cases:

1. **The K Series of Knightscope Robots**: To better secure the areas where people reside, work, study, and visit, Knightscope, a cutting-edge public safety technology business, constructs blue light emergency communications systems and completely autonomous security robots. The robots read licence plates at quick speeds, record high-definition video, and listen for sounds thanks to their built-in GPS, lasers, and infrared cameras. Indoors or out, the robots can navigate any surface, even rough and uneven ones. Robots with similar visual and auditory skills to humans are being considered as a possible addition to hotel personnel (Robinson, 2017; Knightscope, 2020).
2. **Travelmate Autonomous Suitcases (TAS)**: In 2016, the TAS were introduced to the public. By connecting with owners' phones over Bluetooth, these intelligent bags can follow them wherever they go. They navigate smoothly, adjusting speed to match their owners and skilfully avoiding obstacles, showcasing the convenience of autonomous technology in personal travel gear (Travelmate, 2019).
3. **Hilton's Concierge Robot "Connie"**: Connie, who debuted at the Hilton in McLean, Virginia, communicates with visitors through the use of machine learning, computer vision, and natural language processing. It can recognize human guests, comprehend voice queries, and respond in natural languages. Connie's expressive eyes, changing colors to indicate different moods, add a unique touch to guest interactions (Trejos, 2016).
4. **Self-Driving Domino's Pizza Delivery**: Domino's Pizza is at the forefront of using autonomous vehicles for pizza delivery. These specialized vehicles, designed without seats or steering wheels, navigate autonomously to deliver pizzas. The use of Domino's app to place an order, monitor its progress, and retrieve the pizza is an example of autonomous technology in the food delivery industry (Holley, 2019).
5. **The Robot Who Flips Burgers, Flippy**: Flippy, a one-arm robot equipped with computer vision, is revolutionizing the fast-food industry. It accurately determines the perfect timing for flipping burgers, assisting kitchen staff in preparing meals. Management applauds Flippy for its precision and the potential savings in staff training (Caliburger, 2016; Graham, 2018).

3.2.2 Redefining Service With Automation

These instances show that Robots and autonomous things are revolutionizing the hospitality and tourism business. From enhancing guest experiences to optimizing operational efficiency, these technologies are not just futuristic concepts but are actively redefining the standards of service and convenience in the sector.

3.4 Innovative Kiosks and Self-Service Screens in Hospitality

The hospitality sector is witnessing a paradigm shift as self-service kiosks and screens with cutting-edge face recognition technology take centre stage. These systems utilize biometric data to streamline services, enhancing both efficiency and customer experience. Here are two prominent examples:

1. **Marriott International's Facial Recognition Check-In Kiosks**: Marriott International began testing a programme to speed up the check-in process in Sanya and Hangzhou, China, in 2018. Passengers are asked to scan their identification, have their photo taken, sign a contract, and provide their contact details. According to Wang (2018) and Marriott International (2018), the check-in time is reduced from three minutes to just one minute thanks to the facial recognition software that quickly checks personal and reservation details before issuing room keys.
2. **Facial Recognition System with a Smile for Payment**: Launched in 2017 in Hangzhou, China, in collaboration with Alibaba, this system revolutionized payments at KFC stores. Customers complete their order and then smile at the self-service screen for identity verification and transaction processing. Its popularity led to its expansion to over 300 stores by 2018 (Gilchrist, 2017; Meyers, 2017; Burt, 2018).

3.5 Augmented and Virtual Reality Devices Reshaping Tourism

Augmented Reality (AR) and Virtual Reality (VR) technologies are being creatively used in the tourism industry through various devices. While virtual reality typically makes use of head-mounted displays or sensory simulation tools, augmented reality is more commonly used on mobile devices. Below are some key applications:

1. **ETIPS AR Travel App**: The ETIPS AR Travel software has been around since 2009, and it lets users scan their surroundings with their phones to get advice on where to go or interesting facts about the area. The software serves as an interactive guide to certain locations, including hotels, restaurants, and picture places (ETIPS, 2020).
2. **In-Room AR Map at Premier Inn**: Premier Inn, based in London, introduced an in-room AR map in 2014. Guests download the hotel's app and scan a wall map of London in their rooms to access AR information about different areas, including online reviews of restaurants and bars (Huang et al., 2022).
3. **Navitaire's VR Travel Booking Service**: This immersive booking experience transports customers to a virtual globe where they can explore and select destinations. It also allows them to inspect rental cars in VR before booking, providing a comprehensive preview of their choices (Navitaire, 2020).
4. **Marriott VR Honeymoon Headset with Teleporter**: Introduced in 2014, Marriott's VR honeymoon experience offered newlyweds a virtual honeymoon in London or Hawaii. The teleporter boxes provide a four-dimensional experience with the use of sensory simulation techniques such as misting spray and vibrating flooring (Carson, 2015).
5. **The Augmented Reality Athlete Meeting in the Room**: Coinciding with the 2012 London Olympic and Paralympic Games, this AR experience allowed hotel guests to see athletes performing sports

in their rooms. By pointing their mobile devices at hotel amenities, guests could view different sports activities (Martins, 2017).

6. **AR Fine Arts Windows at SFMOMA**: The San Francisco Museum of Modern Art presented "René Magritte: The Fifth Season" in 2018, an AR exhibition that didn't require personal devices. Adding a contemporary spin to the conventional museum experience, visitors interacted directly with augmented reality effects.

Revolutionizing Hospitality and Tourism with Advanced Tech

The integration of kiosks, self-service screens, and AR/VR technologies is reshaping the landscape of the hospitality and tourism sectors. These innovations are not just simplifying operational processes; they're enriching the customer experience with personalized and immersive interactions. From efficient check-in systems to engaging travel planning tools and interactive features within rooms, these technologies are establishing new standards in customer interaction and satisfaction. As these technological advancements continue to progress, they hold the potential to further transform how the hospitality and tourism industries engage with and cater to their clientele, providing a preview of the future direction of these fields (Refer Figure 3).

Figure 3. AI application evaluation criteria for hospitality and tourism

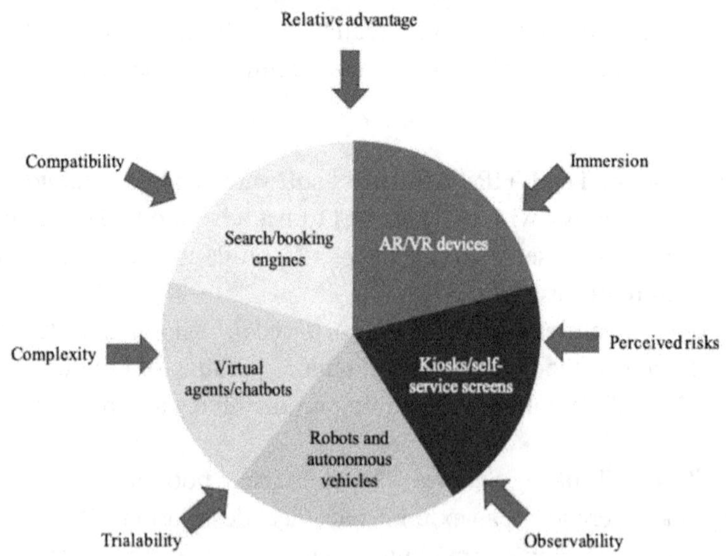

4. THE EVOLUTION AND INTELLIGENCE OF CHATBOTS IN THE DIGITAL ERA

According to Hatwar et al. (2016), chatbots managed by AI are highly significant in the tourism sector. The term "chatbot" was created by combining the words "chat" and "robot," which clearly explains what they are used for. According to Khanna et al. (2015), chatbots are really just computer programmes that mimic human communication by using natural language. These digital assistants are equipped with a knowledge base that includes a variety of dialogue management rules, applying diverse techniques to process and respond to user inputs effectively. As practical and user-centric AI applications, chatbots have witnessed significant market growth. The worldwide market for IT robotic automation is expected to reach $4.98 billion by 2020, up 60.5% from 2014, according to Transparency Market Research. This growth is attributed to the efficiency and cost-effectiveness of chatbots compared to traditional mobile apps. Their decreased dependence on expensive servers allows them to be built and maintained at around half the cost and in a quarter of the time (Waxer, 2016).

4.1 Chatbot Intelligence: The Core of Interactive Technology

The intelligence of a chatbot is primarily measured by its ability to navigate conversations using decision-tree logic. The bot's response is contingent on the keywords identified in the user's input, guiding the conversation based on the questions asked (Skerrett, 2017). However, achieving this seamless interaction is challenging and crucial for the success of a chatbot. An intelligent chatbot is indistinguishable from a human customer service operator, capable of performing functions like arithmetic, logic, learning, heuristics, sensing, and perceiving (Khanna et al., 2015).

In the context of the tourism industry, chatbots follow a specific algorithm to ensure effective and human-like responses (Refer Figure 4). This process begins with the user's input query, which is processed through the chatbot's engine and central processing unit. The response is refined at each step to closely mimic human intelligence and provide the most accurate and relevant information. Hotel room availability and airline itineraries are only two examples of the real-time data that the engine accesses via its connection to the company's database. Thanks to this feature, the chatbot can provide the user with accurate and timely information, leading to a response that meets their demands and closely resembles human customer care.

Figure 4. Tourism bot theory from query to response—tourism and hospitality chatbots

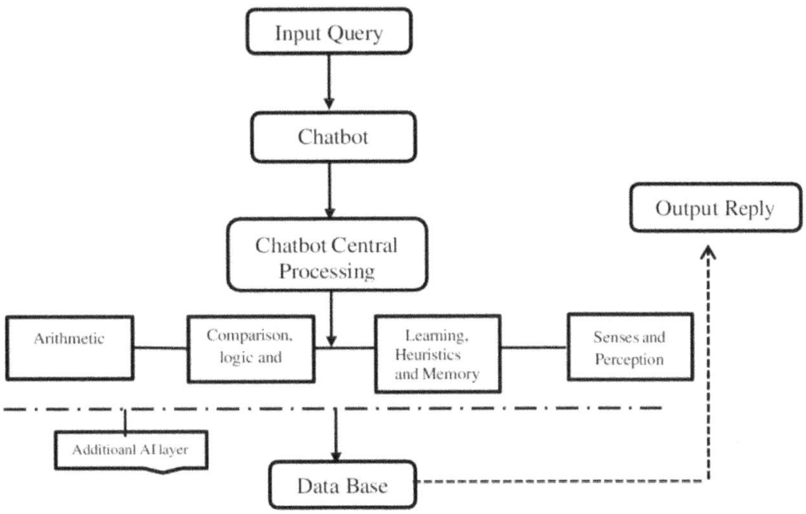

4.2 The Transformative Impact of Chatbots in the Tourism Industry

Chatbots offer significant advantages to the tourism industry. For any business, providing easy access to services is crucial, both before and after a sale. With the growing popularity of instant messaging platforms like Facebook Messenger and WhatsApp, businesses can enhance customer convenience by integrating their services into these commonly used chat channels. It is quite advantageous to use chatbots for common activities like making appointments, sending reminders, purchasing tickets, and giving weather and traffic information. The potential of chatbots in different parts of the tourist business is enormous, notwithstanding a few problems that will be covered later. Restaurants, hotels, vehicle rental services, travel bureaus, and visitor centres can all benefit greatly from this technology.

4.3 Chatbots in the Hotel Industry

Hotels are particularly benefiting from chatbots. For instance, increasing online booking percentages via chatbots directly impacts sales growth (Lasek & Jessa, 2013). Expedia, leveraging Facebook technology, launched a bot for hotel bookings. The Marriott Hotel Chain also launched a chatbot on Facebook to handle guest inquiries and reservations. Chatbots like these not only make it easier to make bookings, but they also let customers schedule extras like spa treatments and dinner reservations before they even arrive (Ukpabi et al., 2018). By interacting with guests throughout their journey, chatbots can gather data used by hotel staff and algorithms to offer personalized services (Bhargava, 2017) (Refer Figure 5).

4.4 Revolutionizing the Restaurant Business

In the restaurant sector, chatbots are making a significant impact. Taco Bell's TacoBot, launched in 2016, exemplifies this, facilitating food ordering with a touch of wit. Following this trend, giants like Burger King, Pizza Hut, and Domino's have also introduced proprietary chatbots (Moharana, 2017). These bots are set to make phone orders obsolete, shifting customer interactions to social media platforms (Refer Figure 6). Additionally, services like MasterCard's Masterpass are enabling chatbots to process payments, streamlining the ordering and payment processes.

4.5 Cost Reduction and Enhanced Service

Chatbots offer economic advantages by reducing communication costs for customers and operational costs for businesses. By eliminating the need for customer service representatives or outsourcing to call centers, companies can achieve significant savings (Ukpabi et al., 2018). Beyond ordering and delivery, chatbots provide additional functionalities like exploring restaurant reviews, managing reservations, and searching for restaurants based on various criteria without the need for additional mobile apps (Gamanyuk, 2017).

4.6 The Rise of Travel Chatbots

In the broader context of tourism, the necessity for reliable information sources is growing. Travel chatbots are designed to meet these needs, guiding tourists through all aspects of their trip, from booking

Figure 5. Sample conversation with a hotel booking chatbot

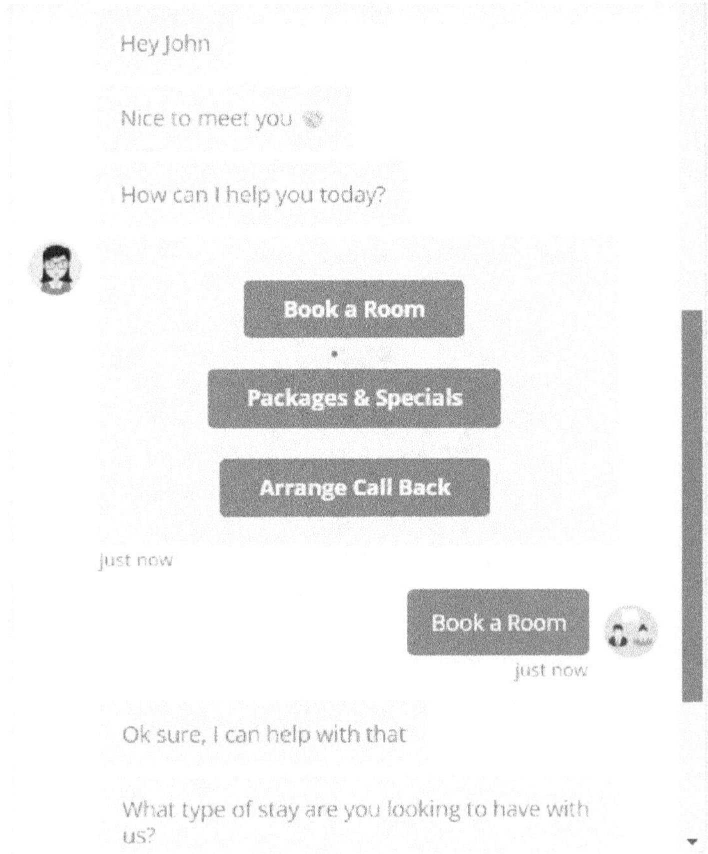

to general travel advice. These bots vary in sophistication and recommendation capabilities, ranging from customer service bots to AI-powered travel bots, each offering unique benefits depending on their platform and functionality.

4.7 Three Types of Travel Chatbots

4.7.1 Customer Service Travel Bots: The Basic Yet Effective AI Tool

Customer service travel bots, the most rudimentary form of chatbots in the travel industry, are embedded in travel companies' websites. These bots, limited to assisting users with website navigation and not equipped for booking processes, rely on a set of predetermined automated answers. Recent trends suggest a decline in their usage as companies like Booking.com, On the Beach, and Tap Portugal have phased them out, acknowledging their limitations. However, some, like Copa Airlines, Amtrak, and Air New Zealand, continue to utilize them, finding value in their basic functionalities (Copa Airlines,2019).

Figure 6. Sample conversation with restaurant chatbot

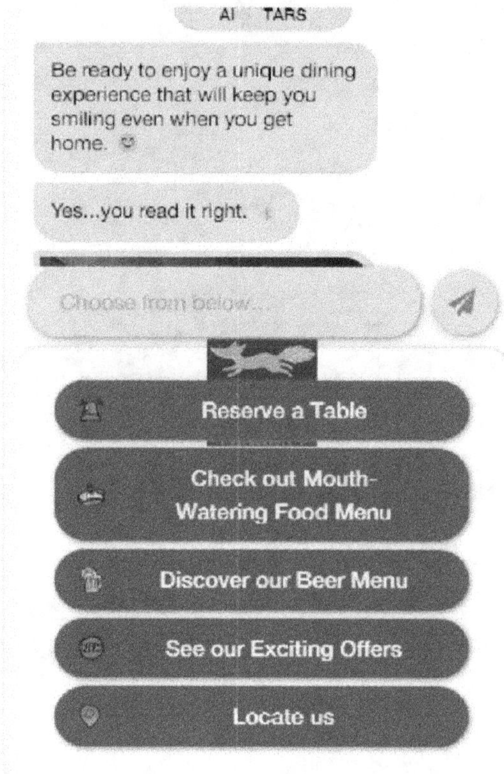

4.7.2 The Rise of Facebook Chatbots in Tourism

Facebook chatbots represent a more advanced and interactive form of AI in tourism. Unlike their simpler counterparts, these bots engage users in two-way conversations, aiding in the booking process. Though users input the same data as they would manually, the convenience and user satisfaction levels are notably higher with these chatbots. In 2018, the number of active chatbots on Facebook Messenger reached 300,000 – a threefold increase from the previous year (Cooper,2019).

Expedia's Facebook chatbot is a prime example, enabling users to initiate chat by simply visiting Expedia's Facebook page (Marques, 2019). However, it's limited to hotel bookings and managing trips, not supporting flight, cruise, or car bookings. Another notable implementation is Skyscanner's chatbot (Facebook, 2019) offering users the cheapest flights from nearby airports and categorizing flights as cheapest, shortest, and best. It also provides travel inspiration when users type "anywhere," offering intriguing destination suggestions. Kayak's chatbot (Facebook, 2019) takes it a step further by remembering past conversations and personalizing searches based on user history. Both Skyscanner and Kayak extend their chatbot services beyond Facebook Messenger to platforms like Slack, Amazon Alexa, Skype, and Google Assistant. These bots are predominantly used by airlines and travel search engines, with few exceptions like the Faroe Island tourist board, which integrates its chatbot both on its official website and Facebook page (The Faroe Islands,2019).

4.7.3 AI Empowered Travel Bots: A Leap in Chatbot Technology

AI-empowered travel bots stand out with their recommendation capabilities, leveraging algorithms and app integrations to provide personalized services. KLM Royal Dutch Airlines' chatbot, BB, not only assists with travel inquiries on Facebook Messenger but also offers packing advice based on destination, travel dates, and duration, available on Google Home Assistant (KLM,2019).

Hello Hipmunk, another sophisticated virtual travel agent, offers comprehensive travel planning and booking services (Hipmunk, 2019). Its standout feature is the integration with users' emails and calendars, enabling personalized travel recommendations and itinerary creation. This bot is accessible via Facebook Messenger and Skype.

HelloGBye travel assistant targets frequent flyers and small businesses (HelloGBuy,2019). Though it's a paid app exclusive to iOS, its ability to process complex, multi-person travel requests in under 30 seconds compensates for the inconvenience of app downloading. Sam, catering to individual users, frequent flyers, and business travelers, excels in booking flights and organizing itineraries (Meet Sam, 2019). It keeps users informed about weather, traffic, and flight delays, and coordinates airport transportation and luggage claim information. Sam's comprehensive services are achieved through integration with apps like Avis, Uber, and Google Maps, available for both iOS and Android users.

4.8 Conclusion: Chatbots as Indispensable Tools in Tourism and Hospitality

In conclusion, chatbots have emerged as a transformative force in the tourism industry, reshaping how companies interact with customers and manage services. These AI-driven digital assistants have proven their worth across various sectors, from hotels and restaurants to travel agencies and tourist information centers. With their ability to handle routine tasks efficiently, chatbots enhance customer experience by offering convenient and quick responses, thereby increasing operational efficiency and reducing costs. Bookings and orders might be expedited and customer experiences could be personalised with the help of chatbots, particularly in the hospitality industry. Chatbots' reach and usefulness have been enhanced with their integration into Facebook Messenger. The result of this shows a shift from conventional to tech-savvy client engagement. Chatbot technology has advanced to the point where AI-powered travel bots can provide customized itineraries and round-the-clock assistance to customers. These chatbots are revolutionizing consumer service by offering tailored travel advice and simplifying complex trip arrangements. Finally, we can say that in travel industry chatbots play a significant role. They are a game-changer in terms of technology and provide real answers to the issues that contemporary travellers face. With the rapid advancement of technology, chatbots are set to play a pivotal role in the tourist and hospitality industries.

REFERENCES

Addady, M. (2016). 'TacoBot' is the newest way to order Taco Bell. *Fortune*. https://fortune.com/2016/04/06/tacobot-taco-bell/.

Alexa, A. (2020). *Alexa for hospitality*. Amazon. https://www.amazon.com/alexahospitality.

Arthur, R. (2016). Macy's teams with IBM Watson for AI-powered mobile shopping assistant. *Forbes*. https://www.forbes.com/sites/rachelarthur/2016/07/20/macys-teams-with-ibmwatson-for-ai-powered-mobile-shopping-assistant/#4c4a1327f415

Aspect. (2020). *Edwardian hotels London launches 'virtual host' designed by aspect software*. Aspect. https://www.aspect.com/company/news/press-releases/edwardian-hotels-londonlaunches- virtual-host-designed-by-aspect-software (accessed 20 June 2020).

Bhargava, V. (2017). Are social chatbots the Future of hassle free travel? *The chatbot magazine*. https://chatbotsmagazine.com/are-social-chatbots-the-future-of-hassle-free-travel-e043c7feea93

Brill, R. (2018). *Resy is using machine learning to help restaurants turn tables more efficiently*. Food Able TV. https://www.foodabletv.com/blog/2018/6/15/resy-is-using-machine-learning-tohelp-restaurants-turn-tables-more-efficiently

Buhalis, D., Harwood, T., Bogicevic, V., Viglia, G., Beldona, S., & Hofacker, C. (2019). Technological disruptions in services: Lessons from tourism and hospitality. *Journal of Service Management*, *30*(4), 484–506. doi:10.1108/JOSM-12-2018-0398

Bulchand-Gidumal, J., & Melián-González, S. (2020). Why are ratings so high in the sharing economy? Evidence based on guest perspectives. *Current Issues in Tourism*, *23*(10), 1248–1260. doi:10.1080/13683500.2019.1602597

Burns, J. (2016). Radisson Blu Edwardian guests can now text Edward the Chatbot for service. *Forbes*. https://www.forbes.com/sites/janetwburns/2016/05/10/radisson-blu-hotel-guestscan-now-text-edward-the-chatbot-for-service/#2f5e8ecd1e23 (accessed 10 June 2020).

Burt, C. (2018). 'Smile-to-Pay' facial recognition system now at 300 locations in China. *Biometric Update*. https://www.biometricupdate.com/201811/smile-to-pay-facial-recognition-system-now-at-300-locations-in-china.

Calfas, J. (2017). You can now order Subway through Facebook. *Fortune*. https://fortune.com/ 2017/04/18/subway-order-facebook-messenger/

Caliburger. (2016). *About Flippy*. Caliburger. https://caliburger.com/flippy

Callaham, J. (2019). *What is Google Duplex and how do you use it?* Android Authority. https://www.androidauthority.com/what-is-google-duplex-869476/

Carson, E. (2015). Marriott Hotels use VR to connect consumers with tech and travel innovation. *Tech Republic*. https://www.techrepublic.com/article/marriott-hotels-use-vr-to-connect-consumerswith-tech-and-travel-innovation/

Chowdhury, G. G. (2003). Natural language processing. *Annual Review of Information Science & Technology*, *37*(1), 51–89. doi:10.1002/aris.1440370103

Cooper, P. (2019). The complete guide to using Facebook messenger bots for business. *Hootsuite*. https://blog.hootsuite.com/facebook-messenger-botsguide/

Dhiman, N., Jamwal, M., & Kumar, A. (2023). Enhancing value in customer journey by considering the (ad) option of artificial intelligence tools. *Journal of Business Research*, *167*, 114142. doi:10.1016/j.jbusres.2023.114142

Doborjeh, Z., Hemmington, N., Doborjeh, M., & Kasabov, N. (2022). Artificial intelligence: A systematic review of methods and applications in hospitality and tourism. *International Journal of Contemporary Hospitality Management*, *34*(3), 1154–1176. doi:10.1108/IJCHM-06-2021-0767

ETIPS. (2020). *Augmented reality*. eTips. https://etips.com/#augmented-reality

Gamanyuk, A. (2017). *Restaurant table reservation chatbot for Facebook bootmaker*. Botmakers. https://blog.botmakers.net/table-eservation-chatbot-for-restaurants 8fb0cf8bd1aa

Gilchrist, K. (2017). Alibaba launches 'smile to pay' facial recognition system at KFC in China. CNBC. https://www.cnbc.com/2017/09/04/alibaba-launches-smile-to-pay-facial-recognitionsystem- at-kfc-china.html (accessed 11 June 2020).

Google. (2020). *Access the Google assistant with your voice*. Google. https://support.google.com/assistant/answer/7394306?co5GENIE.Platform%3DAndroid&hl5en

Graham, J. (2018). Hamburger-making robot Flippy is back at Calif. chain. *USA Today*. https://www.usatoday.com/story/tech/talkingtech/2018/05/28/hamburger-making-robot-flippy-back-serving- 300-burgers-day/649370002/

Grundner, L., & Neuhofer, B. (2021). The bright and dark sides of artificial intelligence: A futures perspective on tourist destination experiences. *Journal of Destination Marketing & Management*, *19*, 100511. doi:10.1016/j.jdmm.2020.100511

Hatwar, P. N., Patil, A., & Gondane, D. (2016). AI based chatbot. *International Journal of Emerging Trends in Engineering and Basic Sciences*. Hello Hipmunk. https://www.hipmunk.com/hello

Holley, P. (2019). Domino's will start delivering pizzas via an autonomous robot this fall. *Washington Post*. https://www.washingtonpost.com/technology/2019/06/17/dominos-will-start-delivering-pizzasvia-an-autonomous-robot-this-fall/

Huang, A., Chao, Y., de la Mora Velasco, E., Bilgihan, A., & Wei, W. (2022). When artificial intelligence meets the hospitality and tourism industry: An assessment framework to inform theory and management. *Journal of Hospitality and Tourism Insights*, *5*(5), 1080–1100. doi:10.1108/JHTI-01-2021-0021

Huang, A., Chao, Y., de la Mora Velasco, E., Bilgihan, A., & Wei, W. (2022). When artificial intelligence meets the hospitality and tourism industry: An assessment framework to inform theory and management. *Journal of Hospitality and Tourism Insights*, *5*(5), 1080–1100. doi:10.1108/JHTI-01-2021-0021

Hutter, F., Kotthoff, L., & Vanschoren, J. (2019). *Automated machine learning: methods, systems, challenges*. Springer Nature. doi:10.1007/978-3-030-05318-5

IBM. (2016). *IBM-Wayblazer*. IBM. https://www.ibm.com/case-studies/g754268s52509183.

Ivanov, D., Dolgui, A., & Sokolov, B. (2019). The impact of digital technology and Industry 4.0 on the ripple effect and supply chain risk analytics. *International Journal of Production Research, 57*(3), 829–846. doi:10.1080/00207543.2018.1488086

Khanna, A., & Pandey, B., & Das, T. (2015). A Study of Today's A.I. through Chatbots and Rediscovery of Machine Intelligence. *International Journal of u- and e- Service. Science and Technology, 8*(7), 277–284.

Knightscope. (2020). *K5 features*. Knightscope. https://www.knightscope.com/knightscope k5.

Lasek, M., & Jessa, S. (2013). Chatbots for customer services on hotel websites. *Information Systems Management, 2*(2), 146–158.

Leviathan, Y. (2018). *Google Duplex: an AI system for accomplishing real-world tasks over the phone*. Google. https://ai.googleblog.com/2018/05/duplex-ai-system-for-naturalconversation. html

Marques, M. (20129). Top 3 chatbots that are changing the travel industry. *Medium*. https://medium. com/hijiff y/top-3-chatbots-that-are-changing-the- travel-industry-d325082c50b8.

Marriott International. (2018). *Joint venture of Alibaba group and Marriott international trials facial recognition check-in technology*. Marriott International. https://news.marriott.com/news/2018/07/11/ jointventure- of-alibaba-group-and-marriott-international-trials-facial-recognition-check-intechnology

Martins, L. M. (2017). Augmented reality in hotels use case - holiday Inn, the first ever. LinkedIn. https://www. linkedin.com/pulse/augmented-reality-hotels-use-case-holiday-inn-first-lu%C3% ADs (accessed 5 June 2020).

Meyers, M. (2017). This Chinese KFC lets you put your money where your mouth is. CNet. https://www. cnet.com/news/smile-to-pay-kfc-facial-recognition-payments-alipay-ant/

Moharana, A. (2017). Why Bots Will Revolutionize the Way Restaurants Work, *Chatbotlife*. https:// chatbotslife.com/why-bots-will-revolutionize-the-way-restaurants-work-11498fb00604

Navitaire. (2020). *Discover the navitaire difference*. Navitaire. https://www.navitaire.com/amadeus

Pereira, V., Hadjielias, E., Christofi, M., & Vrontis, D. (2023). A systematic literature review on the impact of artificial intelligence on workplace outcomes: A multi-process perspective. *Human Resource Management Review, 33*(1), 100857. doi:10.1016/j.hrmr.2021.100857

Perez, S. (2017). Starbucks unveils a virtual assistant that takes your order via messaging or voice. *TechCrunch*. https://techcrunch.com/2017/01/30/starbucks-unveils-a-virtual-assistant-that-takesyour-order-via-messaging-or-voice/

Reid, J. (2018). Amazon's Alexa checks into first Marriott hotel. *Business Traveler*. https://www. businesstraveller.com/business-travel/2018/10/27/amazons-alexa-checks-into-first-marriotthotel/ (accessed 10 June 2020).

Robinson, M. (2017). The tech giants of Silicon Valley are starting to rely on crime-fighting robots for security. *Business Insider*. https://www.businessinsider.com/knightscope-security-robots-microsoftuber- 2017-5

Sakshi, S., Shashi, Cerchione, R., & Bansal, H. (2020). Measuring the impact of sustainability policy and practices in tourism and hospitality industry. *Business Strategy and the Environment, 29*(3), 1109–1126. doi:10.1002/bse.2420

Shankar, V. (2018). How artificial intelligence (AI) is reshaping retailing. *Journal of Retailing*, *94*(4), vi–xi. doi:10.1016/S0022-4359(18)30076-9

Skerrett, D. (2017). Seven reasons why most chatbots launched in 2017 are dead on arrival. *Econtent Mag*. http://www.econtentmag.com/Articles/Editorial/Mobile-Moment/Seven-Reasons-Why-Most-Chatbots-Launched-in-2017-Are-Dead-on-Arrival-119104.htm

Son, L. H., Tripathy, H. K., Acharya, B. R., Kumar, R., & Chatterjee, J. M. (2019). Machine learning on big data: A developmental approach on societal applications. *Big Data Processing Using Spark in Cloud*, 143-165.

Tanpanuwat, A. (2011). *Examining revenue management practices in Las Vegas casino resorts*.

Taulli, T. (2019). *Artificial Intelligence Basics*. APress. https://www.visitfaroeislands. com/

Travelmate. (2019). Travelmate suitcase features. *TravelMate*. https://travelmaterobotics.com/ (accessed 10 June 2020).

Trejos, N. (2016). Introducing Connie, Hilton's new robot concierge. *USA Today*. https://www. usato-day.com/story/travel/roadwarriorvoices/2016/03/09/introducing-connie-hiltons-new-robotconcierge/81525924/

Tussyadiah, I. (2020). A review of research into automation in tourism: Launching the Annals of Tourism Research Curated Collection on Artificial Intelligence and Robotics in Tourism. *Annals of Tourism Research*, *81*, 102883. doi:10.1016/j.annals.2020.102883

Ukpabi, D., Karjaluoto, H., Olaleye, S. A., & Mogaji, E. (2018). Dual Perspectives on the Role of Artificially Intelligent Robotic Virtual Agents in the Tourism, Travel and Hospitality Industries. In D. Vrontis, Y. Weber, & E. Tsoukatos (Eds.), *Proceedings of the 11th Annual Conference of the EuroMed Academy of Business (EMAB)* (pp. 1339–1351). EuroMed Press. https://www.emrbi.org/bop2018.pdf

Ukpabi, D. C., Aslam, B., & Karjaluoto, H. (2019). Chatbot adoption in tourism services: A conceptual exploration. In *Robots, artificial intelligence, and service automation in travel, tourism and hospitality* (pp. 105–121). Emerald Publishing Limited. doi:10.1108/978-1-78756-687-320191006

Wang, J. (2018). You can now check in with a facial scan at Marriott in China. *Forbes*. https:// www.forbes.com/sites/jennawang/2018/07/24/you-can-now-check-in-with-a-facial-scan-atmarriott/#42eeb8a33f7a (accessed 5 June 2020).

Waxer, C. (2016). *Get ready for the bot revolution. Computer World, online link can be. Computer World*. https://www.computerworld.com/article/3126438/emerging-technology/article.html,

Wayblazer. (2017). *About way blazer*. Way Blazer. https://www.wayblazer.ai/about/

Winston, P. H. (1992). *Artificial intelligence*. Addison-Wesley Longman Publishing Co., Inc.

Yao, S. (2018). Categorizing listing photos at Airbnb. *Medium*. https://medium.com/airbnbengineering/categorizing-listing-photos-at-airbnb-f9483f3ab7e3

Chapter 12
Social Media Marketing Strategies for Innovating Relationship Marketing in the Digital Era

Aaruni Batta
Chandigarh Business School of Administration, India

Pallavi Pahuja
Chandigarh Business School of Administration, India

Ruby Sharma
Chandigarh Business School of Administration, India

ABSTRACT

Utilizing social media for real-time communication and feedback is crucial in the evolving landscape of business communication in the digital era. It's not enough to simply acquire new customers through lead generation or sales; you must also foster connections with them on social media and online to ensure their continued loyalty and advocacy for your brand. Traditional word-of-mouth marketing has transformed, and the key to sustaining customer relationships and driving repeat business lies in building strong, lasting connections with your clientele. The absence of verbal marketing underscores the significance of cultivating robust client relationships. Enthusiastic customers who feel a genuine connection to your company will not only continue to patronize your business but will also enthusiastically recommend your products or services to their friends and family. Consequently, both marketing and business operations prioritize the establishment of solid customer connections.

1. SOCIAL MEDIA MARKETING

The rapid advancements in technology have significantly transformed our world, making life more convenient for people. One of the most impactful changes has been the ease of connection through social media platforms. With the evolution of Web 2.0 and the rise of information and communication technol-

DOI: 10.4018/979-8-3693-2019-8.ch012

ogy, businesses now have various online avenues like websites, blogs, and predominantly social media to engage with their customers. Social media, as defined by Wikipedia, is "a communication technology and digital channels facilitating the creation and exchange of knowledge, ideas, hobbies, and various forms of communication within visible groups and networks."

Platforms such as Facebook, Instagram, Twitter, and others have revolutionized how individuals connect and form relationships. Similarly, businesses worldwide are leveraging these platforms to establish and nurture relationships with potential and existing customers. Social media serves as a powerful tool for businesses to enhance brand awareness, address customer concerns, and ultimately increase revenue. By actively engaging with customers, responding to queries, and even recognizing special occasions like birthdays or anniversaries, companies can foster stronger relationships.

Moreover, social media has become a pivotal element in marketers' strategies for promoting products online. It's now imperative for companies to maintain a presence on platforms like Facebook, Instagram, and Twitter, allowing them to gain insights into customer preferences, tastes, and interests. These platforms also facilitate the formation of customer communities, where enthusiasts share experiences and opinions about specific products or services, exemplified by groups such as Harley-Davidson enthusiasts who create blogs and discussions about their experiences with the brand. The primary strength of social media lies in its ability to facilitate global or simultaneous communication with individuals or groups worldwide.

As defined by Kaplan and Haenlein (2010), "social media" encompasses a range of Internet-based applications grounded in Web 2.0 principles, allowing users to create and exchange content. This evolution has altered client relationships, fostering potential collaborations (Cherubini & Pattuglia, 2012; Finotto & Miceli, 2010; Hanna et al., 2011; Lewis & Nichols, 2012; Kietzmann et al., 2011).

The progression of social media has shifted influence away from corporate executives, empowering ordinary individuals and communities (Finotto and Miceli, 2010; Kietzmann et al., 2011; Mangold and Faulds, 2009; Mortara and Sinisi, 2012; O'Reilly; Pastore 2009; Vernuccio et al., 2012).

Social media has become an integral part of modern life, widely adopted as a versatile and dynamic online activity. Its functionalities encompass various technological tasks, including photo-sharing, blogging, sports, dating, video conferencing, business meetings, reviews, virtual worlds, and more. Moreover, even governments and politicians engage with constituents and citizens through social media platforms. Businesses have recognized the potential of social media, leading to the emergence of social media marketing (SMM) as a profitable tool for organizations across various industries.

SMM strategies typically revolve around:

1. Establishing a presence on key platforms for communication.
2. Creating advertisements and shareable content.
3. Collecting consumer feedback through surveys and contests during campaigns.
4. SMM focuses on creating engaging content that sparks conversations, ultimately raising product awareness and expanding customer reach. It's a highly effective form of advertising that significantly contributes to enhancing consumer awareness about products and services.

For small businesses, social media marketing is crucial as it offers immense advantages. Networking and social platforms enable small businesses to thrive without the constraints of hefty advertising budgets.

Chan Irene Cheng Chu et al. (2023) investigated the strategic use of visual elements in social media marketing, emphasizing the importance of creating and employing visual content to engage, motivate, and prompt action from audiences. Their study aimed to expand the understanding of social media marketing by examining how visual concepts like volume, diversity, and vitality influence emotional and behavioral responses in social media users. The research highlighted that consumers' perceptions and actions towards restaurants were significantly impacted by their memories of advertising content, particularly in relation to visual volume, which is influenced by the change and dynamism in the visual environment. This study contributes both theoretically and practically to the realm of visual advertising marketing.

Jacobson et al. (2022), In their research study titled "Social Media Marketing: Who is Watching the Watchers?" sought to comprehend factors that alleviate consumer discomfort regarding emerging data processes in social media advertising. Their aim was to identify strategies employed by advertisers to support and diminish consumer anxiety, thereby maintaining consumer confidence in digital retail processes.

Duyen et al. (2022), assessed the impact of social media marketing (SMM) on customer loyalty within the telecommunications services sector in Vietnam. Their study specifically analyzed the effect of SMM activities on customer loyalty towards Mobifone Telecom's services. The research identified that various SMM activities directly influenced customer loyalty factors such as price balance, link loyalty, and product loyalty, highlighting the significant impact of SMM on customer retention within mobile phone services.

Bipul Kumar & Arun Sharma (2022) conducted a comprehensive analysis of 115 social media articles within the business-to-business sector to understand the landscape of marketing and social media research within these platforms. They categorized the field into four segments: social acceptance, platform usage for business communication, platform utilization within marketing processes and strategies. Their analysis provided insights into various facets of social media application, performance, and frameworks relevant to commercial and communication research.

Sedalo et al. (2022), explored the influence of social media on Small and Medium-sized Enterprises (SMEs) interactions with their clients. Employing the technology affordance theory, they investigated how SMEs in Ghana utilize social media platforms in their relationship marketing strategies. Their findings revealed three primary applications of social media platforms in SMEs: enhancing product visibility, facilitating content sharing, and nurturing customer relationships, resulting in an increased platform for consumer acquisition.

Upadhyay et al. (2022), In their study titled "Effect of Online Social Media Marketing Efforts on Customer Response," uncovered the positive impact of social media marketing on customer responses, particularly in enhancing brand equity and product trust among users of popular smartphone brands in India. The research explored the interaction between social media marketing, brand equity, product trust, and customer behavior, revealing insights into the nuanced relationship between these factors and their influence on consumer feedback and product reliability.

Khoaa Bui Thanh & Huynhb Tran Trong (2023) conducted a study focusing on the influence of social media marketing activities on customer loyalty in the e-commerce industry. Their research underscores the pivotal role of Web 2.0 in fostering customer engagement and collaboration within online commerce. They emphasize the necessity for online businesses to prioritize establishing and maintaining customer trust and loyalty in the digital realm. The study aimed to ascertain whether marketing campaigns enhance e-customer loyalty and trust online. Their survey of 596 participants revealed significant impacts of social media marketing tools on digital channels, affecting customer trust and loyalty towards businesses. These findings aim to aid in developing effective marketing strategies for internet-based companies.

Henceforth, targeting the social networks frequented by your audience is pivotal for success, requiring the right tools and marketing strategies tailored to those platforms. Social media is a powerful tool for businesses of all sizes, offering immense potential for reach, engagement, and growth. But navigating the ever-evolving landscape can be trick. To help you conquer the social media jungle, here's a roadmap packed with effective strategies:

1. **Goal Setting:** Start with the "why": What do you want to achieve with social media? Brand awareness, website traffic, leads, sales? Define SMART goals as Specific, Measurable, Achievable, Relevant, and Time-bound for each platform you use.
2. **Know Your Audience**: Who are you talking to? Understand their demographics, interests, online behavior, and pain points. Research your target audience through surveys, social listening tools, and competitor analysis.
3. **Platform Selection:** Not all platforms are created equal. Choose the ones where your audience spends their time. Focus on quality over quantity, and avoid spreading yourself too thin.
4. **Content is King (and Queen):** Create a compelling mix of content: Informative, educational, entertaining, and inspirational posts. Use visuals like images, videos, and infographics to grab attention.
5. **Engage and Interact:** Don't just broadcast, be social! Respond to comments and messages promptly, participate in conversations, and run contests and polls.
6. **Listen and Learn**: Monitor your social media performance regularly. Use analytics to track engagement, reach, and conversions. Analyze what's working and what's not, and adapt your strategy accordingly.
7. **Be Timely and Relevant:** Post at the right times, and tailor your content to current events and trends. Stay up-to-date on industry news and participate in relevant online conversations.
8. **Experiment and Innovate:** Don't be afraid to try new things. Test different content formats, platforms, and ad campaigns to see what resonates with your audience.
9. **Collaborate and Build Relationships:** Partner with influencers, other businesses, and community leaders. Share each other's content, host joint events, and leverage each other's audiences.
10. **Be Patient and Consistent:** Building a successful social media presence takes time and effort. Don't get discouraged by overnight success stories. Stay consistent with your posting schedule and keep delivering value to your audience.

1.1 Quick Summary

- Utilize automation tools to streamline your workflow.
- Invest in paid advertising for targeted reach and lead generation.
- Integrate social media with your other marketing channels.
- Stay informed about the latest social media trends and algorithms.

Remember, a successful social media strategy is a living document, constantly evolving to fit your brand's needs and the changing landscape. So, get out there, experiment, and connect with your audience! Few examples of the organizations who have used Social Media Marketing strategies to increase their customer base and create a long-lasting relationship with them.

1. **Airbnb:** Showcasing User-Generated Content:

Platform: Instagram
Strategy: Airbnb's Instagram feed is a beautiful tapestry of user-generated content, featuring stunning photos and videos of their unique rentals around the world. This not only inspires wanderlust but also builds trust and authenticity by showcasing real experiences from real guests.

2. **Dollar Shave Club**: Humor and Transparency:

Platform: YouTube
Strategy: Dollar Shave Club rose to fame with their hilarious and transparent YouTube videos. They poked fun at traditional razor companies, offered affordable subscription razors, and built a loyal fanbase through their relatable and down-to-earth approach.

3. **Lush Cosmetics:** Engaging with Social Causes:

Platform: Twitter
Strategy: Lush Cosmetics is known for its activism and commitment to social causes. They use Twitter to raise awareness about environmental issues, animal rights, and ethical sourcing. This resonates with their eco-conscious audience and strengthens their brand identity.

4. **Wendy's:** Master of Twitter Sass:

Platform: Twitter
Strategy: Wendy's Twitter game is on point! They're known for their witty replies, playful banter with other brands, and self-deprecating humor. This unexpected personality has attracted a large following and made them a cultural phenomenon.

5. **GoPro:** User-Generated Adventure:

Platform: Instagram and YouTube
Strategy: GoPro leverages user-generated content to showcase the possibilities of their action cameras. They encourage users to share their adventures through breathtaking videos and photos, capturing the thrill and excitement of extreme sports and travel.

6. **TOMS Shoes:** One for One Movement:

Platform: Facebook and Instagram
Strategy: TOMS Shoes' "One for One" movement, where they donate a pair of shoes to a child in need for every pair purchased, is a powerful social media story. They use platforms like Facebook and Instagram to share heartwarming stories of the impact their shoes have made, connecting with customers on an emotional level.

7. **Slack:** Building a Community:

Platform: Twitter and LinkedIn
Strategy: Slack uses Twitter and LinkedIn to build a community around workplace communication and productivity. They share helpful tips, host live Q&As with experts, and engage in relevant industry conversations. This positions them as thought leaders and attracts potential customers.

8. **Ben & Jerry's:** Chunky Monkey for Change:

Platform: Facebook and Twitter
Strategy: Ben & Jerry's isn't shy about taking a stand on social issues. Their "Chunky Monkey for Change" campaign used their popular ice cream flavor to advocate for racial justice and voting rights. This sparked conversations and showed their commitment to social responsibility.

These are just a few examples of how organizations can use social media marketing creatively and effectively. Remember, the key is to understand your audience, choose the right platforms, and create engaging content that resonates with your brand values.

1.2 Relationship Marketing

Relationship marketing involves establishing and nurturing enduring, cost-effective connections with specific clients, partners, and suppliers for mutual benefit. This approach aims to cultivate long-term relationships by comprehending customer needs, desires, and aspirations, ensuring a personalized and special purchase experience that fosters trust and loyalty towards the company. Renowned marketing expert Peter Drucker aptly expressed that when organizations foster long-term customer relationships, the sale of the product or service naturally follows.

The "millennial generation," as described by Tapscott (2009), expects interactive partnerships with companies due to their upbringing in technology and two-way communication. Relationship marketing, focusing on prolonged relationships over short-term gains, emphasizes customer retention as a priority, prioritizes exceptional customer service, encourages regular interaction, and fosters mutual commitment between customers and the company. It forms the basis for collaborative encounters and building trust.

Acquiring new customers is an expensive and challenging endeavor for businesses. According to business writers Emmett C. Murphy and Mark A. Murphy, acquiring a new customer can cost five times more than retaining an existing one. Therefore, businesses face the crucial decision of allocating resources to retain current clients or attempt to attract new ones. Enhancing client retention by a mere 2% can lead to a substantial 10% cost reduction, underscoring its importance for sustainable growth.

Businesses often differentiate between retaining existing customers and acquiring new ones, often assigning specific sales staff to each task. Relationship marketing techniques are employed to continually engage returning customers while maintaining current clientele. The ultimate objective remains the same: converting new customers into loyal repeat clients.

Various terms, such as interactive marketing, customer relationship management, loyalty marketing, one-to-one marketing, micromarketing, and direct marketing, have been used interchangeably or in conjunction with relationship marketing. However, the distinguishing feature among these methodologies is their transactional rather than relational nature (Egan, 2008). Relationship marketing builds upon traditional marketing concepts but is not an entirely independent ideology (Gordon, 1998).

Researchers view relationship marketing as a "marketing strategy," emphasizing the co-management of the marketing mix using the "4P model" (Grönroos, 1994; Henning-Thurau & Hansen, 2012; 2000; Sheth & Parvatiyar). Retaining and satisfying existing customers is deemed more profitable than acquiring new ones, forming the core principle of relationship marketing - identifying and retaining long-term customers.

Kanapathipillai Kumaran & Sharvena Kumaran (2022), In their research titled "The mediating effect of relationship marketing strategy between digital marketing strategy and consumers' purchase choices in the automotive industry in Malaysia," investigated the impact of online marketing strategies on consumers' decision-making processes in the Malaysian automotive industry. They observed that while not all customers are solely influenced by digital marketing, additional factors, such as social marketing strategies, play a role in consumer purchase decisions. Their study, involving 605 business owners in the automotive sector, analyzed the relationship between digital marketing strategies, social marketing approaches, and consumer choices. Results indicated a correlation between digital and relationship marketing strategies and their influence on consumer decision-making processes, particularly in the Malaysian automotive industry. The study highlights how stores utilizing digital marketing can foster customer communication and relationships, thereby influencing purchasing decisions positively.

Naga V. et al. (2022), investigated the impact of social media engagement on product visibility across various sectors including clothing, travel, jewelry, and mutual funds. They explored the relationships between trust, commitment, communication, and consumer engagement on social media platforms. Utilizing ANOVA analysis, the study focused on the interactions and associations among these variables, contributing insights into marketing relationships and their impact on customer engagement and product visibility on social media.

Badham Mark and Mykkänen Markus (2022), delved into how media entities engage with their audiences via social media platforms, particularly examining newspapers' interactions. They explored how media companies utilize social media to share content and engage audiences. Using the public relations theory of organization-society relations, the study scrutinized the strategies employed by nine leading newspapers from Australia, the USA, and the UK on Twitter and Facebook. The research findings indicated a tendency among media profiles to emphasize social media marketing over direct interaction with audiences, signaling a lack of attention towards audience engagement despite sharing news content.

Meena, P., & Sahu, P. (2021), conducted an extensive literature review on Customer Relationship Management (CRM) research spanning from 2000 to 2020. They examined various themes, theories, and prevalent study areas in CRM research, providing an inclusive overview of research types, data sources, and research areas over this 21-year period. The review encompassed data collection tools, sampling methods, sample countries, statistical analysis techniques, and key terminologies employed in CRM studies, highlighting the emphasis on customer relations, business relations, and information technology in education and research articles.

Durmaz Y. et al. (2020), aimed to elucidate the concept of relationship marketing and its significance. They emphasized the evolution of business relationships, coined by Berry in 1983, encompassing short, medium, and long-term customer relationships and their continuous development. The study highlighted the pivotal role of relationship marketing in ensuring customer satisfaction and success in the international market. The authors underscored the shift in big companies' business models towards prioritizing customer satisfaction, decision-making processes, and production strategies to enhance customer relations and achieve success in the global market.

While traditional marketing principles highlight the functional and procedural aspects, they often overlook the long-term value of the customer. Berry was among the first to introduce the term "social business," emphasizing the significance of attracting, managing, and fostering customer relationships, acknowledging that customer retention is as vital as acquiring new ones. Companies adopting relationship marketing principles focus on forging enduring relationships with their most valuable customers, recognizing the need for different communication approaches based on customer significance and level of engagement. In today's competitive market, it's more important than ever to focus on building lasting relationships with your customers. Here are some key strategies marketers can implement to foster loyalty and engagement:

1. **Personalization is Key**: Go beyond one-size-fits-all campaigns. Use customer data to personalize content, offers, and communication. Address customers by name, recommend products based on their purchase history, and tailor your messaging to their interests and needs.
2. **Customer-Centric Approach**: Shift your focus from product features to customer benefits. Understand their pain points and challenges, and showcase how your solutions can make their lives easier. Show empathy and appreciation for their business.
3. **Deliver Exceptional Service**: Treat every interaction as an opportunity to build trust and loyalty. Offer prompt and helpful customer service, go the extra mile to resolve issues, and proactively address potential concerns.
4. **Create Engaging Content:** Don't just sell, tell stories. Share valuable content that resonates with your audience, educates them, and entertains them. Host webinars, create informative blog posts, and share user-generated content to build a community around your brand.
5. **Build Lasting Connections:** Engage with your customers beyond transactional interactions. Organize events, contests, and loyalty programs to foster deeper connections and encourage advocacy. Respond to their feedback, participate in social conversations, and show you care about their opinions.
6. **Leverage Technology:** Use CRM tools to manage customer data effectively. Segment your audience, personalize campaigns, and track engagement metrics to measure the impact of your efforts. Automated workflows can help streamline communication and nurture leads.
7. **Cultivate Employee Advocacy:** Empower your employees to become brand ambassadors. Train them on your relationship marketing strategy and encourage them to interact with customers authentically. Their passion and enthusiasm can be contagious and build trust in your brand.
8. **Measure and Adapt:** Track key metrics like customer retention, lifetime value, and loyalty program engagement. Analyze your data to identify areas for improvement and adapt your strategies to continually enhance customer relationships.
9. **Celebrate Wins and Milestones:** Show your appreciation for loyal customers. Send personalized birthday messages, offer exclusive discounts, or reward them for repeat purchases. Recognize and celebrate their achievements to solidify the bond and encourage continued engagement.
10. **Build Trust and Transparency:** Be authentic and transparent in your communication. Be upfront about your pricing, acknowledge mistakes, and actively address customer concerns. Building trust will increase loyalty and foster positive word-of-mouth marketing.

Remember, relationship marketing is a long-term journey, not a sprint. By consistently implementing these strategies, you can nurture loyal relationships with your customers, increase customer lifetime value, and build a sustainable brand that thrives on genuine connections. Here are some compelling examples of how organizations across different industries are implementing successful relationship marketing strategies:

1. Starbucks Rewards:

Industry: Coffee
Strategy: A tiered loyalty program rewards frequent customers with free drinks, birthday treats, and exclusive offers. Personalized emails and in-app recommendations further strengthen the connection.

2. Patagonia Worn Wear:

Industry: Outdoor Apparel
Strategy: Patagonia facilitates the resale and repair of used Patagonia gear, extending the life of their products and creating a conscious community. This fosters brand loyalty and environmental responsibility.

3. Southwest Airlines Rapid Rewards:

Industry: Airlines
Strategy: A generous and flexible rewards program allows customers to redeem points for flights, merchandise, and even experiences. Coupled with their fun-loving brand personality and focus on customer service, this creates a loyal following.

4. Lego VIP Club:

Industry: Toys
Strategy: An exclusive club for Lego enthusiasts offers early access to new sets, member-only discounts, and personalized rewards. This builds a community of passionate fans and encourages repeat purchases.

5. Netflix Recommendations:

Industry: Streaming Services
Strategy: A highly personalized recommendation engine suggests shows and movies based on individual viewing habits. This nurtures long-term engagement and keeps users coming back for more.

6. Sephora Beauty Insider:

Industry: Cosmetics
Strategy: A tiered loyalty program with tiered benefits, birthday gifts, and access to exclusive beauty events. Personalized emails and recommendations based on purchase history further cultivate customer relationships.

7. Peloton Community:

Industry: Fitness
Strategy: A virtual fitness platform uses live and on-demand classes, social features, and leaderboards to create a strong sense of community. This motivates users, fosters engagement, and strengthens brand loyalty.

8. Spotify Discover Weekly:

Industry: Music Streaming
Strategy: This personalized playlist, updated weekly, introduces users to new music based on their listening habits. This fosters surprise and delight, encourages exploration, and strengthens user engagement.

9. REI Co-op:

Industry: Outdoor Gear
Strategy: REI focuses on providing expert advice and educational resources, hosting outdoor events, and building a community of outdoor enthusiasts. This goes beyond selling products and creates long-term relationships with customers.

10. Dove Real Beauty Campaign:

Industry: Personal Care
Strategy: Dove emphasizes diversity and inclusivity, celebrating real beauty in all its forms. This authentic storytelling resonates with customers and builds trust through emotional connection.

These examples showcase that effective relationship marketing goes beyond discounts and points. It's about understanding your customers, providing value beyond the product, and building emotional connections that keep them coming back for more.

1.3 Social Media Marketing Strategies for Innovating Relationship Marketing by the Various Organizations in Digital Era

Social Media Marketing users engage in interactions concerning the latest promotions offered by companies, contributing positively to building and strengthening their relationship with these providers. The promotions through social media platforms enable them to stay updated on current schemes and trends available in the market. Consequently, users can compare these trends and make informed decisions. Furthermore, users mentioned that understanding these trends allows for customized offers tailored to their specific usage needs, fostering trust and strengthening their relationship with telecom providers. Moreover, users tend to share the latest trends and promotional offers with their acquaintances, fostering word-of-mouth communication. This kind of interaction among users creates a chain reaction, leading to increased empathy and stronger relationships with companies.

Organizations can leverage social media in exciting ways to foster deeper, more dynamic relationships with their customers. Here are some ideas for innovative strategies:

1. Hyper-personalization:
    a) **Go beyond basic audience segmentation**: Utilize AI and advanced analytics to personalize messaging, content, and offers based on individual preferences, behaviors, and real-time interactions.
    b) **Interactive content & quizzes**: Use polls, quizzes, and personalized product recommendations to engage customers and gather valuable data to refine your personalization efforts.
2. Community building & co-creation:
    a) **Create dedicated online communities**: Foster a space for customers to connect, share experiences, and provide feedback. Host live Q&As, contests, and collaborative projects to encourage participation and build a sense of belonging.
    b) **User-generated content (UGC) amplification:** Share and celebrate customer-created content that showcases your products or services in action. This builds trust, authenticity, and organic reach.
3. Conversational marketing & AI chatbots:
    a) **Implement chatbots for personalized customer service:** Offer 24/7 support, answer questions, and guide customers through their journey. Use AI to personalize interactions and build relationships.
    b) **Interactive storytelling & experiences:** Develop engaging campaigns that allow users to choose their path, influence the narrative, and participate in brand story telling.
4. Gamification & loyalty programs:
    a) **Integrate gamification elements** like points, badges, and leaderboards into your social media presence. Encourage participation, incentivize desired behaviors, and reward loyal customers.
    b) **Exclusive social media** features for loyalty program members: Offer early access to products, VIP experiences, and behind-the-scenes content to solidify loyalty and reward engagement.
5. Social listening & real-time engagement:
    a) **Actively monitor conversations** about your brand and industry on social media. Respond to mentions, address concerns, and participate in relevant discussions to build relationships with potential customers.
    b) **Live video interactions:** Host live Q&As, product demos, or behind-the-scenes tours to connect with your audience in real-time and create a more personal experience.
6. Influencer marketing & social advocacy:
    a) **Partner with relevant influencers** who resonate with your target audience. Leverage their reach and authenticity to build trust and promote your brand in a relatable way.
    b) **Empower your customers as brand advocates**: Encourage them to share their experiences, participate in social campaigns, and promote your brand organically.
7. Social commerce & seamless buying:
    a) **Make it easy for customers** to purchase directly from your social media platforms. Integrate shoppable features, offer exclusive deals, and streamline the checkout process for a seamless omnichannel experience.
    b) **Personalized product recommendations & shopping experiences**: Leverage AI and social media data to recommend products based on individual preferences and browsing history.

8. Social responsibility & cause marketing:
    a) **Align your brand with social causes** that resonate with your audience. Partner with relevant organizations, participate in impactful campaigns, and leverage social media to raise awareness and drive positive change.
    b) **Customer co-creation for social impact**: Allow customers to choose which causes their purchases support, or co-develop products that benefit specific communities.

Remember, the key to success lies in authenticity, relevance, and constant innovation. By understanding your audience and incorporating these creative strategies, you can turn social media into a powerful tool for building meaningful relationships and driving business growth.

2. CONCLUSION

Based on the study findings, several recommendations can be proposed for the telecom industry to enhance their sales and cultivate stronger relationships with customers, aiming to bolster loyalty, trust, and bonding:

1. **Leveraging Social Media Platforms**: Given the surge in active user populations on social media platforms, especially during the COVID-19 pandemic, telecom companies should harness the unique capabilities of these platforms. Engaging with social media effectively can lead to heightened consumer engagement and influence, fostering stronger connections with customers.
2. **Collaboration with Social Media Players**: Collaborating with key social media players can significantly impact various touchpoints in the customer lifecycle for telecom companies. Partnering with these platforms can yield medium to high influence, enhancing engagement and outreach among consumers.
3. **Utilizing Social Media Marketing Strategies:** Employing effective social media marketing strategies will be pivotal for the Telecommunications industry in expanding its customer base. Leveraging these strategies can lead to increased brand visibility, customer engagement, and ultimately, acquisition.
4. **Building Solid Customer Relationships**: Recognizing the significance of robust customer relationships is crucial for the telecom sector. Strengthening relationships through personalized experiences, effective communication, and understanding customer needs can foster loyalty and trust.
5. **Cultivating Devoted Customers**: Understanding the value of cultivating devoted customers who become brand advocates is vital. Satisfied customers are more likely to spread positive word-of-mouth about their experiences, contributing to the industry's reputation and customer acquisition.
6. Social media has emerged as a **viable option** for businesses aiming to adopt a relationship marketing approach. This platform facilitates direct and interactive communication between businesses and their customers, enabling personalized interactions and fostering stronger relationships. Through social media, businesses can engage with their audience in real-time, gather feedback, address concerns, and provide tailored solutions, thereby nurturing long-term relationships and enhancing customer satisfaction. The interactive nature of social media platforms allows businesses to create a sense of community, where customers feel heard, valued, and connected, contributing to the evolution of relationship-based marketing strategies.

Implementing these strategies can empower the various industry to harness the potential of social media platforms, strengthen relationships with customers, and create a loyal customer base, ultimately enhancing their market presence and influence.

REFERENCES

Badham, M., & Mykkänen, M. (2022). A Relational Approach to How Media Engage With Their Audiences in Social Media. *Media and Communication*, *10*(1), 54–65. doi:10.17645/mac.v10i1.4409

Batta A, Kaur S, Jhamb R. (2022). *A literature Review on Social Media Marketing influence on Customer Relationship Management*.

Durmaz, Y., Güvenç, H., & Kaymaz, S. (2020). The Importance and Benefits of Relationship Marketing Concept. *European Journal of Business and Management Research*, *5*(4), 4–5. doi:10.24018/ejbmr.2020.5.4.483

Duyên, P., Công, L., & Duy, N. (2022). The impact of social media marketing on customer loyalty using telecommunications services in Vietnam. *Science & Technology Development Journal: Economics- Law & Management, 6*(2), 2516-2529. https://doi.org/https://doi.org/10.32508/stdjelm.v6i1.916

Finotto V. & Micelli S. (2010). Web e made in Italy: La terra di mezzo della comunicazione d'impresa. *Mercati e Competitività*, (4), 101–119.

Grönroos, C. (2004). The relationship marketing process: Communication, interaction, dialogue, value. *Journal of Business and Industrial Marketing*, *19*(2), 99–113. doi:10.1108/08858620410523981

Hennig-Thurau, T., Gwinner, K. P., & Gremier, D. D. (2002). Understanding relationship marketing outcomes: An integration of relational benefits and relationship quality. *Journal of Service Research*, *4*(3), 230–247. doi:10.1177/1094670502004003006

Irene, C. C. C., Chen, Z., & Leung, D. (2023). The more the better? Strategizing visual elements in social media marketing. *Journal of Hospitality and Tourism Management, 54*.

Jacobson, J., Gruzd, A., & Hernández-García, Á. (2020). Social Media Marketing: Who is Watching the Watchers? *Journal of Retailing and Consumer Services*, *53*, 1–12. doi:10.1016/j.jretconser.2019.03.001

Kaplan, A. M., & Haenlein, M. (2010). Users of the world, unite! The challenges and opportunities of Social Media. *Business Horizons*, *53*(1), 59–68. doi:10.1016/j.bushor.2009.09.003

Kaur, B. (2022). *Literature Review on Relationship Between Types of Purchases and Usage of Digital Payment Methods*. Academy of Marketing Studies.

Khoa, T., & Huynh, T. T. (2023). The influence of social media marketing activities on customer loyalty: A study of e-commerce industry. *International Journal of Data and Network Science.*, *7*(1), 175–184. doi:10.5267/j.ijdns.2022.11.005

Kumar, B., & Sharma, A. (2022). Examining the research on social media in business-to-business marketing with a focus on sales and the selling process. *Industrial Marketing Management, 102*. doi:10.1016/j.indmarman.2022.01.008

Meena, P., & Sahu, P. (2021). Customer Relationship Management Research from 2000 to 2020: An Academic Literature Review and Classification. *Vision (Basel), 25*(2), 136–158. doi:10.1177/0972262920984550

Naga, V., Challa, S. K., Padmalatha, P., & Vamsi, B. (2022). Influence of Relationship Marketing Variables on Social Media Marketing. *The Empirical Economics Letters., 20*, 241–249.

Sedalo, G., Boateng, H., & Kosiba, J. P. (2022). Exploring social media affordance in relationship marketing practices in SMEs. *Digital Business, 2*. doi:10.1016/j.digbus.2021.100017

Upadhyay, Y., Paul, J., & Baber, R. (2022). Effect of online social media marketing efforts on customer response. *Journal of Consumer Behaviour, 21*(3), 554–571. doi:10.1002/cb.2031

Chapter 13
Employer Branding:
Pioneering HR Innovations

Pallavi Pahuja
CGC Landran, India

Ruby Sharma
CBSA, CGC Landran, India

Aaruni Batta
CBSA, CGC Landran, India

ABSTRACT

In today's fiercely competitive job market, establishing a positive image of your company as an employer of choice is paramount. This is the essence of employer branding - a dynamic process that aims to attract and retain top talent by effectively communicating a company's culture, values, and employee value proposition (EVP). HR leaders are pivotal in shaping and sustaining a compelling employer brand. By embracing innovative HR practices, they can craft workplaces that not only lure in the best talent, but also facilitate their growth and development.

1. INTRODUCTION

In today's fiercely competitive job market, establishing a positive image of your company as an employer of choice is paramount. This is the essence of employer branding - a dynamic process that aims to attract and retain top talent by effectively communicating a company's culture, values, and Employee Value Proposition (EVP).

HR leaders are pivotal in shaping and sustaining a compelling employer brand. By embracing innovative HR practices, they can craft workplaces that not only lure in the best talent but also facilitate their growth and development.

DOI: 10.4018/979-8-3693-2019-8.ch013

1.1 Concept of Employer Branding

Employer branding is the process of creating a positive image of your company as a potential employer. It is about attracting and retaining the best talent by communicating your company's culture, values, and employee value proposition (EVP).

Your employer brand is what sets your company apart from other employers and makes it an attractive place to work. It is the sum total of all of the experiences that people have with your company, both as employees and as outsiders.

A strong employer brand is important because it can help you to:

Attract top talent

Reduce employee turnover

Improve employee engagement

Increase employee productivity

Boost brand awareness and reputation

1.2 Theoretical Base of Employer Branding

The theoretical base of employer branding is drawn from a variety of fields, including marketing, human resources, and organizational psychology.

One of the key theories that underpin employer branding is the concept of employee value proposition (EVP). The EVP is the unique set of benefits that your company offers to its employees. It should be clear, concise, and compelling, and it should be communicated to potential employees throughout the recruitment process.

Another important theory that informs employer branding is the concept of employee engagement. Employee engagement is the degree to which employees are committed to their jobs and to their organization. Highly engaged employees are more likely to be productive, satisfied with their jobs, and loyal to their employer.

Employer branding can also be linked to the theory of organizational identity. Organizational identity is the way that an organization sees itself and how it wants to be seen by others. A strong employer brand is one that is aligned with the organization's overall identity. Employer branding is a complex and ever-evolving discipline. However, the core principles remain the same: to create and communicate a positive image of your company as a potential employer. By implementing a strong employer branding strategy, companies can attract and retain the best talent, create a positive employee experience, and build a strong reputation as an employer of choice.

Examples of innovative HR practices for employer branding are:

- **Employee referral programs:** Employee referral programs are a great way to attract and retain top talent. By incentivizing employees to refer their friends and family for jobs at the company, companies can tap into their existing network of employees to find qualified candidates.
- **Employer branding campaigns:** Employer branding campaigns can be used to raise awareness of the company's culture, values, and EVP. These campaigns can be run through a variety of channels, such as social media, job boards, and the company's website.
- **Transparency and feedback:** Transparency and feedback are essential for creating a positive employee experience. Companies can promote transparency by sharing information about the

company's performance, goals, and plans with employees. Companies can also encourage feedback from employees by conducting employee surveys and focus groups.
- **Employee development:** Employee development is a critical component of any strong HR strategy. By offering employees opportunities to learn and grow, companies can help them to reach their full potential and contribute to the company's success.

By implementing innovative HR practices, companies can create a workplace that is attractive to top talent and that helps employees to thrive. This can lead to a number of benefits, such as improved employee engagement, productivity, and retention.

Some of the brands using innovations in HR to enhance Employer Branding are:

- **Netflix:** Netflix is known for its innovative HR practices, such as its unlimited paid time off policy, its focus on employee development, and its strong culture of transparency and feedback.
- **Google:** Google is another company that is known for its innovative HR practices. Google offers its employees a variety of benefits, such as free meals, on-site childcare, and tuition reimbursement. Google also has a strong culture of diversity and inclusion, and it is committed to creating a workplace where all employees feel valued and respected.
- **Spotify:** Spotify is a music streaming company that is known for its innovative HR practices. Spotify offers its employees a variety of benefits, such as free Spotify subscriptions, on-site concerts, and travel allowances. Spotify also has a strong culture of innovation and collaboration, and it encourages its employees to be creative and to take risks.
- **Airbnb:** Airbnb is a short-term rental company that is known for its innovative HR practices. Airbnb offers its employees a variety of benefits, such as unlimited vacation days, travel stipends, and a generous stock grant program. Airbnb also has a strong culture of diversity and inclusion, and it is committed to creating a workplace where all employees feel welcome and respected.
- **HubSpot:** HubSpot is a marketing software company that is known for its innovative HR practices. HubSpot offers its employees a variety of benefits, such as a flexible work schedule, a generous parental leave policy, and a commitment to employee development. HubSpot also has a strong culture of transparency and feedback, and it encourages its employees to be involved in the decision-making process.

These are just a few examples of the many innovative HR practices that companies are using to build and maintain a strong employer brand. By implementing innovative HR practices, companies can attract and retain the best talent, create a positive employee experience, and build a strong reputation as an employer of choice.

2. LITERATURE REVIEW

Sumarsi (2022) stated that an organization's dedication to its employees is significantly influenced by employee competency. Quality of life at work also has a positive impact on employees' organizational commitment, and employee competency has a significant positive impact on organizational citizenship behavior. Association responsibility meaningfully affects hierarchical citizenship conduct, but the nature of the workplace valuably affects it.

Ahmad et al. (2022) directed a concentrate in Public Bank of Pakistan and observed that there is areas of strength for a between representative maintenance and worker inspiration among though representatives' preparation and improvement has extremely less to do with representatives' maintenance. In order to assist the banks in keeping their employees for a longer period of time, it was suggested that they modify their practices and policies regarding training and development .

Barik & Jain (2022) conducted a study during Covid 19 to investigate the impact of employer branding on employee retention. Using Anova, correlation, regression, and employees of academic institutions, the study was conducted. EB factors like culture, WLB, reputation, and job security all have a big effect on ER.

Sindhuja et al. (2020) encompassed that employee retention is positively and directly impacted by the work-life balance of the employees. Additionally, it will aid in increasing employee retention and work satisfaction in the banking sector. 245 banking industry respondents took part in the study.

Gupta et al. (2021) elaborated the concept of Employer branding experience has a direct, favourable relationship with corporate citizenship behavior, according to Additionally, it was discovered that the relationship between corporate citizenship behavior and employer branding experience is mediated by employee engagement.

Scullion, L. (2020) Proposes the concept of "experiential employer branding." This approach focuses on creating positive experiences for employees throughout the entire employee lifecycle, from recruitment and onboarding to development and retention.

Parry, E., & Tracey, P. (2012) Highlight the concept of "employer brand narrative." They suggest that organizations craft a compelling story that articulates their purpose, mission, and values in a way that resonates with potential and current employees.

3. KEY DRIVERS, EMERGING AS DISRUPTION IN HR

3.1 Data-Driven Decision Making

One of the linchpins of modern HR innovation is data-driven decision making. Scholars like Bersin (2013) argue that the integration of data into HR processes has become essential. This paradigm shift enables HR leaders to glean profound insights into their workforce, illuminating areas ripe for improvement in the employee experience. In their seminal work, Davenport, Harris, and Shapiro (2010) emphasize the pivotal role of data analytics in every facet of HR - from recruitment and onboarding to performance management and succession planning. "As Bersin (2013) argues in his article 'The Datafication of HR', utilizing data in HR processes has become increasingly crucial. This is echoed by Davenport, Harris, and Shapiro (2010) in their research on 'Competing on talent analytics', which emphasizes the importance of data-driven decision making in HR practices."

For example, HR leaders can use data to:

- Identify employees who are at risk of leaving the company and develop programs to help them stay.
- Identify employees who are ready for new challenges and promote them into more senior roles.
- Track employee engagement levels and identify areas where they can be improved.
- Measure the effectiveness of training and development programs.

3.2 Artificial Intelligence in HR

Another groundbreaking innovation is the infusion of Artificial Intelligence (AI) into HR practices. Marler and Boudreau (2017) provide a comprehensive review of HR Analytics, shedding light on the rising importance of AI in modern HR. This transformative technology automates myriad HR tasks, liberating HR professionals to focus on strategic endeavors. Amazon's adept use of AI in automating tasks like resume screening and interview scheduling is a testament to its potential (Lepak & Sablynski, 2019).

"Marler and Boudreau (2017) provide an evidence-based review of HR Analytics, emphasizing the growing significance of artificial intelligence in HR practices. Furthermore, Lepak and Sablynski (2019) present a contingency model highlighting the integration of artificial intelligence in talent management."

For example, AI can be used to:

- Screen resumes and schedule interviews.
- Provide personalized employee onboarding experiences.
- Create personalized learning and development plans.
- Provide employee support and coaching.

3.3 Elevating Employee Experience

Prioritizing Employee Experience (EX) is a cornerstone of progressive HR. Albrecht (2010) extensively covers the concept of employee engagement in his work 'Handbook of employee engagement,' emphasizing its pivotal role in organizational success. Companies like Netflix exemplify this approach, offering unparalleled benefits such as unlimited paid time off and an unwavering commitment to employee development. Their culture of transparency and constructive feedback fosters an environment where employees thrive (Albrecht, 2010).

Albrecht (2010) extensively covers the concept of employee engagement in his 'Handbook of employee engagement', shedding light on the critical role of employee experience in organizational success. Moreover, Grant and Parker (2009) in the *Handbook of Organizational Psychology* discuss the evolution of work design towards more relational and proactive forms, emphasizing the importance of employee experience."

For example, HR leaders can:

- Offer employee wellness programs that promote physical, mental, and emotional health.
- Provide flexible work arrangements, such as telecommuting and compressed workweeks.
- Offer opportunities for professional development, such as tuition reimbursement and in-house training programs.
- Create a culture of feedback and recognition, so that employees feel valued and appreciated for their contri

3.4 Championing Diversity, Equity, and Inclusion

Inclusion and diversity have emerged as non-negotiable aspects of a robust employer brand. Cox (1994) delves into the complexities of cultural diversity in organizations in his work 'Cultural diversity in organizations: Theory, research, and practice.' Spotify's commitment to Diversity, Equity, and Inclusion

(DEI) is palpable. Their robust culture of inclusion, complemented by initiatives like unconscious bias training and employee resource groups, stands as a testament to their dedication to DEI (Kalev, Dobbin, & Kelly, 2006).

"Cox (1994) delves into the complexities of cultural diversity in organizations in his work 'Cultural diversity in organizations: Theory, research, and practice'. Additionally, Kalev, Dobbin, and Kelly (2006) critically assess the effectiveness of corporate affirmative action and diversity policies, highlighting the importance of adopting best practices in promoting diversity, equity, and inclusion."

For example, HR leaders can:

- Provide unconscious bias training to all employees, including managers and executives.
- Create employee resource groups for different identity groups
- Implement fair hiring practices that ensure that all qualified candidates are considered for jobs.

3.5 Implementing Innovative Practices

Embarking on these innovative HR practices requires a strategic approach. Firstly, comprehending the intricacies of your workforce is imperative. Employee surveys and focus groups are invaluable tools (Bersin, 2013). Armed with this understanding, harnessing data to make informed decisions becomes the linchpin. It enables targeted interventions to enhance the employee experience (Davenport, Harris, & Shapiro, 2010). Embracing creativity and novelty is essential - be open to exploring new avenues to enthrall and retain top talent.

Collaboration across departments is pivotal. Partnering with marketing and sales amplifies the impact of employer branding efforts. For instance, joint initiatives can target specific audiences, while employee referral programs, a collaborative effort of HR and sales, can be instrumental in attracting potential hires (Bersin, 2013).

3.6 How HR Leaders Can Implement Innovative Practices?

In today's dynamic business landscape, HR leaders play a crucial role in driving innovation and ensuring a competitive edge for their organizations. Implementing innovative practices in HR goes beyond just adopting new technologies; it's about fostering a culture that embraces change, empowers employees, and prioritizes continuous improvement. Here are some key strategies HR leaders can leverage:

3.7 Culture of Innovation

Encourage experimentation and risk-taking: Create a safe space for employees to share ideas, even if they seem unconventional. Celebrate failures as learning opportunities and reward calculated risks.

Foster collaboration and open communication: Break down silos and encourage cross-functional teams to work together on innovative projects. Implement open communication channels where employees feel comfortable voicing their opinions and suggestions.

Empower employees: Give employees ownership of their work and the freedom to make decisions. Provide them with the resources and training they need to be successful.

Recognize and reward innovative behavior: Acknowledge and celebrate employees who contribute to a culture of innovation through awards, bonuses, or other forms of recognition.

3.8 Technology and Data

Embrace HR technology: Utilize HR tech solutions to automate routine tasks, streamline processes, and gain valuable insights into your workforce. This can free up HR professionals' time to focus on strategic initiatives.

Leverage data analytics: Use data to inform your HR decisions and identify areas for improvement. Track employee engagement, performance, and turnover to understand your workforce better and make data-driven decisions.

Implement AI-powered tools: Explore the potential of artificial intelligence (AI) for tasks like resume screening, candidate matching, and performance management. However, ensure ethical implementation and consider potential biases.

3.9 Specific Innovative Practices

Personalized learning and development: Offer customized training and development opportunities based on individual needs and career goals. This can involve microlearning modules, mentorship programs, or tuition reimbursement.

Flexible work arrangements: Implement flexible work policies like remote work, hybrid schedules, and compressed workweeks to improve employee well-being and attract top talent.

Focus on employee experience: Design a positive employee experience from onboarding to offboarding, prioritizing employee well-being, engagement, and recognition.

Diversity and inclusion initiatives: Build a diverse and inclusive workplace by implementing unconscious bias training, promoting equal opportunities, and fostering a culture of belonging.

HR leaders can implement innovative practices for employer branding in a number of ways. Here are a few tips:

- **Start by understanding your workforce:** The first step is to understand your workforce and what they are looking for in an employer. You can do this by conducting employee surveys and focus groups.
- **Use data to make informed decisions:** Once you understand your workforce, you can use data to make informed decisions about how to improve the employee experience. For example, you can use data to identify areas where employees are struggling and to develop programs to help them.
- **Be creative and innovative:** Don't be afraid to try new things. There are many innovative HR practices that you can implement to attract and retain top talent.
- **Partner with other departments:** HR leaders can partner with other departments, such as marketing and sales, to promote the company's employer brand. For example, HR and marketing can work together to create employer branding campaigns that target specific audiences. HR and sales can also work together to develop employee referral programs that encourage employees to refer their friends and family for jobs at the company.

4. CONCLUSION

Employer branding, driven by innovative HR practices, is the cornerstone of a thriving workplace. Through data-driven insights, the integration of AI, a focus on employee experience, and an unwavering commitment to diversity, equity, and inclusion, HR leaders are poised to create environments that not only attract top talent but also inspire them to flourish.

REFERENCES

Ahmad, N., Shahbaz, M., & Ijaz, U. (2022). The impact of employee training and development on employee motivation and retention: Evidence from Public Bank of Pakistan. *Pakistan Journal of Social Sciences*, *14*(1), 172–182.

Albrecht, S. L. (2010). *Handbook of employee engagement: Perspectives, issues, research and practice*. Edward Elgar Publishing. doi:10.4337/9781849806374

Barik, T., & Jain, S. (2022). Employer branding and employee retention during COVID-19: A study of academic institutions. *International Journal of Human Resource Management*, *33*(11), 2505–2533.

Davenport, T. H., Harris, J., & Shapiro, J. (2010). Competing on talent analytics. *Harvard Business Review*. PMID:20929194

Gupta, M., Khan, F., & Gupta, N. (2021). The influence of employer branding experience on corporate citizenship behavior: The mediating role of employee engagement. *Journal of Business Ethics*, *168*(3), 583–602.

Kaur, B. (2022). *Literature Review on Relationship Between Types of Purchases and Usage of Digital Payment Methods*. Academy of Marketing Studies.

Lepak, D. P., & Sablynski, C. J. (2019). A contingency model of artificial intelligence in talent management. *The Journal of Applied Psychology*, *104*(12), 1578–1596.

Marler, J. H., & Boudreau, J. W. (2017). An evidence-based review of HR Analytics. *International Journal of Human Resource Management*, *28*(1), 3–26. doi:10.1080/09585192.2016.1244699

Scullion, L. (2020). Experiential employer branding: A new paradigm for talent attraction and retention. *Journal of Marketing Management*, *36*(9-10), 905–922.

Sharma, R., & Pahuja, P. (2020). A Study on Service Quality of Banks in Tricity. *International Journal of Advanced Science and Technology*, *29*(11s), 1067–1077.

Sindhuja, S., Arora, H., & Kumar, R. (2020). Impact of work-life balance on employee retention and job satisfaction in the banking sector. *International Journal of Business and Social Science*, *11*(2), 350–357.

Sumarsi, A. (2022). The impact of employee competency and quality of life at work on organizational commitment and organizational citizenship behavior. *International Journal of Management and Humanities*, *4*(3), 97–104.

Chapter 14
Robo-Finance Unveiled:
A Bibliometric Analysis of Advisory Services in Financial Management

Divya Goswami
Chitkara Business School, Chitkara University, India

Balraj Verma
https://orcid.org/0000-0002-6542-3261
Chitkara Business School, Chitkara University, India

ABSTRACT

The study aims to correlate financial investment advice with investors, using Scopus and VOS viewer to analyze prominent authors and journals. Gomber emerged as a leading writer, with journals like The Journal of Management Information Systems and Journal of Behavioral and Experimental Finance standing out. These journals have gained significant citations for research on financial advice. Future studies should focus on cognitive biases, financial technology, roboadvisors, financial behavior, and AI. Conducting longitudinal research on market efficiency, decision-making dynamics, information asymmetries, and investor intelligence can enhance financial advice quality. This research provides a foundation and suggestions for future studies in financial advising, especially for investors.

1. INTRODUCTION

According to Beketov et al. (2018), Robo-advisors is a computerized investing portal that use statistical techniques to oversee investor portfolios. Robo-advisors is an advisor in finance that provides an online investing portfolio tracking service using analytics and technology. In the context of financial investment, the term "Robo" can refer to the use of robotic technology in trading or as an advisor. These applications utilize algorithms to automate financial transactions, taking into account factors such as a period of time cost, amount, and other economical features. This approach presents a novel opportunity for prospective financiers (Baek et al., 2020).The rapid development of technological advances drives a shift in human behavior, enabling the establishment of connectivity between devices, faster and more convenient use

DOI: 10.4018/979-8-3693-2019-8.ch014

of information, and reduced transaction costs. Conversely, a robo-advisor can be seen as an upgraded version of the conventional financial consultant, as it leverages technology as its main resource and provides personalized investment options based on an individual's risk profile. Robo-advisors are a perfect tool for novice investors who wish to commence investing. They are particularly beneficial for investors who own surplus savings and have an inclination to vary their holdings. Financial Robo-Advisor has gained popularity leading to a growth in the number of investors, particularly in emerging nations. Several financial services are experiencing rapid growth in order to attract investors, especially younger generations, by providing numerous conveniences, simplicity, and personalized advisors. Robo-advisors have emerged in response to the forward-thinking digitalization, expanding e-commerce industry, and the introduction of algorithmic trading. These automated platforms offer a comprehensive investment experience to a wide range of prospective clients (Jung et al., 2018; Sironi, 2016). These virtual advisers not only construct and allocate funds to a portfolio based on the investor's risk choice, but also actively oversee the investments, taking into account market fluctuations as well as shifts in asset attributes. The robo-advisory idea is perceived as having tremendous upside by entrepreneurs and other stakeholders.

The trend necessitates the development of an in-depth investigation on the latest developments in the field of financial robo-advisors. The present research intends to investigate the current research on financial robo-advisors by a bibliometric evaluation utilizing Scopus database and VOS-viewer programs. *Bibliometric analysis* is a prevalent technique for examining extensive amounts of scientific data, enabling the identification of patterns within a particular scientific discipline (Donthu et al., 2021). In order to achieve this objective, the next section outlines the research methods employed to conduct a bibliometric review. Subsequently, the acquired outcomes are defined from a comprehensive perspective. Ultimately, this study outlines the conclusions that have been drawn, along with the subsequent actions required to conduct a more comprehensive and meticulous investigation.

2. THEORETICAL REVIEW

The initially launched robo-advisor business started in America in 2008, and its enormous popularity drew billions of dollars in funding for this industry (Epperson et al., 2015) Since then, several organizations have entered this sector, including innovative startups, banks, and even technological companies(Fisch et al.,2018). It has been established that the usage of robo-advisors is a great possibility to transform the investment business. The development of modern technology to enable securities trade, processing of transactions, and advisory services to users has been one sector that has steadily evolved over the previous 50 years (Schwinn and Teo, 2017).Although extensive research has been undertaken on robo-advisors as well as additional kinds of digital financial information, there have been little efforts to properly review these results. Bhatia et al. (2021) state that Robo-advisers have a broad acknowledged as a novel tools in the economic-expertise (FinTech) industry, and present research on this subject is limited in its coverage. Furthermore, the robo-advisory services sector is still in its nascent phase and is undergoing ongoing development and advancement. Historically, only wealthy individuals had access to personalized investing guidance, mostly due to the excessively high fees typically associated with such services. However, the financial advisory sector is subject to ongoing change and has recently been accessible to budget-conscious investors (Jung et al., 2017). Yeh et al. (2023) have observed that the rise of robo-advisors is a moderately new occurrence, leading to a scarcity of study focused on investigating the related problems and difficulties. Kraiwanit et al. (2022) did a study investigating how the designs and mechanics of robo-advisers affect individuals' economic decision-making. The findings indicate that only a small group of individuals have comprehended the ways in which these elements can impact the formation of financial choices. This study aims to fill the research gap about research routines and developments in the field of robo-advisory.

Robo Advisor employs advanced learning by yourself Artificial Intelligence investing algorithms that may adapt the investor's categories of assets in real-time based on altering the marketplace and financial requirements. The main objective of the present research was to investigate the impact of artificially intelligent technology on the supervision of emerging initiatives in recent years. *Bibliometric analysis* is a prevalent technique for examining extensive amounts of scientific data, enabling the identification of patterns within a particular scientific discipline (Donthu et al., 2021). In order to achieve this objective, the next section outlines the research methods employed to conduct a bibliometric review Subsequently, the acquired outcomes are defined from a comprehensive perspective. Ultimately, this study outlines the conclusions that have been drawn, along with the subsequent actions required to conduct a more comprehensive and meticulous investigation.

The financing sector was one of the first industries of service to face technological changes. Prior to the financial meltdown of 2008, the sector was known for its "corporate stability and secure jobs". Currently, financial institutions must stay abreast of technology advancements, disruptions in processes, and transformations in services (P.Gomber,et al., 2018). Traditional corporations face a threat from FinTech companies if they do not successfully adjust to these developments Emerging innovations for financial services include artificial intelligence (AI), analysis of data, blockchain technology, and robo-advising (Jiang et al.,2021).Despite the benefits of these technologies, there are also obstacles and hazards that need to be addressed. This can be done by involving humans in the decision-making process and creating novel divisions of labour. However, there is an increasing need for digital service options as clients shift away from conventional human contacts. In order to maintain the involvement of skilled professionals, the sector need a "future-oriented advice provision model" that offers new and appealing services. (Graseck et al.,2020)

3. METHODOLOGY

In this course of research Bibliometric Analysis was utilized to make solid body of data that can be used to make suggestions to the academicians and researchers. The insights for the Bibliometric analysis encompasses two distinct methodologies for analysis: Performance Analysis and Scientific Mapping (Donthu et al., 2021). Performance Analysis examines the different components of research, whereas science mapping investigates the methodologies that explore the connection among these components. The scientific mapping process employs several techniques such as Citations analysis, co-citation evaluation, bibliographical coupling, co-word evaluation, and co-authorship analyses are all methods used in the field of bibliometrics to study the relationships and connections between scholarly publications, researchers, and concepts.. Co-word analysis was employed in this study. This research examines the specific material included in the publication based on the keywords provided by the authors or their frequent appearance in titles, descriptions, or complete texts (Methlagl, 2022). The investigation utilized Scopus as its main source of information. Scopus is an information system that was created to store abstracts and citations in 2004 by Elsevier (2022), and it is recognized as one of the leading bibliographic referral libraries (Baas et al., 2022). Aside from the utilized source, the accuracy of the keyword phrases employed is another crucial factor in bibliometric analysis.

Table 1. Search protocol

Databank	Period	Type of Document	Search Standards	Keywords
Scopus	Untill 14/12/22	Article,ConferencePaper,BookChapter, Review, Book	Article title, Abstract, Keywords	"Robo-Advi*"

3.1 Research Objectives

Formulating the objectives of the study is a crucial step in the methodical review of the literature beginning a research investigation. Formulating research goals demonstrates a thorough comprehension of the entire subject matter and the particular research problem being addressed. An extensive inquiry was conducted to discover relevant scholarly material in order to improve understanding of the research problem. Objectives were established according to the study strategy described in the academic sources listed earlier. The study aims to achieve the following enquiry about "*What is the level of maturity of research on Robo-Advisors? Does the study topic have a specific focus on authors, countries, or journals?*"

Based on the summaries of the publications in our reference collection, we have discerned three primary areas of investigation. One category of papers focuses on issues with relationships and human behavior, while another category focuses on the implementation of new analytical algorithms. These algorithms are related to estimating profitability and risks, interpreting financial parameters, and optimizing portfolios of investments. This article examines the current understanding of Robo-Advisors A by analyzing the information and methods employed. The text provides a concise summary of its primary discoveries, extracting the principal subjects and the most recent developments in research. Ultimately, the document concludes by presenting the findings and outcomes of the investigation.

3.2 Search Strategy

The data that was used was acquired from the SCOPUS data framework, which is extensively employed in academia spheres (Chadegani et al., 2013).The search was done by December 19, 2023 (See Table1). Scopus has been taken for this particular studies to access a vast collection of scholarly literature, track citations, identify trends, and measure research impact. It provides a multidisciplinary perspective, covering journals from various fields, making it a valuable tool for academic and scientific endeavors. This study examines the articles retrieved from the Scopus library database since its inception upto 2023, and 256 initial documents were obtained. The selected publications from the Scopus database limiting it to Journal getting a total of 211 publications in all. Further limiting the articles subject to the language English getting a total of 132 documents. The search criteria encompassed all of the study publications that contained the term "Robo-Advi*" within the title, key phrases, and text. has been limited to English. To have a clear understanding of data, it was a must to clean the data, by fixing the inaccurate or incomplete records.Researchers undertook a thorough study of the research questions to discover the key terms used during the search process or inquiry. The writers engaged in a cooperative discussion to determine and conclude the precise search criteria. In addition, they carefully retrieved the appropriate data from the chosen sources. Diverse varieties of string were produced, finally making noteworthy contributions to scholarly investigation.

("Robo-advisor*" OR "Robo advisor") AND ("Financ*" OR "FinTech")

The keyword strings are formed by employing the "AND" and "OR" expressions to generate relationships between multiple search keywords. The selected digital repositories provide a customized search engine designed to fulfill particular criteria. Search strings are executed by utilizing tailored search techniques within digital information resources.

4. RESULTS AND DISCUSSION

Bibliometric Analysis technique facilitates researchers in identifying the most influential writers, organizations, and studies on topics in a specific field, as well as their interconnections. Bibliometric analysis is a valuable tool for assessing the productivity and impact of investigators, organizations, and scientific domains. It is particularly effective in scientific research assessment, financing distribution, and strategic planning (Costa et al., 2019). In essence, bibliometric analysis serves to enhance scientific investigation making decisions and facilitate the spread of information in a way that is more efficient and effective. The VOS viewer collected reference, bibliographical, and biographical keywords data from a total of 252 publications initially. The VOS-viewer provides researchers with robust capabilities to visualize and analyze bibliometric networks. These capabilities include network visualization, clustering and mapping, cocitation analysis, and bibliographic coupling analysis. As a result, the VOS-viewer is an indispensable tool for researchers who aim to extract valuable insights from extensive datasets (Van Eck &Waltman, 2017). For bibliometric analysis, we employed VOS-viewer to visually represent the connections between scholars and articles. In addition, VOS-viewer visualizes objects in a lower-dimensional space, where the distance between points on the map shows the similarities (Liu et al., 2015). In addition, VOS-viewer is a tool that facilitates the visualization of research dynamism and structure throughout time (Vallaster et al., 2019).

Table 2. Citation of documents

S.No.	Document	Citations	Links
1	Gomber (2018)	648	3
2	Belanche (2019)	252	9
3	Jung (2018a)	114	10
4	Jung (2018b)	95	7
5	Flavi疣 (2022)	83	4
6	Tao (2021)	71	0
7	Hildebrand (2021)	66	2
8	Brenner (2020)	55	0
9	Bhatia (2020)	52	0
10	Giudici (2018)	50	0

Citation serves as a mechanism to give credit where it is due. While citing a document it help the studies to acknowledge the original research contribution but also provides readers with a trail to trace evolutiomn of data.Here in Table 2 the most referred research document among the list that tops the chart

Figure 1. Chart title

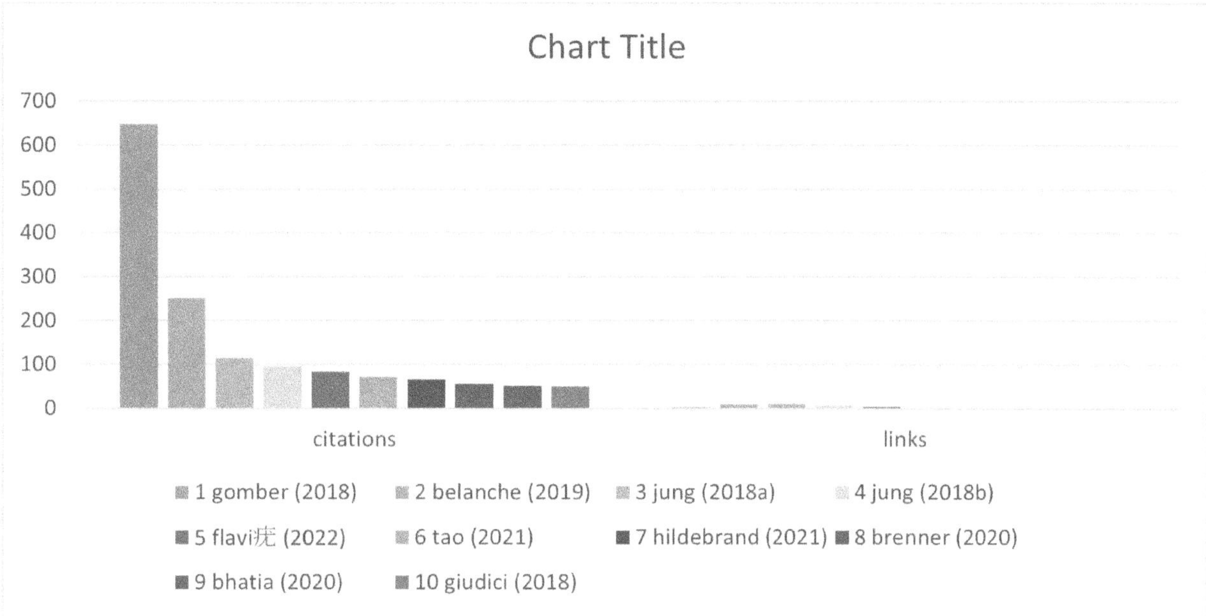

is Gomber (2018) with highest citations of 648.This is further followed by the document by Belanche (2019) with a total of 252 citations and Jung (2018a) with 114 citations.Amon the list the least cited document was provided by Jung (2018a) and Giudici (2018) with 52 and 50 citations.

The following table indicates that the top publications in the study field of financial guidance and individual investor differ in terms of their class, publication rate, and citations score. The Journal of Management Information Systems has the highest number of citations, with a total of 648. The Journal of Industrial Management and Data Systems, on the other hand, has a reasonable number of citations, with a total of 252, placing it in second position among the selected sources. The data indicates that the Journal of the Academy of Marketing Science and Strategic Sciences have the lowest number of cita-

Table 3. Citation of sources

S.No.	Source	Documents	Citations	Total Link strength
1	Journal Of Management Information Systems	1	648	8
2	Industrial Management And Data Systems	2	252	32
3	Journal Of Behavioral And Experimental Finance	4	161	6
4	Business And Information Systems Engineering	1	114	30
5	Electronic Markets	1	95	28
6	Frontiers In Artificial Intelligence	4	85	3
7	Journal Of Service Management	1	83	4
8	Technological Forecasting And Social Change	2	80	3
9	Journal Of The Academy Of Marketing Science	1	66	12
10	Strategic Change	2	49	13

Figure 2. Top publications

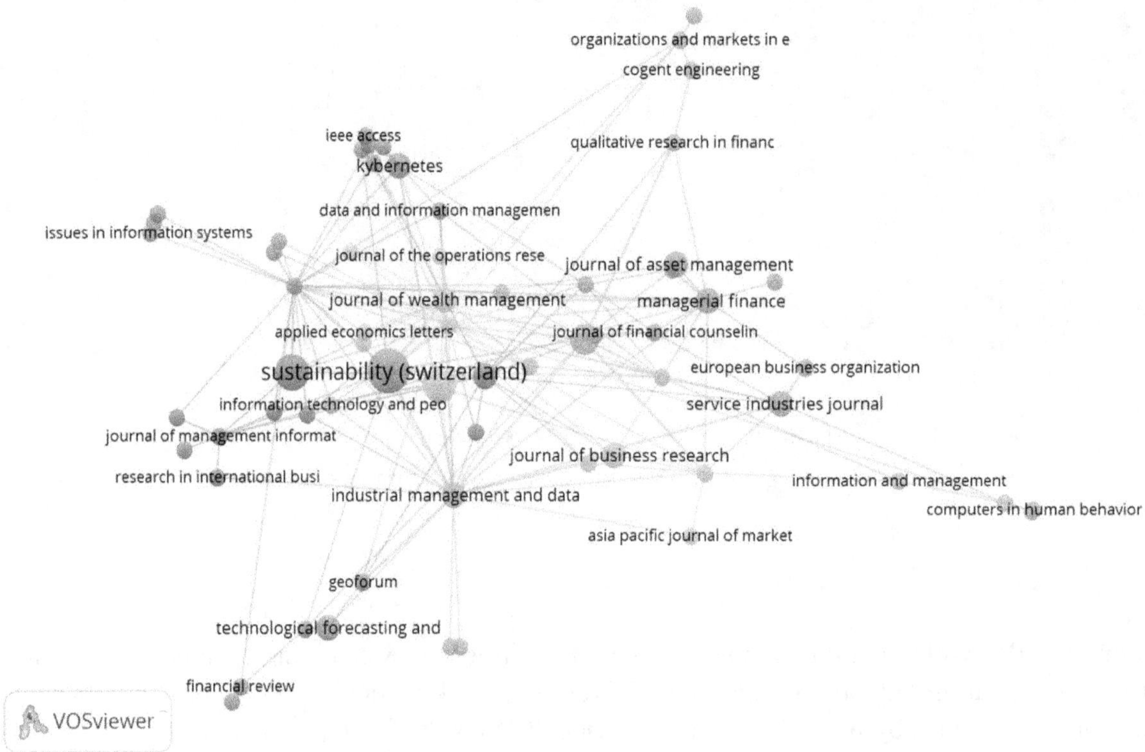

Table 4. Citation of authors

S.No.	Author	Documents	Citations	Total Link Strength
1	Belanche, Daniel	3	337	31
2	Casaló, Luis V.	3	337	31
3	Flavián, Carlos	2	335	30
4	Dorner, Verena	2	209	40
5	Jung, Dominik	2	209	40
6	Morana, Stefan	2	116	21
7	Bhatia, Ankita	4	79	12
8	Chandani, Arti	4	79	12
9	Giudici, Paolo	2	67	0
10	Scherer, Bernd	2	44	12

tions compared to the other eight selected resources that specialize in the subject of Robo-Advice. These figures indicate that journal papers that are based on evidence have varying citation counts, implying their significance and influence.

Figure 3. Chart title

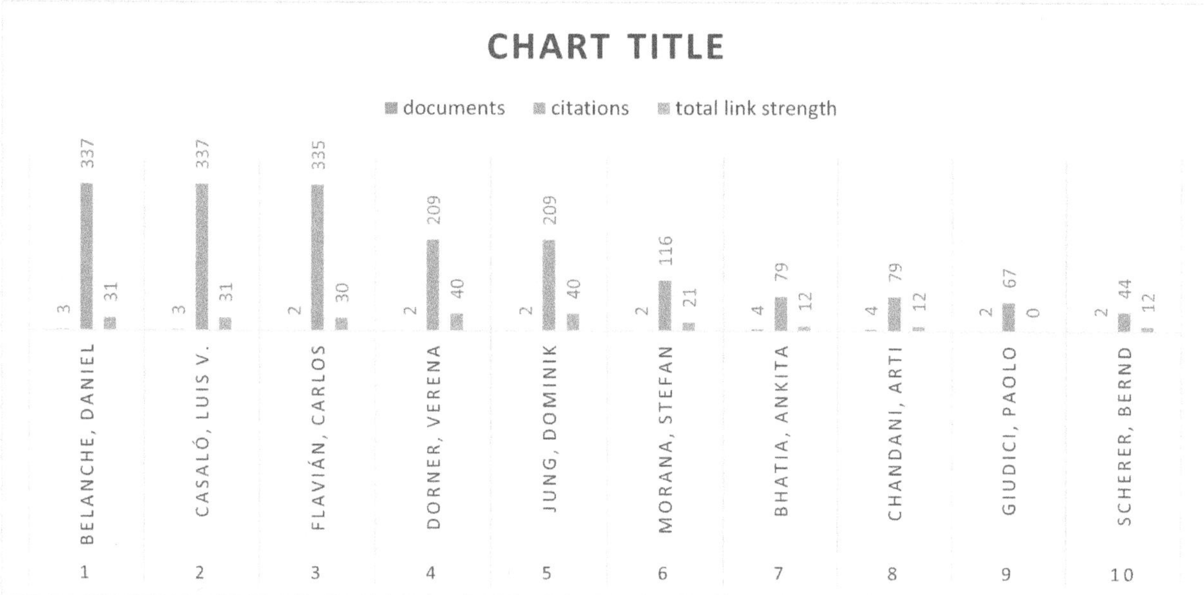

Using VOS-viewer software, Table 5 has been created to identify the pieces with the most impact on the discipline of Robo-Advice in Financial services. The curated database comprises papers, pieces, and evaluations. authored by a total of 2023 individuals by 2023. The writers Daniel Belanche, Luis V. Casaló, and Carlos Flavián are recognized as prominent researchers based on the number of citations they have received and the number of publications they have authored. The scarcity of articles, even from renowned writers, indicates that this field of research is still in its nascent phase. However, the rise in authorship and collaboration has the potential to generate more interest in this discipline.

Table 5. Citation of organisations

S.No.	Organization	Documents	Citations	Total Link Strength
1	DEPARTMENT OF ECONOMICS AND MANAGEMENT, UNIVERSITY OF PAVIA, PAVIA, ITALY	2	67	0
2	SYMBIOSIS INSTITUTE OF MANAGEMENT STUDIES, SYMBIOSIS INTERNATIONAL (DEEMED UNIVERSITY), PUNE, INDIA	2	25	1
3	UCSI GRADUATE BUSINESS SCHOOL, UCSI UNIVERSITY, KUALA LUMPUR, MALAYSIA	2	12	1

VOS-viewer enhances the understanding of unconventional patterns and the field of investigation (Ding & Yang, 2022). In essence, VOS-viewer efficiently compares previous and present actions, revealing the advancements in research fields (Oladinrin et al., 2023).VOSviewer was employed to compare various organizations based on their distinct citation counts, in order to gain further insights. Table 5 provides information on the distribution of literary works among different organizations. It includes citations of organizations that are highly cited. The University of Pavia's Department of Economics and Management in Italy has the most number of citations, with a total of 67. It is followed by Symbosis Institute

Table 6. Citation of countries

S.No.	Country	Documents	Citations	Total Link Strength
1	Germany	17	1051	111
2	United States	21	947	85
3	Spain	6	353	48
4	France	6	111	43
5	China	17	208	36
6	India	7	95	32
7	Malaysia	7	19	27
8	Taiwan	6	34	21
9	Canada	4	19	20
10	Singapore	3	678	19

of Management Studies at Symbosis International in India, which has 25 citations, and UCSI Graduate Business School at UCSI University in Malaysia, which has 12 citations.

According to Table 6, Germany is the leading country with respect of the geographical spread of literary works. It has created 17 documents with a total of 1051 citations, making it first among the top 10 countries. The countries in the forefront of knowledge development in the utilization of finance Robo-Advice in the financial services sector include the USA, Spain, France, China, India, Malaysia, Taiwan, Canada, and Singapore. Germany is ranked first with 17 papers, 1051 citations, and 111 link strength..

The VOSViewer software provides visual representation, grouping, and elucidation of the interconnections between countries. Moreover, each objective study has a distinct methodology to authenticate, investigate, or delineate the research domain. The study methodology employed in a robo-advisor services particularly related to finance can differ based on the investigator's specific goals and level of innovation.

The geographical networking dispersion is produced by analyzing the source nation of publishing and utilizing VOS-viewer freeware. The results are presented in Figure 4. The framework further supports the conclusions derived from the bibliometric evaluation of the leading ten(10) nations in terms of scientific research output in the field of robo-advisory. The diverse clusters of different colors symbolize the distinct fields of research and their interplay with other fields of study within the research's purview.

5. DISCUSSION

Integration with financial planning tools can provide investors with a more holistic view of their financial situation. Studying robo-advisors is valuable for gaining a comprehensive understanding of the evolving landscape of financial technology, investment management, and the broader implications for both professionals and individual. A summary of current research efforts in the European Union about the utilization of automation is given in the article provided by Linaza et al.,2021. It emphasizes that robots can enhance precision and address the various problems related to the investment. The research is pioneering and an original study aiming to investigate the AI approaches employed specially in robo-advisory financial practices, which has not been previously undertaken.

Figure 4. Network visualization

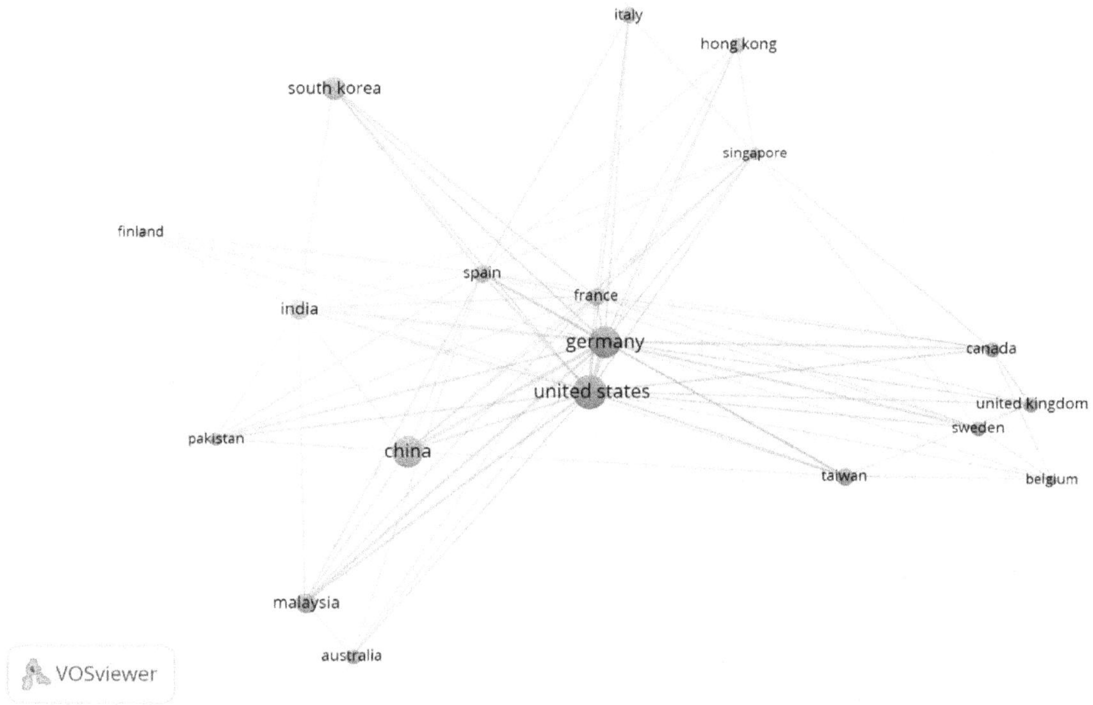

The resulting study structure aims to establish a foundation for future studies in a systematic and streamlined way. This study can serve as a basis for attracting new scholars to explore this field, considering the limited volume of existing scholarly research conducted on robo-advisory services. There is a moral need to encourage more academic interest in the advancement of technology in the financial services chain to guarantee financial Ensuring the security and well-being of subsequent generations due to the swift advancements in technology.

6. CONCLUSION

During our investigation, we categorized the search terms and utilized them to retrieve 252 pertinent papers and reviews. The findings indicate a growing scholarly fascination with the application of automation in banking and financial services, with a significant advancement observed between the years 2021 and 2023. Germany, the United States, and Spain are prominent in the production of exceptional literary works and writers in this field. The findings were acquired through the process of records cleaning and categorizing the collection of data for network evaluation, utilizing the functionalities of MS Excel, VOS-viewer . Through analysis of findings, it is evident that there is significant potential for the utilization of Robo-Advisory services to achieve sustainability, particularly in the fields of finance, managing investments, economics, and technology. This can assist in gaining invaluable insights into the financial and societal effects of these advancements. In order to achieve significant advancements in the discipline, it is imperative for academics and organizations to enhance their collaboration and establish additional connections.

REFERENCES

Baas, J., Schotten, M., Plume, A., Côté, G., & Karimi, R. (2020). Scopus as a curated, high-quality bibliometric data source for academic research in quantitative science studies. *Quantitative Science Studies, 1*(1), 377–386. doi:10.1162/qss_a_00019

Baek, S., Mohanty, S. K., & Glambosky, M. (2020). COVID-19 and stock market volatility: An industry level analysis. *Finance Research Letters, 37*, 101748. doi:10.1016/j.frl.2020.101748 PMID:32895607

Beketov, M., Lehmann, K., & Wittke, M. (2018). Robo Advisors: Quantitative methods inside the robots. *Journal of Asset Management, 19*(6), 363–370. doi:10.1057/s41260-018-0092-9

Belanche, D., Casaló, L. V., & Flavián, C. (2019). Artificial Intelligence in FinTech: Understanding robo-advisors adoption among customers. *Industrial Management & Data Systems, 119*(7), 1411–1430. doi:10.1108/IMDS-08-2018-0368

Bhatia, A., Chandani, A., Atiq, R., Mehta, M., & Divekar, R. (2021). Artificial intelligence in financial services: A qualitative research to discover robo-advisory services. *Qualitative Research in Financial Markets, 13*(5), 632–654. doi:10.1108/QRFM-10-2020-0199

Chadegani, A. A., Salehi, H., Yunus, M. M., Farhadi, H., Fooladi, M., Farhadi, M., & Ebrahim, N. A. (2013). A comparison between two main academic literature collections: Web of Science and Scopus databases. *arXiv preprint arXiv:1305.0377*. Elsevier Scopus.

Costa, D. F., Carvalho, F. D. M., & Moreira, B. C. D. M. (2019). Behavioral economics and behavioral finance: A bibliometric analysis of the scientific fields. *Journal of Economic Surveys, 33*(1), 3–24. doi:10.1111/joes.12262

Ding, X., & Yang, Z. (2020). Knowledge mapping of platform research: A visual analysis using VOSviewer and CiteSpace. *Electronic Commerce Research*, 1–23.

Donthu, N., Kumar, S., Mukherjee, D., Pandey, N., & Lim, W. M. (2021). How to conduct a bibliometric analysis: An overview and guidelines. *Journal of Business Research, 133*, 285–296. doi:10.1016/j.jbusres.2021.04.070

Epperson, T., Hedges, B., Singh, U., & Gabel, M. A. T. (2015). Kearney 2015 Robo-Advisory Services Study. AT Kearney: Bucures,ti, Romania.

Fisch, J. E., Labouré, M., & Turner, J. A. (2018). The Emergence of the Robo-Advisor. *Pension Research Council Working Papers*. Wharton School Pension Research Council, University of Pennsylvania. https://repository.upenn.edu/prc_papers/10

Gomber, P., Kauffman, R. J., Parker, C., & Weber, B. W. (2018). Financial information systems and the fintech revolution. *Journal of Management Information Systems*, *35*(1), 12–18. doi:10.1080/07421222.2018.1440778

Graseck, B. L. (2020). *Wealth Management After the Storm*. MORGAN STANLEY & OLIVER WYMAN.

Jiang, W., Han, B., Habibi, M. A., & Schotten, H. D. (2021). The road towards 6G: A comprehensive survey. *IEEE Open Journal of the Communications Society*, *2*, 334–366. doi:10.1109/OJCOMS.2021.3057679

Jung, D., Dorner, V., Glaser, F., & Morana, S. (2018). Robo-advisory: Digitalization and automation of financial advisory. *Business & Information Systems Engineering*, *60*(1), 81–86. doi:10.1007/s12599-018-0521-9

Jung, D., Dorner, V., Weinhardt, C., & Pusmaz, H. (2018). Designing a robo-advisor for risk-averse, low-budget consumers. *Electronic Markets*, *28*(3), 367–380. doi:10.1007/s12525-017-0279-9

Kraiwanit, T., Jangjarat, K., & Atcharanuwat, J. (2022). The acceptance of financial robo-advisors among investors: The emerging market study. *Journal of Governance and Regulation*, *11*(2), 332–339. doi:10.22495/jgrv11i2siart12

Liu, W., Hu, G., Tang, L., & Wang, Y. (2015). China's global growth in social science research: Uncovering evidence from bibliometric analyses of SSCI publications (1978–2013). *Journal of Informetrics*, *9*(3), 555–569. doi:10.1016/j.joi.2015.05.007

Manohar, S., Mittal, A., & Marwah, S. (2020). Service innovation, corporate reputation and word-of-mouth in the banking sector: A test on multigroup-moderated mediation effect. *Benchmarking*, *27*(1), 406–429. doi:10.1108/BIJ-05-2019-0217

Goyal, J., Singh, M., Singh, R., & Aggarwal, A. (2019). Efficiency and technology gaps in Indian banking sector: Application of meta-frontier directional distance function DEA approach. *The Journal of finance and data science, 5*(3), 156-172.

Methlagl, M. (2022). Mapping inclusive education 1980 to 2019: A bibliometric analysis of thematic clusters and research directions. *Issues in Educational Research*, *32*(1), 225–247.

Oladinrin, O. T., Arif, M., Rana, M. Q., & Gyoh, L. (2023). Interrelations between construction ethics and innovation: A bibliometric analysis using VOSviewer. *Construction Innovation*, *23*(3), 505–523. doi:10.1108/CI-07-2021-0130

Schwinn, R., & Teo, E. (2017). *Robots or Humans: Trends in Robo-Advisory Services and Social Online Trading*. Working paper, Sim Kee Boon Institute.

Sironi, P. (2016). *FinTech innovation: from robo-advisors to goal based investing and gamification*. John Wiley & Sons. doi:10.1002/9781119227205

Vallaster, C., Kraus, S., Lindahl, J. M. M., & Nielsen, A. (2019). Ethics and entrepreneurship: A bibliometric study and literature review. *Journal of Business Research*, *99*, 226–237. doi:10.1016/j.jbusres.2019.02.050

Van Eck, N. J., & Waltman, L. (2017). Citation-based clustering of publications using CitNetExplorer and VOSviewer. *Scientometrics*, *111*(2), 1053–1070. doi:10.1007/s11192-017-2300-7 PMID:28490825

Yeh, H. C., Yu, M. C., Liu, C. H., & Huang, C. I. (2023). Robo-advisor based on unified theory of acceptance and use of technology. *Asia Pacific Journal of Marketing and Logistics*, *35*(4), 962–979. doi:10.1108/APJML-07-2021-0493

Chapter 15
The Power of Cross-Functional Collaboration and Market Knowledge Integration to Achieve Competitive Advantages in the Automobile Sector

Lochan Chavan
Chitkara Business School, Chitkara University, India

Priya Jindal
Chitkara Business School, Chitkara University, India

ABSTRACT

The automotive industry is often regarded as a crucial pillar of the economy in several developed countries. Manufacturers are required to identify and implement strategies aimed at enhancing product quality, enhancing the adaptability of their production facilities, optimizing supply chain networks, managing technical intricacies and variations, and sustaining competitiveness in both developed and emerging nations. This chapter provides insights into the method of collaboration, enhances the utilization of essential automotive technology, and reinforces the fundamental competencies of a manufacturer. Additionally, this emphasizes the crucial roles that cross-functional collaboration and market knowledge integration play in industrial applications as a means to gain competitive advantages. This study highlights the necessity of embracing innovation adoption within the automobile industry to attain competitive advantages and establish sustainable mobility.

DOI: 10.4018/979-8-3693-2019-8.ch015

1. INTRODUCTION

The manufacturing sector in India has experienced significant growth as a result of the country's constantly increasing population. There has been a notabl.,e rise in investments within the industry, with initiatives such as the "Make in India" project seeking to establish the South Asian nation as a global manufacturing hub. In fiscal year 2022, the manufacturing sector saw an annual output growth rate of 11.4% (statista.com, 2022). The automobiles industry encompasses the activities of designing, constructing, manufacturing, and commercialising motor vehicles. It offers a mode of transportation that is comparable to the utilisation of commercial and passenger vehicles in several countries, resulting in substantial financial gains. The implementation of cost-effective manufacturing necessitates the utilisation of a key piece of machinery. The process of transforming unprocessed resources into automobiles and its constituent components is commonly referred to as automotive manufacturing. Manufacturers with superior capabilities will exhibit enhanced competitiveness within the market, resulting in increased sales of their technologically sophisticated and ergonomically superior automobiles. In addition to possessing the most prominent vehicle manufacturers, top-performing organisations also provide a strong framework for marketing and branding initiatives, which are integral elements of the marketing discipline (Gawer & Cusumano, 2014). Certain automotive enterprises perceive a significant treat from the evolving structure of the sector, whilst others perceive a prospect . The automotive sector has seen a substantial transformation due to technical obstacles such as autonomous, connected, electric, and services mobility, stringent emissions regulations, the increasing significance of Asian markets, and evolving customer preferences . As the corporate environment changes, creating new strategies and plans is crucial. The upgrading and integrating of information and ideas from numerous sources to produce a formula for a firm are made possible by market sharing and technological advancements. One of the important economic sectors both internationally and in India is the automobile sector. The industry has a significant multiplier effect on industrial growth as a result of its extensive forward and backward links with several important economic sectors. Through the factor movements of commodities and people in the economy, the increase in efficiency and productivity, directly and indirectly, enhances the efficiency of other sectors. As a result, the sector is acknowledged as one of the main forces behind the economic expansion and a considerable contributor to the country's overall GDP (Burange & Yamini, 2008). Cross- functional collaboration and market knowledge integration include combining experts with knowledge, experience, and skills from several sectors. Additionally, it promotes a more expansive way of thinking. In a manufacturing environment, cross-functional teams can handle a variety of problems, from a lack of talent to boosting productivity. Additionally, Computer-based technology boosts productivity, saves time, and lowers production costs, all of which help businesses gain a competitive edge (Jindal, 2019).

Nevertheless, there has been a notable increase in dynamics and unpredictability attributed to shifts in the market, legislative measures, alterations in consumer behavior, and the emergence of novel product developments. An evaluation of the level of rivalry among Indian automotive businesses has been made possible by understanding the factors that contribute to each company's competitive advantage. To establish and sustain a competitive advantage in the luxury automotive sector, the conventional premium vehicle manufacturer must undergo a transition into a mobility technology firm. To enhance the efficiency of the automotive sector, it must align with contemporary developments by prioritizing digitization. This entails fostering cross-functional collaboration and integrating market knowledge.

1.1 Elements for Implementation of Manufacturing Technologies and Applications

1.1.1 Strategic Planning for Implementing Manufacturing Applications and Technology

Decisions about manufacturing technology should be supported by an examination of how manufacturing might give the business a distinct competitive advantage. Strategic planning is concerned with both business and technological concerns (Zhou et al., 2015). The utilisation of advanced manufacturing technologies (AMT) has a substantial influence on both non-price and price factors, leading to enhanced processes that optimise the utilisation of inputs such as materials, labour, and fuel . These could include production-, finance-, marketing-, design-, and quality-related factors. Manufacturing Technologies & Applications offers greater flexibility in terms of decreased working capital costs, improved delivery responsiveness, decreased rates of rework and scrap, and increased capacity for product customization (Siaminwe et al., 2016).

1.1.2 Product and Process Matching

The design of the vehicle and its parts and their assembly, testing, and eventual delivery to clients are all intricate steps in a lengthy process. The production of automobiles necessitates the use of specialized machinery, highly skilled labour, and a range of raw materials. Auto manufacturers also begin the quick manufacturing of their products. This is because they will be able to evaluate how well the prototypes work under various settings by testing them.

1.1.3 Monitoring Sophisticated Manufacturing Technologies

The manufacturing industry has seen a significant transition as a result of the fourth industrial revolution . The rise of intelligent built-up may be attributed to global enterprises adapting to the prevailing shift towards mechanical automation in conventional production methods (Naghshineh & Carvalho, 2022). The concept of mass customisation was first presented by the proponents of Industry 4.0 . The manufacturing industry is anticipated to benefit from the opportunities brought about by Industry 4.0, which encompasses the use of software-designed networking (SDN), 5G, and machine-to-machine (M2M) communication as emerging networking technologies . The capability of devices that are equipped with software, sensors, and similar computer technologies to establish connections enables the facilitation of real-time monitoring and data transfer. Smartphones, as an example, are being utilised in a growing manner beyond their primary function of communication. They are now being connected to machines to effectively monitor particular machining operations, collect data, and promptly rectify any machining errors that may occur .

1.1.4 Management Commitment and Control

Sutiyem et al. (2020) define organisational commitment as the degree to which employees demonstrate support for the aims of the organisation and exhibit a desire to remain affiliated with it. Organisational commitment refers to the degree to which personnel hold strong beliefs in the aims of the organisation and willingly embrace them, with their intrinsic motivation to be employed within the organisation. The concept of internal control, as stated by, references the Professional Standards of the American Institute of Public Accountants (AICPA). The concept of internal control may be defined as follows: The process undertaken by a company's management, board of directors, and employees to provide assurance that specific objectives will be achieved, including: (A) operational controls, which pertain to the efficient and effective utilisation of the organization's resources; (B) financial reporting controls, which pertain to the generation of reliable and credible financial statements for public use and (C) compliance controls, which pertain to the organization's adherence to applicable laws and regulations. In order to enhance efficiency and expedite the production process, the integration of information from many domains is employed.

1.1.5 Functional Relationship

The fierce rivalry present in the automotive industry is causing generational upheaval as a result of new vehicle technology, accelerating product cycles, and new car ownership patterns. Both the marketing of autos and performing repairs require knowledge transfer. To encourage smooth operations and long-term collaboration, it is necessary for the manufacturer and the dealer to share important information and develop a strong bond. By giving the technicians the right infrastructure, tools, and equipment, we can overcome the technician shortage.

1.1.6 Relationship With the External Environment

The external environment is made up of external forces that impact the industry. The industry goes through significant changes with the aid of environmental considerations. Vehicle development and design are significantly impacted by the arrival of new competition. The sector is now utilizing more cutting-edge driving skills due to technological advancements. The car industry is lucrative, but there are numerous aspects that affect the relationship with the manufacturers, including political, social, economic, cultural, and technological ones.

1.1.7 Measuring the System's Performance

One of the key components of management systems is performance measurement, and performance is determined by the outcomes of actions made. The system makes these decisions using proportional information because of external influences like customers and competitors, the need to regulate the strategy, quality, and customer satisfaction performance substantially impacted the strategic position of the organizations. The integration of performance assessment throughout the entire supply chain enables the evaluation of global performance as well as the identification of internal adjustments that need to be made in order to significantly increase competitiveness (Chand et al., 2022).

1.2 Modern Technologies

Advancements in the use of computer systems within the automotive sector have led to the emergence of more efficient ways for vehicle manufacture. The transition from obsolete to contemporary technology offers several benefits. Several advantages include enhanced speed of product manufacturing, increased operational efficiency, enhanced convenience, and the capacity to tailor items to individual requirements. Among the many technologies, there are a select number that are now in the process of development which are depict in Figure 1.

Figure 1. Modern technologies

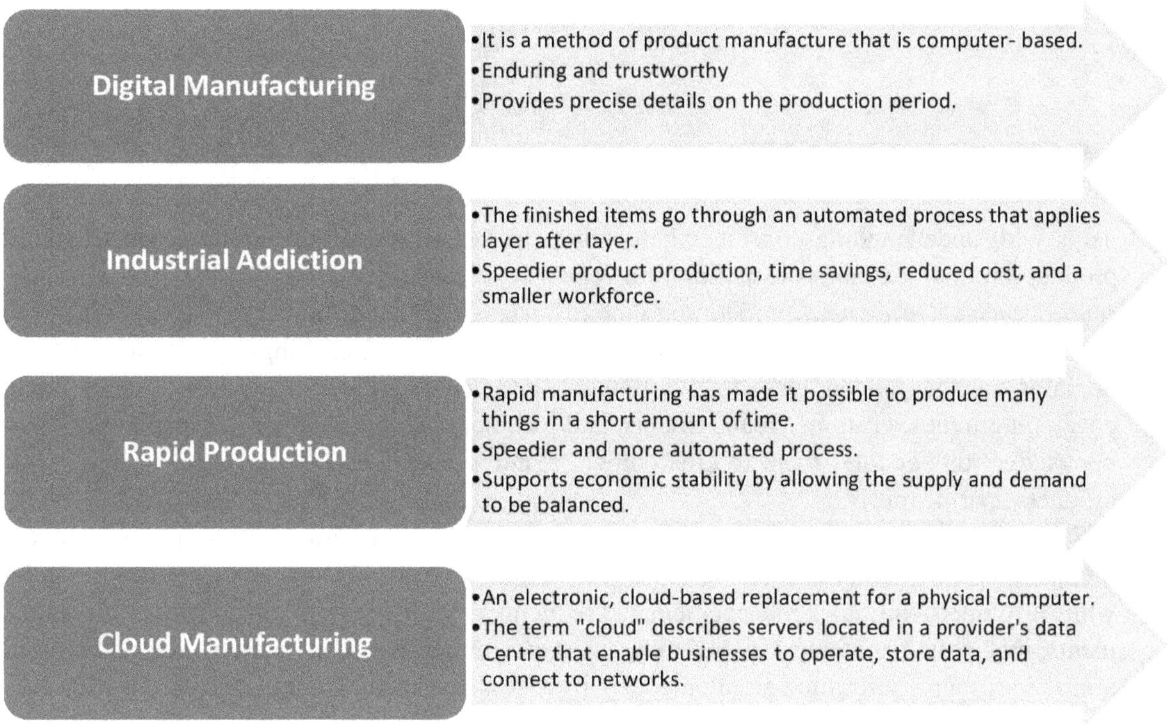

1.3 Manufacturing Techniques

The subsequent production procedures are depicted in Figure 2. The technology employed within the automobile sector exhibits a higher degree of sophistication and advancement. Over the course of time, there has been a notable progression in the production procedure. The use of contemporary technology has accelerated the process of construction, diminished expenses, and enhanced overall efficiency.

2. CROSS-FUNCTIONAL COLLABORATION AND MARKET KNOWLEDGE INTEGRATION ARE CRUCIAL IN THE AUTOMOBILE SECTOR

A. *Product Development*: Cross-functional collaboration shows how several departments work together to generate goods that satisfy consumer demand and cutting-edge technology and are in line with shifting market trends. Different inputs from multiple areas, such as sales, design, marketing, engineering, etc are incorporated to develop a successful vehicle. Integration of market knowledge

Figure 2. Manufacturing techniques

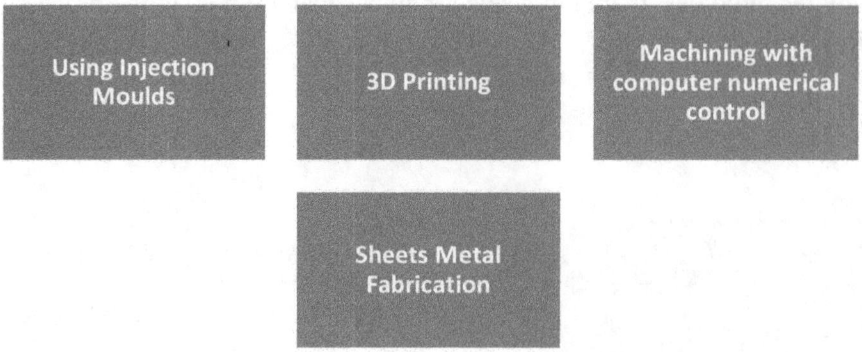

helps with understanding consumer behaviour, market segments, and rivalry, which enhances product development and is essential for a vehicle's success.

B. *Innovation and Differentiation*: The automobile business must constantly innovate if it is to survive in the fiercely competitive market. Cross-functional collaboration brings specialists from many domains together, encourages creative thought, and generates ideas. Companies can recognize developing trends, customer requirements, and technical breakthroughs by incorporating market knowledge; this enables them to create novel features, technologies, and designs that set their products apart from rivals.

C. *Efficient Operations:* Through cross-functional cooperation, it is simpler to coordinate, share and interact with information among the departments, making it possible to carry out activities quickly while also improving stock management and reducing costs. Collaboration enables several departments, including manufacturing, logistics, sales, etc., to operate cooperatively. Market knowledge assists in resource allocation simultaneously by assessing demand, controlling production levels, and adopting adjustments as a result of market conditions.

D. *Customer-Centric Approach:* Knowing the tastes and preferences of the customer is crucial. Businesses engage in R&D to get a better understanding of customer expectations, buying patterns, and emerging trends. Through cross-functional collaboration, data from various departments, including marketing, sales, customer service, research, and development, is provided to the product development team. This aids them in creating consumer-centered vehicles that can meet demand and satisfy needs as the market changes.

E. *Strategic Decision-Making:* For the purpose of making strategic decisions, it is crucial to have strategies for integrating market knowledge and cross-functional collaboration. Teams from different divisions gather to exchange new perspectives, and those in charge of locating resources, managing assets, and laboratories also make decisions regarding the expansion of product portfolios, market acquisitions, and joint ventures.

F. Adaptability to Market Changes: Identifying potential markets for growth, accepting the changes in the government's rules developing strategies, and providing products in accordance with consumer demand and taste is crucial and is accomplished through integrating market knowledge. Collaboration between various divisions enables the company to maintain its flexibility and make quick decisions in response to changes in the market environment.

Overall, cross-functional collaboration and market knowledge integration help automobile firms create innovative products, optimize operations, increase customer happiness, make wise strategic decisions, and compete in a market that is constantly changing as shown in Figure 3.

Figure 3. Importance of cross-functional collaboration and market knowledge integration in the automobile sector

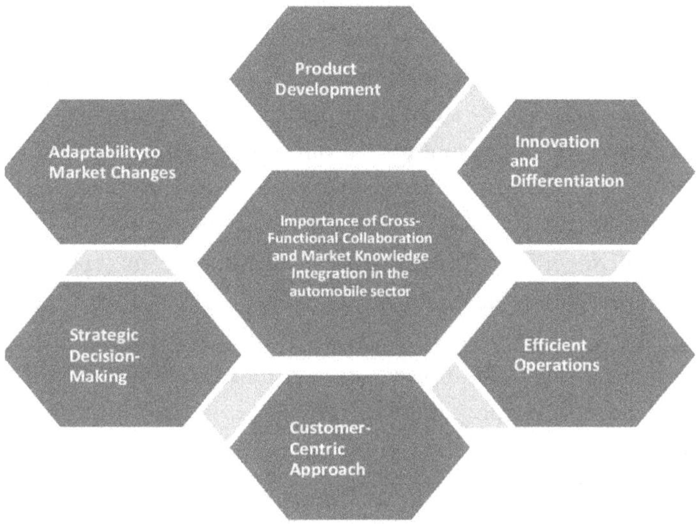

2.1 Sustainable Development in the Automobile Industry

The automotive sector's pursuit of sustainable development involves the incorporation of economic, social, and environmental considerations in order to mitigate the adverse impacts that vehicles have on both the environment and society. The proposal entails the use of environmentally friendly and efficient technologies, the mitigation of greenhouse gas emissions, the advocacy for renewable energy alternatives, and the prioritisation of resource preservation over the whole lifespan of vehicles (Gupta et al., 2021). Recycled materials, recycling initiatives, and sustainable production methods are receiving more attention from the auto industry. Automakers can drastically lower carbon emissions and improve air quality, resulting in a cleaner and healthier environment, by adopting sustainable practices, such as producing electric and hybrid automobiles. To combat climate change, increase energy efficiency, and build a more sustainable and liveable future for everybody, sustainable transportation must be adopted. In order to address environmental issues, save resources, foster economic growth, improve social fairness, and sculpt a sustainable transportation future, the automotive sector must practice sustainable development.

2. SUSTAINABLE DEVELOPMENT IN THE AUTOMOBILE SECTOR THROUGH CROSS-FUNCTIONAL COLLABORATION

Cross-functional collaboration is essential for achieving sustainability goals in the automotive industry by integrating diverse expertise, perspectives, and resources across various departments and customers.

Here are some ways cross-functional collaboration can support sustainable development in the automotive industry:

A. *Design and Innovation:* It is crucial to make eco- friendly and energy-efficient vehicles while designing a product in order to achieve sustainable development. Through cross-functional collaboration, a team of engineers, designers, and sustainability experts come together to create products with innovation and new designs, such as automobiles that use less fuel, emit less carbon dioxide, & are manufactured with the aid of incorporated technological knowledge and sustainability considerations.
B. *Supply Chain Management:* Where departments, such as purchasing, manufacturing, and logistics, work together to develop, much like the automotive industry's supply chain management. Teams collaborate for sustainable development by finding environmentally friendly suppliers, reducing waste, and improving transportation, which will have an effect on the environment and assist to use resources more effectively.
C. *Material Selection and Recycling:* To implement sustainable materials and recycling methods, teams from several departments including R&D technology, and waste management are working together (Nguyen & Hoai, 2023). Striving toward implementing eco-friendly material practices, recycling initiatives, programs, and approaches for the moral disposal of end-of-life vehicles for the advancement of automobile components.
D. Manufacturing Process: Engineers, production managers, and sustainability experts work together to identify and implement energy-efficient technologies, lean manufacturing principles, and sustainable practices throughout the production cycle. This reduces energy consumption, waste production, and emissions, which improves manufacturing operations.
E. Marketing and Consumer Education: Organizations play a significant influence in shaping consumer behavior by educating the public about sustainable forms of transportation that are good for the environment and aid in the production of sustainable automobiles. Collaboration between the marketing, sales, and sustainable departments aids in raising consumer awareness of sustainable automobile choices and their benefits.
F. Policy Advocacy: Externally, cross-functional collaboration engages with NGOs, trade associations, and governmental organizations. Building emissions standards, financial incentives for green technology, and the development of electric vehicle charging stations establish legislation and regulations that will reward eco-friendly behaviour in the auto industry.
G. Data Analysis and Performance Tracking: Utilizing analytical data and information to evaluate Spot opportunities for improvement, and companies' progress, and taking well-informed decisions promotes sustainable development in the organized automobile sector. Information gathered from data analyst engineers and sustainability experts collaborated to evaluate and measure keep performance matrix related to sustainability goals.

Overall, cross-functional collaboration is crucial for fostering long-term growth in the automobile industry. By integrating different knowledge and opinions, businesses can develop creative solutions, enhance processes, and encourage environmental improvements, ultimately leading to a more resilient and sustainable future.

3. SUSTAINABLE DEVELOPMENT IN THE AUTOMOBILE SECTOR THROUGH MARKET KNOWLEDGE INTEGRATION

Market knowledge integration is crucial for achieving sustained growth in the automobile sector. Through the integration of market insights into sustainability initiatives, better strategy alignment in accordance with customer preferences and requirements, outstanding industry trends, and regulatory constants are successfully implemented. Here are a few ways that market knowledge integration can support the automobile industry's long-term expansion:

A. *Market research:* Comprehensive market research must be carried out in order to comprehend and learn about the preferences, attitudes, and expectations of the public regarding sustainable mobility solutions. By combining the results of market research, the company creates vehicles with eco-friendly features, increased fuel efficiency, and decreased carbon emissions.
B. *Consumer Insights:* Through the integration of market knowledge, businesses can get consumer insights and an understanding of sustainable mobility. These businesses then use this information to create effective advertising campaigns and awareness programs that educate and encourage customers to make sustainable mobility decisions.
C. *Regulatory Compliance:* Organizations keep up with rising regulations and standards for environmental impact, emission levels, and energy efficiency. Organizations actively modify their processes and products to comply with regulations and keep an eye on evolving laws, which helps to maintain long-term sustainability and avoid fines or reputational issues.
D. *Competitive Analysis:* Companies may discover opportunities for differentiation, innovation, and market positioning based on sustainability challenges by examining the competitive landscape and evaluating competitors' sustainability programs and approaches (Shaikh et al., 2022). For instance, the generation of renewable energy sources, and the development of supply chains that are carbon neutral.
E. *Partnerships and Collaboration:* Organizations utilize market intelligence to develop strategic alliances with businesses that have complementary skills, resources, or technology to foster long-term innovation in the automotive sector (Mc Anthony & Jindal, 2017). It is simple to identify possible partners and collaborators who are committed to sustainable development through the integration of market knowledge.
F. *Product Lifecycle Management:* Companies may maximize sustainability at every stage, from design to end-of-life disposal, by integrating market insights throughout the product's lifetime. Understanding market demands enables businesses to prioritize eco-friendly materials, adopt effective manufacturing techniques, and create recycling programs that meet regulatory standards and customer expectations.
G. *Customer Feedback and Engagement:* By actively seeking client input on sustainability projects, businesses may incorporate market information into their decision-making processes. Companies can communicate with customers through surveys, focus groups, and online platforms based on shared sustainability principles to gain valuable insights, identify areas for improvement, and create stronger customer relationships.

By effectively integrating market data into sustainability initiatives, the automotive sector may produce and offer goods and services that meet consumer demands, adhere to legal requirements, and help to create a more sustainable future. Integration of market intelligence helps companies stay competitive, build stronger brands, and encourage innovation, all of which eventually result in positive change for the industry and society.

4. LIFECYCLES OF VEHICLES

The end-of-life cycle of vehicles refers to the stage when a vehicle has reached the end of its usable life and needs to be disposed of or recycled. As it entails minimizing the environmental impact and maximizing the resource recovery from vehicles, this phase is essential to sustainable development. Proper disposal and recycling of end-of-life vehicles are essential to prevent environmental pollution. Vehicles contain hazardous materials, such as batteries, oils, and fluids, which must be carefully removed and disposed of according to environmental regulations. Steel, aluminium, plastic, and glass recycling in the production process lowers the need for virgin resources. The end-of-life cycle in the automobile industry presents economic opportunities (Centobelli et al., 2020). The recycling sector helps to create jobs and contribute to the growth of the economy by extracting valuable materials from vehicles and reusing them. To reduce waste and the automobile sector's environmental impact, new strategies, and plans are being implemented to properly manage the end of the lifecycle. The government has put in place rules for ethical waste management, recycling, and environmental standards that make it easier for manufacturers to recycle their products. As a result, these rules aid in responsible environmental management.

5. CONCLUSION

The automotive sector has increasingly prioritised the implementation of sustainable practises, the promotion of sustainable development, and the pursuit of sustainable aims. The primary objectives of the automotive sector are conducting supplier evaluations, procuring sustainable energy sources, and enhancing manufacturing methodologies. The automotive sector had challenges pertaining to supply chain management, delivery disruptions, partial scarcities in automotive components, and sales performance throughout the pandemic. In the year 2018, a total of 86 million automobiles were sold, which accounted for approximately 9% of the global greenhouse gas emissions (forbes.com, 2021). The automotive industry is currently undergoing a significant shift towards a new age characterised by enhanced mobility and a greater emphasis on sustainability.

REFERENCES

Burange, L. G., & Yamini, S. (2008, February). Competitiveness of firms in Indian automobile industry. In *International Conference on Transportation System Studies.* Department of Economics, University of Mumbai, Mumbai.

Centobelli, P., Cerchione, R., Esposito, E., & Shashi. (2020). Evaluating environmental sustainability strategies in freight transport and logistics industry. *Business Strategy and the Environment, 29*(3), 1563–1574. doi:10.1002/bse.2453

Chand, P. K., Kadel, N., Mittal, A., & Mantri, A. (2022). The Relationship of Organizational Ambidexterity and Organizational Virtuousness in the Automobile Industry of India. [IJSKD]. *International Journal of Sociotechnology and Knowledge Development, 14*(1), 1–20. doi:10.4018/IJSKD.301262

Gawer, A., & Cusumano, M. A. (2014). Industry platforms and ecosystem innovation. *Journal of Product Innovation Management, 31*(3), 417–433. doi:10.1111/jpim.12105

Gupta, D., Wadhwa, S., & Moudgil, A. (2021, September). Deploying blockchain based security solutions for vehicular edge computing networks. In *2021 9th International Conference on Reliability, Infocom Technologies and Optimization (Trends and Future Directions)(ICRITO)* (pp. 1-5). IEEE. hipshortage/?sh=78b9cb788b42

Jindal, P. (2019). Special Economic Zones in India: An Instrument for Economic Development. *Mmu Journal Of Management Practices, 10*(1), 8–11.

Mc Anthony, I., & Jindal, P. (2017). Performance Assessment Of Automobile Industry In Japan Using Ratio Analysis. *Impact: International Journal Of Research In Business Management (Impact: Ijrbm), 5*, 89-106.

Naghshineh, B., & Carvalho, H. (2022). The implications of additive manufacturing technology adoption for supply chain resilience: A systematic search and review. *International Journal of Production Economics, 247*, 108387. doi:10.1016/j.ijpe.2021.108387

Nguyen, N. P., & Hoai, T. T. (2023). Internal controls driven by mindfulness toward enhanced ethical behaviors: Empirical evidence from Vietnam. *Heliyon, 9*(7), e18002. doi:10.1016/j.heliyon.2023.e18002 PMID:37483747

Shaikh, T. A., Rasool, T., & Lone, F. R. (2022). Towards leveraging the role of machine learning and artificial intelligence in precision agriculture and smart farming. *Computers and Electronics in Agriculture, 198*, 107119. doi:10.1016/j.compag.2022.107119

Siaminwe, L., Malama, T., Chizyuka, C., Mwenda, H., & Mwanza, M. (2016). Strategic Justification of Advanced Manufacturing Technologies Through Manufacturing Technology Research. *International Journal of Engineering Research & Technology (Ahmedabad), 5*(01), 837–842.

Sutiyem, S., Trismiyanti, D., Linda, M. R., Yonita, R., & Suheri, S. (2020). The impact of job satisfaction and employee engagement on organizational commitment. *Dinasti International Journal of Education Management And Social Science, 2*(1), 55–66. doi:10.31933/dijemss.v2i1.597

Zhou, K., Liu, T., & Zhou, L. (2015, August). Industry 4.0: Towards future industrial opportunities and challenges. In *2015 12th International conference on fuzzy systems and knowledge discovery (FSKD)* (pp. 2147-2152). IEEE.

Chapter 16
Service Quality and Innovation in Air Transport

Ravi Lakshmanan
https://orcid.org/0000-0002-0283-6675
GMR Airports Limited, India

ABSTRACT

Passenger services at airports are coproduced by many organizations - airports, airlines, ground handlers, immigration, customs, aviation security, and commercial establishments. Service performance on subjective parameters is evaluated primarily through customer satisfaction surveys at frequent intervals through third parties with varying parameters and methodology. The objective parameters as defined by the airports are measured and reported by the airports. Thus, there is no standardized set of parameters and methodology for airport services performance. With the increased passenger's awareness about quality of services and reporting platforms like social media, airports have started to innovate the processes and introduce advanced technologies and exceed the service quality paradigm to passenger experience. Also, the importance attached to the services by the passengers differs based on the travel purpose. It is seen that airports compete with each other to add value to passenger services and experience on a continual basis. This book chapter describes these aspects of airport services.

1. INTRODUCTION

Airlines are responsible for transporting passengers and cargo between various locations, with the processing of both occurring at airports. It's essential to note that the following book chapter description focuses solely on passengers, excluding considerations for cargo. Airports furnish the infrastructure, facilities, and systems necessary for processing passengers at passenger terminals. Airlines utilize aircraft parking stands, the runway/taxiway system, and Air Navigation Services provided by airports. Evaluating service delivery and implementing corrective measures not only enhances passenger satisfaction but also enhances an airport's reputation, potentially attracting additional passenger traffic. This, in turn, may lead existing airlines to add more routes/flights, while other airlines may express interest in commencing operations from the airport. Passengers prefer airports offering choices between airlines,

DOI: 10.4018/979-8-3693-2019-8.ch016

seeking positive performance attributes, while airlines aspire to expand their operations based on passenger demand driven by the airport's service quality and performance attributes. Therefore, airlines and airports complement each other.

Service is defined as "a time-perishable, intangible experience performed for a customer acting in the role of co-producer" (Fitzsimmons, 2001). Hill (1977) characterizes service as a change in the condition or state of an economic entity caused by another. Combining Fitzsimmons and Hill's definitions, service emerges as a time-sensitive, intangible experience carried out for a client who also plays the role of a co-producer, transforming the client's state or possession. This amalgamation reveals that clients actively contribute to the co-production of value, often resulting in a transformed state or possession. The concept of responsibility in a co-production activity is exemplified by the check-in process for passengers. The performance of staff at check-in counters or self-service kiosks is integral to service quality, but equally important is how well passengers present documents to facilitate timely process completion.

Airport services, encompassing passenger, baggage, and aircraft processes on apron stands, involve multiple stakeholders such as airports, airlines, ground handlers, fuel suppliers, in-flight caterers, immigration, customs, and aviation security personnel. This intricate network contributes to the challenge of delivering high-quality services while striving to maintain a balance between productivity and performance. It is imperative not to compromise performance quality for increased productivity, and vice versa. The aviation industry, driven by the need to accommodate growing traffic and minimize operational costs, emphasizes service productivity enhancement, transcending mere service delivery to ensure an optimal passenger experience.

This chapter delves into the parameters and methodologies for assessing airport service quality performance, incorporating technologies and innovative approaches to enhance service satisfaction. Noteworthy is the dedication of airport service providers to continually enhance services and distinguish themselves from competitors. Although the term "airport" is used, it encompasses various stakeholders, primarily airports, airlines, and government authorities such as immigration, customs, and aviation security.

The discussion on service performance and productivity includes apron services, with a particular focus about 'On Time Performance' (OTP) of flights as a crucial metric.

Recognizing the diversity in passenger profiles, it becomes essential to understand the specific airport services that passengers deem important.

The subsequent sections of this chapter cover an overview of previous literature (Section 2), methodologies for service assessment (Section 3), results detailing the importance of services based on traveller opinions for domestic passenger processes in Indian airports (Section 4), exploration of service innovations and advanced technologies adopted by airports (Section 5), and the concluding remarks (Section 6).

It's crucial to note that this chapter centers on passenger services while the aircraft is at the airport, excluding in-flight services and their corresponding performance.

Figure 1 illustrates the flow of domestic departure passengers through various processes, and for domestic arrivals, the sole process involves collecting baggage at the arrival baggage carousel. International departures entail an additional immigration process after check-in, while arriving international passengers undergo immigration after deboarding and subsequent baggage reclaim.

2. LITERATURE REVIEW

Literatures reviewed have been grouped together based on the objective of the study as below.

Figure 1. (a) Domestic departure passenger flow; (b) Domestic arrival passenger flow

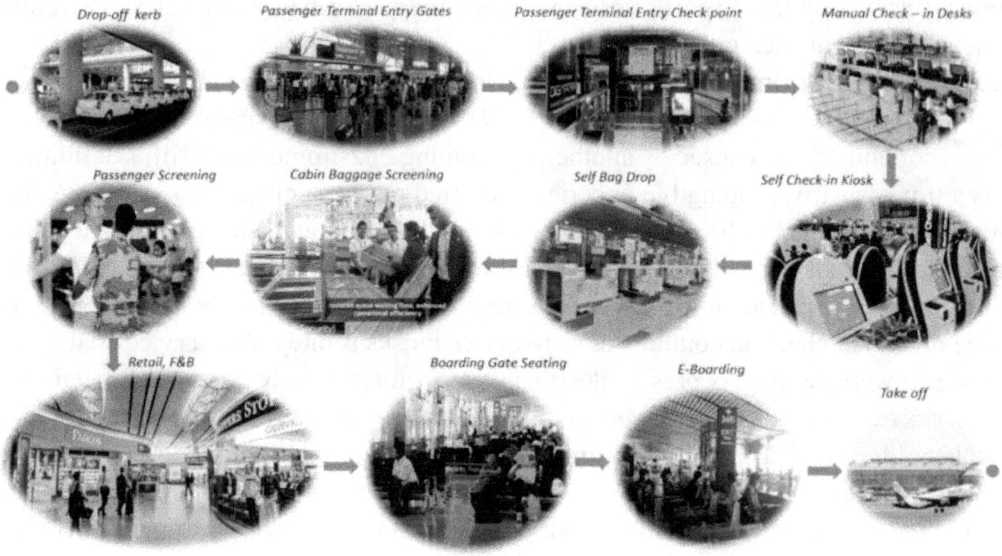

(a)

(b)

2.1 Passengers' Perception of Service Quality

(Widarsyah, 2013) analysed the relationship between seven airport service dimensions (Access, Services and Facilities, Dining, Shopping, Service Personnel and Security, Environment, and Immigration and Customs) and overall passenger perceptions of service quality of four international airports viz. Las Vegas

McCarran International, Los Angeles International, San Francisco International, and Seattle-Tacoma International. Multiple linear regression was employed to analyse the data, revealing that airport environment had the greatest impact on passengers' perceptions, followed by access, dining, and immigration and customs services. (Jiang & Zhang, 2016) using a thirty-seven-parameter evaluated the quality of services provided at Melbourne Airport. The results indicated notable differences in the expectations and perceptions of passengers on the level of service provided. In order for the airport to concentrate on these services, fourteen of the thirty-seven factors were deemed important and satisfactory. The finding was that high income earners, frequent travellers, and business travellers were found to be more demanding on the quality of the services they received than other groups. This survey identified the expectation differences between the type of travellers. (Ejem, 2020) assessed the Airport Service Quality (ASQ) in Nigeria using the SERVQUAL model from both the perspectives of the airlines and airport services at Nnamdi Azikiwe International Airport and Abuja and Murtala Muhammed International Airport, Lagos, in Nigeria. They used questionnaire as survey instrument to elicit the service quality expectations and perceptions of both airlines and air passengers in these airports. The results of the study indicated that ASQ in both airports were low and did not meet the service quality expectations of both passengers as airline users and as airport users. Customer Satisfaction Survey of a small airport in Italy by (Allen et al., 2020) verified and found that latent elements including accessibility to services, control operations, and terminal environment had a substantial impact on total airport service quality. Study by (Chonsalasin et al., 2020) based on a model with seven dimensions of service quality viz. security, check-in, wayfinding, airport environment, access, arrival services, and airport facilities for airport service quality measurement. The selected passengers of Thai airline participated in the survey. The model also used confirmatory factor analysis to identify passenger expectations which can be used for the development plan to align with passengers' needs and requirements. (Halpern & Mwesiumo, 2021) finds that in addition to overall service rating, the services at individual process are also important to get a positive feedback for promotion and service attributes are more important than others. The study also finds that service failures associated with airport front line staff and queueing times have the greatest negative effects on the likelihood of promoting an airport online, while failures associated with airport shopping and Wi-Fi service have the weakest negative effects. (Bellizzi et al., 2018) Using an ordered logit model, illustrates how important it is to look into passengers' views in order to identify the service elements that have the biggest impact on passengers' satisfaction. The study concludes that importance attached to the services by the passengers differ based on the purpose of travel. (Bellizzi et al., 2020) through a literature survey examined the quality of air transport services from the perspective of the passengers, based on customer satisfaction surveys. The study concluded that there are many different approaches to both gathering and analysing data. The above literatures show that common service parameters for assessment of service quality are airport environment, immigration, customs and security services, queuing time and F&B. Passengers' importance parameters are airport environment, access, queuing time and services. Importance differs based on the purpose of travel and even to the extent that how early, before the scheduled flight departure, the passengers arrive the airport. Technique/method commonly used are multiple linear regression, SERVQUAL, MCDM (AHP) and survey through questionnaires.

2.2 Airlines' Perception of Airport Service Quality

In order to understand the airlines preference and importance of airport service quality, (Pabedinskaitė[a] & Akstinaitė, 2014) evaluated the airport service quality for the services provided by airports to airlines, using SERVQUAL model. The survey established the relative importance of airport service quality dimensions in respect of airlines viz., the quality of aircraft landing and parking, while the quality of other services like landside services and non-aviation services is far less important.

2.3 Passengers' Perception of Airline Service Quality

(Samad et al., 2021) evaluated the performance of airline service quality. The authors applied Multi Criteria Decision Making (MCDM) method using Analytic Hierarchy Process (AHP) technique. The key evaluation shows that the airline website, passenger service, and security and reliability are the most crucial quality standards for enhancing airline efficiency. Furthermore, the findings of the AHP analysis demonstrated that the most significant indicators pertaining to services at airports are baggage delivery time, employee courtesy, on-time performance, and handling of delayed flight. (Burapharat et al., 2021) examined managerial views of service quality and customer's satisfaction of hybrid airlines in Suvarnabhumi Airport, Thailand. The five-dimensional SERVQUAL model was used which consists of five factors reliability, responsiveness, assurance, empathy, and tangibles. Most respondents agreed that the service quality of hybrid airlines in Suvarnabhumi Airport, Thailand still in a high level. From the above literatures it is seen that significant indicators for the service performance are waiting time and on-time performance. Airport infrastructure/ system has equal contribution to the performance along with airline staff operating these. Method used are MCDM (AHP) and SERNQUAL.

2.4 Evaluation of Service Attributes to Measure Users' Satisfaction

(Hong et al., 2020)'s study supports the three dimensions - the interactional service (delivery)quality attribute, physical environment quality (servicescape), and outcome quality (convenience) for the service quality of passenger terminals at the selected airport for the study. The study also analysed in two segments viz. service provider and passengers and showed that service providers place more emphasis on physical environment quality (servicescape) while passengers place more emphasis on outcome quality (convenience). However, both emphasis on interactional service quality. The study finds that the importance of the parameter of the service quality are not the same between the service provider and passengers.

2.5 Assessment to Get to Know the Improvements That Are Required

(Pandey, 2016) assessed the level of service at the two busiest airports run by Airport of Thailand and determined where improvements may be made while taking the evolving needs of the customer into consideration. An analysis of the airport's service quality was conducted using the Fuzzy Multi Criteria Decision Making Analysis (MCDM). Additionally, it used fuzzy expert systems for Improvement Performance Analysis (IPA) to investigate ways to improve airport services. The study validated the use of the Fuzzy MCDM approach, which is found to be more accurate in evaluating perception, to assess the airport's service quality. In this study also MCDM approach is used.

2.6 Airport Service Quality Ratings and Its Impact

(Wildan Nugraha dan Direstu Amalia, 2021) analysed if passengers are satisfied with the services at an airport whether they may stay longer in the airport, recommend the airport to other people, or pay higher tax. This also included an assessment the of the ability of ASQ to explain the variation in repeat purchase intention including interaction among variables. The study finds that ASQ has a moderately low effect of purchasing intentions. Thus, only a higher ASQ rating alone will not result in increased commercial revenues.

2.7 Technology and Innovation

(Mohamad Houssam EL Najjar, 2018) conclude that creating new technology is connected to how satisfied customers are and what they intend to do next, and customer satisfaction is linked to their intentions. (Sena Kilic,C.Ucler, 2021) in their systematic literature review on innovation at airports examined the research framework on this subject. It finds that research is mainly focused on product / services, concerned with leveraging Information and Communication Technology, the unplanned implementation with least consolidated strategic approach and lacks the input of external innovation scholars and specialists., The study also finds a rising trend in innovation at airports. (Min Soo Kang, Seung IK Baek, Hyung K.Choi, Yun Young Song, 2008)'s case study at Incheon Airport confirms the use of service Blueprinting as a tool for service innovation by analysing the process flow and identifying improvements that are required. (Gumasing et al., 2020) studied actual waiting time at the immigration process at terminal 1 of Ninoy Aquino International Airport, Manila, which was far more than the time specified by the authorities. The study brought out the factors that contribute the service quality. The authors worked out a revised layout of the immigration counters and the waiting time with revised layout was validated using simulation and found that the waiting time would meet the standard set by the authorities. (Cserdi & Kenesei, 2021) studied the attitude of the users to the forced adoption of new technology. The study used the survey results on the acceptance of introduction of self-service ticket vending machines instead of manual ticket counters by a public transportation company. The study found that positive impact on the acceptance of forced use can be achieved by perceived performance, ease of use of the new kiosks, and the need for interaction by consumers. Also, the acceptance of the new technology has to be tested after some time of the usage as passengers need some time to get used to the new system. (Caetano et al., 2021) Identified and measured the innovation at the airports to quantify what has been done, what all are to be improved and thus, creating opportunities for more innovation. The study resulted in an algorithm for an Airport Integrated Innovation Index (AI^3), composed by 38 measurable variables related to innovation practices, procedures, and infrastructure elements such as new biometric passenger identification systems, real-time passenger flight tracking systems, new types of runway pavement, and actions to reduce airport operational restrictions. Evaluating service quality in air transport sector represents a more stimulating challenge, given the complexity of air transport system in regards to the other systems; in fact, air transport service is characterised by a great variety of service aspects relating to services offered by the airlines and provided by the companies managing airports. The complexity of such a service requires a deep investigation on the methods adopted for collecting and analysing the data regarding passengers' perceptions (Bellizzi et al., 2020). (Thums et al., 2023) examined the current status of digitalization at airports regarding technology implementation, identified impacts of digital transformation and digital technologies especially regarding the specified professional groups of pilots, of cabin crew and of security staff in the context of airports and derived a future research agenda based on the findings. (Weekx & Buyle, 2023) examined the effect of airlines dominance on the airports technical efficiency using the data from 20 medium sized European airports. The study finds that there is a strong relationship between them. Also found that airports operating in an airport group are more efficient. This is because airports' infrastructure is utilised / operated by airlines, and they are expected to operate as per the standards set by the airport operator which complies with the standard set by the regulator or the design basis. Operating below such standards will affect the efficiency of the process and system.

In summary, from the literature review it can be seen that the published papers on the subject is for service performance assessment for specific airports with varying service parameters and varying methodologies. The importance of service parameters opined by the passengers differ based on the type of travellers. Methods adopted for collecting and analysing the data regarding passengers' perceptions require consideration for suitability of the specific airport. Literature review show some studies are empirical, and some are case studies. The recent literatures show that the topic of innovation and application of artificial intelligence also studied. The technology introduction requires proper evaluation for its acceptability to the passengers which should not be done immediately after introduction.

However, it is required to research and comprehensively bring out a research paper with the following contents:-

a) Uniform service performance indicators applicable to all the airports, their measurement methodologies and ranking / rating of the airports based on the actual performance values. Present industry accepted and practiced methods.
b) Passenger preferences in the case of travellers in Indian domestic airports through a survey. It is important since many advanced technologies are being introduced and pax expectations also different than few years back.
c) Practical utilization of the technology and innovation at airports at respective processes as described in this chapter to improve passenger experience and productivity. Added to this certain practical concepts of quality enhancement.

This chapter description is aimed at covering all the above aspects so that readers have an overall view of passenger, baggage and aircraft processes, opportunities and challenges associated with the performance of the services and productivity enhancement through technologies and processes.

3. SERVICE PERFORMANCE MEASUREMENT PRACTICES AT AIRPORTS

The airport provides services to the passengers. It also provides / facilitates airlines and stake holders to perform their functions efficiently. The parameters for the service quality measurement can be broadly classified in to two groups viz.

a) **Objective parameters**- These parameters will have a specific target to achieve, and actual delivery can be measured. Some of the objective parameters are.

Waiting time in the queue for the process

- Check-in, Immigration, Customs and Security
- Delivery time of hold bags at the arrival hall

Availability of equipment / system

- Escalators
- Elevators
- Flight Information Displays

Few examples of the parameters specified in some of the concession agreements between the government and the airport operator.

Waiting time in the Queue for processing

Check-in 95% of business class passengers in 5 min

95% of economy class passengers in 15 min

Security Check 95% of passengers less than 10 min

Immigration 95% of passengers less than 10 min

Baggage delivery **Code C aircrafts** *

First bag in 10 min; last bag in 30 min

Code E aircrafts. *

First bag in 15 min; last bag in 40 min

Availability

Passenger Boarding Bridges 99% availability.

FIDS, PA system, screening machines 99% availability

Escalators, Elevators 98% availability

Apron stands 99% availability.

Passenger facilitation

Baggage trolleys 100% available

Wheelchairs 100% available

Attending complaints 95% of high priority in 4 hours

95% of others in 24 hours

Passenger Boarding Bridges 90% of passengers processed through PBBs (Aircrafts type A-320/B-737 & larger)

*Code C aircrafts- Aircrafts with wingspan less than 36m.

*Code E aircrafts- Aircrafts with wingspan more than 36m but less than 65m.

*Thus, Code E aircrafts' passenger capacity and quantity of checked in bags will be more than Code C aircrafts.

Airports monitor these parameters and report to the regulator, if required.

b) Subjective Parameters- The target values for these parameters are not provided with absolute numbers. The actual quality of service delivery is obtained from the passengers and stakeholders through satisfaction surveys conducted periodically with clear guidelines and a questionnaire identifying the parameters and number of respondents among other specifics. The rating of the passengers for the parameters are perceptions which is required to be considered while structuring the survey and analyzing the ratings.

Examples of subjective **parameters** are.

- Cleanliness of washrooms
- Ambience at the terminal
- Courtesy of staff
- Efficiency of Check-in

4. AIRPORTS COUNCIL INTERNATIONAL (ACI) METHODOLOGY

4.1 Departures and Arrivals ASQ Survey

ACI conducts the following programs for the airports relevant to the subject.

Voice of the customer- these are customer surveys for departure, arrival and commercial.

Voice of the employee- Assess employee commitment and engagement, determine priority improvement areas, Evaluate the success of customer experience measures, and build a positive customer experience culture.

ACI also carries out Airport Customer Experience Accreditation. The Airport Customer Experience Accreditation program by ACI aims to strengthen airports' ability to improve customer experience management in the long term. Engaging airports undergo a thorough evaluation and training regimen, involving stakeholders and staff in development initiatives. Distinguished as the sole accreditation program offering a holistic perspective on customer experience management within the airport sector, it offers a comprehensive 360° assessment.

4.2 Passenger Satisfaction Survey: Voice of the Customer

Departures ASQ is conducted at the departure gates & Arrivals survey is conducted at baggage reclaim belts. The ASQ departures questionnaire is completed by randomly selected passengers at the boarding gates of pre-selected flights. 350- 550 samples per quarter is collected and surveys are conducted every month.

ASQ departure questionnaire consists of thirty-one service-based satisfaction items covering each touchpoint of the airport journey, five emotions to understand how passengers are feeling right after they went through the journey, two for overall satisfaction with the airport and overall experience at the airport, passenger profiling questions (demographic and behavioral) and two open-ended questions. Passengers rate the services on a scale of 1 to 5, 1 being poor and 5 excellent. Some examples of 31 service based parameters are waiting time at the check-in, availability of seats at the boarding gates, availability of flight information, cleanliness of washrooms/ terminal building.

Similarly, ASQ Arrivals investigates 37 service elements across seven segmentation fields, giving the most complete picture of the arrival passenger experience the airport.

Upon successfully conducting the quarterly samples in accordance with ACI's sampling plan, the airport will receive the performance results for each quarter from ACI. Airports that have diligently completed all four quarters of sampling, adhering to ACI's compliance criteria, will be eligible for awards. The ASQ award recognizes airports with the top 20% overall satisfaction score by annual passenger handled and region. For example, for the year 2023, in the Asia- Pacific Region, among airports that handled 15 to 25 million passengers per annum, the three airports awarded are I Gusti Ngurah Rai Airport (Bali, Indonesia), Juanda International Airport (Surabaya, Indonesia), Rajiv Gandhi International Airport (Hyderabad, India).

4.3 SKYTRAX Methodology

Another popular rating is of SKYTRAX which conducts the program for both airlines and airports. For airports, the program consists of Skytrax rating star 1 to 5 and Skytrax ranking of the airports.

Skytrax ranking is based on passenger satisfaction survey with forty-one parameters. The major difference between ACI and Skytrax ranking is that in ACI program the survey questionnaire is given to the passengers and their satisfaction rating is obtained while they are at the airport for their immediate reaction whereas in the case of Skytrax the passengers submit their service evaluation online after the services are performed and away from the airport. 5-Star Airport rating is the highest mark of quality distinction awarded for an airport and recognizes very high standards of Product and Staff service across the different assessment categories in the Airport environment. Top five ranked airports in 2023 are Singapore Changi Airport, Hamad International Airport, Tokyo International Airport (Haneda), Incheon International Airport, Paris Charles de Gaulle Airport.

Whereas Skytrax rating is evaluated by the auditors who assess the infrastructure like availability of flight information displays, signages, seating at the boarding gates etc., and services maintained like cleanliness of the terminal, availability of buggies etc. Skytrax apply ratings for up to eight hundred customer-facing areas of airport product and service, and this spans over thirty different customer contact points. In 2023, there are **twelve 5-Star hub Airports** (Doha Hamad International Airport, Munich Airport among others) and **seven 5-Star Regional Airports**, few airports are rated as **5-Star Terminals** (Terminal B, LaGuardia Airport)

For airline awards, passengers nominate their favorite airline or airline they considered to be best and rank their satisfaction (1 to 5 scale) for aspects of the travel experience, across both the airport and onboard environments. Data weighting is applied to provide equity when evaluating airlines of different sizes. Singapore Airlines was awarded the World's Best Airline at the 2023 World Airline Awards.

4.4 Wall Street Journal (WSJ) Methodology

WSJ publishes an annual list of the best large airports in the US. Assessment by WSJ is slightly different from the others in that there are thirty metrics separated into two categories viz. "reliability" and "value" & "convenience." The metrics to measure "reliability" are on-time arrivals, on-time departures, average arrival delay, average departure delay, flight cancellations, average taxi-in, average taxi-out, security-checkpoint waiting times, and flight delays due to major security issues. These carried more weight than aspects like the quality of washrooms.

For "value," the six metrics are the average domestic fare, cheapest on-site parking, rental car taxes and fees, UberX fare from convention Center to airport, the leading airline's market share, and the cheapest bottle of water. The metrics for "convenience" are J.D. Power customer satisfaction score, nonstop destinations, longest walk, and Yelp restaurant ratings. Based on these metrics, Phoenix's airport was ranked number one in 2023, bolstered by its easy access, airline and flight options, and consistent weather that prevents last-minute flight cancellations and delays, according to the publication. The Arizona hub also had the best taxi-out times of all the airports on this list, which means travelers spend less of their flight waiting on the tarmac.

The mid-sized airports were ranked separately, and the best mid-size airport was Sacramento International Airport.

5. EVALUATION OF IMPORTANCE OF SERVICES BY THE PASSENGERS

As a part of this book chapter, a study was carried out in December 2023 to understand the importance of services for domestic passengers while travelling through airports in India. The services are broadly grouped together the under a) Kerb side b) Terminal facilities c) Way Finding d) Retail and Food and Beverages (F&B)

Each of these services is specified with sub-factors of the services to identify importance over the sub-factors. Multi Criteria Decision Making (MCDM) methodology using fuzzy AHP was adopted to measure the importance of pair-wise comparison. A matrix for seeking passengers input was prepared for comparison between the sub-factors of each of the four services individually.

The matrix was mailed to 58 travellers and were guided how to fill in input for importance in the pair-wise comparison. The received responses were verified for completeness and 50 responses were analysed. Table 1 shows the profile of the respondents.

Table 1. Respondents profile

GENDER	*MALE*	*FEMALE*					
	36	14					
Age Group	*18-24*	*25-34*	*35-45*	*46-56*	*57-67*	*>67*	*DNR*
	1	15	24	5	2		3
Education	*Degree*	*Masters degree*	*Doctoral Degree*	*DNR*			
	17	29	2	2			
Occupation	*Home maker*	*Professional*	*Middle Management*	*Sales Marketing*	*Business Owner*	*Others*	*DNR*
		27	10	3	5	2	3
Travel Type	*Leisure*	*Business*	*Both*	*DNR*			
	14	12	23	1			
No of Trips	*1--2*	*3--4*	*5--6*	*7--8*	*9--10*	*>11*	*DNR*
	8	11	8	3	7	12	1

The linguistic variables of the passengers' judgement were converted to fuzzy triangular numbers. Table 2 presents the linguistic variables and their corresponding triangular fuzzy numbers (TFN). TFN is mostly used for fuzzy numbers.

The importance of the services was analysed in two parts, one with all the 50 responses and 2nd one with only leisure travellers in order to find out if there are any differences in the importance opined by business travellers and leisure travellers, in line with the literatures studied. Table 3 shows the final result.

It is seen that the highest importance rank 1 between leisure travellers and business travellers is the same for terminal facilities, kerb services and way finding. In the case of Retail and F&B, it shows that leisure travellers attach the highest importance to a 'diverse range of F&B' whereas together with business travellers the highest importance is for lounge facilities with F&B, which is realistic. Least

Table 2. Linguistic variables and respective fuzzy numbers

Linguistic variables for the importance	*Triangular fuzzy scale*	*Triangular fuzzy reciprocal scale*
Equal	1, 1, 1	1, 1,1
Moderate	1, 3/2, 2	1/2, 2/3, 1
Strong	3/2, 2, 5/2	2/5,1 /2, 2/3
Very strong	2, 5/2, 3	1/3, 2/5, 1/2
Absolute	5/2, 3, 7/2	2/7, 1/3, 2/5

Table 3. Importance of services opined by the passengers. Rank 1 being the highest importance

Services	Considering all the 50 responses	Considering only the leisure travelers
Terminal Facilities		
Waiting time for different processes	Rank 3	Rank 2
On-time performance of flights	Rank 1	Rank 1
Manually assisted processing	Rank 4	Rank 4
Automation in prassenger processing (DigiYatra, Self Bag Drop, ATRS, E Boarding)	Rank 2	Rank 3
Kerb services		
Availability of sufficient drop off points at kerb	Rank 2	No Change, same as that of 50 respondents
Valet parking facility	Rank 5	
Walking distance between car park and terminal building	Rank 3	
Number of transport options to reach the airport	Rank 1	
Value for Money Car Parking spaces	Rank 4	
Retail and F&B		
Diverse range of food and beverage options	*Rank 2*	*Rank 1*
Exquisite retail offerings	*Rank 4*	*Rank 4*
Value for Money retail offerings	*Rank 3*	*Rank 3*
Lounge facility with F&B	*Rank 1*	*Rank 2*
Availability of business centres/ meeting rooms	*Rank 5*	*Rank 5*
Way Finding		
Dynamic Signage	Rank 5	Rank 5
Easy navigation through the terminal	Rank 1	Rank 1
Interactive maps, and digital guidance systems	Rank 2	Rank 3
Public announcement of flight information	Rank 3	Rank 4
Unlimited free wifi (reliable)	Rank 4	Rank 2

importance is the same for all the sub-factors of the services. 'On Time Performance' (OTP) is of the highest importance for terminal facilities, followed by automated processes.

Travellers attach the highest importance to multiple transport modes to the airport.

The subsequent paragraphs describe the technology / innovation that have been implemented to cater to the importance of passengers derived from the survey as above.

6. SERVICE PERFORMANCE, PRODUCTIVITY THROUGH TECHNOLOGY AND INNOVATION

The reasons for the more focus on performance of service delivery is described herein. The first one being the sustained passenger traffic growth. As per ACI, Global passenger traffic experienced a decline from 9.2 billion in 2019 to 3.6 billion in 2020 due to the Covid pandemic, followed by a recovery to 4.6 billion in 2021 and 6.5 billion in 2022. Over the next five years, a medium-term projection anticipates traffic rebounding from 4.6 billion to 11.0 billion by 2027. In 2024, it is expected to reach the pre-Covid level of 9.2 billion. Long-term forecasts suggest passenger traffic at 19.3 billion in 2041 and 23.9 billion in 2050.

As passenger traffic grows, evolving passenger expectations drive a demand for a distinct experience. Additionally, competition among airports to surpass passenger satisfaction fosters innovation in processes and technology.

6.1 Benefits of Innovation

Due to the increasing volume of passenger traffic, the aviation sector is actively seeking innovative solutions to meet the demand because the airport expansion poses significant financial challenges, encompassing both capital and operational expenses. Additionally, passengers now expect expedited processing and enhanced travel comfort. Limited land availability further compels airports to maximize utilization of their existing infrastructure while adhering to service level standards. This involves implementing inventive processes and technology aimed at minimizing human involvement in passenger and baggage process, given the inherent variability in human performance due to various factors. The overarching goal is to satisfy not only passengers but also all stakeholders within the airport environment.

6.2 Enhancing Overall Passenger Experience

Presently, airports are actively exploring avenues to enhance the overall passenger experience, transcending mere satisfaction. Passengers increasingly anticipate a seamlessly interconnected travel data system, encompassing their journey from entry into the terminal to check-in, security clearance, and boarding the aircraft. The integration of technologies such as biometrics or facial recognition aims to eliminate the need for physically presenting identification and boarding passes at each stage, promising a smoother and more delightful experience for passengers. Not only does this streamline processes for airports and airlines, but it also contributes to increased throughput capacity.

Amidst the heightened hygiene measures necessitated by the COVID-19 pandemic, the aviation industry found itself compelled to innovate, paving the way for touchless and self-processing solutions for passengers. These innovations not only upheld hygiene standards but also alleviated the workload of staff overseeing these processes. Post-pandemic, these automated procedures have become ingrained as the new normal, widely accepted and valued by aviation stakeholders and passengers alike. The current emphasis is on further refining and advancing these automated processes through the integration of cutting-edge technologies and continuous process improvement.

6.3 Productivity Increase Through Technology and Innovation

Service quality or performance measurement alone is not sufficient for the airport, as these are not practicable to carry out daily and these ratings or rankings can be seen as a capability of the airports to deliver service quality. Also, the airports with limited competition try to add value to the passengers while passing through the airport and also differentiate the services from other airports. Today, the airport does not provide services alone; they provide the best experience to the passengers through many means of value added to the services.

Service failure may occur at airports for many reasons. Some of the major failures are congestion in the terminal, long queues and abnormal waiting time in the processes, delayed departure of flights and accurate & timely information not made available for flight status, passengers are not made aware of dos and don'ts at security check, poor environmental condition, and behaviour of staff.

Wait time at the processes is the most irritating and tiring for the passengers, as they would like to be processed quickly. The literature review showed that the wait / queue time is an important service aspect preferred or importance attached to the services. More queue length and waiting time also create tension and stress for the operator manning the process. Certain processes cannot be expedited without adequate care, otherwise may compromise aviation safety, and pose security risks. However, proactive monitoring of the waiting time at each queue of all the processes and giving choices to the passengers with the information requires data collection and processing on time live.

Similarly, OTP is another important service for passengers. This was confirmed in the survey conducted as shown in Section 4.

Service failures fronts mentioned above can be avoided and impact mitigated a) using advanced technology and b) through process improvements. Airports try to innovate the service delivery performance through these two approaches. Another advantage of the innovation is that such interventions help in mitigating unusual conditions at the terminal due to weather related disturbances and as well increase the capacity to meet the passenger traffic growth. For increase in passenger throughput or productivity, the capacity addition with additional infrastructure like extension to terminal building can be postponed until the system gets saturated.

Innovation costs less than increasing additional infrastructure to raise capacity. For example, to increase the throughput of the security check can be achieved either a) by adding more screening machines with same technology as of the current machines or b) can replace screening machines with advanced technology and system which provides higher passenger throughput capacity within the same footprint of the terminal building. In this example, extension to the passenger terminal building in option a) is time consuming, higher capital cost (as small incremental extension is not possible) and impact on operations during the building extension. However, in option b) the stakeholders at the airport and the passengers are to be familiarized with the new system. In the initial stages of the introduction of the new technology or system, staff to be available to help the passengers while they get used to the system.

Data collected through technology increases the trust and confidence of the stakeholders to mitigate the delays in processing time when presented with such data. For example, information about wait time at different queues when collected automatically and made available live and presented to the stakeholders.

6.4 Passengers' Preference to Technology

International Air Transport Association (IATA) conducted Global passenger survey in 2022 and it showed that passengers are willing to take advantage of technology and re-thought processes to improve the convenience of their airport experience and manage their baggage. Specifically, the following were the outcome of the survey.

- 44% of travellers said that their preferred method for processing off-airport was check-in. 93% of travellers are in favour of a background check program designed specifically for reliable travellers in order to speed up the security process.
- Home pick-up and delivery would appeal to 67% of respondents, while remote check-in would appeal to 73%. Eighty percent of travellers stated they would check a bag more frequently if they are able to know the location / status of their bags in the entire trip. And half of those surveyed claimed to have either used or would consider using an electronic bag tag.
- 75% of passengers prefer to use biometric data over boarding passes and passports.
- With an 88% satisfaction score, more than a third have already used biometric identification when traveling. However, over 50% of travellers still have concerns about data protection.

Recent survey by ACI (ASQ 2023 Global Traveler Survey) shows that 58% of the respondents favoured a more technological and automated approach to make their journey fluid. Out of the seamless journey, self service solutions at the airport have scored the highest. Personalization of experience through App is getting popular for the passengers with relevant information about their travel and promotional offers to enhance experience throughout the journey. Emotional engagement is also popular through multimedia experiences, wellness centre, live performances, cultural & art exhibits, movie theatre etc.

The caution in digitalization and automation is that the airports/airlines should evaluate the technology introduction for its longevity, proof of concept firmly cleared, and trial carried out to ensure passengers and stakeholders can operate the new system and are convinced that this will be beneficial. The technology adopted should last for a long period with only upgrades required during its operations and ensure the availability of backup services during the operations. The airports/airlines cannot afford to incur the cost of changing the system frequently. Some of the systems, like security screening, require approval from the regulatory authorities.

6.5 Data Collection, Sharing, and Benefits

The passenger and baggage processes involve more than one stakeholder. Thus, better passenger experience can be achieved only through collaborative efforts among the stakeholders. Data has become more valuable today than a few years before for the reason that the processes use advanced technology as the cost of technology is reducing (on cost benefit analysis basis). At airports, the data collection, analysis, and action required based on the analysis is important and such collected data is to be shared with all the stakeholders so that the objective of providing quality services to the passengers is met. ACI has introduced the data sharing concept through a platform 'Airport Share'.

6.6 Three Horizon Innovation Model (McKinsey)

This approach has been embraced by a certain airport, which employs the metaphor of three horizons—earth, moon, and Mars—as a practical framework. To illustrate,

Amsterdam Schiphol Airport characterizes the "earth" horizon as encompassing daily challenges, typically addressed by operational experts. The "moon" horizon symbolizes imminent opportunities that necessitate a degree of transformation. Meanwhile, the "Mars" horizon signifies more disruptive and exploratory innovations. At Schiphol's Innovation Hub, the primary focus lies on Moon and Mars shots, representing high-risk endeavours with significant potential impact on operations. Consequently, these initiatives extend beyond the aviation sector, seeking innovative solutions from a broader spectrum. For example, automating airside operations by testing automated vehicles to shuttle passengers across airside is an initiative under "Mars". Pre-booking of time slots (described later in the chapter) can be classified under " Moon".

6.7 Examples of Innovation for Processes by Various Airports

Literature review and the survey carried out as explained in 4) show that passengers attach importance to queuing time and On Time Performance (OTP) of flights in the service aspect of services. Reference is made to figures 1 (a) and 1(b) which show the processes involved in passenger flow in an airport. The description below covers the aspect which lessen the queuing time / waiting time and improves the OTP.

6.8 Self-Service by Passengers Through One Digital ID

Passengers use the biometric identification already registered through an app when they enter the airport, and the same is used for verification by the passengers themselves in the subsequent process, enabling the passengers not required to show physical ID proof at every process. This lessens the queuing / waiting time and enhances passenger experience and increases productivity as well. Passengers passing through the process are recorded in the system for easy identification of the location of passengers in the terminal. Indian aviation has introduced one such system named DigiYatra. Presently, it is operational in a few Indian airports. It is a transformative initiative in the realm of air travel, leveraging digital technology to streamline passenger experiences. Revolutionizing the traditional journey, DigiYatra seamlessly integrates biometric authentication, mobile applications, and data analytics. Passengers enjoy a hassle-free experience from airport entry onwards until boarding the aircraft, minimizing processing time and enhancing overall efficiency. This innovative digital platform enhances security, minimizes manual verification of documents, ensuring a smooth and time-efficient travel experience. By harnessing the power of digital advancements, DigiYatra marks a significant leap forward in the aviation industry, promising a future where technology and convenience converge for a more connected and efficient travel landscape.

Similar to above, there are systems provided by various manufacturers. For example, SelfPassTM by M/S Collins Aerospace is an identity management system that allows travellers to move seamlessly through the airport using a facial scan. A secure link is established between passport, boarding pass and biometric identity that enables faster, self-service processing at each stage of the journey. Narita airport has launched 'Face Express', a contactless airport experience for passengers. Through the use of biometric technology, passenger's facial imagery is captured and verified against their passport which can then be used throughout the journey, from check in to the boarding gates.

The above system uses block-chain technology.

6.9 Check-In Process

Most of the major airports have now installed self-service kiosks for check-in and bag drops. Thus, the human performance variation with manual check-in process is avoided. Also, most of the passengers with only cabin bags print out the boarding pass off- airport and thus do not use check-in system at the airports. One of the airports in India innovated the process to reduce the congestion at the security check stations by creating a separate gate entry for cabin baggage passengers with boarding passes already with them so that they do not go through the check-in hall and go straight to the dedicated security check stations and enter the security hold area. This decongested the check-in hall as well as at the security check stations.

6.10 Monitoring Waiting Time and Queue Length

The number of passengers processed in various queues say every 15 min or 30 min can identify queues where there is more than the prescribed time and thus, identify reasons for the less numbers of passengers processed. The reasons may be technical, or staff not trained adequately or fatigue / monotony of the staff manning the process.

The innovation in this aspect is data collection, analysis, sharing with all stakeholders for each one of them to take note of the performance and taking corrective actions if the performance is less than the agreed performance level. For passengers to know in which queue to move depending on the wait time displayed. Wait times in terms of Key Performance Indicators (KPI) are published and made known to the pax to know their rights and to stakeholders for their performance. Less wait time in the process means more time spent on retail and F&B and more revenue for the airport.

Airports, now a days, display the wait time at different queues through a collection of data through cameras or LiDAR technology, and passengers on seeing such timing may move to a queue showing lesser wait times. Also, the stakeholder operating these processes can augment adjust their resources, like increasing the number of manned processors. Also, such data when analysed later in the day may provide information about the efficiency of the staff manning these processes and corrective actions required like training etc.

6.11 Security Check Process

In terms of technology, screening machines for cabin baggage incorporate advanced features such as AI. The latest technological advancement involves the use of Computed Tomography (CT) technology-based screening machines to inspect passengers' cabin baggage. Unlike previous methods, this type of machine eliminates the necessity to remove laptops, power banks, and water for separate scanning. Consequently, this reduces the time passengers spend at security check stations and significantly improves the overall passenger experience.

The bag in feed to the screening machines are through the Automatic Tray Retrieval system (ATR) which diverts the bags found to contain prohibited items so as not to stop the screening process, as well

Figure 2. Terminal entry gate wait time display

Figure 3. Security check wait time display at a central location

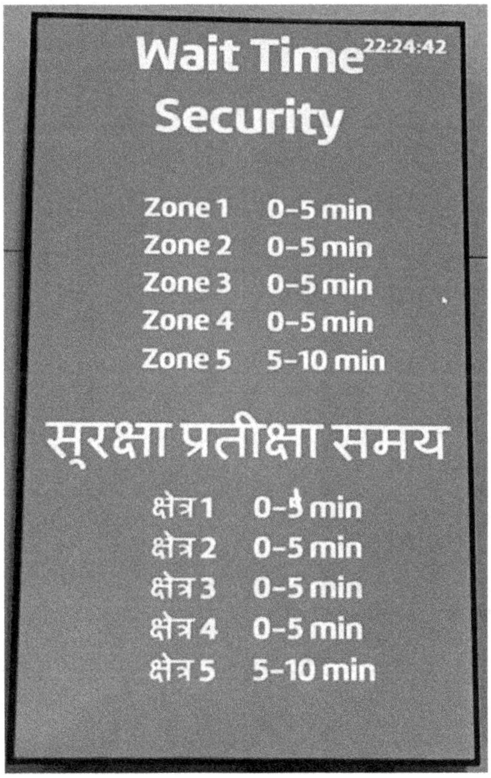

the trays are automatically returned to the infeed location. The screened image of diverted bags will be available at the diverted position and the screening operator will view the image in the presence of the concerned passenger and tell the passenger to show the suspect items to ensure these are permitted or if not remove the item from the bag.

Instead of one machine per operator to view the images of the bag contents, the machines are networked, and the screened bag images are viewed in a centralized image processing room, away from passenger area, and the images are randomly displayed to the operator so that any variation in performance of the

Figure 4. Wait time display zone wise for security check

Figure 5. Cabin baggage screening with automatic tray retrieval system

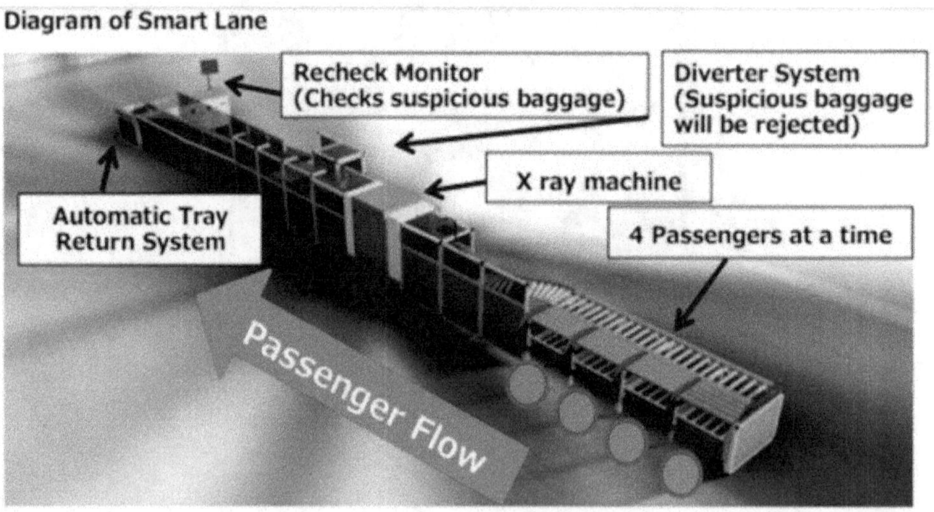

screening operator in terms of time taken to decide the acceptability or otherwise is compensated. Full body scanners are being employed for passenger screening to speed up the screening process as well as for thorough check. Block chain technology can be adopted so that screening results are securely recorded and accessible only to authorized parties, enhancing trust and transparency in the process.

6.12 Pre-Booking Time Slots for Security Check

This facilitation was initiated by a few of the busiest airports. Through this approach, travelers can reserve a security time window up to 72 hours before their departure. When they arrive at the specified queue and timeslot, they can scan the QR code they got, which verifies their position in a virtual line. After that, the passengers can quickly pass through security. Passengers can use this facility with no additional cost. This facilitation will lead to better passenger experience overall, more efficient security procedures, and enhanced passenger sign-in patterns. Airports are also aware of how many passengers will arrive at a particular time window and join the line.

6.13 Baggage Handling

Inbound luggage is unloaded from the aircraft and transported to the baggage unloading area within the airport terminal building via carts. Subsequently, the bags are manually transferred from the carts to conveyors, which then carry them to the carousel in the arrival hall. Passengers gather around the carousel to retrieve their respective bags. This manual offloading process, performed by staff who remove and load bags individually, is labor-intensive. Due to the inherent variability in human performance, this unseen process can result in delays in delivering arrival bags to the carousels, leading to increased wait times for passengers collecting their checked-in luggage.

Efforts are now underway to replace this manual process with robots. Amsterdam Schiphol has introduced a solution involving collaborative robots, or COBOTs, which work in tandem with human personnel. The robot and staff collaborate in offloading bags, with the robot's arms capable of lifting heavy items and placing them on the breakup conveyors. This not only reduces the physical strain on staff but also leverages the intelligence and judgment of human workers. As a result, increased productivity and passenger satisfaction.

Figure 6. Robot assisting unloading of bags

Home pick-up and home delivery of check-in bags are getting the attention of the passengers. Airports arrange to collect the bags from home before the specified time of flight departure. When the passenger arrives at the airport, they need not spend time for check-in bags and after the remaining process can then board the aircraft. Bags at the destination airport will also be handed over at home. This facilitates departing airports free from check-in bags at a time for processing except that the airport has to create space to store and secure the bags.

6.14 Wait Time at the Arrival Carousel to Collect the Bag

A study by SITA finds that positive emotions of passengers drop to below 54% if waiting time at re-claim belts is exceeding 30 minutes. If the waiting time is below 10 minutes, the positive emotions of passengers are 88%.

Passengers wait around the baggage carousel to pick up their bags and they don't know when it will arrive at the carousel. Sometimes this creates congestion around the carousel as passengers wait with the trolley. If the passengers know when their respective baggage will arrive at the carousel, they can relax and wait away from the carousel, till the arrival of the bag. Digital solution has been evolved that provide alerts to passengers on their bag dispatch. After scanning a QR code, users are notified directly on their mobile phone when their baggage is ready to be picked up and thus, they can wait in a less congested area.

Figure 7. Passengers waiting for bags at arrival carousel

6.15 On Time Performance (OTP) of Aircrafts

OTP is an important parameter for service excellence. There are many factors that determine the flights to get delayed. The departure delay could have been if the aircraft had arrived late from the previous sector. Or else the aircraft is not ready for departure as all the services (refuelling, cleaning, unloading, and loading of baggage, maintenance checks, loading of F&B, passengers boarding) are not completed, within the scheduled time or lack of airport infrastructure, air traffic congestion or weather-related delays. It is essential that the airports record the deviation from the scheduled departure and arrival time as per the flight schedule and analyse the reasons thereof.

Figure 8. Aircraft services on apron stand

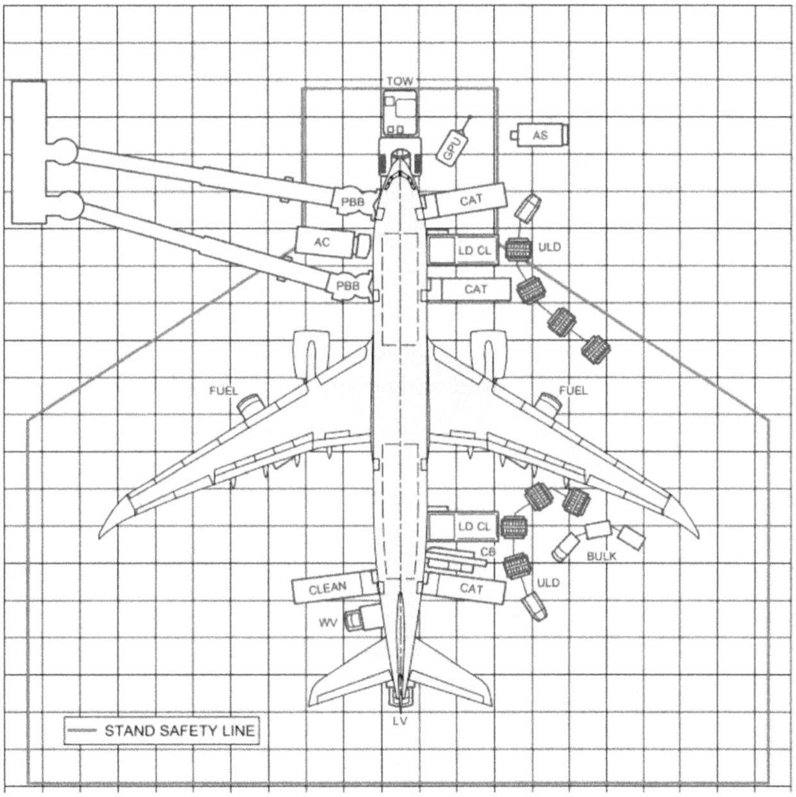

The departure delay will affect the other aircraft in sequence for departure unless the delayed aircraft status is proactively identified so that the subsequent aircraft in sequence can be allowed to leave the stand. If the aircraft is not ready for departure as per the target time to leave the aircraft stand, it means it misses the sequence and it will have a big impact in high volume airports to get into the sequence again later when it is ready for pushback to leave the stand.

If the turnaround time is reduced from 40 min to 30 minutes, aircraft utilization increases by 8% for a point-to-point airline, as per Boeing's research. (OAG, 2023). More utilization of the aircraft means more revenue for the airline. The higher turnaround time of aircraft affects utilization of the apron stands to the extent planned by the airport operator.

Aircraft departure delay in origin station affect its arrival and departure from the next station, meaning a chain reaction to delays throughout the day. Timely operating is crucial if the aircraft is operating in a hub airport as passengers may miss a connecting flight. Sometimes due to delayed departure it may not be possible to land at the destination airport may be due to curfew for certain restrictions like noise and hence, may have to cancel the operation which will result cost to the airline for arranging hotel accommodation for passengers, ticket cancellation without penalty etc. About six minutes into a planned turnaround often recuperate at some stage during a flight, anything beyond this window typically culminates in agonizing delays.(OAG, 2023)

Thus, one of the controllable activities when the aircraft is on the stand is to complete all the services needed in time for the aircraft, unloading/loading of bags and passengers. Instead of monitoring the services at the apron stand manually and storing the data on paper, digitalization helps to monitor as well as catching the data, analysing historical data, and predicting the delays proactively to lessen the impact on operations.

Airport Collaborative Decision Making (A-CDM) is a concept that aims at improving air traffic flow and capacity management at airports by reducing delays, improving the predictability of events, and optimizing the utilization of resources (EUROCONTROL). A-CDM is about stakeholders at an airport working together more efficiently in the way they share and use data. With accurate and prompt provision of time related to the turnaround process, all airport partners will have the same operational information. Most of the busy airports globally have implemented A-CDM which is more of process-oriented innovation. A-CDM helps to reduce delays, improve operational efficiency, and improve customer satisfaction. It also helps to reduce the amount of fuel used and emissions. Thus, A-CDM helps to reduce costs for both the airport and the airline.

6.16 Digitalization of Apron Service Activities Through IoT Application

Amsterdam Schiphol airport has a system called Deep Turnaround. The system uses computer vision techniques gained from thousands of hours of data from aircraft turnarounds at Schiphol, giving it predictive capabilities to detect delays before anyone else can. The system uses machine learning algorithm detects and reports over 70 unique turnaround events in 30 turnaround processes. It detects delays well before the target time to push back from the stand and helps to make informed decisions. The system output can be seen by all the stakeholders online and in real time so that they can accordingly take action to smoothen the operations due to delay by the particular aircraft (s). Gatwick airport uses a system called AirTurn platform with which information can be communicated more quickly on changes to turn events - such as updates on baggage loading, refuelling or other aircraft preparations – giving the control tower a more accurate, real-time departure to feed into the airport's overall flying programme. The AirTurn platform is accessed directly through Gatwick's community app which is already widely used by ground handling staff across the airport.

The timely docking and withdrawal of Passenger Boarding Bridges (PBB) from aircraft can significantly improve the turnaround time. Currently, these bridges are manually operated by an operator stationed at the end of the bridge, remaining on the bridge until it is fully withdrawn. To enhance efficiency, Changi Airport is experimenting with an automatic operation system that allows for control from an operator positioned at the apron stand rather than on the bridge itself.

Figure 9. ACDM concept

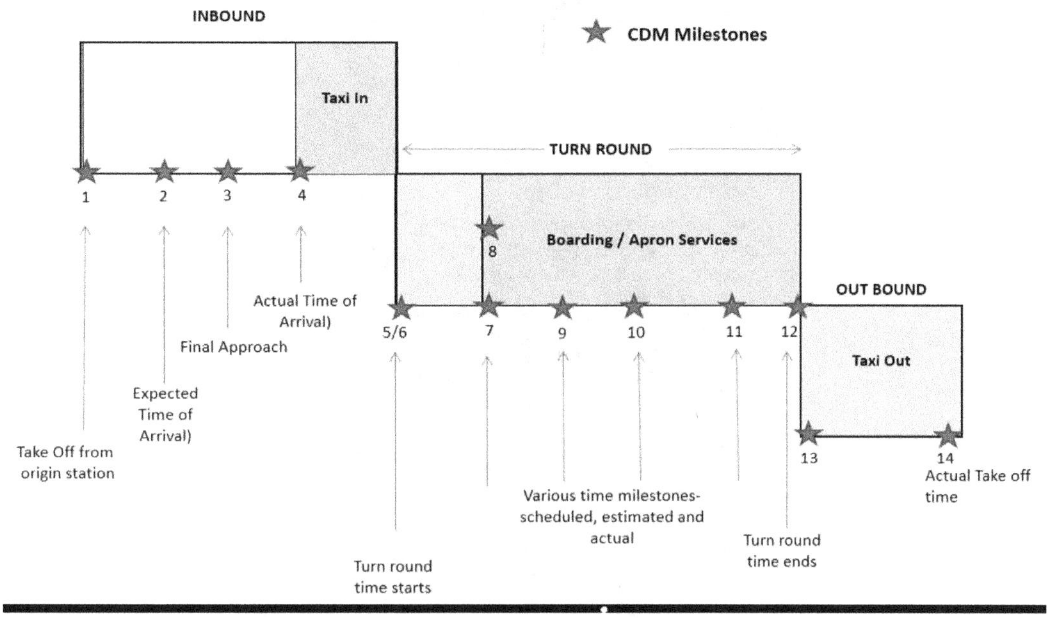

For easy navigation within passenger terminal building, which is one of the importance factor as per the survey described in para 4, one Indian airport has introduced 'Smart Trolleys.' When the passenger scans the boarding pass or enters the flight details on the display of the cabin bag trolley, they can view the gate number of the flight and receive navigation guidance to the gate. Passengers can also enter a specific merchandise, and the display will show in which store the item is available, along with navigation guidance to the shop. The trolley has additional features that are very useful to passengers. Some airports provide such information in the airport's App, which is required to be downloaded. These system use IoT applications.

Fully automatic foreign exchange kiosks without any manual assistance are being implemented. This is just like an ATM for cash withdrawals. One airport has introduced contactless and paperless digital reading experience of favourite magazine and newspaper, for the benefit of departing passengers while at the airport.

6.17 Non-Aeronautical Revenues Through Innovation

The survey described in para 4 show that passenger prefer and attach importance to lounge with F&B / F&B. The following describes the technology and innovation in this aspect of services.

6.17.1 Non-Aeronautical vs. Aeronautical Revenue

Commercial revenues from services such as retail, F&B, duty-free, etc., constitute a significant revenue stream for airports and are categorized as non-aeronautical revenues. This type of revenue is market-driven and falls outside the regulatory purview of aviation regulators. In contrast, aeronautical revenue

Figure 10. Smart trolley

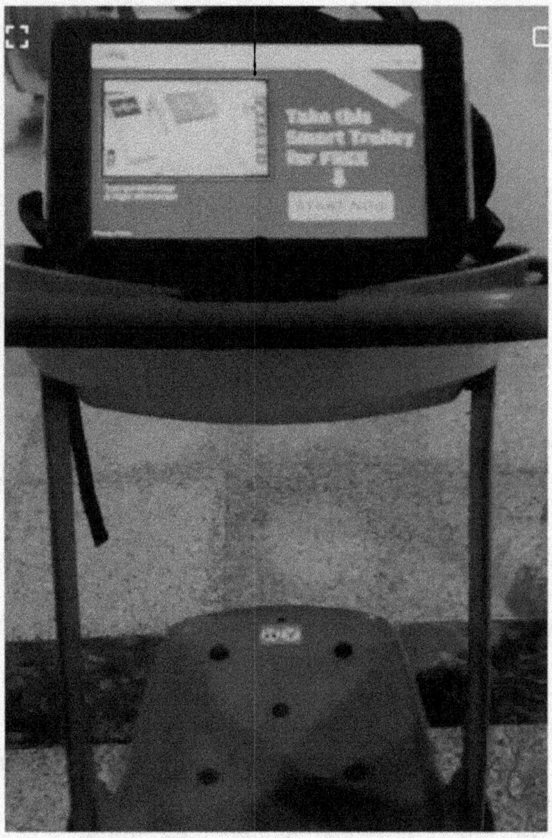

is directly linked to passenger and aircraft movements and is subject to regulation. Airports typically aim to maximize non-aeronautical revenue, emphasizing the need to enhance passengers' satisfaction and overall experience. The strategy involves attracting passengers to engage commercial outlets to boost non-aeronautical revenue. The proportion of aeronautical revenues vs non-aeronautical revenues vary between airports. In smaller airports aeronautical revenues are more than non-aeronautical revenues and larger airports the non-aeronautical revenues are more than aeronautical revenues. On an average globally non-aeronautical revenues constitutes 40% of total revenues. In India, considering six metro airports, non-aeronautical revenues contribute 51% of total revenues. Singapore Changi airport has roughly 55% revenues from non-aeronautical services.

6.17.2 Use of Artificial Intelligence

According to Precedence Research, worldwide artificial intelligence in the aviation market was valued at US$ 653.74 million in 2021. It is predicted to exceed US$ 9,985.86 million by 2030, with a CAGR of 35.38% from 2022 to 2030. By overcoming significant obstacles like siloed data, a lack of customer insights, and inconsistent distribution strategies, AI-centric operations open a new paradigm in airport retailing in the current digital transformation era, where travellers are accustomed to more connected, quick, and personalized engagements in real-time. Businesses can streamline antiquated manual airport procedures, which are frequently sluggish and prone to errors, by utilizing artificial intelligence, which is at the forefront of the aforementioned bottlenecks. It increases operational efficiency in the framework of big data and digital engineering capabilities, resulting in more end-to-end hyper-relevant client experiences. Consequently, this leads to increased client loyalty and new non-aeronautical income growth. (Shaping Airport Retail: Supercharging customer experience and boosting revenue with AI, June 2023).

The advanced AI system employs diverse algorithms to monitor both product movements and customer gestures, additionally ensuring the prevention of shoplifting and accurate recording of purchases.

How airports improve passenger satisfaction in F&B services as well as increase the non-aeronautical revenues?

Passengers can preorder the F&B and get it delivered at the gate. The use of robots for the delivery of F&B and retails to the passengers at the gate is drawing attention. Automatic vending machines are being tried with all merchandise for the passengers to pick them up through contactless system and available 24X7.

As part of the enhancements, the Uber Eats app (Future Travel Experience Oct 2021) now automatically detects when a user is at Toronto Pearson airport and brings up a screen that lets them know the food that is available for pickup at the airport. Schiphol airport allows passengers to view (International Airport Review June 2021) and reserve products online from the comfort of their home. Dubai airport is using digitalization for the retail and F&B.

Cashier-less stores- Passengers can use their credit cards at the payment terminal. Upon completing their shopping, customers can simply leave the store with their selected items, and the credit card will be automatically charged for the purchased items. If desired, customers can print their receipts before exiting, making the entire shopping process swift and uncomplicated. In-store employees are available to address customer needs, ensuring a seamless and enjoyable shopping experience.

Mobile food ordering apps creates the opportunity to increase the quantity of F&B concepts at airports without increasing the commercial space in premium locations, using remote kitchens. This free up the space for operations and processes.

Some airports provide passengers with the ability to collect their purchases at the airport at the beginning or end of their journey. Passengers are therefore able to shop on a tight timeline or travel with their purchases for the entire journey. Thus, airports are able to offer additional products online that would not take up additional commercial space.

Passengers (at Schiphol airport) could browse the airport's website, select the products of their choice and after security checks they would only have to go to the specific store to pay and collect their items.

6.18 Digital Car Parking Facility

One of the survey finding described in para 4 is the walking distance between the car park and the terminal and sufficient drop off points available in the kerb. Transport options availability is the consideration for planning purpose, hence not discussed in this chapter. The other two preferences are taken care by the airports as mentioned herein.

Car parking revenue is one of the major sources of non-aeronautical revenue for the airport. Some airports use robots for the automatic parking of passenger cars. The system works like this: passengers should park their cars in a designated place and in the manner prescribed by the airport. Then, the passenger locks the car and inputs the flight details—both onward and return—into the system before proceeding into the terminal. This designated parking area can be very close to the terminal. As the passenger heads to the terminal, the robot picks up the car and stores it in the parking space. This operation is fully programmed and automated, requiring no manual intervention. Since the passenger's flight details are available in the system, the return flight status is monitored. At the appropriate time, the robot places the car in the designated location for the passenger to access and drive. Thus, the kerb side of the terminal is free of valet parking cars. The advantage to the airport is that a greater number of vehicles can be parked, as the space between them can be minimal without the need for opening and closing doors, trunks, or space for staff/passengers to walk, as is the case in conventional surface manual parking. These robots are battery-powered, and therefore, do not contribute to pollution. Additionally, faster turnaround for passengers is achieved. Airports also offer services to prebook the car park slot on the date of the journey, the passenger makes the payment in advance and when reaches the airport, can park the vehicle at the designated slot with less waiting time/queuing.

6.19 Passenger Experience Through Technology and Innovation

6.19.1 Mishandled Bags

As per the 2023 Baggage IT Insights report, there was a 74.7% increase in the global rate of mishandled baggage per thousand passengers between 2021 and 2022. Transfers, or moving luggage from one aircraft to another, are one of the major problems that contribute to this. Due to the rise in long-haul and international travel, the percentage of improperly handled luggage that were delayed at transfer rose to 42%. The difficulties encountered during the transfer increase the chance of a luggage being mishandled on international travels by approximately eight times when compared to domestic routes.

Recently, Air Canada introduced a new feature to the Air Canada mobile app to enable customers traveling within Canada to track the progress of their baggage and mobility aid in real time at key points as it moves with them throughout their journey. The new tracking feature is designed to provide travellers with added confidence and improve the overall customer experience through greater convenience.

With tracking data on a blockchain, the information remains secure and immutable, reducing the risk of loss or theft.

Changi airport is exploring digital initiative for the passengers to file the missing baggage details, with which they need not wait in queue to submit the form to the airline personnel. The airport is trialling the concept of report filing via the passenger's personal device. This saves time for the passengers as well as improves the experience.

6.19.2 Check in Bag Tags

Currently, the baggage tags affixed to checked-in bags are made of paper and include a barcode that identifies the flight number and passenger details. The bag tag must be scanned at various points in the baggage handling system, including the bag drop/check-in counter, screening machines, diverters, sorters, and up to the baggage make-up area. In the baggage make-up area, the tag is scanned for baggage reconciliation before being placed in the baggage cart for loading onto the aircraft. If, for any reason, some bag tags are not successfully scanned during these processes, they are directed to a designated location for manual reading and flight identification.

In the coming years, most airports are expected to implement self-check-in kiosks and self-bag drop systems, where passengers handle these processes themselves. This could potentially exacerbate the issue of unread bag tags if the tags are not properly attached to the bags. Also, paper tags become wasteful once the bag is retrieved at the arrival airport. Considering an annual count of 4 billion departing passengers and an assumed average of one tag per passenger, this results in the wastage of 4 billion paper tags. In lieu of paper tags, RFID tags have been experimented (Source- M/s Beumer Group) with and are now implemented by airlines as part of a hybrid identification system. For instance, Delta Airlines incorporates RFID tags in their bags. Additionally, Apple and Samsung offer air tags that passengers can use to monitor their bags. Presently, researchers are developing biometric tags, consisting of a series of photos that provide a unique identification by capturing features such as external marks and other distinguishing characteristics of bags. These photos serve as a distinct ID for the bag, offering a means of identification throughout security processes, sortation, loading, unloading, and transfers. This innovative approach has the potential to entirely replace traditional paper tags.

6.19.3 Metaverse Services

The 'Best Innovation in Airport Passenger Related Processes' was won by Incheon International Airport's XR Metaverse Services initiative, which connects virtuality and reality. It consists of a 3D spatial metaverse environment providing an indoor wayfinding service of the actual passenger terminals, covering about 1.4 million square metres. It is based on 3D spatial data and augmented reality (AR) technology and offers a virtual experience of Incheon Airport using VR technology. AR-based indoor wayfinding enables users to visit the digital version of the airport from home and get the necessary information by virtually experiencing various facilities and processes within the airport. (Source ACI).

7. CONCLUSION

When the service parameters are objective, the feedback/assessment for the quality of services supplied can be measured while delivering the services and at the delivery location. However, the subjective parameters must be assessed by the customers and either they can be asked to provide the assessment as soon as the services are delivered or later when they are away from the service location. Of late, achieving a service quality rating alone do not satisfy the passengers and thus, airports' focus is to provide best passenger experience when they travel through the airport. For this, airports compete with each other to innovate processes, introduce advanced technologies continuously. Passenger experience and airport operational efficiency & productivity are significantly improved/increased with the use of innovation and advanced technologies. IoT application and block chain technology have been introduced and gaining attention to improve the services at airports. More processes can be tailored with these advanced technologies. Since the importance of services varies, when compared to each other, depending on passenger profile and it is required to identify these airports in particular region and focus on the identified services.

Future work- With many advanced technologies being introduced at airports and used by the passengers, it is required to carry out a study on technology acceptance by the passengers travelling through major Indian Airports, through a survey. It is also worthwhile to create a framework to assess the cost effectiveness of service quality delivery considering the service delivery rating assessed (for example ASQ), technology innovation rating and the operational cost.

Acknowledgements- The author would like to thank Ms. Charulatha Pasupuleti and Mr. Ashok Yedla for the assistance in the survey conducted.

REFERENCES

Allen, J., Grazia, M., Eboli, L., Forciniti, C., Allen, J., Grazia, M., Forciniti, C., Mazzulla, G., Rica, D. C., Rodrigo, S., & Rica, C. (2020). ScienceDirect ScienceDirect Latent factors on the assessment of service quality in an Italian Latent factors on the assessment of service quality in an Italian peripheral airport peripheral. *Transportation Research Procedia*, *47*, 91–98. doi:10.1016/j.trpro.2020.03.083

Bellizzi, M. G., Eboli, L., Forciniti, C., Mazzulla, G., Grazia, M., Eboli, L., Forciniti, C., & Mazzulla, G. (2018). ScienceDirect ScienceDirect Air Transport Passengers ' Satisfaction : an Ordered Logit Air Transport Passengers ' Satisfaction : an Ordered Logit Model Model. *Transportation Research Procedia*, *33*, 147–154. doi:10.1016/j.trpro.2018.10.087

Bellizzi, M. G., Eboli, L., & Mazzulla, G. (2020). Air Transport Service Quality Factors: A Systematic Literature Review. *Transportation Research Procedia*, *45*, 218–225. doi:10.1016/j.trpro.2020.03.010

Burapharat, Y., Christensen, T. M., & Suthichoti, S. (2021). *How Service Quality Enhances Customer Satisfaction : A Case Study of Hybrid Airlines in Thailand*. 1–10.

Caetano, M., Alves, J. P., Bispo, L., & Alves, O. (2021). *Model for measuring airport innovation* *. 1–29.

Chonsalasin, D., Jomnonkwao, S., & Ratanavaraha, V. (2020). International Journal of Transportation Measurement model of passengers ' expectations of airport service quality. *International Journal of Transportation Science and Technology*, *xxxx*, 1–11. doi:10.1016/j.ijtst.2020.11.001

Cserdi, Z., & Kenesei, Z. (2021). Research in Transportation Business & Management Attitudes to forced adoption of new technologies in public transportation services. *Research in Transportation Business & Management*, *41*, 100611. doi:10.1016/j.rtbm.2020.100611

Ejem, E. A. (2020). *Assessment of Airport Service Quality in Nigeria. December 2020.*

Gumasing, M. J. J., Iii, E. T. G., & Marquez, M. Y. M. (2020). *A Service Quality Model for Bureau of Immigration in NAIA Terminal 1*. 1065–1069.

Halpern, N., & Mwesiumo, D. (2021). Research in Transportation Business & Management Airport service quality and passenger satisfaction : The impact of service failure on the likelihood of promoting an airport online. *Research in Transportation Business & Management*, *41*(May), 100667. doi:10.1016/j.rtbm.2021.100667

Hong, S., Choi, D., & Chae, J. (2020). Journal of Retailing and Consumer Services Exploring di ff erent airport users ' service quality satisfaction between service providers and air travelers. *Journal of Retailing and Consumer Services*, *52*(April 2019), 101917. doi:10.1016/j.jretconser.2019.101917

Jiang, H., & Zhang, Y. (2016). Journal of Air Transport Management An assessment of passenger experience at Melbourne Airport. *Journal of Air Transport Management, 54*, 88–92. doi:10.1016/j.jairtraman.2016.04.002

OAG. (2023). INNOVATIVE AIRLINE OPERATIONS : THE TURNAROUND. *Article in OAG Newsletter*, (November), 2023.

Pandey, M. M. (2016). Journal of Air Transport Management Evaluating the service quality of airports in Thailand using fuzzy multi-criteria decision making method. *Journal of Air Transport Management, 57*, 241–249. doi:10.1016/j.jairtraman.2016.08.014

Samad, S., Nilashi, M., Supriyanto, E., Morshedi, S., Ghabban, F., & Asadi, S. (2021).. . *Journal of Soft Computing and Decision Support Systems Factors Impacting Airport Service Quality Using Multi-Criteria Decision-Making Approach., 8*(2), 2021.

Sena Kilic, C. Ucler, L. M.-D. (2021). *Innovation at Airports: A systematic literature review*. Aviation. https://doi.org/doi.org/10.3846/aviation.2021.14917

Thums, J., Künzel, L., Klumpp, M., Bardmann, M., & Ruiner, C. (2023). Transportation Research Interdisciplinary Perspectives Future air transportation and digital work at airports – Review and developments. *Transportation Research Interdisciplinary Perspectives, 19*(March), 100808. doi:10.1016/j.trip.2023.100808

Weekx, S., & Buyle, S. (2023). Journal of Air Transport Management The effect of airline dominance on airport performance : Empirical evidence from medium-sized European airports. *Journal of Air Transport Management, 107*(November 2022), 102317. doi:10.1016/j.jairtraman.2022.102317

Widarsyah, R. (2013). *The Impact of Airport Service Quality Dimension on Overall Airport Experience and Impression.*

Wildan, M. D. A. (2021). Covid-19 And Implementation Of Airport Health And Safety Procedures The Safety Culture Perception. *Syntax Literate:Jurnal Ilmiah Indonesia.*

Chapter 17
Innovative Technologies for Healthcare Service Productivity

Gaganjot Kaur
Chandigarh University, India

Shalini Sharma
https://orcid.org/0000-0002-1710-1540
Chandigarh University, India

Reepu
https://orcid.org/0000-0002-5607-9825
Chandigarh University, India

ABSTRACT

The world is changing rapidly, especially with a speedy increase in global population. More than ever, for all service-related functions, the organizations are looking for methods to enhance their service throughput. Technological innovations in every industry have been helpful in achieving this growth. In hospitals too, the power of technology has been harnessed for better patient outcomes which directly translates to patient satisfaction. New healthcare technologies have provenly increased the efficiency of care services and operational processes by removing repetitive tasks and providing personalized care to the patients. A successful digital healthcare ecosystem provides clinical decision support which enables both high degree of efficiency (bandwidth and throughput) and high degree of effectiveness (quality patient health outcomes).

1. INTRODUCTION

Advancements in healthcare technology have markedly improved process efficiencies. This has increased the speed of processes and improved patient prognosis and outcomes. Healthcare is considered a challenging service industry where the needs of patients and their families must be taken care of. There is a high degree of complexity in patient care workflows, and the nature of service is considered high-emotion

DOI: 10.4018/979-8-3693-2019-8.ch017

as life is involved. A hospital becomes duty-bound to ensure efficient processes and products with the support of technology and well-trained, technologically savvy staff.

The history of advancement in healthcare technology is a dynamic narrative marked by continuous innovation and progress. The healthcare industry has evolved significantly over the centuries, from ancient healing practices to cutting-edge technologies. This review delves into critical milestones, highlighting pivotal moments that have shaped the trajectory of healthcare technology.

Ancient Healing Practices: The roots of healthcare technology trace back to ancient civilizations, where healing practices were deeply intertwined with religious and spiritual beliefs. In ancient Egypt, medical knowledge was inscribed on papyrus scrolls, documenting remedies for various ailments. The Greeks, particularly Hippocrates, laid the foundation for a more systematic approach to medicine, emphasizing observation and documentation.

Renaissance and the Scientific Revolution: The Renaissance witnessed a resurgence of interest in science and medicine. Anatomical studies and dissections paved the way for a deeper understanding of the human body. The invention of the microscope in the 17th century by Antonie van Leeuwenhoek opened new frontiers in microbiology, enabling the observation of microorganisms.

19th Century: Industrialization and Medical Advances: The 19th century brought about significant advancements in healthcare technology. The Industrial Revolution facilitated the mass production of medical instruments and the development of anesthesia, transforming surgical procedures. Florence Nightingale's contributions to nursing laid the groundwork for modern healthcare management and hygiene practices.

20th Century: Radiology and Antibiotics: The early 20th century marked a paradigm shift with the discovery of X-rays by Wilhelm Roentgen in 1895. Radiology revolutionized diagnostics, allowing physicians to visualize internal structures without invasive procedures. The invention of antibiotics, starting with penicillin in 1928 by Alexander Fleming, transformed the treatment of infectious diseases.

Post-World War II: Technological Boom and Digitalization: The aftermath of World War II witnessed an unprecedented surge in technological innovation. The 1950s saw the development of electronic medical devices such as the electrocardiogram (ECG) and the beginnings of computerized tomography (C.T.) in the 1970s. The 1980s brought forth the widespread adoption of electronic health records (EHR), enhancing information management.

21st Century: Precision Medicine and Digital Health: The 21st century is characterized by the convergence of healthcare and technology. Genomic research has paved the way for precision medicine, tailoring treatments based on individual genetic profiles. Digital health technologies, including telemedicine, wearable devices, and mobile health applications, have become integral to patient care, improving accessibility and monitoring.

1.1 Recent Advances: Artificial Intelligence and Robotics

Electronic Health Records (EHR), Radio Frequency Identification (RFID), telemedicine, device portability, blockchain technology, Picture Archiving and Communication Systems (PACS), robotic surgery, artificial intelligence (A.I.), and Internet of Things (IoT) are among the many technology-supported tools which have transformed healthcare service productivity. EHR is hailed as a highly beneficial technology in healthcare for enhancing operational efficiency and reaching and improving the quality of care. RFID-enabled medication administration and inventory tracking system has improved inventory management and reduced medication stock-outs and expiration. The system is effective in theft prevention, too. During inpatient medication, RFID ensures the correct delivery of drugs to the right patient.

Telemedicine or telehealth uses the telecommunications infrastructure for the remote delivery of healthcare services. It allows healthcare providers to evaluate, diagnose, and treat patients remotely without in-person visits. This offers comfort and convenience to the patient, allowing them better care. The portability of medical devices has revolutionized monitoring of one's health and well-being. These devices non-invasively monitor health parameters and provide real-time updates to healthcare providers. Interventions in case of advancing criticality can be sought sooner.

Picture Archiving and Communication Systems (PACS) have increased the speed of digital acquisition, storage, transmission, and display of radiographs, C.T.s, MRIs, and ultrasound. It has replaced the use of conventional radiological film. Robotic surgery is another high-end technology that has revolutionized surgical procedures in a hospital. It has reduced the total duration of inpatient stays. Post-operative stay of specific procedures using robotic technology has either been reduced drastically, or the procedure has been categorized as ambulatory, requiring no hospital stay. Robotic surgery procedures are more precise, with fewer and smaller scars and faster recovery. Post-surgery pain, blood loss, and rate of infections have also been reduced with robotic technology.

Like every industry, the healthcare industry has been modernized through artificial intelligence (A.I.). A.I. inspects information in real-time and provides answers on a real-time information-linked function, improving the efficiency of care services. Predictive and generative A.I. (ChatGPT) is used in a hospital's day-to-day functioning. A.I. systems mimic human intelligence through pattern recognition and anomaly detection. They perform human-like tasks through visual perception, speech recognition, decision-making based on data patterns, search, and writing. A.I. systems learn over time and provide benefits like foresight (predictive capabilities), assistance (save time), expertise (diagnose disease), explanation (impact on outcomes), and simulations (review all possibilities). Cross-functional AI strategy teams in a healthcare organization help prepare staff for changes in workflow. These include collecting comprehensive data, creating a cloud strategy, strengthening cyber and privacy frameworks, and setting timelines to measure ROI.

AI-supported technologies serve as a "second opinion "to augment doctors' diagnosis decision-making process. Detection of a disease becomes quicker and more efficient, leading to a speedier relief for the patient. Studies have shown that hospital readmission rates for patients are reduced significantly with A.I. Another futuristic technology, which is a subset of A.I., is "Machine Learning" (ML). ML, in conjunction with the "Internet of Things" (IoT), improves decision-making and security in the healthcare ecosystem. Virtual and augmented reality is being used to address the needs of patients with a mental disease. Advanced virtual human avatars are being deployed to conduct conversations for diagnosis and treatment.

Billing processes have become efficient as medical codes are assigned by extracting information from physician notes. Delays are prevented, and administrative errors are reduced. There is an improved assessment of disease onset and treatment success. Technology-aided compilation of clinical research helps formulate appropriate care guidelines, which helps make better clinical decisions. Technology has benefited prominent hospitals and brought cheer to patients in the government-funded public health system through telemedicine in remote and rural areas where there is a shortage of healthcare professionals and access to advanced consultation and treatment is limited. The COVID-19 period saw a gigantic push to telemedicine, which needed to get its fair share of importance earlier.

The massive adoption of advanced digital technologies has improved the cooperation among practitioners. Health professionals effectively work together by sharing their knowledge and coordinating their activities.

2. LITERATURE REVIEW

Advancements in healthcare technology have revolutionized the healthcare industry, enhancing efficiency and improving patient outcomes. This literature review explores the impact of innovative technologies on healthcare service productivity, focusing on Electronic Health Record (EHR), Radio Frequency Identification (RFID), telemedicine, device portability, blockchain technology, Picture Archiving and Communication System (PACS), robotic surgery, artificial intelligence (A.I.), Internet of Things (IoT), Machine Learning (ML), and virtual/augmented reality.

2.1 Electronic Health Record (EHR)

EHR is a cornerstone technology that enhances operational efficiency and care quality. It enables comprehensive patient data management, facilitates information sharing among healthcare providers, and improves patient outcomes (Smith et al., 2017).

2.2 Radio Frequency Identification (RFID)

RFID has transformed medication administration and inventory tracking, reducing stock-outs and theft. It ensures accurate patient medication delivery, enhancing patient safety and inventory management (Kuo et al., 2018).

2.3 Telemedicine

Telemedicine leverages telecommunications for remote healthcare delivery. It provides convenience to patients and allows healthcare providers to diagnose and treat patients remotely. The COVID-19 pandemic accelerated the adoption of telemedicine, especially in remote and rural areas with limited access to healthcare professionals (Bashshur et al., 2020).

2.4 Device Portability

Portable medical devices enable real-time monitoring of health parameters, facilitating early intervention and improved self-care. This technology empowers individuals to actively participate in their healthcare actively, leading to better overall health outcomes (Chan et al., 2015).

2.5 Picture Archiving and Communication System (PACS)

PACS has significantly enhanced the speed of acquiring, storing, and transmitting medical images, replacing traditional film. This technology streamlines radiological processes, contributing to quicker diagnoses and improved patient care (Thrall, 2008).

2.6 Robotic Surgery

Robotic surgery has revolutionized surgical procedures, reducing inpatient stays, minimizing scars, and accelerating post-operative recovery. It has proven efficacy in enhancing precision and minimizing complications, contributing to better patient outcomes (Davila et al., 2019).

2.7 Artificial Intelligence (A.I.) and Machine Learning (ML)

A.I. systems, including predictive and generative A.I., are vital in healthcare. They assist in real-time decision-making and disease detection and even act as a "second opinion" for healthcare professionals. Machine Learning and the Internet of Things enhance decision-making and security in the healthcare ecosystem (Topol, 2019).

2.8 Virtual/Augmented Reality

Virtual and augmented reality technologies address the needs of patients with mental illnesses. Advanced virtual human avatars are deployed for diagnosis and treatment, offering innovative solutions in mental healthcare (Riva et al., 2020).

2.9 Impact on Billing Processes and Administrative Efficiency

Technological advancements have streamlined billing processes by extracting information from physician notes, preventing delays, and reducing administrative errors. This has led to an improved assessment of disease onset and treatment success (Furlong et al., 2015).

2.10 Collaboration Among Practitioners

The adoption of advanced digital technologies has facilitated collaboration among healthcare practitioners. Professionals effectively share knowledge and coordinate activities, contributing to a more integrated and patient-centric healthcare system (Adler-Milstein et al., 2017).

Integrating innovative technologies into healthcare services has significantly enhanced productivity, patient care, and collaboration among healthcare professionals. The multifaceted impact of these technologies underscores the transformative potential they hold for the healthcare industry.

Artificial Intelligence (A.I.) has emerged as a transformative force in healthcare, offering innovative solutions to complex challenges. This literature review aims to explore the significance of A.I. in healthcare by examining critical studies and scholarly works that rigorously back the impact of A.I. on various aspects of the healthcare ecosystem.

2.11 Enhanced Diagnostics and Disease Detection

A.I. has shown remarkable capabilities in enhancing diagnostics and disease detection. A study by Esteva et al. (2017) demonstrated the effectiveness of deep learning algorithms in dermatology, achieving diagnostic accuracy comparable to human experts. A.I.'s ability to analyze vast datasets and identify patterns enables early detection, contributing to improved patient outcomes (Esteva et al., 2017).

2.12 Optimized Treatment Plans and Personalized Medicine

The integration of A.I. in healthcare facilitates the development of optimized treatment plans and personalized medicine. A comprehensive review by Litjens et al. (2017) highlights the role of machine learning in medical imaging, aiding in treatment planning by providing precise insights into the characteristics of individual patients' conditions. Personalized medicine, informed by A.I., promises more effective and tailored interventions (Litjens et al., 2017).

2.13 Predictive Analytics for Patient Outcomes

A.I.'s predictive analytics capabilities contribute significantly to patient outcomes. A study by Rajkomar et al. (2018) utilized deep learning models based on electronic health records to predict patient mortality and readmission risks. The integration of AI-driven predictive analytics assists healthcare providers in proactive decision-making, reducing readmission rates and improving overall patient care (Rajkomar et al., 2018).

2.14 Operational Efficiency and Workflow Enhancement

A.I. applications contribute to operational efficiency and workflow enhancement within healthcare institutions. A systematic review by Krittanawong et al. (2020) highlights the impact of A.I. on streamlining administrative processes, optimizing resource allocation, and reducing operational costs. A.I.'s ability to automate routine tasks allows healthcare professionals to focus on more complex aspects of patient care (Krittanawong et al., 2020).

2.15 Telemedicine and Remote Patient Monitoring

The significance of A.I. is further underscored in telemedicine and remote patient monitoring. A study by Tuckson et al. (2017) emphasizes the role of A.I. in enhancing the capabilities of telemedicine, allowing for more accurate remote diagnostics and monitoring. AI-powered devices facilitate real-time data analysis, enabling timely interventions and improving patient outcomes in remote settings (Tuckson et al., 2017).

2.16 Challenges and Ethical Considerations

Despite the positive impacts, it is essential to acknowledge the challenges and ethical considerations associated with A.I. in healthcare. A review by Char et al. (2018) discusses concerns related to data privacy, algorithm biases, and the need for regulatory frameworks. Understanding and addressing these challenges are crucial to realizing the full potential of A.I. while ensuring ethical and equitable healthcare practices (Char et al., 2018).

The literature reviewed underscores the multifaceted significance of A.I. in healthcare, ranging from enhanced diagnostics and personalized medicine to operational efficiency and remote patient monitoring. While showcasing the positive contributions, it also addresses challenges and ethical considerations. The rigorous backing from diverse studies highlights A.I.'s potential to reshape the future of healthcare, offering more precise, efficient, and patient-centered solutions.

3. INNOVATIVE HEALTHCARE TECHNOLOGIES

Currently, it is an undisputed fact that the operational efficiency of hospitals improves with the use of advanced technologies as these save time and cost, encourage patient participation, and help monitor patient care beyond the hospital premises. Today's HospiTodayare termed Intelligent Hospitals with the integration of diverse technologies into every aspect of care. Here is an insight into the various technologies used in healthcare.

3.1 Electronic Health Records (EHR)

EHR is a digital version of a patient's paper records. It is real-time and patient-centered. It makes patients' medical data available instantly and securely to authorized users. Patients' Medical data includes their diagnoses, medications, radiology images, laboratory results, treatment plans and procedures, immunization dates, and allergies. EHR enables the integration of evidence-based tools for providers to make quicker and better patient care decisions. Such automated systems provide clinical decision support and streamline provider workflow.

EHRs are digital, and information sharing with other healthcare organizations has become more accessible and quicker. A recent study using a data envelopment analysis model indicated that hospitals with EHR outperformed non-EHR hospitals in operational efficiency, profitability, and quality. They chose inputs such as the number of beds, doctors, nurses, and total operating expenses. The outputs were outpatient visits, inpatient days, and total patient revenues. Operating margin was analyzed to measure hospital profitability, patient experience ratings for operational efficiency, and readmission rates to measure hospital quality (Lee et al., 2022).

3.2 Picture Archiving and Communication System (PACS)

PACS is a component of radiology information systems (RIS). It is a digital means of acquiring, storing, transmitting, and displaying radiological images. PACS provides a cost-effective method for image transmission (radiographs, C.T., MR, ultrasound) to be accessed at multiple physically disparate locations. It is interoperable with EHR. PACS has fast-tracked medical care's efficiency and effectiveness, as images can now be quickly and easily accessed from anywhere (Aldosari et al., 2018).

In comparison, before the advent of PACS, much time was lost in the search for images. The unavailability of radiological images delayed the start of treatment as precious time was lost. Despite increased workloads and the complexity of examinations, PACS has reduced turnaround times. Physicians can start the treatment early, and patients can get faster care.

3.3 Radio Frequency Identification (RFID)

RFID is a wireless system comprising two components: tags and readers. The reader is a device that emits radio waves and receives signals back from the RFID tag. RFID technology has revolutionized the effectiveness of service delivery in many industries. In car rental companies, RFID complements the GPS for fleet management. In the supply chain industry, it helps in the accurate counting, tracking, and course correction for individual items and cartons across the supply chain. In healthcare institutions, where EMR and medication administration platforms are already being used to handle large numbers of patients, RFID helps reduce patient-to-staff time, medication errors due to patient identification, and device operating errors.

RFID has also found immense use in the real-time traceability of patients, medical staff, and hospital assets. Due to the traceability of people and assets, theft prevention is taken care of. Medical devices that use RFID traceability features include defibrillators and AEDs, ventilators, vital signs monitors, ECG carts, compression devices, infusion pumps, stretchers, and wheelchairs. In managing patient medication, RFID is essential in ensuring patient safety. Electromagnetic-powered RFID chips on a patient can be worn as an external tag or implanted internally through injection or as a sub-dermal implant. When a nurse has to administer the prescribed drug to the patient, RFID helps match the right patient with the right drug. This reduces the chances of drug administration error and the consequent harm to the patient. Similarly, proper patient identification avoids errors during blood sampling and blood transfusion. An RFID system in a North Carolina hospital was able to timely notify of an infant abduction, allowing immediate action and recovery of the newborn (Wyld, 2009).

Regarding institutional effectiveness and performance improvement, RFID technology helps in decision support, global visualization of medical assets, workflow optimization, clinical and business process validation, and patient throughput improvement. A well-designed and managed RFID setup has continuously improved ROI and operational efficiencies (Frisch, 2019). With numerous advantages, RFID implementation has a few challenges. Abugabah et al., 2020 listed some prominent challenges. Firstly, maintenance of RFID hardware and software is expensive. Secondly, metals and liquids inhibit the electromagnetic wave propagation of RFID. The third challenge is ethical. Privacy breaches may arise if anyone accesses patient data through the RFID reader. There is a risk of misuse of sensitive patient medical data by fraudsters. If such challenges are overcome, RFID technology and machine learning techniques can provide stable healthcare data management.

3.4 Telemedicine

The National Academies of Sciences, Engineering, and Medicine (formerly Institute of Medicine) defines access to health care as the "timely use of personal health services to achieve the best possible health outcomes" (Institute of Medicine, 1993). Equitable healthcare access is the aim of every government in every country because inaccessibility to healthcare leads to poor health outcomes. Healthcare access is disproportionally distributed across various regions of the world. One reason is the maldistribution of physicians geographically, especially in developing regions. People in rural or remote areas also struggle for access to healthcare. De Schutter et al., 2023 in the book chapter "How poverty is perpetuated across generations," explain how the cycle of poor health combined with low levels of education and diminished employment opportunities leading to disregard for preventative healthcare perpetuates poverty. Therefore, promoting good health among the population for a better economy is in the interest of every country. Another emerging reason is the rapid growth in the global elderly population, which has placed greater demands on medical services. Shortly, this will intensify access barriers and burdens on healthcare systems worldwide. There will be a greater need for supporting healthcare infrastructure and processes.

To address the above obstacles in healthcare accessibility, telemedicine has been used to reduce the access gap and promote inequitable access to healthcare. It uses electronic information and communication technology to deliver multimedia via the Internet in real time. Mobile or web applications have been developed for both physician and patient views. Telemedicine provides the advantage of overcoming both distance and time limitations. It has enabled under-resourced communities to receive a preliminary medical diagnosis and corresponding medical consultancy without visiting a physical clinic or hospital.

Moreover, tele-ICU has made inroads into ICU care by providing support to remote intensivists. Intensivists are experts on respiratory failure and ventilation equipment. Many smaller hospitals need to be equipped with such experts. Tele-ICU helps in getting instant access to an intensivist who provides information on a drug or a patient's cardiac rhythm. Tele-ICU support providers highlight the case of venous thromboembolism (VTE) prophylaxis monitoring. VTE is a life-threatening condition that must be quickly addressed when a patient is admitted to the ICU. With tele-ICU, the remote intensivist examines the case and can immediately prescribe anticoagulants or compression stockings. Such advice is crucial for patients in critical care. The advantages of tele-ICU were most evident during the COVID-19 pandemic when there was a shortage of personal protective equipment (PPE) for healthcare workers. Hospitals, through tele-ICU programs, could virtually monitor patients without exposing critical care staff to the coronavirus and were able to save on precious PPE resources. Family members or a chaplain could also be invited into the call for essential psychosocial comfort to the patient.

Access to healthcare is related to healthy aging (McMaughan et al., 2020). Telemedicine has the potential to effectively identify the healthcare needs of older adults and serve them efficiently with quality services. The elderly usually have chronic health conditions which get compounded by deteriorating cognitive health and mental health. It is challenging and sometimes impossible for them to travel to the hospital. Telemedicine, as a preliminary diagnosis or as urgent care, gives patients the comfort, reassurance, and safety of remote medical diagnosis and treatment. Furthermore, telemedicine has shown the potential as a learning tool where physicians from across the globe discuss medical cases and exchange their opinions.

To enumerate, the following are the various advantages provided by telemedicine:

- Healthcare Equality - Access to medical services is possible in underserved remote and rural areas through telemedicine. In smaller hospitals where intensivist support is limited or unavailable, tele-ICU can fill up the gap.
- Cost Reduction - Digital technology integration provides better services at a lower cost. Operational costs such as traveling costs and patient waiting time are reduced. Hospitals benefit from this remote technology, too. Utilizing hospital beds, space, and resources improves as many patients are attended to remotely and do not need to visit the hospital.
- Preventive Health Promotion - Health monitoring through real-time vital sign wearable device readings helps in preliminary diagnosis. This, coupled with telemedicine, helps in early-stage disease detection and prevention.
- Medical Education - Telemedicine is used for continuing medical education, where medical professionals exchange their knowledge and experiences. Novice physicians get the chance to learn from medical specialists.

Along with the various advantages of telemedicine, it has to be borne in mind that a telemedicine technology setup is expensive and time-consuming. Moreover, the setup should adhere to universally pre-defined data formats and protocols. The issues of inaccurate diagnosis and personal data leakage can become legal and ethical subjects. In the absence of regulation, security, and privacy are major concerns.

3.5 Robotic Surgery

Robotic surgery uses a camera and surgeon-controlled mechanical arms to perform surgery. The surgeon seated at a computer console can operate remotely using a high-definition, magnified, 3D view of the surgical site.

The most common robotic surgery procedures are surgical removal of the gallbladder, hip replacement, hysterectomy, coronary artery bypass, transplantation surgeries, and surgical removal of cancerous tissue from sensitive body parts, like nerves or vital organs.

Robotic surgery has the advantage of greater precision, lesser pain, and shorter recovery times compared to traditional surgery, which provides a more hands-on approach and is often more cost-effective. Ultimately, the choice between the two depends on the patient's needs and the surgeon's expertise.

A study concluded that robotic surgery reduces costs (Kneuertz et al., 2019). Robotic and VATS lobectomy were associated with similar costs and improved clinical effectiveness as compared with the open thoracotomy approach. Though robotic surgery appears to be the rapidly evolving segment of minimally invasive surgery, a few studies see no more significant advantages than traditional surgery (Gitas et al., 2022). More data is needed on the advantages and disadvantages of robotic-assisted and laparoscopic surgery. Ongoing technological progress over the next few years may improve robotic-assisted techniques and thus optimize the patient's treatment.

3.6 Artificial intelligence (A.I.)

The healthcare industry has found extensive use of artificial intelligence (A.I.). It is used by doctors, hospitals, insurance companies, and industries linked with the healthcare sector, like life science companies and technology vendors.

A.I. provides answers on a real-time basis and improves the efficiency of care services. As A.I. systems are self-learning systems, they acquire and renew knowledge independently over time. They mimic human intelligence through pattern recognition and anomaly detection. A.I. systems are, in fact, adaptive in nature, meaning their functionalities increase through a learning process. This gives them predictive capabilities, which helps provide foresight into disease diagnosis and impact on outcomes. Hence, AI is assistive and saves time.

There are four broadly interrelated forms of A.I.

1. Machine learning (ML): It uses data sets, such as health records, for categorizing information or predicting outcomes
2. Deep learning: It is a subset of machine learning that is capable of more complex tasks
3. Neural language processing (NLP): It helps interpret medical documentation and published research
4. Robotic process automation (RPA): It automates administrative and clinical workflows

Well-known advantages of A.I. in healthcare are:

a. Collection, storage, and faster retrieval of medical records
b. Reduction in repetitive tasks like analyzing tests and radiological scans
c. Selection of individual customized treatment plan

d. Virtual Nursing: Molly (developed by Sense.ly) helps monitor patients' condition, especially chronic illnesses.
e. Faster drug discovery development
f. Precision medicine: Early detection and prediction of health issues using genetics
g. Health monitoring through wearable trackers
h. Healthcare system analysis: A.I. can highlight errors and reduce workflow inefficiencies

A.I. applications in healthcare can be broadly divided into three main categories: patient-oriented, clinician-oriented, and administration-oriented applications.

1. Patient-oriented AI applications include:
    a. virtual health assistants (Siri, Alexa)
    b. health chatbots (Ada, Your. M.D.)
    c. wearables (Fitbit et al.)
2. Clinician-oriented AI applications include:
    a. Diagnostics (PathAI et al.)
    b. machine learning and radiology (Enlitic)
    c. robot-assisted surgery (Intuitive da Vinci)
    d. new drug discovery (Bioxcel, BERG Health)
    e. medical data mining (IBM Watson)
3. Administration-oriented AI applications include:
    a. appointment scheduling (Althea)
    b. consumer assistants (Olive)
    c. medical dictation (Nuance)
    d. AI-powered EMRs
    e. automated coding (ICD-10)
    f. patient operational flow (LeanTaas)

AI-supported technologies serve as a "second opinion "to augment doctors' diagnosis decision-making process. Detection of a disease becomes quicker and more efficient, leading to a speedier relief for the patient. Studies have shown that hospital readmission rates for a patient are reduced significantly with the use of A.I.

3.7 Internet of Things (IoT)

The Internet of Things (IoT) is a network of physical objects embedded with sensors, software, and other technologies for connecting and exchanging data. These objects could be ordinary household objects like kitchen appliances, refrigerators, cars, thermostats, or sophisticated industrial tools. Using low-cost computing, cloud, and mobile technologies, physical objects now cooperate with the digital world to record, monitor, and adjust. In healthcare, IoT, along with Machine Learning (ML), is improving the clinical decision-making and security of the healthcare ecosystem. These hybrid systems decode hidden patterns in large swathes of data for better disease diagnosis and treatment predictions. In the drug manufacturing industry, IoT has dramatically impacted the computational drug design in pharmaceutical product development, thereby lessening human efforts (Roy & Sengupta, 2020).

IoT-based Electrocardiogram (ECG) monitoring systems are used in reducing sudden death due to heart failure among middle-aged and older adults. Wearable sensors on the patient's body send signals when there is a malfunction of the heart. These signals automatically email the healthcare providers to provide critical care to the patient. It has been proven that such low-cost IoT-based device systems are dependable in collecting real-time ECG data to diagnose heart diseases and reduce mortality (Shaown et al., 2019).

Diabetes mellitus (D.M.) has emerged as a public health problem worldwide. When blood glucose levels are uncontrolled, they cause severe illness, damage multiple organs, and even cause death. Continuous glucose monitoring (CGM) devices that use algorithms supported by IoT architecture prevent complications. CGM devices are noninvasive. They have replaced the traditional painful method of pricking the skin to draw a blood sample. Sensors in the CGM device continuously track the glucose levels and provide greater control over patient health. Real-time tracking enables sending notifications to the doctor and relatives in advance in case of critical conditions (Valenzuela et al., 2020). This approach has improved the quality of life of elderly patients, especially those unable to attend hospital appointments.

Similarly, blood pressure monitoring devices enabled with IoT are helpful in the fast detection of critical blood pressure values in case of hypertension. Hypertension can be a life-threatening disease condition if blood pressure exceeds acceptable values. Early detection through innovative technologies gives better control over patient's health and quality of life. Digital management of hypertension through wearable blood pressure monitoring technology is foreseen as the future (Kario, 2020). First-hand health monitoring through digital devices has brought in greater patient-centricity in services. Citizens, too, feel more in control of their well-being.

3.8 Device Portability

In hospitals, tablet computers and personal digital assistants (PDAs) provide administrative and professional support (e.g., scheduling, electronic prescribing). These are also used for quick clinical and drug references during patient care. Such devices have enhanced productivity and communication. Clinically, the quality of patient care improves with reduced medical errors. Portability in radiography, such as X-ray scanning, is of immense use to patients who cannot leave the ward. Lightweight, portable ultrasound devices provide high-quality, high-resolution imaging. Portable diagnosis is frequently performed in hospitals when patients are in conditions like intubation, medical emergency, severe infection, neutropenic status, etc.

The portability of medical equipment like ECG, Ultrasound, CT scan, and MRI has improved time and cost efficiencies in healthcare settings. When clubbed with futuristic technologies, they provide an added dimension of patient safety and quality of life. When used with IoT-based systems, the portability of ECG devices has been instrumental in reducing mortality during cardiac emergencies. These systems can send real-time critical alerts, which helps in seeking quicker care (Shaown et al., 2019). Portable MRI scanners have enabled point-of-care monitoring applications in patient comfort. This has increased speed and spatial-temporal capabilities in disease detection (Wald et al., 2020). Portable ultrasound and computed tomography (C.T. scan) are great hardware and computational technology advances. These portable devices, being low-cost, have the potential to reach larger patient populations.

3.9 Blockchain Technology

Blockchain is an emerging innovative technology that supports a unique data storage pattern of storing data in blocks linked together in a chain. This helps improve organizational performance by providing decentralization, security, transparency, traceability, incorruptibility, accountability, and data authentication.

Besides providing solutions in various sectors, blockchain technology in healthcare is helpful in:

1. Accurate identification of severe mistakes during medical data exchange as data manipulation is prevented
2. Transparency of prescription process from manufacturing to pharmacy shelves
3. Preventing disruptions and shortages of medicines in the medical supply chain
4. Preventing illicit handling of records and payments
5. Catching deception in clinical trials
6. Quicker access to patient's whole health history by physicians for making correct diagnoses and recommendations
7. Device tracking
8. Eliminating the need for multi-level authentication of time-sensitive procedures
9. Enhancing trust of health insurers
10. Measurement and enforcement of clinical quality management systems

Electronic medical records based on blockchain networks increase efficiencies and promote patient health in the long run. Due to the unified workflow nature of blockchain technology, there is interoperability between the various hospital processes (Haleem et al., 2021). This has enhanced service productivity besides improving patient care.

```
+------------------------------------+
| Healthcare |
| Ecosystem |
+------------------+------------------+
|
|
+-------------------------+------------------------+
| | |
+----------v-----------+ +---------v----------+ +---------v----------+
| Electronic Health | | Radio Frequency | | Telemedicine |
| Records | | Identification | | |
| (EHR System) | | (RFID) | | |
+----------+-----------+ +----------+-----------+ +---------+----------+
| | |
| | |
+----------v-----------+ +----------v-----------+ +---------v----------+
| AI-driven Tools | | AI-driven Tools | | Remote Patient |
| (Decision Support, | |(Patient Monitoring, | | Monitoring, |
| Predictive Analytics)| | Diagnostics, etc.) | | Diagnoses, etc.) |
+---------------------+ +---------------------+ +---------------------+
```

3.10 Explanation

- **Electronic Health Records (EHR):**
- Centralized repository for patient health information.
- Supports real-time data access and integration.
- **Radio Frequency Identification (RFID):**
- Enables tracking and identification of medical assets, patients, and staff.
- Enhances inventory management and patient safety.
- **Telemedicine:**
- Facilitates remote delivery of healthcare services.
- Involves virtual consultations, remote diagnostics, and monitoring.
- **AI-driven Tools:**
- Decision support systems based on A.I. for enhanced diagnostics and treatment planning.
- Predictive analytics for patient outcomes.
- Automation of routine tasks allows healthcare professionals to focus on complex aspects of care.

3.11 Interconnections

- EHR feeds data to AI-driven tools for analysis and decision-making.
- RFID integrates with EHR and A.I. for efficient patient tracking and asset management.
- Telemedicine relies on EHR for access to patient records and A.I. for diagnostics.
- AI-driven tools, including remote patient monitoring, connect with EHR and telemedicine platforms.

This simplified visual representation illustrates how these technologies work in tandem, creating a comprehensive healthcare ecosystem that benefits from the synergies between EHR, RFID, telemedicine, and AI-driven tools.

3.12 Challenges of Innovative Technologies in Healthcare

Data protection is highly relevant even with the benefits of multiple innovative technologies in healthcare. The connectivity of medical devices can have adverse implications for patient's privacy and safety. Though healthcare organizations ensure patient data is stored securely and encrypted, EHR may have cybersecurity concerns.

In places where privacy laws are restrictive, data sharing is a challenge. A lack of protective infrastructure and interoperability standards may cause a system dysfunction. As technology continues to evolve, robust cybersecurity protocols are needed. Med-tech companies, through government regulation, need to ensure ethically safe data-driven devices and equipment. As respect for human rights is paramount, governments must be legally clear on the rules and norms for deploying new digital health technologies (Abbing, 2020).

3.13 Implications of the Study

- **Enhanced Healthcare Delivery:** The integration of advanced technologies outlined in the study implies a potential enhancement in healthcare delivery, leading to improved patient outcomes, reduced errors, and optimized resource utilization.

- **Operational Efficiency and Cost Reduction:** Hospitals adopting these technologies can anticipate increased operational efficiency, streamlined workflows, and potential cost reduction due to optimized resource allocation.
- **Patient-Centric Care:** The focus on patient-oriented technologies, such as telemedicine and wearable devices, suggests a shift towards more patient-centric care, allowing personalized treatment plans and improved accessibility.
- **Data Security and Privacy:** The study highlights the importance of addressing data security and privacy challenges, emphasizing the need for robust regulations and safeguards to protect sensitive healthcare information.
- **Informed Decision-Making:** Incorporating A.I. in healthcare implies a shift toward more informed decision-making processes, enabling healthcare professionals to leverage real-time data for accurate diagnoses and treatment plans.

4. FUTURE RESEARCH DIRECTIONS

- **Interoperability and Integration:** Investigate methods to enhance interoperability and seamless integration of various healthcare technologies, ensuring a holistic and interconnected healthcare ecosystem.
- **Patient-Centered Outcomes:** Conduct research on the impact of innovative technologies on patient-centered outcomes, including patient satisfaction, engagement, and overall quality of life.
- **Ethical Considerations in A.I.:** Delve into the ethical implications of A.I. applications in healthcare, addressing issues such as bias, privacy, and accountability. Develop frameworks for responsible A.I. deployment.
- **Long-Term Effects of Telemedicine:** Explore the long-term effects and sustainability of telemedicine, assessing its impact on healthcare accessibility, patient outcomes, and the overall healthcare system.
- **Human-Machine Collaboration:** Investigate the optimal balance between human and machine collaboration in healthcare settings, considering the role of healthcare professionals alongside A.I. and robotics.

4.1 Limitations of the Study

- **Generalization:** The findings and implications of the study may not be universally applicable across diverse healthcare settings, considering variations in infrastructure, resources, and healthcare practices.
- **Technological Adoption:** The successful implementation of these technologies relies on the willingness and capacity of healthcare institutions to adopt and integrate them into existing workflows, which may face resistance or resource constraints.
- **Ethical Considerations:** While the study acknowledges ethical concerns related to A.I., it does not provide an exhaustive exploration of potential ethical dilemmas and their resolutions in the healthcare context.

- **Long-Term Effects:** The long-term effects of some technologies, especially those recently adopted, may need to be fully understood, and ongoing research is necessary to assess sustainability and evolving challenges.
- **Regulatory Landscape:** The study does not extensively delve into the evolving regulatory landscape governing healthcare technologies, and future research should explore the impact of regulatory changes on technology adoption and patient care.

5. CONCLUSION

Innovative improvements in healthcare product technology for diagnosis, treatments, and care delivery have bettered the quality of patient life and increased their life expectancy. Beyond operational efficiency, hospitals have also seen reduced costs and medical errors. RFID, telemedicine, device portability, PACS, blockchain technology, robotic surgery, artificial intelligence (A.I.), and the Internet of Things (IoT) have substituted repetitive tasks and provided personalized care to patients. A.I. has automated tasks and is delivering faster healthcare at a lower cost. A.I. is helping people stay healthy through early prediction, detection, and decision-making support. This has reduced the dependence on a large number of healthcare providers. These innovative technologies are helpful not only to patients, doctors, nurses, technicians, and administrators but also for regulatory compliance and quality assurance. Health insurance companies, too, have gained confidence with technology that optimizes workflows and positively impacts patient care. It can be confidently deduced that with a slew of technology-based clinical decision support systems, caregivers and patients are in better control of disease management.

REFERENCES

Abbing, H. R. (2020). Innovative Technologies in Healthcare, Beware of the Pitfalls. *European Journal of Health Law*, *27*(1), 1–8. doi:10.1163/15718093-12271453 PMID:33878725

Abugabah, A., Nizamuddin, N., & Abuqabbeh, A. (2020). A review of challenges and barriers to implementing RFID technology in the Healthcare sector. *Procedia Computer Science*, *170*, 1003–1010. doi:10.1016/j.procs.2020.03.094

Adler-Milstein, J., Holmgren, A. J., & Kralovec, P. (2017). Electronic health record adoption in U.S. hospitals: Progress continues, but challenges persist. *Health Affairs*, *36*(8), 1564–1570. PMID:28784734

Aldosari, H., Saddik, B., & Al Kadi, K. (2018). Impact of picture archiving and communication system (PACS) on radiology staff. *Informatics in Medicine Unlocked*, *10*, 1–16. doi:10.1016/j.imu.2017.11.001

Bashshur, R., Doarn, C. R., Frenk, J. M., Kvedar, J. C., Woolliscroft, J. O., & Yellowlees, P. M. (2020). Telemedicine and the COVID-19 pandemic, lessons for the future. *Telemedicine Journal and e-Health*, *26*(5), 571–573. doi:10.1089/tmj.2020.29040.rb PMID:32275485

Chan, M., Esteves, T., & Guo, Y. (2015). Exploring factors influencing individuals' acceptance and use of mobile devices for healthcare. *Journal of the Association for Information Systems*, *16*(11), 796–822.

Char, D. S., Shah, N. H., & Magnus, D. (2018). Implementing machine learning in health care—Addressing ethical challenges. *The New England Journal of Medicine*, *378*(11), 981–983. doi:10.1056/NEJMp1714229 PMID:29539284

Davila, F., Agha, R., & Becker, S. (2019). Robotic technology in surgery: A review. *Surgery Journal (New York, N.Y.)*, *3*(4), e189–e192.

De Schutter, O., Frazer, H., Guio, A. C., & Marlier, E. (2023). How poverty is perpetuated across generations. In *The Escape from Poverty* (pp. 18–60). Policy Press. doi:10.56687/9781447370611-005

Esteva, A., Kuprel, B., Novoa, R. A., Ko, J., Swetter, S. M., Blau, H. M., & Thrun, S. (2017). Dermatologist-level classification of skin cancer with deep neural networks. *Nature*, *542*(7639), 115–118. doi:10.1038/nature21056 PMID:28117445

Fleming, A. (1929). On the Antibacterial Action of Cultures of a Penicillium, with Special Reference to Their Use in the Isolation of B. influenzae. *British Journal of Experimental Pathology*, *10*(3), 226–236.

Frisch, P. H. (2019, September). RFID in today's intelligent hospital enhances patient care and optimizes hospital operations. In *2019, the IEEE International Conference on RFID Technology and Applications (RFID-TA)* (pp. 458-463). IEEE.

Furlong, L. I., Morris, M. E., & Serry, T. (2015). Remote monitoring of Parkinson's disease using inertial sensors. *IEEE Journal of Biomedical and Health Informatics*, *19*(6), 1802–1810.

Gitas, G., Hanker, L., Rody, A., Ackermann, J., & Alkatout, I. (2022). Robotic surgery in gynecology: Is the future already here? *Minimally Invasive Therapy & Allied Technologies*, *31*(6), 815–824. doi:10.1080/13645706.2021.2010763 PMID:34989636

Haleem, A., Javaid, M., Singh, R. P., Suman, R., & Rab, S. (2021). *Blockchain technology applications in healthcare: An overview*. International Journal of Intelligent Networks.

Haux, R. (2006). Health information systems—Past, present, future. *International Journal of Medical Informatics*, *75*(3–4), 268–281. doi:10.1016/j.ijmedinf.2005.08.002 PMID:16169771

Institute of Medicine (U.S.) Committee on Monitoring Access to Personal Health Care Services. (1993). *Access to health care in America* (M. Millman, Ed.). National Academies Press.

Kario, K. (2020). Management of hypertension in the digital era: Small wearable monitoring devices for remote blood pressure monitoring. *Hypertension*, *76*(3), 640–650. doi:10.1161/HYPERTENSIONAHA.120.14742 PMID:32755418

Kneuertz, P. J., Singer, E., D'Souza, D. M., Abdel-Rasoul, M., Moffatt-Bruce, S. D., & Merritt, R. E. (2019). Hospital cost and clinical effectiveness of robotic-assisted versus video-assisted thoracoscopic and open lobectomy: A propensity score–weighted comparison. *The Journal of Thoracic and Cardiovascular Surgery*, *157*(5), 2018–2026. doi:10.1016/j.jtcvs.2018.12.101 PMID:30819575

Krittanawong, C., Zhang, H., Wang, Z., Aydar, M., & Kitai, T. (2020). Artificial intelligence in precision cardiovascular medicine. *Journal of the American College of Cardiology*, *75*(22), 2806–2819. PMID:28545640

Kuo, A. M. H., Borycki, E. M., & Kushniruk, A. (2018). Use of radio-frequency identification (RFID) in a pediatric hospital: A qualitative study. *Studies in Health Technology and Informatics*, *250*, 25–29.

Lee, C. C., Kim, Y., Choi, J. H., & Porter, E. (2022). Does implementing electronic health record systems impact hospital efficiency, profitability, and quality? *Journal of Applied Business & Economics*, *24*(2).

Litjens, G., Kooi, T., Bejnordi, B. E., Setio, A. A. A., Ciompi, F., Ghafoorian, M., van der Laak, J. A. W. M., van Ginneken, B., & Sanchez, C. I. (2017). A survey on deep learning in medical image analysis. *Medical Image Analysis*, *42*, 60–88. doi:10.1016/j.media.2017.07.005 PMID:28778026

McMaughan, D. J., Oloruntoba, O., & Smith, M. L. (2020). Socioeconomic status and access to healthcare: interrelated drivers for healthy aging. *Frontiers in public health*, *8*, 231.

Porter, R. (1998). *The Greatest Benefit to Mankind: A Medical History of Humanity*. W. W. Norton & Company.

Rajkomar, A., Oren, E., Chen, K., Dai, A. M., Hajaj, N., Hardt, M, & Dean, J. (2018). Scalable and accurate deep learning with electronic health records. npj. *Digital Medicine*, *1*(1), 18. PMID:31304302

Riva, G., Gaggioli, A., Villani, D., Cipresso, P., Repetto, C., Serino, S., & Gutiérrez-Maldonado, J. (2020). Positive technology in the clinical setting: A new vision of well-being. *Cyberpsychology, Behavior, and Social Networking*, *13*(5), 651–655.

Roentgen, W. C. (1895). A New Kind of Rays: A Preliminary Communication. *Sitzungsberichte der Würzburger Physik-medizinischen Gesellschaft*, *1895*, 132–141.

Roy, S. N., & Sengupta, T. (2020). Impact of IoT on the Healthcare Producers: Epitomizing Pharmaceutical Drug Discovery Process. Internet of Things Use Cases for the Healthcare Industry.

Shaown, T., Hasan, I., Mim, M. M. R., & Hossain, M. S. (2019, May). IoT-based portable ECG monitoring system for intelligent healthcare. In *2019, the 1st International Conference on Advances in Science, Engineering and Robotics Technology (ICASERT)* (pp. 1-5). IEEE.

Smith, M., Saunders, R., Stuckhardt, L., & McGinnis, J. M. (Eds.). (2017). *Best care at lower cost: The path to continuously learning health care in America*. National Academies Press.

Thrall, J. H. (2008). The next-generation PACS: Implications for radiology. *Journal of the American College of Radiology*, *5*(5), 431–434.

Topol, E. J. (2019). Deep Medicine: How Artificial Intelligence Can Make Healthcare Human Again. Hachette, UK.

Topol, E. J. (2019). High-performance medicine: The convergence of human and artificial intelligence. *Nature Medicine*, *25*(1), 44–56. doi:10.1038/s41591-018-0300-7 PMID:30617339

Tucson, R. V., Edmunds, M., & Hodgkins, M. L. (2017). Telehealth. *The New England Journal of Medicine*, *377*(16), 1585–1592. doi:10.1056/NEJMsr1503323 PMID:29045204

Valenzuela, F., García, A., Ruiz, E., Vazquez, M., Cortez, J., & Espinoza, A. (2020). An IoT-based glucose monitoring algorithm to prevent diabetes complications. *applied sciences, 10*(3), 921.

Wald, L. L., McDaniel, P. C., Witzel, T., Stockmann, J. P., & Cooley, C. Z. (2020). Low-cost and portable MRI. *Journal of Magnetic Resonance Imaging*, *52*(3), 686–696. doi:10.1002/jmri.26942 PMID:31605435

Wyld, D. C. (2009). Preventing the worst-case scenario: Analyzing RFID technology and infant protection in hospitals. *Novel Algorithms and Techniques in Telecommunications and Networking*, *7*(1), 29–33.

Chapter 18
A Review Study on the Challenges and Opportunities in Implementing the Metaverse in Healthcare:
An Asian perspective

Neha Mishra
Chitkara University, India

Krishna Kumar Mishra
Chitkara University, India

ABSTRACT

Recently, metaverse technology has drawn considerable attention in the healthcare industry as a result of multifold technological advancements in the last decade. Metaverse is likely to have a significant impact on our digital lives in the near future by enhancing our interactions, and our working and playing habits. However, it poses a variety of challenges that require special attention and proactive action to be taken. In this study, the authors examine the challenges and opportunities associated with implementing metaverse solutions in Asian healthcare systems. These include infrastructure, cultural considerations, regulatory frameworks, and privacy concerns. These are among the critical factors affecting metaverse solutions development in these systems. China, Bangladesh and Japan. Japan has the highest market size per user in terms of average market size, which was 219.2 dollars in 2022 and will increase to 632.2 dollars in 2030. This study provides essential insights about the metaverse's deployment, acceptance by the young generation, and future recommendations.

DOI: 10.4018/979-8-3693-2019-8.ch018

1. INTRODUCTION

The rising costs of healthcare, substantial infrastructure requirements, growing populations, and an excess of healthcare personnel have revealed the lack of sustainability in healthcare systems for the future. The COVID-19 pandemic has forced healthcare practitioners and entrepreneurs to actively seek solutions for efficiently handling patients outside of conventional healthcare institutions. Technological advancements have made it possible to practice telemedicine and telehealth, which allows for remote connection with healthcare professionals without the need to be physically present in the precise same location. However, the process of transforming the healthcare sector is considerably more intricate. Researchers have been studying the virtualized operation of healthcare within the metaverse. Schroeder (2008) states that there is no concrete universally agreed-upon description for a virtual environment, emphasizing the necessity for a clear and concise definition.

However, on the basis of recent research studies (Weinberger 2022, Park and Kim 2022 Zhang et al., 2022 Ritterbusch and Teichmann 2023) Metaverse represents the convergence of several technological advancements, including artificial intelligence, virtual reality, augmented reality, internet of medical devices, robotics, quantum computing (Singh et al., 202). This combination offers opportunities to identify novel approaches for delivering high-quality healthcare treatment and assures an integrated procedure for patient care (Lee and Yoon 2021, Sharma et al., 2021, Chengoden et al., 2023).

Several countries in Southern Asia are investing heavily in developing the metaverse within their healthcare systems, including India, China, Bangladesh, and Japan, which represents an opportunity to become more innovative. Using virtual consultations and telemedicine can help healthcare providers and patients overcome accessibility barriers. The use of remote consultations and telemedicine can be used to provide remote healthcare without sufficient medical resources (Omboni et al.,2022).

Simulating real-life situations in a metaverse can also improve medical practitioners' competence and knowledge. The use of virtual fascinating environments can improve health literacy of patients and make virtual rooms more realistic (Hamilton et al., 2021). The use of metaverse improve chronic illness management and elder care, as it will allow remote monitoring of patients, which is particularly useful for chronic illnesses (Bansal et al., 2022). Virtual workspaces can be beneficial to doctors and healthcare professionals. Through collaborative research and innovation, healthcare can be advanced throughout the world and support their establishment. Metaverses have the potential to reduce stress and establish a favorable environment for mental health.

Data visualization and pharmaceutical research can be facilitated by using metaverse-based technology in the research world. To achieve the goal of improving care for patients efficiently, effectively, and ethically, technology must be incorporated. Regulatory compliance, data security, and ethical considerations are all key factors in successful implementation of metaverse in healthcare. Health care faces some challenges posed by the metaverse even though it represents a promising future technology. Data privacy and security may be a concern with immersive technologies due to the sensitive nature of patient information.

Data breaches and unauthorized entries must be prevented to maintain confidence in healthcare systems. Additionally, healthcare professionals face significant challenges in compliance with regulatory requirements, as they are required to navigate a complex landscape of rules, standards, and guidelines to comply with ethical norms. Tech giants of China such as Tencent and Alibaba are driving the development of the metaverse (Deloitte report 2021-22). However, a major challenge is in efficiently handling rigorous governmental regulations, particularly concerning content control and ensuring data privacy

(Yeung, 2019). To accomplish successful deployment, it is crucial to guarantee that the metaverse aligns with the government's vision and adheres to its policies.

India possesses a rapidly growing technology sector and a substantial consumer base. However, it must confront obstacles such as inconsistent internet connectivity, disparities in digital literacy, and constraints in infrastructure (Lambrechts and Sinha 2019). Whereas country such as Bangladesh shows great potential but also poses certain difficulties.

Some countries are experiencing rapid advancements in technology, which are laying the foundation for harnessing the metaverse to enhance healthcare services. However, it is essential to thoroughly consider challenges such as insufficient internet infrastructure, varying levels of digital literacy, and even legal barriers. for successfully implement metaverse applications in the healthcare sector, it is essential to find a balanced and harmonic combination of technological progress and the unique socio-economic factors for the ultimate objective to augment the accessibility of healthcare and enhance overall outcomes.

Table 1. Metaverse definitions by different entities

Entity	Metaverse Definitions
Accenture	"Represents a continuum of digitally enhanced world, realities, and business models. It is a dynamic environment that uses spatial computing platforms, generative AI, Web 3, Blockchain technologies to enable augmentation of the real world."
European Parliament	"An immersive and constant virtual 3D world where people interact by means of an avatar to carry out a wide range of activities."
Mathew Ball	"A massively scaled and interoperable network of real time rendered real time 3D virtual world and environments which can be experienced synchronously and persistently by an effectively unlimited number of users with an individual sense of presence and with continuity of data such as identity, history, entitlements, objects, communications, and payments."
Meta	"The next evolution in social connection and the successor to the mobile internet."
XR safety intelligence	"A network of interconnected virtual worlds with the following key characteristics: presence, persistence, immersion and interoperability."
Responsible Metaverse Alliance	"A persistent and immersive simulated or virtual world that is experienced in the first person by large groups of simultaneous users who share a strong sense of mutual presence."
Wikipedia	"A hypothetical iteration of the internet as a single, universal, and immersive virtual world that is facilitated using virtual reality (VR) and augmented reality (AU) headsets. In colloquial usage a metaverse is a network of 3D virtual worlds focused on social and economic connection."
Meriam-Webster Dictionary	"A persistent virtual environment that allows access to and interoperability of multiple individual virtual realities."

2. BACKGROUND

As health data is increasingly important throughout the world, integrating the metaverse with healthcare is a pioneering area with revolutionary potential. The metaverse has been fascinating to discover during covid-19, a mixture of augmented reality, virtual reality, and the internet (Tiwari et al., 2020). Aside from virtual consultations and immersive medical training, the metaverse offers numerous other healthcare innovations such as digital twins. A unique cultural, regulatory, and technological environment exists in Asia, which requires specific consideration. The implementation of the metaverse in Asian healthcare environments presents obstacles and possibilities to understand how it can be efficiently used to improve healthcare processes, patient care, and overall health outcomes. This study examines comprehensively the various aspects of this complex issue, so policymakers, practitioners, and technology developers can gain a deeper understanding of the dynamic relationship between healthcare and the metaverse.

Table 2. Review of literature of metaverse applications in healthcare in a nutshell

S.N.	Article	Authors	Description
1.	*"Metaverse for Healthcare: A Survey on Potential Applications, Challenges and Future Directions"*	Chengoden et al.,2023	The article emphasizes on the state of the art, the enabling technologies to adopt the Metaverse for healthcare.
2.	*"Metaverse beyond the hype: Multidisciplinary perspectives on emerging challenges, opportunities, and agenda for research, practice and policy"*	Dwivedi et al., 2023	By combining the informed narrative with a multi-perspective approach from experts, as well as concerns related to trust, privacy, bias, disinformation, and the application of law, psychological aspects of adoption examined in depth by authors.
3.	*"Metaverse in Healthcare: Applications, Challenges, and Future Directions"*	Musamih et al., 2023	The author explored marketing, healthcare supply chain, healthcare facilities, fitness and wellness.
4.	*"Urology: a trip into metaverse"*	Randazzo et al.,2023	The article described Metaverse benefits to urology and urologic patients.
5.	*"A Bibliometric Study on the Rising Trends of Metaverse Literature in Asia-Pacific"*	Wider et al., 2023	It is the primary purpose of this study to illuminate the research on metaverses and to provide a perspective on the topic of future development in Asia- Pacific Region.
6.	*"On the privacy and security for e-health services in the metaverse: An overview"*	Letafati and Otoum, 2023	The article investigated privacy and security issues of metaverse use in e-health services.
7.	*"Transforming health through the metaverse"*	Qiu et al., 2022	The article defined virtual implications of meta verse in health care.
8.	*"Healthcare in Metaverse: A Survey on Current Metaverse Applications in Healthcare"*	Bansal et al., 2022	The article examined metaverse development in telemedicine, clinical care, education, mental health, physical fitness, veterinary, and pharmaceuticals.
9.	*"Metaverse in medicine"*	Yang et al., 2022	The authors stated that the concept of Medical Internet of Things (metaverse) has been widely accepted and present effective technological support in healthcare problems, and for the future development in Asia-Pacific Region.
10.	*"Applications of Artificial Intelligence, Metaverse and Data Science for Intelligent Healthcare"*	Tyagi and Saxena, 2022	The article gives an overview on artificial intelligence and data science applications in hospital administration, as well as challenges in applying the metaverse, artificial intelligence, and data science within the context of smart health.
11.	*"Metaverse and Virtual Health Care in Ophthalmology: Opportunities and Challenges"*	Tan et al.,2022	The article proposed goodness of metaverse application in ophthalmology along with regulatory and cybersecurity standards.
12.	*"Metaverse phenomenon and its impact on health: A scoping review"*	Garavand and Aslani, 2022	The authors examined and identified the applications of this emerging technology in the health care sector.

3. RESEARCH METHODOLOGY

The analysis of metaverse application in the healthcare sector by Asian countries, followed the Preferred Reporting for Systematic Reviews and Meta-Analyses for Scoping Reviews (PRISMA-ScR) checklist and associated description. The Additional Content incorporates the PRISMA checklist.

The research studies were obtained by doing a comprehensive search of various electronic databases, including JSTOR, PubMed, Scopus, EBSCO, SCIENCE DIRECT, and IEEE Xplore.

3.1 Results

Based on a report by Statista Market Insights, figure 1 below presents a comparison between average market size per user of southern Asian countries such as Japan, India, China, and Bangladesh from the year 2023 to 2030. In 2022, the market size of Japan would reach 219.2 dollars per user, and by 2030, it would reach 632.2 dollars. As of 2022, China has the second highest amount of 58.2 dollars per user, and by 2030 it will reach 171.2%, followed by Bangladesh. The average market size per user in the Indian healthcare market in 2022 was 18.9 dollars, which is quite good and likely to grow further with the hike of 54.9 dollars expected in 2030.

Figure 1. Metaverse health and fitness (average market size per user)

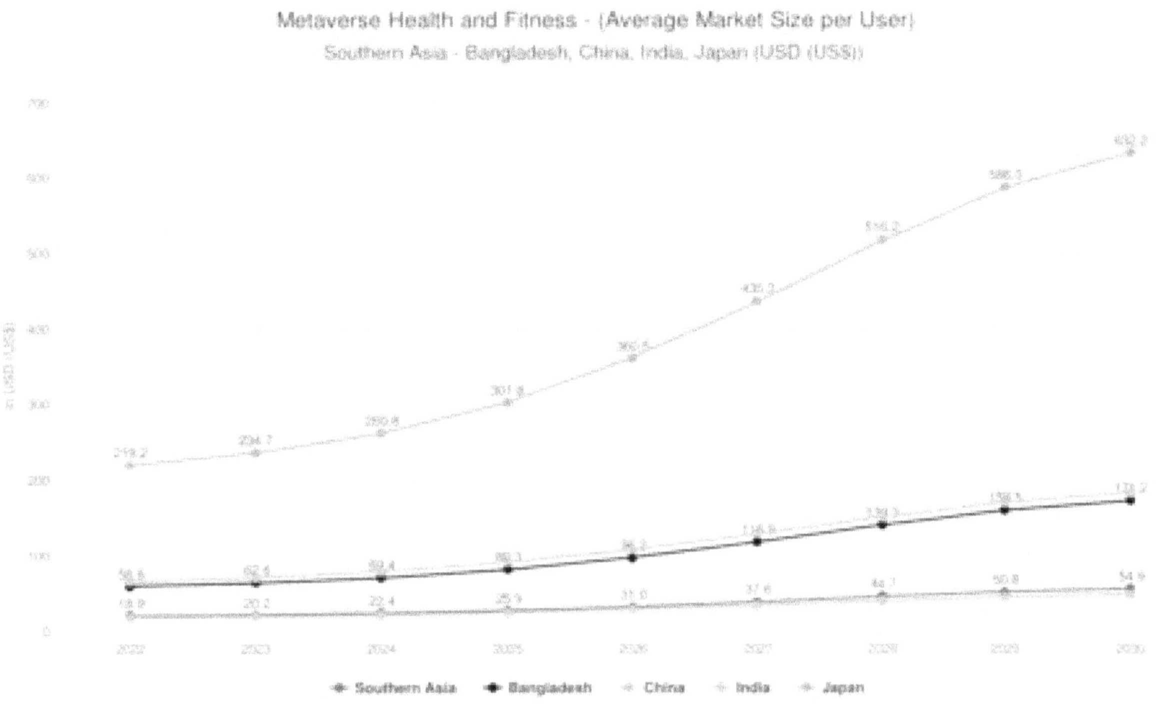

Figure 2 shows the market size growth of metaverse application in healthcare sector among southern Asian countries such as India, Japan, Bangladesh, and China. Bangladesh is shown to have the highest potential growth rate of 50% in 2023, followed by India with a growth rate of 17.6% in 2030 and it is projected that the growth rate will remain the same in 2030 because India has a rapidly growing technology sector and a substantial consumer base. It is important, that training and education are provided to maximize the potential of Metaverse technology in healthcare. In 2023, Japan and China have a growth rate of 13.6% and will reach a growth rate of 17% by 2030.

The potential of healthcare solutions in the metaverse is immense. The core objective of the metaverse is to bring people closer by creating environments that simulate reality.

3.1.1 Practical Implications of the Metaverse in Healthcare

The utilization of the Metaverse facilitates the accumulation and examination of substantial volumes of data, hence potentially yielding advantages in the advancement of novel treatments and therapies.

Figure 2. Metaverse health and fitness (market size change per user)

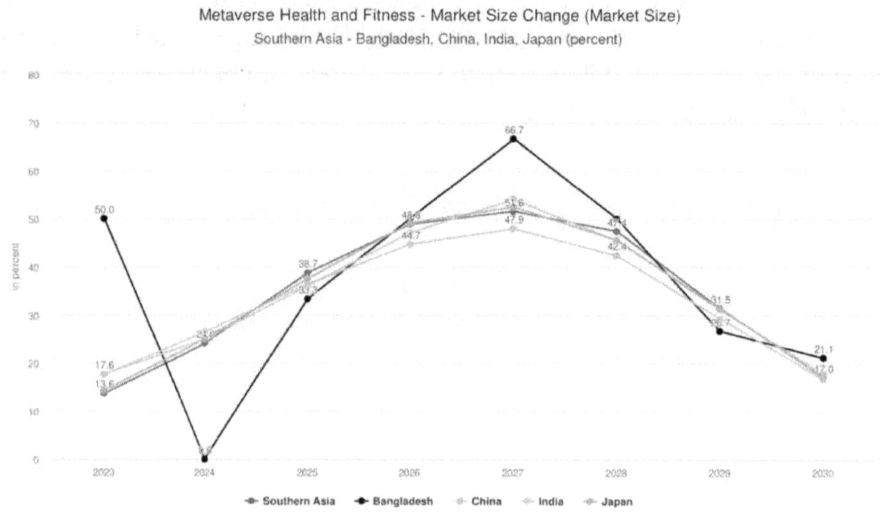

Figure 3. Synchronized and sustainable metaverse

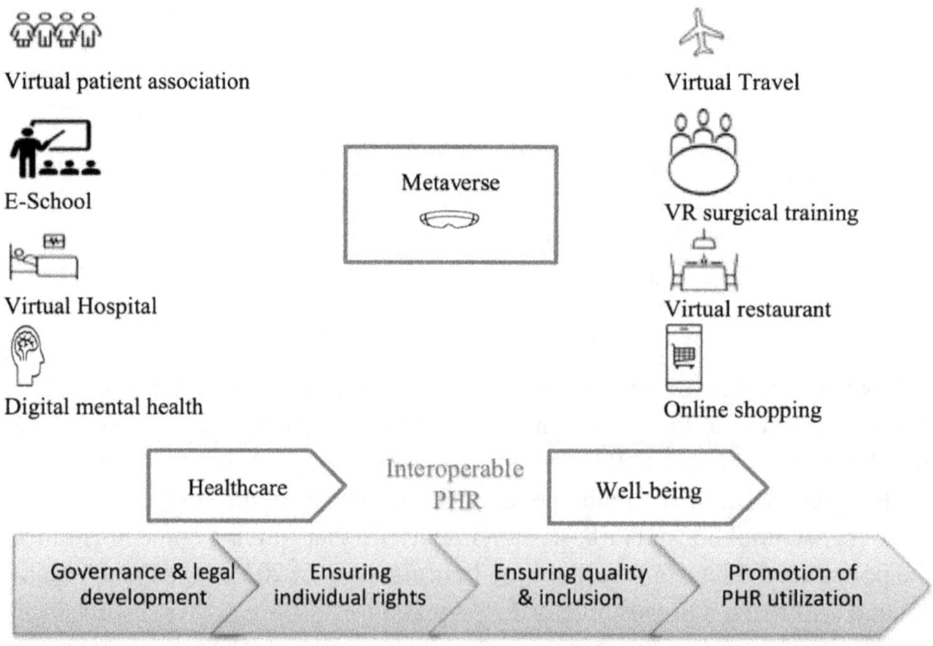

Customized healthcare can greatly benefit from the utilization of individualized data, as it has the potential to enhance diagnostic accuracy and provide customized treatment approaches. As the metaverse is a virtualization of the physical world. Data from the Metaverse includes brainwaves, health information, and biometrics, which allows the Metaverse to collect patient information as well

Figure 4. The amazing benefits of metaverse in healthcare

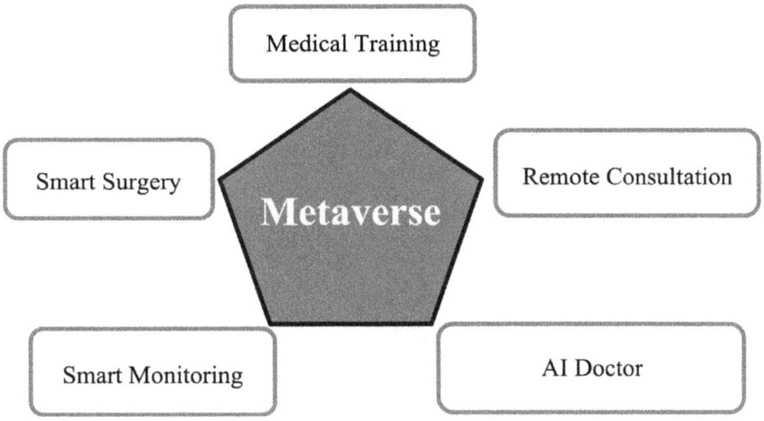

Figure 5. Data processing and privacy in the metaverse

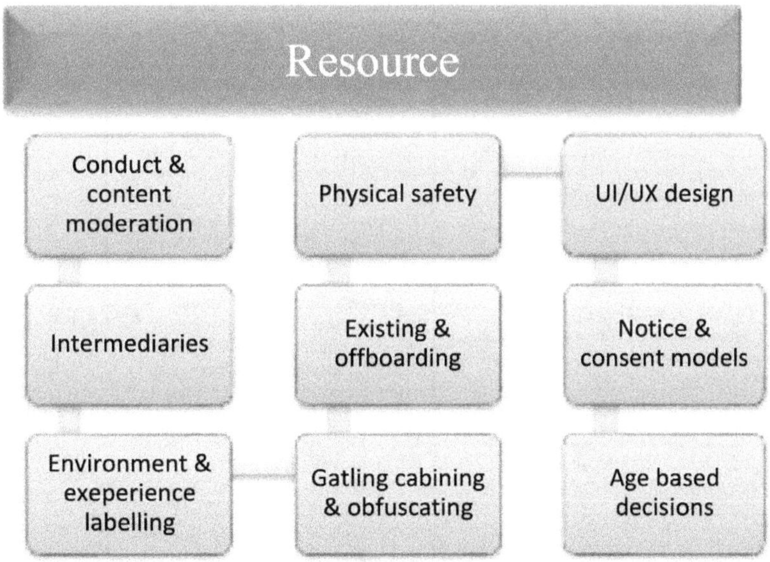

as implement a practical healthcare system that mirrors the real world. The data can also be used to evaluate how the patient's body responded to the treatment, including physiological responses and how their body will respond to the actual treatment. Using metaverse technology has revolutionized how patients are monitored and treated no matter where they are. Creating realistic scenarios is possible with virtual reality. Recovery could be hindered if patients cannot distinguish between reality and virtuality. The best way to maximize the value of virtual assets is to better understand the boundaries between the virtual and real world.

Figure 6. Challenges in applying metaverse

Table 3. Challenges and potential solutions

Challenges	Description	Potential Solutions	Future Directions
Cybersecurity Threats	The transmission of digital data from diverse electronic devices poses a vulnerability to potential unauthorised access by hackers.	1. Utilisation of hardware and software that can detect threats or attacks. 2. The Metaverse network enforces stringent communication protocols. 3. Zero Trust Policy adoption.	Protocols for cyber security, such as network segmentation with ring-fencing. Lightweight Blockchain technology adoption.
Privacy Threats	The exposure of user-sensitive data by contemporary technologies like XR, AI, and IoT is escalating privacy breaches.	1. Encrypt the application layer to assure the security of data throughout the data cycle. 2. Adjust privacy frameworks to give users and developers control over their data. 3. Implement privacy-enhancing technologies (PETs) for the purpose of obscuring sensitive data.	The utilisation of collaborative learning methods to augment data privacy.
Communication Issues	The task of establishing effective communication among various gadgets across the Metaverse is a considerable challenge.	1. Design a Deep Reinforcement Learning auction-based system to enhance communication efficiency. 2. Apply incentive-based mechanisms within the Blockchain technology.	Adoption of 6G networks and service paradigms for healthcare Metaverse efficiency.
Computational Difficulties	The utilisation of artificial intelligence (AI) necessitates substantial computational resources.	1. Design AI models that are effective and optimised. 2. Put AI to use at the edge.	Lean AI models for improved prediction and reduced computational requirements. Adoption of XAI (Explainable AI).
The exorbitant expense	Deployment, maintenance, and the cost of interoperating devices are expensive, driving up infrastructure expenditures.	1. Create gadgets that are reliable and economical. 2. Adopt off-chain blockchain models and decentralised cloud storage systems to reduce storage and computational costs.	Adoption of Web 3.0 infrastructure for the development of the Metaverse.
Standards and ethical considerations	The absence of well-established standards for the Healthcare Metaverse.	1. Adopt a Contextual Approach to investigate the context of the technology and determine information flow constraints. 2. Implement a distinct regulatory framework to strike a balance between user rights and technological development.	The utilisation of enclosures and their impact on consumer behaviour.

4. LIMITATIONS

Security breaches or cyber-attacks can threaten sensitive healthcare information in the application of metaverse. An environment based on virtualization must be secure. Metaverse applications are complex to embed into pre-existing EHRs (Electronic health records) because of wide range of challenges. Integration is essential to maintain an efficient information flow. Prior to its widespread adoption, metaverse technology requires virtual reality headsets (VR), as well as high-speed internet access. As metaverse applications contain essential hardware and software components, their development and deployment can be expensive. Healthcare organizations operating in resource-constrained environments might be most adversely affected. Considering the metaverse in healthcare requires an ethical analysis. According to some researchers, the personalization of the patient-doctor relationship may be a problem and that health data from virtual health systems may be misused. Care and attention must be taken in addressing these ethical issues. Patients and the healthcare community may need time to adopt and understand metaverse applications. It is important to educate and train individuals on how to use and adopt this growing technology.

5. CONCLUSION

On the current scenario of health and fitness market in the South Asia, particularly in (Japan, India, China and Bangladesh), metaverse – virtual reality experiences such as AR and VR, in term of average market size per user Japan is on the highest position which was 219.2$ in 2022 and in 2030 it will become 632.2 $, similarly China with 58.8$ in 2022 and 116.2$ in 2030. However, India and Bangladesh are rapidly growing in the market of metaverse.

As the incorporation of the metaverse in the Asian countries healthcare sector possesses significant promise for transforming the delivery and encounter of healthcare services. However, it also entails noteworthy obstacles and constraints. Key areas of concern include privacy and data security, ensuring compliance with healthcare regulations, seamless integration with existing systems, promoting accessibility and inclusivity, addressing technological barriers, considering economic implications, ensuring user acceptance, and providing enough training, addressing ethical concerns, addressing health inequities, and effectively curating material. The mutual involvement of healthcare professionals, technologists, regulators, and other stakeholders is crucial in addressing and surpassing these limits. Ensuring a harmonious coexistence between technological progress and the preservation of privacy, security, and equitable access is of utmost importance. The careful consideration of these problems will play a pivotal role in fully harnessing the metaverse's potential to enhance healthcare provision, optimize patient results, and foster inclusion within the healthcare domain. Additional investigation, advancement, and formulation of regulations are imperative in order to negotiate the intricacies involved and establish a metaverse that is in accordance with the fundamental principles of healthcare and provides advantages to every stakeholder associated.

REFERENCES

Bansal, G., Rajgopal, K., Chamola, V., Xiong, Z., & Niyato, D. (2022). Healthcare in metaverse: A survey on current metaverse applications in healthcare. *IEEE Access : Practical Innovations, Open Solutions*, *10*, 119914–119946. doi:10.1109/ACCESS.2022.3219845

Chengoden, R., Victor, N., Huynh-The, T., Yenduri, G., Jhaveri, R. H., Alazab, M., Bhattacharya, S., Hegde, P., Maddikunta, P. K. R., & Gadekallu, T. R. (2023). Metaverse for healthcare: A survey on potential applications, challenges and future directions. *IEEE Access : Practical Innovations, Open Solutions*, *11*, 12765–12795. doi:10.1109/ACCESS.2023.3241628

Garavand, A., & Aslani, N. (2022). Metaverse phenomenon and its impact on health: A scoping review. *Informatics in Medicine Unlocked*, *32*, 101029. doi:10.1016/j.imu.2022.101029

Hamilton, D., McKechnie, J., Edgerton, E., & Wilson, C. (2021). Immersive virtual reality as a pedagogical tool in education: A systematic literature review of quantitative learning outcomes and experimental design. *Journal of Computers in Education*, *8*(1), 1–32. doi:10.1007/s40692-020-00169-2

Lambrechts, W., & Sinha, S. (2019). *Last mile internet access for emerging economies*. Springer International Publishing. doi:10.1007/978-3-030-20957-5

Lee, D., & Yoon, S. N. (2021). Application of artificial intelligence-based technologies in the healthcare industry: Opportunities and challenges. *International Journal of Environmental Research and Public Health*, *18*(1), 271. doi:10.3390/ijerph18010271 PMID:33401373

Letafati, M., & Otoum, S. (2023). On the privacy and security for e-health services in the metaverse: An overview. *Ad Hoc Networks*, *150*, 103262. doi:10.1016/j.adhoc.2023.103262

Musamih, A., Yaqoob, I., Salah, K., Jayaraman, R., Al-Hammadi, Y., Omar, M., & Ellahham, S. (2022). Metaverse in healthcare: Applications, challenges, and future directions. *IEEE Consumer Electronics Magazine*.

Oleksy, T., Wnuk, A., & Piskorska, M. (2023). Migration to the metaverse and its predictors: Attachment to virtual places and metaverse-related threat. *Computers in Human Behavior*, *141*, 107642. doi:10.1016/j.chb.2022.107642

Omboni, S., Padwal, R. S., Alessa, T., Benczúr, B., Green, B. B., Hubbard, I., Kario, K., Khan, N. A., Konradi, A., Logan, A. G., Lu, Y., Mars, M., McManus, R. J., Melville, S., Neumann, C. L., Parati, G., Renna, N. F., Ryvlin, P., Saner, H., & Wang, J. (2022). The worldwide impact of telemedicine during COVID-19: Current evidence and recommendations for the future. *Connected Health*, *1*, 7. doi:10.20517/ch.2021.03 PMID:35233563

Özkaynar, K. (2022). Marketing strategies of banks in the period of Metaverse, Block-chain, and Crypto-currency in the context of consumer behavior theories. *International Journal of Insurance and Finance*, *2*(1), 1–12.

Park, S. M., & Kim, Y. G. (2022). A metaverse: Taxonomy, components, applications, and open challenges. *IEEE Access : Practical Innovations, Open Solutions*, *10*, 4209–4251. doi:10.1109/ACCESS.2021.3140175

Qiu, C. S., Majeed, A., Khan, S., & Watson, M. (2022). Transforming health through the metaverse. *Journal of the Royal Society of Medicine*, *115*(12), 484–486. doi:10.1177/01410768221144763 PMID:36480946

Randazzo, G., Reitano, G., Carletti, F., Iafrate, M., Betto, G., Novara, G., ... Zattoni, F. (2023). Urology: A trip into metaverse. *World Journal of Urology*, 1–11. PMID:37552265

Ritterbusch, G. D., & Teichmann, M. R. (2023). Defining the metaverse: A systematic literature review. *IEEE Access : Practical Innovations, Open Solutions*, *11*, 12368–12377. doi:10.1109/ACCESS.2023.3241809

Schroeder, R. (2008). Defining virtual worlds and virtual environments. *Journal of Virtual Worlds Research*, *1*(1). doi:10.4101/jvwr.v1i1.294

Sharma, A., Kaur, S., & Singh, M. (2021). A comprehensive review on blockchain and Internet of Things in healthcare. *Transactions on Emerging Telecommunications Technologies*, *32*(10), e4333. doi:10.1002/ett.4333

Singh, G., Mantri, A., Sharma, O., & Kaur, R. (2021). Virtual reality learning environment for enhancing electronics engineering laboratory experience. *Computer Applications in Engineering Education*, *29*(1), 229–243. doi:10.1002/cae.22333

Tan, T. F., Li, Y., Lim, J. S., Gunasekeran, D. V., Teo, Z. L., Ng, W. Y., & Ting, D. S. (2022). Metaverse and virtual health care in ophthalmology: Opportunities and challenges. *Asia-Pacific Journal of Ophthalmology*, *11*(3), 237–246. doi:10.1097/APO.0000000000000537 PMID:35772084

Thomason, J. (2021). Metahealth-how will the metaverse change health care? *Journal of Metaverse*, *1*(1), 13–16.

Tiwari, S., Kumar, S., & Guleria, K. (2020). Outbreak trends of coronavirus disease–2019 in India: A prediction. *Disaster Medicine and Public Health Preparedness*, *14*(5), e33–e38. doi:10.1017/dmp.2020.115 PMID:32317044

Tyagi, Y., & Saxena, S. (2022). Applications of Artificial Intelligence, Metaverse and Data Science for Intelligent Healthcare. *AAYAM: AKGIM Journal of Management*, *12*(2), 141–149.

Wang, G., Badal, A., Jia, X., Maltz, J. S., Mueller, K., Myers, K. J., Niu, C., Vannier, M., Yan, P., Yu, Z., & Zeng, R. (2022). Development of metaverse for intelligent healthcare. *Nature Machine Intelligence*, *4*(11), 922–929. doi:10.1038/s42256-022-00549-6 PMID:36935774

Weinberger, M. (2022). What Is Metaverse?—A Definition Based on Qualitative Meta-Synthesis. *Future Internet*, *14*(11), 310. doi:10.3390/fi14110310

Wider, W., Jiang, L., Li, J., Tanucan, J. C. M., & Fauzi, M. A. (2023). *A Bibliometric Study on the Rising Trends of Metaverse Literature in Asia-Pacific Countries*.

Yang, D., Zhou, J., Song, Y., Sun, M., & Bai, C. (2022). Metaverse in medicine. *Clinical eHealth*, *5*, 39-43.

Yeung, K. (2019). 'Hypernudge': Big Data as a mode of regulation by design. In *The social power of algorithms* (pp. 118–136). Routledge. doi:10.4324/9781351200677-8

Zhang, X., Chen, Y., Hu, L., & Wang, Y. (2022). The metaverse in education: Definition, framework, features, potential applications, challenges, and future research topics. *Frontiers in Psychology*, *13*, 6063. doi:10.3389/fpsyg.2022.1016300 PMID:36304866

Chapter 19
Green Shoots of Agriculture:
Nurturing Agri Start-Ups in Jammu and Kashmir and Punjab – An Incubation Center Perspective

Ashish Kumar Isher
Mittal School of Business, Lovely Professional University, Phagwara, India

Veer P. Gangwar
Mittal School of Business, Lovely Professional University, Phagwara, India

Sabbey Sharma
Sher-e-Kashmir University of Agricultural Sciences and Technology of Jammu, India

ABSTRACT

This research investigates the challenges and opportunities confronted by startups in Jammu & Kashmir, and Punjab, with a specific focus on those engaged in agriculture and allied sectors within business incubators. Employing an interpretivist and inductive approach, the study adopts a cross-sectional design and collects data from 90 startups in six business incubators. The study uniquely examines challenges within agriculture startups under incubation. It offers distinctive insights into perceptions on entrepreneurial skills and assesses the relationship between incubation services and startup success. Employing a mixed-methods approach, the study collects data from startups using a structured questionnaire. Entrepreneurs agree on the importance of skills like education but show variations in softer skills. The study reveals a positive link between incubation services and startup success, outlining risk factors and challenges like fund disbursement and regulatory compliance.

DOI: 10.4018/979-8-3693-2019-8.ch019

1. INTRODUCTION

1.1 Navigating the Start-Up Landscape: A Global and Indian Perspective

Entrepreneurial pursuits are often fueled by a desire to address existing gaps in business or consumer needs and streamline processes (Henry, 2020). Driven by innovation and creativity, entrepreneurs are typically young, highly educated, socially connected, and bring extensive experience to their ventures (Picken, 2017). The success of these endeavors, defined by the achievement of set objectives, hinges on factors such as the scale of the start-up and the leadership style employed (Zaech & Baldegger, 2017).

Start-ups face myriad internal and external constraints, including market dynamics, institutional factors, and broader ecosystem challenges. These constraints become particularly pronounced as start-ups venture into solving novel problems in ambiguous circumstances, often in unnamed markets with unknown demand and funding sources (Tehseen & Ramayah, 2015).

Distinguishing between two uses of the term "start-up" is crucial. It can denote an innovative micro-enterprise from its inception to market maturity, covering the entire entrepreneurial growth process. Alternatively, it can refer to a specific phase between other developmental stages (Autio, 2016). Start-ups evolve through various stages, broadly categorized as Standup, Startup, and Scaleup, with a unique category of unicorns or scalers boasting valuations exceeding 1 billion USD.

Economically, start-ups contribute significantly to innovation and societal advancement, fostering increased income levels and improved quality of life over the long term (Cockayne, 2019; Barbulescu et al., 2021; Skawinska & Zalewski, 2020).

1.2 India's Rising Start-Up Horizon

India has emerged as a prominent and rapidly growing hub for start-ups, hosting over 79,000 registered ventures across the country. The government, through initiatives like Start-up India, launched in 2015, has actively supported and promoted this vibrant ecosystem. The demographic dividend, with a substantial youth population, coupled with an expanding middle class and increased disposable income, has fueled the growth of the market. India's digital initiatives and widespread internet usage, further accelerated by affordable data services introduced by Reliance Jio in 2016, have opened new avenues for start-ups.

Regulatory support, a robust higher education system producing skilled graduates, and a surge in angel investments and venture capital funds have all contributed to India's position as a preferred investment destination. However, challenges such as multi-stakeholder involvement, evolving consumer behavior, prolonged gestation periods, and cash burn have slowed down reforms in comparison to other global counterparts like China (Sharma and TN, 2018).

While India's start-up ecosystem continues to evolve dynamically, it faces ongoing challenges that necessitate strategic reforms and collaborative efforts to maintain its growth trajectory in the global start-up landscape.

India's prowess in Information and Communication Technology (ICT) has propelled its remarkable economic progress through digital transformation. The nation stands as one of the world's largest start-up ecosystems, a testament to its robust entrepreneurial landscape. This growth is attributed to increased angel investments and government initiatives like Make in India, Made in India, Smart City Missions, Digital India, and Start-up India, fostering entrepreneurial activities across sectors. The surge in start-ups, including new Unicorns, is fueled by factors such as increased purchasing power, widespread internet usage, adoption of digital social media, tech innovations, and a favorable demographic with a sizable young working population.

Recent years have witnessed a significant surge in India's start-up landscape, with investments steadily increasing across diverse sectors such as e-commerce, mobility, transportation, logistics, adtech, digital banking, finance, online aggregation, and analytics. In August 2019 alone, Indian start-ups secured an impressive funding amount of $1.4 billion, marking a substantial increase from the previous year's $182 million (IVCA-EY, 2019). India is home to over 80,000 start-ups, with 50% experiencing an annual growth rate of 30%, solidifying its position as the world's 3rd largest start-up ecosystem, closely trailing behind the United States and China.

India's commitment to augmenting agricultural production, enhancing food processing capabilities, and optimizing marketing strategies has opened substantial opportunities for Agri-tech start-ups. These ventures, characterized by innovation and dedication to the agricultural sector, capitalize on technology integration, fostering agricultural innovation and business development.

1.3 Start-Ups Incubation in India

Start-ups, especially in their initial days, require a supportive ecosystem to survive and sustain. Incubators and incubation centers are crucial components of the overall entrepreneurial ecosystem, playing a pivotal role in facilitating the journey of innovative ventures to the marketplace. All start-ups, including Agricultural technology entrepreneurs, benefit from an integrated ecosystem comprising innovators, incubators, and other supporting stakeholders. Identifying suitable incubation centers for Agri-tech entrepreneurs is essential to ensure optimal assistance and a shorter gestation period.

The perceived value that start-ups assign to an incubator is influenced by expectations from the incubation process and the incubator services. Evaluation criteria encompass external and internal factors, with empirical investigations relying on chosen performance criteria (Bergek and Norrman, 2008; Hackett and Dilts, 2004). External influences include project type, characteristics, human capital, and the surrounding environment, while internal criteria comprise the selection procedure, services offered, support delivered, and incubator staff's skill sets.

1.4 Research Gap

Existing literature has predominantly focused on the founding, objectives, planning, and administration of incubators, with an emphasis on theories and models (Becker and Gassmann, 2006; Ahmad and Ingle, 2013; Tavoletti, 2013). Evaluation areas include economic, financial, and technological objectives, the creation of new businesses and jobs, and the development of an entrepreneurial society (McAdam and McAdam, 2008; Al-Mubaraki, 2015). This study aims to contribute empirical insights into how budding Agri-tech entrepreneurs perceive the business incubation services provided by incubators.

In the agri-tech landscape of Jammu and Kashmir and Punjab, start-ups face unique challenges and opportunities. The research article also explores the growth, innovations, and hurdles encountered by these agri-tech ventures, shedding light on the incubation support they receive. The article aims to provide insights into the potential for nurturing agri start-ups in these regions and the crucial role played by incubation centers in fostering agricultural innovation and business development.

2. THE EMERGENCE OF START-UPS IN AGRICULTURAL AND ALLIED ACTIVITIES

2.1 Global Importance of Agriculture

Agriculture, supporting livelihoods in developing nations and fostering economic development in industrialized ones, holds global significance. The international food systems employ 29% of the global workforce and use 38% of all arable land for food production (The global risks report 2020). Out of 570 million farms worldwide, 500 million are smallholder farms generating 80% of food crops. With the projected global population of 10 billion by 2050, meeting the demand for food, feed, fuel, and industry is critical (FAO, 2017).

By 2050, a 59 to 89% increase in world food demand is anticipated, necessitating a 50% increase in agricultural production by 2050 compared to 2012 (FAO, 2020). The majority of this demand is expected from areas with rapid population expansion, including India, the Middle East, North Africa, and Sub-Saharan Africa. By 2027, India is projected to surpass China as the most populated nation (United Nations, 2019).

2.2 Start-Ups in Agri-Tech

The urgency for sustainable agrarian value chains arises from factors like the increasing global population, limited arable land, labor shortages, higher per capita consumption, changing dietary patterns, and growing Green House Gas (GHG) emissions. Despite improvements in the agricultural sector, the potential of digital technologies remains untapped for addressing these challenges.

Farmers face various productivity and return on investment challenges, including subpar agri-input quality, poor decision-making, marketing difficulties, unpredictable weather conditions, reliance on intermediaries, and a lack of labor, financing, and insurance options. Digital technologies, including drones, mobile applications, cloud computation, big data, IoT, remote sensing, machine learning, image analytics, AI, blockchain, and agricultural robots, offer real-time data and transformative opportunities. The pandemic has accelerated the adoption of these solutions, providing greater control over various aspects of the agricultural value chain.

The surge in digital and technology-based opportunities has led to significant entrepreneurial ideas and investments in the agricultural and related value chains over the past decade. Agri-tech start-ups leverage these opportunities to offer specialized services and products, enhancing the profitability and efficiency of the agricultural value chain. Governments and the corporate sector emphasize the importance of leveraging scientific data and technology in farming practices.

2.3 Incubators and the Incubation Ecosystem in India

Business incubators, as centralized hubs for entrepreneurs, provide essential services, including office spaces, shared facilities, peer support, seed funding, mentoring, capacity building, and training (Business Dictionary, 2020). A well-designed incubator, according to Hackett and Dilts (2004), leads to financial success and innovation, or at least increases survival chances. However, the effectiveness of incubators varies based on local entrepreneurial climate, infrastructure, government policies, and market potential.

Incubators offer diverse services to support start-up development, including office spaces, IT infrastructure, mentorship, legal assistance, and various forms of support. They assist in securing funding and facilitate networking opportunities among entrepreneurs. Incubators aim to establish robust venture and social networks, providing academic and financial resources (Cooper *et al.,* 2012). The Indian government's initiatives, along with the presence of numerous incubators, underscore the commitment to creating a sustainable start-up environment. In the Union Territory of Jammu and Kashmir (JK-UT) alone, more than ten incubators are in operation (Start-up India Report, 2022).

3. START-UP ECOSYSTEM EVALUATION: JAMMU & KASHMIR VS. PUNJAB

3.1 Jammu & Kashmir

J&K participated in 18 out of 26 Action Points of the Startup Ranking Framework 2020. The region excelled in 'Institutional Support,' 'Fostering Innovation and Entrepreneurship,' and 'Incubation Support.' Despite challenges, it demonstrated growth with approximately 500 start-ups registered in the valley since the abrogation of Article 370.

3.1.1 Government Initiatives to Support Agri-tech Entrepreneurs in Jammu & Kashmir

The government has launched several programs in collaboration with the Ministry of Agriculture and Startup India Hub to bolster Agri-tech entrepreneurs in Jammu & Kashmir. These initiatives aim to empower aspiring Agri innovators, recognizing the immense potential for growth and innovation in the agricultural sector.

3.1.2 Demographic Dividend and Economic Productivity

With over 58% of the population in the working-age demographic, Jammu & Kashmir holds a significant demographic dividend. The government sees this as a promising opportunity to enhance the UT's economic productivity. Efforts are underway to shift the mindset of the young population from job seekers to job creators.

3.1.3 Start-Up Policy Implementation

The Start-up policy of Jammu & Kashmir, implemented in 2018, plays a pivotal role in fostering the growth of start-ups. The policy aims to promote an innovative culture and establish a thriving entrepreneurial ecosystem within the UT. Both the Jammu & Kashmir government and the union government are actively involved in initiatives to create a start-up-friendly environment in the region.

3.1.4 Start-Up Environment Development

The UT is actively working towards cultivating a conducive start-up environment, encouraging its youth to venture into entrepreneurship. The goal is to create a generation of job creators who contribute to economic growth. According to the "States' Startup Ranking 2021-Jammu & Kashmir-Top Performer" report on the Startup India portal, the UT boasts more than 250 DPIIT registered start-ups (Startup India Report, 2022).

3.1.5 Creating a Start-Up Friendly Ecosystem

The collaborative efforts between the Jammu & Kashmir government and the union government focus on creating a conducive ecosystem for start-ups. This involves providing necessary support, resources, and incentives to nurture the growth of innovative ventures. The aim is to eliminate barriers and challenges faced by Agri-tech entrepreneurs, ensuring they have the tools and support needed for success.

3.2 Punjab

Punjab actively engaged with 25 out of the 26 Action Points, demonstrating its commitment to the 'Startup India' initiative. The Industrial and Business Development Policy (IDBP) 2017, alongside subsequent schemes and operating guidelines, underscores the state's focus on establishing an enabling environment for startups. The provision of incubation support is facilitated through fiscal incentives and dedicated efforts towards infrastructure development. Punjab has garnered recognition as a leader among states, surpassing others such as Assam, Tamil Nadu, Uttar Pradesh, and Uttarakhand in fostering a conducive startup ecosystem (Start-up Ranking Report 2021). This advancement is noteworthy, especially considering that the state was previously acknowledged as an "Aspiring Leader" in the 2019 rankings.

4. UNLOCKING SUCCESS: THE DYNAMICS OF BUSINESS INCUBATORS

A business incubator serves as a crucial support system for entrepreneurs, providing a range of services essential for running a successful company. These services encompass affordable workspace, shared facilities, peer support, seed capital, mentoring, and capacity building (Business Dictionary, 2020). According to Hackett and Dilts (2004), the effective setup of an incubator is correlated with the financial success and innovation of the companies it nurtures, enhancing their likelihood of survival.

However, the impact of incubators on local businesses may vary, influenced by factors like the local entrepreneurial climate, infrastructural development, government policies, and market potential. Incubators extend beyond physical spaces, creating communities of entrepreneurs who collaborate, share knowledge and resources, expand networks, and inspire each other (Maria 01, 2019; Aura Bear, 2019).

4.1 Balancing Support and Autonomy

Incubators must strike a balance between providing support and allowing entrepreneurial autonomy. Saltzman (2018) emphasizes the importance of understanding this equilibrium. While support is essential for shaping the startup environment, it's equally crucial to empower entrepreneurs to pursue their passions and express creativity.

4.2 Incubators as Network Facilitators

Entrepreneurial ecosystems often require a support network to foster economic growth. Incubators act as intermediaries, addressing weak network issues. Van Rijnsoever's (2020) study sheds light on how incubators function as middlemen in entrepreneurial ecosystems, offering fresh theoretical perspectives on network emergence and innovation systems.

4.3 Publicly Supported Incubators for Societal Goals

Incubators play a pivotal role in achieving Sustainable Development Goals (SDGs), especially in developing nations. Surana et al. (2020) explored how publicly supported incubators, using India as an example, go beyond conventional activities to enable entrepreneurship for societal goals. Government involvement becomes imperative to support market failures, and publicly sponsored incubators fulfill this role.

4.4 Incubators and Start-Up Performance

Lukes, Longo, and Zouhar (2019) delved into the short-term and long-term effects of business incubators on innovative start-ups' performance. The study revealed an initial negative effect on sales revenue that turns positive over time. It also explored the influence of incubator ownership and size on the development of incubated startups.

4.5 Promoting Gender-Inclusive Entrepreneurship

Research by Gupta & Etzkowitz (2021) based on post-structural feminist theory demonstrated that academic incubators can improve emerging entrepreneurial cultures and gender dynamics. Albort-Morant & Oghazi (2016) focused on incubator tenants' characteristics, revealing that young individuals with social skills, professional expertise, and family experience found incubator services most helpful.

4.6 Challenges and Opportunities in Developing Nations

Jamil et al. (2016) highlighted the positive impact of business incubators on commercialization goals, new business creation, entrepreneurial culture, creativity, and revenue generation. However, challenges in developing nations include a lack of technological and human skills and financial limitations. Van Weele (2016) proposed the concept of "systemic incubators" to address institutional problems limiting start-up activity.

4.7 Founders' Characteristics and Incubator Resources

Blank's (2020) study emphasized the role of founders' characteristics in the relationship between incubator resources and start-up success. The findings indicated that the founders' experience moderates the effectiveness of mentoring programs provided by incubators.

4.8 Incubation Experience and Resource Access

Van and Eveleens (2021) explored the impact of incubation experience on entrepreneurs' evaluation of resources provided by incubators. Their research concluded that incubators contribute significantly to enhancing entrepreneurs' access to valuable resources.

The existing literature supports the multifaceted role of Business incubators in nurturing startups, from providing physical spaces to shaping entrepreneurial cultures, fostering gender-inclusive entrepreneurship, and addressing challenges in developing nations. Understanding the dynamics of incubators and tailoring support to founders' characteristics can optimize their effectiveness and contribute to the success of early-stage ventures.

Figure 1. Role of business incubators

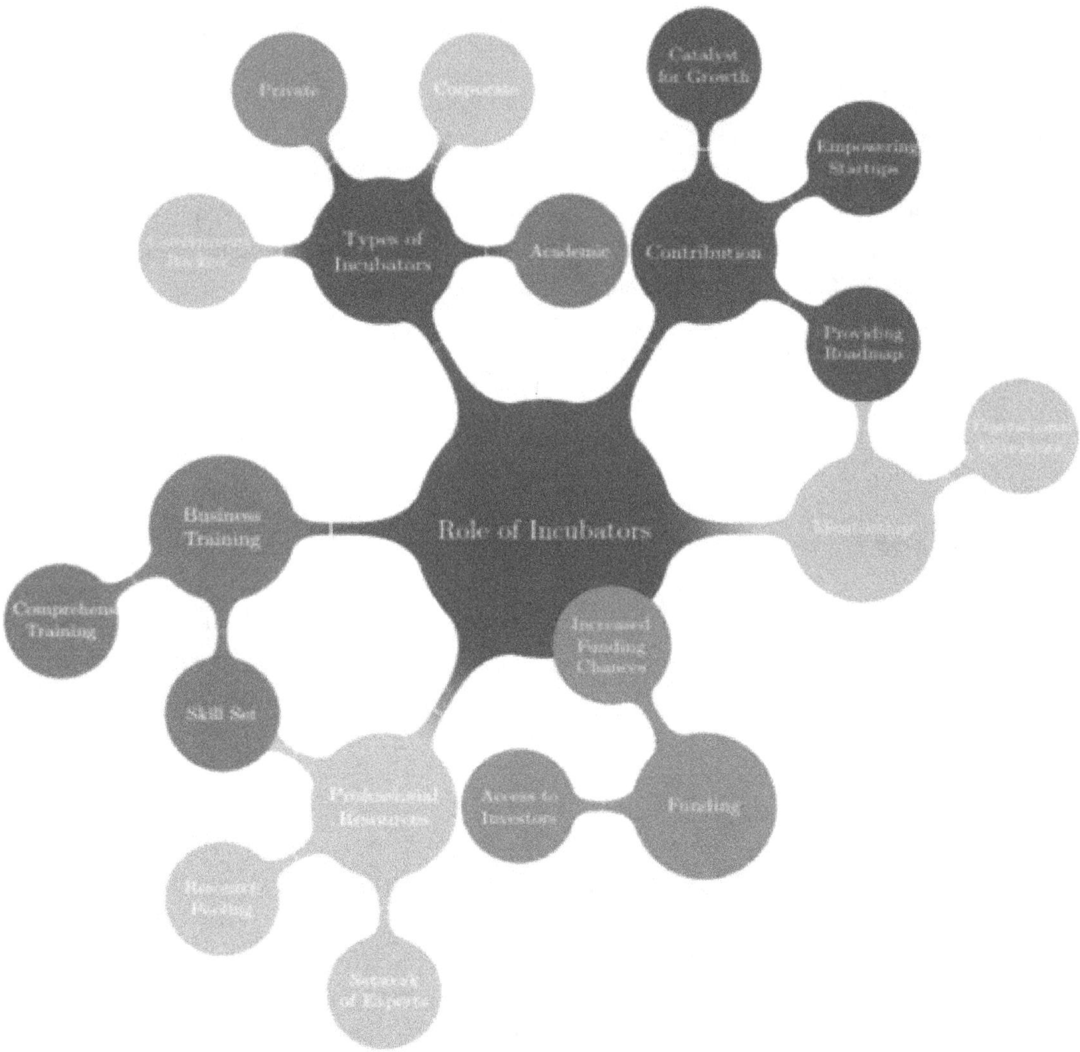

5. CASE STUDY: FROM JOBLESSNESS TO ENTREPRENEURSHIP - KULDEEP VERMA'S FISH FARMING JOURNEY

5.1 Introduction and Background

Kuldeep Verma's trajectory from joblessness to successful entrepreneurship through fish farming exemplifies the transformative power of agri-entrepreneurship in providing sustainable livelihoods. Amid challenges to traditional agriculture in Jammu, Kuldeep, former military personnel, faced unemployment in 2001. Undeterred by initial family resistance and financial constraints, he ventured into fish farming, marking a pivotal shift in his career path.

5.2 The Entrepreneurial Journey-Challenges and Struggles

Endowed with limited education and a military background, Kuldeep encountered initial resistance from his family. Overcoming financial constraints and societal pressures became integral to his entrepreneurial journey.

5.3 Turning Point-Family Support

Marriage and steadfast support from his wife, coupled with successful persuasion of his parents to allocate land, marked a turning point. Utilizing wedding funds to dig the fishpond became a strategic move that set the stage for Kuldeep's entrepreneurial endeavors.

5.4 The Startup- Initiation of Fish Farming

Commencing independently in 2017 without external funding, Kuldeep faced initial challenges, with low fish production (200-300 kg/year).

5.5 Training and Development

Seeking guidance from KVK SKUAST Jammu, Kuldeep followed scientific recommendations, resulting in a significant production increase to 400 kg in 2020. Integrating poultry and Sahiwal cow further diversified his income streams.

5.6 Present Scenario

Operating a 1000 m2 fish pond, Kuldeep generates a net profit of Rs. 59000/year from fish sales. Technological integration includes perforated pipes for oxygen supply and localized fish feed production.

5.7 Constraints and Learning

Kuldeep's Initial challenges included familial and societal resistance, a lack of awareness about government schemes, and gaps in technical and scientific knowledge. Kuldeep acquired technical knowledge through KVK Jammu, emphasizing the importance of changing societal attitudes and advocating for government support.

5.8 Lessons for Other Farmers

Highlighting the profitability of fish farming in high-demand areas, Kuldeep encourages unemployed youth to explore the sector. Advocating for government support, especially through initiatives like Pradhan Mantri Matsya Sampada Yojana, remains a key takeaway.

5.9 Future Plans

Kuldeep envisions expanding the fish farm, expecting government subsidy support. His plans include value addition through a fish cutlet and food shop, showcasing his entrepreneurial vision and commitment to diversification.

Kuldeep Verma's journey stands as a testament to the transformative potential of agri-entrepreneurship. His determination, strategic acumen, and integration of scientific practices offer valuable insights and underscore the need for ongoing support from agricultural institutions and the government for sustained success in agri-ventures.

6. RESEARCH DESIGN

6.1 Research Methodology

The research adopts an interpretivist approach, aiming to understand the experiences and perspectives of startups incubated in business incubators in Jammu & Kashmir and Punjab. The research follows an inductive approach, allowing insights to emerge from the data collected during the study and is an exploratory study to gain insights into the challenges and opportunities faced by startups, particularly those focusing on agriculture and allied sectors.

The study adopts a cross-sectional design, collecting data at a specific point in time from startups incubated in business incubators.

The primary data source comprises startups incubated in business incubators. Data collection is based on a structured questionnaire developed for this purpose. The respondent includes 90 startups in total, with 45 startups each from Jammu & Kashmir and Punjab. These startups are selected from six business incubators, three in each state.

A structured questionnaire is developed to collect quantitative and qualitative data from startups. The questionnaire is designed to gather information on startup characteristics, challenges faced, support received from the incubators, and the overall impact of the incubation process.

The target population includes startups in the selected business incubators focusing on agriculture and allied sectors. A combination of stratified and convenience sampling is used to ensure representation from diverse startups within the agriculture and allied sectors.

6.2 Data Analysis

A mixed-methods approach is employed, combining quantitative analysis of survey responses and qualitative analysis of open-ended questions. Quantitative data is analyzed using statistical tools, while qualitative data is subjected to thematic analysis.

Limitations: Include potential biases in self-reported data and the cross-sectional nature of the study.

Future Recommendations: Future research may explore longitudinal aspects and conduct in-depth case studies to complement the findings of this study.

7. RESULT AND DISCUSSION

RQ1: Skills & Traits that are required to be a successful incubate/entrepreneur.

The table provides a comprehensive overview of the perceived importance of various skills and traits necessary for success as an incubatee or entrepreneur, as rated by respondents. Each skill or trait is rated on a scale, with a mean score indicating the average perceived significance and a standard deviation reflecting the degree of variability in responses.

Table 1. Skills and traits to be a successful incubate/entrepreneur

Sr no	Skills & Traits that are required to be a successful incubate/entrepreneur	Mean	SD
1	Age of the Entrepreneur	3.367	1.328
2	Gender of the Entrepreneur	2.800	1.124
3	Education of the Entrepreneur	3.767	1.050
4	Accountability (Willingness to accept responsibility for our actions)	3.622	1.147
5	Building buy-in to an idea (Convincing Others)	3.533	1.367
6	Business Plan & Technical Report Writing	3.089	1.363
7	Coordinating Resources	3.678	1.381
8	Creative Thinking (An ability to consider something in a new way)	3.489	1.247
9	Critical Thinking (An objective analysis and evaluation of an issue to form a judgement)	3.422	1.315
10	Decision Making	3.756	1.275
11	Interpersonal Skills	3.056	1.212
12	Problem Solving	3.611	1.251
13	Project Management (Application of processes, methods, skills, knowledge, and experience to achieve the specific objectives of the project)	3.178	1.167
14	Relationship Building (Developing social connections with others)	3.389	1.187
15	Resilience (Capacity to recover quickly from difficulties)	3.278	1.341
16	Risk-Taking Ability	3.278	1.290
17	Self-Esteem (An opinion about one's character and abilities)	3.044	1.357
18	Stress Management	3.044	1.365
19	Entrepreneurial Skills & Traits are required to be a successful incubate or entrepreneur.	3.656	1.342

Entrepreneurs exhibit varying perspectives on the importance of different factors contributing to success, as indicated by survey responses. Age is generally perceived as moderately important, with opinions differing among respondents. Gender, on the other hand, is rated lower in significance, suggesting a prevailing sentiment that success is not strongly influenced by gender.

In contrast, education stands out as relatively crucial, with a high mean score reflecting a consensus among respondents on its importance. Convincing others is viewed as moderately important, with a broader range of opinions indicated by the standard deviation, highlighting diverse perspectives on the significance of this skill.

Business plan and technical report writing skills are perceived with moderate importance, but there is higher variability in opinions, suggesting a lack of consensus among respondents. Decision-making emerges as highly valued, with a strong consensus, underlining its critical role in entrepreneurial success. Problem-solving skills are considered highly important, with a consistent opinion among respondents, emphasizing their significance in navigating challenges.

Project management skills receive a moderate valuation, and opinions vary among respondents, indicating a lack of unanimous consensus. Resilience is also moderately valued, with a broad range of opinions, suggesting differing perspectives on its importance. Stress management is perceived with moderate importance, and opinions vary among respondents, highlighting a divergence in views on the significance of this skill.

Entrepreneurial skills and traits, overall, are emphasized as highly important, with a high mean score indicating a consensus on their significance for success. This aligns with the understanding that a combination of skills, traits, and education contributes to the holistic success of an entrepreneur, emphasizing the multifaceted nature of entrepreneurial success.

RQ2: There is a relation between incubation services offered and startup success.

- **Start-up Perspective**

This table outlines the descriptive statistics for "Incubation Services" and "Startup Success" from the perspective of startups. The key findings are as follows:

The mean score for "Incubation Services" is 74.6667, with a standard deviation of 14.27026, indicating that startups, on average, have received a relatively high level of incubation services.

"Startup Success" has a mean score of 136.1778, with a standard deviation of 16.46827, implying that startups, on average, have experienced a substantial degree of success.

This table presents the correlation analysis between "Incubation Services" and "Startup Success" for startups. The following insights can be derived:

Table 2. Descriptive statistics

Descriptive Statistics			
	Mean	**Std. Deviation**	**N**
Incubation Services	74.66	14.27	90
Startup success	136.17	16.46	90

Table 3. Correlation between incubation services and startup success (startup perspective)

Correlations			
		Incubation Services	Startup success
Incubation Services	Pearson Correlation	1	.338**
	Sig. (2-tailed)		.001
	N	90	90
Startup success	Pearson Correlation	.338**	1
	Sig. (2-tailed)	.001	
	N	90	90

**. Correlation is significant at the 0.01 level (2-tailed).

The Pearson Correlation between "Incubation Services" and "Startup Success" is 0.338. This positive correlation suggests a statistically significant relationship between the level of incubation services received and the level of startup success.

The associated two-tailed significance (Sig.) is 0.001, indicating that the correlation is significant at the 0.01 level. This implies a strong association between the two variables.

Table 4. Descriptive statistics

Descriptive Statistics			
	Mean	Std. Deviation	N
Incubator Services	70.20	19.48	10
Startup/ Incubation Success	56.20	14.31	10

- **For Incubator Perspective**

This table provides the descriptive statistics for "Incubator Services" and "Startup/ Incubation Success" from the perspective of the incubation team:

"Incubator Services" has a mean score of 70.2000, with a standard deviation of 19.48675, indicating that the incubation team has provided a relatively high level of services to startups.

"Startup/ Incubation Success" has a mean score of 56.2000, with a standard deviation of 14.31239, suggesting that startups in the incubation program have achieved a moderate level of success.

This table presents the correlation analysis between "Incubator Services" and "Startup/ Incubation Success" from the perspective of the incubation team:

The Pearson Correlation between "Incubator Services" and "Startup/ Incubation Success" is 0.806. This strong positive correlation indicates a statistically significant relationship between the level of incubation services provided and the level of startup/incubation success.

The two-tailed significance (Sig.) is 0.005, confirming that the correlation is significant at the 0.01 level. This emphasizes the strong association between the variables.

Table 5. Correlation between incubation services and startup success (incubator perspective)

Correlations			
		Incubator Services	Startup Success
Incubator Services	Pearson Correlation	1	.806**
	Sig. (2-tailed)		.005
	N	10	10
Startup/ Incubation Success	Pearson Correlation	.806**	1
	Sig. (2-tailed)	.005	
	N	10	10

**. Correlation is significant at the 0.01 level (2-tailed).

Table 6. Problems faced by the startups

Sr no	Problems Faced by the Startups	Mean	SD
1	Disbursement of Grant-in Aid/Fund Raising/Loan	3.39	1.00
2	Rigid Exit Policy of the Business Incubator	3.37	1.34
3	Documentation/Paperwork	3.19	1.13
4	Incubator Selection Process	3.61	0.86
5	Regulatory Environment	3.57	1.08
6	Filling IPR applications	3.98	1.08
7	Registration Process Support	3.58	0.98
8	Family/Social Support	3.64	1.20
9	Customer Retention	3.47	0.97
10	Profitability	3.50	1.07

This table outlines the problems faced by startups, along with the associated mean scores and standard deviations. These problems are crucial indicators of challenges in the startup environment, and their interpretations are as follows:

Startups encounter a spectrum of challenges as they navigate the dynamic entrepreneurial landscape. Among the array of obstacles, a prominent concern surfaces in the form of Filling Intellectual Property Rights (IPR) Applications, garnering the highest mean score of 3.98. This underscores a significant hurdle in safeguarding intellectual property, necessitating streamlined processes and accessible mechanisms for startups to protect their innovations effectively. Additionally, startups express moderate challenges in Disbursement of Grant-in Aid/Fund Raising/Loan and perceive the incubator selection process and Rigid Exit Policy of Business Incubators as a noteworthy concern. The intricacies associated with Documentation and Paperwork and the registration process support also emerge as areas warranting attention. Collectively, these challenges shed light on key pain points within the startup ecosystem, urging for tailored support, streamlined processes, and a conducive environment for entrepreneurial growth.

8. CONCLUSION

In conclusion, the interpretation reveals a general alignment among entrepreneurs on the importance of crucial skills like education, decision making, and problem-solving. However, there is noticeable variability in perceptions, particularly for softer skills like interpersonal skills and stress management. This suggests that while certain skills are widely acknowledged as vital, there is room for diverse opinions on the significance of others, reflecting the multifaceted nature of entrepreneurship. The data from both the startup and incubation team perspectives suggest a positive and statistically significant relationship between the level of incubation services and startup success. Additionally, the risk assessment factors provide insights into the risk management practices and strategic considerations of startups in the context of incubation services. The data brings to light the myriad challenges faced by startups across various operational facets, spanning from financial matters like fund disbursement and fundraising to compliance with regulatory standards and achieving profitability. A particularly noteworthy concern surfaces in the realm of Filling Intellectual Property Rights (IPR) Applications, attaining the highest mean score of 3.98. The mean scores provide insights into the perceived difficulty of each challenge. Addressing these challenges is crucial for the growth and success of startups in their journey toward sustainability and profitability.

REFERENCES

Acs, Z. J., Armington, C., & Zhang, T. (2007). The determinants of new-firm survival across regional economies: The role of Human Capital Stock and knowledge spillover. *Papers in Regional Science*, *86*(3), 367–391. doi:10.1111/j.1435-5957.2007.00129.x

Ahmad, A., & Ingle, S. (2013). Business incubators and HTSF development: setting an agenda forfurther research. In R. Oakey, A. Groen, G. Cook, & P. Van Der Sijde (Eds.), *New Technology-based Firms in the New Millennium* (Vol. 10, pp. 119–140). Emerald Group. doi:10.1108/S1876-0228(2013)0000010009

Akçomak, İ. S. (2009). *Working Paper Series*. UNU. https://collections.unu.edu/eserv/UNU:62/wp2009-054.pdf

Al-Mubaraki, H. M., Muhammad, A. H., & Busler, M. (2015). 'Categories of incubator success: Acase study of three New York incubator programmes', *World Journal of Science. Technology and Sustainable Development*, *12*(1), 2–12.

Audretsch, D., & Keilbach, M. (2004). Entrepreneurship Capital and Economic Performance. *Regional Studies*, *38*(8), 949–959. doi:10.1080/0034340042000280956

Autio, E. (2016). Entrepreneurship Support in Europe: Trends and Challenges for EU Policy. *Report Prepared for EU DG Growth*. https://www.researchgate.net/profile/Erkko-Autio/publication/304659214_Entrepreneurship_Support_in_Europe_Trends_and_Challenges_for_EU_Policy/links/577649a408ae4645d60d5b8e/Entrepreneurship-Support-in-Europe-Trends-and-Challenges-for-EU-Policy.pdf

Barbulescu, O., Tecău, A. S., Munteanu, D., & Constantin, C. P. (2021). Innovation of startups, the key to unlocking post-crisis sustainable growth in Romanian entrepreneurial ecosystem. *Sustainability (Basel), 13*(2), 671. doi:10.3390/su13020671

Becker, B., & Gassmann, O. (2006). Corporate incubators: Industrial R&D and what universities can learn from them. *The Journal of Technology Transfer, 31*(4), 469–483. doi:10.1007/s10961-006-0008-6

Bergek, A., & Norrman, C. (2008). Incubator best practice: A framework. *Technovation, 28*(1/2), 20–28. doi:10.1016/j.technovation.2007.07.008

Startup Business. (2019). What is Deep Tech and which startups are marking the road (not Uber)? Startup Business. https://www.startupbusiness.it/what-is-deep-tech-and-which-startups-are-marking-the-road-not-uber/96448/

Chandra, A., & Chao, A. C. (2011). Growth and Evolution of high technology business incubation in China. *Human Systems Management, 30*(1-2), 55–69. doi:10.3233/HSM-2011-0739

Chandra, A., & Medrano Silva, M. A. (2012). Business Incubation in Chile: Development, Financing and Financial Services. Journal of Technology Management &Amp. *Innovation, 7*(2), 1–13. doi:10.4067/S0718-27242012000200001

Cockayne, D. (2019). What is a startup firm? A methodological and epistemological investigation into research objects in economic geography. *Geoforum, 107*, 77–87. doi:10.1016/j.geoforum.2019.10.009

Cooper, C. E., Hamel, S. A., & Connaughton, S. L. (2010). Motivations and obstacles to networking in a University Business Incubator. *The Journal of Technology Transfer, 37*(4), 433–453. doi:10.1007/s10961-010-9189-0

Department for Promotion of Industry and Internal Trade: MOCI: GOI. (2022). Department for Promotion of Industry and Internal Trade. https://dpiit.gov.in/publications/annual-report

Dewangan, V., & Godse, M. (2014). Towards a holistic enterprise innovation performance measurement system. *Technovation, 34*(9), 536–545. doi:10.1016/j.technovation.2014.04.002

Doing business 2020. (2020). World Bank. https://documents1.worldbank.org/curated/en/688761571934946384/pdf/Doing-Business-2020-Comparing-Business-Regulation-in-190-Economies.pdf

Establishment of Atal Innovation Mission and Self Employment and talent utilisation in Niti Aayog. (2016). PIB. https://www.pib.gov.in/newsite/PrintRelease.aspx?relid=136754

Establishment of Atal Innovation Mission and Self Employment and talent utilisation in Niti Aayog. (2016). PIB. https://www.pib.gov.in/newsite/PrintRelease.aspx?relid=136754

Grant Thornton and Assocham India. (2016). *Startups India – An Overview*. Grant Thornton and Assocham. https://www.grantthornton.in/ globalassets/1.-member-firms/india/assets/pdfs/grant_thornton-startups _report.pdf

Hackett, M., & Dilts, D. M. (2004). A systematic review of business incubation research. *The Journal of Technology Transfer, 29*(1), 55–82. doi:10.1023/B:JOTT.0000011181.11952.0f

Hansen, M. T., Chesbrough, H. W., Nohria, N., & Sull, D. N. (2000). Networked incubators—Hothouses of the new economy. *Harvard Business Review*, *78*(5), 74. PMID:11143156

Henry, M., Bauwens, T., Hekkert, M., & Kirchherr, J. (2020). A typology of circular start-ups: An analysis of 128 circular business models. *Journal of Cleaner Production*, *245*, 118528. doi:10.1016/j.jclepro.2019.118528

IBM Institute for Business Value and Oxford Economics. (2016). *Entrepreneurial India: how startups redefine India's economic growth.* IBM. https://d1iydh3qrygeij.cloudfront.net/Media/Default/New%20release%20images%20and%20reports/Entrepreneurial%20India%20IBV%20mid%202016

IVCA-EY. (2019). Year-to-date PE/VC investments in India at a new all-time high of US$36.7 billion: *IVCA-EY Report.* EY. https://www.ey.com/en_in/news/2019/09/year-to-date-pe-vc-investments-in-india-at-new-all-time-high-of-us-dollar-36-7-billion-ivca-ey-report

Jha, L. (2019). Most of India's Digitally Monetizable Users Want Vernacular Content: Report. *Livemint.com.* https://www.livemint.com/industry/media/most-of-india-s-digitally-monetizable-users-want-vernacular-content-report-1565097932712.html

Kato, M., Onishi, K., & Honjo, Y. (2022). Does patenting always help new firm survival? Understanding heterogeneity among exit routes. *Small Business Economics*, *59*(2), 449–475. doi:10.1007/s11187-021-00481-w

KrAsia Writers. (2019). *A part of the third-largest startup ecosystem, Indian companies enjoy investors attention.* KrAsia.com. https://kr-asia.com/a-part-of-the-third-largest-startup-ecosystem-indian-companies-enjoy-investors-attention

Lalkaka, R. (2002). Technology business incubators to help build an innovation-based economy. *Journal of Change Management*, *3*(2), 167–176. doi:10.1080/714042533

McAdam, M., & McAdam, R. (2008). High tech Startups in university science park incubators: The relationship between the Startup's life cycle progression and use of the incubator's resources. *Technovation*, *28*(5), 277–290. doi:10.1016/j.technovation.2007.07.012

Nanda, R., Sharma, L. K., & Sharma, R. (2020). *Farm Innovators of Jammu: A Compendium of Success Stories*. Sher-e-Kashmir University of Agricultural Sciences and Technology of Jammu.

NASSCOM and Zinnov. (2019). *Indian tech startup ecosystem: leading tech in the 20s*. Nasscom. https://www.nasscom.in/knowledge-center/ publications/indian-tech-start-ecosystem-leading-tech-20s

National Business Incubation Association. (February 2019). *Business Incubation FAQ*. National Business Incubation Association. http://nbia.org/resource_library/faq/index.php

Naudé, W., Gries, T., Wood, E., & Meintjies, A. (2008). Regional determinants of entrepreneurial Startups in a developing country. *Entrepreneurship and Regional Development*, *20*(2), 111–124. doi:10.1080/08985620701631498

NITI. (2019). Guidelines for setting up of incubation centres under Atal Innovation Mission – 'Atal Incubation Centres'. *Government of India NITI Aayog Atal Innovation Mission May 2016*. NITI. https://niti.gov.in/writereaddata/files/Guidelines %20to%20setup%20AIC%20May%202016.

Outlook. (2019). 54 tech unicorns expected in India by 2024. *Outlook, The News Scroll*. https://www.outlookindia.com/newsscroll/54-tech-unicorns-expected-in-india-by-2024-lead-correcting-headline/1587697 [Accessed June 12, 2022].

PIB. (2017). Startup: Definition changes. Press Information Bureau, *Government of India, Ministry of Commerce & Industry*. PIB. https://pib.gov.in/newsite/PrintRelease.aspx?relid=162140

Picken, J. C. (2017). From startup to scalable enterprise: Laying the Foundation. *Business Horizons*, *60*(5), 587–595. doi:10.1016/j.bushor.2017.05.002

Press Information Bureau. (2020). *Press Release*. PIB. https://pib.gov.in/PressReleseDetail.aspx?PRID=1605956

Press Information Bureau, Government of India. (2019). *Suresh Prabhu clears proposal to encourage investments in Startups*. PIB. https://pib.gov.in/newsite/PrintRelease.aspx? relid=188720

Press Trust of India. (2019, April 25). DPIIT proposes Startup India Vision 2024, Proposes tax sops for new ventures. *The Economic Times*. https://economictimes.indiatimes.com/small-biz/startups/newsbuzz/dpiit-proposesstartup-india-vision-2024-proposes-tax-sops-for-new-ventures/ articleshow/69043102.cms

Rajan, P. (2019). *The startup ecosystem in India is scaling new heights. Here's why*. Yourstory.com. https://yourstory.com/2019/12/indian-startup-ecosystem-priyan-rajan-silicon-valley-bank?utm_pageloadtype=scroll

Sa, C., & Lee, H. (2012). Science, business, and Innovation: Understanding Networks in technology-based incubators. *R & D Management*, *42*(3), 243–253. doi:10.1111/j.1467-9310.2012.00681.x

Saltzman, J. (2018). *The Importance of Creating Incubator Programs for Entrepreneurs*. Entrepreneur Europe. https://www.entrepreneur.com/article/320670

Sen, A. (2019). Government looking at deploying larger funds for startups: Piyush Goyal. *The Hindu Business Line*. https://www.thehindubusinessline.com/economy/policy/govt-looking-at-deploying-larger-funds-for-startups-piyush-goyal/article30229659.ece

Sharma, S. K., & Meyer, K. E. (2019). *Industrializing innovation-the next revolution*. Springer Books. doi:10.1007/978-3-030-12430-4

Sharma, S. & Hari, T.N. (2018). The decade that was: how India's startup landscape has evolved. *YS Journal*. Your Story. https://yourstory.com/journal/the-decade-that-was-india-part-1

Skawińska, E., & Zalewski, R. I. (2020). Success factors of startups in the EU—A comparative study. *Sustainability (Basel)*, *12*(19), 8200. doi:10.3390/su12198200

Smilor, R. W. (1987). Managing the Incubator System: Critical Success Factors to Accelerate New Company Development. *IEEE Transactions on Engineering Management*, *34*(4), 146–156.

Startup India. (2019). Startup engagement: Best practices for large organizations. *Startup India*. https://www.startupindia.gov.in/content/dam/invest-india/Templates/public/incubator_page_content/Startup%20Engagement%20Best%20Practices%20for%20%20Large%20Organizations.pdf

Startup India kit. (2019). Startup India. https://www.startupindia.gov.in/content/dam/investindia/Templates/public/Startup%20India%20Kit_2021_V2.pdf

State Ranking System. (2021). Startup India. https://www.startupindia.gov.in/srf/

Tan, K. G., Gopalan, S., & Sharma, J. (2019). Impact of exchange rates on exports from India's sub-national economies. *South Asian Journal of Business Studies*, *8*(2), 166–184. doi:10.1108/SAJBS-09-2018-0100

Tang, M. F., Lee, J., Liu, K., & Lu, Y. (2014). Assessing government-supported technology-based business incubators: Evidence from China. *International Journal of Technology Management, 65*(1/2/3/4), 24. doi:10.1504/IJTM.2014.060956

Tavoletti, E. (2013). Business incubators: Effective infrastructures or waste of public money? Looking for a theoretical framework, guidelines and criteria. *Journal of the Knowledge Economy*, *4*(4), 423–443. doi:10.1007/s13132-012-0090-y

Tehseen, S., & Ramayah, T. (2015). Entrepreneurial Competencies and SMEs Business Success: The Contingent Role of External Integration. *Mediterranean Journal of Social Sciences*, *6*(1), 50. https://www.richtmann.org/journal/index.php/mjss/article/view/5434. doi:10.5901/mjss.2015.v6n1p50

The Comprehensive Guide to Finnish startup ecosystem - P1/2. (2019). Aurabear. https://www.aurabear.com/blog/the-comprehensive-guide-to-finnish-startup-ecosystem-p1-2

The Economist. (2019). India's missing middle class. *Economist*. https://www.economist.com/briefing/2018/01/ 11/Indias-missing-middle-class

The Future of Food and Agriculture – Trends and challenges. (2017). The Food and Agriculture Organization (FAO). https://www.fao.org/3/i6583e/i6583e.pdf

The global risks report 2020. (2020). World Economic Forum. https://www.weforum.org/reports/the-global-risks-report-2020

The State of World Fisheries and Aquaculture 2020. (2020). The Food and Agriculture Organization (FAO). https://www.fao.org/3/ca9229en/CA9229EN.pdf

United Nations. (2019). *World population prospects 2019: Highlights | multimedia library - united nations department of economic and social affairs*. United Nations. https://www.un.org/development/desa/publications/world-population-prospects-2019-highlights.html

United Nations. (2021). *Goal 2: Zero Hunger - United Nations Sustainable Development*. United Nations. https://www.un.org/sustainabledevelopment/hunger/#:~:text=Current%20estimates%20show%20that%20nearly,achieve% 20Zero%20Hunger%20by%202030.

van Rijnsoever, F. J., & Eveleens, C. P. (2021). Money Don't matter? How incubation experience affects start-up entrepreneurs' resource valuation. *Technovation*, *106*, 102294. doi:10.1016/j.technovation.2021.102294

Vijayan, B., & Shivkumar, P. S. (2020). Pro-AgripreneurialFactorsfortheFormationofAgri-startupsinIndia. *Asian Journal of Agricultural Extension. Economia e Sociologia*, *38*(8), 1–8. doi:10.9734/ajaees/2020/v38i830381

Water and agriculture in India. (2017). OAV. https://www.oav.de/fileadmin/user_upload/5_Publikationen/5_Studien/170118_Study_Water_Agriculture_India.pdf

Zaech, S., & Baldegger, U. (2017). Leadership in start-ups. *International Small Business Journal*, *35*(2), 157–177. doi:10.1177/0266242616676883

Chapter 20
The Impact of Innovative Strategies on a Small-Scale Service Industry in Ghana

Richard H. Afedzie
Pentecost University College, Ghana

ABSTRACT

A lot of research studies have shown that a direct and positive relationship exists between innovative strategies (IS) and an organisational performance. However, the relationship may not be simple and clear to understand. This study used a qualitative, simple descriptive case study approach to critically investigate the level of innovative strategies approach to the growth of Compressor Techniques Limited, Ghana. A semi-structured questionnaire was utilised to interview employees (participants) at Compressor Techniques Limited to gather primary data for the study. Purposeful sampling was used to select twenty (20) participants who have worked in the organisation five years and above to gather rich data for the data analysis. The research findings showed the company organizes workshops and seminars to improve upon the abilities of employees. It was recommended that the organization should regularly review and update their internal structures and decision-making processes for approving innovative projects so that the company can reach its productivity goals.

1. BACKGROUND OF THE STUDY

Innovative strategies (IS) have become associated with our 21st century world of business and has gained significant traction because of advancement in technology and creativity (Kiyabo & Isaga, 2020). Scholars in the field of innovative strategies and management have given much focus on the meteoric rise of business in both developing and developed country because of innovative strategies (Meekaewkunchorn, Szczepaska-Woszczyna, Muangmee, Kassakorn, & Khalid, 2021). Innovative strategies can be defined as the decision-making styles and practices initiated by management to foster creativity and growth within the organisation's growth (Okangi, 2019). In essence, innovative strategies seek to promote organisational creativity and commitment. The quest to achieve enhanced organisational performance is often

DOI: 10.4018/979-8-3693-2019-8.ch020

derived from intentional internal behaviour that support critical change process. Over the past decade, there has been a growing number of research exploring the notion of IS and the impact the concept has on organisational performance of varying sizes (Abu-Rumman et al., 2021; Jeong et al., 2019). There has been some evidence linking IS to expansion, but the investigations have had mixed outcomes (Kiyabo & Isaga, 2020). Specifically, the internal behaviour is focused on producing exceptional results and a distinct and long-lasting advantage (Abu-Rumman, Al Shraah, Al-Madi & Alfalah, 2021). Similarly, Hossain and Al Asheq (2019) stated that the primary goal of IS is to create a new inner drive that enables the creation of organisational structure and ensures the organization's survival.

Underpinning any organisation's competitiveness, superior performance and corporate development is the desire by management to create a proactive and risk-taking innovative strategy (Okangi, 2019). There are ample research highlighting the relationship between innovative strategies and an organisational productivity (Kiyabo & Isaga, 2020; Galbreath et al., 2020; Abu-Rumman et al., 2021). However, studies show that the efficiency implications of IS are not uniform and rely on a wide range of internal and external contingency factors, such as a company's resources and capabilities, its industry, and its environment (Jeong, Ali, Zacca, & Park, 2019). (Zhang, Wang, & Jia, 2021).

There have been a lot of scholars who have claimed that it is not enough to only evaluate how each person's innovative attitude effects the performance of an organisation. Additionally, recent scholarly works articulate that IS should be combined with other innovative strategies, such as market innovative strategies, learning innovative strategies, and employee innovative strategies, in order to achieve the highest possible level of performance (Eshima & Anderson, 2017).

This study was conducted within the context of a small-scale size organisation that has utilised innovative strategies in its approach to its growth since its birth in 2009. It has contributed substantially in terms of jobs, the generation of tax income, the generation of money from exports and imports, the facilitation of the distribution of commodities, and the development of human resources. Specifically, several medium organisations have contributed significantly to employment opportunities available to persons living in both rural and urban regions with lower incomes and their role cannot be ignored (Galbreath et al., 2020).

Scholars in entrepreneurship have highlighted the value and importance of innovative strategies in organisations and its benefits on small and medium size organisations growth (Abu-Rumman et al., 2021). The growth of many organisations that have become multinational organisations began from a small beginning of small size and have grown with many subsidiaries across the globe. The intention of this paper was primarily to study how medium size organisations have employed innovative strategies to ensure continuous growth and sustainability. While many of the studies on medium size organisations grow to multinational organisations in developed countries, this study examined the case of a Compressor Technique Services and how it has made remarkable growth over the past decade in a developing country (Shirokova, Bogatyreva, Beliaeva, & Puffer, 2016). Innovative strategies has been a good indicator of the success of organisations growth and the success of such a process have been studied over the past two decades. As such this study sought to articulate that there is a direct correlation between a company's capacity to embrace innovative concepts and practises, including proactivity, risk-taking, and opportunity-seeking, and the company's ability to perform at a higher level.

In particular, research aimed at learning more about the impacts of IS is necessary since the findings on the IS-growth relationship are not clear and IS is a resource-consuming approach (Galbreath et al., 2020). Undertaking this study helped to provide light on whether or not implementing an IS on this small-scale organisation would be worthwhile. Similarly, our 21st century world of business contends that dynamic business environment requires organisations of all sizes to continually look for methods to improve their operations. It has been suggested that an IS may be helpful in this situation (Lekmat, Selvarajah & Hewege, 2018). The ability to think creatively, to take risks in the pursuit of new goods, services, and markets, and to seize opportunities before the competition are all hallmarks of IS (Altinay, Madanoglu, De Vita, Arasli & Ekinci, 2016). Academics and business leaders have paid close attention to IS because of its potential advantages (Ribau, Moreira & Raposo, 2017). Although, the importance of innovative strategies is crucial in any organisation, not much has been given attention in sub-Saharan Africa and especially in Ghana. This study addresses the gap by examining how IS influences the growth of the organisation. For management, it is greatly important to review the extent to which their organisation is innovative and creative in order to identify how it relates to the internal factors in the organisation. This is because a critical understanding of this internal factors permits management to keep their organisations more creative and resourceful.

The purpose of this research which used Compressor Techniques Services Limited as a case study is to add to the existing body of knowledge about the connection between an innovative mindset and successful company expansion. By examining the extent of innovative innovative strategies, its impact on growth, and the challenges related with its implementation, this study provided valuable insights and practical suggestions for CTS and other organisations operating in analogous conditions. The study's overarching objective was to provide useful information that will help CTS sustain development and gain an advantage in the fast-paced service industry.

1.1 Research objectives

The main objective of the research is to assess the effect of innovative strategies on business expansion at Compressor Techniques Services Limited.

- To assess Compressor Techniques Service Limited level of innovative strategies.
- To examine the effect of an innovative strategies on business expansion at Compressor Techniques Service Limited.
- To identify internal barriers to implementing an innovative strategy at Compressor Techniques Service Limited

1.2 Research Questions

This study would be guided by the following research questions.

- What is Compressor Techniques Service Limited level of innovative strategy approach?
- What is the effect of an innovative strategies on business expansion at Compressor Techniques Service Limited?
- What are the internal barriers to implementing an innovative strategy at Compressor Techniques Service Limited?

This research aims to contribute significantly to the body of knowledge and provide useful recommendations for CTS and other organisations in the service sector by investigating the extent to which CTS is innovatively oriented, the effect that innovative strategies have on firm growth, and the challenges associated with implementing innovative strategies. Understanding how an innovative mindset contributes to a successful business is the primary goal of this research. The case study of CTS will provide light on the unique conditions in which a service business operates. How an organization's culture encourages or discourages innovative behaviour and how that impacts its ability to innovate and develop will also be highlighted.

2. LITERATURE REVIEW

Small and medium-sized businesses (SMEs) are extremely important to the development of many countries across the world, especially in emerging economies. In emerging economies, small and medium-sized businesses (SMEs) must struggle with surroundings that are changing, continually shifting, and less developed institutionally. Small and medium-sized enterprises (SMEs) in developing nations mainly rely on informal, interpersonal, and political relationships because of their small size and absence of industrial opportunities. Growth in sales, workers, profit, resources, and equity are five popular business growth indicators that have previously been employed in the innovate strategies literature (Koe et al., 2016). Entrepreneurs in developed countries are driven by the availability of possibilities that may be taken advantage of, but entrepreneurs in developing countries are driven by needs (Arshad & Rasli, 2018). While profits from innovative enterprises in Western countries can only be used to assist company expansion, a portion of profits in least-developed nations are used to cover the entrepreneurs' private expenses.

2.1 Small and Medium-Sized Organisations in Developing Countries

The SMEs are regarded as the foundation of the economy. Considering the SME sector's substantial impact on socioeconomic growth, it is well known on a global scale. This industry has made a substantial contribution to increased growth in labour output, export promotion, as well as entrepreneurshiParticipant Micro, small, and medium-sized businesses have received enough attention from many nations, who have recognized them as a foundation for their national economic growth. It has become crucial for organisations to set themselves apart based on talents and competences to remain competitive in today's market and satisfy consumers. They must compete on a variety of fronts, including product development, production, price, distribution, communication, and creative marketing strategies. SME innovation creation, use, and introduction are essential for economic growth (Nkwabi & Mboya, 2019). The SME sector accounted for 60% of inventions in the past century, but many of them failed because of lack of competence and an unwillingness to work with other businesses (Scuotto et al., 2021). Product creation, manufacturing, pricing, distribution, interaction, and innovative marketing techniques are just a few of the areas in which they must contend. These issues call for a complete reorganization of SMEs to fulfil the demand for high energy, flexibility, and creativity.

Economic growth depends on the development, adoption, and implementation of SME innovations (Koirala, 2019). 60% of inventions in the last century came from the SME sector, however most of them failed due to a lack of skill and a reluctance to collaborate with other companies (Denicolai et al., 2021). Typically, SMEs have been characterized as privately held companies with a small number of workers.

2.2 Research Design

A simple descriptive case study utilising a semi-structured interview approach was employed. The type of research questions, the kind of data to be gathered, and the study design all influence the research approach chosen. The descriptive case study shed lighter on the origins and trend of events that has occurred within the organisational setting. The internal and external factors that has contributed to the benefits and challenges in the organisation (O'Gorman & MacIntosh, 2015).

2.3 Research Approach

The study aims to assess the impact of innovative stratagies on firm growth with a specific focus on Compressor Techniques Services Limited. Qualitative method will give a better understanding of the topic. This approach was used so that one develops more interest for a particular subject by way of interacting with the participants who are cognisant of the history and stages of growth within the organisation. Allwood (2012) asserts that using qualitative methodology does not just answer the questions of how much and how many participants are interviewed, but it involves a subjective inquiry of the meaning of experiences and words by observing behaviours, going through documents and interviewing participants so that whatever responses they give can be noted. The main advantage of using a qualitative approach is that, it generates more information on the subject and this is exactly what the study wanted.

2.4 Population

In this study, the total number of fifty-three workers in Compressor Techniques Services Limited made up the study population. Out of the fifty-three employees, twenty of them were engaged in semi-structured interview on the questionnaire set for the study. The participants were interviewed on questions relating on innovative strategies on the organisation's growth. Before the interview with employees of Compressor Technique Services, a pilot study was done to ascertain the appropriate of the questionnaires set for the study. The rational for the pilot study was conducted to purposefully to test the meaningfulness of the questionnaire as it relates to the research questions.

2.5 Sampling Technique

Purposeful sampling is the best method for a qualitative approach to target the participants who have the best knowledge on the research topic. Participants that are selected for the study were employees who had rich information and were able to provide adequate knowledge on the topic. A purposive sampling technique has the ability to use reasoning to choose participants based on the field of study. The study wanted to find out about the growth process of the company over the years and in so doing, only employees who have been working in the company for five years or more were chosen for the study. They provided rich information for better understanding of the topic. The interviews were undertaken until the point of saturation when no new information shared by participants. The interviews reached the saturation point with the twentieth (20th) participant.

2.6 Data Collection

In gathering the primary data, the study relied on semi-structured interviews to answer the study's research questions. This form of data collection enabled the researcher to directly confirm if primary data meets the quality, availability, sample size and sample criteria for a particular study subject. The majority of the secondary data sources came from Compressor Techniques Services Limited. The information consisted of documents on IS from Compressor Techniques Services Limited. Research books and journals were used to collect secondary data.

2.7 Data Collection Tool

Interviews were used to collect data for the study. The researcher chose twenty (20) participants which included managers, supervisors and lower-level employees of Compressor Techniques Limited. The purpose of using the semi-structured interview to gather data was to gain more information from the participants about the research topic (Anugwom, 2011). Semi-structured interview allowed the researcher to ask questions in a flexible manner. During the interviews, the researcher made sure to observe the participants as well. Each of the participants were interviewed for twenty minutes so that they were able to share a good amount of information. The interview was held in serene environment with little to no distractions.

2.8 Data Analysis

Thematic analysis was used to analyse the responses from the interviews. Braun & Clarke (2021), defined thematic analysis as the method used for the systematic identification, organisation and offering of insights into patterns about meaning across a set of data. Thematic was utilised and this brought about the salient themes within the context of innovative innovative stratagies and organisational growth. Statements from participants were reviewed for key themes and subthemes that occurred frequently in the data gathered on innovative strategies within the organisation.

Braun & Clarke (2021), proposed six steps to thematically analyse data which were as follows, (i) being familiar with the data by making notes of the responses made by the participants, (ii) coming up with codes in an attempt to answer the research questions, (iii) the researcher must explore themes by reviewing and grouping the codes according to their similarities, (iv) continue with brainstorming themes that are appropriate for the study and labelling them, (iv) analyse the data by listening to the audio recordings from the interview, and (v) transcribing them into word text format. This took a lot of time for the researcher to listen to the audio on repeated number of times just to pick up ideas correctly. To eliminate any errors, the word text was edited and then data was coded into themes and subthemes under the specific objectives of the study. Themes were given proper headings for easy identification. Data was also presented in relation to the literature review and compared to the data collected from the field. It highlighted key statements that were made by the participants in answering research questions.

2.9 Findings of Research Questions

This section highlights the demographics and discusses the findings from the research questions. Participants' age range, gender, highest level of education, departments they work in, positions held in the office and how many years they have worked in the organization were gathered to in the initial analysis before the findings.

Gender: Participants were made up of thirteen (13) men and (7) women with the men constituting a larger part of the total number of participants for the study.

Age Range: The study inquired about the age range of the participants in the questionnaire. One (1) of the participants indicated that he is within the 58 years and above range. Four (4) of them was between the 48-57 years range and four (4) of the participants belonged to the 38-47 years range whilst eight (8) of them belong to the 28-37 years range and three (3) of them belong to the 23-27 years range and this gave a total of twenty (20) participants who took part in the study.

The interview was conducted from 21/8/23 to 28/8/23 with 20 participants and each participant was interviewed for about 20 minutes. Participants were eager to take part in the study and the organization allowed the researcher to conduct the interviews in seven days so that employees could go back to their work duties. Research question one is as follows;

2.9.1 What is Compressor Techniques Service Limited level of innovative approach?

For research question one, participants were asked about existing programs in place that promote intrapreneurship and the participants shared their opinions in the statements below;

An interview conducted on 21/8/23 with the IT manager who has been working for seven (7) years expressed that, *"Compressor Techniques Service Limited has established a number of initiatives and programmes to encourage intrapreneurship within the company because it understands how important it is. Employees are invited to submit creative ideas through our "Innovation Challenge" programme, and those that are chosen receive funding and support for implementation".* (Participant 1).

An interview conducted on 21/8/23 with the Store Assistant who has worked for six (6) years in the company said that, "*Compressor Techniques Service Limited has programs and activities to encourage employees to think creatively and come up with new ideas. We have workshops, brainstorming sessions, and forums where people can share their innovative thoughts*" (Participant 4).

The HR manager for Compressor Techniques Services was interviewed on 21/8/23 and she also said that, "*In our company, we have special programs and activities that encourage employees to think creatively and come up with new ideas. We organize brainstorming sessions, innovation contests, and workshops to inspire innovation and entrepreneurship"* (Participant 5).

On 23/8/23, The operations manager who has worked for 10 years also said during the interview that, "*Compressor Techniques Service Limited has programs and activities to encourage employees to think creatively and come up with new ideas. We have brainstorming sessions, suggestion boxes, and innovation contests to foster an innovative spirit*" (PARTICIPANT 7).

The company is concerned about instilling an innovative culture in the organization so initiating creativity programs is a good way to go but this cannot end here since there has to be support for this initiative so participants were asked if they were supported to be innovative and some of their responses are as follows;

An interview was conducted on 21/8/23 with the Account Manager who has been in the company for a good number of 14 years offering his expertise said that, "*Compressor Techniques Service Limited actively encourages and supports employees to generate and pursue innovative ideas through various means such as open communication and training and development"* (Participant 2).

A Technical assistant who has been working in the company for 5 years during an interview scheduled on 23/8/23 also said, *"The company supports employees by providing them with the necessary tools and resources to explore their innovative ideas. We have mentors and experts who guide employees and help them bring their ideas to life"* (Participant 8).

The Store Manager who has worked for 11 years was interviewed on 23/8/23 also said, *"The organization actively encourages and supports employees to generate and pursue innovative ideas. We have an open-door policy where employees can share their ideas with leadership and receive feedback and guidance. Additionally, there are innovation grants and internal competitions that provide funding and recognition for innovative projects."* (Participant 9).

On 24/8/23, the General Supervisor for the engineering department was interviewed and he said, *"We support our employees by giving them the tools and things they need to explore their cool ideas. We have special people called mentors who help and guide employees to make their ideas happen"* (Participant 12).

Participants were also asked if leadership supports the organization's innovative culture and specifically what form of support employees get from leadership.

On 24/8/23, an interview was conducted with the Assistant Operations Manager who opined that, *'"Leaders in the company encourage everyone to take risks and be brave in trying new things. They guide and support employees to make their ideas successful and celebrate their achievements"* (Participant 13).

An interview was conducted with a 37-year-old engineer who has worked for 8 years on 28/8/23 and he said, *"Leadership plays a vital role in promoting an innovative culture at Compressor Techniques Service Limited. They set the vision and values that encourage risk-taking, creativity, and innovation. Leaders empower employees, provide mentorship, and create a supportive environment that rewards innovative thinking and initiative."* (Participant 16).

Another technical assistant who has worked for 6 years was interviewed on 23/8/23 and she expressed that, *'They provide support, guidance, and resources to help employees turn their ideas into reality. They also recognize and reward employees for their innovative contributions." (Participant 10).*

The Assistant manager also said during an interview on 24/8/23 that, *"They set the vision and direction for the organization, communicate the importance of innovation and entrepreneurship, and lead by example. They also provide support and guidance to employees, empowering them to take risks and explore new opportunities* He also said, *" We believe in investing in innovative projects to help them grow." (Participant 13).*

Participants were then asked how the organization allocates funding for innovative projects and some of the responses are stated the following. On 24/8/23, the Assistant HR manager expressed during the interview that, *"The company sets aside money and special people to help with new projects. They give the things they need to make their ideas happen" (Participant 11).*

On 21/8/23, during the same interview with the CEO who has worked for Compressor Technique Services for 14 years he said that, *"At Compressor Techniques Service Limited, we ensure the provision of resources required for innovative initiatives. This includes allocating sufficient financial support and other necessary resources to turn innovative ideas into reality" (Participant 3).*

Another 27-year-old engineer who has been working for 5 years was interviewed on the 28/8/23 and he also said that, *"The company has a budget for research and development and provide teams with the resources they need to work on innovative initiatives" (Participant 15)*

2.9.2 What is the effect of an innovative strategies on business expansion at Compressor Techniques Service Limited?

Research question two was to find out what effects innovative strategies has on business expansion at Compressor Techniques Service Limited. Participants were asked to give practical examples of how innovative strategies has contributed to the company's growth. During the same interview on 28/8/23, the 37-year-old engineer said, *"By creating new product lines based on customer feedback, forming strategic partnerships with other companies, and exploring new markets. These initiatives have helped the company expand its customer base and increase its presence." And because of this the organization "has increased revenue, improved its reputation, and made it more competitive. It has also boosted employee morale and engagement (Participant 16).*

The Assistant IT manager was interviewed on 28/8/23 and she said,

Specific initiatives driven by innovative strategies that have led to organizational expansion include the development of cutting-edge IT solutions, the introduction of innovative service offerings, and the establishment of strategic partnerships and collaborations. "This has led to increased market share, improved competitiveness, enhanced brand reputation, and higher profitability. The organization's ability to adapt to changing market dynamics and seize opportunities has contributed to its sustained growth and success (Participant 17).

During the same interview on 24/8/23, the technical assistant who has worked for 5 years mentioned that, *"launching new product lines based on customer feedback and market trends, exploring partnerships with other companies to expand our reach, and investing in research to develop cutting-edge technologies. These initiatives have contributed to our company's expansion."* Additionally, there is a positive impact on organizational performance because, *"It has resulted in increased revenue, improved customer satisfaction, and strengthened our position in the market. It has also fostered a sense of innovation and collaboration among employees"* (Participant 13).

In the same interview on 23/8/23, with the Store Manager who has worked for 11 years said, *"introduction of energy-efficient compressor systems, expansion into emerging markets, and the development of predictive maintenance solutions. These initiatives have opened up new revenue streams and enhanced our competitive edge."* She went on to say that this has a positive impact on organizational performance *"We have experienced increased profitability, higher customer satisfaction, and improved brand reputation due to our innovative products and services"* (Participant 9).

2.10 What are the internal barriers to implementing an innovative strategies at Compressor Techniques Service Limited?

For research question three, participants were asked to state some of the internal barriers to implementing innovative stratagies at Compressor Technique Services. A Technical assistant who has worked for six (6) years said, *"Yes, there are structures and processes in place that make it difficult to implement innovative practices. Hierarchical structures, lack of cross-department collaboration, and slow decision-making can be barriers to innovative initiatives"* (Participant 10). In the same interview on 23/8/23, a technical assistant who has worked for 5 years said, *"Hierarchical decision-making, rigid workflows, and limited communication between departments can slow down the implementation of innovative ideas."* In the interview (Participant 8).

In the same interview on 21/8/23, the HR manager also expressed that, *"Yes, there are existing structures and processes that can make it challenging to implement innovative practices. For example, rigid hierarchies and lengthy decision-making processes can slow down the implementation of innovative ideas."* (Participant 5).

To overcome the challenges participants also gave their opinions and some of them are stated as follows;

On 23/8/23, the operations manager said that, *'To overcome internal challenges, the company can foster a culture that values innovation and experimentation. We can promote open communication, establish cross-functional teams, and provide training and resources to empower employees to take calculated risks and pursue innovative ideas."* (Participant 7).

On 24/8/23, the general supervisor of the engineering department said that, *"To overcome challenges, we can change our ways a bit. We can encourage everyone to keep learning and trying new things. We can also make it easier for different teams to work together and make decisions faster. This will help us be more innovative."* (Participant 12).

On 24/8/23, the Assistant HR manager also opined that, *"To overcome challenges, we can encourage everyone to be creative and try new things. We can also make it easier for different teams to work together and make decisions faster. This will help us be more innovative."* (Participant 11).

On 23/8/23, in the same interview, the technical assistant said, *"To overcome challenges, fostering a culture that promotes risk-taking, streamlining decision-making, and providing training and development opportunities is recommended"* (Participant 10).

The general administrator on 28/8/23 said that, *"To overcome internal challenges, the company can promote a culture of continuous learning and experimentation. Encouraging cross-department collaboration, providing training on innovation and creative problem-solving, and streamlining decision-making processes can help foster an innovative strategy"* (Participant 18).

The data in this research were analysed using a thematic approach. The participants were initially given access to the categories to access the researcher's perspective and analysis in order to verify the data.

3. DISCUSSION OF THE FINDINGS

After analysing the interview data, codes were extracted from the interview and finally the Intrapreneurship programs, encouragement and support of employees to be innovative, promoting or innovative culture by leadership, allocation of resources for innovative projects, company growth due to entrepreneurship, impact of company expansion on organizational performance, hindrances to the development of innovative strategies and measures to address innovative challenges have been categorized into eight (8) main themes, 16 Sub category themes and 21 codes for research question 1, 11 codes for research question 2 and 10 codes for research question 3. The categorization of the findings is presented in Table 4.2.

Buli (2017), believes that companies are progressively using innovative strategies for creativity, expansion, and revitalization of approach to address business difficulties. Wach (2015), also opines that companies with high innovative approach keep an eye on market shifts and act swiftly to seize new possibilities. Innovation puts businesses one step ahead of their rivals, and by acquiring a competitive edge, they can achieve better financial outcomes. This agrees with what participants discussed concerning the growth of Compressor Techniques Service as a result of creating new products from the feedback they

Table 1. Categorization of findings

Main theme	Sub category theme	Codes extracted from interviews
Intrapreneurship	Implementation of innovation contests to foster intrapreneurial spirit	Establishing programs such as innovation challenges, idea incubation labs to encourage Intrapreneurship (1), we have fun activities and workshops to help employees to be innovative (2), programs make us feel empowered to come up with new ideas (3) employees are invited to submit creative ideas through innovation challenges (4).
Entrepreneurship	Organizing workshops, seminars and conferences to expose employees to new industry development	Programs consist of workshops and Entrepreneurship training to improve innovative abilities (5) participation in workshops and seminars exposes employees to new developments in the industry (6).
Encouragement and Support for employees	Training and mentorship programs for employees	We have special people called mentors who guide and support employees (7), training and development programs for employees to pursue innovative ideas (8).
Encouragement and Support for employees	Innovation grants or bonus structures	Implementing rewards and recognition programs for successful innovation (9), innovation grants and internal competitions with funding for innovative projects (10).
Support for employees	Open door policy for employees to share their ideas with leadership	Leaders encourage us to brave and try new things (11). Employees are given time and resources to explore ideas independently (12), regular brainstorming sessions are held to help with idea generation (13), open communication channels for employees to share their ideas (14).
Promoting innovative culture by leadership	Leadership allocates resources to support innovative culture	Leadership believes in investing in innovative projects (15).
Promoting innovative culture by leadership	Actively engage with employees and offer guidance	Leadership sets the tone for encouraging risk-taking (16), leadership prioritizes innovation (17), leadership sets a clear vision that encourages innovation (18).
Allocation of resources for innovative projects	Dedicated budget for research, technology and talent development	The company sets aside money to help with new projects (19), The company distributes resources to support innovative projects (20), A separate budget is maintained for innovation (21).
Company growth due to innovative strategies	Creation of different products	Launching new product lines based on customer feedback and market trends (1) introducing new technologies to improve our products (2)
	Increase in customers	Customers have increased (3), more people like the company's products and this has increased our customer base (4)
Impact of company expansion on organizational performance	Increased employee engagement	Employees have become innovative (5), there has been a boost in employee morale (6), employees are happy and excited to work (7).
	The organization has a good brand image	We are known as a good company (8), The company's standing in the market has improved (9), improved brand reputation due to our innovative products and services (10).
	Increased revenue	The company makes more money (11), we have expanded our service offerings and this has increased revenue (12).
Hindrance to the development of innovative strategies	Lengthy approval process for innovative ideas to be put into practice	Lengthy approval process sometimes slows down the implementation of innovative ideas (1), bureaucratic decision making and excessive red tape (2), rules that make innovative programs to take a long time to be implemented
Measures to overcome the challenges	Streamlining decision making process for approval of innovative ideas	Deciding on which innovative programs to approve should be in a timely manner (5), decision making should be faster (6), decision making process should be more efficient and hasten the approval of innovative projects (7).
Measures to overcome the challenges	Encourage cross-department collaboration	Create platforms for knowledge sharing and idea exchange amongst departments (8), encourage everyone to be creative and try new things so that it will be easier for everyone to work as a team (9), promote open communication amongst various departments (10).

Source; Field work, 2023

receive from the markets, it has increased the customer base, increased the company's revenue, increased employee engagement and enhanced the good reputation of the business.

Besides this, (Cho & Lee, 2018) encouraging and fostering novel concepts, in addition to experimentation and imagination, which are likely to produce new goods, services, or procedures, are all aspects of innovation. This study agrees with (Cho & Lee, 2018) because the company has established a number of initiatives and programmes to encourage intrapreneurship within the company because it understands how important it is. Employees are invited to submit creative ideas through the "Innovation Challenge" programme. It is from this program that workers produce new products which has given them a competitive advantage in the service industry. as was stated by (Rodríguez-Gutiérrez et al., 2015) that, being proactive enables businesses to provide new goods and services to the market before rivals, which offers them an edge over their rivals.

For (Ribau et al., 2017), businesses should be willing to invest in innovative projects and the readiness to invest in initiatives with ambiguous results is referred to as a risk-taking propensity. Compressor Technique Service has a dedicated budget which is set aside for research, acquiring technology and developing the talents of employees so that they can be more innovative. The company also organizes training workshops and seminars for all workers so that they are exposed top new technologies that aid in carrying out their duties. Compressor Technique Service is not discouraged to fund innovative projects even if the projects may fail and doing this shows that the company has a risk-taking component in its innovative approach. (Wahyuni & Sara, 2020) stated that, the importance of the risk-taking component is that it directs the company towards an accepting of ambiguity instead of a paralysing dread of it.

The study agrees with Quagrainie (2016) who examined the innovative strategies dimensions and business performance of women entrepreneurs in three Ghanaian cities which were; Accra, Kumasi and Takoradi and argued that the performance of businesses requires that leaders should be autonomous, strong and creative without any restrictions from the bureaucracy of the business. Participants mentioned that the hierarchy of Compressor Technique Service is bureaucratic and this makes it challenging for the company to have a high level of innovative approach.

This study agrees with Liping (2022), who conducted a study in Thailand to find out the link between innovative strategies and performance of the firm. It was revealed that a positive relationship exists between perceptions of innovative strategies and perceptions of firm performance. Knowledge creation processes and competitive strategy also play a role in how best a firm performs. On the basis of the findings and discussions, recommendations are offered to support the innovative strategies of Compressor Technique Service.

3.1 Summary

The general objective of the study was to assess the effect of innovative approach on business expansion of Compressor Technique Service. The study took a look at some of the innovative activities and programs of Compressor Technique Service, how relevant these practices are to the employees of Compressor Technique Service and finally the hindrance to the development of innovative strategies. The background of the study was done by studying literature on innovative strategies. The statement of the problem covered innovative strategies and organizational performance. Specific objectives of the study included; to assess Compressor Techniques Service Limited level of innovative approach, to examine the effect of an innovative strategies on business expansion at Compressor Techniques Service Limited, to identify internal barriers to implementing an innovative strategy at Compressor Techniques Service Limited.

The research was guided by this set of objectives in order to achieve the ultimate goal of the study and they informed the themes for the literature review; both known and new concepts were reviewed to give further clarity to the study. Next to this was the methodology which gave directions on how data was to be gathered.

The study used the qualitative research design and participants consisted of employees of Compressor Techniques Service. The sampling method used in the study was the purposive sampling method, as it was believed that most important information to answer the research questions could be obtained using this sample. The number of respondents who took part in the study were 20. Interviews were conducted with each of the participants who were audio recorded. The data was analysed using thematic analysis. The findings were presented and discussed in chapter 4. The findings revealed that the majority of the respondents were aged between 28-57 years and both genders were almost equally represented to avoid being biased. Most of the respondents have been to school especially the university.

The study assessed Compressor Techniques Service Limited level of innovative approach and the findings revealed that the respondents had a very good knowledge of the innovative approach of Compressor Techniques Service. The research findings showed the company organizes workshops, seminars to improve upon the abilities of employees. Participants also made it clear that when they attend the workshops and seminars, they are exposed to new technologies and developments in their line of work. Organizing these programs are mostly done in a formal setting but this does not end here as Compressor Techniques Service also initiates fun activities for employees to come out with new ideas in a more relaxed manner. According to the findings, participants agreed that management has a dedicated budget which is money set aside for innovative projects. This budget is for research, technology acquisition and developing the talent of employees for the purpose of innovative strategies. Employees also receive support from management in the form of mentorship. Managers are assigned to workers to guide them on how to carry out their innovative projects. This allows employees to share their ideas freely.

The study also examined the effect of an innovative strategies on business expansion at Compressor Techniques Service Limited and it was revealed that innovative strategies has led to the expansion of Compressor Techniques Services and there has been an increase in the company's revenue, customer base, employee engagement, creation of different products and a good brand image in the industry. The innovative culture of the company allows the employees to come out with new ideas on how can be done.

Finally, the study identified internal barriers to implementing an innovative strategies at Compressor Techniques Service Limited. It was revealed it takes a long time for management to approve innovative programs in the company. Participants also opined that the hierarchy of the organization was also a hindrance to the development of innovative projects. In order to address this hindrance, there is the need for management to streamline decision making process on approving innovative projects. This should be done in a timely manner. A section of the participants also believe that it is better to work in a team so management should create platforms for knowledge sharing and idea exchange amongst departments in the organization and also promote open communication across the company.

The findings of the study have demonstrated that there are associations between innovative strategies and organizational performance in Compressor Techniques Service just as was found in Liping (2022). Very little research focused on this association of service companies in Ghana. This study also extends the research on innovative strategies and organizational performance.

4. CONCLUSION

The concept of innovative strategies has emerged as acritical factor in understanding and predicting organizational performance. Through a combination of innovative, proactive and risk-taking behaviours, innovative-oriented organizations have demonstrated the ability to adapt very well to changing market conditions, seize opportunities and have competitive advantage. Empirical research has showed that there is positive relationship between innovative strategies and various dimensions of organizational performance. this includes profitability, growth etc. by fostering a culture of creativity, encouraging experimentation and empowering employees to take risks, companies can enhance their innovative strategies and gain many benefits. Organizations should focus on creating an environment that encourages and supports innovative behaviour. Providing resources, training employees and establishing rewards systems for innovative projects helps organizations to have a high level of innovative approach.

4.1 Recommendations

In view of the research findings, the recommendations were made;

- In as much as such activities is mostly initiated from the leadership of Compressor Technique Service to the various departments, it may not agree with the needs of specific departments since everyone performs different function for the organization. It is therefore important for unit heads and officers to also share their ideas on what innovative programs will best suit their operations.
- Compressor Techniques Service needs to assess the employees' skills and training needs and then structure the way that the innovative training programs must be carried out and department heads will also assist with this. Workers' personal strengths and capabilities, aims and desires and special talents must also be assessed, so that they can be understood and given opportunities to be innovative in the organization. Workers should also know that they are not limited to only their job role, but they should also develop their skills.
- Compressor Techniques Service should consider fostering a culture of continuous learning and experimentation, promoting knowledge sharing and cross-functional collaboration amongst the various departments in the company. There should also be an innovation fund to support innovative projects and provide mentorship and guidance to employees pursuing innovative initiatives. In addition to this, the company should adapt its strategies to align with emerging trends and opportunities.
- Given the large number of skills and other capabilities which can be developed in people, it is useful for organizations to prioritize innovative programs which focus on yielding the best results for the organization. The organization should make sure to have dedicated team responsible for driving innovation and innovative projects. They should also regularly review and update their internal structures and decision-making processes for approving innovative projects so that the company can reach its innovative goals.

4.2 Areas for Further Study

This research is limited to only the Compressor Technique Service using a qualitative approach. Further research should be conducted into innovative approach of other companies in the service sector. Also, further research can be done using a quantitative approach that involves the themes that were found in this research to measure the extent to which the findings can be applied. The quantitative approach can use a larger number of participants as compared to the study.

REFERENCES

Abu-Rumman, A., Al Shraah, A., Al-Madi, F., & Alfalah, T. (2021). Innovative networks, innovative strategies, and performance of small and medium enterprises: Are dynamic capabilities the missing link? *Journal of Innovation and Entrepreneurship*, *10*(1), 1–16. doi:10.1186/s13731-021-00170-8

Acheampong, G. (2017). Beyond the EJ model: Innovative strategies and industry choice of Ghanaian entrepreneurs. *Journal of Global Entrepreneurship Research*, *7*(1), 28. doi:10.1186/s40497-017-0086-y

Aftab, J., Veneziani, M., Sarwar, H., & Ishaq, M. I. (2022). Organizational ambidexterity, firm performance, and sustainable development: Mediating role of innovative strategies in Pakistani SMEs. *Journal of Cleaner Production*, *367*, 132956. doi:10.1016/j.jclepro.2022.132956

Allwood, C. M. (2012). The distinction between qualitative and quantitative research methods is problematic. *Quality & Quantity*, *46*(5), 1417–1429. doi:10.1007/s11135-011-9455-8

Altinay, L., Madanoglu, M., De Vita, G., Arasli, H., & Ekinci, Y. (2016). The interface between organizational learning capability, innovative strategies, and SME growth. *Journal of Small Business Management*, *54*(3), 871–891. doi:10.1111/jsbm.12219

Alvarez-Torres, F. J., Lopez-Torres, G. C., & Schiuma, G. (2019). Linking innovative strategies to SMEs' performance: Implications for entrepreneurship universities. *Management Decision*, *57*(12), 3364–3386. doi:10.1108/MD-11-2018-1234

Amarteifio, E., & Agbeblewu, S. (2020). Innovative strategies and Firm Performance of Tourist Accommodation Establishment in Ghana. *Open Journal of Business and Management*, *4*(9), 78–98.

Anderson, B. S., Kreiser, P., Kuratko, D. F., Hornsby, J. S., & Eshima, Y. (2015). Reconceptualizing innovative strategies. *Strategic Management Journal*, *36*(10), 1579–1596. doi:10.1002/smj.2298

Anugwom, E. E. (2011). Women Entrepreneurs and the Niger Delta conflict. *Journal of Small Business and Entrepreneurship*, *24*(2), 243–252. doi:10.1080/08276331.2011.10593536

Arshad, A. S., & Rasli, A. (2018). Innovative strategies of technology-based SMEs in Malaysia. In *Proceedings of the 2nd Advances in Business Research International Conference: ABRIC2016* (Participant 23-30). Springer Singapore. 10.1007/978-981-10-6053-3_3

Bhattacharyya, D. K. (2009). *Research methodology*. Excel Books India.

Biney, C. O. (2018). *Impact of Venture Capital Financing on SMEs' Growth and Development in Ghana* [Doctoral dissertation, Lincoln University].

Boohene, R. (2018). Innovative strategies, strategic innovative strategies and performance of small family firms in the Kumasi Metropolis. *Academy of Entrepreneurship Education*, *24*(2), 501–529.

Braun, V. & Clarke, V. (2021). *Conceptual and design thinking for thematic analysis*. doi:. doi:10/1080/2159676X.2019.1704846

Buli, B. M. (2017). Innovative strategies, market innovative strategies and performance of SMEs in the manufacturing industry: Evidence from Ethiopian enterprises. *Management Research Review*, *40*(3), 292–309. doi:10.1108/MRR-07-2016-0173

Cho, Y. H., & Lee, J. H. (2018). Innovative strategies, innovative education and performance. *Asia Pacific Journal of Innovation and Entrepreneurship*, *12*(2), 124–134. doi:10.1108/APJIE-05-2018-0028

Covin, J. G., & Lumpkin, G. T. (2011). Innovative strategies theory and research: Reflections on a needed construct. *Entrepreneurship Theory and Practice*, *35*(5), 855–872. doi:10.1111/j.1540-6520.2011.00482.x

Criado-Gomis, A., Iniesta-Bonillo, M. Á., & Cervera-Taulet, A. (2018). Sustainable innovative strategies within an intrapreneurial context: Effects on business performance. *The International Entrepreneurship and Management Journal*, *14*, 295–308. doi:10.1007/s11365-018-0503-x

Cuevas-Vargas, H., Parga-Montoya, N., & Fernández-Escobedo, R. (2019). Effects of innovative strategies on business performance: The mediating role of customer satisfaction—A formative–Reflective model analysis. *SAGE Open*, *9*(2), 2158244019859088. doi:10.1177/2158244019859088

Denicolai, S., Zucchella, A., & Magnani, G. (2021). Internationalization, digitalization, and sustainability: Are SMEs ready? A survey on synergies and substituting effects among growth paths. *Technological Forecasting and Social Change*, *166*, 120650. doi:10.1016/j.techfore.2021.120650

Eshima, Y., & Anderson, B. S. (2017). Firm growth, adaptive capability, and innovative innovative stratagies. *Strategic Management Journal*, *38*(3), 770–779. doi:10.1002/smj.2532

Galbreath, J., Lucianetti, L., Thomas, B., & Tisch, D. (2020). Innovative strategies and firm performance in Italian firms: The moderating role of competitive strategy. *International Journal of Innovative Behavior & Research*, *26*(4), 629–646.

Galbreath, J., Lucianetti, L., Thomas, B., & Tisch, D. (2020). Innovative strategies and firm performance in Italian firms: The moderating role of competitive strategy. *International Journal of Innovative Behavior & Research*, *26*(4), 629–646.

Gherhes, C., Williams, N., Vorley, T., & Vasconcelos, A. C. (2016). Distinguishing micro-businesses from SMEs: A systematic review of growth constraints. *Journal of Small Business and Enterprise Development*, *23*(4), 939–963. doi:10.1108/JSBED-05-2016-0075

Goktan, A. B., & Gupta, V. K. (2015). Sex, gender, and individual innovative strategies: Evidence from four countries. *The International Entrepreneurship and Management Journal*, *11*, 95–112. doi:10.1007/s11365-013-0278-z

Gruber-Muecke, T., & Hofer, K. M. (2015). Market innovative strategies, innovative innovative strategies and performance in emerging markets. *International Journal of Emerging Markets*, *10*(3), 560–571. doi:10.1108/IJoEM-05-2013-0076

Gupta, V. K., & Batra, S. (2016). Innovative strategies and firm performance in Indian SMEs: Universal and contingency perspectives. *International Small Business Journal*, *34*(5), 660–682. doi:10.1177/0266242615577708

Herlinawati, E., Ahman, E., & Machmud, A. (2019). The effect of innovative strategies on SMEs business performance in Indonesia. *Journal of Entrepreneurship Education, 22*(5), 1–15.

Hess, T. J., McNab, A. L., & Basoglu, K. S. (2016). Reliability generalization of perceived ease of use, perceived usefulness, and behavioural intentions. *International Journal of Management Studies, 5*(12), 401–433.

Hooi, H. C., Ahmad, N. H., Amran, A., & Rahman, S. A. (2016). The functional role of innovative strategies and innovative bricolage in ensuring sustainable entrepreneurshiParticipant. *Management Research Review, 39*(12), 1616–1638. doi:10.1108/MRR-06-2015-0144

Hossain, M. U., & Al Asheq, A. (2019). The role of innovative strategies to SME performance in Bangladesh. *International Journal of Entrepreneurship, 23*(1), 1–6.

Hossain, M. U., & Al Asheq, A. (2019). The role of innovative strategies to SME performance in Bangladesh. *International Journal of Entrepreneurship, 23*(1), 1–6.

Hussain, J., Rahman, W., & Shah, F. A. (2016). Market innovative strategies and performance: The interaction effect of innovative strategies. [PJCSS]. *Pakistan Journal of Commerce and Social Sciences, 10*(2), 388–403.

Jalali, A., Thurasamy, R., & Jaafar, M. (2017). The Moderating effect of social capital in relation to innovative strategies and firm performance. In Handbook of Research on Small and Medium Enterprises in Developing Countries (pParticipant 82-115). IGI Global.

Jeong, Y. M., Ali, M., Zacca, R., & Park, K. (2019). The effect of entrepreneurship innovative strategies on firm performance: A multiple mediation model. *Journal of East-West Business, 25*(2), 166–193. doi:10.1080/10669868.2018.1536013

Jogaratnam, G. (2017). The effect of market innovative strategies, innovative strategies and human capital on positional advantage: Evidence from the restaurant industry. *International Journal of Hospitality Management, 60*, 104–113. doi:10.1016/j.ijhm.2016.10.002

Kajalo, S., & Lindblom, A. (2015). Market innovative strategies, innovative strategies and business performance among small retailers. *International Journal of Retail & Distribution Management, 43*(7), 580–596. doi:10.1108/IJRDM-04-2014-0044

Karmann, T., Mauer, R., Flatten, T. C., & Brettel, M. (2016). Innovative strategies and corruption. *Journal of Business Ethics, 133*, 223–234. doi:10.1007/s10551-014-2305-6

Kiyabo, K., & Isaga, N. (2020). Innovative strategies, competitive advantage, and SMEs' performance: Application of firm growth and personal wealth measures. *Journal of Innovation and Entrepreneurship, 9*, 1–15. doi:10.1186/s13731-020-00123-7

Koe, W. L. (2016). The relationship between individual innovative strategies (IEO) and innovative intention. *Journal of Global Entrepreneurship Research, 6*, 1–11. doi:10.1186/s40497-016-0057-8

Lekmat, L., Selvarajah, C., & Hewege, C. (2018). Relationship between Market Innovative strategies, Innovative strategies, and Firm Performance in Thai SMEs: The Mediating Role of Marketing Capabilities. *European Journal of Pediatric Dermatology : PD, 28*(4), 89–109.

Liping, Y. & Vesarach, A. (2022). *The Impact of Innovative strategies on Firm Performance: The Multiple Mediating Roles of Competitive Strategy and Knowledge Creation Process.*

Lisboa, A., Skarmeas, D., & Saridakis, C. (2016). Innovative strategies pathways to performance: A fuzzy-set analysis. *Journal of Business Research*, *69*(4), 1319–1324. doi:10.1016/j.jbusres.2015.10.099

Love, J. H., & Roper, S. (2015). SME innovation, exporting and growth: A review of existing evidence. *International Small Business Journal*, *33*(1), 28–48. doi:10.1177/0266242614550190

MacIntosh, R., & O'Gorman, K. (2015). Research methods for business and management. *A guide to writing your dissertation,* 558 -578.

Mantok, S., Sekhon, H., Sahi, G. K., & Jones, P. (2019). Innovative strategies and the mediating role of organisational learning amongst Indian S-SMEs. *Journal of Small Business and Enterprise Development*, *26*(5), 641–660. doi:10.1108/JSBED-07-2018-0215

Martens, C. D., Lacerda, F. M., Belfort, A. C., & de Freitas, H. M. R. (2016). Research on innovative strategies: Current status and future agenda. *International Journal of Innovative Behavior & Research*, *22*(4), 556–583.

Mason, M. C., Floreani, J., Miani, S., Beltrame, F., & Cappelletto, R. (2015). Understanding the impact of innovative strategies on SMEs' performance. The role of the financing structure. *Procedia Economics and Finance*, *23*, 1649–1661. doi:10.1016/S2212-5671(15)00470-0

Meekaewkunchorn, N., Szczepańska-Woszczyna, K., Muangmee, C., Kassakorn, N., & Khalid, B. (2021). Innovative strategies and SME performance: The mediating role of learning innovative strategies. *Economia e Sociologia*, *14*(2), 294–312.

Mthanti, T., & Ojah, K. (2017). Innovative strategies (EO): Measurement and policy implications of entrepreneurship at the macroeconomic level. *Research Policy*, *46*(4), 724–739. doi:10.1016/j.respol.2017.01.012

Muchiri, M., & McMurray, A. (2015). Innovative strategies within small firms: A critical review of why leadership and contextual factors matter. *Small Enterprise Research*, *22*(1), 17–31. doi:10.1080/13215906.2015.1017076

Naldi, L., Larsson, J., & Westlund, H. (2020). Policy entrepreneurship and innovative strategies in vulnerable Swedish municipalities. *Entrepreneurship and Regional Development*, *32*(7-8), 473–491. doi:10.1080/08985626.2020.1798557

Neneh, B. N., & Van, Z. J. (2017). Innovative strategies and its impact on firm growth amongst SMEs in South Africa. *Problems and Perspectives in Management*, (15), 166–178. doi:10.21511/ppm.15(3).2017.14

Nkwabi, J., & Mboya, L. (2019). A review of factors affecting the growth of small and medium enterprises (SMEs) in Tanzania. *European Journal of Business and Management*, *11*(33), 1–8.

O'Gorman, K., & MacIntosh, R. (2015). Mapping research methods. *Research methods for business and management: A guide to writing your dissertation*, 50-74.

Octavia, A., Indrawijaya, S., Sriayudha, Y., & Hasbullah, H. (2020). Impact on E-commerce adoption on innovative strategies and market innovative strategies in business performance of SMEs. *Asian Economic and Financial Review*, *10*(5), 516. doi:10.18488/journal.aefr.2020.105.516.525

Okangi, F. P. (2019). The impacts of innovative innovative strategies on the profitability growth of construction firms in Tanzania. *Journal of Global Entrepreneurship Research*, *9*(1), 14. doi:10.1186/s40497-018-0143-1

Oluwatayo, J. A. (2017). Validity and Reliability issues in education research. *Journal of Educational and Social Research*, *2*, 391–399.

Oni, O., Agbobli, E. K., & Iwu, C. G. (2019). Innovative strategies and performance of small business in Vryburg region North West province South Africa. *Journal of Reviews on Global Economics*. doi:10.6000/1929-7092.2019.08.07

Osei, A., Forkuoh, K. S., Shao, Y., & Osei, M. A. (2016). The impact of institutional support in SMEs marketing, and growth—A case study of retail SMEs in Ghana. *Open Journal of Business and Management*, *4*(03), 408–426. doi:10.4236/ojbm.2016.43043

Pratono, A. H., & Mahmood, R. (2015). Mediating effect of marketing capability and reward philosophy in the relationship between innovative strategies and firm performance. *Journal of Global Entrepreneurship Research*, *5*, 1–12. doi:10.1186/s40497-015-0023-x

Quagrainie, A. F. (2016). *Innovative strategies dimensions and business performance of Women Entrepreneurs in three Ghanaian cities.*

Rajasekar, D., & Verma, R. (2013). *Research methodology*. Archers & Elevators Publishing House.

Rezaei, J., & Ortt, R. (2018). Innovative innovative strategies and firm performance: The mediating role of functional performances. *Management Research Review*, *41*(7), 878–900. doi:10.1108/MRR-03-2017-0092

Ribau, C. P., Moreira, A. C., & Raposo, M. (2017). SMEs innovation capabilities and export performance: An innovative innovative strategies view. *Journal of Business Economics and Management*, *18*(5), 920–934. doi:10.3846/16111699.2017.1352534

Ribau, C., Moreira, A. C., & Raposo, M. (2017). SMEs innovation capabilities and export performance: An innovative strategies view. *Journal of Business Economics and Management*, *18*(5), 920–934. doi:10.3846/16111699.2017.1352534

Rodríguez-Gutiérrez, M. J., Moreno, P., & Tejada, P. (2015). Innovative innovative strategies and performance of SMEs in the services industry. *Journal of Organizational Change Management*, *28*(2), 194–212. doi:10.1108/JOCM-01-2015-0020

Scuotto, V., Nicotra, M., Del Giudice, M., Krueger, N., & Gregori, G. L. (2021). A micro foundational perspective on SMEs' growth in the digital transformation era. *Journal of Business Research*, *129*, 382–392. doi:10.1016/j.jbusres.2021.01.045

Shan, P., Song, M., & Ju, X. (2016). Innovative strategies and performance: Is innovation speed a missing link? *Journal of Business Research*, *69*(2), 683–690. doi:10.1016/j.jbusres.2015.08.032

Shirokova, G., Bogatyreva, K., Beliaeva, T., & Puffer, S. (2016). Innovative strategies and firm performance in different environmental settings: Contingency and configurational approaches. *Journal of Small Business and Enterprise Development*, *23*(3), 703–727. doi:10.1108/JSBED-09-2015-0132

Šlogar, H. (2021). Longitudinal research-Innovative innovative strategies impact, innovativeness, and business performance in Croatian companies. *Entrepreneurship and Sustainability Issues*, *9*(2), 152. doi:10.9770/jesi.2021.9.2(10)

Snyder, H. (2019). Literature review as a research methodology: An overview and guidelines. *Journal of Business Research*, *104*, 333–339. doi:10.1016/j.jbusres.2019.07.039

Stenholm, P. A., Pukkinen, T., & Heinonen, J. (2016). Firm growth in family businesses—The role of innovative strategies and the innovative activity. *Journal of Small Business Management*, *54*(2), 697–713. doi:10.1111/jsbm.12166

Su, Z., Xie, E., & Wang, D. (2015). Innovative strategies, managerial networking, and new venture performance in China. *Journal of Small Business Management*, *53*(1), 228–248. doi:10.1111/jsbm.12069

Theriou, N., Maditinos, D. I., & Theriou, G. (2017). Management control systems and strategy: A resource-based perspective. Evidence from Greece. *International Journal of Business and Economic Sciences Applied Research*, *10*(2), 35–47. doi:10.25103/ijbesar.102.04

Wach, K. (2015). Innovative strategies and business internationalisation process: The theoretical foundations of international entrepreneurshiParticipant *Innovative. Business and Economic Review*, *3*(2), 9–24.

Wahyuni, N. M., & Sara, I. M. (2020). The effect of innovative strategies variables on business performance in the SME industry context. *Journal of Workplace Learning*, *32*(1), 35–62. doi:10.1108/JWL-03-2019-0033

Zarrouk, H., Sherif, M., Galloway, L., & El Ghak, T. (2020). Innovative strategies, access to financial resources and SMEs' business performance: The case of the United Arab Emirates. *Journal of Asian Finance. Economics and Business*, *7*(12), 465–474.

Zhang, Z., Wang, X., & Jia, M. (2021). Echoes of CEO innovative strategies: How and when CEO innovative strategies influence dual CSR activities. *Journal of Business Ethics*, *169*, 609–629. doi:10.1007/s10551-020-04553-x

Compilation of References

Abass, M. (2023). Artificial Intelligence Techniques in Egyptian Hotels: Current Status and Prospective. *Egyptian Journal of Tourism and Hospitality*, *30*(1), 1–53. doi:10.21608/ejth.2023.303527

Abbing, H. R. (2020). Innovative Technologies in Healthcare, Beware of the Pitfalls. *European Journal of Health Law*, *27*(1), 1–8. doi:10.1163/15718093-12271453 PMID:33878725

Abduljabbar, R., Dia, H., Liyanage, S., & Bagloee, S. A. (2019). Applications of artificial intelligence in transport: An overview. *Sustainability (Basel)*, *11*(1), 189. doi:10.3390/su11010189

Abu-Abed, F., & Zhironkin, S. (2023). New Game Artificial Intelligence Tools for Virtual Mine on Unreal Engine. *Applied Sciences (Basel, Switzerland)*, *13*(10), 6339. doi:10.3390/app13106339

Abugabah, A., Nizamuddin, N., & Abuqabbeh, A. (2020). A review of challenges and barriers to implementing RFID technology in the Healthcare sector. *Procedia Computer Science*, *170*, 1003–1010. doi:10.1016/j.procs.2020.03.094

Abu-Rumman, A., Al Shraah, A., Al-Madi, F., & Alfalah, T. (2021). Innovative networks, innovative strategies, and performance of small and medium enterprises: Are dynamic capabilities the missing link? *Journal of Innovation and Entrepreneurship*, *10*(1), 1–16. doi:10.1186/s13731-021-00170-8

Acheampong, G. (2017). Beyond the EJ model: Innovative strategies and industry choice of Ghanaian entrepreneurs. *Journal of Global Entrepreneurship Research*, *7*(1), 28. doi:10.1186/s40497-017-0086-y

Acs, Z. J., Armington, C., & Zhang, T. (2007). The determinants of new-firm survival across regional economies: The role of Human Capital Stock and knowledge spillover. *Papers in Regional Science*, *86*(3), 367–391. doi:10.1111/j.1435-5957.2007.00129.x

Addady, M. (2016). 'TacoBot' is the newest way to order Taco Bell. *Fortune*. https://fortune.com/2016/04/06/tacobot-taco-bell/.

Adler-Milstein, J., Holmgren, A. J., & Kralovec, P. (2017). Electronic health record adoption in U.S. hospitals: Progress continues, but challenges persist. *Health Affairs*, *36*(8), 1564–1570. PMID:28784734

Adner, R., & Kapoor, R. (2010). Value creation in innovation ecosystems: How the structure of technological interdependence affects firm performance in new technology generations. *Strategic Management Journal*, *31*(3), 306–333. doi:10.1002/smj.821

Aftab, J., Veneziani, M., Sarwar, H., & Ishaq, M. I. (2022). Organizational ambidexterity, firm performance, and sustainable development: Mediating role of innovative strategies in Pakistani SMEs. *Journal of Cleaner Production*, *367*, 132956. doi:10.1016/j.jclepro.2022.132956

Agrawal, D. K. (2012). Demand chain management: Factors enhancing market responsiveness capabilities. *Journal of Marketing Channels*, *19*(2), 101–119. doi:10.1080/1046669X.2012.667760

Ahmad, A., & Ingle, S. (2013). Business incubators and HTSF development: setting an agenda forfurther research. In R. Oakey, A. Groen, G. Cook, & P. Van Der Sijde (Eds.), *New Technology-based Firms in the New Millennium* (Vol. 10, pp. 119–140). Emerald Group. doi:10.1108/S1876-0228(2013)0000010009

Ahmadi, S., Shokouhyar, S., Amerioun, M., & Tabrizi, N. S. (2024). A social media analytics-based approach to customer-centric reverse logistics management of electronic devices: A case study on notebooks. *Journal of Retailing and Consumer Services*, *76*, 103540. doi:10.1016/j.jretconser.2023.103540

Ahmad, N., Shahbaz, M., & Ijaz, U. (2022). The impact of employee training and development on employee motivation and retention: Evidence from Public Bank of Pakistan. *Pakistan Journal of Social Sciences*, *14*(1), 172–182.

Ahrne, G., & Brunsson, N. (2005). Organizations and meta-organizations. *Scandinavian Journal of Management*, *21*(4), 429–449. doi:10.1016/j.scaman.2005.09.005

Akarsu, T. N., Marvi, R., & Foroudi, P. (2023). Service failure research in the hospitality and tourism industry: A synopsis of past, present and future dynamics from 2001 to 2020. *International Journal of Contemporary Hospitality Management*, *35*(1), 186–217. doi:10.1108/IJCHM-11-2021-1441

Akçomak, İ. S. (2009). *Working Paper Series*. UNU. https://collections.unu.edu/eserv/UNU:62/wp2009-054.pdf

Albrecht, S. L. (2010). *Handbook of employee engagement: Perspectives, issues, research and practice*. Edward Elgar Publishing. doi:10.4337/9781849806374

Aldosari, H., Saddik, B., & Al Kadi, K. (2018). Impact of picture archiving and communication system (PACS) on radiology staff. *Informatics in Medicine Unlocked*, *10*, 1–16. doi:10.1016/j.imu.2017.11.001

Alexa, A. (2020). *Alexa for hospitality*. Amazon. https://www.amazon.com/alexahospitality.

Alexis, P. (2017). R-Tourism: Introducing the Potential Impact of Robotics and Service Automation in Tourism. *Ovidius University Annals: Economic Sciences Series*, 211-216.

Al-Hyari, H. S., Al-Smadi, H. M., & Weshah, S. R. (2023). The impact of artificial intelligence (ai) on guest satisfaction in hotel management: An empirical study of luxury hotels. *Geo Journal of Tourism and Geosites*, *48*(2, supplement), 810–819. doi:10.30892/gtg.482spl15-1081

Aliyah, L., Lukita, C., Pangilinan, G. A., Chakim, M. H. R., & Saputra, D. B. (2023). Examining the Impact of Artificial Intelligence and Internet of Things on Smart Tourism Destinations: A Comprehensive Study. [ATT]. *Aptisi Transactions on Technopreneurship*, *5*(2sp), 135–145. doi:10.34306/att.v5i2sp.332

Alkaabi, K. (2023). Exploring logistics service providers for small and medium-sized enterprises and large corporations: benefits and challenges. *European Business Review*.

Alkhatib, A. W., & Valeri, M. (2024). Can intellectual capital promote the competitive advantage? Service innovation and big data analytics capabilities in a moderated mediation model. *European Journal of Innovation Management*, *27*(1), 263–289. doi:10.1108/EJIM-04-2022-0186

Allen, J., Grazia, M., Eboli, L., Forciniti, C., Allen, J., Grazia, M., Forciniti, C., Mazzulla, G., Rica, D. C., Rodrigo, S., & Rica, C. (2020). ScienceDirect ScienceDirect Latent factors on the assessment of service quality in an Italian Latent factors on the assessment of service quality in an Italian peripheral airport peripheral. *Transportation Research Procedia*, *47*, 91–98. doi:10.1016/j.trpro.2020.03.083

Allwood, C. M. (2012). The distinction between qualitative and quantitative research methods is problematic. *Quality & Quantity*, *46*(5), 1417–1429. doi:10.1007/s11135-011-9455-8

Al-Mubaraki, H. M., Muhammad, A. H., & Busler, M. (2015). 'Categories of incubator success: Acase study of three New York incubator programmes', *World Journal of Science. Technology and Sustainable Development*, *12*(1), 2–12.

Alsahafi, R., Alzahrani, A., & Mehmood, R. (2023). Smarter Sustainable Tourism: Data-Driven Multi-Perspective Parameter Discovery for Autonomous Design and Operations. *Sustainability (Basel)*, *15*(5), 4166. doi:10.3390/su15054166

Altinay, L., Madanoglu, M., De Vita, G., Arasli, H., & Ekinci, Y. (2016). The interface between organizational learning capability, innovative strategies, and SME growth. *Journal of Small Business Management*, *54*(3), 871–891. doi:10.1111/jsbm.12219

Álvarez-Carmona, M. Á., Aranda, R., Rodrı́guez-Gonzalez, A. Y., Fajardo-Delgado, D., Sánchez, M. G., Pérez-Espinosa, H., Martínez-Miranda, J., Guerrero-Rodrı́guez, R., Bustio-Martínez, L., & Díaz-Pacheco, Á. (2022). Natural language processing applied to tourism research: A systematic review and future research directions. *Journal of King Saud University. Computer and Information Sciences*, *34*(10), 10125–10144. doi:10.1016/j.jksuci.2022.10.010

Alvarez-Torres, F. J., Lopez-Torres, G. C., & Schiuma, G. (2019). Linking innovative strategies to SMEs' performance: Implications for entrepreneurship universities. *Management Decision*, *57*(12), 3364–3386. doi:10.1108/MD-11-2018-1234

Amarteifio, E., & Agbeblewu, S. (2020). Innovative strategies and Firm Performance of Tourist Accommodation Establishment in Ghana. *Open Journal of Business and Management*, *4*(9), 78–98.

Amit, R., & Zott, C. (2001). Value creation in e-business. *Strategic Management Journal*, *22*(6-7), 493–520. doi:10.1002/smj.187

Analytics, D., & Mccarthy, G. (2020). Transforming Business Using Digital Innovations : The Application of AI. *Transforming Business Using Digital Innovations*, 1–33.

Anderson, B. S., Kreiser, P., Kuratko, D. F., Hornsby, J. S., & Eshima, Y. (2015). Reconceptualizing innovative strategies. *Strategic Management Journal*, *36*(10), 1579–1596. doi:10.1002/smj.2298

Anderson, M., & Anderson, S. L. (2007). Machine ethics: Creating an ethical, intelligent agent. *AI Magazine*, *28*(4), 15–15.

Andriole, S. J. (2017). Five myths about digital transformation. *MIT Sloan Management Review*, *58*(3), 20–22.

António, N., & Rita, P. (2021). COVID 19: The catalyst for digital transformation in the hospitality industry? *Tourism & Management Studies*, *17*(2), 41–46. doi:10.18089/tms.2021.170204

Anugwom, E. E. (2011). Women Entrepreneurs and the Niger Delta conflict. *Journal of Small Business and Entrepreneurship*, *24*(2), 243–252. doi:10.1080/08276331.2011.10593536

Aranda, D. A. (2003). Service operations strategy, flexibility, and performance in engineering consulting firms. *International Journal of Operations & Production Management*, *23*(11), 1401–1421. doi:10.1108/01443570310501907

Arshad, A. S., & Rasli, A. (2018). Innovative strategies of technology-based SMEs in Malaysia. In *Proceedings of the 2nd Advances in Business Research International Conference: ABRIC2016* (Participant 23-30). Springer Singapore. 10.1007/978-981-10-6053-3_3

Arthur, R. (2016). Macy's teams with IBM Watson for AI-powered mobile shopping assistant. *Forbes*. https://www.forbes.com/sites/rachelarthur/2016/07/20/macys-teams-with-ibmwatson-for-ai-powered-mobile-shopping-assistant/#4c4a1327f415

Arthur, W. B. (2009). *The nature of technology: What it is and how it evolves*. Simon and Schuster.

Ashurov, D. Z., Makhmudova, G., & Razakova, B. (2022). *Development of digital ecosystem and formation of digital platforms in Uzbekistan*. Research Gate.

Aspect. (2020). *Edwardian hotels London launches 'virtual host' designed by aspect software*. Aspect. https://www.aspect.com/company/news/press-releases/edwardian-hotels-londonlaunches- virtual-host-designed-by-aspect-software (accessed 20 June 2020).

Atsalakis, G. S., Atsalaki, I. G., & Zopounidis, C. (2018). Forecasting the success of a new tourism service by a neuro-fuzzy technique. *European Journal of Operational Research*, *268*(2), 716–727. doi:10.1016/j.ejor.2018.01.044

Attaran, M. (2020). Digital technology enablers and their implications for supply chain management. *Supply Chain Forum*, *21*(3), 158–172. 10.1080/16258312.2020.1751568

Attaran, M., & Woods, J. (2018). *Cloud computing technology : improving small business performance using the Internet*. Taylor & Francis. doi:10.1080/08276331.2018.1466850

Audretsch, D., & Keilbach, M. (2004). Entrepreneurship Capital and Economic Performance. *Regional Studies*, *38*(8), 949–959. doi:10.1080/0034340042000280956

Aula, P. (2010). Social media, reputation risk and ambient publicity management. *Strategy and Leadership*, *38*(6), 43–49. doi:10.1108/10878571011088069

Autio, E. (2016). Entrepreneurship Support in Europe: Trends and Challenges for EU Policy. *Report Prepared for EU DG Growth*. https://www.researchgate.net/profile/Erkko-Autio/publication/304659214_Entrepreneurship_Support_in_Europe_Trends_and_Challenges_for_EU_Policy/links/577649a408ae4645d60d5b8e/Entrepreneurship-Support-in-Europe-Trends-and-Challenges-for-EU-Policy.pdf

Awasthi, S., Bathla, D., & Singh, S. (2023). A Literature Review on H.R. Analytics: Trends and Future Challenges. Tyagi, P., Chilamkurti, N., Grima, S., Sood, K. and Balusamy, B. (Ed.) The Adoption and Effect of Artificial Intelligence on Human Resources Management, Part B. Emerald Publishing Limited. doi:10.1108/978-1-80455-662-720230014

Baas, J., Schotten, M., Plume, A., Côté, G., & Karimi, R. (2020). Scopus as a curated, high-quality bibliometric data source for academic research in quantitative science studies. *Quantitative Science Studies*, *1*(1), 377–386. doi:10.1162/qss_a_00019

Baden-Fuller, C., & Haefliger, S. (2013). Business models and technological innovation. *Long Range Planning*, *46*(6), 419–426. doi:10.1016/j.lrp.2013.08.023

Badham, M., & Mykkänen, M. (2022). A Relational Approach to How Media Engage With Their Audiences in Social Media. *Media and Communication*, *10*(1), 54–65. doi:10.17645/mac.v10i1.4409

Baek, S., Mohanty, S. K., & Glambosky, M. (2020). COVID-19 and stock market volatility: An industry level analysis. *Finance Research Letters*, *37*, 101748. doi:10.1016/j.frl.2020.101748 PMID:32895607

Baesens, B., Van Vlasselaer, V., Verbeke, W., & Vanthienen, J. (2015). Big data analytics in the fight against cybercrime. *Journal of Management Information Systems*, *32*(2), 319–346.

Bai, C., Quayson, M., & Sarkis, J. (2021). COVID-19 pandemic digitization lessons for sustainable development of micro-and small- enterprises. *Sustainable Production and Consumption*, *27*, 1989–2001. doi:10.1016/j.spc.2021.04.035 PMID:34722843

Baig, U., Hussain, B. M., Meidute-Kavaliauskiene, I., & Davidavicius, S. (2022). Digital entrepreneurship: Future research directions and opportunities for a new business model. *Sustainability (Basel)*, *14*(9), 5004. doi:10.3390/su14095004

Balasubramanian, N., Ye, Y., & Xu, M. (2022). Substituting human decision-making with machine learning: Implications for organizational learning. *Academy of Management Review*, *47*(3), 448–465. doi:10.5465/amr.2019.0470

Baldwin, C. Y., & Clark, K. B. (2003). Managing in an age of modularity. Garud, R., Kumaraswamy, A.,& Langlois, R.N.(Eds), Managing in the modular age: Architectures, networks, and organizations. (pp.149-158). Blackwell Publishing: UK.

Balsalobre-Lorente, D., Abbas, J., He, C., Pilař, L., & Shah, S. A. R. (2023). Tourism, urbanization and natural resources rents matter for environmental sustainability: The leading role of AI and ICT on sustainable development goals in the digital era. *Resources Policy*, *82*, 103445. doi:10.1016/j.resourpol.2023.103445

Banipal, I. S., Asthana, S., & Mazumder, S. (2023). Sustainable AI - Standards, Current Practices and Recommendations. In K. Arai (Ed.), *Proceedings of the Future Technologies Conference (FTC) 2023,* (*Vol. 813*, pp. 271–289). Springer Nature Switzerland. 10.1007/978-3-031-47454-5_21

Bansal, G., Rajgopal, K., Chamola, V., Xiong, Z., & Niyato, D. (2022). Healthcare in metaverse: A survey on current metaverse applications in healthcare. *IEEE Access : Practical Innovations, Open Solutions*, *10*, 119914–119946. doi:10.1109/ACCESS.2022.3219845

Barbulescu, O., Tecău, A. S., Munteanu, D., & Constantin, C. P. (2021). Innovation of startups, the key to unlocking post-crisis sustainable growth in Romanian entrepreneurial ecosystem. *Sustainability (Basel)*, *13*(2), 671. doi:10.3390/su13020671

Barik, T., & Jain, S. (2022). Employer branding and employee retention during COVID-19: A study of academic institutions. *International Journal of Human Resource Management*, *33*(11), 2505–2533.

Barney, N., & Nolle, T. (2023). Service-oriented architecture (SOA). *Tech Target.* https://www.techtarget.com/searchapparchitecture/definition/service-oriented-architecture-SOA

Barzaeva, M. & Ilyasov, R., (2022). Sustainable Development Of The Global Labor Market In The Context Of The Transformation Of The Industrial Complex Of The Digital Economy. *Reliability: Theory & Applications, 17*(70), 476-484.

Bashshur, R., Doarn, C. R., Frenk, J. M., Kvedar, J. C., Woolliscroft, J. O., & Yellowlees, P. M. (2020). Telemedicine and the COVID-19 pandemic, lessons for the future. *Telemedicine Journal and e-Health*, *26*(5), 571–573. doi:10.1089/tmj.2020.29040.rb PMID:32275485

Basiri, A., Amirian, P., Winstanley, A., & Moore, T. (2018). Making tourist guidance systems more intelligent, adaptive and personalised using crowd sourced movement data. *Journal of Ambient Intelligence and Humanized Computing*, *9*(2), 413–427. doi:10.1007/s12652-017-0550-0

Bass, B. M., & Riggio, R. E. (2006). *Transformational leadership* (2nd ed.). Psychology Press. doi:10.4324/9781410617095

Batta A, Kaur S, Jhamb R. (2022). *A literature Review on Social Media Marketing influence on Customer Relationship Management.*

Battour, M., Mady, K., Salaheldeen, M., Elsotouhy, M., Elbendary, I., & Boğan, E. (2023). AI-enabled technologies to assist Muslim tourists in Halal-friendly tourism. *Journal of Islamic Marketing*, *14*(5), 1291–1309. doi:10.1108/JIMA-01-2022-0001

Bauernhansl, T., Ten Hompel, M., & Vogel-Heuser, B. (Eds.). (2014). *Industrie 4.0 in Produktion, Automatisierung und Logistik: Anwendung-Technologien-Migration* (pp. 1–648). Springer Vieweg. doi:10.1007/978-3-658-04682-8

Baunsgaard, V. V., & Clegg, S. R. (2015). Innovation: A critical assessment of the concept and scope of literature. Agarwal, R., Selen, W., Roos, G., Green, R. (Eds). The Handbook of Service Innovation. (pp. 5-25). Springer. doi:10.1007/978-1-4471-6590-3_1

Becker, B., & Gassmann, O. (2006). Corporate incubators: Industrial R&D and what universities can learn from them. *The Journal of Technology Transfer*, *31*(4), 469–483. doi:10.1007/s10961-006-0008-6

Bejtlich, R. (2013). *The Practice of Network Security Monitoring: Understanding Incident Detection and Response*. No Starch Press.

Beketov, M., Lehmann, K., & Wittke, M. (2018). Robo Advisors: Quantitative methods inside the robots. *Journal of Asset Management*, *19*(6), 363–370. doi:10.1057/s41260-018-0092-9

Belanche, D., Casaló, L. V., & Flavián, C. (2019). Artificial Intelligence in FinTech: Understanding robo-advisors adoption among customers. *Industrial Management & Data Systems*, *119*(7), 1411–1430. doi:10.1108/IMDS-08-2018-0368

Belanche, D., Casaló, L. V., Flavián, C., & Schepers, J. (2020). Service robot implementation: A theoretical framework and research agenda. *Service Industries Journal*, *40*(3-4), 203–225. doi:10.1080/02642069.2019.1672666

Belhadi, A., Mani, V., Kamble, S. S., Khan, S. A. R., & Verma, S. (2021). Artificial intelligence-driven innovation for enhancing supply chain resilience and performance under the effect of supply chain dynamism: An empirical investigation. *Annals of Operations Research*, 1–26. PMID:33551534

Bellizzi, M. G., Eboli, L., Forciniti, C., Mazzulla, G., Grazia, M., Eboli, L., Forciniti, C., & Mazzulla, G. (2018). ScienceDirect ScienceDirect Air Transport Passengers ' Satisfaction : an Ordered Logit Air Transport Passengers ' Satisfaction : an Ordered Logit Model Model. *Transportation Research Procedia*, *33*, 147–154. doi:10.1016/j.trpro.2018.10.087

Bellizzi, M. G., Eboli, L., & Mazzulla, G. (2020). Air Transport Service Quality Factors: A Systematic Literature Review. *Transportation Research Procedia*, *45*, 218–225. doi:10.1016/j.trpro.2020.03.010

Bergek, A., & Norrman, C. (2008). Incubator best practice: A framework. *Technovation*, *28*(1/2), 20–28. doi:10.1016/j.technovation.2007.07.008

Berman, S. J. (2012). Digital transformation: Opportunities to create new business models. *Strategy and Leadership*, *40*(2), 16–24. doi:10.1108/10878571211209314

Berry, L. L. (1995). Relationship Marketing of Services—Growing Interest, Emerging Perspectives. *Journal of the Academy of Marketing Science*, *23*(4), 236–245. doi:10.1177/009207039502300402

Berry, L. L., Zeithaml, V. A., & Parasuraman, A. C. S. Q. (1990). Five imperatives for improving service quality. *MIT Sloan Management Review*, *31*(4), 29.

Bertsimas, D., & Paschalidis, I. C. (2018). The Price of Fairness. *Operations Research*, *66*(5), 1283–1300.

Bessant, J., & Davies, A. (2007). Managing service innovation. *Innovation in services, 9,* 61-96.

Bhargava, V. (2017). Are social chatbots the Future of hassle free travel? *The chatbot magazine*. https://chatbotsmagazine.com/are-social-chatbots-the-future-of-hassle-free-travel-e043c7feea93

Bhaskar, A., Yadav, P., Singh, S. P., Kumar, V., Srivastava, S., Singh, S. K., Singh, B., & Dutt, A. (2023). Role of Artificial Intelligence in Healthcare Management. In A. Garg, V. Emilia Balas, R. Pratap Ojha, & P. Kumar Srivastava (Eds.), Reinventing Technological Innovations with Artificial Intelligence (pp. 26–47). Bentham science publishers. do i:10.2174/9789815165791123010006

Bhatia, A., Chandani, A., Atiq, R., Mehta, M., & Divekar, R. (2021). Artificial intelligence in financial services: A qualitative research to discover robo-advisory services. *Qualitative Research in Financial Markets*, *13*(5), 632–654. doi:10.1108/QRFM-10-2020-0199

Bhattacharyya, D. K. (2009). *Research methodology*. Excel Books India.

Bigné, E. (2023). Artificial Intelligence in Tourism. In L. Moutinho, L. Cavique, & E. Bigné (Eds.), (pp. 98–114). Advances in Human and Social Aspects of Technology. IGI Global. doi:10.4018/978-1-6684-9591-9.ch006

Bilynets, I., Trkman, P., & Knežević Cvelbar, L. (2023). Virtual tourism experiences: Adoption factors, participation and readiness to pay. *Current Issues in Tourism*, 1–18. doi:10.1080/13683500.2023.2268809

Biney, C. O. (2018). *Impact of Venture Capital Financing on SMEs' Growth and Development in Ghana* [Doctoral dissertation, Lincoln University].

Bitner, M. J., & Wirtz, J. (2019). *Services Marketing: Integrating Customer Focus Across the Firm*. McGraw-Hill Education.

Blackburn, O., Ritala, P., & Keränen, J. (2023). Digital platforms for the circular economy: Exploring meta-organizational orchestration mechanisms. *Organization & Environment*, *36*(2), 253–281. doi:10.1177/10860266221130717

Blodgett, J. G., Granbois, D. H., & Walters, R. G. (1993). The effects of perceived justice on complainants' negative word-of-mouth behavior and repatronage intentions. *Journal of Retailing*, *69*(4), 399–428. doi:10.1016/0022-4359(93)90015-B

Blodgett, J. G., Hill, D. J., & Tax, S. S. (1997). The effects of distributive, procedural and interactional justice on post-complaint behavior. *Journal of Retailing*, *73*(2), 185–210. doi:10.1016/S0022-4359(97)90003-8

Boberskogo, I. (2023). Marketing technologies of personalization in tourism based on artificial intelligence. *Eastern Europe: Economy. Business and Management*, *2*(39). doi:10.32782/easterneurope.39-4

Boohene, R. (2018). Innovative strategies, strategic innovative strategies and performance of small family firms in the Kumasi Metropolis. *Academy of Entrepreneurship Education*, *24*(2), 501–529.

Borgschulte, M., Molitor, D., & Zou, E. Y. (2022). Air pollution and the labor market: Evidence from wildfire smoke. *The Review of Economics and Statistics*, 1–46. doi:10.1162/rest_a_01243

Boss, G., Malladi, P., Quan, D., Legregni, L., & Hall, H. (2007). Cloud computing. *IBM white paper, 321*, 224-231.

Böttcher, T. P., Phi, D. A., Flötgen, R. J., Weking, J., & Krcmar, H. (2021). What Makes an Innovative Business Model? Evidence From the 70 Most Innovative Firms. In AMCIS.

Boudreau, K. J., & Hagiu, A. (2009). *Platform rules: Multi-sided platforms as regulators*. Edward Elgar.

Bowersox, D. J., & Closs, D. J. (1974). *Logistical management*. Macmillan New York.

Boyd, D., & Crawford, K. (2012). Critical questions for big data: Provocations for a cultural, technological, and scholarly phenomenon. *Information Communication and Society*, *15*(5), 662–679. doi:10.1080/1369118X.2012.678878

Braglia, M., Gabbrielli, R., Marrazzini, L., & Padellini, L. (2022). Key Performance Indicators and Industry 4.0 - A structured approach for monitoring the implementation of digital technologies. *Procedia Computer Science, 200*(2019), 1626–1635. doi:10.1016/j.procs.2022.01.363

Brás, J., Pereira, R., & Moro, S. (2023). Intelligent Process Automation and Business Continuity: Areas for Future Research. *Information (Basel)*, *14*(2), 122. doi:10.3390/info14020122

Braun, V. & Clarke, V. (2021). *Conceptual and design thinking for thematic analysis*. doi:. doi:10/1080/2159676X.2019.1704846

Braun, A. T., Schöllhammer, O., & Rosenkranz, B. (2021). Adaptation of the business model canvas template to develop business models for the circular economy. *Procedia CIRP*, *99*, 698–702. doi:10.1016/j.procir.2021.03.093

Bresciani, S., Ferraris, A., Romano, M., & Santoro, G. (2021). Building a Digital Transformation Strategy. In *Digital Transformation Management for Agile Organizations: A Compass to Sail the Digital World* (pp. 5–27). Emerald Publishing Limited. doi:10.1108/978-1-80043-171-320211002

Brettel, M., Friederichsen, N., Keller, M., & Rosenberg, M. (2014). How virtualization, decentralization and network building change the manufacturing landscape: An Industry 4.0 Perspective. *International journal of mechanical, industrial science and engineering, 8*(1), 37-44.

Brewer, P. C., & Speh, T. W. (2000). Using the balanced scorecard to measure supply chain performance Brewer, Peter CSpeh, Thomas W. *Journal of Business Logistics*, *21*(1), 75–93.

Brill, R. (2018). *Resy is using machine learning to help restaurants turn tables more efficiently.* Food Able TV. https://www.foodabletv.com/blog/2018/6/15/resy-is-using-machine-learning-tohelp-restaurants-turn-tables-more-efficiently

Brown, S. L., & Eisenhardt, K. M. (1998). *Competing on the Edge: Strategy as Structured Chaos.* Harvard Business Press.

Brynjolfsson, E., & McAfee, A. (2014). *The Second Machine Age: Work, Progress, and Prosperity in a Time of Brilliant Technologies*. W. W. Norton & Company.

Buckley, S., Ettl, M., Jain, P., Luss, R., Petrik, M., Ravi, R. K., & Venkatramani, C. (2014). Social media and customer behavior analytics for personalized customer engagements. IBM Journal of Research and Development, 58(5/6), 7:1-7:12. doi:10.1147/JRD.2014.2344515

Buhalis, D., Harwood, T., Bogicevic, V., Viglia, G., Beldona, S., & Hofacker, C. (2019). Technological disruptions in services: Lessons from tourism and hospitality. *Journal of Service Management*, *30*(4), 484–506. doi:10.1108/JOSM-12-2018-0398

Bulchand-Gidumal, J. (2022). Impact of artificial intelligence in travel, tourism, and hospitality. In *Handbook of e-Tourism* (pp. 1943–1962). Springer International Publishing. doi:10.1007/978-3-030-48652-5_110

Bulchand-Gidumal, J., & Melián-González, S. (2020). Why are ratings so high in the sharing economy? Evidence based on guest perspectives. *Current Issues in Tourism*, *23*(10), 1248–1260. doi:10.1080/13683500.2019.1602597

Bulchand-Gidumal, J., William Secin, E., O'Connor, P., & Buhalis, D. (2023). Artificial intelligence's impact on hospitality and tourism marketing: Exploring key themes and addressing challenges. *Current Issues in Tourism*, 1–18. doi:10.1080/13683500.2023.2229480

Buli, B. M. (2017). Innovative strategies, market innovative strategies and performance of SMEs in the manufacturing industry: Evidence from Ethiopian enterprises. *Management Research Review*, *40*(3), 292–309. doi:10.1108/MRR-07-2016-0173

Burange, L. G., & Yamini, S. (2008, February). Competitiveness of firms in Indian automobile industry. In *International Conference on Transportation System Studies.* Department of Economics, University of Mumbai, Mumbai.

Burapharat, Y., Christensen, T. M., & Suthichoti, S. (2021). *How Service Quality Enhances Customer Satisfaction : A Case Study of Hybrid Airlines in Thailand.* 1–10.

Burns, J. (2016). Radisson Blu Edwardian guests can now text Edward the Chatbot for service. *Forbes.* https://www.forbes.com/sites/janetwburns/2016/05/10/radisson-blu-hotel-guestscan-now-text-edward-the-chatbot-for-service/#2f5e8ecd1e23 (accessed 10 June 2020).

Burt, C. (2018). 'Smile-to-Pay' facial recognition system now at 300 locations in China. *Biometric Update*. https://www.biometricupdate.com/201811/smile-to-pay-facial-recognition-system-now-at-300- locations-in-china.

Butt, J. (2020). *A Conceptual Framework to Support Digital Transformation in Manufacturing Using an Integrated Business Process Management Approach.*

Bygstad, B., & Dulsrud, A. (2020). *Digital ecosystems as a unit of scientific analysis. A sociological investigation.* Research Gate.

Cabanas-Abascal, A., Rodríguez-González, A., Casado-Lumbreras, C., Fernández-González, J., & Jiménez-López, D. (2013). POST-VIA: Develop Individualized Marketing Strategies for Tourists. In T. Matsuo & R. Colomo-Palacios (Eds.), *Electronic Business and Marketing. Studies in Computational Intelligence* (Vol. 484). Springer. doi:10.1007/978-3-642-37932-1_4

Caetano, M., Alves, J. P., Bispo, L., & Alves, O. (2021). *Model for measuring airport innovation* *. 1–29.

Calfas, J. (2017). You can now order Subway through Facebook. *Fortune.* https://fortune.com/ 2017/04/18/subway-order-facebook-messenger/

Caliburger. (2016). *About Flippy*. Caliburger. https://caliburger.com/flippy

Callaham, J. (2019). *What is Google Duplex and how do you use it?* Android Authority. https://www. androidauthority.com/what-is-google-duplex-869476/

Cardonha, C., Herrmann, R., & Avegliano, P. (2013). Theoretical aspects of the integrated route planning problem. *IFAC Proceedings Volumes, 46*(24), 427-432. 10.3182/20130911-3-BR-3021.00082

Carlini, N. & Wagner, D. (2017). Towards evaluating the robustness of neural networks. In *2017, the IEEE symposium on security and privacy* (pp. 39–57). IEEE.

Carson, E. (2015). Marriott Hotels use VR to connect consumers with tech and travel innovation. *Tech Republic.* https://www.techrepublic.com/article/marriott-hotels-use-vr-to-connect-consumerswith-tech-and-travel-innovation/

Castelo, N. (2019). *Blurring the line between human and machine: marketing artificial intelligence*. Columbia University.

Castelo, N., Bos, M. W., & Lehmann, D. R. (2019). Task-dependent algorithm aversion. *JMR, Journal of Marketing Research, 56*(5), 809–825. doi:10.1177/0022243719851788

Catanzaro, P. F., & Hamunen, K. (2019). Extension and Education Services: Applying Service-Dominant Logic Through Peer-to-Peer Learning. In: Hujala, T., Toppinen, A., J. Butler, B. (eds) Services in Family Forestry. World Forests, 24. Springer, Cham. doi:10.1007/978-3-030-28999-7_11

Cavoukian, A., & Castro, D. (2012). *Privacy by Design: The 7 Foundational Principles*. Information and Privacy Commissioner of Ontario.

Centeno, M. A., Nag, M., Patterson, T. S., Shaver, A., & Windawi, A. J. (2015). The emergence of global systemic risk. *Annual Review of Sociology, 41*(1), 65–85. doi:10.1146/annurev-soc-073014-112317

Centobelli, P., Cerchione, R., Esposito, E., & Shashi. (2020). Evaluating environmental sustainability strategies in freight transport and logistics industry. *Business Strategy and the Environment, 29*(3), 1563–1574. doi:10.1002/bse.2453

Chadegani, A. A., Salehi, H., Yunus, M. M., Farhadi, H., Fooladi, M., Farhadi, M., & Ebrahim, N. A. (2013). A comparison between two main academic literature collections: Web of Science and Scopus databases. *arXiv preprint arXiv:1305.0377*. Elsevier Scopus.

Chand, P. K., Kadel, N., Mittal, A., & Mantri, A. (2022). The Relationship of Organizational Ambidexterity and Organizational Virtuousness in the Automobile Industry of India. [IJSKD]. *International Journal of Sociotechnology and Knowledge Development, 14*(1), 1–20. doi:10.4018/IJSKD.301262

Chandra, A., & Chao, A. C. (2011). Growth and Evolution of high technology business incubation in China. *Human Systems Management, 30*(1-2), 55–69. doi:10.3233/HSM-2011-0739

Chandra, A., & Medrano Silva, M. A. (2012). Business Incubation in Chile: Development, Financing and Financial Services. Journal of Technology Management &Amp. *Innovation, 7*(2), 1–13. doi:10.4067/S0718-27242012000200001

Chan, M., Esteves, T., & Guo, Y. (2015). Exploring factors influencing individuals' acceptance and use of mobile devices for healthcare. *Journal of the Association for Information Systems, 16*(11), 796–822.

Char, D. S., Shah, N. H., & Magnus, D. (2018). Implementing machine learning in health care—Addressing ethical challenges. *The New England Journal of Medicine, 378*(11), 981–983. doi:10.1056/NEJMp1714229 PMID:29539284

Chengoden, R., Victor, N., Huynh-The, T., Yenduri, G., Jhaveri, R. H., Alazab, M., Bhattacharya, S., Hegde, P., Maddikunta, P. K. R., & Gadekallu, T. R. (2023). Metaverse for healthcare: A survey on potential applications, challenges and future directions. *IEEE Access : Practical Innovations, Open Solutions, 11*, 12765–12795. doi:10.1109/ACCESS.2023.3241628

Chen, I. J., & Popovich, K. (2003). Understanding Customer Relationship Management (CRM): People, Process and Technology. *Business Process Management Journal, 9*(5), 672–688. doi:10.1108/14637150310496758

Chen, L., & Wei, K. K. (2001). The impact of the individual's perceived market orientation on the acceptance of new technology. *The Journal of High Technology Management Research, 12*(2), 183–209.

Chen, X., & Kim, H. (2021). Security and reliability analysis of real-time applications in 5G network environment. *Wireless Communications and Mobile Computing, 2021*, 1–12. https://pubmed.ncbi.nlm.nih.gov/28276134/

Chen, Y. C., Lin, G., Chan, Y. H., & Shih, M. J. (2014). *Mining frequent patterns with multiple item support thresholds in tourism information databases. Technologies and Applications of Artificial Intelligence*. Springer.

Chen, Y., & Bellavitis, C. (2020). Blockchain disruption and decentralized finance: The rise of decentralized business models. *Journal of Business Venturing Insights, 13*, e00151. doi:10.1016/j.jbvi.2019.e00151

Chesbrough, H. W. (2003). *Open innovation: The new imperative for creating and profiting from technology*. Harvard Business Press.

Chin, H., Marasini, D. P., & Lee, D. (2023). Digital transformation trends in service industries. *Service Business, 17*(1), 11–36. doi:10.1007/s11628-022-00516-6

Cho, D. W., Lee, Y. H., Ahn, S. H., & Hwang, M. K. (2012). A framework for measuring the performance of service supply chain management. *Computers & Industrial Engineering, 62*(3), 801–818. doi:10.1016/j.cie.2011.11.014

Choi, B., & Choi, B. J. (2014). The effects of perceived service recovery justice on customer affection, loyalty, and word-of-mouth. *European Journal of Marketing, 48*(1/2), 108–131. doi:10.1108/EJM-06-2011-0299

Choi, J., Nazareth, D. L., & Jain, H. K. (2010). Implementing service-oriented architecture in organizations. *Journal of Management Information Systems, 26*(4), 253–286. doi:10.2753/MIS0742-1222260409

Chonsalasin, D., Jomnonkwao, S., & Ratanavaraha, V. (2020). International Journal of Transportation Measurement model of passengers ' expectations of airport service quality. *International Journal of Transportation Science and Technology, xxxx*, 1–11. doi:10.1016/j.ijtst.2020.11.001

Choo, K.-K. R. (2011). The Cyber Threat Landscape: Challenges and Future Research Directions. *Computers & Security*, *30*(8), 719–731. doi:10.1016/j.cose.2011.08.004

Choudhury, A., Behl, A., Sheorey, P. A., & Pal, A. (2021). Digital supply chain to unlock new agility: A TISM approach. *Benchmarking*, *28*(6), 2075–2109. doi:10.1108/BIJ-08-2020-0461

Chowdhury, G. G. (2003). Natural language processing. *Annual Review of Information Science & Technology*, *37*(1), 51–89. doi:10.1002/aris.1440370103

Cho, Y. H., & Lee, J. H. (2018). Innovative strategies, innovative education and performance. *Asia Pacific Journal of Innovation and Entrepreneurship*, *12*(2), 124–134. doi:10.1108/APJIE-05-2018-0028

Cichosz, M., Wallenburg, C. M., & Knemeyer, A. M. (2020). Digital transformation at logistics service providers: Barriers, success factors and leading practices. *International Journal of Logistics Management*, *31*(2), 209–238. doi:10.1108/IJLM-08-2019-0229

Cipolla Ficarra, F. V. (2011). Human-computer interaction, tourism and cultural heritage. Lecture Notes in Computer Science (including subseries Lecture Notes in Artificial Intelligence and Lecture Notes in Bioinformatics). Springer. doi:10.1007/978-3-642-18348-5_5

Cockayne, D. (2019). What is a startup firm? A methodological and epistemological investigation into research objects in economic geography. *Geoforum*, *107*, 77–87. doi:10.1016/j.geoforum.2019.10.009

Coding Env. (2023, November 5). *Service Oriented Architecture (SOA) simplified* [Video]. YouTube. https://www.youtube.com/watch?app=desktop&v=PA9RjHI463g

Collins, H. M. (2018). Expert systems, artificial intelligence, and the behavioral coordinates of skill. In *The question of artificial intelligence* (pp. 258–281). Routledge. doi:10.4324/9780429505331-6

Cook, D. J., Augusto, J. C., & Jakkula, V. R. (2009). Ambient intelligence: Technologies, applications, and opportunities. *Pervasive and Mobile Computing*, *5*(4), 277–298. doi:10.1016/j.pmcj.2009.04.001

Cooper, P. (2019). The complete guide to using Facebook messenger bots for business. *Hootsuite*. https://blog.hootsuite.com/facebook-messenger-botsguide/

Cooper, C. E., Hamel, S. A., & Connaughton, S. L. (2010). Motivations and obstacles to networking in a University Business Incubator. *The Journal of Technology Transfer*, *37*(4), 433–453. doi:10.1007/s10961-010-9189-0

Coreynen, W., Matthyssens, P., Vanderstraeten, J., & van Witteloostuijn, A. (2020). Unravelling the internal and external drivers of digital servitization: A dynamic capabilities and contingency perspective on firm strategy. *Industrial Marketing Management*, *89*, 265–277. doi:10.1016/j.indmarman.2020.02.014

Costa, D. F., Carvalho, F. D. M., & Moreira, B. C. D. M. (2019). Behavioral economics and behavioral finance: A bibliometric analysis of the scientific fields. *Journal of Economic Surveys*, *33*(1), 3–24. doi:10.1111/joes.12262

Covin, J. G., & Lumpkin, G. T. (2011). Innovative strategies theory and research: Reflections on a needed construct. *Entrepreneurship Theory and Practice*, *35*(5), 855–872. doi:10.1111/j.1540-6520.2011.00482.x

Cranor, L. F., & McDonald, A. M. (2012). Building the Future of Privacy Notices: A Survey of Plans for Change and Barriers to Change. *International Journal of Human-Computer Studies*, *70*(10), 711–722.

Crevani, L., Palm, K., & Schilling, A. (2011). Innovation management in service firms: A research agenda. *Service Business*, *5*(2), 177–193. doi:10.1007/s11628-011-0109-7

Criado-Gomis, A., Iniesta-Bonillo, M. Á., & Cervera-Taulet, A. (2018). Sustainable innovative strategies within an intrapreneurial context: Effects on business performance. *The International Entrepreneurship and Management Journal*, *14*, 295–308. doi:10.1007/s11365-018-0503-x

Crosby, M., Pattanayak, P., Verma, S., & Kalyanaraman, V. (2016). Blockchain technology: Beyond bitcoin. *Applied Innovation*, *2*(6-10), 71–81.

Cserdi, Z., & Kenesei, Z. (2021). Research in Transportation Business & Management Attitudes to forced adoption of new technologies in public transportation services. *Research in Transportation Business & Management*, *41*, 100611. doi:10.1016/j.rtbm.2020.100611

Cuellar, M. (2023). A virtue ethical approach to the use of artificial intelligence. *Data and Information Management*, 100037. doi:10.1016/j.dim.2023.100037

Cuevas-Vargas, H., Parga-Montoya, N., & Fernández-Escobedo, R. (2019). Effects of innovative strategies on business performance: The mediating role of customer satisfaction—A formative–Reflective model analysis. *SAGE Open*, *9*(2), 2158244019859088. doi:10.1177/2158244019859088

Cui, R., Li, M., & Zhang, S. (2022). A.I. and Procurement. *Manufacturing & Service Operations Management*, *24*(2), 691–706. doi:10.1287/msom.2021.0989

D'Alvano, L., & Hidalgo, A. (2012). Innovation management techniques and development degree of innovation process. *R & D Management*, *42*(1), 60–70. doi:10.1111/j.1467-9310.2011.00663.x

Danks, D., Zhao, M., & Smith, L. (2021). Algorithmic bias and ethical implications of artificial intelligence. *Journal of Technology and Human Affairs*, *41*(3), 207–220. https://dr.lib.iastate.edu/bitstreams/4ccd635c-aa0b-475e-8de1-8175fb09fff3/download

Dapp, T., & Slomka, L. AG, D. B., & Hoffmann, R. (2015). Fintech reloaded–Traditional banks as digital ecosystems. Publication of the German original, 261-274.

Davenport, T. H. (1993). *Process innovation: reengineering work through information technology*. Harvard Business Press.

Davenport, T. H., & Harris, J. (2007). *Competing on Analytics: The New Science of Winning*. Harvard Business Press.

Davenport, T. H., Harris, J., & Shapiro, J. (2010). Competing on talent analytics. *Harvard Business Review*. PMID:20929194

Davenport, T. H., & Kalakota, R. (2019). The potential for artificial intelligence in healthcare. *Future Healthcare Journal*, *6*(2), 94–98. doi:10.7861/futurehosp.6-2-94 PMID:31363513

Davenport, T., Guha, A., Grewal, D., & Bressgott, T. (2020). How artificial intelligence will change the future of marketing. *Journal of the Academy of Marketing Science*, *48*(1), 24–42. doi:10.1007/s11747-019-00696-0

Davila, F., Agha, R., & Becker, S. (2019). Robotic technology in surgery: A review. *Surgery Journal (New York, N.Y.)*, *3*(4), e189–e192.

De Brentani, U. (2001). Innovative versus incremental new business services: Different keys for achieving success. *Journal of Product Innovation Management*, *18*(3), 169–187. doi:10.1111/1540-5885.1830169

De Jong, J. P., & Vermeulen, P. A. (2003). Organizing successful new service development: a literature review. *Management decision*, *41*(9), 844-858. http://doi.org/ (" 3A < 6@0 @/ 64$

De Schutter, O., Frazer, H., Guio, A. C., & Marlier, E. (2023). How poverty is perpetuated across generations. In *The Escape from Poverty* (pp. 18–60). Policy Press. doi:10.56687/9781447370611-005

Delfanti, A. (2021). *The warehouse. Workers and robots at Amazon.* Pluto Books. doi:10.2307/j.ctv2114fnm

Deloitte. (2023). *Platform Business Model explained…in under 100 words.* Deloitte.com https://www2.deloitte.com/ch/en/pages/innovation/articles/platform-business-model-explained.html

Demir, S., Yilmaz, I., & Paksoy, T. (2020). Augmented Reality in SCM. *Logistics 4.0: Digital Transformation of Supply Chain Management*, 136.

den Hertog, P., van der Aa, W., & de Jong, M. W. (2010). Capabilities for managing service innovation: Towards a conceptual framework. *Journal of Service Management, 21*(4), 490–514. doi:10.1108/09564231011066123

Denicolai, S., Zucchella, A., & Magnani, G. (2021). Internationalization, digitalization, and sustainability: Are SMEs ready? A survey on synergies and substituting effects among growth paths. *Technological Forecasting and Social Change, 166*, 120650. doi:10.1016/j.techfore.2021.120650

Denison, D. R. (1990). *Corporate Culture and Organizational Effectiveness.* Wiley.

Department for Promotion of Industry and Internal Trade: MOCI: GOI. (2022). Department for Promotion of Industry and Internal Trade. https://dpiit.gov.in/publications/annual-report

Dewangan, V., & Godse, M. (2014). Towards a holistic enterprise innovation performance measurement system. *Technovation, 34*(9), 536–545. doi:10.1016/j.technovation.2014.04.002

Dhiman, N., Jamwal, M., & Kumar, A. (2023). Enhancing value in customer journey by considering the (ad) option of artificial intelligence tools. *Journal of Business Research, 167*, 114142. doi:10.1016/j.jbusres.2023.114142

Diaferia, L., Blohm, I., De Rossi, L.M. & Salviotti, G. (2022). *When Standard Is Not Enough: A Conceptualization of A.I. Systems' Customization and Antecedents.*

Dietvorst, B. J., Simmons, J. P., & Massey, C. (2015). Algorithm aversion: People erroneously avoid algorithms after seeing them err. *Journal of Experimental Psychology. General, 144*(1), 114–126. doi:10.1037/xge0000033 PMID:25401381

Dietvorst, B. J., Simmons, J. P., & Massey, C. (2018). Overcoming algorithm aversion: People will use imperfect algorithms if they can (even slightly) modify them. *Management Science, 64*(3), 1155–1170. doi:10.1287/mnsc.2016.2643

Ding, S., Cui, T., Wu, X., & Du, M. (2022). Supply chain management based on volatility clustering: The effect of CBDC volatility—*research in International Business and Finance, 62*, 101690.

Ding, B., Ferràs Hernández, X., & Agell Jané, N. (2023). Combining lean and agile manufacturing competitive advantages through Industry 4.0 technologies: An integrative approach. *Production Planning and Control, 34*(5), 442–458. doi:10.1080/09537287.2021.1934587

Ding, X., & Yang, Z. (2020). Knowledge mapping of platform research: A visual analysis using VOSviewer and CiteSpace. *Electronic Commerce Research*, 1–23.

Doborjeh, Z., Hemmington, N., Doborjeh, M., & Kasabov, N. (2022). Artificial intelligence: A systematic review of methods and applications in hospitality and tourism. *International Journal of Contemporary Hospitality Management, 34*(3), 1154–1176. doi:10.1108/IJCHM-06-2021-0767

Doing business 2020. (2020). World Bank. https://documents1.worldbank.org/curated/en/688761571934946384/pdf/Doing-Business-2020-Comparing-Business-Regulation-in-190-Economies.pdf

Dönmez, N. (2022). Metaverse bankaciliği yolunda değişen müşteri beklentilerine hitaben gelişen pazarlama anlayişlari üzerine bir inceleme. *Uluslararası Bankacılık Ekonomi ve Yönetim Araştırmaları Dergisi, 5*(1), 97–132. doi:10.52736/ubeyad.1119156

Donthu, N., Kumar, S., Mukherjee, D., Pandey, N., & Lim, W. M. (2021). How to conduct a bibliometric analysis: An overview and guidelines. *Journal of Business Research*, *133*, 285–296. doi:10.1016/j.jbusres.2021.04.070

Dremel, C., Herterich, M. M., Wulf, J., Waizmann, J.-C., & Brenner, W. (2017). How AUDI AG established big data analytics in its digital transformation. *MIS Quarterly Executive*, *16*(2), 81–100.

Duleepa, D., Hasini, J., & Ruwan, R. (2023). Potentials of developing artificial intelligence technology in the sri lankan hotel industry with special reference to colombo district. *cactus, 5*(1). doi:10.24818/CTS/5/2023/1.04

Durmaz, Y., Güvenç, H., & Kaymaz, S. (2020). The Importance and Benefits of Relationship Marketing Concept. *European Journal of Business and Management Research*, *5*(4), 4–5. doi:10.24018/ejbmr.2020.5.4.483

Dutta, K., Venkatesh, U., & Parsa, H. G. (2007). Service failure and recovery strategies in the restaurant sector: An Indo-US comparative study. *International Journal of Contemporary Hospitality Management*, *19*(5), 351–363. doi:10.1108/09596110710757526

Duyên, P., Công, L., & Duy, N. (2022). The impact of social media marketing on customer loyalty using telecommunications services in Vietnam. *Science & Technology Development Journal: Economics- Law & Management, 6*(2), 2516-2529. https://doi.org/https://doi.org/10.32508/stdjelm.v6i1.916

Edström, A., Nylander, B., Molin, J., Ahmadi, Z., & Sörqvist, P. (2022). Where service recovery meets its paradox: Implications for avoiding overcompensation. *Journal of Service Theory and Practice*, *32*(7), 1–13. doi:10.1108/JSTP-06-2021-0120

Edwards, D., & Griffin, T. (2013). Understanding tourists' spatial behaviour: GPS tracking as an aid to sustainable destination management. *Journal of Sustainable Tourism*, *21*(4), 580–595. doi:10.1080/09669582.2013.776063

Einav, L., Farronato, C., & Levin, J. (2016). Peer-to-peer markets. *Annual Review of Economics*, *8*(1), 615–635. doi:10.1146/annurev-economics-080315-015334

Ejem, E. A. (2020). *Assessment of Airport Service Quality in Nigeria. December 2020.*

Enoch, M., Potter, S., Parkhurst, G., & Smith, M. (2004). *Internode: Innovations in Demand Responsive Transport.* Department for Transport and Greater Manchester Passenger Transport Executive.

Entenam, K., & Ahmed, U. (2014). Cloud Computing for Enterprise Architectures. *Identity and Access Management in Cloud Computing*, (May). doi:10.1007/978-1-4471-2236-4

Epperson, T., Hedges, B., Singh, U., & Gabel, M. A. T. (2015). Kearney 2015 Robo-Advisory Services Study. AT Kearney: Bucures,ti, Romania.

Escalante, J., Pack, A., & Barrett, A. (2023). AI-generated feedback on writing: Insights into efficacy and ENL student preference. *International Journal of Educational Technology in Higher Education*, *20*(1), 57. doi:10.1186/s41239-023-00425-2

Eshima, Y., & Anderson, B. S. (2017). Firm growth, adaptive capability, and innovative innovative stratagies. *Strategic Management Journal*, *38*(3), 770–779. doi:10.1002/smj.2532

Essen, A., Frishammar, J., & Cenamor, J. (2023). Entering non-platformized sectors: The co-evolution of legitimacy debates and platform business models in digital health care. *Technovation*, *121*, 102597. doi:10.1016/j.technovation.2022.102597

Establishment of Atal Innovation Mission and Self Employment and talent utilisation in Niti Aayog . (2016). PIB. https://www.pib.gov.in/newsite/PrintRelease.aspx?relid=136754

Esteva, A., Kuprel, B., Novoa, R. A., Ko, J., Swetter, S. M., Blau, H. M., & Thrun, S. (2017). Dermatologist-level classification of skin cancer with deep neural networks. *Nature*, *542*(7639), 115–118. doi:10.1038/nature21056 PMID:28117445

Etemad, H. (2023). The increasing prevalence of multi-sided online platforms and their influence on international entrepreneurship: The rapid transformation of entrepreneurial digital ecosystems. *Journal of International Entrepreneurship*, *21*(1), 1–30. doi:10.1007/s10843-023-00331-8

ETIPS. (2020). *Augmented reality*. eTips. https://etips.com/#augmented-reality

Evans, D. S., Hagiu, A., & Schmalensee, R. (2008). *Invisible engines: How software platforms drive innovation and transform industries*. The MIT Press.

Farchi, F., Farchi, C., Touzi, B., & Mabrouki, C. (2023). A comparative study on AI-based algorithms for cost prediction in pharmaceutical transport logistics. *Acadlore Trans. Mach. Learn*, *2*(3), 129–141. doi:10.56578/ataiml020302

Fehrer, J. A., Woratschek, H., & Brodie, R. J. (2018). A systemic logic for platform business models. *Journal of Service Management*, *29*(4), 546–568. doi:10.1108/JOSM-02-2017-0036

Ferguson, N., & Schneier, B. (2003). *Practical Cryptography*. Wiley Publishing.

Fernando, Y., Chidambaram, R. R. M., & Wahyuni-TD, I. S. (2018). The impact of Big Data analytics and data security practices on service supply chain performance. *Benchmarking*, *25*(9), 4009–4034. doi:10.1108/BIJ-07-2017-0194

Ferreira, R. P., Vilarinho, L. O., & Scotti, A. (2023). Enhanced-pixel strategy for wire arc additive manufacturing trajectory planning: Operational efficiency and effectiveness analyses. *Rapid Prototyping Journal*, *30*(11), 1–15. doi:10.1108/RPJ-12-2022-0413

Figueroa, R. B. Jr. (2023). Immersive capability and spatial presence in virtual reality photo-based tours: Implications for distance education. *Asian Association of Open Universities Journal*, *18*(3), 201–217. doi:10.1108/AAOUJ-12-2022-0171

Filieri, R., D'Amico, E., Destefanis, A., Paolucci, E., & Raguseo, E. (2021). Artificial intelligence (AI) for tourism: A European-based study on successful AI tourism start-ups. *International Journal of Contemporary Hospitality Management*, *33*(11), 4099–4125. doi:10.1108/IJCHM-02-2021-0220

Finotto V. & Micelli S. (2010). Web e made in Italy: La terra di mezzo della comunicazione d'impresa. *Mercati e Competitività*, (4), 101–119.

Fisch, J. E., Labouré, M., & Turner, J. A. (2018). The Emergence of the Robo-Advisor. *Pension Research Council Working Papers*. Wharton School Pension Research Council, University of Pennsylvania. https://repository.upenn.edu/prc_papers/10

Fitzgerald, M., Kruschwitz, N., Bonnet, D., & Welch, M. (2014). Embracing digital technology: A new strategic imperative. *MIT Sloan Management Review*, *55*(2), 1.

Fitzsimmons, J. A., & Fitzsimmons, M. J. (2013). *Service Management: Operations, Strategy, Information Technology*. McGraw-Hill Education.

Fitzsimmons, J., & Fitzsimmons, M. J. (1999). *New service development: creating memorable experiences*. Sage Publications.

Flavián, C., & Casaló, L. V. (2021). Artificial intelligence in services: Current trends, benefits and challenges. *Service Industries Journal*, *41*(13-14), 853–859. doi:10.1080/02642069.2021.1989177

Fleming, A. (1929). On the Antibacterial Action of Cultures of a Penicillium, with Special Reference to Their Use in the Isolation of B. influenzae. *British Journal of Experimental Pathology*, *10*(3), 226–236.

Flood, D., West, T., & Wheadon, D. (2013). Trends in mobile payments in developing and advanced economies. *Bulletin, 2013*, 71–80.

Floridi, L. (2013). *The Ethics of Information*. Oxford University Press. doi:10.1093/acprof:oso/9780199641321.001.0001

Fogel, G. B., & Bonissone, P. (2023). Conference Report on the Inaugural 2023 IEEE Conference on Artificial Intelligence (IEEE CAI 2023) [Conference Reports]. *IEEE Computational Intelligence Magazine, 18*(4), 5–7. 10.1109/MCI.2023.3306149

Ford, R. C., & Sturman, M. C. (2018). *Managing hospitality organizations: Achieving excellence in the guest experience*. SAGE Publications.

Fox, G. (2001). Peer-to-peer networks. *Computing in Science & Engineering, 3*(3), 75–77. doi:10.1109/5992.919270

Frisch, P. H. (2019, September). RFID in today's intelligent hospital enhances patient care and optimizes hospital operations. In *2019, the IEEE International Conference on RFID Technology and Applications (RFID-TA)* (pp. 458-463). IEEE.

Frow, P., Nenonen, S., Payne, A., & Storbacka, K. (2015). Managing co-creation design: A strategic approach to innovation. *British Journal of Management, 26*(3), 463–483. doi:10.1111/1467-8551.12087

Furlong, L. I., Morris, M. E., & Serry, T. (2015). Remote monitoring of Parkinson's disease using inertial sensors. *IEEE Journal of Biomedical and Health Informatics, 19*(6), 1802–1810.

Fu, W., Wang, Q., & Zhao, X. (2018). Platform-based service innovation and system design: Research opportunities. *Industrial Management & Data Systems, 118*(5), 975–997. doi:10.1108/IMDS-03-2017-0130

Fu, X., Ghauri, P., Ogbonna, N., & Xing, X. (2023). Platform-based business model and entrepreneurs from Base of the Pyramid. *Technovation, 119*, 102451. doi:10.1016/j.technovation.2021.102451

G2. (2023). *Best Digital Customer Service Platforms*. G2.com. https://www.g2.com/categories/digital-customer-service-platforms

Gadrey, J., Gallouj, F., & Weinstein, O. (1995). New modes of innovation: How services benefit the industry. *International Journal of Service Industry Management, 6*(3), 4–16. doi:10.1108/09564239510091321

Galaz, V., Centeno, M. A., Callahan, P. W., Causevic, A., Patterson, T., Brass, I., Baum, S., Farber, D., Fischer, J., Garcia, D., McPhearson, T., Jimenez, D., King, B., Larcey, P., & Levy, K. (2021). Artificial intelligence, systemic risks, and sustainability. *Technology in Society, 67*, 101741. doi:10.1016/j.techsoc.2021.101741

Galbreath, J., Lucianetti, L., Thomas, B., & Tisch, D. (2020). Innovative strategies and firm performance in Italian firms: The moderating role of competitive strategy. *International Journal of Innovative Behavior & Research, 26*(4), 629–646.

Gallo, P., Gallo, P. Jr, Timková, V., Šenková, A., & Karahuta, M. (2018). Use of dashboards in predicting the development of the company using neural networks in hotel management. *Geo Journal of Tourism and Geosites, 22*(2), 307–316.

Gallouj, F., & Savona, M. (2009). Innovation in services: A review of the debate and a research agenda. *Journal of Evolutionary Economics, 19*(2), 149–172. doi:10.1007/s00191-008-0126-4

Gallouj, F., & Weinstein, O. (1997). Innovation in services. *Research Policy, 26*(4-5), 537–556. doi:10.1016/S0048-7333(97)00030-9

Gamanyuk, A. (2017). *Restaurant table reservation chatbot for Facebook bootmaker*. Botmakers. https://blog.botmakers.net/table-eservation-chatbot-for-restaurants 8fb0cf8bd1aa

Gandomi, A., & Haider, M. (2015). Beyond the hype: Big data concepts, methods, and analytics. *International Journal of Information Management*, *35*(2), 137–144. doi:10.1016/j.ijinfomgt.2014.10.007

Ganeshan, M. K. (2021). New Agriculture Technology in Modern Farming. *International Journal of Management Research and Social Science (IJMRSS) ISSN 2394-6407(Print)*, *8*(3).

Garavand, A., & Aslani, N. (2022). Metaverse phenomenon and its impact on health: A scoping review. *Informatics in Medicine Unlocked*, *32*, 101029. doi:10.1016/j.imu.2022.101029

García-Pablos, A., Cuadros, M., & Linaza, M. T. (2016). Automatic analysis of textual hotel reviews. *Information Technology & Tourism*, *16*(1), 45–69. doi:10.1007/s40558-015-0047-7

Garcia, S., Gutierrez, R., & Barbero, E. (2023). User experience and inclusivity in augmented reality applications: A human-centered design approach. *Interacting with Computers*, *35*(2), 319334. https://www.researchgate.net/publication/337160678_User_Experience_Design_With_Augmented_Reality_AR

Gasparini, A. A., & Kautonen, H. (2023). Determinants of using AI-powered discovery services. *Septentrio Conference Series*, *1*(1). doi:10.7557/5.7164

Gawer, A., & Cusumano, M. A. (2014). Industry platforms and ecosystem innovation. *Journal of Product Innovation Management*, *31*(3), 417–433. doi:10.1111/jpim.12105

Gayathiri, R., Ramakrishnan, L., Babatunde, S. A., Banerjee, A., & Islam, M. Z. (2013). Quality of work life–Linkage with job satisfaction and performance. *International Journal of Business and Management Invention*, *2*(1), 1–8.

Gerth, A. B., & Peppard, J. (2016). The dynamics of CIO derailment: How CIOs come undone and how to avoid it. *Business Horizons*, *59*(1), 61–70. doi:10.1016/j.bushor.2015.09.001

Gherhes, C., Williams, N., Vorley, T., & Vasconcelos, A. C. (2016). Distinguishing micro-businesses from SMEs: A systematic review of growth constraints. *Journal of Small Business and Enterprise Development*, *23*(4), 939–963. doi:10.1108/JSBED-05-2016-0075

Ghouse, S. M., Duffett, R. G., & Chaudhary, M. (2022). How Twitter advertising influences the purchase intentions and purchase attitudes of Indian millennial consumers? *International Journal of Internet Marketing and Advertising*, *16*(1-2), 142–164. doi:10.1504/IJIMA.2022.120973

Gilchrist, K. (2017). Alibaba launches 'smile to pay' facial recognition system at KFC in China. CNBC. https://www.cnbc.com/2017/09/04/alibaba-launches-smile-to-pay-facial-recognitionsystem- at-kfc-china.html (accessed 11 June 2020).

Ginting, N. C. A., Sianturi, M., & Ariesa, Y. (2023). The influence of service quality and price on guest loyalty during the COVID-19 pandemic with guest satisfaction as an intervening variable at Hotel Grand Cityhall Medan. *Priviet Social Sciences Journal*, *3*(7), 1–8. doi:10.55942/pssj.v3i7.227

Gitas, G., Hanker, L., Rody, A., Ackermann, J., & Alkatout, I. (2022). Robotic surgery in gynecology: Is the future already here? *Minimally Invasive Therapy & Allied Technologies*, *31*(6), 815–824. doi:10.1080/13645706.2021.2010763 PMID:34989636

Gobble, M. M. (2018). Digitalization, digitization, and innovation. *Research Technology Management*, *61*(4), 56–59. doi:10.1080/08956308.2018.1471280

Goktan, A. B., & Gupta, V. K. (2015). Sex, gender, and individual innovative strategies: Evidence from four countries. *The International Entrepreneurship and Management Journal*, *11*, 95–112. doi:10.1007/s11365-013-0278-z

Gölzer, P., & Fritzsche, A. (2017). Data-driven operations management: Organisational implications of the digital transformation in industrial practice. *Production Planning and Control*, *28*(16), 1332–1343. doi:10.1080/09537287.2017.1375148

Gomber, P., Kauffman, R. J., Parker, C., & Weber, B. W. (2018). Financial information systems and the fintech revolution. *Journal of Management Information Systems*, *35*(1), 12–18. doi:10.1080/07421222.2018.1440778

Google. (2020). *Access the Google assistant with your voice*. Google. https://support.google.com/assistant/answer/7394306?co5GENIE.Platform%3DAndroid&hl5en

Gosjen, D. I., Haryadi, K. H., Nicholas, Gunawan, A. A. S., Djuwita, C. M., & Adiati, M. P. (2023). Implementation e-concierge in hotel. *Procedia Computer Science*, *216*, 485–498. doi:10.1016/j.procs.2022.12.161

Gössling, S. (2020). Technology, ICT and tourism: From big data to the big picture. *Journal of Sustainable Tourism*, *29*(5), 849–858. doi:10.1080/09669582.2020.1865387

Goyal, J., Singh, M., Singh, R., & Aggarwal, A. (2019). Efficiency and technology gaps in Indian banking sector: Application of meta-frontier directional distance function DEA approach. *The Journal of finance and data science, 5*(3), 156-172.

Graham, J. (2018). Hamburger-making robot Flippy is back at Calif. chain. *USA Today*. https://www. usatoday.com/story/tech/talkingtech/2018/05/28/hamburger-making-robot-flippy-back-serving- 300-burgers-day/649370002/

Grant Thornton and Assocham India. (2016). *Startups India – An Overview*. Grant Thornton and Assocham. https://www.grantthornton.in/ globalassets/1.-member-firms/india/assets/pdfs/grant_thornton-startups _report.pdf

Graseck, B. L. (2020). *Wealth Management After the Storm*. MORGAN STANLEY & OLIVER WYMAN.

Gray, P., El Sawy, O. A., Asper, G., & Thordarson, M. (2013). Realizing strategic value through center-edge digital transformation in consumer-centric industries. *MIS Quarterly Executive*, *12*(1), 1–17.

Greenleaf, G., & Waters, N. (2017). The EU General Data Protection Regulation: What Change Will It Bring? *International Data Privacy Law*, *7*(2), 122–145.

Grennan, J., & Michaely, R. (2021). Fintechs and the market for financial analysis. *Journal of Financial and Quantitative Analysis*, *56*(6), 1877–1907. doi:10.1017/S0022109020000721

Grönroos, C. (1988). Service quality: The six criteria of good perceived service quality. *Review of Business*, *9*(3), 10–13.

Grönroos, C. (2004). The relationship marketing process: Communication, interaction, dialogue, value. *Journal of Business and Industrial Marketing*, *19*(2), 99–113. doi:10.1108/08858620410523981

Grönroos, C. (2007). *Service Management and Marketing: Customer Management in Service Competition*. John Wiley & Sons.

Gruber-Muecke, T., & Hofer, K. M. (2015). Market innovative strategies, innovative innovative strategies and performance in emerging markets. *International Journal of Emerging Markets*, *10*(3), 560–571. doi:10.1108/IJoEM-05-2013-0076

Grundner, L., & Neuhofer, B. (2021). The bright and dark sides of artificial intelligence: A futures perspective on tourist destination experiences. *Journal of Destination Marketing & Management*, *19*, 100511. doi:10.1016/j.jdmm.2020.100511

Gubbi, J., Buyya, R., Marusic, S., & Palaniswami, M. (2013). Internet of Things (IoT): A Vision, Architectural Elements, and Future Directions. *Future Generation Computer Systems*, *29*(7), 1645–1660. doi:10.1016/j.future.2013.01.010

Gumasing, M. J. J., Iii, E. T. G., & Marquez, M. Y. M. (2020). *A Service Quality Model for Bureau of Immigration in NAIA Terminal 1*. 1065–1069.

Gunasekaran, A., & Ngai, E. W. T. (2005). Build-to-order supply chain management: A literature review and framework for development. *Journal of Operations Management, 23*(5), 423–451. doi:10.1016/j.jom.2004.10.005

Gunasekaran, A., Patel, C., & McGaughey, R. E. (2004). A framework for supply chain performance measurement. *International Journal of Production Economics, 87*(3), 333–347. doi:10.1016/j.ijpe.2003.08.003

Gunasekaran, A., Patel, C., & Tirtiroglu, E. (2001). Performance measures and metrics in a supply chain environment. *International Journal of Operations & Production Management, 21*(1/2), 71–87. doi:10.1108/01443570110358468

Gündüz, C. (2023). Customised Holiday Experiences through Artificial Intelligence: Case Studies from the Aviation and Hospitality Sectors. *Journal of Aviation, 7*(3), 337–345. doi:10.30518/jav.1351472

Gupta, D., Wadhwa, S., & Moudgil, A. (2021, September). Deploying blockchain based security solutions for vehicular edge computing networks. In *2021 9th International Conference on Reliability, Infocom Technologies and Optimization (Trends and Future Directions)(ICRITO)* (pp. 1-5). IEEE. hip-shortage/?sh=78b9cb788b42

Gupta, M., Khan, F., & Gupta, N. (2021). The influence of employer branding experience on corporate citizenship behavior: The mediating role of employee engagement. *Journal of Business Ethics, 168*(3), 583–602.

Gupta, R., Mejia, C., & Kajikawa, Y. (2019). Business, innovation and digital ecosystems landscape survey and knowledge cross sharing. *Technological Forecasting and Social Change, 147*, 100–109. doi:10.1016/j.techfore.2019.07.004

Gupta, S., Lehmann, D. R., & Stuart, J. A. (2004). Valuing customers. *JMR, Journal of Marketing Research, 41*(1), 7–18. doi:10.1509/jmkr.41.1.7.25084

Gupta, V. K., & Batra, S. (2016). Innovative strategies and firm performance in Indian SMEs: Universal and contingency perspectives. *International Small Business Journal, 34*(5), 660–682. doi:10.1177/0266242615577708

Haaker, T., Ly, P. T. M., Nguyen-Thanh, N., & Nguyen, H. T. H. (2021). Business model innovation through the application of the Internet-of-Things: A comparative analysis. *Journal of Business Research, 126*, 126–136. doi:10.1016/j.jbusres.2020.12.034

Hackett, M., & Dilts, D. M. (2004). A systematic review of business incubation research. *The Journal of Technology Transfer, 29*(1), 55–82. doi:10.1023/B:JOTT.0000011181.11952.0f

Hagberg, J., Sundstrom, M., & Egels-Zandén, N. (2016). The digitalization of retailing: An exploratory framework. *International Journal of Retail & Distribution Management, 44*(7), 694–712. doi:10.1108/IJRDM-09-2015-0140

Hagiu, A. (2014). Strategic decisions for multisided platforms. *MIT Sloan Management Review, 55*(2), 71.

Haleem, A., Javaid, M., Singh, R. P., Suman, R., & Rab, S. (2021). *Blockchain technology applications in healthcare: An overview*. International Journal of Intelligent Networks.

Halpern, N., & Mwesiumo, D. (2021). Research in Transportation Business & Management Airport service quality and passenger satisfaction : The impact of service failure on the likelihood of promoting an airport online. *Research in Transportation Business & Management, 41*(May), 100667. doi:10.1016/j.rtbm.2021.100667

Halstead, D., Morash, E. A., & Ozment, J. (1996). Comparing objective service failure and subjective complaints: An investigation of domino and halo effects. *Journal of Business Research, 36*(2), 107–115. doi:10.1016/0148-2963(95)00170-0

Hamelin, N., & Chaudhary, M. (2023). Assessing the Impact of Sustainability News Clips on Fast-Fashion Brands Purchase Intention: A Neuromarketing Study. In Luxury Marketing, Sustainability and Technology (pp. 116-134). Routledge. doi:10.4324/9781003321378-7

Hamilton, D., McKechnie, J., Edgerton, E., & Wilson, C. (2021). Immersive virtual reality as a pedagogical tool in education: A systematic literature review of quantitative learning outcomes and experimental design. *Journal of Computers in Education*, *8*(1), 1–32. doi:10.1007/s40692-020-00169-2

Hanelt, A., Bohnsack, R., Marz, D., & Antunes Marante, C. (2021). A Systematic Review of the Literature on Digital Transformation. *Journal of Management Studies*, *58*(July), 1159–1197. doi:10.1111/joms.12639

Hang, H. and Chen, Z., 2022. How do we realize artificial intelligence's (A.I.) full potential in the digital economy? A literature review. *Journal of Digital Economy*.

Hansen, M. T., Chesbrough, H. W., Nohria, N., & Sull, D. N. (2000). Networked incubators—Hothouses of the new economy. *Harvard Business Review*, *78*(5), 74. PMID:11143156

Hansen, R., & Sia, S. K. (2015). Hummel's digital transformation toward omnichannel retailing: Key lessons learned. *MIS Quarterly Executive*, *14*(2), 51–66.

Hao, J. X., Yu, Y., Law, R., & Fong, D. K. C. (2015). A genetic algorithm-based learning approach to understand customer satisfaction with OTA websites. *Tourism Management*, *48*, 231–241. doi:10.1016/j.tourman.2014.11.009

Harrington, R. J., & Ottenbacher, M. C. (2009). Decision-making tactics and contextual features: Strategic, tactical and operational implications. *International Journal of Hospitality & Tourism Administration*, *10*(1), 25–43. doi:10.1080/15256480802557259

Harrison, R., Fischer, S., Walpola, R. L., Chauhan, A., Babalola, T., Mears, S., Le-dao, H., Harrison, R., Fischer, S., Walpola, R. L., & Chauhan, A. (2022). Where Do Models for Change Management, Improvement and Implementation Meet? *A Systematic Review of the Applications of Change Management Models in Healthcare*. IEEE. 10.2147/JHL.S289176

Hart, C., Heskett, J. L., & Sasser, W. E. (2003). The profitable art of service recovery. *Harvard Business Review*, *81*(7), 148–156. PMID:10106796

Harvey, J., Lefebvre, L. A., & Lefebvre, E. (1997). Flexibility and technology in services: A conceptual model. *International Journal of Operations & Production Management*, *17*(1), 29–45. doi:10.1108/01443579710157970

Hasselfeld, B. W. (2023). *Benefits of Telemedicine*. Hopkins Medicine. https://www.hopkinsmedicine.org/health/treatment-tests-and-therapies/benefits-of-telemedicine

Hatwar, P. N., Patil, A., & Gondane, D. (2016). AI based chatbot. *International Journal of Emerging Trends in Engineering and Basic Sciences*. Hello Hipmunk. https://www.hipmunk.com/hello

Haux, R. (2006). Health information systems—Past, present, future. *International Journal of Medical Informatics*, *75*(3–4), 268–281. doi:10.1016/j.ijmedinf.2005.08.002 PMID:16169771

Helbing, D. (2013). Globally networked risks and how to respond. *Nature*, *497*(7447), 51–59. doi:10.1038/nature12047 PMID:23636396

Helfat, C. E., & Raubitschek, R. S. (2018). Dynamic and integrative capabilities for profiting from innovation in digital platform-based ecosystems. *Research Policy*, *47*(8), 1391–1399. doi:10.1016/j.respol.2018.01.019

Hennessey, J. (2013). Location Technologies: Risks and Threats to Privacy. *The Journal of Privacy and Confidentiality*, *5*(2), 51–68.

Hennig-Thurau, T., Gwinner, K. P., & Gremier, D. D. (2002). Understanding relationship marketing outcomes: An integration of relational benefits and relationship quality. *Journal of Service Research*, *4*(3), 230–247. doi:10.1177/1094670502004003006

Henry, M., Bauwens, T., Hekkert, M., & Kirchherr, J. (2020). A typology of circular start-ups: An analysis of 128 circular business models. *Journal of Cleaner Production*, *245*, 118528. doi:10.1016/j.jclepro.2019.118528

Herlinawati, E., Ahman, E., & Machmud, A. (2019). The effect of innovative strategies on SMEs business performance in Indonesia. *Journal of Entrepreneurship Education*, *22*(5), 1–15.

Hermann, M., Pentek, T., & Otto, B. (2016, January). Design principles for industries 4.0 scenarios. In *2016 49th Hawaii international conference on system sciences (HICSS)* (pp. 3928-3937). IEEE.

Heskett, J. L., Sasser, W. E., & Schlesinger, L. A. (1997). *The Service Profit Chain*. Free Press.

Hess, T. J., McNab, A. L., & Basoglu, K. S. (2016). Reliability generalization of perceived ease of use, perceived usefulness, and behavioural intentions. *International Journal of Management Studies*, *5*(12), 401–433.

Hess, T., Benlian, A., Matt, C., & Wiesböck, F. (2016). Options for formulating a digital transformation strategy. *MIS Quarterly Executive*, *15*(2), 123–139.

Hinings, B., Gegenhuber, T., & Greenwood, R. (2018). Digital innovation and transformation: An institutional perspective. *Information and Organization*, *28*(1), 52–61. doi:10.1016/j.infoandorg.2018.02.004

Hinze, A., & Quan, Q. (2009). Trust- and location-based recommendations for tourism. Lecture Notes in Computer Science (including subseries Lecture Notes in Artificial Intelligence and Lecture Notes in Bioinformatics. Springer. doi:10.1007/978-3-642-05148-7_31

Hoch, N. B., & Brad, S. (2021). Managing business model innovation: An innovative approach towards designing a digital ecosystem and multi-sided platform. *Business Process Management Journal*, *27*(2), 415–438. doi:10.1108/BPMJ-01-2020-0017

Holley, P. (2019). Domino's will start delivering pizzas via an autonomous robot this fall. *Washington Post*. https://www.washingtonpost.com/technology/2019/06/17/dominos-will-start-delivering-pizzasvia- an-autonomous-robot-this-fall/

Holmes, W., Persson, J., Chounta, I. A., Wasson, B., & Dimitrova, V. (2022). *Artificial intelligence and education: A critical view of human rights, democracy and the rule of law*. Council of Europe.

Holmes, W., & Porayska-Pomsta, K. (Eds.). (2022). *The Ethics of Artificial Intelligence in education: Practices, challenges, and debates*. Taylor & Francis. doi:10.4324/9780429329067

Holmes, W., Porayska-Pomsta, K., Holstein, K., Sutherland, E., Baker, T., Shum, S. B., Santos, O. C., Rodrigo, M. T., Cukurova, M., Bittencourt, I. I., & Koedinger, K. R. (2021). Ethics of A.I. in education: Towards a community-wide framework. *International Journal of Artificial Intelligence in Education*, 1–23.

Holsapple, C. W., & Wu, J. (2011). Modeling customer knowledge for customer relationship management. *Decision Support Systems*, *51*(4), 1064–1074.

Hong, S., Choi, D., & Chae, J. (2020). Journal of Retailing and Consumer Services Exploring di ff erent airport users ' service quality satisfaction between service providers and air travelers. *Journal of Retailing and Consumer Services*, *52*(April 2019), 101917. doi:10.1016/j.jretconser.2019.101917

Hooi, H. C., Ahmad, N. H., Amran, A., & Rahman, S. A. (2016). The functional role of innovative strategies and innovative bricolage in ensuring sustainable entrepreneurshiParticipant. *Management Research Review*, *39*(12), 1616–1638. doi:10.1108/MRR-06-2015-0144

Hossain, M. U., & Al Asheq, A. (2019). The role of innovative strategies to SME performance in Bangladesh. *International Journal of Entrepreneurship*, *23*(1), 1–6.

Hu, B. (2014). Linking business models with technological innovation performance through organizational learning. *European Management Journal, 32*(4), 587-595.https://doi.org/ rights and content doi:10.1016/j.emj.2013.10.009Get

Huang, A., Chao, Y., de la Mora Velasco, E., Bilgihan, A., & Wei, W. (2022). When artificial intelligence meets the hospitality and tourism industry: An assessment framework to inform theory and management. *Journal of Hospitality and Tourism Insights*, *5*(5), 1080–1100. doi:10.1108/JHTI-01-2021-0021

Huang, H. C. (2013). The construction of a visitor number forecasting model for the Shihmen reservoir recreation area using artificial intelligence technology. *Journal of Theoretical and Applied Information Technology*, *54*(1), 4–19.

Hu, H., & Li, C. (2023). Smart tourism products and services design based on user experience under the background of big data. *Soft Computing*, *27*(17), 12711–12724. doi:10.1007/s00500-023-08851-0

Hussain, J., Rahman, W., & Shah, F. A. (2016). Market innovative strategies and performance: The interaction effect of innovative strategies. [PJCSS]. *Pakistan Journal of Commerce and Social Sciences*, *10*(2), 388–403.

Hutter, F., Kotthoff, L., & Vanschoren, J. (2019). *Automated machine learning: methods, systems, challenges*. Springer Nature. doi:10.1007/978-3-030-05318-5

IBM Institute for Business Value and Oxford Economics. (2016). *Entrepreneurial India: how startups redefine India's economic growth*. IBM. https://d1iydh3qrygeij.cloudfront.net/Media/Default/New%20release%20images%20and%20reports/Entrepreneurial%20India%20IBV%20mid%202016

IBM. (2016). *IBM-Wayblazer*. IBM. https://www.ibm.com/case-studies/g754268s52509l83.

IBM. (2021). *SOA vs. Microservices: What's the Difference?* IBM.com. https://www.ibm.com/blog/soa-vs-microservices/?mhsrc=ibmsearch_a&mhq=soa

Institute of Medicine (U.S.) Committee on Monitoring Access to Personal Health Care Services. (1993). *Access to health care in America* (M. Millman, Ed.). National Academies Press.

Io, H. N., & Lee, C. B. (2020). Social media comments about hotel robots. *Journal of China Tourism Research*, *16*(4), 606–625. doi:10.1080/19388160.2020.1769785

Irene, C. C. C., Chen, Z., & Leung, D. (2023). The more the better? Strategizing visual elements in social media marketing. *Journal of Hospitality and Tourism Management, 54.*

Ivanov, S., & Webster, C. (2019). Perceived appropriateness and intention to use service robots in tourism. In *Information and Communication Technologies in Tourism 2019: Proceedings of the International Conference in Nicosia,* (pp. 237-248). Springer International Publishing. 10.1007/978-3-030-05940-8_19

Ivanov, D., Dolgui, A., & Sokolov, B. (2019). The impact of digital technology and Industry 4.0 on the ripple effect and supply chain risk analytics. *International Journal of Production Research*, *57*(3), 829–846. doi:10.1080/00207543.2018.1488086

Ivanov, D., Dolgui, A., & Sokolov, B. (2022). Cloud supply chain: Integrating Industry 4.0 and digital platforms in the "Supply Chain-as-a-Service.". *Transportation Research Part E, Logistics and Transportation Review*, *160*, 102676. doi:10.1016/j.tre.2022.102676

IVCA-EY. (2019). Year-to-date PE/VC investments in India at a new all-time high of US$36.7 billion: *IVCA-EY Report.* EY. https://www.ey.com/en_in/news/2019/09/year-to-date-pe-vc-investments-in-india-at-new-all-time-high-of-us-dollar-36-7-billion-ivca-ey-report

Jacobson, J., Gruzd, A., & Hernández-García, Á. (2020). Social Media Marketing: Who is Watching the Watchers? *Journal of Retailing and Consumer Services*, *53*, 1–12. doi:10.1016/j.jretconser.2019.03.001

Jain, D. K., Kumar, A., Sangwan, S. R., Nguyen, G. N., & Tiwari, P. (2019). A Particle Swarm Optimized Learning Model of Fault Classification in Web-Apps. *IEEE Access : Practical Innovations, Open Solutions*, *7*, 18480–18489. doi:10.1109/ACCESS.2019.2894871

Jain, H., Padmanabhan, B., Pavlou, P. A., & Raghu, T. S. (2021). Editorial for the special section on humans, algorithms, and augmented intelligence: The future of work, organizations, and Society. *Information Systems Research*, *32*(3), 675–687. doi:10.1287/isre.2021.1046

Jalali, A., Thurasamy, R., & Jaafar, M. (2017). The Moderating effect of social capital in relation to innovative strategies and firm performance. In Handbook of Research on Small and Medium Enterprises in Developing Countries (pParticipant 82-115). IGI Global.

Jamaluddin, Z., & Rahmat, A. K. (2023). Artificial Intelligence Technology in Travel, Tourism and Hospitality: Current and Future Developments. In A. Hassan & N. A. A. Rahman (Eds.), *Technology Application in Aviation, Tourism and Hospitality* (pp. 169–177). Springer Nature Singapore. doi:10.1007/978-981-19-6619-4_12

Jannapureddy, R., Vien, Q.-T., Shah, P., & Trestian, R. (2019). An auto-scaling framework for analyzing big data in the cloud environment. *Applied Sciences (Basel, Switzerland)*, *9*(7), 1417. doi:10.3390/app9071417

Janssen, M., & Wagenaar, R. (2017). Big and Open Linked Data (BOLD) in government: A challenge to transparency and privacy? *Government Information Quarterly*, *34*(3), 355–364.

Jeong, Y. M., Ali, M., Zacca, R., & Park, K. (2019). The effect of entrepreneurship innovative strategies on firm performance: A multiple mediation model. *Journal of East-West Business*, *25*(2), 166–193. doi:10.1080/10669868.2018.1536013

Jha, L. (2019). Most of India's Digitally Monetizable Users Want Vernacular Content: Report. *Livemint.com*. https://www.livemint.com/industry/media/most-of-india-s-digitally-monetizable-users-want-vernacular-content-report-1565097932712.html

Jiang, H., & Zhang, Y. (2016). Journal of Air Transport Management An assessment of passenger experience at Melbourne Airport. *Journal of Air Transport Management*, *54*, 88–92. doi:10.1016/j.jairtraman.2016.04.002

Jiang, W., Han, B., Habibi, M. A., & Schotten, H. D. (2021). The road towards 6G: A comprehensive survey. *IEEE Open Journal of the Communications Society*, *2*, 334–366. doi:10.1109/OJCOMS.2021.3057679

Jiang, Y., & Balaji, M. S. (2022). Getting unwired: What drives travellers to take a digital detox holiday? *Tourism Recreation Research*, *47*(5–6), 453–469. doi:10.1080/02508281.2021.1889801

Jindal, P. (2019). Special Economic Zones in India: An Instrument for Economic Development. *Mmu Journal Of Management Practices*, *10*(1), 8–11.

Jobin, A. (2019). *The Ethics of AI Ethics: An Evaluation of Guidelines*. arXiv preprint arXiv:1903.03425.

Jogaratnam, G. (2017). The effect of market innovative strategies, innovative strategies and human capital on positional advantage: Evidence from the restaurant industry. *International Journal of Hospitality Management*, *60*, 104–113. doi:10.1016/j.ijhm.2016.10.002

Johne, A., & Storey, C. (1998). New service development: A review of the literature and annotated bibliography. *European Journal of Marketing*, *32*(3/4), 184–251. doi:10.1108/03090569810204526

Johnson, S. P. (2000). A critical evaluation of the new services development process: integrating service innovation and service design. Fitzsimmon, J. A. & Fitzsimmon, M.J. (Eds). New service development, creating memorable experiences. Sage: USA. doi:10.4135/9781452205564.n1

Johnson, M. D., Morgeson, F. P., Ilgen, D. R., Meyer, C. J., & Lloyd, J. W. (2019). Multiple professional identities: Examining differences in identification across work-related targets. *The Journal of Applied Psychology*, *104*(5), 649–661. PMID:16551201

Jones, A., & Wang, F. (2020). Cybersecurity challenges in the era of cloud computing: A need for robust security measures. *Journal of Network and Computer Applications*, *168*, 102815. https://www.sciencedirect.com/science/article/abs/pii/S1084804516301060

Jung, D., Dorner, V., Glaser, F., & Morana, S. (2018). Robo-advisory: Digitalization and automation of financial advisory. *Business & Information Systems Engineering*, *60*(1), 81–86. doi:10.1007/s12599-018-0521-9

Jung, D., Dorner, V., Weinhardt, C., & Pusmaz, H. (2018). Designing a robo-advisor for risk-averse, low-budget consumers. *Electronic Markets*, *28*(3), 367–380. doi:10.1007/s12525-017-0279-9

Kagermann, H., Wahlster, W., Helbig, J., Hellinger, A., & Karger, R. (2012). *Fokus: das Zukunftsprojekt Industrie 4.0.* Handlungsempfehlungen zur Umsetzung. Bericht der Promotorengruppe Kommunikation. Forschungsunion.

Kajalo, S., & Lindblom, A. (2015). Market innovative strategies, innovative strategies and business performance among small retailers. *International Journal of Retail & Distribution Management*, *43*(7), 580–596. doi:10.1108/IJRDM-04-2014-0044

Kamalaldin, A., Linde, L., Sjödin, D., & Parida, V. (2020). Transforming provider-customer relationships in digital servitization: A relational view on digitalization. *Industrial Marketing Management*, *89*, 306–325. doi:10.1016/j.indmarman.2020.02.004

Kanagavalli, G. & Arumugam, U. (2020). Effect of Social Media on Purchase Decision, 2020/3. *Aegaeum, 8*(3), 787-793.

Kaplan, A. M., & Haenlein, M. (2010). Users of the world, unite! The challenges and opportunities of Social Media. *Business Horizons*, *53*(1), 59–68. doi:10.1016/j.bushor.2009.09.003

Kaplan, A., & Haenlein, M. (2019). Siri, Siri, in my hand: Who's the fairest in the land? On the interpretations, illustrations, and implications of artificial intelligence. *Business Horizons*, *62*(1), 15–25. doi:10.1016/j.bushor.2018.08.004

Karakuş, G., Karşıgil, E., & Polat, L. (2019). In *Proceedings of the International Symposium for Production Research 2018*. Springer International Publishing. 10.1007/978-3-319-92267-6

Kario, K. (2020). Management of hypertension in the digital era: Small wearable monitoring devices for remote blood pressure monitoring. *Hypertension*, *76*(3), 640–650. doi:10.1161/HYPERTENSIONAHA.120.14742 PMID:32755418

Karmann, T., Mauer, R., Flatten, T. C., & Brettel, M. (2016). Innovative strategies and corruption. *Journal of Business Ethics*, *133*, 223–234. doi:10.1007/s10551-014-2305-6

Kato, M., Onishi, K., & Honjo, Y. (2022). Does patenting always help new firm survival? Understanding heterogeneity among exit routes. *Small Business Economics*, *59*(2), 449–475. doi:10.1007/s11187-021-00481-w

Katz, M. L., & Shapiro, C. (1985). Network Externalities, Competition, and Compatibility. *The American Economic Review*, *75*(3), 424–440. https://www.jstor.org/stable/1814809

Kaur, B. (2022). *Literature Review on Relationship Between Types of Purchases and Usage of Digital Payment Methods*. Academy of Marketing Studies.

Kayabay, K., Gökalp, M. O., Eren, P. E., & Koçyiğit, A. (2018). [WiP] A Workflow and Cloud-Based Service-Oriented Architecture for Distributed Manufacturing in Industry 4.0 Context. *2018 IEEE 11th Conference on Service-Oriented Computing and Applications (SOCA).* IEEE. 10.1109/SOCA.2018.00020

KAYAK. (2023). *Welcome, robots: KAYAK is now integrated on ChatGPT.* Kayak.com. https://www.kayak.com/news/kayak-chatgpt/

Kelley, S. W., & Davis, M. A. (1994). Antecedents to customer expectations for service recovery. *Journal of the Academy of Marketing Science, 22*(1), 52–61. doi:10.1177/0092070394221005

Kemer, E., & Tyagi, P. K. (2023). Application of Artificial Intelligence and Robotics in Tourism and Hospitality Marketing. In P. K. Tyagi, V. Nadda, V. Bharti, & E. Kemer (Eds.), (pp. 125–140). Advances in Business Strategy and Competitive Advantage. IGI Global. doi:10.4018/978-1-6684-6732-9.ch008

Khanna, A., & Pandey, B., & Das, T. (2015). A Study of Today's A.I. through Chatbots and Rediscovery of Machine Intelligence. *International Journal of u- and e- Service. Science and Technology, 8*(7), 277–284.

Khoa, T., & Huynh, T. T. (2023). The influence of social media marketing activities on customer loyalty: A study of e-commerce industry. *International Journal of Data and Network Science., 7*(1), 175–184. doi:10.5267/j.ijdns.2022.11.005

Kim, J. (2014). Platform business and network strategy. *STI Policy Review, 5*(1), 57–74.

Kim, J. (2016). The platform business model and business ecosystem: Quality management and revenue structures. *European Planning Studies, 24*(12), 2113–2132. doi:10.1080/09654313.2016.1251882

Kitsios, F., & Kamariotou, M. (2021). Service innovation process digitization: Areas for exploitation and exploration. *Journal of Hospitality and Tourism Technology, 12*(1), 4–18. doi:10.1108/JHTT-02-2019-0041

Kiyabo, K., & Isaga, N. (2020). Innovative strategies, competitive advantage, and SMEs' performance: Application of firm growth and personal wealth measures. *Journal of Innovation and Entrepreneurship, 9*, 1–15. doi:10.1186/s13731-020-00123-7

Kneuertz, P. J., Singer, E., D'Souza, D. M., Abdel-Rasoul, M., Moffatt-Bruce, S. D., & Merritt, R. E. (2019). Hospital cost and clinical effectiveness of robotic-assisted versus video-assisted thoracoscopic and open lobectomy: A propensity score–weighted comparison. *The Journal of Thoracic and Cardiovascular Surgery, 157*(5), 2018–2026. doi:10.1016/j.jtcvs.2018.12.101 PMID:30819575

Knightscope. (2020). *K5 features.* Knightscope. https://www.knightscope.com/knightscope k5.

Koe, W. L. (2016). The relationship between individual innovative strategies (IEO) and innovative intention. *Journal of Global Entrepreneurship Research, 6*, 1–11. doi:10.1186/s40497-016-0057-8

Kohavi, R., Deng, A., Frasca, B., Longbotham, R., Walker, T., & Xu, Y. (2012). Trustworthy Online Controlled Experiments: Five Puzzling Outcomes Explained. *Proceedings of the 18th ACM SIGKDD International Conference on Knowledge Discovery and Data Mining*, (pp. 786-794). IEEE. 10.1145/2339530.2339653

Komunda, M., & Osarenkhoe, A. (2012). Remedy or cure for service failure? Effects of service recovery on customer satisfaction and loyalty. *Business Process Management Journal, 18*(1), 82–103. doi:10.1108/14637151211215028

Koolen, C., & van Cranenburgh, A. (2017). These are not the stereotypes you are looking for: Bias and fairness in authorial gender attribution. In *Proceedings of the First ACL Workshop on Ethics in Natural Language Processing* (pp. 12-22). ACL. 10.18653/v1/W17-1602

Kozlov, D. A. (2017). The concept of neuro-agents in hospitality industry and tourism. *Journal of Environmental Management and Tourism*, *8*(4), 835–842.

Kraiwanit, T., Jangjarat, K., & Atcharanuwat, J. (2022). The acceptance of financial robo-advisors among investors: The emerging market study. *Journal of Governance and Regulation*, *11*(2), 332–339. doi:10.22495/jgrv11i2siart12

KrAsia Writers. (2019). *A part of the third-largest startup ecosystem, Indian companies enjoy investors attention*. KrAsia.com. https://kr-asia.com/a-part-of-the-third-largest-startup-ecosystem-indian-companies-enjoy-investors-attention

Krause, D. R., Handfield, R. B., & Tyler, B. B. (2007). The relationships between supplier development, commitment, social capital accumulation and performance improvement. *Journal of Operations Management*, *25*(2), 528–545. doi:10.1016/j.jom.2006.05.007

Kraus, S., Jones, P., Kailer, N., Weinmann, A., Chaparro-Banegas, N., & Roig-Tierno, N. (2021). Digital Transformation: An Overview of the Current State of the Art of Research. *SAGE Open*, *11*(3). doi:10.1177/21582440211047576

Kraus, S., Palmer, C., Kailer, N., Kallinger, F. L., & Spitzer, J. (2019). Digital entrepreneurship: A research agenda on new business models for the twenty-first century. *International Journal of Entrepreneurial Behaviour & Research*, *25*(2), 353–375.

Krittanawong, C., Zhang, H., Wang, Z., Aydar, M., & Kitai, T. (2020). Artificial intelligence in precision cardiovascular medicine. *Journal of the American College of Cardiology*, *75*(22), 2806–2819. PMID:28545640

Kulesz, O. (2011). *Digital publishing in developing countries*. International Alliance of Independent Publishers.

Kulkarni, G., Gambhir, J., & Palwe, R. (2012). Cloud computing-software as a service. *International Journal of Cloud Computing and Services Science*, *1*(1), 11–16.

Kumar, B., & Sharma, A. (2022). Examining the research on social media in business-to-business marketing with a focus on sales and the selling process. *Industrial Marketing Management, 102*. doi:10.1016/j.indmarman.2022.01.008

Kumar, A., & Joshi, A. (2017, March). Ontology driven sentiment analysis on social web for government intelligence. In *Proceedings of the Special Collection on eGovernment Innovations in India* (pp. 134-139). ACM. 10.1145/3055219.3055229

Kumar, A., & Khorwal, R. (2017). Firefly algorithm for feature selection in sentiment analysis. In *Computational Intelligence in Data Mining* (pp. 693–703). Springer. doi:10.1007/978-981-10-3874-7_66

Kumar, A., Khorwal, R., & Chaudhary, S. (2016). A survey on sentiment analysis using swarm intelligence. *Indian Journal of Science and Technology*, *9*(39), 1–7. doi:10.17485/ijst/2016/v9i39/100766

Kumar, A., & Sebastian, T. M. (2012). Machine learning assisted sentiment analysis. In *Proceedings of International Conference on Computer Science & Engineering (ICCSE'2012)* (pp. 123-130). IEEE.

Kumar, M., Mamgain, P., Pasumarti, S. S., & Singh, P. K. (2024). Organizational IT support and knowledge sharing behaviour affecting service innovation performance: Empirical evidence from the hospitality industry. *VINE Journal of Information and Knowledge Management Systems*, *54*(2), 256–279. doi:10.1108/VJIKMS-07-2021-0124

Kumar, S., Talukder, M. B., Kabir, F., & Kaiser, F. (2024). Challenges and Sustainability of Green Finance in the Tourism Industry: Evidence from Bangladesh. In S. Taneja, P. Kumar, S. Grima, E. Ozen, & K. Sood (Eds.), (pp. 97–111). Advances in Finance, Accounting, and Economics. IGI Global. doi:10.4018/979-8-3693-1388-6.ch006

Kuo, A. M. H., Borycki, E. M., & Kushniruk, A. (2018). Use of radio-frequency identification (RFID) in a pediatric hospital: A qualitative study. *Studies in Health Technology and Informatics*, *250*, 25–29.

Kyung, N. & Kwon, H.E. (2022). Rationally trust, but emotionally? The roles of cognitive and affective trust in laypeople's acceptance of A.I. for preventive care operations. *Production and Operations Management.*

LabdaouiD. (2023). *(The role of startups in promoting digital and smart tourism in the era of artificial intelligence).* doi:10.13140/RG.2.2.16097.68964

Lalkaka, R. (2002). Technology business incubators to help build an innovation-based economy. *Journal of Change Management, 3*(2), 167–176. doi:10.1080/714042533

Lambrechts, W., & Sinha, S. (2019). *Last mile internet access for emerging economies.* Springer International Publishing. doi:10.1007/978-3-030-20957-5

Lanzolla, G., & Anderson, J. (2008). Digital transformation. *Business Strategy Review, 19*(2), 72–76. doi:10.1111/j.1467-8616.2008.00539.x

Lapidus, R. S., & Pinkerton, L. (1995). Customer complaint situations: An equity theory perspective. *Psychology and Marketing, 12*(2), 105–118. doi:10.1002/mar.4220120203

Larson, B. (2017, April). Gender as a variable in natural-language processing: Ethical considerations. In *Proceedings of the First ACL Workshop on Ethics in Natural Language Processing* (pp. 1–11). ACL. 10.18653/v1/W17-1601

Lasek, M., & Jessa, S. (2013). Chatbots for customer services on hotel websites. *Information Systems Management, 2*(2), 146–158.

Laskey, K. B., & Laskey, K. (2009). Service-oriented architecture. *Wiley Interdisciplinary Reviews: Computational Statistics, 1*(1), 101–105. doi:10.1002/wics.8

LeCun, Y., Bengio, Y., & Hinton, G. (2015). Deep learning. *Nature, 521*(7553), 436-444.

Le, D. N., Nguyen, H. T., & Truong, P. H. (2020). Port logistics service quality and customer satisfaction: Empirical evidence from Vietnam. *The Asian Journal of Shipping and Logistics, 36*(2), 89–103. doi:10.1016/j.ajsl.2019.10.003

Lee, C. C., Kim, Y., Choi, J. H., & Porter, E. (2022). Does implementing electronic health record systems impact hospital efficiency, profitability, and quality? *Journal of Applied Business & Economics, 24*(2).

Lee, D., & Yoon, S. N. (2021). Application of artificial intelligence-based technologies in the healthcare industry: Opportunities and challenges. *International Journal of Environmental Research and Public Health, 18*(1), 271. doi:10.3390/ijerph18010271 PMID:33401373

Lee, H. L., & Billington, C. (1992). Managing supply chain inventory: Pitfalls and opportunities. *MIT Sloan Management Review.*

Lee, H. L., & Whang, S. (2000). Information sharing in a supply chain. *International Journal of Manufacturing Technology and Management, 1*(1), 79–93. doi:10.1504/IJMTM.2000.001329

Lee, J., Suh, T., Roy, D., & Baucus, M. (2019). Emerging technology and business model innovation: The case of artificial intelligence. *Journal of Open Innovation, 5*(3), 44. doi:10.3390/joitmc5030044

Lee, S., & Lee, K. (2021). Human-centered design principles for augmented reality applications. *International Journal of Human-Computer Studies, 148*, 102605. https://www.sciencedirect.com/science/article/abs/pii/S1084804516301060

Leibold, M., & Voelpel, S. C. (2007). *Managing the aging workforce: Challenges and solutions.* John Wiley & Sons.

Lekmat, L., Selvarajah, C., & Hewege, C. (2018). Relationship between Market Innovative strategies, Innovative strategies, and Firm Performance in Thai SMEs: The Mediating Role of Marketing Capabilities. *European Journal of Pediatric Dermatology : PD*, *28*(4), 89–109.

Lenuwat, P., & Boon-itt, S. (2022). Information technology management and service performance management capabilities: An empirical study of the service supply chain management process. *Journal of Advances in Management Research*, *19*(1), 55–77. doi:10.1108/JAMR-01-2021-0039

Lepak, D. P., & Sablynski, C. J. (2019). A contingency model of artificial intelligence in talent management. *The Journal of Applied Psychology*, *104*(12), 1578–1596.

Letafati, M., & Otoum, S. (2023). On the privacy and security for e-health services in the metaverse: An overview. *Ad Hoc Networks*, *150*, 103262. doi:10.1016/j.adhoc.2023.103262

Leviathan, Y. (2018). *Google Duplex: an AI system for accomplishing real-world tasks over the phone*. Google. https://ai.googleblog.com/2018/05/duplex-ai-system-for-naturalconversation. html

Lewis, B. R., & McCann, P. (2004). Service failure and recovery: Evidence from the hotel industry. *International Journal of Contemporary Hospitality Management*, *16*(1), 6–17. doi:10.1108/09596110410516516

Liao, Z., Jin, M., Luo, Y., Ren, P., & Gao, H. (2013). Research on prediction of tourists' quantity in Jiuzhaigou valley scenic based on ABR integration model. *International Journal of Environment and Pollution*, *51*(3/4), 176–191. doi:10.1504/IJEP.2013.054028

Liaw, S. Y., Tan, J. Z., Lim, S., Zhou, W., Yap, J., Ratan, R., Ooi, S. L., Wong, S. J., Seah, B., & Chua, W. L. (2023). Artificial intelligence in virtual reality simulation for interprofessional communication training: Mixed method study. *Nurse Education Today*, *122*, 105718. doi:10.1016/j.nedt.2023.105718 PMID:36669304

Liedtka, J. (2018). Why Design Thinking Works. *Harvard Business Review*, *96*(5), 72–79.

Li, H., Suomi, R., & Törnroos, J. A. (2019). Customer engagement through big data analytics. *Industrial Management & Data Systems*, *119*(9), 1877–1897.

Li, J., Xu, L., Tang, L., Wang, S., & Li, L. (2018). Big data in tourism research: A literature review. *Tourism Management*, *68*, 301–323. doi:10.1016/j.tourman.2018.03.009

Li, M., Chen, Y., & Zhang, W. (2023). Research on 5G network security challenges and countermeasures. *Journal of Computer Networks and Communications*, *2023*, 1–10. https://ieeexplore.ieee.org/document/10039654/

Liping, Y. & Vesarach, A. (2022). *The Impact of Innovative strategies on Firm Performance: The Multiple Mediating Roles of Competitive Strategy and Knowledge Creation Process*.

Li, S., Xu, L. D., & Zhao, S. (2015). The Internet of things: A survey. *Information Systems Frontiers*, *17*(2), 243–259. doi:10.1007/s10796-014-9492-7

Lisboa, A., Skarmeas, D., & Saridakis, C. (2016). Innovative strategies pathways to performance: A fuzzy-set analysis. *Journal of Business Research*, *69*(4), 1319–1324. doi:10.1016/j.jbusres.2015.10.099

Litjens, G., Kooi, T., Bejnordi, B. E., Setio, A. A. A., Ciompi, F., Ghafoorian, M., van der Laak, J. A. W. M., van Ginneken, B., & Sanchez, C. I. (2017). A survey on deep learning in medical image analysis. *Medical Image Analysis*, *42*, 60–88. doi:10.1016/j.media.2017.07.005 PMID:28778026

Liu, B. (2012). Sentiment Analysis and Opinion Mining. *Synthesis Lectures on Human Language Technologies*, *5*(1), 1–167. doi:10.1007/978-3-031-02145-9

Liu, D., Chen, S., & Chou, T. (2011). Resource fit in digital transformation: Lessons learned from the CBC Bank global e-banking project. *Management Decision*, *49*(10), 1728–1742. doi:10.1108/00251741111183852

Liu, P., Zhang, P., & Nie, G. (2010, October). Business modelling for service ecosystems. In *Proceedings of the International Conference on Management of Emergent Digital EcoSystems* (pp. 102-106). ACM. 10.1145/1936254.1936272

Liu, W., Hu, G., Tang, L., & Wang, Y. (2015). China's global growth in social science research: Uncovering evidence from bibliometric analyses of SSCI publications (1978–2013). *Journal of Informetrics*, *9*(3), 555–569. doi:10.1016/j.joi.2015.05.007

Liu, X., Jiang, Y., Wang, Z., Zhong, R. Y., Cheung, H. H., & Huang, G. Q. (2023). imseStudio: Blockchain-enabled secure digital twin platform for service manufacturing. *International Journal of Production Research*, *61*(12), 3984–4003. doi:10.1080/00207543.2021.2003462

Liu, Z. (2021). Sociological perspectives on artificial intelligence: A typological reading. *Sociology Compass*, *15*(3), e12851. doi:10.1111/soc4.12851

Li, W., Badr, Y., & Biennier, F. (2012, October). Digital ecosystems: challenges and prospects. In *Proceedings of the International Conference on Management of Emergent Digital EcoSystems* (pp. 117-122). ACM. 10.1145/2457276.2457297

Li, W., Liu, K., Belitski, M., Ghobadian, A., & O'Regan, N. (2016). e-Leadership through strategic alignment: An empirical study of small- and medium-sized enterprises in the digital age. *Journal of Information Technology*, *31*(2), 185–206. doi:10.1057/jit.2016.10

Li, X., Liu, D., Hu, X., & Yu, P. S. (2020). Chatbot in customer service and e-commerce: State-of-the-art and research directions. *IEEE Access : Practical Innovations, Open Solutions*, *8*, 191625–191648.

Li, X., Tan, A. J. H., Wang, X., & Yuen, K. F. (2023). Investigating gig workers' commitment to crowdsourced logistics platforms: Fair employment and social exchange perspectives. *Technology in Society*, *74*, 102311. doi:10.1016/j.techsoc.2023.102311

Li, Y., Ge, Y., & Zhang, Y. (2021, July). Tutorial on the fairness of machine learning in recommender systems. In *Proceedings of the 44th international ACM SIGIR conference on research and development in information retrieval* (pp. 2654–2657). ACM. 10.1145/3404835.3462814

Llopis-Albert, C., Rubio, F., & Valero, F. (2021). Impact of digital transformation on the automotive industry. *Technological Forecasting and Social Change*, *162*, 120343. doi:10.1016/j.techfore.2020.120343 PMID:33052150

Logistics 4.0 and Smart supply chain management in Industry 4.0. (2020). iScoop. https://www.i-scoop.eu/industry-4-0/supply-chain-managementscm-logistics/

Longoni, C., Cian, L. and Kyung, E., 2022. A.I. in the Government: Responses to Failures.

Longoni, C., & Cian, L. (2022). Artificial intelligence in utilitarian vs. hedonic contexts: The "word-of-machine" effect. *Journal of Marketing*, *86*(1), 91–108. doi:10.1177/0022242920957347

Loutas, N., Kamateri, E., Bosi, F., & Tarabanis, K. (2011, November). Cloud computing interoperability: the state of play. In *2011 IEEE Third International Conference on Cloud Computing Technology and Science* (pp. 752-757). IEEE. 10.1109/CloudCom.2011.116

Love, J. H., & Roper, S. (2015). SME innovation, exporting and growth: A review of existing evidence. *International Small Business Journal*, *33*(1), 28–48. doi:10.1177/0266242614550190

Lu, H., Li, Y., Chen, M., Kim, H., & Serikawa, S. (2018). Brain intelligence: Go beyond artificial intelligence. *Mobile Networks and Applications*, *23*(2), 368–375. doi:10.1007/s11036-017-0932-8

Lukanova, G., & Ilieva, G. (2019). Robots, Artificial Intelligence, and Service Automation in Hotels. In S. Ivanov & C. Webster (Eds.), Robots, Artificial Intelligence, and Service Automation in Travel, Tourism and Hospitality (pp. 157–183). Emerald Publishing Limited. doi:10.1108/978-1-78756-687-320191009

Lusch, R. F., & Nambisan, S. (2015). Service innovation. *Management Information Systems Quarterly*, *39*(1), 155–176. https://www.jstor.org/stable/26628345. doi:10.25300/MISQ/2015/39.1.07

Luspo, C., Remetio, A. C., Sadial, B. P., & Pabatang, M. (2021). Guest Service Management among Hotels and Restaurants in Butuan City. *SMCC Higher Education Research Journal*, *2*(1). doi:10.18868/hrm-v2-a5

Lu, Y. (2019). Artificial intelligence: A survey on evolution, models, applications and future trends. *Journal of Management Analytics*, *6*(1), 1–29. doi:10.1080/23270012.2019.1570365

Luz Martín-Peña, M., Díaz-Garrido, E., & Sánchez-López, J. M. (2018). The digitalization and servitization of manufacturing: A review on digital business models. *Strategic Change*, *27*(2), 91–99. doi:10.1002/jsc.2184

MacIntosh, R., & O'Gorman, K. (2015). Research methods for business and management. *A guide to writing your dissertation,* 558 -578.

Maglio, P. P., & Spohrer, J. (2008). Fundamentals of service science. *Journal of the Academy of Marketing Science*, *36*(1), 18–20. doi:10.1007/s11747-007-0058-9

Manohar, S., Mittal, A., & Marwah, S. (2020). Service innovation, corporate reputation and word-of-mouth in the banking sector: A test on multigroup-moderated mediation effect. *Benchmarking*, *27*(1), 406–429. doi:10.1108/BIJ-05-2019-0217

Mantok, S., Sekhon, H., Sahi, G. K., & Jones, P. (2019). Innovative strategies and the mediating role of organisational learning amongst Indian S-SMEs. *Journal of Small Business and Enterprise Development*, *26*(5), 641–660. doi:10.1108/JSBED-07-2018-0215

Manyika, J., Lund, S., Chui, M., Bughin, J., Woetzel, J., Batra, P., & Sanghvi, S. (2017). *Jobs lost, jobs gained: What the future of work will mean for jobs, skills, and wages.*

Marković, S., Raspor Janković, S., & Zubović, V. (2020). The impacts of robots and artificial intelligence on service quality in the hotel industry. *Balkans Journal of Emerging Trends in Social Sciences*, *3*(2), 163–170. doi:10.31410/Balkans.JETSS.2020.3.2.163-170

Marler, J. H., & Boudreau, J. W. (2017). An evidence-based review of HR Analytics. *International Journal of Human Resource Management*, *28*(1), 3–26. doi:10.1080/09585192.2016.1244699

Marques, M. (20129). Top 3 chatbots that are changing the travel industry. *Medium.* https://medium. com/hijiff y/top-3-chatbots-that-are-changing-the- travel-industry-d325082c50b8.

Marrese-Taylor, E., Velasquez, J. D., & Bravo-Marquez, F. (2013). Modular tool to explore tourism opinions on the web. *Proceedings – 2013 IEEE/WIC/ACM International Joint Conference on Web Intelligence and Intelligent Agent Technology – Workshops, WI-IATW 2013.* IEEE. 10.1109/WI-IAT.2013.193

Marriott International. (2018). *Joint venture of Alibaba group and Marriott international trials facial recognition check-in technology.* Marriott International. https://news.marriott.com/news/2018/07/11/jointventure- of-alibaba-group-and-marriott-international-trials-facial-recognition-check-intechnology

Martens, C. D., Lacerda, F. M., Belfort, A. C., & de Freitas, H. M. R. (2016). Research on innovative strategies: Current status and future agenda. *International Journal of Innovative Behavior & Research*, *22*(4), 556–583.

Martins, L. M. (2017). Augmented reality in hotels use case - holiday Inn, the first ever. LinkedIn. https://www.linkedin.com/pulse/augmented-reality-hotels-use-case-holiday-inn-first-lu%C3% ADs (accessed 5 June 2020).

Marton, A. (2022). Steps toward a digital ecology: Ecological principles for the study of digital ecosystems. *Journal of Information Technology*, *37*(3), 250–265. doi:10.1177/02683962211043222

Marz, N., & Warren, J. (2015). *Big Data: Principles and best practices of scalable realtime data systems*. Manning Publications.

Mason, M. C., Floreani, J., Miani, S., Beltrame, F., & Cappelletto, R. (2015). Understanding the impact of innovative strategies on SMEs' performance. The role of the financing structure. *Procedia Economics and Finance*, *23*, 1649–1661. doi:10.1016/S2212-5671(15)00470-0

Masuda, Y., Shirasaka, S., Yamamoto, S., & Hardjono, T. (2018). Architecture board practices in adaptive enterprise architecture with digital platform: A case of global healthcare enterprise. *International Journal of Enterprise Information Systems*, *14*(1), 1–20. doi:10.4018/ijeis.2018010101

Matt, C., Hess, T., & Benlian, A. (2015). Digital transformation strategies. *Business & Information Systems Engineering*, *57*(5), 339–343. doi:10.1007/s12599-015-0401-5

Maxham, J. G. III, & Netemeyer, R. G. (2003). Firms reap what they sow: The effects of shared values and perceived organizational justice on customers' evaluations of complaint handling. *Journal of Marketing*, *67*(1), 46–62. doi:10.1509/jmkg.67.1.46.18591

Ma, Y., Xiang, Z., Du, Q., & Fan, W. (2018). Effects of user-provided photos on hotel review helpfulness: An analytical approach with deep leaning. *International Journal of Hospitality Management*, *71*, 120–131. doi:10.1016/j.ijhm.2017.12.008

Mc Anthony, I., & Jindal, P. (2017). Performance Assessment Of Automobile Industry In Japan Using Ratio Analysis. *Impact: International Journal Of Research In Business Management (Impact: Ijrbm)*, *5*, 89-106.

McAdam, M., & McAdam, R. (2008). High tech Startups in university science park incubators: The relationship between the Startup's life cycle progression and use of the incubator's resources. *Technovation*, *28*(5), 277–290. doi:10.1016/j.technovation.2007.07.012

McAfee, A., & Brynjolfsson, E. (2012). Big Data: The Management Revolution. *Harvard Business Review*, *90*(10), 60–68. PMID:23074865

McMaughan, D. J., Oloruntoba, O., & Smith, M. L. (2020). Socioeconomic status and access to healthcare: interrelated drivers for healthy aging. *Frontiers in public health*, *8*, 231.

Meekaewkunchorn, N., Szczepańska-Woszczyna, K., Muangmee, C., Kassakorn, N., & Khalid, B. (2021). Innovative strategies and SME performance: The mediating role of learning innovative strategies. *Economia e Sociologia*, *14*(2), 294–312.

Meena, P., & Sahu, P. (2021). Customer Relationship Management Research from 2000 to 2020: An Academic Literature Review and Classification. *Vision (Basel)*, *25*(2), 136–158. doi:10.1177/0972262920984550

Mende, M., Scott, M. L., van Doorn, J., Grewal, D., & Shanks, I. (2019). Service robots rising: How humanoid robots influence service experiences and elicit compensatory consumer responses. *JMR, Journal of Marketing Research*, *56*(4), 535–556. doi:10.1177/0022243718822827

Menezes, A. J. (1996). *Handbook of Applied Cryptography*. CRC press.

Mergel, I., Edelmann, N., & Haug, N. (2019). Defining digital transformation: Results from expert interviews. *Government Information Quarterly*, *36*(4), 101385. doi:10.1016/j.giq.2019.06.002

Meta, A. I. (2023). *We're advancing AI for a more connected world*. Meta. https://ai.meta.com/resources/

Methlagl, M. (2022). Mapping inclusive education 1980 to 2019: A bibliometric analysis of thematic clusters and research directions. *Issues in Educational Research*, *32*(1), 225–247.

Meyer, M. H., & Lehnerd, A. P. (1997). *The power of product platforms*. Simon and Schuster.

Meyers, M. (2017). This Chinese KFC lets you put your money where your mouth is. CNet. https://www.cnet.com/news/smile-to-pay-kfc-facial-recognition-payments-alipay-ant/

Michel, S., & Meuter, M. L. (2008). The service recovery paradox: True but overrated? *International Journal of Service Industry Management*, *19*(4), 441–457. doi:10.1108/09564230810891897

Miles, I. (2010). Service innovation. Handbook of Service Science. In P. P. Maglio, C. A. Kieliszewski, & J. C. Spohrer (Eds.), *Service Science: Research and Innovation* (pp. 511–533). Springer.

Milojicic, D. S., Kalogeraki, V., Lukose, R., Nagaraja, K., Pruyne, J., Richard, B., & Xu, Z. (2002). *Peer-to-peer computing*.

Miloud, T., Aspelund, A., & Cabrol, M. (2012). Startup valuation by venture capitalists: An empirical study. *Venture Capital*, *14*(2-3), 151–174. doi:10.1080/13691066.2012.667907

Min, H., & Zhou, G. (2002). Supply chain modeling: Past, present and future. *Computers & Industrial Engineering*, *43*(1–2), 231–249. doi:10.1016/S0360-8352(02)00066-9

Minz, N. K., & Saluja, A. (2024). Developing Skills with Team-Based Learning. In Cases on Economics Education and Tools for Educators (pp. 25-53). IGI Global. doi:10.4018/978-1-6684-7583-6.ch002

Minz, N. K., Mushir, N., Tanwar, S., & Chaffai, M. (2024). Islamic Finance and Fintech: A Scoping Review. In M. Irfan, S. Kadry, M. Sharif, & H. Khan (Eds.), *Fintech Applications in Islamic Finance: AI, Machine Learning, and Blockchain Techniques* (pp. 150–170). IGI Global. doi:10.4018/979-8-3693-1038-0.ch010

Minz, N. K., Prakash, A., Shrivastava, S., & Nangia, R. (2024). Leveraging Technology-Based Innovation for Business Model Innovation. In V. Gupta (Ed.), *Fostering Global Entrepreneurship Through Business Model Innovation* (pp. 115–133). IGI Global. doi:10.4018/978-1-6684-6975-0.ch005

Mishra, D. B., Haider, I., Gunasekaran, A., Sakib, M. N., Malik, N., & Rana, N. P. (2023). "Better together": Right blend of business strategy and digital transformation strategies. *International Journal of Production Economics*, *266*, 109040. doi:10.1016/j.ijpe.2023.109040

Mittelstadt, B. D., & Floridi, L. (2016). The Ethics of Algorithms: Mapping the Debate. *Big Data & Society*, *3*(2), 1–21. doi:10.1177/2053951716679679

Mohammad, B. T., & Mokarram Hossain, M. (2021). Prospects of future tourism in bangladesh: An evaluative study. *I-Manager's. Journal of Management*, *15*(4), 31. doi:10.26634/jmgt.15.4.17495

Mohammed, C. M., & Zeebaree, S. R. (2021). Sufficient comparison among cloud computing services: IaaS, PaaS, and SaaS: A review. *International Journal of Science and Business*, *5*(2), 17–30.

Moharana, A. (2017). Why Bots Will Revolutionize the Way Restaurants Work, *Chatbotlife*. https://chatbotslife.com/why-bots-will-revolutionize-the-way-restaurants-work-11498fb00604

Morrison, A. M. (2022). *Hospitality and travel marketing*. Taylor & Francis. doi:10.4324/9781003292616

Mthanti, T., & Ojah, K. (2017). Innovative strategies (EO): Measurement and policy implications of entrepreneurship at the macroeconomic level. *Research Policy*, *46*(4), 724–739. doi:10.1016/j.respol.2017.01.012

Muchiri, M., & McMurray, A. (2015). Innovative strategies within small firms: A critical review of why leadership and contextual factors matter. *Small Enterprise Research*, *22*(1), 17–31. doi:10.1080/13215906.2015.1017076

Munirathinam, S. (2020). Chapter Six - Industry 4.0: Industrial Internet of Things (IIOT). In P. Raj & P. B. T.-A. in C. Evangeline (Eds.), *The Digital Twin Paradigm for Smarter Systems and Environments: The Industry Use Cases* (*Vol. 117*, Issue 1, pp. 129–164). Elsevier.

Murphy, J., Hofacker, C., & Gretzel, U. (2017). Dawning of the age of robots in hospitality and tourism: Challenges for teaching and research. *European Journal of Tourism Research*, *15*, 104–111. doi:10.54055/ejtr.v15i.265

Musamih, A., Yaqoob, I., Salah, K., Jayaraman, R., Al-Hammadi, Y., Omar, M., & Ellahham, S. (2022). Metaverse in healthcare: Applications, challenges, and future directions. *IEEE Consumer Electronics Magazine*.

Naga, V., Challa, S. K., Padmalatha, P., & Vamsi, B. (2022). Influence of Relationship Marketing Variables on Social Media Marketing. *The Empirical Economics Letters.*, *20*, 241–249.

Naghshineh, B., & Carvalho, H. (2022). The implications of additive manufacturing technology adoption for supply chain resilience: A systematic search and review. *International Journal of Production Economics*, *247*, 108387. doi:10.1016/j.ijpe.2021.108387

Naldi, L., Larsson, J., & Westlund, H. (2020). Policy entrepreneurship and innovative strategies in vulnerable Swedish municipalities. *Entrepreneurship and Regional Development*, *32*(7-8), 473–491. doi:10.1080/08985626.2020.1798557

Nambisan, S. (2017). Digital entrepreneurship: Toward a digital technology perspective of entrepreneurship. *Entrepreneurship Theory and Practice*, *41*(6), 1029–1055. doi:10.1111/etap.12254

Nanda, R., Sharma, L. K., & Sharma, R. (2020). *Farm Innovators of Jammu: A Compendium of Success Stories*. Sher-e-Kashmir University of Agricultural Sciences and Technology of Jammu.

Narayanan, A., & Shmatikov, V. (2008). Robust De-anonymization of Large Sparse Datasets." *IEEE Symposium on Security and Privacy*, (pp. 111-125). IEEE.

NASSCOM and Zinnov. (2019). *Indian tech startup ecosystem: leading tech in the 20s*. Nasscom. https://www.nasscom.in/knowledge-center/ publications/indian-tech-start-ecosystem-leading-tech-20s

National Business Incubation Association. (February 2019). *Business Incubation FAQ*. National Business Incubation Association. http://nbia.org/resource_library/faq/index.php

Naudé, W., Gries, T., Wood, E., & Meintjies, A. (2008). Regional determinants of entrepreneurial Startups in a developing country. *Entrepreneurship and Regional Development*, *20*(2), 111–124. doi:10.1080/08985620701631498

Navitaire. (2020). *Discover the navitaire difference*. Navitaire. https://www.navitaire.com/amadeus

Nayyar, A., Jain, R., Mahapatra, B., & Singh, A. (2019). Cyber Security Challenges for Smart Cities. In Driving the Development, Management, and Sustainability of Cognitive Cities (pp. 27-54). IGI Global. doi:10.4018/978-1-5225-8085-0.ch002

Nayyar, A. K. (Ed.), *A Roadmap to Industry 4.0: Smart Production*. Sharp Business and Sustainable Development, Advances in Science, Technology & Innovation. doi:10.1007/978-3-030-14544-6_1

Nayyar, A., Puri, V., & Le, D. N. (2017). Internet of nano things (IoNT): Next evolutionary step in nanotechnology. *Nanoscience and Nanotechnology*, *7*(1), 4–8.

Nedumaran, G. & Kumar, M. (2019). Effect of Mobile Applications on Farming in Virudhunagar District - A Study. *Our Heritage, 68*(1), 12718-12727.

Negash, S. (2004). Communications of the Association for Information Systems. Business Intelligence, 13. doi:10.17705/1CAIS.01315

Neneh, B. N., & Van, Z. J. (2017). Innovative strategies and its impact on firm growth amongst SMEs in South Africa. *Problems and Perspectives in Management*, (15), 166–178. doi:10.21511/ppm.15(3).2017.14

Nguyen, N. P., & Hoai, T. T. (2023). Internal controls driven by mindfulness toward enhanced ethical behaviors: Empirical evidence from Vietnam. *Heliyon*, *9*(7), e18002. doi:10.1016/j.heliyon.2023.e18002 PMID:37483747

Nieto, D., Quesada-Arencibia, A., García, C. R., & Moreno-Díaz, R. (2014). A social robot in a tourist environment. *International Conference on Ubiquitous Computing and Ambient Intelligence*. Springer, Cham. 10.1007/978-3-319-13102-3_5

Niroula, B. (2023). *The Impact of AI on the Future of Voice Acting* [Preprint]. Open Science Framework. doi:10.31219/osf.io/wn5y3

NITI. (2019). Guidelines for setting up of incubation centres under Atal Innovation Mission – 'Atal Incubation Centres'. *Government of India NITI Aayog Atal Innovation Mission May 2016*. NITI. https://niti.gov.in/writereaddata/files/Guidelines %20to%20setup%20AIC%20May%202016.

Nkwabi, J., & Mboya, L. (2019). A review of factors affecting the growth of small and medium enterprises (SMEs) in Tanzania. *European Journal of Business and Management*, *11*(33), 1–8.

Nour, R. (2022). Enhancing the Logistics 4.0 Firms through Information Technology. *Sustainability (Basel)*, *14*(23), 15860. doi:10.3390/su142315860

O'Gorman, K., & MacIntosh, R. (2015). Mapping research methods. *Research methods for business and management: A guide to writing your dissertation*, 50-74.

OAG. (2023). INNOVATIVE AIRLINE OPERATIONS : THE TURNAROUND. *Article in OAG Newsletter*, (November), 2023.

Obschonka, M., & Audretsch, D. B. (2020). Artificial intelligence and big data in entrepreneurship: A new era has begun. *Small Business Economics*, *55*(3), 529–539. doi:10.1007/s11187-019-00202-4

Octavia, A., Indrawijaya, S., Sriayudha, Y., & Hasbullah, H. (2020). Impact on E-commerce adoption on innovative strategies and market innovative strategies in business performance of SMEs. *Asian Economic and Financial Review*, *10*(5), 516. doi:10.18488/journal.aefr.2020.105.516.525

Ogbeide, G. C. A., Böser, S., Harrinton, R. J., & Ottenbacher, M. C. (2017). Complaint management in hospitality organizations: The role of empowerment and other service recovery attributes impacting loyalty and satisfaction. *Tourism and Hospitality Research*, *17*(2), 204–216. doi:10.1177/1467358415613409

Okangi, F. P. (2019). The impacts of innovative innovative strategies on the profitability growth of construction firms in Tanzania. *Journal of Global Entrepreneurship Research*, *9*(1), 14. doi:10.1186/s40497-018-0143-1

Okano, M. T., Antunes, S. N., & Fernandes, M. E. (2021). Digital transformation in the manufacturing industry under the optics of digital platforms and ecosystems. *Independent Journal of Management & Production*, *12*(4), 1139–1159. doi:10.14807/ijmp.v12i4.1375

Oke, A. (2007). Innovation types and innovation management practices in service companies. *International Journal of Operations & Production Management*, *27*(6), 564–587. doi:10.1108/01443570710750268

Oladinrin, O. T., Arif, M., Rana, M. Q., & Gyoh, L. (2023). Interrelations between construction ethics and innovation: A bibliometric analysis using VOSviewer. *Construction Innovation*, *23*(3), 505–523. doi:10.1108/CI-07-2021-0130

Olavarrieta, S., & Ellinger, A. E. (1997). Resource-based theory and strategic logistics research. *International Journal of Physical Distribution & Logistics Management*, *27*(9/10), 559–587. doi:10.1108/09600039710188594

Oleksy, T., Wnuk, A., & Piskorska, M. (2023). Migration to the metaverse and its predictors: Attachment to virtual places and metaverse-related threat. *Computers in Human Behavior*, *141*, 107642. doi:10.1016/j.chb.2022.107642

Oliinyk, I.Kherson State Agrarian and Economic University. (2023). Prospects for implementing generative artificial intelligence in marketing and trade. *Scientific Bulletin of Flight Academy. Section: Economics. Management and Law*, *8*, 110–115. doi:10.33251/2707-8620-2023-8-110-115

Oluwatayo, J. A. (2017). Validity and Reliability issues in education research. *Journal of Educational and Social Research*, *2*, 391–399.

Omboni, S., Padwal, R. S., Alessa, T., Benczúr, B., Green, B. B., Hubbard, I., Kario, K., Khan, N. A., Konradi, A., Logan, A. G., Lu, Y., Mars, M., McManus, R. J., Melville, S., Neumann, C. L., Parati, G., Renna, N. F., Ryvlin, P., Saner, H., & Wang, J. (2022). The worldwide impact of telemedicine during COVID-19: Current evidence and recommendations for the future. *Connected Health*, *1*, 7. doi:10.20517/ch.2021.03 PMID:35233563

Ondrus, J., Gannamaneni, A., & Lyytinen, K. (2015). The impact of openness on the market potential of multi-sided platforms: A case study of mobile payment platforms. *Journal of Information Technology*, *30*(3), 260–275. doi:10.1057/jit.2015.7

Oni, O., Agbobli, E. K., & Iwu, C. G. (2019). Innovative strategies and performance of small business in Vryburg region North West province South Africa. *Journal of Reviews on Global Economics*. doi:10.6000/1929-7092.2019.08.07

Oosthuizen, K., Botha, E., Robertson, J., & Montecchi, M. (2021). Artificial intelligence in retail: The AI-enabled value chain. *Australasian Marketing Journal*, *29*(3), 264–273. doi:10.1016/j.ausmj.2020.07.007

Opara, O., Nsirim, O., & Irokah, P. L. (2023). Technological Methods and Security of Information Resources in Dame Patience Goodluck Jonathan Automated Library, Ignatius Ajuru University of Education. *Southern African Journal of Security*, *1*. doi:10.25159/3005-4222/14506

Osei, A., Forkuoh, K. S., Shao, Y., & Osei, M. A. (2016). The impact of institutional support in SMEs marketing, and growth—A case study of retail SMEs in Ghana. *Open Journal of Business and Management*, *4*(03), 408–426. doi:10.4236/ojbm.2016.43043

Osterwalder, A., & Pigneur, Y. (2013). *Business Model Generation: A Handbook for Visionaries, Game Changers, and Challengers. Almanya*. Wiley.

Osterwalder, A., Pigneur, Y., Bernarda, G., & Smith, A. (2014). *Value Proposition Design: How to Create Products and Services Customers Want*. John Wiley & Sons.

Outlook. (2019). 54 tech unicorns expected in India by 2024. *Outlook, The News Scroll*. https://www.outlookindia.com/newsscroll/54-tech-unicorns-expected-in-india-by-2024-lead-correcting-headline/1587697 [Accessed June 12, 2022].

Özkaynar, K. (2022). Marketing strategies of banks in the period of Metaverse, Block-chain, and Cryptocurrency in the context of consumer behavior theories. *International Journal of Insurance and Finance*, *2*(1), 1–12.

Pandey, M. M. (2016). Journal of Air Transport Management Evaluating the service quality of airports in Thailand using fuzzy multi-criteria decision making method. *Journal of Air Transport Management*, *57*, 241–249. doi:10.1016/j.jairtraman.2016.08.014

Panesar, S., & Markeset, T. (2008). Development of a framework for industrial service innovation management and coordination. *Journal of Quality in Maintenance Engineering*, *14*(2), 177–193. doi:10.1108/13552510810877674

Parasuraman, A., & Colby, C. L. (2015). An Updated and Streamlined Technology Readiness Index: TRI 2.0. *Journal of Service Research*, *18*(1), 59–74. doi:10.1177/1094670514539730

Parasuraman, A., Zeithaml, V. A., & Berry, L. L. (1985). A conceptual model of service quality and its implications for future research. *Journal of Marketing*, *49*(4), 41–50. doi:10.1177/002224298504900403

Parasuraman, A., Zeithaml, V. A., & Berry, L. L. (1988). Servqual: A Multiple-Item Scale for Measuring Consumer Perceptions of Service Quality. *Journal of Retailing*, *64*(1), 12–40.

Parida, V., Sjödin, D., & Reim, W. (2019). Reviewing literature on digitalization, business model innovation, and sustainable industry: Past achievements and future promises. *Sustainability (Basel)*, *11*(2), 391. doi:10.3390/su11020391

Parker, G. (2016). *Platform Revolution MIT Information and Communications Technologies Conference*. MIT.

Park, S. M., & Kim, Y. G. (2022). A metaverse: Taxonomy, components, applications, and open challenges. *IEEE Access : Practical Innovations, Open Solutions*, *10*, 4209–4251. doi:10.1109/ACCESS.2021.3140175

Peca, A., Coeckelbergh, M., Simut, R., Costescu, C., Pintea, S., David, D., & Vanderborght, B. (2016). Robot enhanced therapy for children with autism disorders: Measuring ethical acceptability. *IEEE Technology and Society Magazine*, *35*(2), 54–66. doi:10.1109/MTS.2016.2554701

Pechlaner, H., Thees, H., Manske-Wang, W., & Scuttari, A. (2021). Local service industry and tourism development through the global trade and infrastructure project of the New Silk Road–the example of Georgia. *Service Industries Journal*, *41*(7-8), 553–579. doi:10.1080/02642069.2019.1623204

Pereira, V., Hadjielias, E., Christofi, M., & Vrontis, D. (2023). A systematic literature review on the impact of artificial intelligence on workplace outcomes: A multi-process perspective. *Human Resource Management Review*, *33*(1), 100857. doi:10.1016/j.hrmr.2021.100857

Perez, S. (2017). Starbucks unveils a virtual assistant that takes your order via messaging or voice. *TechCrunch*. https://techcrunch.com/2017/01/30/starbucks-unveils-a-virtual-assistant-that-takesyour-order-via-messaging-or-voice/

PIB. (2017). Startup: Definition changes. Press Information Bureau, *Government of India, Ministry of Commerce & Industry*. PIB. https://pib.gov.in/newsite/PrintRelease.aspx?relid=162140

Piccinini, E., Hanelt, A., Gregory, R. W., & Kolbe, L. M. 2015. Transforming industrial business: the impact of digital transformation on automotive organizations. In: T Paper Presented at the *2015 International Conference on Information Systems: Exploring the Information Frontier, ICIS 2015* IEEE.

Picken, J. C. (2017). From startup to scalable enterprise: Laying the Foundation. *Business Horizons*, *60*(5), 587–595. doi:10.1016/j.bushor.2017.05.002

Porter, R. (1998). *The Greatest Benefit to Mankind: A Medical History of Humanity*. W. W. Norton & Company.

Potter, S., Valdez, A. M., & Cook, M. (2020). Autonomous vehicles and the urban mobility ecosystem. In W. J. Nuttall, D. V. Gibson, D. M. Trzmielak, & A. Ibarra-Junez (Eds.), *Energy and Mobility in Smart Cities* (pp. 83–98). ICE Publishing London.

Pourebrahimi, B., Bertels, K., & Vassiliadis, S. (2005, November). A survey of peer-to-peer networks. In *Proceedings of the 16th annual workshop on Circuits, Systems and Signal Processing* (pp. 570-577). IEEE.

Powell, W. W., White, D. R., Koput, K. W., & Owen-Smith, J. (2005). Network dynamics and field evolution: The growth of inter-organizational collaboration in the life sciences. *American Journal of Sociology*, *110*(4), 1132–1205. doi:10.1086/421508

Pratono, A. H., & Mahmood, R. (2015). Mediating effect of marketing capability and reward philosophy in the relationship between innovative strategies and firm performance. *Journal of Global Entrepreneurship Research*, *5*, 1–12. doi:10.1186/s40497-015-0023-x

Press Information Bureau, Government of India. (2019). *Suresh Prabhu clears proposal to encourage investments in Startups.* PIB. https://pib.gov.in/newsite/PrintRelease.aspx? relid=188720

Press Information Bureau. (2020). *Press Release.* PIB. https://pib.gov.in/PressReleseDetail.aspx?PRID=1605956

Press Trust of India. (2019, April 25). DPIIT proposes Startup India Vision 2024, Proposes tax sops for new ventures. *The Economic Times.* https://economictimes.indiatimes.com/small-biz/startups/newsbuzz/dpiit-proposesstartup-india-vision-2024-proposes-tax-sops-for-new-ventures/ articleshow/69043102.cms

Provost, F., & Fawcett, T. (2013). *Data Science for Business: What You Need to Know about Data Mining and Data-Analytic Thinking*. O'Reilly Media.

Puthal, D., Malik, N., Mohanty, S. P., Kougianos, E., & Yang, C. (2018). The blockchain as a decentralized security framework [future directions]. *IEEE Consumer Electronics Magazine*, *7*(2), 18–21. doi:10.1109/MCE.2017.2776459

Putri, D. R., Zamheri, A., Ridho, S. L. Z., Paisal, P., & Africano, F. (2022). The Mediation of Tourist Engagement on The Effect of Destination Quality on Tourist Loyalty. [IJABIM]. *International Journal of Applied Business and International Management*, *7*(1), 1–16. doi:10.32535/ijabim.v7i1.1437

Qiu, C. S., Majeed, A., Khan, S., & Watson, M. (2022). Transforming health through the metaverse. *Journal of the Royal Society of Medicine*, *115*(12), 484–486. doi:10.1177/01410768221144763 PMID:36480946

Quagrainie, A. F. (2016). *Innovative strategies dimensions and business performance of Women Entrepreneurs in three Ghanaian cities.*

Quinn, J. B., & Paquette, P. C. (1990). Technology in services: Creating organizational revolutions. *MIT Sloan Management Review*, *31*(2), 67.

Raikwar, M., Gligoroski, D., & Kralevska, K. (2019). SoK of used cryptography in blockchain. *IEEE Access : Practical Innovations, Open Solutions*, *7*, 148550–148575. doi:10.1109/ACCESS.2019.2946983

Rajan, P. (2019). *The startup ecosystem in India is scaling new heights. Here's why.* Yourstory.com. https://yourstory.com/2019/12/indian-startup-ecosystem-priyan-rajan-silicon-valley-bank?utm_pageloadtype=scroll

Rajkomar, A., Oren, E., Chen, K., Dai, A. M., Hajaj, N., Hardt, M, & Dean, J. (2018). Scalable and accurate deep learning with electronic health records. npj. *Digital Medicine*, *1*(1), 18. PMID:31304302

Rammer, C., Fernández, G. P., & Czarnitzki, D. (2022). Artificial intelligence and industrial innovation: Evidence from German firm-level data. *Research Policy*, *51*(7), 104555. doi:10.1016/j.respol.2022.104555

Randazzo, G., Reitano, G., Carletti, F., Iafrate, M., Betto, G., Novara, G., ... Zattoni, F. (2023). Urology: A trip into metaverse. *World Journal of Urology*, 1–11. PMID:37552265

Rane, N., Choudhary, S., & Rane, J. (2023). Sustainable tourism development using leading-edge Artificial Intelligence (AI), Blockchain, Internet of Things (IoT), Augmented Reality (AR) and Virtual Reality (VR) technologies. SSRN *Electronic Journal*. doi:10.2139/ssrn.4642605

Rani, D., & Ranjan, R. K. (2014). A comparative study of SaaS, PaaS, and IaaS in cloud computing. *International Journal of Advanced Research in Computer Science and Software Engineering*, *4*(6).

Ranjan, R., & Sharma, A. (2019). *Evaluation of Frequent Item set Mining Platforms using Apriori and FP-Growth Algorithm.* arXiv preprint arXiv:1902.10999.

Ransbotham, S., Kiron, D., & Palmer, D. (2017). The Benefits—and Limits—of Cyber Value-at-Risk. *MIT Sloan Management Review*, *58*(3), 1–10.

Rao, B., & Jimenez, B. (2011, July). A comparative analysis of digital innovation ecosystems. In *2011 Proceedings of PICMET'11: Technology management in the energy smart world (PICMET)* (pp. 1-12). IEEE.

Rebecca Yen, H., Gwinner, K. P., & Su, W. (2004). The impact of customer participation and service expectation on Locus attributions following service failure. *International Journal of Service Industry Management*, *15*(1), 7–26. doi:10.1108/09564230410523312

Rehman, S. U., Usman, M., Fernando, Y., Kamarudin, D., & Waheed, A. (2023). Improving manufacturing supply chain performance: nexus of industrial Internet of Things, blockchain technology and innovativeness. *Journal of Science and Technology Policy Management.*

Reichheld, F. F., & Schefter, P. (2000). E-loyalty: Your Secret Weapon on the Web. *Harvard Business Review*, *78*(4), 105–113.

Reid, J. (2018). Amazon's Alexa checks into first Marriott hotel. *Business Traveler.* https://www. businesstraveller.com/business-travel/2018/10/27/amazons-alexa-checks-into-first-marriotthotel/ (accessed 10 June 2020).

Reim, W., Andersson, E., & Eckerwall, K. (2023). Enabling collaboration on digital platforms: A study of digital twins. *International Journal of Production Research*, *61*(12), 3926–3942. doi:10.1080/00207543.2022.2116499

Reinhardt, F. L., Casadesus-Masanell, R., & Nellemann, F. (2012). Maersk Line and the Future of Container Shipping. *Harvard Business School Case Study*, 9–712.

Reisman, N. R. (2022). Commentary on: Fake News, Defamation, and Online Reviews and Their Potential Devastating Consequences for Aesthetic Plastic Surgeons. *Aesthetic Surgery Journal*, *42*(8), NP554–NP555. doi:10.1093/asj/sjac097 PMID:35439283

Rezaei, J., & Ortt, R. (2018). Innovative innovative strategies and firm performance: The mediating role of functional performances. *Management Research Review*, *41*(7), 878–900. doi:10.1108/MRR-03-2017-0092

Ribau, C. P., Moreira, A. C., & Raposo, M. (2017). SMEs innovation capabilities and export performance: An innovative innovative strategies view. *Journal of Business Economics and Management*, *18*(5), 920–934. doi:10.3846/16111699.2017.1352534

Ritterbusch, G. D., & Teichmann, M. R. (2023). Defining the metaverse: A systematic literature review. *IEEE Access : Practical Innovations, Open Solutions*, *11*, 12368–12377. doi:10.1109/ACCESS.2023.3241809

Ritter, C. (2016). *Tarred and Floral: Femininity.* Race, and the Abject in Bayou.

Riva, G., Gaggioli, A., Villani, D., Cipresso, P., Repetto, C., Serino, S., & Gutiérrez-Maldonado, J. (2020). Positive technology in the clinical setting: A new vision of well-being. *Cyberpsychology, Behavior, and Social Networking*, *13*(5), 651–655.

Rivera Otero, J. M., Lagares Díez, N., Pereira López, M., & López-López, P. C. (2021). Transparency Policies in European Public Broadcasters: Sustainability, Digitalisation and Fact-Checking. *Social Sciences (Basel, Switzerland)*, *10*(6), 217. doi:10.3390/socsci10060217

Robinson, M. (2017). The tech giants of Silicon Valley are starting to rely on crime-fighting robots for security. *Business Insider.* https://www.businessinsider.com/knightscope-security-robots-microsoftuber- 2017-5

Rodríguez-Gutiérrez, M. J., Moreno, P., & Tejada, P. (2015). Innovative innovative strategies and performance of SMEs in the services industry. *Journal of Organizational Change Management*, *28*(2), 194–212. doi:10.1108/JOCM-01-2015-0020

Roentgen, W. C. (1895). A New Kind of Rays: A Preliminary Communication. *Sitzungsberichte der Würzburger Physik-medizinischen Gesellschaft*, *1895*, 132–141.

Rojko, A. (2017). Industry 4.0 concept: Background and overview. [IJIM]. *International Journal of Interactive Mobile Technologies*, *11*(5), 77–90. doi:10.3991/ijim.v11i5.7072

Romagnoli, S., Tarabu', C., Maleki Vishkaei, B., & De Giovanni, P. (2023). The Impact of Digital Technologies and Sustainable Practices on Circular Supply Chain Management. *Logistics*, *7*(1), 1. doi:10.3390/logistics7010001

Rose, K., Eldridge, S., & Chapin, L. (2015). The internet of things: An overview. [ISOC]. *The Internet Society*, *80*, 1–50.

Rosenberg, D. (2008). Inside Risks: Supply Chain Security. *Communications of the ACM*, *51*(4), 136–140.

Roy, S. N., & Sengupta, T. (2020). Impact of IoT on the Healthcare Producers: Epitomizing Pharmaceutical Drug Discovery Process. Internet of Things Use Cases for the Healthcare Industry.

Rupeika-Apoga, R., & Petrovska, K. (2022). Barriers to Sustainable Digital Transformation in Micro-, Small-, and Medium-Sized Enterprises. *Sustainability (Basel)*, *14*(20), 13558. doi:10.3390/su142013558

Sa, C., & Lee, H. (2012). Science, business, and Innovation: Understanding Networks in technology-based incubators. *R & D Management*, *42*(3), 243–253. doi:10.1111/j.1467-9310.2012.00681.x

Safi, M., Chung, J., & Pradhan, P. (2019). Review of augmented reality in aerospace industry. *Aircraft Engineering and Aerospace Technology*, *91*(9), 1187–1194. doi:10.1108/AEAT-09-2018-0241

Sakhuja, S., Jain, V., Kumar, S., Chandra, C., & Ghildayal, S. K. (2016). Genetic algorithm-based fuzzy time series tourism demand forecast model. *Industrial Management & Data Systems*, *116*(3), 483–507. doi:10.1108/IMDS-05-2015-0165

Sakshi, S., Shashi, Cerchione, R., & Bansal, H. (2020). Measuring the impact of sustainability policy and practices in tourism and hospitality industry. *Business Strategy and the Environment*, *29*(3), 1109–1126. doi:10.1002/bse.2420

Saltzman, J. (2018). *The Importance of Creating Incubator Programs for Entrepreneurs*. Entrepreneur Europe. https://www.entrepreneur.com/article/320670

Samad, S., Nilashi, M., Supriyanto, E., Morshedi, S., Ghabban, F., & Asadi, S. (2021).. . *Journal of Soft Computing and Decision Support Systems Factors Impacting Airport Service Quality Using Multi-Criteria Decision-Making Approach.*, *8*(2), 2021.

Samara, D., Magnisalis, I., & Peristeras, V. (2020). Artificial intelligence and big data in tourism: A systematic literature review. *Journal of Hospitality and Tourism Technology*, *11*(2), 343–367. doi:10.1108/JHTT-12-2018-0118

Saraswat, M., & Tripathi, R. C. (2020, December). Cloud computing: Analysis of top 5 CSPs in SaaS, PaaS, and IaaS platforms. In *2020 9th International Conference System Modeling and Advancement in Research Trends (SMART)* (pp. 300-305). IEEE.

Sautter, B. (2021). Shaping Digital Ecosystems for Sustainable Production: Assessing the Policy Impact of the 2030 Vision for Industrie 4.0. *Sustainability (Basel)*, *13*(22), 12596. doi:10.3390/su132212596

Schad, J., Dittrich, J., & Quiané-Ruiz, J. A. (2010). Runtime measurements in the cloud: Observing, analyzing, and reducing variance. *Proceedings of the VLDB Endowment International Conference on Very Large Data Bases*, *3*(1-2), 460–471. doi:10.14778/1920841.1920902

Schneier, B. (2004). *Secrets and Lies: Digital Security in a Networked World.* Wiley.

Schollmeier, R. (2001, August). A definition of peer-to-peer networking for the classification of peer-to-peer architectures and applications. In *Proceedings first international conference on peer-to-peer computing* (pp. 101-102). IEEE. 10.1109/P2P.2001.990434

Schroeder, R. (2008). Defining virtual worlds and virtual environments. *Journal of Virtual Worlds Research*, *1*(1). doi:10.4101/jvwr.v1i1.294

Schumpeter, J. A., & Nichol, A. J. (1934). Robinson's economics of imperfect competition. *Journal of Political Economy*, *42*(2), 249–259. doi:10.1086/254595

Schwinn, R., & Teo, E. (2017). *Robots or Humans: Trends in Robo-Advisory Services and Social Online Trading*. Working paper, Sim Kee Boon Institute.

Scullion, L. (2020). Experiential employer branding: A new paradigm for talent attraction and retention. *Journal of Marketing Management*, *36*(9-10), 905–922.

Scuotto, V., Nicotra, M., Del Giudice, M., Krueger, N., & Gregori, G. L. (2021). A micro foundational perspective on SMEs' growth in the digital transformation era. *Journal of Business Research*, *129*, 382–392. doi:10.1016/j.jbusres.2021.01.045

Sedalo, G., Boateng, H., & Kosiba, J. P. (2022). Exploring social media affordance in relationship marketing practices in SMEs. *Digital Business, 2*. doi:10.1016/j.digbus.2021.100017

Sen, A. (2019). Government looking at deploying larger funds for startups: Piyush Goyal. *The Hindu Business Line*. https://www.thehindubusinessline.com/economy/policy/govt-looking-at-deploying-larger-funds-for-startups-piyush-goyal/article30229659.ece

Sena Kilic, C. Ucler, L. M.-D. (2021). *Innovation at Airports: A systematic literature review*. Aviation. https://doi.org/doi.org/10.3846/aviation.2021.14917

Seyedghorban, Z., Samson, D., & Tahernejad, H. (2020). Digitalization opportunities for the procurement function: Pathways to maturity. *International Journal of Operations & Production Management*, *40*(11), 1685–1693. doi:10.1108/IJOPM-04-2020-0214

Shaikh, T. A., Rasool, T., & Lone, F. R. (2022). Towards leveraging the role of machine learning and artificial intelligence in precision agriculture and smart farming. *Computers and Electronics in Agriculture*, *198*, 107119. doi:10.1016/j.compag.2022.107119

Shamim, S., Cang, S., Yu, H., & Li, Y. (2017). Examining the feasibilities of Industry 4.0 for the hospitality sector with the lens of management practice. *Energies*, *10*(4), 499. doi:10.3390/en10040499

Shams, G., Rehman, M. A., Samad, S., & Rather, R. A. (2020). The impact of the magnitude of service failure and complaint handling on satisfaction and brand credibility in the banking industry. *Journal of Financial Services Marketing*, *25*(1-2), 25–34. doi:10.1057/s41264-020-00070-0

Shankar, V. (2018). How artificial intelligence (AI) is reshaping retailing. *Journal of Retailing*, *94*(4), vi–xi. doi:10.1016/S0022-4359(18)30076-9

Shan, P., Song, M., & Ju, X. (2016). Innovative strategies and performance: Is innovation speed a missing link? *Journal of Business Research*, *69*(2), 683–690. doi:10.1016/j.jbusres.2015.08.032

Shaown, T., Hasan, I., Mim, M. M. R., & Hossain, M. S. (2019, May). IoT-based portable ECG monitoring system for intelligent healthcare. In *2019, the 1st International Conference on Advances in Science, Engineering and Robotics Technology (ICASERT)* (pp. 1-5). IEEE.

Sharma, S. & Hari, T.N. (2018). The decade that was: how India's startup landscape has evolved. *YS Journal.* Your Story. https://yourstory.com/journal/the-decade-that-was-india-part-1

Sharma, A., & Borle, S. (2020). Sustainable service innovation: Conceptualization, measurement, and managerial implications. *Journal of Business Research*, *109*, 55–67.

Sharma, A., & Jain, D. K. (2020). Development of Industry 4.0, Advances in Science. *Technology and Innovation*, 23–38. doi:10.1007/978-3-030-14544-6_2

Sharma, A., Kaur, S., & Singh, M. (2021). A comprehensive review on blockchain and Internet of Things in healthcare. *Transactions on Emerging Telecommunications Technologies*, *32*(10), e4333. doi:10.1002/ett.4333

Sharma, A., Sharma, S., & Chaudhary, M. (2020). Are small travel agencies ready for digital marketing? Views of travel agency managers. *Tourism Management*, *79*, 104078. doi:10.1016/j.tourman.2020.104078

Sharma, R., & Pahuja, P. (2020). A Study on Service Quality of Banks in Tricity. *International Journal of Advanced Science and Technology*, *29*(11s), 1067–1077.

Sharma, S. K., & Meyer, K. E. (2019). *Industrializing innovation-the next revolution*. Springer Books. doi:10.1007/978-3-030-12430-4

Shirokova, G., Bogatyreva, K., Beliaeva, T., & Puffer, S. (2016). Innovative strategies and firm performance in different environmental settings: Contingency and configurational approaches. *Journal of Small Business and Enterprise Development*, *23*(3), 703–727. doi:10.1108/JSBED-09-2015-0132

Shi, X., Yao, S., & Luo, S. (2023). Innovative platform operations with the use of technologies in the blockchain era. *International Journal of Production Research*, *61*(11), 3651–3669. doi:10.1080/00207543.2021.1953182

Siaminwe, L., Malama, T., Chizyuka, C., Mwenda, H., & Mwanza, M. (2016). Strategic Justification of Advanced Manufacturing Technologies Through Manufacturing Technology Research. *International Journal of Engineering Research & Technology (Ahmedabad)*, *5*(01), 837–842.

Silber, I., Israeli, A., Bustin, A., & Zvi, O. B. (2009). Recovery strategies for service failures: The case of restaurants. *Journal of Hospitality Marketing & Management*, *18*(7), 730–740. doi:10.1080/19368620903170273

Simatupang, T. M., & Sridharan, R. (2002). The collaborative supply chain. *International Journal of Logistics Management*, *13*(1), 15–30. doi:10.1108/09574090210806333

Sindhuja, S., Arora, H., & Kumar, R. (2020). Impact of work-life balance on employee retention and job satisfaction in the banking sector. *International Journal of Business and Social Science*, *11*(2), 350–357.

Singh, A., & Hess, T. (2017). How chief digital officers promote the digital transformation of their companies. *MIS Quarterly Executive*, *16*(1), 1–17.

Singh, G., Mantri, A., Sharma, O., & Kaur, R. (2021). Virtual reality learning environment for enhancing electronics engineering laboratory experience. *Computer Applications in Engineering Education*, *29*(1), 229–243. doi:10.1002/cae.22333

Singh, P., Gupta, P., Jyoti, K., & Nayyar, A. (2019). Research on Auto-Scaling of Web Applications in Cloud: Survey, Trends and Future Directions. Scalable Computing. *Practice and Experience*, *20*(2), 399–432. doi:10.12694/scpe.v20i2.1537

Singh, S. P., Nayyar, A., Kumar, R., & Sharma, A. (2019). Fog computing: From architecture to edge computing and big data processing. *The Journal of Supercomputing*, *75*(4), 2070–2105. doi:10.1007/s11227-018-2701-2

Sironi, P. (2016). *FinTech innovation: from robo-advisors to goal based investing and gamification*. John Wiley & Sons. doi:10.1002/9781119227205

Skawińska, E., & Zalewski, R. I. (2020). Success factors of startups in the EU—A comparative study. *Sustainability (Basel)*, *12*(19), 8200. doi:10.3390/su12198200

Skerrett, D. (2017). Seven reasons why most chatbots launched in 2017 are dead on arrival. *Econtent Mag*. http://www.econtentmag.com/Articles/Editorial/Mobile-Moment/Seven-Reasons-Why-Most-Chatbots-Launched-in-2017-Are-Dead-on-Arrival-119104.htm

Slattery, J.P. (2022). We Must Find a Stronger Theological Voice: A Copeland Dialectic to Address Racism, Bias, and Inequity in Technology. *Journal of Moral Theology, 11*(Special Issue 1), 112-131

Šlogar, H. (2021). Longitudinal research-Innovative innovative strategies impact, innovativeness, and business performance in Croatian companies. *Entrepreneurship and Sustainability Issues*, *9*(2), 152. doi:10.9770/jesi.2021.9.2(10)

Smilor, R. W. (1987). Managing the Incubator System: Critical Success Factors to Accelerate New Company Development. *IEEE Transactions on Engineering Management*, *34*(4), 146–156.

Smith, A. K., Bolton, R. N., & Wagner, J. (1999). A model of customer satisfaction with service encounters involving failure and recovery. *JMR, Journal of Marketing Research*, *36*(3), 356–362. doi:10.1177/002224379903600305

Smith, M., Saunders, R., Stuckhardt, L., & McGinnis, J. M. (Eds.). (2017). *Best care at lower cost: The path to continuously learning health care in America*. National Academies Press.

Smith, R. (2022). Navigating the ethical minefield of artificial intelligence: Privacy, bias, and accountability. *AI Magazine*, *43*(3), 42–53. https://arxiv.org/abs/2306.01800

Snyder, H. (2019). Literature review as a research methodology: An overview and guidelines. *Journal of Business Research*, *104*, 333–339. doi:10.1016/j.jbusres.2019.07.039

Solanki, A., & Nayyar, A. (2019). Green Internet of Things (G-IoT): ICT Technologies, Principles, Applications, Projects, and Challenges. In Handbook of Research on Big Data and the IoT (pp. 379-405). IGI Global.

Solove, D. J. (2008). *Understanding Privacy*. Harvard University Press.

Son, L. H., Tripathy, H. K., Acharya, B. R., Kumar, R., & Chatterjee, J. M. (2019). Machine learning on big data: A developmental approach on societal applications. *Big Data Processing Using Spark in Cloud*, 143-165.

Sople, V. V. (2009). *Logistics Management, 2/E*. Pearson Education India.

Sreekanth, S Shakeel. (2020). A Study on Online Shopping Behaviour of College Students in Hyderabad Region. *Aegaeum Journal*, *8*(4), 911–919.

Startup Business. (2019). What is Deep Tech and which startups are marking the road (not Uber)? Startup Business. https://www.startupbusiness.it/what-is-deep-tech-and-which-startups-are-marking-the-road-not-uber/96448/

Startup India kit. (2019). Startup India. https://www.startupindia.gov.in/content/dam/investindia/Templates/public/Startup%20India%20Kit_2021_V2.pdf

Startup India. (2019). Startup engagement: Best practices for large organizations. *Startup India.* https://www.startupindia.gov.in/content/dam/invest-india/Templates/public/incubator_page_content/Startup%20Engagement%20Best%20Practices%20for%20%20Large%20Organizations.pdf

State Ranking System. (2021). Startup India. https://www.startupindia.gov.in/srf/

Staudenmayer, N., Tripsas, M., & Tucci, C. L. (2005). Interfirm modularity and its implications for product development. *Journal of Product Innovation Management, 22*(4), 303–321. doi:10.1111/j.0737-6782.2005.00128.x

StaykovaK. S.DamsgaardJ. (2015, May). A Typology of Multi-sided Platforms: The Core and the Periphery. In ECIS. http://doi.org/ doi:10.18151/7217486

Stenholm, P. A., Pukkinen, T., & Heinonen, J. (2016). Firm growth in family businesses—The role of innovative strategies and the innovative activity. *Journal of Small Business Management, 54*(2), 697–713. doi:10.1111/jsbm.12166

Stodt, J., Stodt, F., Reich, C., & Clarke, N. (2022, December). Verifiable Machine Learning Models in Industrial IoT via Blockchain. In *Proceedings of the 12th International Advanced Computing Conference, Hyderabad, Telangana* (pp. 16–17). IEEE.

Strønen, F. (2020). Drivers for digitalization in retail and service industries. In: *Proceedings of the 16th European conference on management leadership and governance.* ACPI

SubburayanB. (2023). *The Artificial Intelligence (AI) Odyssey: Redefining Travel and Tourism for Modern Explorers.* doi:10.13140/RG.2.2.22816.15362

Sumarsi, A. (2022). The impact of employee competency and quality of life at work on organizational commitment and organizational citizenship behavior. *International Journal of Management and Humanities, 4*(3), 97–104.

Sum, C., & Teo, C. (1999). Strategic posture of logistics service providers in Singapore. *International Journal of Physical Distribution & Logistics Management, 29*(9), 588–605. doi:10.1108/09600039910287538

Sundaram, D. S., Jurowski, C., & Webster, C. (1997). Service failure recovery efforts in restaurant dining: The role of criticality of service consumption. *Hospitality Research Journal, 20*(3), 137–149.

Sussan, F., & Acs, Z. J. (2017). The digital entrepreneurial ecosystem. *Small Business Economics, 49*(1), 55–73. doi:10.1007/s11187-017-9867-5

Sutiyem, S., Trismiyanti, D., Linda, M. R., Yonita, R., & Suheri, S. (2020). The impact of job satisfaction and employee engagement on organizational commitment. *Dinasti International Journal of Education Management And Social Science, 2*(1), 55–66. doi:10.31933/dijemss.v2i1.597

Su, Z., Xie, E., & Wang, D. (2015). Innovative strategies, managerial networking, and new venture performance in China. *Journal of Small Business Management, 53*(1), 228–248. doi:10.1111/jsbm.12069

Sweeney, L. (2002). K-Anonymity: A Model for Protecting Privacy. *International Journal of Uncertainty, Fuzziness and Knowledge-based Systems, 10*(5), 557–570. doi:10.1142/S0218488502001648

Syara, A. S., & Fauzan, T. R. (2023). Does Halal Tourism Matter? A Study About Implementation of Sharia-based Hotel in Bandung, West Java, Indonesia. *AL-MANHAJ: Jurnal Hukum Dan Pranata Sosial Islam*, *5*(2), 2045–2058. doi:10.37680/almanhaj.v5i2.3992

Tabudlo, J., Kuan, L., & Garma, P. F. (2022). Can nurses in clinical practice ascribe responsibility to intelligent robots? *Nursing Ethics*, *29*(6), 1457–1465. doi:10.1177/09697330221090591 PMID:35727571

Talukder, M. B. (2020a). An Appraisal of the Economic Outlook for the Tourism Industry, Specially Cox's Bazar in Bangladesh. *i-manager's Journal on Economics & Commerce, 2*(1), 23-35. doi:10.26634/jecom.2.1.17285

Talukder, M. B., & Kumar, S. (2023). *The Effect of Food Service Quality onCustomer Satisfaction in the Hotel Industry: A Conceptual Paper*. ResearchGate. https://www.researchgate.net/publication/371503829_The_Effect_of_Food_Service_Quality_on_Customer_Satisfaction_in_the_Hotel_Industry_A_Conceptual_Paper

Talukder, M., Shakhawat Hossain, M., & Kumar, S. (2022). Blue Ocean Strategies in Hotel Industry in Bangladesh: A Review of Present Literatures' Gap and Suggestions for Further Study. SSRN Electronic Journal. https://doi.org/doi:10.2139/ssrn.4160709

Talukder, M. B. (2020b). The Future of Culinary Tourism: An Emerging Dimension for the Tourism Industry of Bangladesh. I-Manager's. *Journal of Management*, *15*(1), 27. doi:10.26634/jmgt.15.1.17181

Talukder, M. B. (2021). An assessment of the roles of the social network in the development of the Tourism Industry in Bangladesh. *International Journal of Business, Law, and Education*, *2*(3), 85–93. doi:10.56442/ijble.v2i3.21

Talukder, M. B., Kumar, S., Sood, K., & Grima, S. (2023). Information Technology, Food Service Quality and Restaurant Revisit Intention. *International Journal of Sustainable Development and Planning*, *18*(1), 295–303. doi:10.18280/ijsdp.180131

Tang, M. F., Lee, J., Liu, K., & Lu, Y. (2014). Assessing government-supported technology-based business incubators: Evidence from China. *International Journal of Technology Management, 65*(1/2/3/4), 24. doi:10.1504/IJTM.2014.060956

Tan, K. G., Gopalan, S., & Sharma, J. (2019). Impact of exchange rates on exports from India's sub-national economies. *South Asian Journal of Business Studies*, *8*(2), 166–184. doi:10.1108/SAJBS-09-2018-0100

Tanpanuwat, A. (2011). *Examining revenue management practices in Las Vegas casino resorts.*

Tan, T. F., Li, Y., Lim, J. S., Gunasekeran, D. V., Teo, Z. L., Ng, W. Y., & Ting, D. S. (2022). Metaverse and virtual health care in ophthalmology: Opportunities and challenges. *Asia-Pacific Journal of Ophthalmology*, *11*(3), 237–246. doi:10.1097/APO.0000000000000537 PMID:35772084

Tao. F., Sun, X., CHENG, J., Zhu, Y., Liu, W., Wang, Y., & Xiaohui, J. I. N. (2023). makeTwin: A reference architecture for digital twin software platform. *Chinese Journal of Aeronautics 37*(1), 1-18. doi:10.1016/j.cja.2023.05.002

Tashman, L. (2000). Out-of-sample tests of forecasting accuracy: An analysis and review. *International Journal of Forecasting*, *16*(4), 437–450. doi:10.1016/S0169-2070(00)00065-0

Taulli, T. (2019). *Artificial Intelligence Basics*. APress. https://www.visitfaroeislands. com/

Tavoletti, E. (2013). Business incubators: Effective infrastructures or waste of public money? Looking for a theoretical framework, guidelines and criteria. *Journal of the Knowledge Economy*, *4*(4), 423–443. doi:10.1007/s13132-012-0090-y

Teece, D. J. (2010). Business models, business strategy, and innovation. *Long Range Planning*, *43*(2-3), 172–194. doi:10.1016/j.lrp.2009.07.003

Tehseen, S., & Ramayah, T. (2015). Entrepreneurial Competencies and SMEs Business Success: The Contingent Role of External Integration. *Mediterranean Journal of Social Sciences*, *6*(1), 50. https://www.richtmann.org/journal/index.php/mjss/article/view/5434. doi:10.5901/mjss.2015.v6n1p50

Teixeira, T., Patrício, L., Nunes, N. J., Nóbrega, L., Fisk, R. P., & Constantine, L. (2012). Customer experience modeling: From customer experience to service design. *Journal of Service Management*, *23*(3), 362–376. doi:10.1108/09564231211248453

Tene, O., & Polonetsky, J. (2013). Big Data for All: Privacy and User Control in the Age of Analytics. *Northwestern Journal of Technology and Intellectual Property*, *11*, 239.

The Comprehensive Guide to Finnish startup ecosystem - P1/2 . (2019). Aurabear. https://www.aurabear.com/blog/the-comprehensive-guide-to-finnish-startup-ecosystem-p1-2

The Economist. (2019). India's missing middle class. *Economist*. https://www.economist.com/briefing/2018/01/ 11/Indias-missing-middle-class

The Future of Food and Agriculture – Trends and challenges. (2017). The Food and Agriculture Organization (FAO). https://www.fao.org/3/i6583e/i6583e.pdf

The global risks report 2020. (2020). World Economic Forum. https://www.weforum.org/reports/the-global-risks-report-2020

The State Council of the People's Republic of China. (2016). *Made in China 2025*. SCPRC. http://english.gov.cn/2016special/ madeinchina2025/.

The State of World Fisheries and Aquaculture 2020. (2020). The Food and Agriculture Organization (FAO). https://www.fao.org/3/ca9229en/CA9229EN.pdf

The World Bank. (2018) *Digital Platforms and the Future of Tourism*. Retrieved October 20, 2023, from https://www.worldbank.org/en/news/feature/2018/09/25/digital-platforms-and-the-future-of-tourism-a-world-tourism-celebration

Theriou, N., Maditinos, D. I., & Theriou, G. (2017). Management control systems and strategy: A resource-based perspective. Evidence from Greece. *International Journal of Business and Economic Sciences Applied Research*, *10*(2), 35–47. doi:10.25103/ijbesar.102.04

Thomas, L. D., Autio, E., & Gann, D. M. (2014). Architectural leverage: Putting platforms in context. *The Academy of Management Perspectives*, *28*(2), 198–219. doi:10.5465/amp.2011.0105

Thomason, J. (2021). Metahealth-how will the metaverse change health care? *Journal of Metaverse*, *1*(1), 13–16.

Thovex, C., & Trichet, F. (2013). Opinion mining and semantic analysis of touristic social networks. *Proceedings of the 2013 IEEE/ACM International Conference on Advances in Social Networks Analysis and Mining - ASONAM '13*. IEEE. 10.1145/2492517.2500235

Thrall, J. H. (2008). The next-generation PACS: Implications for radiology. *Journal of the American College of Radiology*, *5*(5), 431–434.

Thums, J., Künzel, L., Klumpp, M., Bardmann, M., & Ruiner, C. (2023). Transportation Research Interdisciplinary Perspectives Future air transportation and digital work at airports – Review and developments. *Transportation Research Interdisciplinary Perspectives*, *19*(March), 100808. doi:10.1016/j.trip.2023.100808

Timmermans, J., Stahl, B. C., Ikonen, V., & Bozdag, E. 2010, November. The ethics of cloud computing: A conceptual review. In *2010, IEEE hosted its second international conference on cloud computing technology and science* (pp. 614-620). IEEE. 10.1109/CloudCom.2010.59

Tinkham, M. A., & Kleiner, B. H. (1993). New developments in service operations management. *Work Study, 42*(1), 16–19. doi:10.1108/EUM0000000002691

Tiwari, S., Kumar, S., & Guleria, K. (2020). Outbreak trends of coronavirus disease–2019 in India: A prediction. *Disaster Medicine and Public Health Preparedness, 14*(5), e33–e38. doi:10.1017/dmp.2020.115 PMID:32317044

Topol, E. (2020). Telemedicine is essential amid the COVID-19 crisis and after it. *The Economist.*

Topol, E. J. (2019). Deep Medicine: How Artificial Intelligence Can Make Healthcare Human Again. Hachette, UK.

Topol, E. J. (2019). High-performance medicine: The convergence of human and artificial intelligence. *Nature Medicine, 25*(1), 44–56. doi:10.1038/s41591-018-0300-7 PMID:30617339

Tortorella, G. L., Giglio, R., & Van Dun, D. H. (2019). Industry 4.0 adoption as a moderator of the impact of lean production practices on operational performance improvement. *International Journal of Operations & Production Management, 39*(6/7/8), 860–886.

Trabucchi, D., Buganza, T., Muzellec, L., & Ronteau, S. (2021). Platform-driven innovation: Unveiling research and business opportunities. *Creativity and Innovation Management, 30*(1), 6–11. doi:10.1111/caim.12428

Travelmate. (2019). Travelmate suitcase features. *TravelMate.* https://travelmaterobotics.com/ (accessed 10 June 2020).

Trejos, N. (2016). Introducing Connie, Hilton's new robot concierge. *USA Today.* https://www. usatoday.com/story/travel/roadwarriorvoices/2016/03/09/introducing-connie-hiltons-new-robotconcierge/ 81525924/

Tronvoll, B., Sklyar, A., Sörhammar, D., & Kowalkowski, C. (2020). Transformational shifts through digital servitization. *Industrial Marketing Management, 89*, 293–305. doi:10.1016/j.indmarman.2020.02.005

Trzmielak, D. M., Shonia, D., & Skoneczna, M. (2021). Marketing, Start-Ups and Innovation: A Framework for Understanding the Possibilities for Harnessing Technological Innovations in Tourism (Based on the Example of the Georgian Tourism Sector and Russian Start-Ups). *Marketing of Scientific and Research Organizations, 40*(2), 93–113. doi:10.2478/minib-2021-0011

Tsaih, R. H., & Hsu, C. C. (2018). *Artificial intelligence in smart tourism: A conceptual framework.*

Tsai, W., Bai, X., & Huang, Y. (2014). Software-as-a-service (SaaS): Perspectives and challenges. *Science China. Information Sciences, 57*(5), 1–15. doi:10.1007/s11432-013-5050-z

Tucson, R. V., Edmunds, M., & Hodgkins, M. L. (2017). Telehealth. *The New England Journal of Medicine, 377*(16), 1585–1592. doi:10.1056/NEJMsr1503323 PMID:29045204

Tung, V. W. S., & Au, N. (2018). Exploring customer experiences with robotics in hospitality. *International Journal of Contemporary Hospitality Management, 30*(7), 2680–2697. doi:10.1108/IJCHM-06-2017-0322

Tussyadiah, I. P., & Park, S. (2018). Consumer evaluation of hotel service robots. In *Information and Communication Technologies in Tourism 2018: Proceedings of the International Conference in Jönköping,* (pp. 308-320). Springer International Publishing.

Tussyadiah, I. (2020). A review of research into automation in tourism: Launching the Annals of Tourism Research Curated Collection on Artificial Intelligence and Robotics in Tourism. *Annals of Tourism Research, 81*, 102883. doi:10.1016/j.annals.2020.102883

Tussyadiah, I., & Miller, G. (2019). Nudged by a robot: Responses to agency and feedback. *Annals of Tourism Research, 78*, 102752. doi:10.1016/j.annals.2019.102752

Tyagi, Y., & Saxena, S. (2022). Applications of Artificial Intelligence, Metaverse and Data Science for Intelligent Healthcare. *AAYAM: AKGIM Journal of Management*, *12*(2), 141–149.

Uhodnikova, O., Sokolenko, A., Ryabev, A., Abramov, V., Pokolodna, M., Kravtsova, S., Shevchenko, V., & Miroshnichenko, Yu. (2022). Innovative approaches to the management of effective communications in tourism and the hotel and restaurant industry. *Municipal Economy of Cities*, *7*(174), 9–13. doi:10.33042/2522-1809-2022-7-174-9-13

Ukpabi, D. C., Aslam, B., & Karjaluoto, H. (2019). Chatbot adoption in tourism services: A conceptual exploration. In *Robots, artificial intelligence, and service automation in travel, tourism and hospitality* (pp. 105–121). Emerald Publishing Limited. doi:10.1108/978-1-78756-687-320191006

Ukpabi, D., Karjaluoto, H., Olaleye, S. A., & Mogaji, E. (2018). Dual Perspectives on the Role of Artificially Intelligent Robotic Virtual Agents in the Tourism, Travel and Hospitality Industries. In D. Vrontis, Y. Weber, & E. Tsoukatos (Eds.), *Proceedings of the 11th Annual Conference of the EuroMed Academy of Business (EMAB)* (pp. 1339–1351). EuroMed Press. https://www.emrbi.org/bop2018.pdf

United Nations. (2019). *World population prospects 2019: Highlights | multimedia library - united nations department of economic and social affairs*. United Nations. https://www.un.org/development/desa/publications/world-population-prospects-2019-highlights.html

United Nations. (2021). *Goal 2: Zero Hunger - United Nations Sustainable Development*. United Nations. https://www.un.org/sustainabledevelopment/hunger/#:~:text=Current%20estimates%20show%20that%20nearly,achieve%20Zero%20Hunger%20by%202030.

UNWTO. (2020) *Tourism and Covid-19*. UNWTO. https://www.unwto.org/tourism-covid-19-coronavirus

Upadhyay, Y., Paul, J., & Baber, R. (2022). Effect of online social media marketing efforts on customer response. *Journal of Consumer Behaviour*, *21*(3), 554–571. doi:10.1002/cb.2031

Ustymenko, R. (2023). Trends and innovations in cosmetic marketing. *Economics & Education*, *8*(3), 12–17. doi:10.30525/2500-946X/2023-3-2

Vacca, J. R. (2017). *Computer and Information Security Handbook*. Morgan Kaufmann.

Valdez-De-Leon, O. (2019). How to develop a digital ecosystem: A practical framework. *Technology Innovation Management Review*, *9*(8), 43–54. doi:10.22215/timreview/1260

Valenzuela, F., García, A., Ruiz, E., Vazquez, M., Cortez, J., & Espinoza, A. (2020). An IoT-based glucose monitoring algorithm to prevent diabetes complications. *applied sciences, 10*(3), 921.

Vallaster, C., Kraus, S., Lindahl, J. M. M., & Nielsen, A. (2019). Ethics and entrepreneurship: A bibliometric study and literature review. *Journal of Business Research*, *99*, 226–237. doi:10.1016/j.jbusres.2019.02.050

Van der Aa, W., & Elfring, T. (2002). Realizing innovation in services. *Scandinavian Journal of Management*, *18*(2), 155–171. doi:10.1016/S0956-5221(00)00040-3

Van Eck, N. J., & Waltman, L. (2017). Citation-based clustering of publications using CitNetExplorer and VOSviewer. *Scientometrics*, *111*(2), 1053–1070. doi:10.1007/s11192-017-2300-7 PMID:28490825

Van Riel, A. C., Lemmink, J., & Ouwersloot, H. (2004). High-technology service innovation success: A decision-making perspective. *Journal of Product Innovation Management*, *21*(5), 348–359. doi:10.1111/j.0737-6782.2004.00087.x

van Rijnsoever, F. J., & Eveleens, C. P. (2021). Money Don't matter? How incubation experience affects start-up entrepreneurs' resource valuation. *Technovation*, *106*, 102294. doi:10.1016/j.technovation.2021.102294

Van Vaerenbergh, Y., & Orsingher, C. (2016). Service recovery: An integrative framework and research agenda. *The Academy of Management Perspectives*, *30*(3), 328–346. doi:10.5465/amp.2014.0143

Van Wassenhove, L. N. (2006). Humanitarian aid logistics: Supply chain management in high gear. *The Journal of the Operational Research Society*, *57*(5), 475–489. doi:10.1057/palgrave.jors.2602125

Vargo, S. L., & Lusch, R. F. (2004). Evolving to a New Dominant Logic for Marketing. *Journal of Marketing*, *68*(1), 1–17. doi:10.1509/jmkg.68.1.1.24036

Vargo, S. L., & Lusch, R. F. (2008). Service-dominant logic: Continuing the evolution. *Journal of the Academy of Marketing Science*, *36*(1), 1–10. doi:10.1007/s11747-007-0069-6

Vargo, S. L., & Lusch, R. F. (2016). Institutions and axioms: An extension and update of service-dominant logic. *Journal of the Academy of Marketing Science*, *44*(1), 5–23. doi:10.1007/s11747-015-0456-3

Varma, P., Nijjer, S., Kaur, B., & Sharma, S. (2022). *Blockchain for Transformation in Digital Marketing. Handbook of Research on the Platform Economy and the Evolution of E-Commerce*. IGI Global. doi:10.4018/978-1-7998-7545-1.ch012

Verhoef, P. C., Broekhuizen, T., Bart, Y., Bhattacharya, A., Dong, J. Q., Fabian, N., & Haenlein, M. (2021). Digital transformation: A multidisciplinary reflection and research agenda. *Journal of Business Research*, *122*, 889–901. doi:10.1016/j.jbusres.2019.09.022

Verhoef, P. C., Kannan, P. K., & Inman, J. J. (2015). From Multi-Channel Retailing to Omni-Channel Retailing: Introduction to the Special Issue on Multi-Channel Retailing. *Journal of Retailing*, *91*(2), 174–181. doi:10.1016/j.jretai.2015.02.005

Verma, A. K., Raval, P. D., Rajagopalan, N., Khariya, V., & Sudha, R. (2022). Development of an AI-based FSA for real-time condition monitoring for industrial machines. *Neural Computing & Applications*, *34*(11), 8597–8615. doi:10.1007/s00521-021-06741-w

Vermesan, O., & Friess, P. (2014). *Internet of things: Converging technologies for smart environments and integrated ecosystems*. River Publishers.

Vijayan, B., & Shivkumar, P. S. (2020). Pro-AgripreneurialFactorsfortheFormationofAgri-startupsinIndia.*Asian Journal of Agricultural Extension. Economia e Sociologia*, *38*(8), 1–8. doi:10.9734/ajaees/2020/v38i830381

Wach, K. (2015). Innovative strategies and business internationalisation process: The theoretical foundations of international entrepreneurshiParticipant *Innovative. Business and Economic Review*, *3*(2), 9–24.

Wahyuni, N. M., & Sara, I. M. (2020). The effect of innovative strategies variables on business performance in the SME industry context. *Journal of Workplace Learning*, *32*(1), 35–62. doi:10.1108/JWL-03-2019-0033

Wald, L. L., McDaniel, P. C., Witzel, T., Stockmann, J. P., & Cooley, C. Z. (2020). Low-cost and portable MRI. *Journal of Magnetic Resonance Imaging*, *52*(3), 686–696. doi:10.1002/jmri.26942 PMID:31605435

Wang, J. (2018). You can now check in with a facial scan at Marriott in China. *Forbes*. https:// www.forbes.com/sites/jennawang/2018/07/24/you-can-now-check-in-with-a-facial-scan-atmarriott/#42eeb8a33f7a (accessed 5 June 2020).

Wang, G., Badal, A., Jia, X., Maltz, J. S., Mueller, K., Myers, K. J., Niu, C., Vannier, M., Yan, P., Yu, Z., & Zeng, R. (2022). Development of metaverse for intelligent healthcare. *Nature Machine Intelligence*, *4*(11), 922–929. doi:10.1038/s42256-022-00549-6 PMID:36935774

Wang, G., Gunasekaran, A., Ngai, E. W. T., & Papadopoulos, T. (2016). Big data analytics in logistics and supply chain management: Certain investigations for research and applications. *International Journal of Production Economics*, *176*, 98–110. doi:10.1016/j.ijpe.2016.03.014

Wang, J., Li, Y., Wu, B., & Wang, Y. (2021). Tourism destination image based on tourism user generated content on internet. *Tourism Review*, *76*(1), 125–137. doi:10.1108/TR-04-2019-0132

Wang, R., & Zhang, Y. (2022). Blockchain technology for supply chain transparency: Challenges and opportunities. *International Journal of Logistics Management*, *33*(3), 596–612. https://www.emerald.com/insight/content/doi/10.1108/K-05-2021-0384/full/html

Wang, Y., Lo, H. P., Chi, R., & Yang, Y. (2004). An integrated framework for customer value and customer-relationship-management performance: A customer-based perspective from China. *Managing Service Quality*, *14*(2/3), 169–182. doi:10.1108/09604520410528590

Water and agriculture in India. (2017). OAV. https://www.oav.de/fileadmin/user_upload/5_Publikationen/5_Studien/170118_Study_Water_Agriculture_India.pdf

Waxer, C. (2016). *Get ready for the bot revolution. Computer World, online link can be. Computer World.* https://www.computerworld.com/article/3126438/emerging-technology/article.html,

Wayblazer. (2017). *About way blazer*. Way Blazer. https://www.wayblazer.ai/about/

Weekx, S., & Buyle, S. (2023). Journal of Air Transport Management The effect of airline dominance on airport performance : Empirical evidence from medium-sized European airports. *Journal of Air Transport Management*, *107*(November 2022), 102317. doi:10.1016/j.jairtraman.2022.102317

Weerasinghe, M., Kodikara, N.D., Dammika, N., Nisansala, A., Keppitiyagama, C., Buddhika, I., & Perera, C. (2016). *Poster: Virtual Eye-A smarter mode of interaction to virtual tours*. doi:10.1145/2938559.2948861

Wei, C., Li, J., & Guo, X. (2022). Influence Analysis of Hotel and Tourism Economic Development Based on Computational Intelligence. *Security and Communication Networks*, *2022*, 1–9. doi:10.1155/2022/7549628

Weill, P., & Woerner, S. L. (2015). Thriving in an increasingly digital ecosystem. *MIT Sloan Management Review*.

Weinberger, M. (2022). What Is Metaverse?—A Definition Based on Qualitative Meta-Synthesis. *Future Internet*, *14*(11), 310. doi:10.3390/fi14110310

Wei, Y., & Blake, M. B. (2010). Service-oriented computing and cloud computing: Challenges and opportunities. *IEEE Internet Computing*, *14*(6), 72–75. doi:10.1109/MIC.2010.147

Wei, Z., Yang, D., Sun, B., & Gu, M. (2014). The fit between technological innovation and business model design for firm growth: Evidence from China. *R & D Management*, *44*(3), 288–305. doi:10.1111/radm.12069

Weng, G., & Li, L. (2015). Study of tourism flow forecasting based on a seasonally adjusted particle swarm optimization-support vector regression model. *Journal of Information and Computational Science*, *12*(7), 2747–2757. doi:10.12733/jics20105860

Westerman, G., Tannou, M., Bonnet, D., & Ferraris, P. (2011). *The Digital Advantage: How Digital Leaders Outperform Their Peers in Every Industry*. Capgemini Consulting.

White, M. (2012). Digital workplaces: Vision and reality. *Business Information Review*, *29*(4), 205–214. doi:10.1177/0266382112470412

Whitman, M. E., & Mattord, H. J. (2018). *Principles of Information Security*. Cengage Learning.

Widarsyah, R. (2013). *The Impact of Airport Service Quality Dimension on Overall Airport Experience and Impression.*

Wider, W., Jiang, L., Li, J., Tanucan, J. C. M., & Fauzi, M. A. (2023). *A Bibliometric Study on the Rising Trends of Metaverse Literature in Asia-Pacific Countries.*

Wiener, N. (2017). Some moral and technical consequences of automation. In *Computer Ethics* (pp. 13–16). Routledge. doi:10.4324/9781315259697-3

Wildan, M. D. A. (2021). Covid-19 And Implementation Of Airport Health And Safety Procedures The Safety Culture Perception. *Syntax Literate:Jurnal Ilmiah Indonesia.*

Winston, P. H. (1992). *Artificial intelligence*. Addison-Wesley Longman Publishing Co., Inc.

Wirtz, J., & Mattila, A. S. (2004). Consumer responses to compensation, speed of recovery and apology after a service failure. *International Journal of Service Industry Management*, *15*(2), 150–166. doi:10.1108/09564230410532484

WrightA.De FilippiP. (2015). Decentralized blockchain technology and the rise of lex cryptographia. SSRN 2580664. doi:10.2139/ssrn.2580664

Wu, F., Yeniyurt, S., Kim, D., & Cavusgil, S. T. (2006). The impact of information technology on supply chain capabilities and firm performance: A resource-based view. *Industrial Marketing Management*, *35*(4), 493–504. doi:10.1016/j.indmarman.2005.05.003

Wyld, D. C. (2009). Preventing the worst-case scenario: Analyzing RFID technology and infant protection in hospitals. *Novel Algorithms and Techniques in Telecommunications and Networking*, *7*(1), 29–33.

Xie, L., & Lee, Y.-J. (2015). Hotels at Our Fingertips: Understanding Consumer Conversion from Search, Click-Through, to Book. SSRN *Electronic Journal*. doi:10.2139/ssrn.2609514

Yang, D., Zhou, J., Song, Y., Sun, M., & Bai, C. (2022). Metaverse in medicine. *Clinical eHealth, 5*, 39-43.

Yang, C., & Liu, H. (2012). Boosting firm performance via enterprise agility and network structure. *Management Decision*, *50*(6), 1022–1044. doi:10.1108/00251741211238319

Yang, L., Holtz, D., Jaffe, S., Suri, S., Sinha, S., Weston, J., Joyce, C., Shah, N., Sherman, K., Hecht, B., & Teevan, J. (2022). The effects of remote work on collaboration among information workers. *Nature Human Behaviour*, *6*(1), 43–54. doi:10.1038/s41562-021-01196-4 PMID:34504299

Yang, X., & De Veciana, G. (2006). Performance of peer-to-peer networks: Service capacity and role of resource sharing policies. *Performance Evaluation*, *63*(3), 175–194. doi:10.1016/j.peva.2005.01.005

Yan, X., Melkote, S., Mishra, A. K., & Rajagopalan, S. (2022). A digital apprentice for chatter detection in machining via human–machine interaction. *Journal of Intelligent Manufacturing*, 1–14.

Yao, S. (2018). Categorizing listing photos at Airbnb. *Medium.* https://medium.com/airbnbengineering/categorizing-listing-photos-at-airbnb-f9483f3ab7e3

Yeh, H. C., Yu, M. C., Liu, C. H., & Huang, C. I. (2023). Robo-advisor based on unified theory of acceptance and use of technology. *Asia Pacific Journal of Marketing and Logistics*, *35*(4), 962–979. doi:10.1108/APJML-07-2021-0493

Yeniyurt, S., Wu, F., Kim, D., & Cavusgil, S. T. (2019). Information technology resources, innovativeness, and supply chain capabilities as drivers of business performance: A retrospective and future research directions. *Industrial Marketing Management*, *79*, 46–52. doi:10.1016/j.indmarman.2019.03.008

Yeung, K. (2019). 'Hypernudge': Big Data as a mode of regulation by design. In *The social power of algorithms* (pp. 118–136). Routledge. doi:10.4324/9781351200677-8

Yixian, L., & Xiao, T. (2023). *Digital platforms and digital ecosystems in the digital economy.*

Yu, H., Shum, C., Alcorn, M., Sun, J., & He, Z. (2022). Robots can't take my job: Antecedents and outcomes of Gen Z employees' service robot risk awareness. *International Journal of Contemporary Hospitality Management, 34*(8), 2971–2988. doi:10.1108/IJCHM-10-2021-1312

Zaech, S., & Baldegger, U. (2017). Leadership in start-ups. *International Small Business Journal, 35*(2), 157–177. doi:10.1177/0266242616676883

Zarrin, J., Wen Phang, H., Babu Saheer, L., & Zarrin, B. (2021). Blockchain for decentralization of internet: Prospects, trends, and challenges. *Cluster Computing, 24*(4), 2841–2866. doi:10.1007/s10586-021-03301-8 PMID:34025209

Zarrouk, H., Sherif, M., Galloway, L., & El Ghak, T. (2020). Innovative strategies, access to financial resources and SMEs' business performance: The case of the United Arab Emirates. *Journal of Asian Finance. Economics and Business, 7*(12), 465–474.

Zeithaml, V. A., Berry, L. L., & Parasuraman, A. (1996). The Behavioral Consequences of Service Quality. *Journal of Marketing, 60*(2), 31–46. doi:10.1177/002224299606000203

Zemke, R., & Bell, C. (1990). Service recovery: Doing it right the second time. *Training (New York, N.Y.), 27*(6), 42–49.

Zhai, S., Yang, Y., Li, J., Qiu, C., & Zhao, J. (2019, February). Research on the Application of Cryptography on the Blockchain. In Journal of Physics: Conference Series (Vol. 1168, p. 032077). IOP Publishing. doi:10.1088/1742-6596/1168/3/032077

Zhang, C., & Huang, Z. (2015). Mining tourist motive for marketing development via TwiceLearning. *Applied Artificial Intelligence, 29*(2), 119–133. doi:10.1080/08839514.2015.993554

Zhang, X., Chen, Y., Hu, L., & Wang, Y. (2022). The metaverse in education: Definition, framework, features, potential applications, challenges, and future research topics. *Frontiers in Psychology, 13*, 6063. doi:10.3389/fpsyg.2022.1016300 PMID:36304866

Zhang, Y., Xiong, Y., Lee, T. J., Ye, M., & Nunkoo, R. (2021). Sociocultural Sustainability and the Formation of Social Capital from Community-based Tourism. *Journal of Travel Research, 60*(3), 656–669. doi:10.1177/0047287520933673

Zhang, Z., Wang, X., & Jia, M. (2021). Echoes of CEO innovative strategies: How and when CEO innovative strategies influence dual CSR activities. *Journal of Business Ethics, 169*, 609–629. doi:10.1007/s10551-020-04553-x

Zhao, L., Li, S., & Xu, M. (2023). Research on the application of blockchain technology in supply chain traceability. *IEEE Access : Practical Innovations, Open Solutions, 11*, 23056–23068. https://ieeexplore.ieee.org/document/9730966

Zhou, K., Liu, T., & Zhou, L. (2015, August). Industry 4.0: Towards future industrial opportunities and challenges. In *2015 12th International conference on fuzzy systems and knowledge discovery (FSKD)* (pp. 2147-2152). IEEE.

Zhou, W., & Liu, Z. (2022). Design and Optimization of Hotel Management Information System Based on Artificial Intelligence. *Scientific Programming, 2022*, 1–9. doi:10.1155/2022/2445343

Zhu, S., Yu, T., Xu, T., Chen, H., Dustdar, S., Gigan, S., & Pan, Y. (2023). Intelligent computing: the latest advances, challenges, and future. *Intelligent Computing, 2*, 0006.

About the Contributors

Sridhar Manohar, currently working In Doctoral Research Center, Chitkara University, completed his doctorate in the area of Services Marketing from VIT Business School, VIT University. He has a Bachelor of Technology and Dual Masters in Business Administration and Organization Psychology. Dr. Sridhar further certified with FDP at IIM-A. He is expertise in Service Marketing, Innovation and Entrepreneurship, Scale Development Process and Multivariate Analytics and interests in teaching Business Analytics, Innovation and Entrepreneurship, Research Methodology and Marketing Management. He has published around 20 research papers that includes Scopus listed and ABDC ranked International Journals like – Society and Business Review, Benchmarking-An International Journal, Electronics Market, Corporate Reputation Review, International Journal of Services and Operations Management, International journal of Business Excellence and presented papers and ideas in numerous international conferences.

Amit Mittal is a Professor of Management / Dean at Chitkara University, Punjab, India, and Dean, Doctoral Research Centre. He has over 19 years of experience in teaching, research, consulting, and academic administration. His areas of research and consulting expertise are graduate employability, leadership, emerging market studies, business research methods, etc. Eight scholars have been awarded a PhD under his supervision. He has published in reputable journals such as Frontiers in Psychology; Benchmarking; European Business Review; Business: Theory & Practice; International Journal of Quality Research; South Asian Journal of Business Management Cases; International Journal of Human Capital & Information Technology Professionals; International Journal of e-Services & Mobile Applications; International Journal of Business & Globalisation; International Journal of Socio-technology & Knowledge Development, etc. He is also a reviewer for the International Journal of Consumer Studies; International Journal of Quality Research; Frontiers in Psychology; Higher Education, Skills & Work-based Learning; Business: Theory & Practice, etc.

***

Arun Aggarwal is an Assistant Professor at Chitkara University, Punjab, India. He currently holds prestigious editorial roles, including Senior Editor of Global Business and Organizational Excellence (Wiley) and Editorial Board Member of the International Journal of Work Innovation. Under his supervision, seven PhD candidates have been awarded the degree of PhD in Business Management. He has been ranked as top 100 researchers by P-ranking, an international rating agency, not only in India but also in Southern Asia. He has authored an international book "Adjustment Problem and Attributional Style among Adolescents". He has served as session chair in various conferences. He has also acted as resource person in various workshops related to research methods at national and international levels. He has also served as the Guest Editor for two Scopus international journals. Dr. Aggarwal's expertise spans Human Resource Management, Organizational Behaviour, Industrial Relations, Labor Laws, and Research Methodology. With an impressive publication record, he has more than 45 papers in high-impact journals. Email ID- arunagagrwal.mba@gmail.com ORCID- 0000-0003-3986-188X

Terrance Ancheary is a young researcher and author in the field of Hospitality under tourism, being a Master's student in hospitality administration at the National Council for Hotel Management, Noida(India), he navigates the realms of academia, seamlessly blending passion and scholarly rigor. With an insatiable curiosity, he delve into the intricacies of cultural exchange, sustainable tourism, and innovative hospitality practices. His work reflects a commitment to unravelling the industry's complexities, offering fresh perspectives and contributing to the evolving narrative of tourism. Terrance envisions a future where his insights shape the trajectory of hospitality & tourism, leaving an indelible mark on the industry's sustainable and transformative growth

Esha Bansal has a vast academic and administrative experience of 16 years in various academic institutions. She is also experienced as a teacher administrator. Over the years, she has served the University in diverse roles and has headed several committees. She has been teaching courses like Operation Research, Strategic Management, Security Analysis and Investment Management, Financial Services, Insurance Management, Operations Management. She has publications in reputed national and international journals, attended FDPs/workshops to her credit and has presented papers in conferences and seminars too. She is outcome-oriented and positively motivates her students to come up with innovative ideas for their enrichment.

Aaruni Batta is a renowned academician working in the field of management education.

Nisha Chanana has more than 16 Years of teaching experience with reputed Universities. She holds a Doctor of Philosophy (Ph.D.) in Management from the University School of Management, Kurukshetra University, Kurukshetra (2015). She has also qualified for the UGC- NET in Management twice, in June 2007 and December 2010. She holds an MBA in Human Resource Management and Marketing Management from Chaudhary Charan Singh Haryana Agricultural University, Hisar (2007) where she achieved excellent academic performance. Her current research interests include Organizational Behaviour, Recent HR practices, Organizational Change and Development, Training and Development, and Strategic HRM. She has published papers in National and International Journals, published/presented papers in National Conferences and Seminars. Attended various Faculty Development Programmes and Workshops. She has been invited to deliver her expertise and insights in various seminars and workshops. She has organized various conferences, workshops, management development programmes and seminars.

Monica Chaudhary is an Associate Professor, Dept. of Marketing, SP Jain School of Global Management, Sydney, Australia. Her research interests lies in the areas of consumer behaviour, tourism and entrepreneurship. She has published several research papers in high impact factor and top ranked business journals.

Lochan Chavan is currently working as an Assistant Professor at Transstadia Institute, School of Management, Mumbai, India and holds Master Degree in Commerce and is also a Law Graduate. She is currently pursuing her PhD in Business Management from Chitkara Business School, Chitkara University, Punjab, India. She has contributed more than 5 years in teaching. Also published 2 book chapters in Scopus Indexed Journal.

Tammy Cowart is a lecturer in Business Law and Business Ethics at the Soules College of Business, The University of Texas at Tyler since 1999. She earned her law degree from Texas Tech University and Has practiced law in a variety of areas including tort law, business law and employment law.

Saurav Dixit is the Dean of the Division of Research and Development Cell at Lovely Professional University, India. He specialises in Self-healing building materials, Advanced building technology, Waste management, Automation in construction, Circular Economy, Supply chain management, E-waste modified concrete, Green concrete, Green manufacturing, Sustainable building, Lean construction, and Sustainable construction. Prof Saurav has an impressive academic record, evidenced by his H-index of 26 and the i-10 index 57. He has also edited several corrosion-related books indexed in the Scopus database and contributed to numerous book chapters for renowned publishers such as Elsevier, Springer, IGI Global, and CRC Press. Prof Saurav has served as a reviewer for several international journals. He has presented his research findings at various conferences and workshops, showcasing his commitment to staying at the forefront of advancements in his field.

G. Chamdramowleeswaran is currently working as Assistant Professor in Department of Commerce and business administration, VelTech Rangarajan Dr. Sagunthala R&D Institute of Science and Technology (Deemed to be University), Avadi, Chennai. He has more than 11 years 5 months of industry experience and 1 year and 11 months of teaching experience with specialization in HR and Marketing. He Holds a B.Com., M.B.A., M. Phil., and Ph.D. in Management from Bharathidasan University, Trichy.

G. Manoj is currently working as Associate Professor in Department of Management Studies, VelTech Rangarajan Dr. Sagunthala R&D Institute of Science and Technology (Deemed to be University), Avadi, Chennai. He has more than 10 years 5 months of teaching experience with specialization in HR and Marketing. He Holds a B.Sc., M.B.A., M. Phil., and Ph.D. in Management from Bharathidasan University, Trichy.

Suhail Ghouse has a PhD in Marketing with more than twelve years of experience in academics. Research interest in the areas of internationalization, consumer behavior, entrepreneurship, social media marketing, etc.

Priya Jindal is currently working as an Associate Professor at Chitkara Business School, Chitkara University, Punjab, India and holds a master degree in commerce and economics. She earned her doctorate in management. She has contributed more than 16 years in teaching. She supervised four Ph.D. research scholars and two M.Phil candidates. There are numerous research papers to her credit in leading journals among them seven research paper has been published in Scopus Indexed Journal. Her areas of research included Banking, Finance and insurance. She has filed more than 21 patents and two copyrights. She is the editor of two books under IGI publications and both the books got indexed in Scopus.

Ravi Lakshmanan holds a postgraduate degree in electrical engineering, a Master of Science in Quality Management, and a PhD in Management. With a professional career spanning over 46 years, including 33 years dedicated to the aviation industry, he possesses extensive expertise in airport planning, design, development, commissioning, as well as airport operations and management. Notably, he served as the CEO of GMR Airport Developers Limited in his most recent full-time role and currently serves as an advisor for GMR Airports Ltd following his retirement. Beyond his corporate roles, he contributes to academia as a visiting faculty member and guest lecturer at prominent business schools in India. Ravi Lakshmanan has authored research articles, two university course books, and has provided guidance to two research scholars. His latest publication, titled "Fundamentals of Airport Planning- Theory and Practice," focuses on airport planning and was published by Taylor and Francis (UK)..He is a member of University academic council and research advisory committee.

Nitish Kumar Minz, an exemplary Bachelor of Commerce student specializing in Business Administration and Management at K.R. Mangalam University, has made significant contributions to several research papers and book chapters currently in the final stages of publication. Holding the esteemed position of Secretary of Extension and Outreach Activity in the Student Council of K.R. Mangalam University, Mr. Minz has showcased a remarkable work ethic, unwavering commitment to excellence, and honed skills in project management and strategic planning through his internship at KEIC (KRMU Entrepreneurship & Incubation Center). He has also been chosen as NEP SAARTHI- Student Ambassador for Academic Reforms in Transforming Higher Education at K.R. Mangalam University and recently achieved the CHANCELLOR'S EXCELLENCE AWARD.

K. K. Mishra holds a Ph.D. Degree in Solid State Electronics and Master Degree in Physics with specialisation in Electronics. Dr. Mishra has a rich experience of teaching, research about 15 years with more than 30 research papers to his credit published in various journals and conferences at national & international level. Dr. Mishra has been instrumental in accreditation & quality assurance parameter and and has a well proven track record about his expertise in ranking system in India. He has been reviewer of various reputed journal and member of various governing bodies and professional societies during his tenure. Currently, he is serving as Pro Vice Chancellor (Quality Assurance) at Chitkara University, Punjab. He has visited UK, Indonesia, Kuwait and UAE for presenting his research and as a speaker in various events of reputed ranking agencies.

Neha Mishra hold Ph.D Degree in Business Management and working as Assistant Professor in Chitkara Business School at Chitkara University, India.

Mune Moğol Sever started working in the service sector after working in the manufacturing industry for a short time. Mune Moğol Sever is Assistant Professor in Anadolu University. She has a double major in industrial engineering and economics, a master's degree in tourism management, and a doctoral degree in the same field. Mune Moğol Sever has written a book titled "Industry 5.0 = Industry 4.0 + Society 5.0 Technology for People" and various research articles on service operation management and digitalization. Mune Moğol Sever conducts undergraduate courses on production management and quality management in service enterprises and master's courses on operations management and marketing research in service processing.

Anish Mondal is a dedicated and passionate individual who is currently pursuing a Masters in Hospitality Administration from NCHM IH Noida and a Masters in Tourism and Travel Management (MTTM) from IGNOU simultaneously. He completed his graduation from IHM Mumbai. He has a strong understanding of the industry's nuances and a keen interest in exploring and contributing to its ever-evolving landscape. His work reflects a commitment to unravelling the industry's complexities, offering fresh perspectives on cultural exchange, sustainable tourism, and innovative hospitality practices.

Pallavi Pahuja boasts 12 years in management, making substantial strides with numerous case studies, book chapters, books, and articles. A respected figure in her field, her work offers deep insights into managerial challenges and proposes practical solutions, enhancing academic and practical understandings of management. Dr. Pahuja is committed to shaping future leaders, sharing her knowledge and passion to inspire and guide. Her contributions not only advance the field but also pave the way for innovative management practices, underscoring her role as a pivotal influence in the discipline.

R. Kandavel, an Associate Professor at the School of Management, Jeppiaar University, Chennai, With a solid foundation of 2 years and 6 months as an HR Executive in the corporate sector, with a commendable track record of more than 8 years and 6 months in teaching management courses with specialization in HR, Marketing, Organizational Behavior and Entrepreneurship Development. He Holds an M.B.A., M. Phil., and Ph.D. in Management. He has published 15 articles including Scopus Journals and UGC Care Journals globally and has presented papers in many National and International Conferences. He having authored and Published Books "Training on Employee Development and Productivity," published by Lambert Academic Publishing, Germany (ISBN: 978-613-8-39027-5). He has published a patent titled "Device to track Tax Lien". He also holds membership in various Professional Bodies. He has attended and also organized more than 15 Seminars, FDP and Workshops. Where he invited speakers from esteemed higher educational institutions and the corporate sector. He has been honored by the Best Faculty Award in 2023 from the South India Press Club and the Outstanding Researcher Award in 2020 from the Puducherry Academic Researchers Association (PARA).

Shashank Rajauria is lecturer in Institute of hotel management, Ahmedabad. With an academic background spanning ten years, he brings a wealth of theoretical knowledge in tandem with a practical understanding gained through three years of hands-on experience in the hotel industry with specialisation in housekeeping. His unique blend of academic prowess and industry insight positions them as well-rounded professional capable of applying theoretical concepts to real-world hospitality challenges.

Ishani Sharma is a Research Scholar at Chitkara Business School, Chitkara University, Punjab, India. Her current teaching and research interest areas include Tourist Psychology & Behavior, Tourism Marketing, Tourism Advertising and Corporate Travel Management. ORCID- 0009-0009-3439-5980

Renuka Sharma is a Professor (Finance) at Chitkara Business School at Chitkara University in Punjab. She has over 18 years of teaching and research experience (more than ten years post-doctoral and eight years before to obtaining her PhD). She has authored numerous research papers, a few of which have been published in international/national journals (Taylor&Francis, Emerald, Sage, Inderscience, etc.) and the rest have been presented at international/national conferences (IIM Bangalore, Shillong, Calcutta, Indore, and Kozhikode, among others), with numerous papers selected for Best Paper Awards. She also serves as a reviewer for numerous prestigious journals published by Emerald, Elsevier, and Inderscience, among others. Currently, she is guiding two PhD scholars and has successfully defended five others. She has been a consultant for several start-ups and MSMEs. She is the author of two textbooks for Cengage Pub. and Vikas Pub. Additionally, she has developed study materials for a variety of business-related courses for prominent Indian universities and institutions She has served as a resource person for several MDPs and FDPs related to research and finance. She is an entrepreneur too.

Ruby Sharma is a senior academician working in the field of management for more than 15 years.

Rishi Shukla Associate Professor AIT-Management, Centre of Excellence Chandigarh University Chandigarh, India Rishi.pshukla@gmail.com

Sujay Vikram Singh is a Senior Research Fellow currently pursuing a doctorate from Banaras Hindu University graduated and post-graduated from IHM Lucknow. His research interests include hospitality, CRM, service marketing, service quality, and systematic literature reviews. Published papers in various handbooks and journals. His Recent journal publications include International Journal of Market Research (Sage publishing), ABDC-A, and the Scopus Journal of Global Information Management (IGI Publishing), Scopus, ABDC-A. Presented and published papers at various national and international conferences, seminars. Achieved the best papers in various conferences .

Yuvika Singh has about 13 years of work experience in both industry as well as academic areas and has been associated with reputed B-Schools in Punjab and Haryana in the past. Currently she is working as an Assistant Professor at The ICFAI University, Himachal Pradesh. She is a B.Tech graduate and have pursued her MBA with HR and Marketing as the areas of specializations. Currently she is pursuing PhD from Punjabi University, Patiala. She has published about 25 research papers in reputed journals along with 4 chapters (one SCOPUS Indexed) in IGI Global Publication and other reputed publication house. She has presented 30 research papers in national and international conferences and attended more than 30 workshops/FDP in reputed organizations. She is not only connected with the research area but also actively engaged in organizing developmental programmes such as industrial visits, guest lectures, business plan and placement activities for the students along with the coordination for different committees. Her teaching and research areas are Human resource management, Organizational behavior, Employee engagement, Business research methodology and Psychology.

Mohammad Badruddoza Talukder is an Associate Professor & Head of the Department, Department of Tourism and Hospitality Management, Daffodil Institute of Information Technology (at the National University), Dhaka, Bangladesh. He holds PhD in Hotel Management from India. He has been teaching various courses in the Department of Tourism and Hospitality at various universities in Bangladesh since 2008. His research areas include tourism management, hotel management, hospitality management, food & beverage management, and accommodation management, where he has published research papers in well-known journals in Bangladesh and abroad. Mr. Talukder is one of the executive members of the Tourism Educators Association of Bangladesh. He has led training and consulting for a wide range of hospitality organizations in Bangladesh. He just became an honorary facilitator at the Bangladesh Tourism Board's Bangabandhu international tourism and hospitality training institution.

Sanjay Taneja is currently an Associate Professor in Research at Graphic Era University, Dehradun, India. His significant thrust areas are Banking Regulations, Banking and Finance (Fin Tech, Green Finance), Risks, Insurance Management, Green Economics and Management of Innovation in Insurance. He holds a double master's degree (MBA &M.Com.) in management with a specialization in Finance and Marketing. He received his PG degrees in Management (Gold Medalist) from Chaudhary Devi University, Sirsa, India in 2012. He earned his Doctor of Philosophy (Sponsored By ICSSR) in Banking and Finance entitled"An Appraisal of financial performance of Indian Banking Sector: A Comparative study of Public, Private and Foreign banks in 2016 from Chaudhary Devi University, Sirsa, India. He received his Post Doctoral Degree from faculty of Social Sciences, Department of Banking and Insurance, Usak University, Turkey entitled on "Impact of the European Green Deal on Carbon (CO2) Emission in Turkey" in 2023. He has published research papers in reputed SCOPUS/Web of Science/SCI/ABDC/UGC Care Journals. Prof. Taneja has more than fifty publications in total (Scopus/ABDC/Web of Science- 27)

Balraj Verma serves as an Assistant Professor at the esteemed Chitkara Business School-Doctoral Research Centre, affiliated with Chitkara University in Rajpura, Punjab. Holding a Ph.D. earned from Jaypee University of Information Technology (JUIT), Waknaghat, and a master's degree in Business Administration, he brings to the academic arena more than 16 years of rich experience in both academia and the corporate world. His qualifications extend to successfully passing the National Eligibility Test (NET) for teaching in the field of management, a testament to his dedication to education. He possesses a remarkable teaching portfolio, which includes courses such as Marketing Management, Strategic Management, Business Statistics, and Research Methodology. Furthermore, he is a strong advocate for rigorous research, as reflected in his extensive publication record. His research contributions encompass numerous papers published in SCI, ABDC-listed and Scopus Index journals, as well as authorship and editorial work for books and book chapters, published by renowned major presses. Notably, he is not just an academic but also an active contributor to the academic community. He has played a pivotal role in organizing workshops and conferences, contributing significantly to the academic growth and development of his department and university.

Index

S

T

V

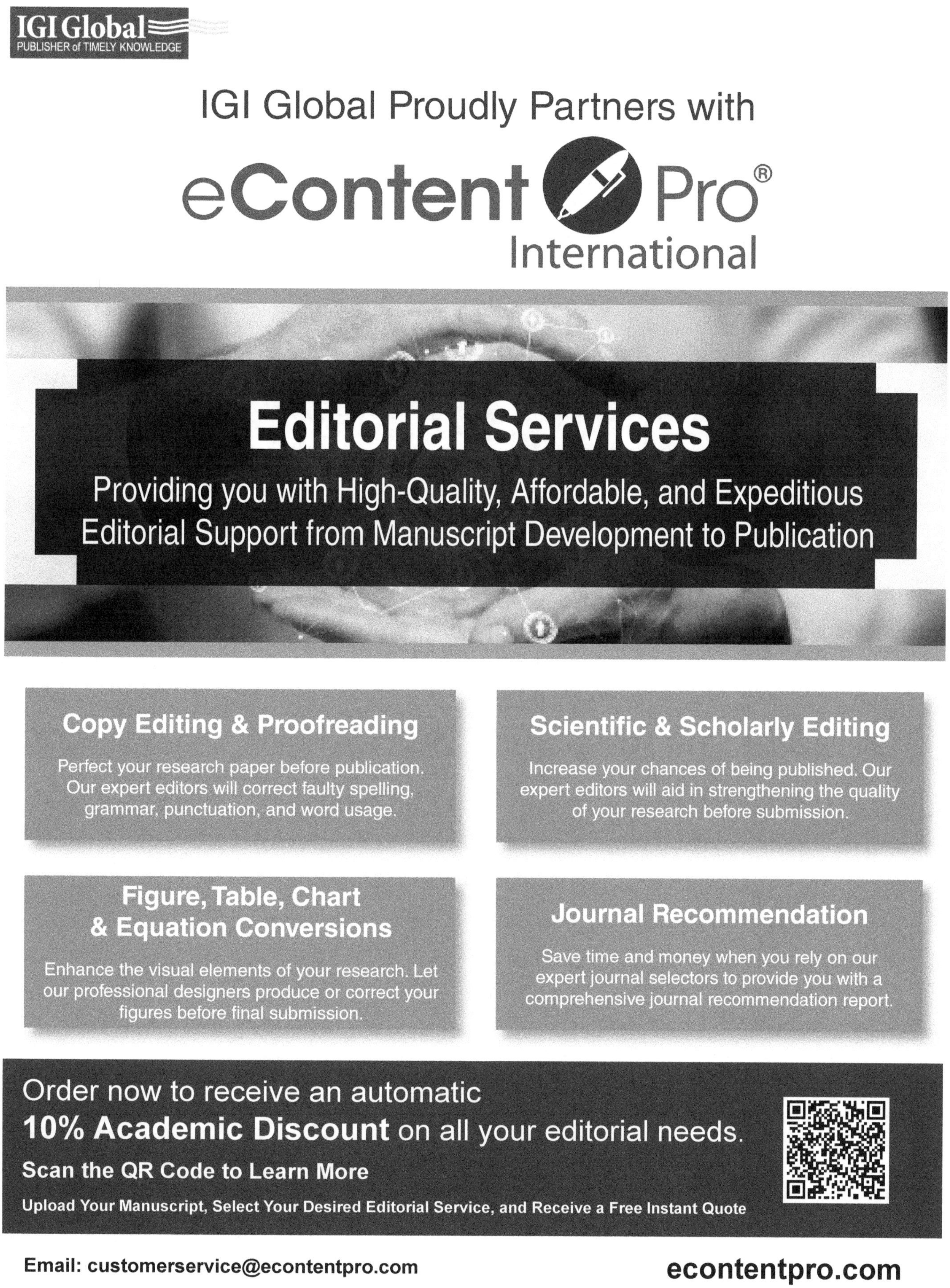
IGI Global
PUBLISHER of TIMELY KNOWLEDGE
IGI Global Proudly Partners with
eContent Pro®
International
Editorial Services
Providing you with High-Quality, Affordable, and Expeditious Editorial Support from Manuscript Development to Publication
Copy Editing & Proofreading
Perfect your research paper before publication. Our expert editors will correct faulty spelling, grammar, punctuation, and word usage.
Scientific & Scholarly Editing
Increase your chances of being published. Our expert editors will aid in strengthening the quality of your research before submission.
Figure, Table, Chart & Equation Conversions
Enhance the visual elements of your research. Let our professional designers produce or correct your figures before final submission.
Journal Recommendation
Save time and money when you rely on our expert journal selectors to provide you with a comprehensive journal recommendation report.
Order now to receive an automatic
10% Academic Discount on all your editorial needs.
Scan the QR Code to Learn More
Upload Your Manuscript, Select Your Desired Editorial Service, and Receive a Free Instant Quote
Email: customerservice@econtentpro.com
econtentpro.com

www.ingramcontent.com/pod-product-compliance
Lightning Source LLC
LaVergne TN
LVHW080122011026
849160LV00013B/1156